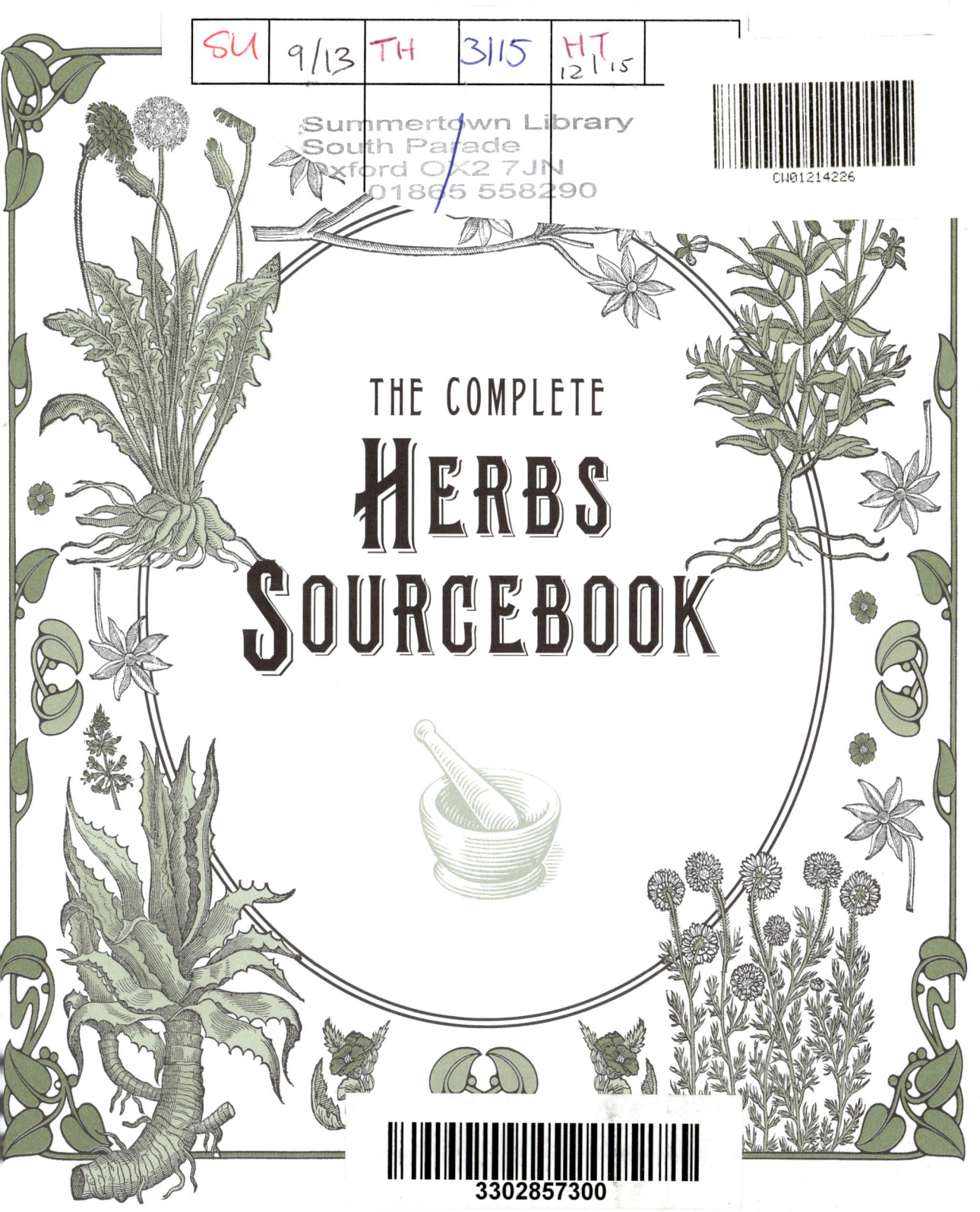

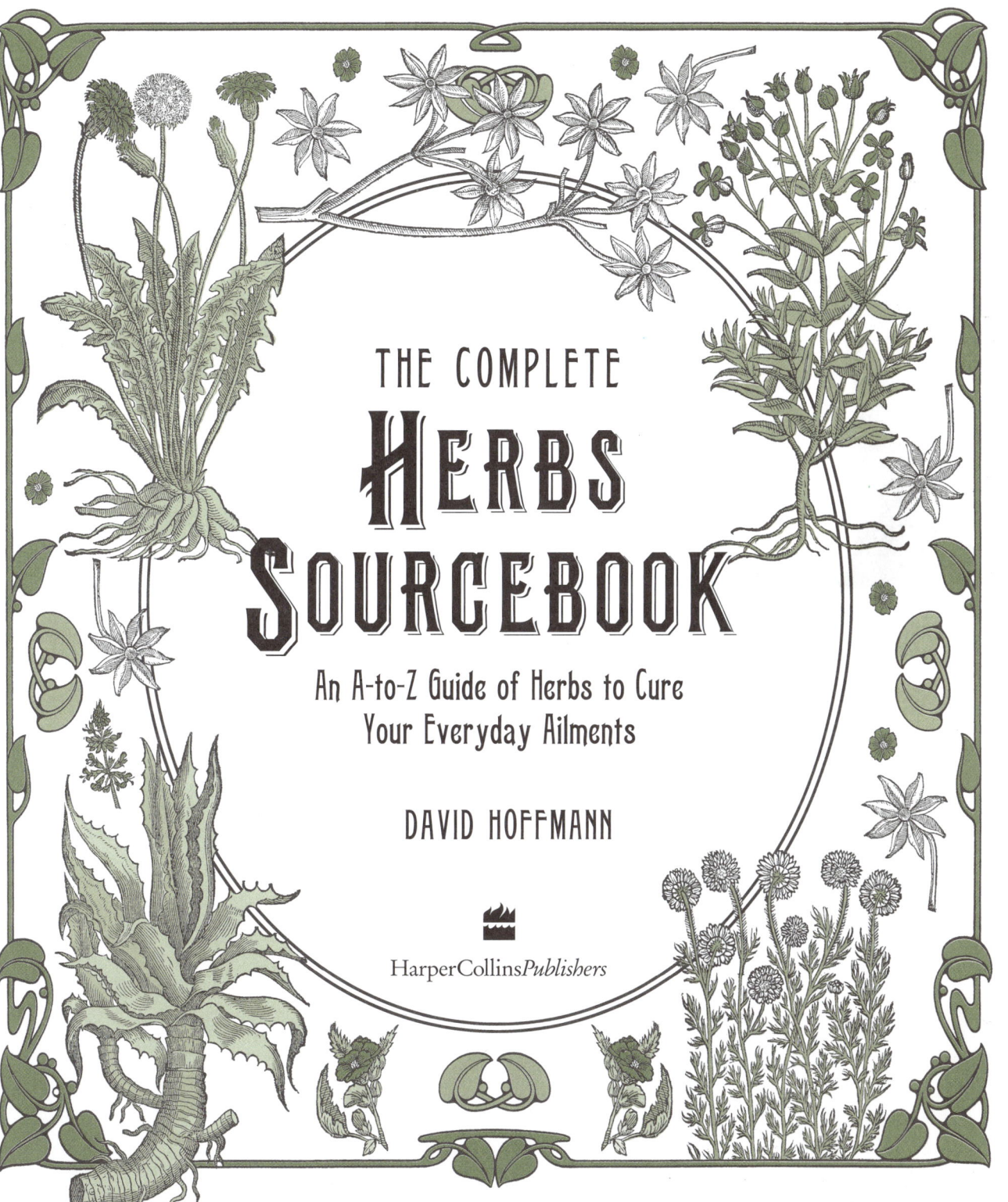

THE COMPLETE HERBS SOURCEBOOK

An A-to-Z Guide of Herbs to Cure Your Everyday Ailments

DAVID HOFFMANN

HarperCollins*Publishers*

TO LOLO, FOR NOW AND ALWAYS

APPRECIATIONS

I would like to thank my family at Findhorn for all their help and encouragement, especially Peter Königs, Robyn Gaston, and John Button in Publications. Also Kathy Thormod, Jane Crosen, Taras and Moia, Sabrina Dearborn, Doc. Monocle, Erica Cook, Michael and Linda Gardiner, Joy Drake, Kathy Tyler, Angé Stephens, Phoebe Reeves, The Game Deva, Michael Lindfield, and Binka Popov and the Angel of Findhorn.

And to Linda; without you it would never have got finished!

HarperCollins*Publishers*
77–85 Fulham Palace Road
Hammersmith, London W6 8JB
www.harpercollins.co.uk

First published in USA in 1983 by Findhorn

Published as *New Holistic Herbal* in Great Britain in 1990 by
Element Books Limited

Published as *Complete Herbs Sourcebook* by HarperCollins*Publishers* 2013

1 3 5 7 9 10 8 6 4 2

Text © David Hoffmann 1983, 1990, and 2013
Drawings and artwork © Ronald Morton and John Button 1983

David Hoffmann asserts the moral right to
be identified as the author of this work

Illustrations by Miranda Gray
Illustration on page 120 by Jennifer Jones
Illustrations on pages 84, 154, 223, 232, 235, 241, 247, 281, 285, 305, 311, 314,
319, 321, 328, 336, and 345 by Joe Bright

A catalogue record for this book
is available from the British Library

ISBN 978-0-00-793196-5

Printed and bound in China

All rights reserved. No part of this publication may be
reproduced, stored in a retrieval system, or transmitted,
in any form or by any means, electronic, mechanical,
photocopying, recording, or otherwise, without the prior
permission of the publishers.

CONTENTS

Preface 7
Introduction to This Edition 8
How to Use This Book 11
An Herbal Medicine Chest for the Home 13

THE HOLISTIC APPROACH ... 16
Gaia—the Living Earth 17
Herbs and Ecology 20
Ecosystems and the Biosphere 21
Herbs in Healing 22
Homeostasis 23
Self-Healing 24

THE CIRCULATORY SYSTEM 30
Prevention of Circulatory Disease 30
Herbs for the Circulatory System 32
Patterns of Disease 35
The Lymphatic System 40

THE RESPIRATORY SYSTEM 42
Prevention of Respiratory Disease 42
Herbs for the Respiratory System 44
Patterns of Disease of the Respiratory System .. 45

EARS, NOSE, THROAT, AND EYES 50
Herbs for Ears, Nose, Throat, and Eyes 50

The Ears 51
The Nose 52
The Throat 55
The Eyes 56

THE DIGESTIVE SYSTEM 58
Prevention of Disease 59
Herbs for the Digestive System 59
Patterns of Digestive Disease 62
The Mouth 64
The Stomach 65
The Small Intestine 68
The Large Intestine 70
Liver and Gallbladder 72

THE NERVOUS SYSTEM 76
Herbs for the Nervous System 77
Patterns of Disease of the
Nervous System 80

THE SKIN 92
Herbs for the Skin 93
Patterns of Skin Disease 94
Internal Causes 94
Internal Reactions to External Causes 96
External Causes 99

THE MUSCULAR AND
SKELETAL SYSTEM..................102
  Herbs for the Muscular and Skeletal System..102
  Patterns of Muscular and Skeletal Disease....105

THE GLANDULAR SYSTEM..........112
  Health and the Glands..................113
  Herbs for the Glands....................113
  Patterns of Disease of the Glandular System..114
  The Pancreas..........................114
  The Thyroid...........................115
  The Adrenal Glands....................116

THE REPRODUCTIVE SYSTEM.......120
  Herbs for the Female Reproductive System...121
  Patterns of Disease of the Female
  Reproductive System..................123
  The Menstrual Cycle...................123
  Pregnancy and Childbirth..............125
  Menopause...........................128
  Infections............................129
  Herbs and Sexuality...................130

THE URINARY SYSTEM..............132
  Herbs for the Urinary System............133
  Patterns of Disease of the Urinary System....134

INFECTIONS AND INFESTATIONS....140
  Antibiotics...........................141
  Herbs for Infections and Infestations......141
  Treating Infections....................143
  Treating Infestations..................144

CANCER..........................148
  Herbs and Cancer.....................149
  Nutrition and Cancer..................150
  Psychological Factors and Cancer........151

WHOLENESS AND PREVENTION.....154

THE CHEMISTRY OF HERBS.........162

THE ACTIONS OF HERBS.............174

THE PREPARATION OF HERBS.......182
  Internal Remedies.....................183
  External Remedies....................189

GATHERING HERBS................196
  When to Gather Herbs.................198

THE HERBAL 208

ABOUT THE AUTHOR...............339

RESOURCES AND SUPPLIERS........341

BIBLIOGRAPHY....................343

REPERTORY......................347

INDEX...........................357
  General Index........................357
  Index of English Names................385
  Index of Botanical Names..............393

PREFACE

THIS IS A BEAUTIFUL AND FASCINATING book, an enthralling gateway into a wonderful field. The beginner can understand, and the expert can really use it. David is to be congratulated on his achievement.

The Hermetic Wisdom laid down as first principle that the universe is Mind, an ocean of living Intelligence; and as second principle the Law of Correspondences—as above, so below; as in the greatest, so in the smallest; as in the macrocosm, so in the microcosm.

Holistic healing reveals the great truth. Thus reflexology can discover all imbalances in the bodily organism from the feet, iridology from the eye, and true phrenology from the conformation of the cranium. Every part contains the whole, as is so beautifully demonstrated by the shattered holographic plate. And now herbalism reveals all the secret gifts of nature for holistic healing.

Our minds are still overcoming centuries of conditioning to "apartness" thinking. The holistic world view lifts beyond such separation. We learn to see Truth as a hovering crystalline structure of many facets. You pick up one glint, I another, and the separatist reason can too easily conclude that, since I know and can prove I'm right, you must be wrong. All the glints together make up the Truth, and we are finding that true "conversation" (a "turning-about together") is an art of helping each other to see the wonder of the whole revealed in every part. This lifts it above intellectual discussion or that debased form of exchange called argument.

In holistic thinking we become eclectic and learn to draw our truth from many complementary sources. Thus herbalism opens up a wonderful field for natural healing, and this beautiful book by David Hoffmann will guide many into it, for it is an essential aspect of natural therapy.

In our age of drugs and chemicals, here is a path to safe treatment that respects the Oneness of Life. This book is delightfully illustrated and produced. All who are drawn into our movement for regeneration will want to possess it.

GEORGE TREVELYAN

Introduction to This Edition

TRANSFORMATION IS IN THE AIR. It is the keynote of all we see, do, and hear. Our lives are being transformed from within and without, sometimes positively growing and other times painfully changing, but always in flux. The purpose of our lives and the direction of society are no longer what they were, as the basis of our collective reality and beliefs changes. It is a time of chaos, crisis, and great opportunity. A fundamental change in perspective and context is occurring throughout society, and as a result much has happened in the field of herbalism and holistic healing in the short time since the first edition of this book appeared, as *The New Holistic Herbal*.

Herbalism is based on relationship—relationship between plant and human, plant and planet, human and planet. Using herbs in the healing process means taking part in an ecological cycle. This offers us the opportunity to be consciously present in the living, vital world of which we are part; to invite wholeness and our world into our lives through awareness of the remedies being used. The herbs can link us into the broader context of planetary wholeness, so that while they are doing their physiological/medical job, we can do ours and build an awareness of the links and mutual relationships.

Consider, for example, the treatment of a stomach ulcer with herbs and with drugs. Comfrey, Marshmallow Root, Meadowsweet, and Golden Seal can all be used to soothe and heal an ulcer, and with the help of the right diet and lifestyle it need not return. But there is also the chance here for people to become aware of the way in which the environment through plants is actively healing them, so that they can be more *present* in their world. Perhaps they can attune to the plants, visit the places where they grow, and establish a deeper rapport with nature through their healing process. Thus the treatment of the ulcer becomes part of a deeper transformative process.

If drug treatment is considered in the same way, problems arise. One of the drugs frequently used for ailments related to overproduction of stomach acid is Tagamet or cimetidine. This is effective for changing rapidly some of the biochemistry that leads to ulcer formation and irritation, reducing discomfort, and making life more bearable. However, looking at it in a broader context, we soon become aware that difficulties intervene. The chemical process whereby this drug is made is renowned for pollution production. So instead of linking with nature's wholeness, there is an immediate relationship with nature's pain—a direct connection between your stomach and dead fish in a polluted

river. Consider also the laboratory animals that died in the development of the drug and the dependence on a multinational pharmaceutical industry not renowned for its selfless service!

If holism embraces broader perspectives than simply internal pathology and individual lifestyle, then the choice posed here between two kinds of ecological relationships is a meaningful one in healing.

Holistic medicine can only be truly holistic if the perspectives it embraces acknowledge the social and cultural context in which the "illness" and the desired healing take place. It is a therapeutic and moral mistake to use herbalism to relieve people's physical distress and illness only for them to return to and continue in patterns of thought, behavior, work, and culture that are the sources of the disease.

By the nature of things it is often extremely difficult to affect change in these broader fields of nonherbal therapy! However, it is becoming increasingly important for the holistic therapist to speak out, to take a stand, to take risks. Things either change through action or degenerate through inaction. The insights gained through exploring holistic medicine add to the momentum for positive, loving change. I would suggest it is right and appropriate for practitioners of holistic medicine to contribute to the issues of our time. The perspectives gained through ecologically oriented herbalism have much to contribute to the issues of environment, nuclear power, nuclear weapons, and a stance of fear, aggression, alienation, and oppression. We are at home on this planet—we have but to recognize it. From the ills of humanity through the gift of herbal remedies comes a clue, a signpost, to this reality. We are part of a wonderfully integrated whole. This is not the stuff of vague idealism and mysticism but a solid reality. It is the basis of this book and the whole of herbal medicine.

HOLISTIC PARADIGM

Herbalism is practiced holistically, as orthodox medicine and other complementary therapies can be. But what is holistic medicine, other than the latest buzzword?

As people in all fields of life explore the implications of a holistic and ecological world view, medicine is at the forefront. We have gone beyond the ideal of "treating the whole person and not the symptoms" to begin to articulate a definition of a holistic approach to health.

Holistic medicine addresses itself to the physical, mental, and spiritual aspects of those who come for care. It views health as a positive state, not as the absence of disease. It emphasizes the uniqueness of the individual and the importance of tailoring treatment to meet each person's needs. The promotion of health and the prevention of disease is a priority, while emphasis is placed on the responsibility of each individual for his or her own health. The therapeutic approaches employed are aimed at mobilizing the person's innate capacity for self-healing.

While not denying the occasional necessity for swift medical or surgical intervention, holistic medicine puts the emphasis on assisting people to understand and help themselves, on education and self-care rather than treatment and dependence. Illness may be an opportunity for discovery as well as a misfortune.

A holistic approach to health care includes understanding and treating people in the context of their culture and community. An understanding of and a commitment to change those social and economic conditions that perpetuate ill health are as much a part of holistic medicine as its emphasis on individual responsibility. Most importantly, holistic medicine transforms its practitioners as well as its patients.

Such holistic perspectives suggest exciting ways in which health care can develop across the globe. There is a need, however, to develop the relationship between the complementary therapies and orthodox medicine. This is the way forward to create the framework that will fulfill our expectations of health and well-being.

Herbal medicine has much to contribute to the development of a holistic health service using the healing plants provided by nature. The use of herbs for healing brings us immediately into contact with our world in a profound and uplifting way. Many ills of our culture stem from our sense of separation from Earth, the ground of our being. Herbal medicine, while being a valid and effective therapeutic tool, can also be part of a personal and even social transformation.

A NEW EXPECTATION

During the years since this book was first published there have been great changes in attitudes toward herbalism and complementary medicine in general. Why are people turning to such alternative therapies as medical herbalism? There is a growing recognition that concern with health and well-being is not the same as one with illness and cure. What this means and how anything can be achieved in practice is vague in the public mind, but expectations have been raised and important questions have been asked.

There is a multitude of reasons, ranging from abject desperation to a positive and active quest for transformation, as to why people will consider consulting an herbalist or other alternative therapists. An increasingly important trigger is the fear, real or imaginary, of drugs and their side effects or of the trauma of operations. The herbalist is often called upon to act as a surrogate counselor, advising or guiding in place of the doctor. The question of safety and even the need for drug therapy is an enormous one, and this is not the place to air it. However, fears about side effects are often well founded. While not wishing to belittle potentially life-saving drugs or surgery, I feel the limitations of such methods are becoming increasingly apparent and will often unintentionally direct people toward safer alternatives.

In Great Britain in particular, another prompt to try alternatives is increasing exasperation with the organizational monolith of the National Health Service. This is not a criticism of the nurses, ancillary workers, and doctors valiantly endeavoring to care for their patients but simply an acknowledgment of the faults of the system. An atmosphere of alienation and impersonalization pervades many waiting rooms, hospital wards, and consultations. The field of health and wholeness is the epitome of where small really is beautiful.

Those who have been told that they must learn to live with their illness, or that there is nothing else orthodox medicine can do, will often turn to medical herbalism in the hope that something can be done. Herbal medication may very well help, but it is a great pity that such help is not sought earlier. Often it will be in such extreme cases that doctors themselves may even consider alternative therapies, and if little or nothing can be done they will then conclude the approach has no value. The flaws in this attitude are obvious.

The Green movement is growing strong, holism is no longer simply the domain of the fringe, and herbalism is thriving throughout the industrialized West. At long last the world view that this book is embedded in is increasingly seen as the only perspective that offers hope for the future of our society. Whether in health care, politics, economics, or any of the multitudinous facets of human endeavor, a change is manifesting that moves us to cooperation, both with each other and with the world we are part of. This transformation is not easy or comfortable but is very, very real. I feel deeply blessed to be able to make this small contribution to the field of Herbal Medicine, one aspect of the dawning human awareness of the embrace of Gaia.

How to Use This Book

THE COMPLETE HERBS SOURCEBOOK consists of three parts. "The Holistic Approach to Herbalism" places herbalism into its context, showing plants in their relationship to healing and humanity. The central part of the book discusses herbs and the herbal treatment of the systems of the body. The third part is a traditional herbal, which discusses the herbs in detail and provides information about their chemistry and actions, as well as information on gathering and preparing them.

The book can be used in several ways. It can be read from cover to cover as an introduction to herbalism; it can be used as a textbook; it can be used as a source for finding out about the holistic treatment of specific conditions and problems; or it can be used as a traditional herbal to find out more about a particular herb.

The approach to herbalism in this book uses herbs, according to their actions, that work synergistically to provide the body with the most appropriate help to work against disease. In this book the synergistic use of herbs is recommended. A combination of the actions of each herb or herbs must be carefully worked out so that the most appropriate aid is provided in combating disease. A uniform approach to the problem is necessary. The reader needs to decide which actions are needed to counteract a disease, and then to consult either "The Herbal" section, which provides a general description of each herb and its actions, or the section on "The Actions of Herbs."

To find information about specific diseases, the reader should consult the contents pages for the chapter in which the problem occurs, or look in the "General Index" for references.

"The Herbal" section is arranged alphabetically by English names. If the reader knows only the Latin name, the "Index of Botanical Names" will help in finding the English derivation. A particular herb can be located throughout the book by using the "General Index," the "Index of English Names," and the "Index of Botanical Names."

To find out which herbs might be useful in a particular disease, the reader should look to the "Repertory" section, and then to "The Herbal" section for more detailed information. When it says in this book, "This may be helpful" or "That may be considered," it is for the reader to look up the particular herbs and make the decision.

When to Use Herbs

Herbs can be used freely and safely as part of one's lifestyle without thinking of them as "medicines." For specific health needs, their best use would be preventative—to prevent problems from appearing. There are specific herbs that strengthen and tone specific organs and systems. These may be used where a tendency toward illness is recognized but no overt disease is present. By using herbs, it may well be possible to overcome any weakness.

While each person should find their own herbal "ally," the following may be safely used over extended periods of time:

Circulatory system	*Hawthorn Berries*
Respiratory system	*Mullein*
Digestive system	*Meadowsweet*
Nervous system	*Skullcap*
Skin	*Nettles*
Muscular and skeletal system	*Celery Seed*
Reproductive system	*Raspberry Leaves*
Urinary system	*Buchu*

Apart from prophylactic and culinary uses, herbs are used in specific conditions. Suggestions are given throughout the book for such cases, but self-diagnosis is not advisable. Consult an herbalist, if there is one available, or a doctor to ascertain the nature of your problem.

DURATION OF TREATMENT

Where a specific condition is being treated, the duration of the appropriate treatment will vary. Constipation should respond quickly, while osteoarthritis will take some time. In general, however, allow two to three weeks before any marked improvement can be expected. If in doubt, see an herbalist.

DOSAGE

The normal dosage for an adult is given for each herb in "The Herbal" section, and similarly where a mixture is given in the text. For children under 12 this should be reduced by a quarter, and for children under seven by a half. For adults over 65, there should be a quarter reduction, and a reduction to half the full dose for people over 70. These are very broad guidelines and will be less important for a very large, strong person of 75 than for a small, frail person of 65.

DRUGS

There is usually little to fear in combining herbs with chemical drugs, but there are a number of important exceptions, so consult your doctor *and* an herbalist. Unfortunately, the doctor will be unlikely to know anything about herbs!

PREPARATION AND DOSAGE OF MIXTURES

Throughout the book herbal mixtures are suggested that can support the body in healing itself. Depending on the specific case, those mixtures can be adapted accordingly.

With each mixture, recommendations are made as to the way they should be prepared. Their respective properties are given in *parts*, meaning proportions of weight of dried herbs, and instructions for their preparation are given accordingly. (Dried herbs can be substituted by other preparations, for instance by tinctures, in which case the same proportions apply. For details on the dosage of tinctures, see the specific dosage information in "The Herbal" section.) Detailed information on how to prepare an infusion or decoction can be found in the section "The Preparation of Herbs."

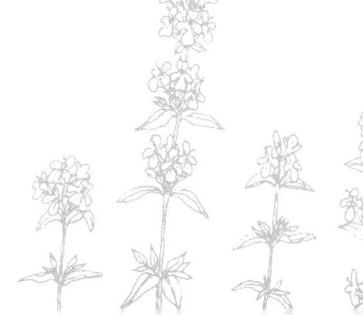

An Herbal Medicine Chest for the Home

There are well over 2,000 plants that can be used in herbal medicine in the Western world. The planet-wide list is far greater. So what can you realistically provide in the home? A daunting prospect faces the fledgling herbalist, yet by using the actions approach presented in this book, it is possible to stock a small herbal medicine chest that will fulfill most day-to-day needs. The following list of herbs includes representatives of all the main actions, plus specific ones as well. If you are going to stock such a medicine chest, become thoroughly familiar with these 25 plants and use them at your discretion. They may be stored as dried herbs or as tinctures.

In addition to these specific herbs, it will be helpful to have the following in the form of ointments:

Arnica
Chickweed
Comfrey
Marigold

Distilled *Witch Hazel*, obtainable from pharmacies and some health food stores, should also be included.

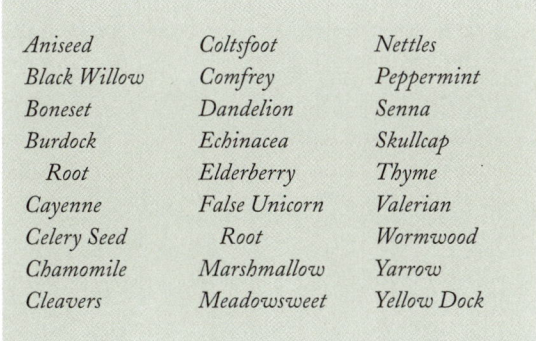

Aniseed
Black Willow
Boneset
Burdock Root
Cayenne
Celery Seed
Chamomile
Cleavers
Coltsfoot
Comfrey
Dandelion
Echinacea
Elderberry
False Unicorn Root
Marshmallow
Meadowsweet
Nettles
Peppermint
Senna
Skullcap
Thyme
Valerian
Wormwood
Yarrow
Yellow Dock

THE HOLISTIC APPROACH

"We are on a quest, individually and collectively, to create wholeness within ourselves and within all of our life, to find it within ourselves and to release it—a process of communion and education. What is created will not be separation, conflict, and diversity among peoples, but wholeness, oneness, peace, a new earth for humankind that reflects the oneness and wholeness of the Earth that has always been."

DAVID SPANGLER

The Holistic Approach

IN THE HANDS OF A HOLISTIC HEALER, who works with the life force and with the integrated whole that the body represents, herbs are a powerful tool. In this book I would like to present a context for holistic herbalism. There is the need for a new kind of herbal that goes beyond the more common medicinal approach where herbs are listed alphabetically, prior knowledge is assumed, or symptoms are listed with their appropriate remedies. While herbs can be used effectively to treat symptoms, such an approach is just an organic form of drug therapy if we do not take the whole person into account. I offer this book to all who use herbs, all who work in healing, and all who are growing in ecological awareness.

In the holistic approach to healing we can see how "all disease is the result of inhibited soul life, and that is true of all forms in all kingdoms. The art of the healer consists in releasing the soul so that its life can flow through the . . . form."[*] Any illness is a manifestation of disease within the whole being. To truly heal, we need to look at the interconnectedness and the dynamic play of all the parts in the whole—the physical, emotional, and mental bodies and the enlivening presence of the soul. And then we need to further expand our view and see this wholeness as part of a greater whole: the person's group, humanity, the entire planet, as all these work together in a dynamic, integrated system.

This ideal may be daunting, but it is an opportunity and a gift to explore this vision and to bring it through into reality. There are many new approaches today to healing, with differing attitudes and terminologies, and together they contribute to a planetary change. As the Tibetan in Alice Bailey's mystical writing says: "There is no school in existence today which should not be retained. All of them embody some useful truth, principle, or idea. I would point out that a synthetic group would still be a separative and separate entity, and no such group is our goal. It is the synthesis of the life and of the knowledge that is desirable. There will be eventually, let us hope, hundreds and thousands of groups all over the world who will express this new attitude to healing, who will be bound together by their common knowledge and aims, but who will express this to the best of their ability in their own particular fields, in their own peculiar way and with their own peculiar terminologies."[*]

Herbs are part of our total ecology and as such lend themselves to us to integrate and heal our physical bodies. By taking the wider context of the whole being into consideration, we see how this inner shift toward holism reflects a global shift, a realignment throughout. As we move into the New Age, a great exploration of consciousness is underway, an exploration we are all

---

[*] Alice Bailey, *Esoteric Healing*, Lucis Press, 1953

[*] *Ibid*

involved in. The use of herbs can be a tool of growing consciousness, to recognize holism. In healing we must take the whole being of the patient into our awareness, including the context of their life. We ask patients to look at how to make their environment, habits, and activities life-supporting, and by doing this we contribute to a change of consciousness. And we realize more and more that we have the capacity to create our reality and relationships consciously. As our awareness grows, we contribute to the illumination of ourselves and of our world. Our planetary companions, the plants, offer themselves in service to humanity. Perhaps through the recognition of this gift, humanity will at last start to serve our planet appropriately, to bring healing and renewal. I write *The Complete Herbs Sourcebook* in the light of this vision.

Gaia—the Living Earth

The great work of today is the recognition of our wholeness, as individuals, as groups, as humanity, and as a planetary whole. Perhaps the most exciting symbol of the birth of this vision of wholeness in the heart and mind of humanity was the first photograph of our world taken from space by the *Apollo* astronauts. This has been with us for over a decade now, acting as a "raising agent" to leaven the consciousness of humanity.

Seeing our world as a whole helps us recognize that we are at a turning point in humanity's "groping toward the light," as Teilhard de Chardin has described it. It is now apparent that our world is not just a passive geophysical object where things happen in random-but-fortuitous ways. In fact Planet Earth can be seen as an active participant in the creation of its own story, a living being now given the name of *Gaia*, a name from Greek mythology for the goddess of Earth. Gaia has been described as ". . . a complex entity involving the earth's biosphere, atmosphere, oceans, and soil; the totality constituting a feedback or cybernetic system which seeks an optimal chemical and physical environment for life on this planet. This maintenance of relatively constant conditions by *active control* may be conveniently described by the term 'homeostasis'."*

What this description implies is that our world is acting as a whole to create and maintain optimum conditions for life to thrive and evolve. An integral part of this development is the evolution of consciousness in its many forms. The opportunity before us now is to consciously recognize and embrace our role within the greater being of Gaia. This realization is not new to us; it has been embraced by the mystics of all religions for as long as humanity has searched for mystical truth. However, we have reached a point in the unfolding of human culture where these insights are becoming the stuff of science, where the "spiritualization of the mundane" is truly happening.

The revelation of our unity with Gaia provides a new context within which to view our world and our human actions. While the details of our reality as such are not changing, this broadening of perspective changes everything as we become conscious of interrelationships between parts within the whole. A parallel can be seen in what happened to physics when the theory of relativity was introduced; it did not change the laws of thermodynamics or the specifics of Newtonian physics, but these laws and world view came to be seen within a much wider and more encompassing perception of the world, the implications of which are still not fully grasped.

*J. E. Lovelock, *Gaia, a New Look at Life on Earth*, Oxford University Press, 1979

The very ability to perceive the Earth as living, as Gaia, is an indication of the expansion of consciousness that humanity as a whole is experiencing. Until recently, the only field of human endeavor that was inclusive and holistic enough to grasp the insights that point toward our unity has been that of mysticism and spirituality. Some of these ideas have permeated the teachings of spiritually enlightened people, or the expression of poets, artists, and musicians. It is now clear that even in that most materialistic science, physics, the limits of reductionism have been reached. To explore the nature of our world further, it is necessary to expand parameters to embrace the whole of any system. The whole is always more than the sum of its parts. Analyzing or reducing something to its constituent parts can only tell us so much, and to find out more, these parts need to be seen in a broader picture that includes function and relationship. Whether it be an atom, a daisy, a worker in a car factory, it can only be perceived and understood when seen in relationship to the greater whole of which it is a part. This is the heart of holism.

The work of the theoretical physicist David Bohm provides a good example of the way science is starting to approach reality as a dynamic web of relationships that cannot be comprehended unless consciousness is taken as an integral part of the universe.[*] Bohm's theory explores the order he believes to be inherent at a "nonmanifest" level in the cosmic web of relationships that make up the "unbroken wholeness." This order he has called "implicate" or "enfolded," as opposed to the "explicate" or "unfolded" structure of the universe. A useful analogy is that of the hologram, a specially constructed transparent plate that, when illuminated by a laser beam, produces a three-dimensional image. The extraordinary property of a hologram is that each part of the holographic plate contains the information for the entire picture. If any part of the holographic plate is illuminated by a laser, the entire image will be produced (although in less detail). The information of the whole is contained, or enfolded, in each of its parts.

This is the nature of our world and universe, an implicit unity and wholeness that is the basis and nature of creation. This perception also recognizes the dynamic nature of the universe through the concept of the "olomovement," by looking at the dynamic phenomena out of which all forms of the material universe flow. The focus of study has shifted from the structure of objects to the structure of movement, revealing the order enfolded in the holomovement. Implicit in this perception of reality is the essential role played by consciousness. The correlation and interdependence of mind and matter is not a causal relationship. Mind and matter are mutually enfolded projections of a higher reality that are neither matter nor consciousness.

With such developments in physics and the recognition of Gaia in the life sciences, it is clear that profound changes are afoot in the world view embraced by science. This world view is becoming closely attuned to the insights given to humanity by mystics and the spiritual philosophies of the East.[*] The word "holistic" describes integrated wholes whose properties cannot be reduced to those of smaller units. Holistic attitudes and perceptions are appearing in all fields of life, from agriculture and medicine to politics. The word has its roots in the Greek *holos* or whole, and was used by Arthur Koestler to coin the word "holon" in an attempt to grasp how systems act as wholes while still being parts of yet greater wholes. So we find that each holon has two opposite tendencies; an integrative tendency to function as part of a greater whole and a self-assertive tendency

---

[*] David Bohm, *Wholeness and the Implicate Order*, Routledge & Kegan Paul, 1980

[*] These parallels are explored by Fritjof Capra in his excellent book *The Tao of Physics*, Fontana/Collins, 1975

to preserve its individual autonomy. The subsystems that are described as holons may be individuals, ecosystems, or individual cells, showing that for health at any level of organization these opposite but complementary tendencies must be in dynamic balance. There must be a harmony between integration and self-assertion that makes the whole system flexible and open to change.

It becomes clear that when one considers the whole topic of healing, whether medical or societal, one must view the needs of the individual, or the organ, in the context of the greater whole in which they exist. One must focus on the relationship between the individual and society, between organs and organism. This dynamic relationship between part and whole can be demonstrated as crucial in any field of endeavor, and its implications for healing are explored in this book; but broader and more profound conclusions can be reached.

It is becoming apparent that a fundamental change in perspective and context is occurring. The transition into the holistic world view is but a manifestation of a profound reorientation within human consciousness. It is perhaps a response to an inner change in the very fabric of humanity. If evolution is interpreted as the unfolding story of consciousness in our planet, then the point humanity has reached is the threshold of deep and profound expansions in the content and context of consciousness. The vast array of crises that faces us can be seen as the result of human limitation and are only solvable by the expansion into deeper, broader, more inclusive realms of meaning. The perception of Gaia and one world is part of the transition into planetary consciousness where our problems are approachable. Whether we then solve them is another question!

At this point of change and crisis there are no convenient maps, no guide books, only the occasional road sign suggesting directions. The limitations of thought and perception that have proved so useful for so long are now only a source of pain and crisis. But crisis is opportunity, and through the pressure and discomfort of our individual and social lives, the cracks are appearing in the shell of human life. A quantum leap in consciousness and possibility is occurring, and, as Marilyn Ferguson puts it: "Our past is not our potential."*

A wind of change is blowing from deep within the spiritual roots of humanity, moving us forward, waking us up. What this change means is hard to say, although certain outlines may be discernible. While the problems remain the same, the quality of our approach to them will be enhanced by viewing them as wholes within wholes. The key may be in working with a nonjudgmental inclusiveness, discriminating between what is or is not *appropriate* among parts of the whole rather than criticizing differences. As humanity has been told for millennia, love is the key. And we each have a role to play in this exploration of the new, in the revealing of our new parameters, in humanity's groping toward the light.

One of the ways in which this profound spiritual transformation is manifesting is in the area of cultural values and attitudes, leading to a "paradigm shift," a shift in the pattern of thoughts, perceptions, and values that form our particular vision of reality. It encompasses the complete vision of what society considers its reality. The way science is being transformed by this shift has been briefly touched upon, but the cultural impact is profound and often painful. The whole of our world—whether individuals, civilizations, or the biosphere—is undergoing a crisis of birth and transition. The pain of this growth should not be avoided; the cultural transformation cannot be prevented. It would seem that through the trauma of the birth process lies the escape from crisis and collapse.

Within the chaos that seems to be surrounding this time of transition, our response to it can be completely free and open. In some fields there is an active growth

---

* Marilyn Ferguson, *The Aquarian Conspiracy*, Granada, 1980

toward the new vision that shows itself in certain areas of science and the arts, in the development of communities, and the broad expansion of human growth and spirituality. However, in other areas the old vision and old paradigm are grimly being held on to, causing much pain and suffering as the old patterns no longer provide help or guidance within the new situation. Politics and economics, while trying valiantly to stem the tide, are fields of thought stuck in the old fragmented perceptions. Unless there is a movement toward more inclusive policies and attitudes, an embracing of the fact of our one world, there seems little hope of cure for our mega crisis. However, from within the new paradigm the outlook is totally different. While not being easy, there are many directions in which our culture can move. The spirit of wholeness that holism offers to humanity can act as a beacon lighting our way as we stumble home.

The vision of Gaia offers a way in which the consciousness of humanity can resonate with the planetary whole. The vision and purpose of the spiritual drive of humanity can consciously synthesize scientific striving and allow a dynamic interaction between humanity and other realms of nature, within the embrace of the being which is the planet, which is Gaia.

Through the right flow of energies within a system, a body, an ecosystem, comes ecological harmony, comes healing. In this book I wish to share a vision of herbal medicine as a manifestation of Gaia at work, providing that which we need to ensure health and vitality in our physical bodies, which in turn allows us greater involvement in the whole. Holistic healing offers an abundance of relevant, valid techniques—something that simply reflects the diversity of human consciousness. There is no need to separate herbal medicine from other holistic forms or even allopathic medicine; they are all valid as agents of healing. This book focuses on herbs as a healing tool, as ecological healers that are gifts from Gaia to humanity.

Herbs and Ecology

"He causeth the grass to grow for the cattle, and herbs for the service of man"
Psalm 104:14

Herbs, which comprise much of the realm of plants, are an interface within the body of Gaia. They are an interface between two realms of nature. Where humanity and plants meet, a synergistic energy can be created and exchanged. At such a point inner and outer ecology may resonate and become attuned. We have then an ecologically integrated process that heals and harmonizes the inner environment (the human body) while being produced by an outer, harmonized environment (nature).

Flowering plants first appeared in geological history during the Cretaceous period, about 135 million years ago. It took them only a very short period of time to diversify into the main flowering plant families we know today. This baffled botanists for a long time until they recognized that the plants evolved within the context of an ecological whole and not as isolated individuals. They evolved within the ecosystem they lived in. The rapid diversification took place through the interaction of plants and insects. The interface between plant and animal realms provided the evolutionary drive.

With the concept of Gaia in mind, we can see that evolution is an exercise in cooperation as well as one of competition, both processes forming a web of interactions and producing the complex tapestry of today's ecology, an interwoven dynamic system. The ecosystem can only be understood as a whole—as one integrated and self-maintaining unit. All that is needed for the maintenance of any part of the whole is supplied by it; in fact, it *has* to be supplied by the system, since there is nothing outside it. If the system did not take care of itself, it would not be viable and could not survive.

A specific example is the phenomenon of secondary plant products. A number of plants produce a range of complex chemicals that play no identifiable role within the metabolism of that plant; we call them secondary plant products. The only way to explain their function within the individual plant scientifically is to assume that it is a very complex way of isolating waste matter accumulated from the metabolic process of the plant, and this would be totally out of keeping with the genius of the realm of plants for efficiency and design.

Secondary plant products, such as the alkaloids, the glycosides, and many other groups, have a strong and marked influence on human and animal physiology. They are the agents that distinguish herbs from other plants, as pharmaceutical chemists are finding out. This is not merely a fortuitous accident. It is in fact the hallmark of Gaia. By eating plants, we are linked to a circulatory system within the biosphere and to the energy source of the sun, since plants synthesize their own nutrition via sunlight. The secondary plant products are taking part in this circulation to reach us and to facilitate homeostasis. In a profound and ingenious way, our food can be our healing.

The realm of plants provides everything our body needs for a balanced and integrated existence. However, we are more than just a body; we also have consciousness, which brings other factors onto the stage. We not only have to take our animal body into consideration, but also our emotions, our mind, and our spiritual nature. Harmony is no longer simply a matter of right diet or even right herbs, but also a matter of right feelings, right thoughts, lifestyle, attunement, actions—harmony of right relationship to our world and ourselves. Choice comes into the healing process when we see which of these areas we need to work with most.

It is impossible to generalize about the relative value of techniques that work with the physical body, with the emotions or spiritual energies. All have their role and can work together for healing to take place. It can be said that health lies in correct diet, or right use of allopathic drugs, or a free flow of soul energy. All these statements are correct and all of them are relative.

Where does herbal medicine fit into this picture? By the nature of the plant form, herbs work on the physical body. They are acting to integrate and balance its physiological function and to augment its innate vitality. When the body is balanced, the process of integrating the other aspects of our being is helped and catalyzed. While herbs will not replace relevant techniques like counseling or meditation, they will help the chalice of the body to be strong, receptive, and supportive of the subtler aspects of human life.

Ecosystems and the Biosphere

Every culture throughout the world—until very recently—used healing plants as the basis for their medicine. The therapeutic philosophy and rationale for plant use varies, but for thousands of years plants have demonstrated their efficiency and significance.

Each culture had a basic healing flora from which remedies were selected. This range of plants would vary from area to area depending on the local ecosystem. It is remarkable, however, to look at Wales, Southern India, the North American plains, or any other area, and find herbs with equivalent actions. The plant species, or even the botanical types, might be totally different, but the range of human problems that can be dealt with botanically is the same. While this supports the idea of Gaia providing a context for healing with the aid of herbs, it raises the question of whether today we should always stick to the flora provided by the local ecosystem within which we live.

The ecosystem available to us is no longer a local one, just as our human culture and consciousness is no longer a local one. We have become planetary beings, though not necessarily yet out of our own choice. Our food may come from anywhere in the world, and modern information technology brings the world into our homes, opening our thoughts and emotional lives to a wide range of influences. We are already in many ways planetary citizens. As planetary beings within the body of Gaia, the whole of the world's flora is available to us, and rightly so.

We also have to consider human impact on local ecosystems. In Wales, for example, it used to be possible to obtain a large range of plants in natural habitats. Nowadays, due to intensive agriculture, to deforestation and reafforestation with foreign conifers, and the expansion and industrialization of towns, there are few truly natural and wild habitats left; the range of plants available to us locally is therefore greatly reduced. This has been part of the ecological impact of humanity, unaware as it has been of whole systems and the value of their interrelationships.

Herbs in Healing

The potent healing qualities of herbs have been used in different therapeutic philosophies throughout history. We find plants used within the Indian ayurvedic system and in Chinese medicine alongside acupuncture and other techniques. They play a very important role in the spiritual healing ecology of the Native Americans. We see them being used as a source of drugs in the highly scientific and technological approach of modern pharmacy and allopathic medicine.

In fact, allopathic medicine, now often called "orthodox" medicine, has its roots in the use of herbs. Until about 50 years ago, nearly all the entries in pharmacopoeias describing the manufacture of drugs indicated an herbal origin. Only since the refinement of chemical technology and developments in chemotherapy has the use of herbs apparently diminished. Nonetheless, it should be recognized that a majority of drugs still have their origin in plant material. Some very simple examples will illustrate this.

The amphetamines, which are based on the alkaloid ephedrine, supply stimulants and anti-asthmatic drugs and play an important role in medicine. Their exploitation followed the discovery of the active ingredient ephedrine in the Chinese herb Ma Huang, *Ephedra sinica*. The steroid drugs, the wonder drugs of the 1960s, now known to have unfortunate side effects, are still synthesized from a chemical extracted from the West African Wild Yam, *Dioscorea spp.* Aspirin, too, was discovered in the nineteenth century from a number of plants like Meadowsweet and Black Willow. In fact, its name comes from the old botanical name of Meadowsweet, *Spirea*.

So we see that allopathic medicine still uses herbs, if in a limited way. Plants are approached as a source of active ingredients, specific bioactive chemicals that can be analyzed, synthesized, and used in the form of potent drugs. The body is seen as being essentially biochemical in nature, so when something goes wrong, it does so on the level of chemical processes and molecules. To get it to work correctly, we thus have to use chemicals. If such an attitude is correct, why not use isolated constituents from plants? After all, nature provides powerful agents like morphine, still one of the best painkillers known, so why not approach plants this way? In the context of the scientific approach, to view the human being as a biochemical laboratory where specific chemicals have specific effects seems justified and valid.

But can we really reduce a human being to the level of molecules? The human being surpasses description in its beauty and dynamic complexity of form and function, in potential expression and creativity. Of course on the level of physical form our body is *also* biochemical, but its organization transcends by far the realms of biochemistry textbooks. Even if we were to fully comprehend the molecular complexities, we would not find what makes us human. There is a powerful and synergistic force at work within us—call it life, life force, vital force, or other names—that *is* us and is involved with the whole of us on all levels, not just the biochemical. At death the same chemicals are present but this energy of life and synthesis has gone. It is impossible to define this force, but the holistic approach is based on and works with a vision of humanity as animated by it.

Herbal medicine in its holistic sense recognizes humanity as an expression of life, enlivened with life force, and herbs can work with this whole being, not just specific symptoms. They do function through biochemical interactions and specific applications, but they do so in a way that augments the vital processes of the body. On the biochemical level, the numerous ingredients in an herb work in a synergistic way, with elements involved in the process that chemotherapy would not even consider as being active. In later chapters we will hear more about this—for instance, in a comparison of *Foxglove* and *Lily of the Valley*, in the section on circulation.

If we just looked at herbs as a source of valuable chemicals, we would limit their healing power, for beyond the physical level they can also work on the level of the life force. As they heal our bodies, they may also heal our hearts and minds, for they open the body to a clear flow of integrating and synergizing vital energy.

Homeostasis

The body maintains a steady internal state, where temperature, blood sugar level, and other variables are kept within narrow limits, this process being known as homeostasis. This ability is fundamental to life, an expression of a force within working toward harmony and integration. If the body were not able to maintain this state of homeostasis, we would not survive long.

This principle of homeostasis also applies to our environment. Our environment adapts to changes, but, like us, it is only able to do this within narrow limits. Beyond those, it dies.

As human beings, we live in contact with two environments, the outer ecological one and the inner physiological one. Herbs can be seen as a bridge between the outer and inner environment, augmenting health by facilitating harmony and resonance between the two. Once we are in balance, we can radiate our higher state of health back into the ecosystem from which the herbs came.

If we slightly shift our view, we can see that we are really part of the whole of ecology, not separate from it. When we are healed with the help of plants, a part of the ecology is healed. By healing our bodies and our minds, we will be more present as whole beings. And it is hoped that health will enable the growth of new awareness so that we can become conscious cocreators with nature and not remain the abusers and rapists that recent history shows us to be. A state of wholeness and health can affect our whole environment. It can affect our relationships, which affect society, and so potentially act to heal all humanity.

If we consider the concept of Gaia and remember that the Earth constantly works toward staying in a state of homeostasis, we can see how herbs act as homeostatic agents. Their purpose is to keep an element of the ecology—humanity—integrated and in harmony with the whole ecology. We can compare it to the purpose of hormones. Hormones released in one part of the body lead to a specific action in another part, integrating and harmonizing our inner environment.

Chemotherapy cannot be substituted for this work of herbs. Chemicals do not work toward the integration of a system; at their best they bring some elements back into alignment. We can look at health as at any ecological system aiming for homeostasis. It is always in motion, with varying elements from outside influencing the system, which does its best to stay in balance and thus to stay alive. Health is when the personal ecosystem, the inner space that has been called the *milieu interieur*, is in balance with the outer space, and both of them are one. As J. Z. Young says: "The entity that is maintained intact, and of which we all form a part, is not the life of any one of us, but in the end the whole of life upon the planet."

Self-Healing

The word "healing" has its roots in the Greek word *holos*, the same word that has given us "whole" and "holistic." Healing is the expression of wholeness; health *is* wholeness. The experience and expression of this quality can only come from within the individual; it never comes from an outer source such as a therapist or teacher. Just as all paths of spiritual development tell us to look within, so for our healing we must look to our inner selves.

Health is also the expression of integrated being that a person embodies. The emotions, thought-life, and spiritual flow are as important to health as is the state of organs and tissues within the body. Whether we are concerned about being healthy, regaining health, or moving to greater health, the whole of the being is involved.

The person who is "sick" is in fact the healer. Aid can be sought from "experts" whether allopaths or herbalists, psychotherapists or witch doctors, but the responsibility for healing can never be truly handed to anyone other than the person desiring the healing. Healing comes from within, from truly embracing the life that flows within us. Herbs will aid in this process, but healing is inherent in being alive. It is our gift and our responsibility. This may come as a surprise to most of us, conditioned as we are to hand our power over to "experts," whether they are doctors or politicians. In healing as in all life, we are free, and we are the divinely empowered authority for the process of our unfolding lives.

Healing is rarely an act of consciously harnessing inner energy and light, but is always a release and expression of this inner power. While the healing process is unique, an expression of life in a person, this miraculous event can be facilitated by various tools and techniques. Numerous therapies have been developed throughout the unfolding of human culture that have much to offer as healing arts. However, these do not heal. They cannot heal; they can only aid the body with its own innate healing power.

The apparent multitude of healing techniques, often appearing to contradict each other, can be seen as an interrelating ecology of approaches. I call it therapeutic ecology. Seeing the connections between the different schools of healing makes it clear that a unique blend of therapies may ideally suit one person while a different blend would be right for someone else. This provides us with a choice as to the best way to aid the self-healing process.

The diagram on the following page places the individual—the heart and center of self-healing—in the middle of an array of therapies. The foundation is Gaia, our beloved planet, sustaining and supporting us. The overlighting presence is that of grace, embracing and

---

[*] J. Z. Young, *Introduction to the Study of Man*, Oxford University Press, 1979

illuminating us with the mystery of God's loving presence.

I suggest four branches of healing techniques: medicine, body work, psychotherapies, and methods of spiritual integration. Each of these is divided to show individual paths that represent many more, but there are limitations to this diagram as it is two-dimensional, suggesting that the relationships of the tools of self-healing are linear. This could not be further from the truth, for the actual relationships are complex and numerous, creating a rich diversity. It is best to view this diagram as part of a three-dimensional web, creating a geodesic pattern of healing possibilities. An example would be an approach based upon herbs, massage, psychosynthesis, and meditation. This combination might offer the person involved exactly what they need to facilitate self-healing. However, it may be that homeopathy by itself is appropriate. The combinations offer great subtlety and diversity of approach.

MEDICINE

The word "medicine" here is used to describe anything that is taken—anything that is a gift from the Earth. At first sight, it might seem strange that drugs are in the same group with herbs and homeopathy. They are all *things*, and as such, they are part of the diversity and richness of our planet. Whether it be hydrocortisone, False Unicorn Root, or a Bach Flower Remedy, all are produced from the body of the Earth. It would be a mistake to judge one against another. All have their place. What is needed is clear discrimination as to the appropriate treatment for each unique individual. There is nothing universally bad about chemotherapy or universally good about herbs. Let us be thankful for the choice.

BODY WORK

The physical body has a deep wisdom, far outstretching the mind's ability to conceive of it. A whole range of ways for freeing this wisdom and releasing the healing activity of the body have been developed. Perhaps the most limited and primitive method is surgical manipulation. But then there are times when all that can be done is to remove diseased tissue. This is necessary far less often than our surgeons believe, but it is still a valid and occasionally appropriate form of body work. Acupuncture, the ancient Chinese therapy of balancing body energy, is a most useful way of working with the body. In addition to these two very different types of body work, we can include the manipulative techniques of physiotherapy, osteopathy, chiropractic, massage, and Rolfing. Added to these things done *to* us are those we ourselves do. This would include Yoga, jogging, dance, and all forms of physical exercise and expression.

PSYCHOTHERAPIES

Much of the pain and trauma that we experience in our lives is the result of emotional and mental problems. There are a range of therapies that help us move toward an inner knowing and an integrative realignment of our psychological selves. It is not just the emotionally traumatized or mentally confused person that benefits from an exploration and healing of the recesses of their emotional and mental nature. There is much that can be learned by the ordinary individual to promote wholeness. Liberating the potential of a person can holistically transform them, which in turn affects their whole world. Reviewing belief systems, self-image, patterns of behavior, and deep-seated drives or motivations within a clear context can liberate great reserves of healing energy and affirm an individual's life and purpose.

Within the range of therapies there may be differing views of a human being's psychic makeup that focus upon different parts of our "inner geography." But they can all aid in the release of mental and emotional blocks. Approaches range from traditional psychoanalysis to the humanistic therapies and those called transpersonal, which recognize and work with the spiritual dimension as well as other aspects of our being.

SPIRITUAL INTEGRATION

Inherent in the holistic view of humanity is the perception of an integrating center, a spiritual core, a source of life and love. Healing can be brought about by integrating the experiences of daily existence with the inner core of our lives. There are many varieties of spiritual paths. The paths to God are as numerous as the people going there. In approaching human spirituality from the angle of healing, there are ways in which we can open to our higher selves and ways in which others can affect our "spiritual bodies." One approach would be prayer or a variety of meditation, and another spiritual healing or the techniques that work with what has been called the "subtle body." A factor that must not be overlooked is the possibility of miracles, a profound form of healing, and perhaps the only time that healing is done *for* a person and then it is only done by the spirit.

In all this we can see how the inner process of healing can be helped by a multiplicity of approaches. Many are the ways to free up and liberate the body's innate powers of wholeness and regeneration. However, no matter how sincere the attempts at healing, if we don't also look at

26   THE COMPLETE HERBS SOURCEBOOK

our lifestyle and way of being in the world to see what changes are indicated—the healing won't really work.

An important first step in the process of healing is the removing of value judgments. Being sick is not "bad" and being well is not "good." This is not to deny that one is more preferable and appropriate, but the rigidity and pressure contained within any judgment of good and bad will itself contribute to the disease. Illness may often be an opportunity created within one's life to change and transform, and seen this way, it may be approached with less resistance and disapproval. There are times when the problem is an opportunity to use strong will and fight the illness, and times to be still and at peace with the process. It is impossible to generalize as to the way of approaching the lesson offered. To judge it—and yourself—is a mistake.

It is worth remembering that we are what we eat, but also what we breathe, what we think, what we say, what we see. So while all of what has been said concerns our inner lives, the interaction with the environment we choose to live in is just as important. The important word here is *choose*. We can choose to change. We are powerful and free in our lives. If we cannot change the outer situation, then we can change our attitude to it.

The belief system through which we interpret the world colors our experience of both the world and ourselves. Beliefs can limit our expression and the clear flow of energy and consciousness through us. It is good to examine our beliefs to see if they support our life and purpose. In tandem with this goes self-image. The way we see ourselves, our gifts and limitations, needs and strengths, physical appearance and health, will largely create us. Self-image can have a profound impact on health, as skin and weight problems demonstrate, although other factors may be involved, too.

If our relationships are not healthy, we won't be. We can create relationships that affirm us, that reinforce our movement toward health and wholeness. Consciously choose the people with whom you share your life and work. Do your home, work place, and recreational space reflect to you joy and positivity? If not, then change it or yourself. This may be very difficult, but then that is what healing is about, transforming ourselves and our world.

The most important relationship of all is possibly the one we have with nature and the planet. Well-being is dependent upon our interaction with Gaia, and wholeness can be expressed through a conscious interplay with the greater whole of which humanity is part. The spirit of life can freely flow from nature to humanity when given the opportunity. A mutuality of life is then created, the context within which all healthy relationships are built. This experience of nature may be climbing mountains or sitting under a tree. The form is not important. The openness to a communion with nature *is*.

What about the books we read, the movies and television we watch, the billboards we see, the politics we support? Is the music we listen to good for our health? Are your friends good for you? These are all relevant questions, none of which have assumed answers. Healthy music is that which helps you experience your wholeness. For some people this may be Bach, while for others it may be The Grateful Dead. The task is taking responsibility for our own lives. We can choose who we want to be and then create ourselves!

A key to all self-healing is compassion. Expressing compassion for oneself creates an inner ease and clear perspective from which much can change and heal. Compassion grows in an openness to spirit in one's life. The form is not important. The ineffable must be part of one's life; meaning and significance, no matter how indefinable or subtle, must be actively present in one's experience and expression. This may take the form of meditation, prayer, or whatever works for each of us. The form is irrelevant; the content and attitude are crucial. Openness to the experience of soul and spirit is healing and affirms wholeness of being.

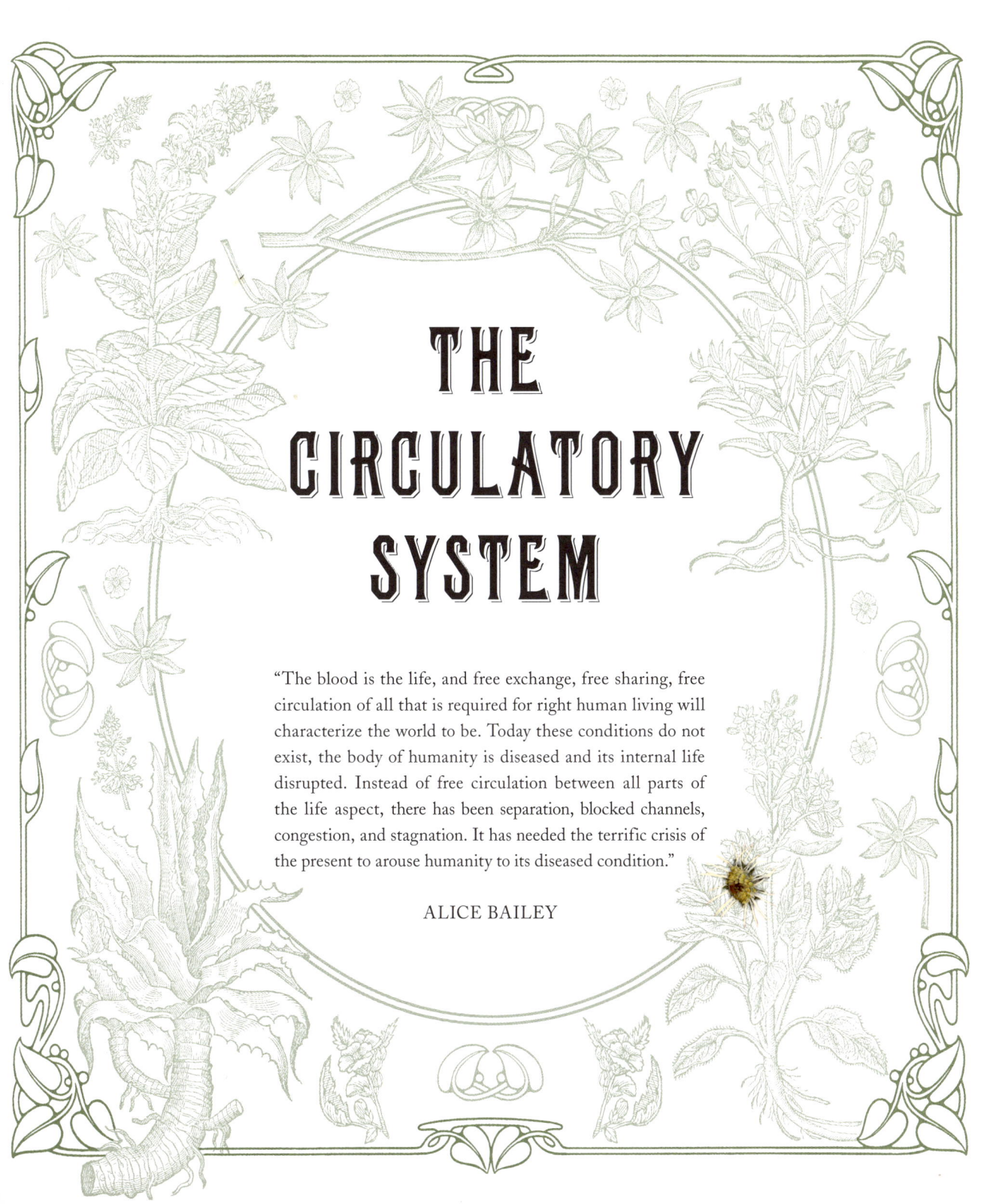

THE CIRCULATORY SYSTEM

"The blood is the life, and free exchange, free sharing, free circulation of all that is required for right human living will characterize the world to be. Today these conditions do not exist, the body of humanity is diseased and its internal life disrupted. Instead of free circulation between all parts of the life aspect, there has been separation, blocked channels, congestion, and stagnation. It has needed the terrific crisis of the present to arouse humanity to its diseased condition."

ALICE BAILEY

The Circulatory System

WE BEGIN OUR TRIP THROUGH THE systems of the body by having a look at the circulatory system, as it is one that connects all the others and affects all of them.

While considering the circulatory system, let us keep in mind that it is a *transportation system* that we are looking at. In this section, we are not yet concerned with what is being transported, namely the blood, which is a combination of various substances made up in different parts of the body. In this section, we will be talking about the health and the right function of the *heart* and the *blood vessels*.

The vitality and tone of the whole circulatory system is fundamental to life and to the integration of all the parts of the body. If there is weakness or congestion present, it will have profound effects on the tissues and organs involved. The blood may be in perfect condition, but if the supply of this blood to the organs is not adequate, there will be problems. Similarly, if waste materials produced in the metabolic process are not removed properly, damage to tissue will quickly result.

From this we can conclude that any disease focused in any organ may have its roots in an insufficiency of the circulatory system, either because the organ is not being properly supplied with blood or because the waste it produces is not being drained off well enough.

When we look at the body in a holistic way and treat any disease from this perspective, we recognize that all organs and systems are connected and influence each other. We have to look at what each one individually contributes to the whole picture. The heart vessels may be involved in any condition and must be helped and aided in the healing process.

In our society the circulatory system is a common site for illnesses, often fatal ones, as we do not take proper care of our heart and blood vessels by our way of living and by our approach to life. Prevention of circulatory problems is easy, and a number of guidelines are set out below.

When major heart problems are already apparent, the matter is somewhat different and care must be taken. Herbal medicine has a lot to offer in the healing of heart failure and cardiac conditions, but any treatment has to be under qualified supervision.

Prevention of Circulatory Disease

Prevention is far better than having to resort to curing a disease that has developed, and prevention means finding ease for body, mind, and spirit.

We call a condition a disease when the body is so worn out that it begins to manifest symptoms. With most people it takes a number of years to get to such a state, as the body is usually able to handle quite a lot for a long time without breaking down. There is often a steady decline: we are not quite as strong and vigorous as last year; our health is not quite as good as it could be.

It is declining toward a state of disease, but we don't notice it until something breaks down and we are sick.

There are specific details relating to the cardiovascular system that should be borne in mind. They apply not only to anyone who already has problems with this particular system, or whose way of life puts them into a "high-risk" category for developing cardiovascular conditions. They also apply to anyone who does not want to develop problems in that area.

There are four factors that need to be considered:

Exercise: It is vital for the whole system that it is used and at least occasionally stretched. The only way to ensure that heart and blood vessels are truly used is to exercise so the heartbeat sped up and we become short of breath. This does not mean that people should jog themselves into exhaustion every day! Regular exercises that feel right and are enjoyable are the key. Moderation in all things, exercise included.

Diet: As far as the circulatory system is concerned, the most important single factor that causes problems is the intake of fat, which most of us eat far too much of. Over the last couple of years, we have heard a lot about a relationship between the consumption of saturated fats and the level of cholesterol (one of these fats) in the blood, leading to various cardiovascular problems. One recommended way out was to eat unsaturated fats instead of the dangerous saturated ones, mainly by changing from animal fats to vegetable fats. According to new research, however, it is not all that simple. The evidence is pointing to dangers in the consumption of unsaturated fats, too, and the only safe way out is to reduce your total fat intake, which in general means cutting it out altogether. And this means a decrease in the consumption of visible fat (in meat, butter, oils) and also of invisible fat (in cake, pastries, thick soups, mayonnaise, cheese, milk, and other dairy products, including eggs), which often makes up the bulk of our fat intake. Instead, most of our food should consist of plenty of fresh fruit and vegetables, whole grains, beans, and peas—the latter two being considered capable of reducing the cholesterol level in the blood. The minimum of salt should be used.

Tobacco and Alcohol: It is vital that anyone with concerns about their health, and especially about the heart and blood vessels, should stop smoking and keep the intake of alcohol to a reasonable amount.

Stress: There is a close correlation between the level of stress in your life and the occurrence of health problems, particularly with problems in the cardiovascular system. "Stress" is a relative concept. It would be more appropriate to consider the individual's ability to deal with the stress in their life rather than to look at the stress itself. There are a number of tools available to us today to help take responsibility in our lives and to deal with stress and emotional tensions. It is possible to help with tension by using herbal remedies, but it is far better and more realistic to go to the underlying cause within us and change it. This involves consciousness and sometimes courage. Relaxation therapy, re-evaluation cocounseling, and humanistic and transpersonal psychology all have much to offer. Disease can be prevented by bringing ease into one's life. Psychological and spiritual harmony will create the inner environment for bodily harmony.

Herbs for the Circulatory System

As with all systems of the body, an identification of herbs for that system is a necessary simplification. The body is an integrated whole, and the herbal approach to healing recognizes this. Any problems arising in a particular system may be caused by the state of health and vitality in any other part of the body, and therefore any herb can have a role to play in the treatment of any system. However, to enable our limited human comprehension to grasp the basics of herbalism, it is valid to identify herbs that have a specific role to play in this system.

To keep things simple and to avoid complex groupings, the herbs will be differentiated into those that have a direct action on the heart and those that affect the peripheral vessels.

Heart Tonics

The most important herbal agents for the heart include *Broom, Bugleweed, Figwort, Hawthorn, Lily of the Valley, Motherwort,* and *Night-Blooming Cereus.*

You will notice that herbs such as *Foxglove (Digitalis)* and *Mediterranean Squill* have been left out of the list, even though these plant remedies are used extensively by orthodox medicine as effective treatments for heart failure. However, as there are marked dangers with the use of *Foxglove*, this poisonous plant has been left out. This does not mean that effective heart remedies are not available to us. By far the most important one on the list is *Lily of the Valley*. We shall digress slightly here to discuss the action of this herb and compare it to *Foxglove*, as there are some important lessons involved.

As mentioned in the chapter on plant constituents, the remedies often used to treat the heart are rich in a group of chemicals called cardiac glycosides. These complex chemicals have the astounding ability to stimulate the muscles of the heart in a way that strengthens its contraction and ensures that more blood is pumped through the body. The efficiency of the heart is thereby increased, but with the help of these chemicals the oxygen required by the heart muscle for this work is not increased and thus we do not have to worry about any oxygen deficiency.

With *Foxglove*, however, there is an added danger, as some of its constituents can accumulate in the body and lead to poisoning, which does not happen with *Lily of the Valley*. As pharmacological analysis shows, there are a number of different cardiac glycosides present in *Lily of the Valley*, such as Convallatoxin, Convallatoxol, Convallarin, Convallatoxin, Convallaside, and Convallatoxoloside. (The root of all these outlandish words is the Latin name of the herb, *Convallaria majalis*.) While these many biochemicals are present, only two act directly on the heart, and of these the most important one is Convallatoxin.

To a pharmacist this would imply that the rest are useless, which could not be further from the truth, as the other glycosides have been found to increase the solubility of the active ones by up to 500 times. The obvious value of this is that a smaller dose is necessary, as an increase in solubility will also increase the "bioavailability." Furthermore, it was found that though Convallatoxin has a fast effect and is oxidized and excreted rapidly, the whole plant has a longer effective time in the body. Others of the apparently inactive glycosides are being converted by the body into the directly active ones as and when needed. A danger of poisoning does not exist with *Lily of the Valley*, as its glycosides have a unique chemical structure that ensures that they are easily excreted and do not build up in the body.

In *Lily of the Valley* we have a good example of the synergistic way in which herbs can work. From all this analytical and biochemical study, we can see that the whole is indeed more than the sum of its parts. The action of the whole plant cannot be predicted by knowing the separate chemical constituents, as the effects are brought about through complex, integrated interactions. All this goes to show that ancient wisdom about this herb, passed down to us through the generations, can be supported by modern science when a wide enough perspective is used.

Let us now have a closer look at the specific heart tonics mentioned previously. They all act in a way that tones and strengthens heart function and will be given here with some brief indications of their use in the circulatory system. Please consult "The Herbal" section for more details.

Lily of the Valley: This can be used where the strength of the heart is insufficient, as in angina or in the treatment of the aging heart, especially when there are deposits in the blood vessels.

Night-Blooming Cereus: This can be used similarly to *Lily of the Valley* and is especially useful where there is any change in the rhythm of the heartbeat.

Hawthorn Berries: These constitute one of the most valuable remedies for the cardiovascular system, strengthening the force of the contraction of the heart muscle while also acting to dilate the vessels of the coronary circulation. They can be used in most circulatory problems, as they are amphoteric (i.e., they will relax or stimulate the heart according to its need) and normalize the heart function.

Motherwort: This herb is a relaxing nervine and a valuable emmenagogue. Its value for the circulatory system is even noted in its Latin name, *Leonurus cardiaca*. It will greatly strengthen and normalize the function of the heart.

Broom: It can be considered as the primary heart diuretic. While it strengthens and normalizes the heartbeat, it also rids the body of any buildup of water that is due to insufficient heart strength. Care has to be taken, though, as it may increase blood pressure.

Figwort: Although this is primarily an herb known for skin problems, it also increases the strength of the heart contractions.

Bugleweed: While this herb increases the strength of the heartbeat, it also reduces its rate. It is a valuable relaxant as well.

HERBS FOR THE CIRCULATION

As with herbs for the heart, there is a vast range of remedies available to help and heal the vessels of the circulatory system, but here we limit ourselves to specific ones.

The most important herbal agents for the circulation include *Broom, Buckwheat, Cayenne, Dandelion, Ginger, Hawthorn, Horse Chestnut, Lime Blossom, Mistletoe*, and *Yarrow*.

As you can see, some of these are also heart tonics, while some are diaphoretics and stimulate the peripheral circulation (*Cayenne, Ginger*), and yet others are diuretics (*Yarrow*). This again goes back to the fact that the body will manifest problems in an area because of a whole range of causes and contributing factors stemming from the interdependence of all the systems.

DIURETICS

When circulatory problems arise, there is often a need to aid the body in the removal of water from the system. When the heart is weak and fails to circulate the blood efficiently through the kidneys or when the blood vessels (particularly in the venous system of the legs) are weak, a buildup of water in parts of the body can occur and in such conditions diuretics such as *Broom, Dandelion, Lily of the Valley*, and

THE CIRCULATORY SYSTEM

Yarrow can help. Perhaps the most important diuretic for circulatory problems is *Dandelion*. When any other remedy is used to increase the power of the heart, there is always the danger of causing a potassium deficiency in the body, which in turn would aggravate the heart problem. Therefore, whenever a diuretic is prescribed in orthodox medicine, there is also a potassium supplement added. However, as *Dandelion* already contains a high level of potassium, there is an overall gain of it whenever *Dandelion* is used as a diuretic, which makes its value apparent.

The cardioactive herbs *Broom* and *Lily of the Valley* are included here, as *Broom* is a strong diuretic and because *Lily of the Valley* also acts as a strong diuretic if the root of the problem lies in the heart.

NERVINES

Anxiety and stress can lead to cardiovascular problems, and it is often impossible to pinpoint any particular cause. Any specific problem is a manifestation of the whole interacting web of lifestyle, inner reality, and physical tendencies. Whenever there is a cardiovascular problem, the use of relaxing nervines has to be considered, as in many cases anxiety and stress are involved, and sometimes even caused by the problem.

The most useful nervines for cardiovascular problems are *Balm*, *Hops*, *Lime Flowers*, *Motherwort*, *Pasque Flowers*, *Skullcap*, and *Valerian*. The appropriate ones to be used by any individual should be selected by comparing their associated actions in "The Herbal" section of this book.

Patterns of Disease

The conscious and holistic use of herbal medicine has much to offer in the treatment of circulatory problems. It must be emphasized, however, that the more serious heart problems should be treated under medical observation.

While considering these specific conditions and patterns of illness, we have to bear in mind that each person is unique. People are not textbooks!

Heart Weakness

Conventional medicine divides heart problems into many categories, but when using herbs it is not usually necessary to do this, as we are working with herbs that have an overall strengthening effect. Again it must be emphasized that chronic heart failure has to be treated by trained professionals.

To strengthen the heart, the following mixture should be taken over an extended period of time:

Hawthorn Berries	2 parts
Motherwort	2 parts
Lily of the Valley	1 part

Drink a cup of this three times a day.

At the same time, an adequate intake of potassium has to be ensured—for instance, by eating grapes and tomatoes. If there is any water retention, one part of *Dandelion* should be added to the mixture. If tension or anxiety is present, use the following:

Balm	1 part
Lime Blossom	1 part

This tea should also be drunk three times a day or as often as needed.

If this does not prove strong enough, use *Skullcap* and *Valerian* instead, as described in the chapter on the nervous system.

Palpitations

Quite separate from any organic heart disease, racing of the heartbeat can occur and can be caused by a whole range of factors, from menopause and allergies to fear and sexual excitement.

Apart from doing something about the specific cause whenever it is appropriate, there are a number of effective remedies that will reduce erratic and fast heartbeats without affecting the heart in an adverse way. In addition to the remedies described for normalizing heart activity, *Broom, Bugleweed, Mistletoe, Motherwort, Passion Flower*, and *Valerian* are indicated.

A common occurrence is the speeding up of the heart rate due to anxiety and stress, which has been given the label "nervous tachycardia." An excellent basic mixture for this problem is the following:

Motherwort	2 parts
Mistletoe	1 part
Valerian	1 part

This should be drunk three times a day or as needed.

If there is any suggestion of heightened blood pressure or heart problems, *Hawthorn Berries* should be added.

Angina Pectoris

This painful and distressing condition is brought about when the blood supply to the heart itself is deficient and leads to a lack of usable oxygen in the heart tissue, often brought about by physical exertion or emotional stress. This problem can be treated effectively and reversed if the treatment is spread over an adequate period of time.

The aim of the therapy is to bring more blood, rich in oxygen, to the heart via the coronary arteries. A two-fold process has to bring this about. Initially, the vessels can be dilated to allow more blood to flow through, but as a long-term treatment, any blockage that is present in the vessels has also to be cleared. The key to this is the use of *Hawthorn Berries*, which will do both, given enough time and taken regularly.

An addition of *Lime Blossom* leads to excellent results, as it has the unique ability to clear any cholesterol deposits in vessels and guard against any further buildup. A basic mixture:

Hawthorn Berries	3 parts
Motherwort	2 parts
Lime Blossom	2 parts
Lily of the Valley	1 part

This tea should be drunk three times a day over a long period; it will not immediately relieve the pain of an attack.

If there is an additional problem with high blood pressure, *Mistletoe* should be added to the mixture.

Angina has to be treated within the context of the complete state of health; the individual must be treated as a whole being and any other problem should also be taken into account. The state of the nervous system should be considered and treated appropriately. Further, the condition of the digestive system can have a profound effect. Constipation has to be treated as a priority, as any chronic constipation can put unnecessary pressure on the heart.

The guidelines at the beginning of the chapter regarding prevention should be taken into account, particularly the dietary limitations, which are vital, as is the recognition of stress. Exercise has to be moderate and gentle until the condition has been brought under control, otherwise an attack might be triggered off even though herbal medicine is taken. Raw *Garlic* in the diet can be most helpful in this problem as in all cardiovascular conditions.

HIGH BLOOD PRESSURE

High blood pressure (hypertension) is a very common problem in our society. It can be caused by a range of primarily physical problems, in which case these must be seen to as appropriate, but it may also occur without any clear cause. It is this so-called "essential hypertension" that will be discussed here. While no specific cause is found with this very common variety of heightened blood pressure, there are some easily identifiable contributing factors. There is often a genetic disposition, stemming from a hereditary gift from one's parents, but this tendency need not actually manifest physically if steps for its prevention are taken.

Stress and anxiety play a large part in this condition. Emotional problems, work pressure, and the state of the world (*especially* the state of the world!) can all contribute to a state of mind that is reflected in the body in a pattern of tension, inflexibility and constriction, a tightening of the whole being, so raising the blood pressure. There is a direct relationship mediated through the nerves, leading to a constriction of the peripheral blood vessels and influencing the heartbeat. Relaxation therapy and body-work techniques such as massage are very valuable in such cases, as they ease up the body. (See the section on "Relaxation Exercises" in the chapter on the nervous system.)

Dietary factors can also be involved in two ways. When the diet is too rich in fats and carbohydrates, there is a strong chance that some of the extra fat is deposited on the walls of the blood vessels. This atheroma, the fatty deposit, will directly raise the blood pressure. High blood pressure can also be caused by an allergy to certain foods. Whereas sometimes the allergy may be obvious and overt, in many cases it is subclinical and not easy to detect. Such mild reactions often show themselves through an elevation of blood pressure. A common cause is an allergy to dairy products. This can easily be checked by withdrawing all milk products for one to two weeks, and seeing what happens, then reintroducing them and comparing blood pressures, as well as any subjective impressions.

The level of blood pressure in the body is maintained by a complex mechanism. Complex as it is, we can draw valuable conclusions by comparing it to basic hydraulics: if there is an increase of fluid in the system, the pressure will go up as through water retention; similarly, if the volume decreases by constriction of vessels or "furring" by deposits; or if the force of the pumping goes up if there are heart problems.

There are a number of herbs that will dilate the peripheral blood vessels, thereby increasing the total volume of the system. Similarly, there are herbs that will help the kidneys pass more water, thus reducing the amount of fluid in the system. There are others to normalize the activity of the heart, safely decreasing the force with which the blood is pumped through the body. The most important remedies are *Buckwheat, Cramp Bark, Garlic, Hawthorn Berries, Lime Blossom, Mistletoe,* and *Yarrow.*

As always, the actual approach to each individual will vary according to their unique needs. As a basic guide, this mixture is effective:

Hawthorn Berries	2 parts
Lime Blossom	2 parts
Yarrow	2 parts
Mistletoe	1 part

This tea should be drunk three times a day.

In addition to this, *Garlic* may be eaten, preferably raw. If there is a lot of tension in the body, one part of *Cramp Bark* should be included in the mix. If there is much anxiety and stress, include *Skullcap* and *Valerian*. When headaches accompany high blood pressure, include one part of *Wood Betony* in the mixture.

> **CAUTION:**
> Do not use *Broom* as a diuretic in cases of raised blood pressure.

By using this mixture over a period of time, blood pressure will return to a normal level. The mixture is safe and does not artificially depress the blood pressure. None of these herbs are able to do that, because they are normalizers and will not lower blood pressure to an inappropriate level.

LOW BLOOD PRESSURE

When the blood pressure drops below the individual's normal level, it can cause as much distress as when heightened. Apart from being directly related to organic problems, there is often an association with debility and exhaustion.

The herbal approach to such a problem combines help for physical and nervous exhaustion with remedies that tone up the circulatory system and return the blood pressure to a normal level. Depending on the cause, different herbs are appropriate. Where stress and nervous exhaustion are involved, the nervine tonics should be used—most important in this case being *Oats*, otherwise either *Kola* or *Skullcap*, depending on the individual need. Bitters such as *Gentian* and *Wormwood* should be considered to help activate the digestive process with a strengthening effect. A basic mixture:

Broom	1 part
Hawthorn Berries	1 part
Kola Nut	1 part

This tea can be drunk three times a day.

When there is any degree of debility present, it is valuable to take *Ginseng* regularly.

THE CIRCULATORY SYSTEM

ARTERIOSCLEROSIS

Arteriosclerosis is characterized by a thickening and hardening of the artery walls, caused in the early stages by a gradual deposit of calcium, restricting the flow of blood to the cells of the body. In further stages, this can develop into a buildup of cholesterol and fatty deposits in the artery walls, leading to a speedy degeneration of the vessels and causing profound problems. These fatty deposits are called atheromas. They can build up in the aorta, in the arteries of the heart, and in the brain. Arteriosclerosis is one of the most common causes of death in the Western world.

Arteriosclerosis is a primary product of inappropriate lifestyle, and a lot can be done to heal the body by making necessary changes. Diet, stress, and lack of exercise are critical factors usually requiring change, as is the use of tobacco and alcohol. A major part of the treatment of arteriosclerosis can be found in the section on prevention of cardiovascular problems.

There are also a number of herbs that can help in this condition, above all *Lime Blossom*, as it has a specific anti-atheroma action and in long-term use will guard against the deposition of cholesterol, also helping the body in the removal of any that has already built up. The long-term use of *Garlic* has a similar effect.

Specific herbs for this condition include *Garlic, Hawthorn Berries, Lime Blossom, Mistletoe,* and *Yarrow*. As you may notice, these are also herbs found to be most effective in the treatment of raised blood pressure, which often accompanies arteriosclerosis. The same mixture as for high blood pressure can be used, if the proportion of *Lime Blossom* is raised to three parts.

THROMBOSIS AND PHLEBITIS

When there is a buildup of atheromas, there is an added danger that a piece of it or clotted blood may enter the bloodstream. Both can cause a vessel to be blocked, which leads to a deficiency of oxygen downstream from the blocked vessel. The seriousness of this thrombosis depends on where in the body the block occurs. It can be a minor problem, but it also is a possible cause of death. It must be treated to make sure that no new focus for thrombus formation develops. The treatment should be based on herbs that ensure a healthy circulatory system, together with following the advice given for arteriosclerosis.

When a clot occurs in the veins of the legs, the condition is labeled phlebitis. In cases of local inflammations and pains, lotions, compresses, or poultices are most effective. Herbs such as *Arnica, Comfrey, Hawthorn Berries,* and *Marigold* should be used in the external treatment of these conditions.

VARICOSE VEINS

Lack of exercise, obesity, pregnancy, and anything that reduces the circulation in the legs, such as tight clothing or sitting with crossed legs, can contribute to the development of varicose veins, a name for veins that have become enlarged, twisted, and swollen. They can appear anywhere in the body, but are most commonly found in the legs, as the heart on its own is not strong enough to return the venous blood from the lower part of the body without the pumping action of the leg muscles, which only happens when these muscles are used and exercised. It is essential that adequate exercise be undertaken and that the feet are elevated when sitting for a long time, to counteract the effects of gravity.

Herbal medicine has a lot to offer for this condition, as long as its action is supported by exercise. The diet should be rich in fruit and green vegetables. Constipation has to be avoided. Vitamin B-complex, C, and E should be added to the diet. The herbs to be used for this condition should stimulate the peripheral circulation and thereby aid the flow of blood in the legs. Appropriate herbs are *Cayenne*, *Ginger*, and *Prickly Ash Bark* or *Berries*. Furthermore, herbs that strengthen the blood vessels have to be included—for example, *Buckwheat*, *Hawthorn Berries*, or *Horse Chestnut*. If there is any water retention that leads to swelling of the ankles or legs, a diuretic such as *Dandelion* or *Yarrow* has to be included.

This mixture approaches the problem from all angles:

Hawthorn Berries	3 parts
Horse Chestnut	3 parts
Prickly Ash Bark (or *Berries*)	2 parts
Yarrow	2 parts
Ginger	1 part

This should be drunk three times a day.

When there is a local inflammation with pain, a lotion or compress of *Witch Hazel* will often ease the discomfort, otherwise *Marigold*, *Comfrey*, or *Hawthorn Berries* can be used.

VARICOSE ULCERS

There is a very close connection between the development of varicose ulcers and the condition of the veins, their activity, and tone, which is also reflected in varicose veins. When the legs are not sufficiently drained of blood and tissue fluid—due to the factors described for varicose veins—the water-logging leads to the tissue breaking down and ulcers developing. They are notoriously difficult to heal. Here it is even more important that adequate exercise be undertaken and that the feet are elevated, to counteract the effect of gravity on the legs.

The herbs to be used here are the same as for varicose veins, but a higher proportion of diuretics and alteratives have to be used. External treatment is vital here. If there is any secondary infection, it can be treated by a compress made from *Marigold*, *Marshmallow*, and *Echinacea*, which has to be changed often. When the infection has subsided, change the compress for a poultice of powdered *Comfrey*, *Marigold*, and *Marshmallow* made into a thick paste and applied to the surrounding tissue of the ulcer and kept in place with the aid of an elastic bandage.

BAD CIRCULATION AND CHILBLAINS

When the circulation of the extremities is not adequate, leading to cold hands and feet, the following mixture can be very helpful:

Prickly Ash Bark	3 parts
Hawthorn Berries	3 parts
Ginger	1 part

This should be drunk three times a day.

When there are any unbroken chilblains, they can be treated successfully by the application of a thin layer of *Cayenne* ointment, applied very sparingly.

The Lymphatic System

The lymphatic system is a series of vessels whose job it is to return intercellular and intracellular fluid back to the bloodstream from whence it came. However, in the process of this apparently passive job of transportation, much vital work goes on. It is through the lymphatic drainage of the cells, tissues, and organs that cleansing largely occurs. The proper flow and coherence of the lymphatic system is thus vital to the body function and must be considered when approaching the body from a holistic point of view. A second major function of this system occurs in the lymphatic glands, as the antimicrobial activity of the body is partially located there. This function has been considered in various parts of the book, but especially in the chapter on ears, nose, throat, and eyes. Swollen glands may occur wherever there are lymph glands, common sites being the throat, under the arms, the breasts, and the tops of the legs in the groin. Herbs like *Cleavers, Echinacea, Golden Seal, Marigold*, and *Pokeweed Root* may be considered to be lymphatic cleansers and may be used as such wherever they are needed.

A cleansing diet is called for wherever there is any suspicion of lymphatic trouble. A fruit-based cleansing diet would be best. In such a diet, the following sources of food should be avoided or kept to a minimum. This will give the lymphatic system a rest from overload of the following inappropriate foods:

—Red meats
—Greasy, fatty foods and fried foods
—Cheese, butter, cream, milk
—Vinegar and pickles
—Alcohol
—Sugar and sugar-based products
—Artificial additives, preservatives, colorings, flavorings

Avoidance of these foods will help the body, but with the use of the right foods, an active cleansing through the diet can take place. Fresh fruit and vegetables provide the basis here. For a thorough cleansing, it is best to go on a fruit diet for a while and then reintroduce other foods. The following is a short list of appropriate foods:

—Fresh fruit, especially oranges, grapes, and apples
—Fresh green vegetables
—White meat and white fish, if desired

An herbal mixture that will aid the lymphatic system wherever the problem arises is the following:

Echinacea	2 parts
Cleavers	1 part
Golden Seal	1 part
Pokeweed Root	1 part

This should be drunk three times a day.

This sort of mixture could be used in other conditions wherever it is thought that the lymphatic drainage needs support.

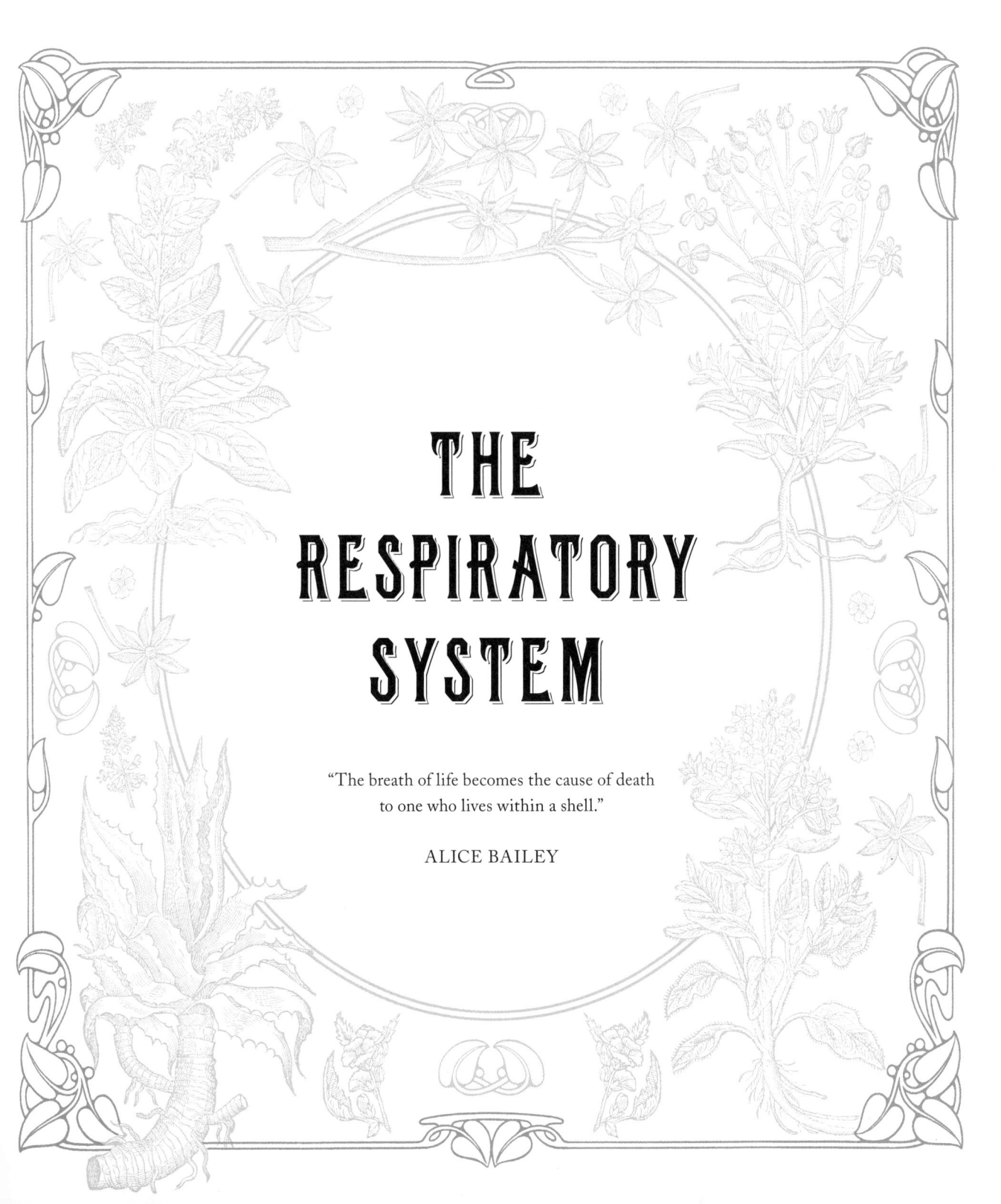

THE RESPIRATORY SYSTEM

"The breath of life becomes the cause of death
to one who lives within a shell."

ALICE BAILEY

The Respiratory System

THE AIR WE BREATHE IS SPIRITUAL ecology in action. When we draw in the breath of life, we share that air with all other human beings, all life on our planet. It is through respiration that our oneness with the trees becomes a manifest fact and our communion with the oceans has immediate impact. Through the circulation of the gases and energy of the atmosphere, the reality of the planetary whole reveals itself, with implications for all human life. This vision underlies holistic healing as much as it does ecology—the science of the whole. From the perspective of spiritual ecology, we can repeat the question of the mystics: *"Who is breathing?"*

Every minute, usually unconsciously, we breathe in and out between 10 and 15 times. We move enough air back and forth every day to blow up several thousand balloons. In this way, the body can extract the oxygen it needs from the air and discharge waste carbon dioxide from the blood.

While only one-fifth of the air is oxygen, this is the part our body needs for our survival, as oxygen is needed by every cell in the body to release the energy that is locked in food reserves. Many cells can survive for a period of time without oxygen; others need a constant supply. Brain cells die—and cannot be replaced—if they lack oxygen for more than a few minutes.

Supplying the cells of the body with oxygen is the responsibility of the respiratory and circulatory systems. This process is controlled by the brain via the *medulla oblongata* in the brain stem, where messages concerning blood composition are integrated with other information, thus regulating the appropriate breathing rhythm.

The ebb and flow of the breath draws life energy into the being. Thus if there are respiratory disturbances that inhibit gaseous exchange, they can lead to a lowering of the body's vitality, an increase in metabolic disorders, and degeneration of tissue.

The anatomy and physiology of the respiratory system is a complex and beautiful embodiment of integration and wholeness.

Prevention of Respiratory Disease

We are not only what we eat, but also what we breathe. Any problem with breathing will not only affect other organs and systems, but may well cause disease in these systems. However, as the body is a whole, the reverse is also true. When the lungs need to be treated, we also have to look at the circulatory system; much of what has been said about the heart and the circulation is relevant to the lungs. We should also look at the condition of the digestive system and especially of the organs of elimination, as the lungs share the role of removing waste with the bowels, the kidneys, and the skin. If a problem develops in any of these systems, the body compensates by increasing the load on the others. There are limits to the amount of waste the lungs can put up with if, for instance, the bowels are clogged.

Most pathological changes in tissues can be prevented if the environmental milieu of the cells is constantly rich in oxygen. The amount of oxygen the circulation supplies to the tissue is largely controlled by respiration.

From all this, it is apparent that the best preventative measures for this system are regular exercise and good breathing. While we take breathing for granted, conscious and proper breathing is regarded, even in orthodox medical circles, as invaluable. The central role of the breath in many spiritual paths should perhaps give us a clue here.

As with all disease, the best prophylactic is a positive lifestyle. Diet, exercise, and quality of life all have a profound influence on the health of the lungs.

To ensure healthy lungs, the inner environment must be in harmony, and so too must be the outer environment. If the air we breathe is polluted, it will disrupt the ecology of the lungs just as it disrupts the ecology of any forest. Air contaminated with chemicals and particles, gases and smoke, should be avoided. This brings us to tobacco. Smoking puts a wall of tar and ash between the individual and the world so that a free ecological flow cannot take place in the lungs. This can lead to an impressive host of problems, from bronchitis to cancer, without taking into account all the effects of a diminished oxygen supply to the rest of the body. If we are to heal ourselves and our world, here is a good place to start. Eating a whole food diet and living in the country pales a bit when faced with 20 cigarettes a day!

There are other specific dangers that can be recognized and avoided. In the case of infections, the simplest answer is to just avoid contact with it. However, as this is often socially impossible, we need to maintain our natural defenses at their peak. A word is in place here about the questionable use of immunization. The body, if given the chance, is capable of great feats of self-defense, as long as we provide a balanced, vitamin-rich diet in combination with a lifestyle that is healthy in thought and feeling as much as in action. In this context, it is vital to curb the misuse of antibiotics. While these drugs, used at the right time in the right way, can save lives, they can also reduce the innate defense systems of the body to impotence. In addition to the reduction of our defense, they also in the long run create—in an evolutionary sense—highly resistant bacteria, so that problems become more and more difficult to be treated. Over the last 50 years, doctors have had to watch alarming developments in this direction. With correct lifestyle and the use of herbal remedies when needed, antibiotics can often be avoided.

Herbs for the Respiratory System

All aspects of the respiratory system can benefit from appropriate herbal remedies. Herbs can aid the activity of the mucous membranes and ensure that gaseous exchange through these membranes can occur; they can activate the secretion of lung tissue so that the air is sufficiently moistened and the membranes protected; they can augment neurological responses regulating the breath; they can tone up the circulation and ensure that blood bathes the tissues properly, and help by stimulating the whole of the glandular and excretory processes to ensure a clean and harmonious inner environment.

As we view the respiratory system in the context of the whole, it is evident that to truly heal any condition focused in that area we have to look at and be prepared to treat the whole of the body. Nature has been bountiful in the range of actions of the "pectoral" herbs available to us, thus giving us the possibility of working within a wide context.

While it is inadvisable to classify herbs strictly by their actions, it may be of value to lay some broad guidelines. We will look at respiratory stimulants, respiratory relaxants, amphoteric remedies, and respiratory demulcents.

RESPIRATORY STIMULANTS

Herbs in this category act as stimulants to the nerves and muscles of the respiratory system by triggering a neurological reflex via the sensory endings in the digestive system. This causes "expectoration." Expectorants encourage the loosening and subsequent expulsion of mucus from the respiratory system. Plants that fit into this category include *Bittersweet*, *Cowslip*, *Daisy*, *Senega*, *Bouncing Bet (aka Soapwort)*, *Squill*, and *Thuja*.

RESPIRATORY RELAXANTS

The primary action of these plants is to relax the tissue of the lungs, which will be most useful in any problem connected with tension and overactivity. In a seemingly paradoxical way, the easing of tension promotes the flow of mucus and thus allows expectoration to occur. Many plants can be included in this group, but *Angelica*, *Aniseed*, *Coltsfoot*, *Elecampane*, *Ephedra*, *Flaxseed*, *Grindelia*, *Hyssop*, *Plantain*, *Pill-Bearing Spurge*, *Sundew*, *Thyme*, *Wild Cherry Bark*, and *Wild Lettuce* are representatives.

AMPHOTERIC REMEDIES

The concept of amphotericity is of great value when we deal with the apparently contradictory actions of many plants. The term is borrowed from chemistry, where it is used to describe a substance that is capable of acting as either an acid or an alkali. Amphoterics, which are normalizers, change and adapt their action, depending on the conditions. That such a concept should find a place in herbal medicine might at first seem odd. In orthodox medicine a remedy is expected to have a clearly definable effect, which should be related to the dosage and easily controlled. If we see the body as essentially mechanical, this makes sense. However, in a holistic view it must be remembered that the body is seen as an integrated, synergistic whole, and that the work of the healer is to augment and aid the vital recuperative processes naturally at work. Thus we find that the amphoteric herbs work in a way that suits the systems at a particular time, using the body's wisdom to do that which is appropriate.

The best respiratory amphoterics are *Bloodroot, Lobelia, Mullein, Pleurisy Root*, and *White Horehound*.

DEMULCENTS

Demulcents soothe, relieve, and soften irritated or inflamed mucous membranes, as their mucilaginous, slippery characteristics enable them to coat, protect, and lubricate the membranes and other tissue surfaces. Under their protective help, healing can take place.

Many of the already mentioned herbs are demulcents, the most valuable ones for the lungs being *Coltsfoot, Comfrey Root, Flaxseed, Licorice, Lungwort Moss, Marshmallow Leaf*, and *Mullein*.

Patterns of Disease of the Respiratory System

In practice, the various respiratory diseases and syndromes that have been labeled with a name can be viewed as the manifestation of two sorts of respiratory defects: congestion or spasm. Congestion is brought about by an overburdening of the lungs with mucus, either excessive production or inadequate excretion of it, which in time leads to degenerative effects. Spasms of the bronchial muscles constitute the other group of respiratory problems and can be caused by a number of factors.

While some conditions do not fit into either category (such as lung cancer), they provide a useful frame for a holistic treatment of the lungs.

CONGESTION

Orthodox medicine often considers infection by bacteria or viruses to be the cause of a congestive state of the lungs, ears, nose, or throat. It may be more appropriate, however, to regard the infection as the *result* of a congested condition of the lung tissue. Organisms can only thrive within the body if the "soil" is right. In the case of the lungs, congestion provides the right soil for infection, but this is not a healthy and normal state of affairs. Removing only the infection does nothing for the underlying problem; instead, the congestion has also to be treated to prevent a recurrence of the symptoms.

One factor that is most often related to congestion is the mucus content of the diet. If the body's need for mucus-forming foods is exceeded, it will get rid of it by increasing secretion—for instance, into the lungs. If this natural cleansing process is inhibited by antibiotics, the seeds are sown for chronic and perhaps degenerative diseases as the result of congestion.

Therefore, in any respiratory condition where there is excessive mucus, it is essential that a diet low in mucus-forming foods be embarked upon. Whenever there is a buildup of catarrh, such as sinus congestion, a diet that limits the intake of food that feeds the catarrh-forming metabolic paths would help. Even in normal conditions, some people think that accumulations of catarrh, or mucus, are sites in which metabolic waste and toxic material build up, which may eventually overload the body and lead to degenerative disease. There is nothing inherently wrong with mucus; it is a natural body carbohydrate acting as a lubricant and a waste-disposal medium. It is only the excess that we need to watch, and the dietary sources of mucus, which are:

—Dairy products, including goat's milk and yogurt
—Eggs
—Grains, especially gluten-rich ones such as wheat, oats, rye, and barley
—Sugar
—Potatoes and other starchy root vegetables, like rutabagas and turnips

Replace these foods with fresh fruit and juices when following a mucus-free diet.

COUGHS

Coughs can be treated herbally in many ways, and every herbalist will have a favorite herb or mixture. *Coltsfoot* is by far the best standard remedy to have available. Sometimes a combination can be more effective. A basic one with a quite pleasant taste can be made from equal parts of:

> *Coltsfoot*
> *Licorice*
> *Mullein*

Potter's *New Cyclopaedia* contains a mixture of flowers that is not only effective but looks and tastes exquisite.

Potter's Pectoral No. 1:

> *Marshmallow Flowers*
> *Mallow Flowers*
> *Coltsfoot Flowers*
> *Violet Flowers*
> *Mullein Flowers*
> *Red Poppy Flowers*

are combined in equal parts and made into an infusion.

Both of the above mixtures can be taken up to every three hours, although three times a day would be best. Another highly effective remedy is *White Horehound*, but because of its unpleasant taste it needs to be well masked by combining it with *Licorice* or *Aniseed*. This herb was the original constituent of cough drops—an infusion of *White Horehound* plus sugar—lots of it.

If the cough is causing any pressure on a weak heart, it might be useful to add *Motherwort* to the tea. This will help cardiac activity without forcing the heart.

A dry, irritable cough would benefit from respiratory relaxants and demulcents. *Wild Lettuce* and *Coltsfoot* are useful here. Sometimes such coughs can be nervous in origin, in which case it is more advisable to use nervine relaxants.

BRONCHITIS

Bronchitis is an infection of the bronchi, the tube that takes air to the lungs. It may describe any mild pulmonary infection, but, as already said, these fine details and differentiations are not crucial when using herbal medicine. The best herbs to use are pectorals that combine expectorant action to clear the sputum with demulcent properties to soothe the inflamed tissue. The best ones include *Angelica Root, Aniseed, Bloodroot, Coltsfoot, Comfrey Root, Elecampane Root, Flaxseed, Hyssop, Lobelia, Lungwort, Mouse-Ear, Mullein, Senega, Thyme,* and *White Horehound*. Consult "The Herbal" section for more details on each of these, in order to choose the most appropriate herb or combination for your own case.

Antimicrobial herbs are also indicated to fight against any infection. Perhaps the most important one among the many available is *Garlic*, which may be taken in any form, either raw or as *Garlic* oil in capsules. The antiseptic oil in *Garlic* is excreted through the lungs and so directly affects any bacteria there. If *Garlic* is rubbed into the feet, it can still be smelled on the breath. There is now a new Japanese variety of *Garlic* that has the properties without the smell! It is available as KYLORIC capsules. Other good antimicrobials for bronchitis are *Echinacea*, *Eucalyptus*, and *Thyme*. The antiseptic volatile oils contained in *Eucalyptus* and *Thyme* can also be of value in the form of inhalations or baths. For a healing bath in bronchitis and other respiratory infections, take equal parts of *Eucalyptus* and *Thyme* leaves to make a total of four or five tablespoons. Pour 2 pints (1 liter) of boiling water over the mixture and let it stand for 30 minutes. Strain and add the liquid to the bathwater. Bathe at 100°F (38°C) for about 15 minutes.

In addition to the above, it might be helpful to aid the lymphatic system, especially if there are swollen glands. As it would be beneficial to stimulate elimination as well, *Cleavers* and *Pokeweed Root* can be recommended.

PLEURISY

When an infection has given rise to pleurisy or developed into pneumonia, the most important thing is to treat the person for fever, thus helping the whole body and specifically the chest. To this end, diaphoretics are invaluable, usually combined with respiratory demulcents. *Boneset*, *Cayenne*, *Comfrey Root*, *Hyssop*, *Garlic*, *Mullein*, and *Pleurisy Root* will be found to be especially useful. Choose the appropriate ones, depending on the condition of the whole body, and combine them into an infusion.

In addition to this internal help, pleurisy is a condition where a poultice or a compress is called for. A poultice made from *Flaxseed* is excellent in chest complaints:

Take a handful of *Flaxseed* and stir thoroughly with boiling water, until it reaches the consistency of thick paste. Spread the paste about ½ inch (1 centimeter) thick on linen, leaving the sides of the linen free from *Flaxseed* and avoiding lumps from forming. Apply it as hot as possible, covering the whole chest, and leave it on for two hours. Renew it some hours later or the next day. After removing the poultice, sponge the area with warm water, then dry well. To increase its power, sprinkle some *Mustard* powder on the poultice, but do not use *Mustard* for young children or those with sensitive skin.

Alternatively, a compress using an infusion of *Cayenne* may be of value. See the "Preparation of Herbs" section.

WHOOPING COUGH

As this condition can lead to unfortunate complications and to a constitutional weakness in later life, it should be treated thoroughly. The herbs *Sundew* (it may make the urine darker than usual) and *Mouse-Ear* can be regarded as specific remedies and should be included in a mixture:

Mouse-Ear	2 parts
Sundew	1 part
Coltsfoot	1 part
Thyme	1 part
White Horehound	1 part

This should be drunk three times a day.

The mixture may be flavored with *Aniseed* or *Licorice*. If vomiting is accompanying the coughing attacks, it is best to give the drink after a spasm to ensure that it stays down. A *Flaxseed* poultice may be helpful.

In cases of more serious or chronic respiratory conditions—such as emphysema or bronchiectasis—herbal therapy can play a major part in the treatment. Particularly remedies that clear sputum—like *Elecampane* or *Comfrey Root*—should be considered. The herbs recommended for asthma will be useful to regain tissue tone, but above all there is the need for breathing exercises.

SPASM

Besides congestion, the other important kind of respiratory problem is characterized by spasms of the bronchial tube, and the most common "disease" showing this pattern is asthma. The spasms are not the cause of the problem, they are always the result of complex bodily processes—the tip of an iceberg—and treatment has to consider the condition of the whole body.

ASTHMA

Asthma can stem from a combination of causes. There is often an allergic component that triggers asthmatic attacks. In some cases the cause is purely genetic, while in others it may be an aquired reaction due to exposure to an irritant. The state of the nervous tone of the body can also lead to bronchial spasms. In predisposed people, tension, anxiety, hyperactivity, or exhaustion can cause so much stress that an asthma attack is triggered. Similarly, spasms or difficulty in breathing could be caused by osteopathic problems that happen to affect the spot where the thoracic nerve comes out of the spine.

The body is usually able to compensate for and balance a lot of influences, but our lifestyle, diet, posture, and attitude to life are all powerful contributing factors and have to be taken into account in a treatment.

Asthma will respond well to herbal treatment, but it is impossible to give a prescription that is appropriate in all cases, as the various factors involved must be identified and the remedies chosen accordingly. Herbs that help reduce spasm and ease breathing include *Grindelia*, *Lobelia*, *Mouse-Ear*, *Pill-Bearing Spurge*, *Sundew*, and *Wild Cherry*.

If there is production of sputum—which of course must be eliminated—expectorants like *Aniseed*, *Bloodroot*, *Coltsfoot*, *Comfrey Root*, *Licorice*, and *Senega* will help.

Where there is an allergic component, it is good to remember the use of the Chinese herb *Ephedra*.

If the attacks tax the strength of the heart—which they often do—*Motherwort* will be invaluable with its gentle strengthening action.

If any hypertension is involved, *Hawthorn* and *Lime Blossom* will be useful. Anxiety and tension are best treated with *Hops*, *Skullcap*, or *Valerian*.

Occasionally one finds that asthma will respond well to the use of nervines alone, as fear is one of the most potent triggers for an asthma attack. It can even be fear of the attack itself. As such, anything that will augment the person's inner strength and self-image is called for. The nervines will help this process, but a psychotherapeutic approach can be invaluable in addition. Relaxation techniques can help, and some are described in the "Relaxation Exercises" section in the chapter on the nervous system.

A word about dairy products: in many cases of childhood asthma and eczema, milk has been shown to be a trigger for allergic reactions. Such causes may lie at the heart of many adult problems as well. It is vital that our children are breast-fed for as long as possible. When they are weaned, they should not be put on a diet of cow's milk with its various additions. Instead, dairy products should be kept from the diet, as well as overrefined foods, especially sugar. Red meat is inadvisable. The milk and cheese from goats cause none of the problems that cow's milk does and can be used as a substitute.

EARS, NOSE, THROAT, AND EYES

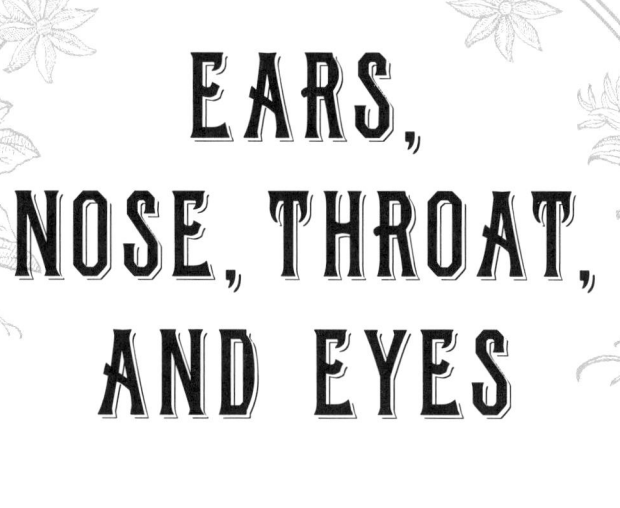

"The senses have often been mistrusted by disciples on the path; it is the world of sense that must be transcended. And in our modern cities these precious qualities are daily assaulted by garish images, noxious air, a cacophony of inharmonious sound. Yet through the gentle use of the senses we can experience joy on the earth plane, encounter beauty, develop sensitivity and discrimination. With right use of the senses we know the immanence of spirit in matter."

HEINRICH S. RIPSZAM

Ears, Nose, Throat, and Eyes

All the organs considered in this section share an anatomical closeness and a functional relationship and are a major interface between the inner and outer environments. This interface is physical, in that there is an exchange of gas in respiration and an input of food in eating, for instance, but there is also the interface of awareness and communication. With our ears we hear the sounds of our world, a sense that reflects the spiritual quality of comprehension. With our nose we smell, an outer reflection of spiritual discernment and idealism. Through the mouth the world of taste opens to us, itself a doorway to discrimination. The voice, generated in the throat, facilitates communication. Through the eyes light is revealed to us, and also the doorway to divinity.

This interaction with the outer environment, and the close connection between these organs through the continuous layer of mucous membranes they share, explains many of the conditions that may occur. It is possible to simply say that a bacterial infection has occurred, or that an allergy reaction is due to a particular grass pollen, but this is a very limited way of looking at symptoms. The systemic roots for a reduction of innate resistance must be sought, as must the cause of an immunological sensitivity.

There is a strong connection between the respiratory system and the ears, nose, and throat. A beautiful example of the body's synergy and self-healing is given by the way that mucus is dealt with by the mucous membranes. Part of the function of the mucus is to trap particles and protect the underlying membranes from invasion. The mucus is disposed of by the "mucociliary escalator." The cells lining the nose and throat have little hairs on them called cilia. These beat in one direction, moving material inexorably downward toward the esophagus and thus into the sterilizing stomach. The lining of the bronchial tubes has cilia that move material upward to the same fate. Under healthy conditions, this works perfectly. However, if there is a change in the consistency of the mucus, the mechanism cannot operate efficiently. Much of the herbal treatment of mucous conditions is therefore based on changing the consistency of the mucus; the cilia will do the rest.

Herbs for Ears, Nose, Throat, and Eyes

As most of the diseases that manifest in this system stem from problems with the mucous membranes, we usually have to deal with catarrh and infections. While we have to remember that these conditions can only be treated in the context of the whole body, certain groups of remedies are especially indicated. For any catarrhal problem, astringents and anticatarrhal plants should be used, but herbs rich in volatile oils can also be very useful. As there is often a microbial involvement, antimicrobials should be considered, as should alteratives to aid the lymphatic system in its defensive and cleansing work.

Especially suited for use in this system are *Balm of Gilead, Boneset, Echinacea, Elderberry Flower, Eucalyptus, Eyebright, Golden Rod, Golden Seal, Hyssop, Marshmallow Leaf, Peppermint, Pokeweed Root, Sage, Silverweed,* and *Wild Indigo.*

The Ears

We are most familiar with the ears' responsibility for hearing, but besides this perception of sound waves they send impulses to the brain that tell which way up we are, as well as information about the movement of the body in the three dimensions of space. To fulfill all these functions, the body has evolved an architecturally beautiful structure that facilitates these complex activities in a miraculously efficient way.

It is beyond the scope of this book to explore problems of the inner ear. We shall concern ourselves with conditions due to infections and catarrh that are within the field of home treatment.

INFECTIONS

Infections of the middle ear often originate in the throat and spread via the eustachian tube. The most important herbs to use are antimicrobial remedies like *Blue Flag, Echinacea, Garlic,* and *Wild Indigo,* which are also anticatarrhal and alterative, with *Echinacea* being the most useful one in all infections of the ears, nose, and throat. The herbs rich in antiseptic oils may be useful but are more indicated in throat or nose complaints. The lymphatic tonics such as *Cleavers* and *Pokeweed Root* have to be considered, as should the anticatarrhal and mucous membrane tonics *Elderberry Flower, Golden Rod,* and *Golden Seal.*

The appropriate herbs should be combined into a tea (except maybe for *Golden Seal,* which because of its bitter taste often has to be given as a powder in capsules, particularly for children). While this internal treatment will be effective, in cases of earaches there can also be the need for an external treatment. An earache can be very painful, particularly in children, and can cause much distress, but there are a number of ways to ease such pain.

EARACHES

The quickest way I know to relieve an earache is to use *Pennywort* juice. Collect some of the round leaves of *Pennywort.* It can occasionally be found growing in walls and on rocks in many places. (More than one herb has the common name of *Pennywort.* This one is unmistakable, as the stem goes down from the center of the round leaf.) Crush a couple of leaves in a sieve and collect the expressed juice. Put a couple of drops (which have to be at body temperature) of this green juice into the painful ear and plug it with a cotton ball.

Mullein oil can be used in the same way, as can warm *Almond* oil or the tincture of *Lobelia.* If none of these are available, make a strong infusion of *Chamomile, Hyssop,* or *Yarrow* and use a couple of drops in the same way.

While any of these remedies will relieve the earache, we have to remember that the infection itself that is causing the pain also needs to be treated.

MASTOIDITIS

A not uncommon condition is an infection of the mastoid process, just behind the ear, which may produce an abscess or a boil that affects the outer or middle ear. This condition should be treated in the same way as boils, as a systemic infection (see the chapter on the skin).

DEAFNESS AND HEARING PROBLEMS

Deafness may be due to neurological causes or due to a catarrhal blockage of the middle ear. Such blockage can be successfully treated with the approach described for nasal catarrh. A buildup of wax in the outer ear canal can also contribute to deafness and should be removed by a competent practitioner.

TINNITUS

Tinnitus is a condition in which one hears a noise within the ear. It can be caused by catarrhal congestion, but regardless of the cause it may be treated effectively by the use of *Black Cohosh* or *Golden Seal*, taken as a tea or in capsules over a period of time.

The Nose

The nasal passages are lined with mucous membranes. They constantly produce some mucus, to protect the underlying membranes from drying out and to remove and sterilize any irritant that enters the nose when we breathe. This natural production of mucus can be stimulated by various factors and lead to problems of excess mucus, such as catarrh and colds. The reason can lie in external irritants, like tobacco or gasoline fumes, dust particles, or bacteria, but most commonly stems from internal problems, from a state of internal buildup of toxins due to an inappropriate lifestyle, particularly an inappropriate diet (see the section on mucus-free diet in the chapter on the respiratory system under congestion). If this is the cause, the body will use the mucus of the upper respiratory tract as one of its vehicles for waste removal. The first step in a treatment of such conditions is to examine one's diet. In all the following suggestions for herbal treatment, it is assumed that a diet low in mucus is followed.

CATARRH

As already pointed out, nasal catarrh may be the result of systemic factors and can also involve infections and allergies. To treat this sometimes intransigent problem effectively, we can use herbs that work on the mucous membranes in the nose, while we also treat the body in a wider context. Herbs like *Elderberry Flower*, *Eyebright*, and *Golden Rod* bring specific relief, as they are anti-catarrhal and astringent, with *Golden Rod* normally being the most useful. *Golden Seal* is another specific remedy for nasal catarrh, but should be used with discretion as some people find that it has too much of a drying action on the mucous membranes. Catarrh is often accompanied by an infection, so antimicrobial remedies like *Echinacea*, *Garlic* (best taken raw or as oil in capsules), or *Wild Indigo* should be used.

As the lymphatic system will be under stress, *Pokeweed Root* should be included, which is a good tonic for the system and at the same time an anticatarrhal.

Besides using a mixture of these herbs as a tea, we can also make an excellent balm of antiseptic, volatile oils to relieve nasal congestion. It may be applied in a very small amount to the nostril and so be inhaled, or it can be rubbed on the chest at night so that the vapors will be breathed in. Combine:

Peppermint Oil	0.5 fl. oz. (15 ml)
Eucalyptus Oil	0. 5 fl. oz. (15 ml)
Pine Oil	0.5 fl. oz. (15 ml)
Vaseline	1 lb. (500 g)

Melt the Vaseline, without overheating it. When it just turns liquid, add the oils and stir them in. Pour the mixture into pots and seal them when the balm has reached room temperature.

Another way to inhale volatile oils is to use the method of steam inhalation. We can either use some of the balm or an aromatic herb like *Eucalyptus, Pine Needles*, or even *Chamomile*. For a steam inhalation of *Eucalyptus*, put three teaspoonfuls of leaves in a basin and pour 4 pints (2 liters) of boiling water on them. Put your head over the basin and cover with a towel, to prevent a loss of the volatile oils. For about 10 minutes, inhale through the nose. Do not go out immediately afterward, as the mucous membranes will be very sensitive for a while. Repeat the process two or three times a day.

COLDS

The common cold is usually seen as an inconvenience that should be suppressed as soon as possible. It is a typical example of the way we perceive an "illness"; we see it as something that has to be combated, rather than taking it as an indicator that points to something being out of balance in the body. The aim should not be to suppress the indicator and to stay out of balance, but rather to find our way back to inner harmony and thus make the indicator unnecessary. We "catch" a cold when the conditions in our body are right for a virus to thrive. If our inner environment were sound and in harmony, we would not "catch" a cold, no matter how many viruses were "thrown" at us.

The first step in the treatment of a cold is to work on the causes of mucus buildup (see under catarrh). In most cases, it will mean cutting out all mucus-forming foods from the diet. If you normally "catch colds" all through the winter, a mucus-free diet is advisable all the time.

The next step is to treat the cold herbally. The herbs described for nasal catarrh may all be beneficial, but there are also many specific cold remedies. Every area has its own specifics, but all are useful. My favorite is a combination of *Elderberry Flower, Peppermint*, and *Yarrow* in equal parts, a tea that combines the anticatarrhal and mucous membrane-toning properties of *Elderberry Flower* with the stimulating, decongestant action of *Peppermint* and the diaphoretic and diuretic powers of *Yarrow*. The tea should be drunk at least three times daily as hot as possible. If the cold is accompanied by feverishness, use an additional diaphoretic such as *Boneset*.

Besides embarking on a mucus-free diet and using herbs, vitamin C should be considered. Its value cannot be overstressed, both in the treatment and in a long-term prophylaxis of a cold. The exact dosage of vitamin C has been argued about a lot. I recommend taking 1 ounce (2 grams) of the vitamin—divided over the day—at the first sign of a cold until a few days after it clears, then to lower the dosage to 500 milligrams. Ideally it should be taken in the form of *Acerola Berries* or *Rosehips* or as extracts from these, since both are also rich in bioflavonoids, necessary for the absorption and action of vitamin C.

INFLUENZA

A herb that should be in every home in case of the flu is *Boneset*, as it will relieve the aches and pains while also easing some of the malaise of this unpleasant infection. A useful mixture is:

Boneset	2 parts
Elderberry Flower	1 part
Peppermint	1 part

Drink a cup as hot as can be taken every two hours. If the tea is found to be too bitter, especially for children, it may be sweetened with *Licorice*.

The depression that sometimes accompanies the flu or follows it may be eased by taking *Skullcap* or *Vervain*.

If antibiotics have been taken, it is good to take vitamin C and eat yogurt afterward. Vitamin C eases the stress caused to the body by the antibiotics and by the fever. The yogurt is taken as the antibiotics tend to kill bacteria in our intestines that are necessary for well-functioning digestion. By eating a live yogurt (not one that has been pasteurized), we can help the new growth of beneficial bacteria in the intestines.

SINUSITIS

Sinusitis, an infection of the sinus cavities, often turns from an acute state into a chronic one and can, with some people, develop into a very persistent and almost constant state. For a short-term treatment, an effective mixture is:

Echinacea	1 part
Golden Rod	1 part
Golden Seal	1 part
Marshmallow Leaf	1 part

Drink a cup of this tea every two hours.

This mixture combines the antimicrobial properties of *Echinacea*, the anticatarrhal actions of *Golden Rod*, the tonic and anticatarrhal actions of *Golden Seal*, and the invaluable demulcent contribution of *Marshmallow Leaf*. Besides using the tea, the balm and the steam inhalation mentioned for catarrh can also prove very beneficial, along with the general recommendations given there.

As a long-term treatment, particularly in persistent cases, the diet has to be examined, again with emphasis on mucus-forming foods, as sinusitis depends on the state of the mucous membranes. The diet should be supplemented with vitamin C and with *Garlic*, either eaten raw in the diet or as oil in capsules.

HAY FEVER

Hay fever and other conditions, such as allergic rhinitis, are caused by an immunological reaction to an external allergenic substance. It is debatable why the body reacts in this oversensitive fashion. Is the allergy due to the allergen or an internal process triggered by it? A classical chicken and egg situation! I feel that there is a spectrum of reasons from purely genetic causes to purely inappropriate lifestyle. If the lifestyle is right and the inner environment is in harmony, a genetic weakness might not even show itself.

To treat and alleviate the symptoms of hay fever, the following combination of herbs can be most effective:

Elderberry Flower	2 parts
Ephedra	1 part
Eyebright	1 part
Golden Seal	1 part

A cup of this tea should be drunk two or three times a day.

To prevent hay fever occurring and to be really effective, the treatment should start at least a month before the person's particular hay fever season begins, as the tonic and anti-allergenic properties need time to take effect. The low-mucus diet may be beneficial here (see the section under the respiratory system on congestion), as will vitamin C and *Garlic*.

POLYPS

Nasal polyps can be a recurring problem and have to be examined and treated in the context of the condition of the whole body. Locally, they can best be treated with a snuff made from equal parts of *Bloodroot* and an astringent such as *Rhatany* (or *Krameria*), which should be made into a fine powder. The snuff should be used twice a day over a long period. Additionally, the polyps may also be painted twice daily with the fluid extract of *Thuja* by using a fine brush.

NOSEBLEED

Nosebleed is purely a symptom of something else that is wrong in the body. It may be a minor sign or can indicate a serious problem—for example, high blood pressure—but if it is a recurring event, the patient should get professional advice.

The symptom itself can easily be treated by the use of an astringent. A simple and convenient way is to use *Witch Hazel*: soak a cotton ball in distilled *Witch Hazel* and put a small plug into the nostril.

SKIN CONDITIONS

A variety of skin conditions affect the nose—for example, impetigo, herpes, and eczema. They are dealt with in the chapter on the skin.

THE THROAT

The throat may be affected by problems originating in the lungs, nose, sinuses, stomach, and mouth, and also by systemically based problems. They may take the form of tonsillitis, pharyngitis, or laryngitis, but these conditions must always be seen in the wider context. A good example of this wider view is the holistic approach to tonsillitis.

TONSILLITIS

The glandular tissue that is called the tonsils is a variety of the lymphatic tissue and shares with other lymphatic glands a role in the defense of the body from infection. The inflammation of the tonsils—tonsillitis—demonstrates that the glands fulfill their purpose of protecting the body. The appropriate treatment aims at supporting the body herbally, to aid the glands in the work they are doing. They should not be removed by surgery as is done so often, unless there is very good reason.

To this end, antimicrobial remedies like *Echinacea*, *Myrrh*, or *Red Sage* are called for, together with lymphatic alterative tonics like *Cleavers*, *Golden Seal*, *Marigold*, or *Pokeweed Root*. Astringents and demulcents may also be used. A good mixture for internal use is:

Echinacea	2 parts
Pokeweed Root	2 parts
Red Sage	2 parts
Balm of Gilead	1 part

Take a cup every two hours; this may be sweetened with *Licorice*.

Agrimony and *Raspberry* have a good reputation in tonsillitis. An infusion of equal parts drunk three times a day may help. Use the infusion as a gargle as well.

A gargle of *Golden Seal* or *Red Sage* can be used, and this can also be sprayed onto the tonsils using a hand sprayer obtainable from drugstores.

LARYNGITIS

The advice given for tonsillitis is also applicable for laryngitis. *Red Sage*—or, if not available, *Garden Sage*—makes an especially invaluable mouthwash and gargle. Put two tablespoons of *Sage* leaves into 1 pint (0.5 liters) of cold water and bring it to the boil. Cover it and let it infuse for a further 10 minutes. Reheat the mixture whenever needed and gargle often.

SWOLLEN GLANDS

This condition, also known as lymphadenitis, is considered in the chapter on the circulatory system.

THE EYES

The treatment of the eye is beyond the scope of this book. However, conditions that affect the eyelids and tear glands may be treated herbally.

The herb par excellence for the treatment of the eyes is *Eyebright*. It can be used internally and externally in all eye problems and will help the eyeball and the surrounding tissue, but it can also be combined with other herbs. When treating styes, inflammation of the eyelids or other infections such as conjunctivitis, it is best to treat the problem both internally and externally. Internally, the herbs should be antimicrobial, detoxifying and toning for the whole body, to strengthen it to the point where it can "throw off" the infection itself. A good example of such a combination would be a mixture of equal parts of:

Blue Flag
Cleavers
Echinacea
Eyebright
Pokeweed Root

A cup of this should be drunk three times a day.

Externally, an eyewash or a compress may be made with *Eyebright*. Put one tablespoon of the dried herb in 1 pint (0.5 liters) of water, boil it for 10 minutes, and let it cool. It can either be used as an eyewash or applied as a compress by moistening a cotton ball, gauze, or muslin in the warm liquid and placing it over the eyes for about 15 minutes. This should be repeated several times a day. Other remedies that may be used in a similar way externally are *Golden Seal* and *Marigold*.

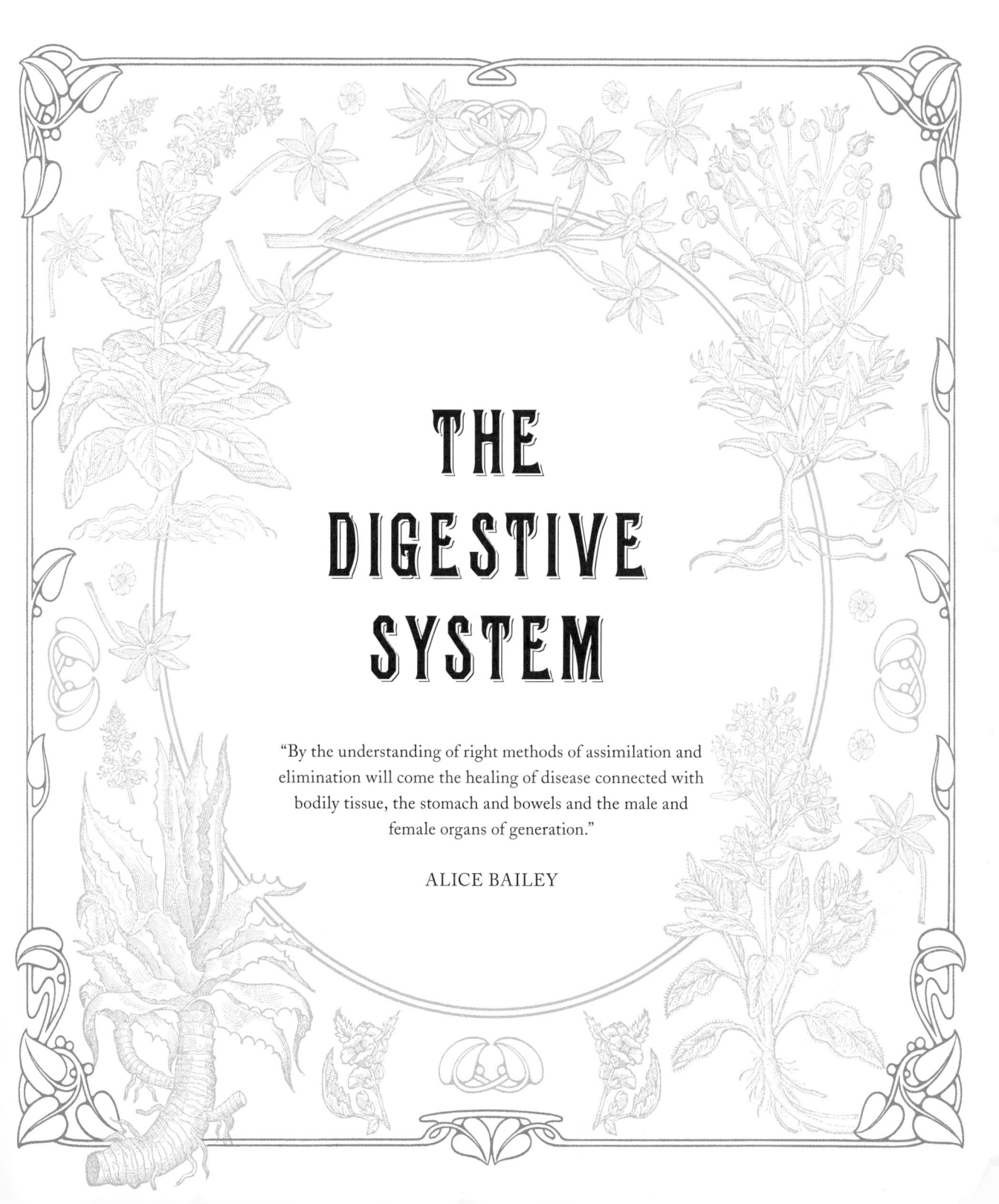

THE DIGESTIVE SYSTEM

"By the understanding of right methods of assimilation and elimination will come the healing of disease connected with bodily tissue, the stomach and bowels and the male and female organs of generation."

ALICE BAILEY

The Digestive System

THE DIGESTIVE SYSTEM BEGINS WITH the mouth and ends with the rectum, some 36 feet (11 meters) later! It has been described as a tube passing through the body, as a sort of factory where food is processed and made available for the body to use. This description indicates how narrow our awareness of our bodies often is today. In fact, the digestive system is one of the major interfaces between our inner world and the outer, with a total surface that is some hundred times larger than our skin, with a complexity of reactions that are still beyond our understanding. For instance, the number of living microbes that inhabit the digestive system equals the total number of cells in the body, but how exactly the mixture of these microbes influences our well-being, and how our state of health influences their condition, is still largely unresearched.

The digestive system is richly supplied with nerves, a whole network of integrated control that works in conjunction with a wide array of hormones, both local and systemic. This has been described as a web of enteric brains. Enteric means to do with the gut and in this context means the local nervous system of the digestive system. This gut-level intelligence can usually run the digestive system quite adequately. The degree of interaction and synergy between the various parts of the digestive tract is quite astounding, and the more research done by the physiologists, the more is revealed.

As we are what we eat, our health and vitality depends to a large degree on how well our digestive system functions in providing the building blocks for our physical body. It is not just a matter of what substance we put into our mouth, but also essentially one of what is properly processed so that it can be assimilated and used by the body, as we are really what we assimilate.

If there is a functional problem in the digestion, then no matter what is being eaten it will not be properly absorbed, and deficiency is experienced. An example of a functional, as opposed to an organic, problem in this system would be tension during irregular and rushed meals, leading to indigestion. The food will enter an unprepared gut too fast and eventually cause malabsorption and so discomfort. The fault can lie either in the eating habits, the content or amount of digestive juices, or in a dysfunction of the intestinal walls, so that the food is not properly absorbed through the lining of the gut. These problems can give rise to a whole range of diseases. It must be stressed that this refers to functional problems, where the system does not work as well as it could, not to organic conditions caused by injury or a structural abnormality of the organs and tissues involved.

An excellent example of the complex functioning of the digestive process is the action of the digestive bitter herbs. It is often said jokingly that the nastier the medicine, the better it is for you. In the case of bitters this is so! It has been found that the taste of bitterness on the tongue will stimulate, via reflex circuits in the brain, the secretions and activity of the esophagus, the secretions of the stomach, duodenum, and gallbladder, and stimulate the production of insulin by the pancreas. All this from a nasty taste in the mouth!

Besides its function of assimilation, an equally important activity of the digestive system is elimination. Not all the food that is eaten is absorbed. Some is not digestible and needs to be disposed of. The body also produces a lot of metabolic waste products that it has to eliminate, partly through the digestive system. The condition of the bowels and the state of their content will fundamentally affect the rest of the body. The focus of naturopaths on the bowels is understandable, and the nature of the food we eat is of great importance.

In addition to the physiological influences that affect the functioning and health of the digestive system, there is a constant interplay between the state of mind and digestion. Emotions profoundly influence both the functioning and structure of tissue in the stomach and intestines. There is an immediate response to anger, anxiety, fear, and all forms of stress and worry. To approach the healing of digestive problems in a holistic way, an appreciation of these psychological influences must be included.

Prevention of Disease

Most of the digestive problems that commonly occur are easily avoidable by changes of lifestyle and habits. Some clear guidelines to follow in preventing problems include our attitudes toward alcohol, tobacco, stress, and diet.

It is clear that excess alcohol acts as a major irritant on the walls of the intestine and is a specific threat to the liver. It should ideally be kept to a minimum. Tobacco presents a similar problem. It has been proven that nicotine slows the healing of gastric ulcers and may promote the development of duodenal ulcers. The tar that gets swallowed acts as an irritant. DON'T SMOKE!

Stress and anxiety are major contributors to illness and impede the healing process. Their effect is particularly strong on the digestive system via the influence of the autonomic nervous system. Such states of stress and anxiety should be actively reduced. Create peace and stillness within yourself. The stress is unnecessary. Change your job. BE AT PEACE!

The diet should be as mixed, natural, and as high in roughage as possible. It should contain fruit, vegetables, and natural cereals in preference to starches, sugar, and highly refined flour. Artificial chemical additives should be avoided. The specific details of diet should be determined individually according to personal needs and philosophical approach.

Herbs for the Digestive System

There are a multitude of plant remedies that have a use in the treatment of digestive disorders. This is not surprising if herbs are viewed as food—as vegetables. Most herbs are taken by mouth and therefore absorbed through the digestive system, where their healing powers will start to be effective immediately.

Rather than give an endless list of digestive herbs, they will be reviewed by their actions with a few outstanding examples given. A more exhaustive list of herbs is given in the chapter on actions.

Actions can be broadly grouped into those that stimulate various parts of the system to increase or better activity—the digestive stimulants—and those that relax the tissue or reduce any overactivity in the system—the digestive relaxants.

STIMULANTS

BITTERS

While having a large range of other properties and chemical constituents, the bitter herbs all have in common an intensely bitter taste. This bitterness promotes appetite and in a complex way aids digestion. As I explained earlier, this action is entirely via the taste buds and a reflex action in the brain. If these herbs are given in capsule form and cannot be tasted, their digestive properties do not come into play. Out of the many bitters, the most valuable ones are *Barberry, Centaury, Gentian Root, Golden Seal, White Horehound*, and *Wormwood*.

Of course a large range of other actions are also represented here. For example, *White Horehound* can be used in a bronchitic condition where the appetite is weak and the digestion sluggish or as a digestive remedy in cases where there is a lung weakness.

SIALAGOGUES

The importance of the saliva in the digestive process cannot be overstressed. Digestion starts in the mouth and initiates a process that is continued in the gut. The saliva breaks down large carbohydrates into smaller units, which can then be processed in other parts of the system. If time is not taken to chew food properly, the saliva does not get to mix thoroughly enough with it and the whole digestive process is affected. Besides the bitters, which all stimulate the flow of saliva, other sialagogues are *Cayenne, Ginger, Licorice, Tamarind*, and *Turkey Rhubarb Root*.

HEPATICS

Hepatics are herbs that strengthen, tone, and stimulate the secretive functions of the liver. This causes an increase in the flow of bile. Remedies that also promote the discharge of this bile into the duodenum are called cholagogues. In treating the whole body, it is often beneficial to aid the liver and its function, as this most important organ is intimately involved in all body functions and the health of all tissues. The liver is involved in digestive problems via the bile. As its importance would suggest, there are many hepatic herbs available to us, and the most useful are *Balmony, Barberry, Black Root, Blue Flag, Boldo, Dandelion Root, Fringetree Bark, Golden Seal, Vervain, Wild Yam, Winged Elm*, and *Yellow Dock*.

LAXATIVES AND EVACUANTS

Many herbs can promote the evacuation of the bowels, ranging from very mild laxatives to more violent and drastic purgatives. Such strong purgatives should only be used in extreme cases and under qualified supervision. The best laxatives are those that stimulate the natural secretion of digestive juices such as bile (the cholagogues), thus promoting evacuation. Some of these are *Balmony, Barberry, Dandelion Root, Licorice, Winged Elm*, and *Yellow Dock*.

For a more powerful evacuant, consider *Rhubarb Root*, which in small dosage is also a mild astringent. Other valuable ones to consider are *Aloe, Buckthorn, Cascara Sagrada*, and *Senna*. These stronger evacuants work mainly by chemical or neurological stimulation, irritating the lining of the intestines and causing an active expulsion of material.

EMETICS

There are situations where expulsion of the content of the stomach is highly desirable, as in poisoning, where vomiting is often the appropriate treatment. Many plants can cause this reflex by either acting on the controlling nerves or by irritating the gastric lining. Good ones to use would be *Balm*, *Ipecac*, *Lobelia*, and *Senega*.

ANTHELMINTICS

The anthelmintics are a group of stimulating herbs that do not really act on the digestive system itself but rather against parasitic worms that might be present. Please refer to the chapter on infections and infestations for more information.

RELAXANTS

Following the stimulants, we shall consider a group of properties that relax the tissue of the digestive system or reduce the overactivity of normal functions.

DEMULCENTS

When the membranes of the digestive tract are irritated or inflamed, demulcent herbs can soothe and protect them. Out of the many demulcents that are active in different parts of the body, *Comfrey Root*, *Hops*, *Iceland Moss*, *Irish Moss*, *Marshmallow Root*, *Oats*, *Quince Seed*, and *Slippery Elm* are most effective for the digestive system.

CARMINATIVES

Many aromatic herbs contain volatile oils that affect the digestive system by relaxing the stomach muscles, increasing the peristalsis of the intestine, and reducing the production of gas in the system. They thus support the movement of material through the system and relieve distension due to gas. Of the many carminatives, *Angelica*, *Aniseed*, *Calamus*, *Caraway*, *Cardamom*, *Cayenne*, *Chamomile*, *Coriander Seed*, *Fennel*, *Ginger*, *Peppermint*, and *Thyme* are among the best ones for the digestive system.

ASTRINGENTS

The action of astringents lies mainly in their ability to contract cell walls, thus condensing the tissue and making it firmer and arresting any unwanted discharge. Of the many astringents provided by the plant kingdom, *Agrimony*, *Bayberry*, *Geranium*, *Lesser Celandine*, *Meadowsweet*, *Nettles*, *Oak Bark*, and *Tormentil* are suitable for the digestive system.

ANTISPASMODICS

Antispasmodics are remedies that rapidly relax any nervous tension that may be causing digestive spasms or colic. The tension of our current lifestyle can manifest in many digestive conditions that necessitate the use of relaxing nervines or muscular antispasmodics. The best ones to use in cases of digestive problems are *Chamomile*, *Hops*, *Lobelia*, *Mistletoe*, *Pasqueflower*, *Skullcap*, and *Valerian*. See "The Herbal" section for more details on each of these, in order to choose the best herb or combination for the individual case.

ANTIMICROBIALS

Infections can be the cause of digestive problems; they can also arise easily if the digestive system has been weakened by a disease. In either case, the use of antimicrobials will be helpful. Many of the herbs already mentioned are antimicrobials, such as *Pasqueflower*, *Thyme*, and *Wormwood*, but the two outstanding ones are *Echinacea* and *Myrrh*.

Patterns of Digestive Disease

In this section, we shall review the digestive system starting from the mouth and ending with the rectum, referring to the common conditions but explaining their treatment in terms of the whole. It is valuable first to recognize a number of symptoms that are common to many diseases affecting the whole system but that have a particular relevance to digestion. These are constipation, diarrhea, vomiting, pain, and loss of appetite.

CONSTIPATION

Contrary to common belief, constipation is not a disease but a symptom of some underlying problem. This could be inappropriate diet, a liver problem, or even a physical blockage in the system. In any case, the cause must be identified and treated, as the long-term use of laxatives in chronic constipation can eventually lead to other symptoms, such as headaches, colic, or even jaundice. Most constipation would not occur if the body were given a well-balanced diet with adequate levels of roughage.

In cases of chronic constipation, the muscles of the intestines have to be retrained to move the bowel content. The movement of the intestinal wall is a complex and highly integrated example of muscle control, designed to push the content onward at the right time and with the right force. This natural peristaltic movement can be blocked by the long use of laxatives. Two things should be done to retrain the intestines: care should be taken that meals are eaten regularly (at the same time each day) and small amounts of appropriate herbs should be used to restimulate the peristalsis—for instance, *Cascara Sagrada*.

A further factor that should not be underestimated is the attitude and state of mind of the person who is constipated. Somebody who is tense and tight, who wants to hold on to everything and everyone, who cannot relax and let go, whose attitude toward the world is one of taking and keeping rather than of giving and staying open, will often also be constipated. In such cases, relaxation exercises or meditation can be the best laxatives.

When constipation is the result of a disease process, it is important to relieve the symptom while treating the cause, otherwise the body might absorb some of the stagnant material from the intestine.

Of all the evacuant herbs available, perhaps the most widely applicable is *Rhubarb Root*, as it is a prime example of a normalizing herb. While in a large dose it is a purgative, taken in small doses it tones and astringes the intestine wall, promotes appetite, and can disperse any gas that develops.

Any of the evacuant herbs will work well on their own, but the following mixture combines a number of valuable actions. *Barberry* aids the liver and the gallbladder, *Boldo* stimulates the digestive process, *Cascara Sagrada* acts on the peristaltic movement, *Licorice* is mainly included to mask the bitter taste of some of the herbs, *Rhubarb Root* is included in a small dose for the above mentioned reasons, and *Ginger* will guard against any colic:

Barberry	2 parts
Boldo	2 parts
Cascara Sagrada	1 part
Licorice	1 part
Rhubarh Root	1 part
Ginger	1 part

Take a cup of this tea before going to bed.

As an alternative to *Boldo*, *Dandelion* can be used and *Fennel* can be substituted for *Ginger*, both in the same quantities.

DIARRHEA

A bout of diarrhea that does not last more than a day or two is a very common symptom and can be caused by an acute infection or inflammation of the intestine wall or by psychological stress—for instance, by overexcitement or by a long journey. In most cases, diarrhea sets in when the body has to remove digestive poisons from its system, and as such it should not be suppressed. However, it can be useful to control the process and help the system with herbs that tone the lining of the intestine wall and that are mildly astringent. For persistent, long-standing diarrhea, seek the advice of a skilled practitioner. By far the best mild digestive astringent is *Meadowsweet*, which can safely be used in all cases of diarrhea. In cases of childhood diarrhea, a good remedy is a tea made of equal parts of *Lady's Mantle* and *Meadowsweet*, which can be sweetened with some honey and should be taken often. For an acute attack in adults, a very good mixture would be a tea of equal parts of:

Bayberry
Geranium
Meadowsweet
Oak Bark

This tea should be drunk every hour until the symptoms subside and then before every meal until the digestion is normal.

PAIN

Pain in the digestive system is an indicator of the type of illness present. Any extreme, acute abdominal pain necessitates immediate medical supervision. Less acute pain will often accompany digestive disorders. Colic and griping pains are due to intense muscle spasms in the gut and usually indicate an attempt to remove a blockage that could be caused by wind or fecal matter, or perhaps a muscle spasm of nervous origin. Flatulent colic will be relieved by the carminative herbs, but all causes must be treated to clear the pain. Useful antispasmodics in this case are *Caraway, Ginger, Valerian*, and *Wild Yam*. Pain from stomach ulcers and similar problems can be eased by using demulcents such as *Comfrey* or *Marshmallow*. Of course, the roots of the problem must be treated in all cases where pain is a symptom.

LOSS OF APPETITE

The appetite can be a good indicator for the state of the digestive system. If there is, for instance, a gastric problem, the appetite will often diminish for a period of time. This way the stomach will have a better chance to recover, as it has to process less food. A similar pattern can evolve with liver problems when the liver is overburdened.

If there is a loss of appetite in the recovery phase of an illness such as influenza, digestive stimulants like *Gentian* or *Wormwood* should be used to restore healthy function.

ANOREXIA NERVOSA

Anorexia nervosa is characterized by an extreme loss of appetite, practically an aversion to food, and often the inability to eat anything, which consequently leads to a drastic loss of weight. Anorexia nervosa is caused by psychological problems and has thus to be approached psychotherapeutically. Herbally, the process can be aided with the use of digestives and nervines—for instance, with a tea of equal parts of:

Chamomile
Condurango
Gentian
Skullcap

This should be drunk three times daily.

The Mouth

As the beginning of the digestive system, the health of the mouth will affect the whole of the system. If there is a chronic tooth problem that makes proper chewing painful, or if there is an infection like an abscess, the system downstream will be affected and polluted. Similarly, if there is not enough saliva or if the composition of saliva is not adequate, the digestive process will be slowed down. Oral hygiene therefore cannot be stressed too much. Problems in the gut can also give mouth problems, such as bad breath or recurrent mouth ulcers.

TEETH

When problems arise, teeth must be treated by a dentist, but herbs can be helpful to prevent tooth decay.

Long before toothbrushes made of bristle or plastic were developed, roots like *Marshmallow, Licorice, Alfalfa,* or *Horseradish* were used to clean teeth. *Licorice Root*, for instance, can be prepared very easily, simply by peeling the bark off one end and flaying the fibers. *Marshmallow Root* needs somewhat more preparation: choose a straight root and cut it into 5-inch (13-centimeter) pieces. Peel the ends and boil in water, together with *Cinnamon* sticks and *Cloves*, until the sticks are tender. Put them carefully—as they break easily—into brandy and let them soak for a day. Take them out and let them dry. Before you use them, soak the end for a short time in hot water. You will not even need to use toothpaste, since all the necessary ingredients are in the root. It has a nice taste, too.

If you want to use toothpaste, many herbal ones are now available, the best being those that contain the antimicrobial herbs *Echinacea* and *Myrrh*.

For a first-aid treatment of toothache, chew some *Cloves*, as they are rich in the analgesic oil eugenol. Alternatively, you can soak a cotton pad in *Clove* oil and place it by the tooth. *Peppermint* oil also acts as an analgesic, but it is not as effective.

GINGIVITIS

Gingivitis is a common infection of the surface tissue of the gums, caused by a lack of oral hygiene and by an inappropriate diet. Particularly sugar and refined, processed foods have to be avoided. The herbal antimicrobials like *Echinacea, Eucalyptus,* and *Myrrh*, can be used very effectively in the form of tinctures. Depending on the severity of the infection, you can either wash the gums daily with a tincture of *Myrrh* or if a stronger remedy is needed, you can use a mixture of equal parts of tincture of *Myrrh* and tincture of *Echinacea*. While not being very pleasant to taste, it will be very effective. Alternatively, massage the gums before going to bed with oil of *Eucalyptus* and wash out the mouth in the morning with distilled *Witch Hazel*.

PYORRHEA

This chronic degenerative disease of the gums must be treated systemically with the use of alteratives that are antimicrobials and lymphatic cleansers as well. For a treatment, use the approach described under gingivitis to treat the gums themselves and combine this with taking a high dosage of vitamin C. Most important is the use of a mixture of:

Echinacea	2 parts
Blue Flag	1 part
Cleavers	1 part
Pokeweed Root	1 part

This tea should be drunk three times daily for a number of weeks until the condition clears.

ABSCESS

This very painful condition can be best helped by the use of the tea described under pyorrhea. This treatment will also protect the whole system from a spreading of the infection which could occur, as the existence of the abscess indicates that the defense capacity of the body is reduced. Any treatment that aims at encouraging the body to absorb the abscess should be avoided.

MOUTH ULCERS

Mouth ulcers are usually indicators of a generally run-down condition and are best treated by increasing general health. They commonly occur after the use of antibiotics or during recovery from influenza. In both cases the body has been exposed to considerable physiological stress, resulting in a general weakening. This in turn affects the normal ecology of the mouth and of other areas, and, as one symptom, the ulcer appears. They can also arise during a period of psychological stress. Whether the cause is physical or psychological, it obviously has to be treated by increasing general health.

To treat the ulcer, *Red Sage* (in the form of a mouthwash, made preferably from the infusion of fresh leaves) is very simple and effective. The fresh leaves can also be chewed. Alternatively, a mouthwash of tincture of *Myrrh* in an equal amount of water will be effective.

At the same time, vitamin B-complex and vitamin C should be taken to help deal with the stress involved, whatever the cause.

THE STOMACH

The stomach is the organ that takes the brunt of the liberties we sometimes take with the food and drink we consume. Too much alcohol, too much refined food, too many cigarettes, too many aspirins, all will affect the stomach.

The main task of the stomach is to prepare the food for further processing in the small intestine, which it accomplishes by mixing it with hydrochloric acid and powerful enzymes.

Before we look at the stomach, two problems with the esophagus (the tube down which swallowed food travels) will be examined. If there is a burning sensation in the esophagus or acid rising into the mouth, the symptom is due to a problem in the stomach. It can be treated with the help of demulcents, but the condition of the stomach has also to be examined. If there is a problem with swallowing, the problem (dysphagia) should be examined professionally. It is often due to nervous tension and anxiety and may be relieved by the use of nervines like *Hops*, *Valerian*, or *Wild Lettuce*.

INDIGESTION

The label "indigestion" is used for a wide range of symptoms, all of which are due to a functional problem in the stomach caused by inappropriate eating habits. Indigestion (or dyspepsia) can be accompanied by pain, flatulence, heartburn, and other symptoms. The causes of these symptoms can be grouped into four categories:

Irregular eating. The functioning of the body is characterized by rhythms, and the stomach—and, in fact, the whole digestive system—is no exception to this. If meals are taken irregularly, these rhythms are disturbed and functional problems may result. Shift workers, for instance, are very prone to this.

Overeating and eating too quickly. If too much food goes into the stomach, either at any one time or in total over the day, the stomach will be overloaded and thus work with reduced efficiency. Overloading causes problems in the stomach that may affect the whole system. Obesity is the most common result. Also when food is eaten too quickly and not chewed thoroughly, it causes problems; food will not be digested properly and may pass through the system in an undigested state.

Eating the wrong food. Many people are allergic to certain foods, even though the symptoms might not be very obvious. Any food that causes a problem should be eliminated from the diet altogether. A typical example is food containing gluten, such as brown bread. Another common allergen may be cow's milk.

Nervous tension. The stomach, like the whole digestive system, is easily affected by stress and anxiety.

By taking all these factors into account and by changing one's diet and lifestyle accordingly, indigestion can be treated. There are a number of herbs that will speed up the healing process, but obviously they will have to be chosen according to the cause. The most important remedy is *Meadowsweet*, which will settle the stomach and reduce any excess acidity.

The demulcents can be very useful, a good one being *Irish Moss*, though the other digestive demulcents will also do.

If the digestion is sluggish, bitters like *Gentian*, *Golden Seal*, and *Wormwood* will help.

If there is flatulence, the carminatives should be used as well. Good ones for the stomach are *Aniseed*, *Balm*, *Cardamom*, *Fennel*, and *Peppermint*.

If there is nervous tension involved, the nervine relaxants are indicated, especially those that also aid digestion, such as *Chamomile*, *Hops*, *Lavender*, *Rosemary*, and *Valerian*. In all cases consult "The Herbal" section to choose the most appropriate herb or combination of them to use in the individual case.

GASTRITIS

When a disturbance in the stomach changes from a functional one like indigestion to a structural one, the first stage is an inflammation of the lining of the stomach wall. It may last only for a short time and can be due to an infection or a reaction to food, or it might be more chronic. If it lasts for a while, the causes that should be looked at are: eating the wrong foods, alcohol, cigarettes (swallowed tar), and stress. Usually a combination of these factors will be involved. The treatment of gastritis is based on diet and herbs.

As far as diet is concerned, the primary short-term need is to avoid irritants that may cause or aggravate the inflammation. These may involve temperature or irritants of a chemical or mechanical nature:

—Very hot foods or drinks should be abstained from, as these will directly aggravate the inflammation. Cold things will usually have a similarly painful effect.
—Chemical irritants will have an immediate impact. Commonly used foodstuffs that contain vinegar, which is diluted acetic acid, must be avoided. Vinegar

should not be added to food; pickles must similarly be avoided. Alcohol in any form is out, as this acts on the stomach lining in a similar way to vinegar. Tobacco will also aggravate the problem, as much of the tar is swallowed. Spicy food, curries, and rich and greasy foods will all have an unpleasant effect.
—Mechanical irritants will cause discomfort as well.

When there is acute inflammation, it is best to have a diet that is very low in fiber, as fiber may have a similar effect to sandpaper on a cut! A bland diet is called for: no coarse bread, nuts, tomatoes, etc. As soon as an improvement is established, then reintroduce roughage, as it is an essential component of a healthy diet.

Herbally, the following mixture will effectively soothe and heal the stomach lining:

Comfrey Root	2 parts
Marshmallow Root	2 parts
Meadowsweet	2 parts
Golden Seal	1 part

Take this tea after each meal, until the condition clears.

If a lot of flatulence accompanies the inflammation, add one part of *Calamus* to the mixture. Similarly, if stress is part of the problem, *Valerian* may be added as a suitable nervine.

GASTRIC ULCER

When abuse of the stomach has continued, perhaps unconsciously, for too long, an inevitable breakdown occurs in the lining of the stomach. As the mucous membranes of the wall no longer deal with the unhealthy condition, the acid and the digestive enzymes can reach the wall and take their toll. A gastric ulcer develops.

The herbal treatment of these ulcers is quite straightforward and apparently fast. However, a relief of the pain must not be confused with the healing of the underlying problem. The herbal remedies will ease the symptoms and start the healing process, but a complete healing will take time and has to include a close look at one's lifestyle. By developing a gastric or a duodenal ulcer, the body is telling us that something in the whole web of our lifestyle is inappropriate. It may just be the diet, but it may also often be the work pattern, our relationships, or even our country's defense policy!

Herbs can heal the ulcer, but it may return very quickly, unless the lessons being offered are recognized consciously and acted upon.

The treatment is based on a careful diet and on the use of herbs. A useful herbal tea consists of equal parts of:

Comfrey Root
Golden Seal
Marshmallow Root
Meadowsweet

The *Comfrey* and *Marshmallow* provide excellent soothing demulcent action combined with a healing effect upon the mucous membranes. A cold infusion of the demulcents is more mucilaginous and soothing than tea or tincture. For details, see the chapter on preparing herbs. *Slippery Elm* may be added to the diet or taken as tablets. The *Meadowsweet* will settle the stomach content and reduce the impact of overacidity. The *Golden Seal* will prove beneficial for the membranes and act to tone the tissue while providing a general tonic action upon the body. If bleeding occurs within the stomach, *Geranium* may be added to the mixture. If there is a stress component—and there usually is—*Valerian* or perhaps *Hops* may be considered.

The diet should be very low in fiber during the acute phase of the illness. In addition there should be little protein, thereby giving the stomach less work to do. When the symptoms recede, fiber and a variety of proteins may slowly be reintroduced. Of great importance is the avoidance of alcohol and also the avoidance of tobacco. With tobacco, withdrawal may produce nervous tension and therefore make things worse. If this is the case, then stop smoking as soon as you can; you're hooked.

The Small Intestine

The long stretch of the small intestine is the site where most nutrition is absorbed into the body. Thus any problems in the small intestine will affect the nutritional state, causing apparent deficiencies that are really malabsorption problems. Stress has a marked impact on this part of the body, as is demonstrated by duodenal ulcers. The small intestines make up the longest part of the digestive system, with a total length of about 20 feet (6 meters), which is divided into three sections, the duodenum, the jejunum, and the ileum.

Duodenal Ulcers

The duodenum, the first stretch of the small intestine, starts at the pyloric sphincter, a valve at the end of the stomach. This valve controls the release of parts of the stomach content into the duodenum, and if it does not function properly, too much stomach acid can get into the duodenum and cause problems. When too much of the highly acidic stomach juices seeps into the alkaline duodenum, the walls of the duodenum will become inflamed and ultimately develop ulcers. A number of factors can cause the seepage, but by far the most common one stems from the fact that the function of the valve is influenced by stress and tension. Considering the highly competitive and charged environment many people live in, it is surprising that more people do not develop duodenal ulcers.

The approach to healing a duodenal ulcer is threefold, consisting of an herbal treatment, dietary changes, and a consideration of the cause, which in most cases means a consideration of the factors causing stress and tension.

The herbal treatment is based on a number of actions. Demulcents are called for to soothe the ulcer and the surrounding tissue. If a vulnerary action can be added to speed the healing process, then so much the better. This may be done with *Comfrey Root* and *Marshmallow*. The specific mucous membrane healing properties of *Golden Seal* will aid the healing of the lining of the intestine. An appropriate astringent like *Geranium* should be used to strengthen the tissue. As a duodenal ulcer is often accompanied by a general debility and a reduction in vitality due to toxins from the ulcer entering into the blood and lymph system, appropriate alteratives and lymphatic tonics like *Echinacea* should be used. A good basic mixture would therefore consist of:

Comfrey Root	2 parts
Marshmallow Root	2 parts
Geranium	1 part
Echinacea	1 part
Golden Seal	1 part

This tea should be drunk three times a day before meals. If you are fasting, drink it at the times you would usually eat.

The diet should be low in fiber and low in proteins as long as the symptoms persist and must be followed by a gradual return to a normal whole-food diet. An excellent soothing food to take during the peak of the problem is *Slippery Elm*. It can be made into the consistency of a thick gruel and will provide nutrition as well as a demulcent action on the ulcerated tissue.

To deal with stress and tension, nervines are indicated for a short-term treatment. But the body is sending a signal and giving a clue by developing a symptom like an ulcer, and it is best to take the hint. Take a look at your lifestyle and purpose in life. Is your life fulfilling and meaningful? Many valuable techniques are available to help you re-evaluate your life and clear these problems, ranging from simple relaxation techniques to psychotherapy. Stress management and relaxation is discussed in the next chapter.

Herbally, a good nervine mixture to treat tension can be made of equal parts of *Skullcap* and *Valerian*, which should be made into a tea and drunk whenever needed. Other appropriate relaxing herbs, though not as strong, are *Balm*, *Chamomile*, *Lavender*, and *Lime Blossom*, which can also be made into a tea and drunk whenever needed.

ENTERITIS

This name is given to an inflammation that can occur in any section of the small intestine and sometimes even over its whole length. When it appears in one of the sections, it can be called accordingly: duodenitis, jejuvinitis, or ileitis; but the treatment will always be the same. In most cases, the guidelines and treatment suggested for duodenal ulcers will be found sufficient. However, it would be good to add one part of *Wild Yam* to the mixture to further ease the inflammation and pain.

MALABSORPTION

A very common—though frequently unrecognized—condition is a diminished ability of the small intestine to absorb food in general or specific components, like minerals. This can lead to symptoms of malnutrition, to apparent mineral or vitamin deficiencies, to anemia and weight loss, to abdominal pain, or to a more insidious state of vague ill health.

Most commonly the malabsorption stems from an allergic reaction to particular foods that leads to problems in the lining of the intestine wall. The allergic reaction might be extreme and obvious, as in the case of celiac disease due to a strong allergy to gluten, or it can take a mild form and not produce obvious symptoms. But in any case of suspected malabsorption, it is always worth removing potential allergens from the diet. A complete list of potential allergens would include any food, as everything can trigger an allergic reaction, but the majority of cases are found to be caused by just four types of foods. The gluten-containing foods should be avoided. They include primarily all products made from wheat. Another major cause for allergic reactions is milk and milk products, like cheese and butter. Sugar and foods rich in sugar should also be considered, as should eggs. Eliminate these foods from your diet for a number of weeks and see if anything changes. If so, leave the food that is causing the allergy out of your diet; if not, see if your diet contains other foods you might suspect, like coffee or tea, or tomatoes. It is worth experimenting for a while to find out.

Herbal remedies can help soothe, heal, and renew the lining of the intestine. Demulcents like *Comfrey Root*, *Marshmallow Root*, and *Slippery Elm* will soothe the mucous membranes. Anti-inflammatory herbs, such as *Meadowsweet* and *Wild Yam*, should be considered, as well as astringents like *Agrimony*, *Bayberry*, and *Meadowsweet*. Carminatives such as *Cardamom*, *Chamomile*, and *Hops* will be invaluable, with the last two also acting as relaxing nervines. It may be necessary to guard against infection, thus *Echinacea* would be used. For more serious problems in this category, such as celiac disease or Crohn's disease, seek the help of a qualified practitioner.

The Large Intestine

The main function of the large intestine—or colon— is to absorb water and minerals. Little or no other food is extracted, as this has occurred in the small intestine. The bacteria in the gut, or gut flora as they are known, make some of our vitamins here and protect against some toxic bacteria.

APPENDICITIS

An infection of the appendix can manifest in two ways, either in an acute and severe attack or in a more chronic form. A sudden and acute attack calls for immediate medical attention as it can develop into peritonitis, a condition in which the appendix bursts, which is very dangerous.

The symptoms of a chronic infection can take the form of recurring attacks of abdominal pain on the lower right side, accompanied by a rise in temperature, by nausea, and perhaps vomiting. This can be treated with a mixture of:

Echinacea	2 parts
Wild Yam	2 parts
Agrimony	1 part
Chamomile	1 part

This tea should be drunk three times a day over a period of time. It should be found that the condition gradually improves.

While this mixture may also ease the symptoms of acute appendicitis, proper medical attention is called for in the case of a sudden attack. Even though constipation often accompanies appendicitis, laxatives should not be used, as they may aggravate the condition.

COLITIS

Colitis, an inflammation of part of the colon, is the most common complaint affecting the large intestine. The intensity and the particular symptoms depend on the extent of the inflammation. While the symptoms vary to some extent from person to person, colitis is characterized by alternating bouts of diarrhea and constipation, by a general lowering of vitality, and often depression. This distressing condition will usually respond well to herbal medication and the use of an appropriate diet. A useful mixture is:

Wild Yam	3 parts
Bayberry	2 parts
Agrimony	1 part
Comfrey Root	1 part
Golden Seal	1 part
Marshmallow Root	1 part

This tea should be drunk three times a day.

This combination of herbs soothes and heals the lining of the large intestine with demulcents (*Comfrey, Marshmallow*), astringents (*Agrimony, Bayberry, Comfrey*), and an anti-inflammatory herb (*Wild Yam*). Other astringents like *Geranium, Oak Bark, Periwinkle,* and *Shepherd's Purse* may also be considered. It may also be necessary to include alteratives and antimicrobials, such as *Echinacea* or *Garlic*, depending on the condition.

When stress and anxiety accompany the colitis, relaxing nervines like *Lime Blossom, Skullcap,* and *Valerian* should also be used. The key to diet in the treatment of colitis is the avoidance of anything that will irritate the colon wall, either by physical irritation, by its temperature, because of a chemical action, or because it an causes allergic reaction.

Physical irritation can be avoided by excluding any fibrous food from the diet. Bran and whole-wheat flour, raw vegetables, fruit skins, fruit with pips (like raspberries), nuts, and cooked fibrous vegetables (like the brassica group) should all be avoided. The temperature of food should be medium; hot or cold foods or drinks (hot coffee, ice cream, or beer) should be avoided.

Chemical irritants should be avoided, namely alcohol, vinegar and vinegar products (like pickles), spicy condiments, strong cheese, and fried foods.

The main food causing allergic reactions in the colon are cow's milk products. Coffee and pork products should be avoided.

Instead, goat's milk or soy milk can be substituted. Other permissible foods include eggs, tender and light meats, fish, liver and poultry, bland soups, lightly cooked vegetables and fruit (bananas and avocados may be eaten raw), products of unbleached white flour, fine cereals, and *Slippery Elm* food (see under duodenal ulcer), which also has a very healing action.

Meals should be small and eaten often, rather than large and eaten three times daily. The diet should be followed while the inflammation is acute, but once the symptoms are eased, high-fiber foods should be slowly reintroduced. The chemical irritants and foods causing allergies should be avoided permanently.

DIVERTICULITIS

Through the unnatural and unhealthy food that is the usual diet of so many in the "civilized" world today, there is a high occurrence of weakness of the colon wall. This weakness can lead to the development of a pouch in the wall, called a "diverticulum." Sometimes only a number of small ones develop, sometimes a lot, and in many cases they can also grow into large ones. Often these diverticula cause little or no apparent trouble, but they can also be the site for inflammations and for the buildup of waste material. Once an inflamed state is reached, any fibrous or indigestible material like tomato skins can cause intense pain and discomfort.

Diverticulitis—the inflamed state—can be treated by a combined herbal and dietary approach. An efficient basic herbal mixture can be made from:

Wild Yam	3 parts
Chamomile	2 parts
Marshmallow	1 part
Calamus	1 part

This tea should be drunk three times a day.

If the diverticulitis is accompanied by flatulence, more carminatives like *Calumba* and *Ginger* should be added, and if there is also constipation, laxatives like *Rhubarb Root* or *Senna* may be included. The dietary approach seems paradoxical. Even though the problem arises from a lack of roughage in the diet over a period of time, when the inflammation is acute, roughage would aggravate the problem and has to be avoided. Instead, the diet should be bland and low in fiber and rich in demulcent food, such as *Slippery Elm*. Only when the inflammation has been brought under control should whole foods and roughage gradually be reintroduced. A natural and healthy diet is the best way to control diverticulitis in the long run.

HEMORRHOIDS

Hemorrhoids, or piles, is a distressing condition of the rectum and anus. They may be internal or external. In most cases they respond well and quickly to the use of herbal remedies, taken internally and used as external applications. It is of paramount importance to trace the cause of this problem and treat it as a priority. If this is not done, the hemorrhoids will recur. The most common cause is chronic constipation. The treatment of this has already been reviewed. Another common cause is a congested liver.

The following herbal approach will usually help in the most intransigent cases. The most important herbs needed here are astringents, especially ones that also tone the vessels involved. The herb to choose is *Lesser Celandine* (also known as *Pilewort*, of course!). In addition, *Witch Hazel*, *Periwinkle*, and *Tormentil* may be considered, if a simple infusion of *Lesser Celandine* should not suffice. If constipation is caused, hepatics may help through their gentle laxative and tonic actions. Consider *Barberry*, *Dandelion Root*, *Golden Seal*, or *Yellow Dock*.

A very soothing ointment can be made from *Lesser Celandine*, which should be applied after each motion.

LIVER AND GALLBLADDER

The liver is the largest organ of the human body, and it is involved, directly or indirectly, in all physiological processes. It plays a vital part in the digestive process—for instance, by facilitating the secretion of bile into the duodenum. Here is not the place to investigate in depth the workings of this incredible organ, but it is appropriate to mention briefly its main functions, to show how vital its health is to the body. The liver is involved in the metabolism of carbohydrates and is the most important organ for the maintenance of blood sugar levels. The liver is involved in the metabolism of proteins and is the main site for the breakdown of amino acids and for the synthesis of blood plasma proteins like globulins and clotting factors. The liver is involved with the metabolism of fats—for instance, with the synthesis of cholesterol and its subsequent breakdown into the bile salts. The liver is involved in the storage and metabolism of vitamins. The fat-soluble vitamins depend on bile for their absorption, the vitamins A, D, K, and B12 are stored in the liver, and many of the vitamins are metabolized in the liver. The liver is involved in inactivating hormones like the estrogens, corticosteroids, and other steroids. The liver is involved in the detoxification of drugs to protect our inner ecology from disruption by drugs, pollutants, artificial food additives, and other potentially poisonous substances. This function will put the liver under stress from constant work. The liver produces and excretes bile, a digestive juice essential for the digestive process.

These few examples demonstrate that the liver plays an integral part in maintaining the health of the blood, in the proper function of the endocrine system, and of the digestive process and in metabolism in general. As the liver is connected with many other functions of the body, any dysfunction or disease will affect the liver and reflect in its activity. Similarly, a state of minor liver dysfunction may show itself as a symptom elsewhere in the body. Skin disorders are a good example of this.

The liver can be helped by the use of hepatics, the most important of which include *Balmony, Barberry, Black Root, Blue Flag, Boldo, Dandelion, Fringetree Bark, Golden Seal, Vervain, Wild Yam, Winged Elm*, and *Yellow Dock*.

There is often the need to aid the liver even when no specific "disease" is present. A wide spectrum of functional problems can occur, which may be described as "liverishness." Folk remedies that were used as "spring tonics" were often based upon liver stimulants, to ensure that after a winter of bad food the liver would be strengthened and could thus help in cleansing and toning the whole body. While the modern diet in developed countries can be well balanced and nutritious throughout the year, it is nevertheless contaminated with a range of chemicals with which the body has great difficulties in dealing. Thus we can need a "spring tonic" at any time of the year.

The simplest way of helping the liver and the whole digestive process is to use bitters, like *Gentian, Golden Seal*, or *Wormwood*. A more specific decongestant action on the liver is supplied by all the hepatics mentioned above. *Dandelion* is the simplest and most widely applicable one. The root or leaves of the *Dandelion* are excellent hepatics that also work on the kidney and so help the cleansing of the body through that organ. While treating the liver in this way, it is helpful to aid the stomach as well by using *Meadowsweet*. Similarly, any other aspect of the whole system that needs aid should be taken into account. A useful liver tonic is:

Dandelion	2 parts
Meadowsweet	2 parts
Fringetree Bark	1 part
Golden Seal	1 part

This tea should be drunk after each meal.

DIET FOR LIVER AND GALLBLADDER

In any problem related to the function of the liver or the gallbladder, it is vital that strict dietary guidelines are followed, to ease the digestive burden on the liver and to ensure that there is no unnecessary pain caused. The dietary guidelines are simple: avoid all fried and roasted foods and reduce all fats and fatty foods to an absolute minimum. Drink alcohol only in moderation.

JAUNDICE

Jaundice is a symptom, not a disease. It indicates congestion within the liver that leads to a buildup of bile in the blood. The cause for the congestion has to be identified to guarantee real healing. It can be caused by an overburden of chemicals, it can be due to an infection, or it can be due to physical damage and thus has to be treated accordingly. However, the treatment can be supported by a mixture that will aid the recovery in most forms of jaundice:

Balmony	1 part
Black Root	1 part
Dandelion	1 part
Fringetree Bark	1 part
Golden Seal	1 part

A small cup of this decoction should be drunk every two hours during the day while the symptoms last.

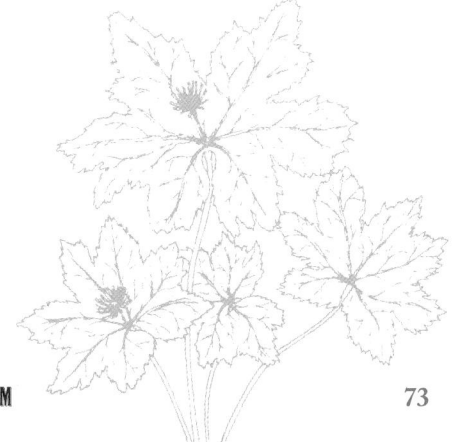

GALLSTONES

The cause of the development of gallstones is not entirely clear. Herbs can, in some cases, help the body eliminate the stones with a minimum of pain. However, this may take time. A mixture that can do this is:

Marshmallow Root	2 parts
Balmony	1 part
Boldo	1 part
Fringetree Bark	1 part
Golden Seal	1 part

This tea should be drunk three times daily.

The *Golden Seal* in this mixture may be substituted with *Barberry* or *Mountain Grape*, as all contain very similar alkaloids that work on the gallbladder. The whole of the digestive system must be aided in gallstones, so it has to be treated with the appropriate digestive herbs. If the nervous system is under stress, it should be treated accordingly.

GALLBLADDER INFLAMMATION

This extremely painful condition usually responds well to herbal remedies. The diet must be carefully examined and the recommendations given above must be strictly followed. A mixture that will ease the pain and reduce the inflammation can be made from:

Marshmallow Root	2 parts
Dandelion	1 part
Fringetree Bark	1 part
Winged Elm	1 part
Mountain Grape	1 part

This tea should be drunk three times a day.

With the extreme pain that often accompanies this condition, relaxing nervines like *Valerian* might be useful.

In addition, it is essential to take the whole state of health into account and to use the above suggestions in that context.

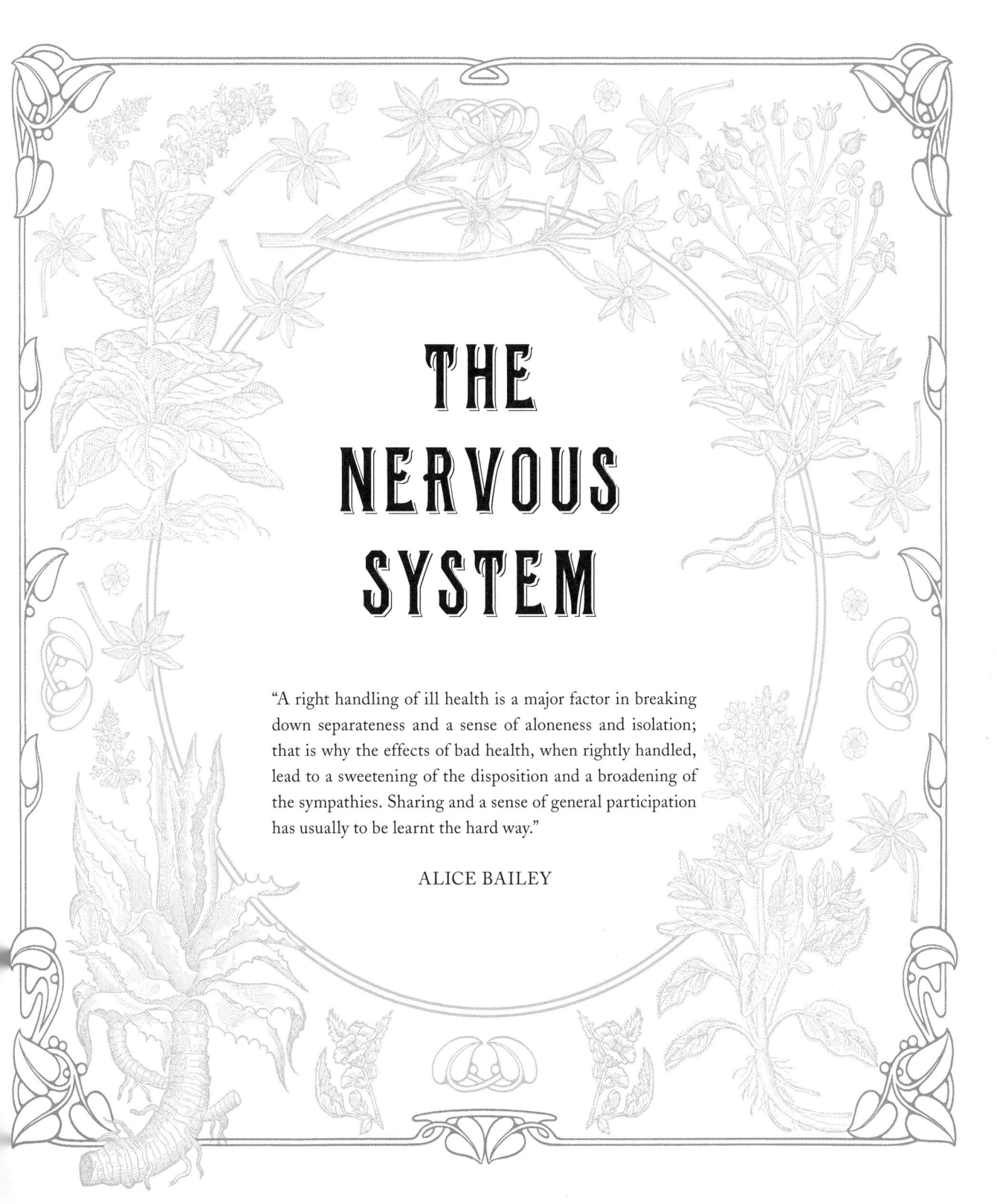

THE NERVOUS SYSTEM

"A right handling of ill health is a major factor in breaking down separateness and a sense of aloneness and isolation; that is why the effects of bad health, when rightly handled, lead to a sweetening of the disposition and a broadening of the sympathies. Sharing and a sense of general participation has usually to be learnt the hard way."

ALICE BAILEY

The Nervous System

IN NO OTHER SYSTEM OF THE BODY IS the connection between the physical and the psychological aspects of our being as apparent as in the nervous system. Clearly, the nervous system is part of the physical makeup of the body, and, just as clearly, all psychological processes take place in the nervous system. Therefore, if there is disease on the psychological level, it will reflect in the physical; and when there is disease on the physical level, this will reflect in the psychological. One wonders why the physical side of being was ever regarded as separate from the psychological.

A holistic approach to herbal healing acknowledges this interconnectedness and regards nervous tissue and its functions as a vital element in the treatment of the whole being.

Traditional allopathic medicine tends to reduce psychological problems to the mere biochemical level and assumes that "appropriate" drugs will sort out or at least hide the problem sufficiently to allow "normal" life to continue.

Interestingly enough, many techniques in the field of alternative medicine assume or imply the other extreme, namely that psychological factors are the cause of any disease and that treatment of the psyche is the only appropriate way of healing and will take care of any physical problem.

By bringing these two reductionist views together, we come closer to a holistic approach; with herbal medicine, we can treat the nervous system as part of the whole body and can feed and strengthen it and help the psyche. For our being to be wholly healthy, we have to take care of our physical health through right diet and right lifestyle, but we are also responsible for a healthy emotional, mental, and spiritual life. The emotional atmosphere we live in should be fulfilling, nurturing, and support emotional stability. Our thoughts should be creative and life-enhancing, open to the free flow of intuition and imagination, not conceptually rigid. And equally, we have to stay open to the free flow of the higher energies of our soul, without which health is impossible.

We therefore view any disease that manifests in the body in an emotional, mental, and spiritual, as well as a physical, context. We must also remember that we are part of the greater whole of humanity and are thus connected with humanity's diseases and immersed in a sea of impulses and factors not directly under our control. Many neuroses we meet in today's Western society are normal responses to an abnormal environment, sane reactions of the psyche to the insanities of a diseased society.

In this sense, there is a limit to the healing of an individual, when the disease is really a reflection of society's disease. To be a healer today involves an awareness of the whole, plus a certain amount of political insight, if not activity.

For us to be whole, our society must be whole. For our society to be whole, we must be whole. For our society to truly reflect our highest aspirations, we have to live, embody, and reflect those aspirations.

Herbal medicine can be an ecological and spiritually integrated tool to aid the nervous system of humanity, so that humanity can help itself. On the physical level, it is an ideal counterpart for therapeutic techniques on the psychological level, to help people embrace their wholeness.

Herbs for the Nervous System

There are a number of ways in which herbs can benefit the nervous system, in addition to the rather simplistic ones of stimulation and relaxation.

NERVINE TONICS

Perhaps the most important contribution herbal medicine can make in this area is in strengthening and feeding the nervous system. In cases of shock, stress, or nervous debility, the nervine tonics strengthen and feed the tissues directly; there is no need to resort to tranquilizers or other drugs to ease anxiety or depression. In many "nerve" problems, the aid of nervine tonics can be invaluable.

Surprising as it may seem, one of the best and certainly the most widely applicable remedy to feed nervous tissue is *Oats*, which can either be taken in the form of tinctures, combined as needed with relaxants, stimulants, or any other indicated remedy, or can simply be eaten, in the form of old-fashioned porridge, not instant oatmeal.

Other nervine tonics that have, in addition, a relaxing effect include *Damiana, Skullcap, Vervain,* and *Wood Betony*. Of these, *Skullcap* is often the most effective, particularly for problems related to stress.

NERVINE RELAXANTS

In cases of stress and tension, the nervine relaxants can help a lot to alleviate the condition. A representative list of the nervine relaxants include *Black Cohosh, Black Haw, California Poppy, Chamomile, Cramp Bark, Hops, Hyssop, Jamaican Dogwood, Lady's Slipper, Lavender, Lime Blossom, Mistletoe, Motherwort, Pasqueflower, Passion Flower, Rosemary, St. John's Wort, Skullcap,* and *Valerian*. As can be seen from this list, many of the relaxants also have other properties and can be selected to aid in related problems.

In addition to the herbs that work directly on the nervous system, the antispasmodic herbs—which affect the peripheral nerves and the muscle tissue—can have an indirect relaxing effect on the whole system. When the physical body is at ease, ease in the psyche is promoted.

The demulcents can also help in conjunction with nervines, as they soothe irritated tissue and promote healing.

NERVINE STIMULANTS

Direct stimulation of the nervous tissue is not very often indicated. In most cases, it is more appropriate to stimulate the body's innate vitality with the help of nervine or even digestive tonics, which work by augmenting bodily harmony and thus have a much deeper and longer-lasting effect than nervine stimulants.

When direct nervine stimulation is indicated, the best herb to use is the *Kola Nut*, although Coffee, Maté Tea, and Black Tea should also be remembered. A problem with these commonly used stimulants is the fact that they have a number of side effects and can be involved in causing many minor psychological problems, such as anxiety and tension.

Some of the herbs rich in volatile oils are also valuable stimulants, the best being *Peppermint*.

BACH FLOWER REMEDIES

The Bach Flower Remedies represent an approach to herbalism that is an alchemical amalgam of the spiritual essence of the flower in cooperation with the emotional/mental need of the person.

They are not used directly for physical illness, but for the individual's worry, apprehension, hopelessness, fear, irritability, etc. The state of someone's psychic being has a major bearing on the causation, development, and cure of any physical illness. The remedies appear to work with the life force, allowing it to flow freely through or around the blockage and so speed healing and a return to wholeness.

Thirty-eight remedies were developed by the late Dr. Edward Bach. The story of how he found them is wonderful indeed and worth reading. The contact details for any information about the Remedies is:

United States:
The Original Bach Flower Remedies
California, U.S.A.
Phone: (1-800) 214-2850
Website: www.bachflower.com

United Kingdom:
Dr. E. Bach Centre
Mount Vernon, Sotwell, Wallingford, Oxon OX10 0PZ, England
Phone: +44 (0)1491 834678
Website: www.bachcentre.com/centre/remedies.htm

Bach found 38 flowers to cover the negative states of mind from which we so often suffer, categorizing them under seven major headings with further subdivisions. These headings are Apprehension, Indecision, Loneliness, Insufficient Interest in Circumstances, Oversensitivity, Despondency and Despair, and Overccare for Others.

These flower remedies are ideal for self-use. Supplies and much more information are obtainable from the Bach Centre or its websites. The remedies are inherently benign in action with no unpleasant reactions and can be used by anyone. The dose is simply a few drops of the special extracts in water.

I shall quote from a brief guide to the remedies produced by the center to give a taste of their uses.

Agrimony: for those who suffer inner torture that they try to hide behind a facade of cheerfulness
Aspen: for apprehension and foreboding; fears of unknown origin
Beech: for those who are arrogant, critical, and intolerant of others
Centaury: for weakness of will in those who let themselves be imposed upon and become subservient, who have difficulty in saying "no"
Cerato: for those who doubt their own judgment and overly seek the advice of others. Often influenced and misguided

Cherry Plum: for a fear of mental collapse, desperation, or loss of control. Vicious rages

Chestnut Bud: for those who refuse to learn by experience and continually repeat the same mistakes

Chicory: for overpossessiveness and demanding attention; selfishness; those who like others to conform to their standards and will often make martyrs of themselves

Clematis: for indifference, inattentiveness, dreaminess, and absentmindedness; mental escape from reality

Crab Apple: a cleanser for those who feel unclean or ashamed of ailments. For self-disgust and the house-proud

Elm: for those temporarily overcome by responsibility or inadequacy, although normally very capable

Gentian: for the despondent, easily discouraged, and dejected

Gorse: for extreme hopelessness

Heather: for people who are obsessed with their own troubles and experiences. Poor listeners

Holly: for those who are jealous, envious, revengeful, and suspicious. For those who hate

Honeysuckle: for those with nostalgia who constantly dwell in the past. Also homesickness

Hornbeam: for procrastination; "Monday morning" feeling

Impatiens: for impatience and irritability

Larch: for despondency due to lack of self-confidence. An expectation of failure, so failing to make an attempt. Feeling inferior although having the ability

Mimulus: for fear of known things; shyness and timidity

Mustard: for deep gloom that descends for no known reason but can lift just as suddenly; melancholy

Oak: for those who struggle on in illness and against adversity despite setbacks; plodders

Olive: for exhaustion—feeling of being drained of energy and everything being an effort

Pine: for feelings of guilt; people who blame themselves for mistakes of others and feel unworthy

Red Chestnut: for excessive fear and overcaring for others held dear

Rock Rose: for terror, extreme fear, or panic

Rock Water: for those who are hard on themselves, rigid-minded, and self-denying

Scleranthus: for uncertainty, indecision, or vacillation

Star of Bethlehem: for all the effects of bad news or fright following an accident

Sweet Chestnut: for the anguish of those who have reached the limits of endurance and absolute dejection

Vervain: for overenthusiasm, overeffort, and straining; fanaticism

Vine: for those who are dominating, inflexible, ambitious, autocratic, arrogant, and proud

Walnut: a protection remedy against powerful influences and helps adjustment to any transition or change, e.g., menopause or divorce

Water Violet: for those who are proud, reserved, or "superior"

White Chestnut: for persistent unwanted thoughts; preoccupation with a worry or event; mental arguments

Wild Oat: helps determine one's intended path in life

Wild Rose: for resignation, apathy. For drifters who accept their lot, making little effort for improvement

Willow: for resentment and bitterness with a "poor me" attitude

Rescue Remedy: a combination of *Cherry Plum, Clematis, Impatiens, Rock Rose, Star of Bethlehem.* An all-purpose emergency composite for cases of trauma, anguish, bereavement, and any stress

Rescue Remedy treats the effect that a sufferer may experience through serious news, bereavement, terror, severe mental trauma, a feeling of desperation, or a numbed, bemused state of mind. Every home should have a dropper bottle of it, and it is worth traveling with it. It is taken orally, at a dose of about four drops in water.

Patterns of Disease of the Nervous System

The connection between physical and psychological factors in illness is recognized by orthodox medicine in the concept of psychosomatic and somatopsychic illness. Psychological factors can predispose or aggravate physical problems (psychosomatic concept), or physical factors can affect the psychological state (somatopsychic concept). It is perhaps far more appropriate to view all illness as part of a profound relationship between body, mind, and soul. Wherever a nervine treatment is appropriate to support the healing of a condition, this has been pointed out.

A number of conditions have an especially strong relationship with the nervous system, while not producing neurological symptoms. These conditions can often be helped greatly by strengthening the nerves and toning the whole system. A representative list includes:

—The circulatory system: high blood pressure and coronary disease
—The respiratory system: asthma, hay fever, and irritable coughs
—The digestive system: peptic ulcer, colon disorder, flatulence, and dyspepsia
—The skin: skin problems
—The glandular system: thyroid problems and other endocrine disorders
—The reproductive system: many problems associated with menstruation

This list suggests conditions in which nervines are often appropriate, which does not imply that the conditions are "all in the mind." It means that to promote healing in the whole being, the nervous system may need more help here than usual.

The nervous system is perhaps the easiest system in the body in which to see the relevance of discussing disease rather than disease. It may seem like a quibble, but this usage demonstrates the holistic view that the proper functioning of the whole body can be seen in terms of harmony and energy flow. By viewing disease from this standpoint, it is possible to differentiate between psychological and neurological problems without resorting to a dualistic separation of mind and body.

There is a plethora of relaxation and meditation techniques to help attain a relaxed state. We each have to find those most suitable for us. For some of us complex relaxation programs work best, while for others it might be a walk in the woods. Meditation can range from a gentle inner stilling to a profound process of inner transcendence. While in an herbal of this kind it is not possible to explore these in depth, here are a couple of simple but effective methods.

Relaxation Exercises

Breathing is of great value in relaxation, particularly during the initial stages. People who are at ease with themselves and their world breathe slowly, deeply, and rhythmically. Breathing is the only autonomic function we are capable of controlling consciously, and by doing so it is possible to influence all autonomic and, to a degree, emotional responses.

Here is a basic and safe breathing relaxation technique:

—Ideally this should be done twice a day for 5 to 15 minutes in a quiet room free of disturbance.
—Rest on your back with head and neck comfortably supported.
—Rest hands on upper abdomen, close your eyes, and settle into a comfortable position.

— Avoid distractions such as sunlight, a clock, animals, etc.
— The aim is to breathe slowly, deeply, and rhythmically. Inhalation should be slow, unforced, and unhurried. Silently count to 4, 5, or 6, whatever is comfortable for you. When inhalation is complete, slowly exhale through the nose. Count this breathing out, as when breathing in. *The exhalation should take as long as the inhalation.*
— There should be no sense of strain. If initially you feel you have breathed your fullest at a count of 3, that is all right. Try gradually to slow down the rhythm until a slow count of 5 or 6 is possible, with a pause of 2 or 3 between the in and out breath.
— This pattern of breathing should be repeated 15 to 20 times, and, since each cycle should take about 15 seconds, this exercise should occupy a total of about 5 minutes.
— Once the mechanics of this exercise have been mastered, introduce thoughts at different parts of the cycle. An example would be trying on inhalation to sense a feeling of warmth and energy entering the body with the air. On exhalation, sense a feeling of sinking and settling deeper into the surface you are lying on.
— On completion, do not get up immediately but rest for a minute or two, allowing the mind to become aware of any sensations of stillness, warmth, heaviness, etc.
— Once mastered, this exercise can be used in any tense situation with the certainty that it will defuse the normal agitated response and should result in a far greater ability to cope.

Often tension is focused in the muscles of the body itself, and this following exercise can release such tightness and so allow the mind to be at ease.

It is best to precede this exercise with a few cycles of deep breathing.

— Either lie down or sit in a reclining chair.
— Avoid distractions and wear clothes that do not constrict.
— Starting with the feet, try to sense or feel that the muscles of the area are not actively tense.
— Then deliberately tighten the muscles, curling the toes under and holding the tension for 5 or 10 seconds. Then tense them *even more strongly* for a further few seconds before letting all the tension go and sensing the wonderful feeling of release.
— Try consciously to register what this feels like, especially in comparison with the tense state in which they were held.
— Progress to the calf muscles and exercise in the same way. *First sense the state the muscles are in, then tense them, hold the position, and then tense them even more before letting go.* Positively *register the sense of relief.*
— There is a slight possibility of inducing a cramp doing this. If this occurs, stop tensing that area immediately and go on to the next.
— After the calf, go on to exercise the knees, then the upper leg, thighs, buttocks, back, abdomen, chest, shoulders, arms, hands, neck, head, and face.
— The precise sequence is irrelevant, as long as all these areas are "treated" to the same process.
— Some areas may need extra attention. For example, in the abdomen the tensing of muscles can be achieved either by contracting (pulling in the stomach) or by stretching (pushing outward). This variation in tensing is applicable to many muscles in the body.
— There are between 20 and 25 of these "areas," depending upon how you go about it. Each should be given at least 5 to 10 seconds of tensing and a further 5 to 10 seconds of letting go and passively sensing the feeling.
— Thus 8 to 10 minutes should cover the whole technique. This should be followed by several minutes of an unhurried feeling of warm, relaxed tranquillity.

— Focus the mind on the whole body. Sense it as heavy and content, free of tension or effort. This can be enhanced by a few cycles of deep breathing.
— Have a good stretch and then carry on with your daily life.

PSYCHOLOGICAL DISEASE

Our society is plagued by self-doubt, by fear and alienation, by dehumanization and violence. It is perhaps understandable that an epidemic of stress-related conditions characterizes the casebooks of most doctors.

While the trauma and chaos of our times seems to weigh heavily, there is the profound support that comes from the Spirit that dwells within us all. Herbal medicine is an expression of God's love for all of life. The new age is already thriving in our hearts. Our task is to reveal it.

STRESS

"Stress" can be seen as any stimulus or change in the internal or external environment that disturbs homeostasis or inner harmony. This can be many things, from work conditions, relationships, and bodily health to the state of the weather. The body responds in a similar way to any stress with hormonal and behavioral reactions.

A certain degree of stress reaction is essential to survive in a modern city; the problems arise when an individual stress response moves beyond that which aids, to a state that detracts.

By definition, stress itself cannot be treated, as it is a natural response to prevailing conditions. What can be done, however, is to aid the body as it responds. This is possible with the use of herbs and with the help of vitamins, but perhaps more important are relaxation exercises to give the body some chance for recovery. In addition, the situation causing the stress should be re-evaluated. Rather than alter the response to a situation, change the situation.

When stress does lead to a problem, the treatment can be based on a number of approaches. It is vital that the body's nutrition is adequate. It is often appropriate to supply the body with additional vitamin C and the vitamin B-complex, as it needs more of both when stressed. The nervine tonics will feed and tone the nervous system. The best ones in this case are *Oats* and *Skullcap*, but others may also be indicated, if there are related physical symptoms. *Ginseng* is an excellent herb to increase one's ability to cope with stress, when it is taken over a period of time. Of equal relevance and potency as an adaptogen is *Siberian Ginseng*. It is worth exploring the concept of adaptogens here.

This is a relatively new concept to Western medicine and herbalism. However, in China and the East, such ideas are the very basis of their preventative approach to health and well-being. Adaptogens act in such a way as to improve the body's adaptability. In other words, by helping it to adapt "around" the problem, they enable it to avoid reaching a point of collapse or overstress.

There is now much research into these potentially astounding remedies. The core of their action appears to lie in helping the body deal with stress. As we know, an inability to cope with external pressures leads to many internal repercussions. Thus many diverse forms of illness can develop. Adaptogens seem to increase the threshold of damage via support of adrenal gland and possibly pituitary gland function.

By stretching the meaning of the word, it can come to mean what in the past was called a tonic. This is especially true where an herb can have a normalizing effect, that is, contradictory actions depending on the body's needs. This restorative quality is a common and unique feature of herbal medicines.

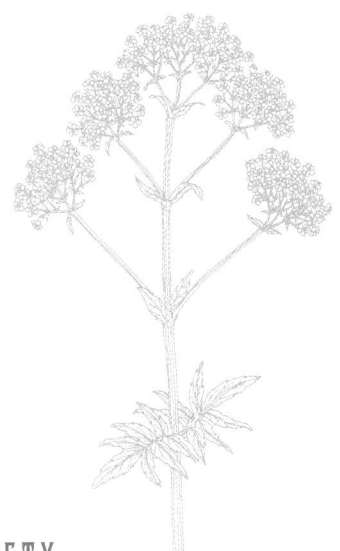

ANXIETY

We have all at some point in our life experienced anxiety. Normally, the feeling lasts only for a short time and is caused by some relevant external problem. Sometimes, though, it becomes a habitual pattern, influencing our thoughts and behavior. We then perceive the world filtered through our attitude of anxiety and we act accordingly. We enter a vicious circle where anxiety produces more anxiety. It has become a truism in the growth movement that "we create our own reality" and are responsible for what we create. We often need help in appreciating this and incorporating the insight into our lives. Therapeutic counseling techniques and herbal medicine can ease the process.

All the nervine relaxants will ease anxiety and tension, the specific ones varying with each individual, as some are more effective with a particular mind than others. The most effective ones are *Lady's Slipper, Lime Blossom, Mistletoe, Skullcap,* and *Valerian.*

In addition to the nervine relaxants, the antispasmodic herbs are useful, as often in cases of anxiety there is also muscle tension, the relief of which helps the whole being to move to a state of ease and well-being, the perfect inner state within which to bring about healing.

A mixture of equal parts of *Skullcap* and *Valerian* is usually best; the one drawback of this effective mixture is that its taste is not very pleasant.

| *Skullcap* | 1 part |
| *Valerian* | 1 part |

This tea can be drunk three times a day or when needed. Since it is safe at a higher dosage for most people, take it in the amount that is effective for *you*.

PREMENSTRUAL SYNDROME

This distressing problem, connected with the menstrual cycle, can create emotional and psychological disruption. To ease PMS in the short term, *Skullcap* and *Valerian* can be very effective. However, to really solve the problem, the state of hormonal balance in general has to be examined and treated. This is discussed in depth in the chapter on the reproductive system.

HYPERACTIVITY

A growing phenomenon is that of hyperactivity, particularly in children. Hyperactivity is not easy to define or diagnose, and many normal, healthy children have been classed as hyperactive just because they are more alive than their peers or parents. The latter may suffer from low energy due to a bad diet, including the consumption of large amounts of sugar. Sugar acts like a sedative with a number of harmful side effects.

If a child has been correctly diagnosed as hyperactive, a number of steps should be taken. One of the central factors leading to hyperactivity is an accumulation of heavy metals in the body. Due to increased industrialization, our atmosphere and diet have become rather polluted by these substances. The first step to combat hyperactivity is to provide a diet that is as pure and natural as possible, without any synthetic chemicals. You might also consider joining Friends of the Earth, the environmental action group, to work for the reduction of pollution in our environment. The growing problem of hyperactivity is a microcosmic reflection of the condition we are creating in the world.

In this growing area of concern, it is clear that artificial food additives have a lot to answer for. It appears that young, developing nervous systems are particularly prone to the damage or irritation that many food additives can cause. The effect is one of excessive activity with only a few hours' sleep each night, and because of the overactivity such children are more prone to accidents. There is some association with eczema and asthma, both of which will be aggravated by the overactivity. There may be difficulties with speech, balance, and learning, even if the child has a high IQ.

Anyone with a child suspected of having this problem will be under extreme stress themselves. So there are two things to look at: ways to help the child and ways for the parents to cope.

Excellent support and help groups exist, and these can provide a resource of useful information on this problem. Look for one in your area.

A treatment that can be quite effective is based on a diet by Dr. Feingold and cuts out all food and drink containing synthetic additives of any kind and certain natural chemicals.

However, there are specific food additives to avoid, and these are by law marked on any package containing them. They are:

E102	Tartrazine
E104	Quinoline Yellow
107	Yellow 2G
E110	Sunset Yellow
E120	Cochineal
E122	Carmoisine
E123	Amaranth
E124	Ponceau 4R
E127	Erythrosine
128	Red 2G
E132	Indigo Carmine
E133	Brilliant Blue
E150	Caramel
E151	Black PN
154	Brown FK
155	Brown HT
E210	Benzoic Acid
E211	Sodium Benzoate
E250	Sodium Nitrite
E251	Sodium Nitrate
E320	Butylated Hydroxyanisole
E321	Butylated hydroxytoluene

These are additives that there is little doubt about, but the complete list of possible culprits is almost endless.

A combination of the diet and good herbal treatment for any bodily symptoms the child has developed should be able to clear the problem.

To rid the body of the chemicals that have already been accumulated, alteratives should be used over a long period of time. The best one in this case is *Red Clover*, as it is also a nervine relaxant. For a short-term alleviation of the problem, other strong relaxants might be added and the person should also be treated for stress (as their body will be in a constant state of alert) with the aid of

Oats and *Vervain* and the vitamins C and B-complex. Gentle bitter tonics such as *Centaury* or *Dandelion* will quicken this return to stability.

DEPRESSION

Depression can be a reaction to external factors or it can be an internally created state of mind, and often it is a combination of the two. In either case, herbs can help to lift the depression, but at the same time the basic cause has to be treated.

An honest look at the factors involved and a courageous reappraisal of one's life is called for, as herbs by themselves will not solve the underlying problem. They may, however, create the space and ease of mind to do so. The best antidepressive herbs include *Damiana, Ginseng, Kola Nut, Lady's Slipper, Lavender, Lime Blossom, Oats, Rosemary, Skullcap, Valerian,* and *Vervain*.

When the depression is connected with a general debility of the whole body, affecting the nervous system, the following mixture is indicated:

Kola Nut	2 parts
Damiana	1 part
Lavender	1 part
Oats	1 part
Rosemary	1 part

This should be drunk three times a day.

Where there is not so much debility involved, use the following mixture:

Kola Nut	1 part
Lime Blossom	1 part
Skullcap	1 part

This tea should be drunk three times a day as well. If a more powerful approach is needed, *Valerian* may be added to the mixture.

As with all the mixtures recommended, remember that they may not be the ones you need. As all the herbs in this book are safe to use (within normal dosage), try out different mixtures. Read in "The Herbal" section about the herbs that can be used and choose accordingly. Use the teas over two or three days to give them time to work. And if in doubt, consult an herbalist in your area. You may want to talk to someone confidentially about your problems, and a worthy herbalist will be a good listener.

INSOMNIA

At one time or another everyone has a sleepless night; stress during the day or anxiety about the next day can keep us awake and restless all through the night or keep us from finding deep peaceful sleep. When this occurs only once in a while, there is little wrong. However, it can become a repeated situation in which the whole body will suffer, as it is during sleep that most healing and revivifying takes place. There are many useful and powerful herbal hypnotics that aid a restful night's sleep, but often a gentle relaxation with the help of nervine relaxants is enough to allow the natural sleep process to take over.

The most effective sleep inducers are *Californian Poppy, Hops, Jamaican Dogwood, Passion Flower,* and *Valerian,* with *Jamaican Dogwood* being particularly useful when sleeplessness is due to pain. A useful mixture is:

Passion Flower	1 part
Valerian	1 part

This tea should be drunk just before going to bed. The strength needed will vary from person to person, so experiment. The mixture is safe, and it is impossible to overdose with these herbs.

Most of the nervine relaxants will promote a restful, natural sleep. *Chamomile, Lime Blossom,* and *Red Clover* are especially good and make delicious teas. They should be drunk last thing at night to relax any tension left over from the day and ease one into sleep.

Another very pleasant and excellent way to imbibe these herbs is through the skin when having a bath. This is a particularly good way to help children sleep better. Thus, a *Lime Blossom* bath last thing at night will promote sleep, while a *Chamomile* one will, too, in addition to helping with teething.

This recipe is for a *Valerian* bath, but it can be used as a guideline for any of the herbs mentioned. Pour 2 pints (1 liter) of boiling water onto one or two handfuls of the dried root of *Valerian*, leave it to stand for half an hour, then strain the liquid and add it to the hot bath, which should be taken just before going to bed. The bath may be a whole bath, a foot bath, or a hand bath. Light a candle, leave the lights off, read a fairytale (no thrillers or newspapers!), and relax.

NEUROLOGICAL DISEASES

So far we have discussed problems manifesting mainly through psychological causes. We now turn to the herbal treatment of problems that manifest themselves within the nerve tissue itself. These can be overt organic ones, such as multiple sclerosis, or minor functional ones, such as headaches.

HEADACHES

Headaches can be caused by a variety of psychological and physical dysfunctions, from stress and tension to digestive disorders and postural problems. The list of herbs potentially useful for headaches is therefore extensive and includes *Balm, Cayenne, Chamomile, Elderberry Flower, Ground Ivy, Jamaican Dogwood, Lady's Slipper, Lavender, Marjoram, Peppermint, Rosemary, Rue, Skullcap, Tansy, Thyme, Valerian, Wood Betony,* and *Wormwood*. From this list, it is apparent that actions other than that of pain relief (anodyne) will aid in the relief of headaches. This, of course, reflects the diversity of possible causes, which range from pollution, bad lighting, or domestic gas leaks (no matter how minute) to neck tension, eye strain, postural problems, bad diet, allergies, or other factors.

First, some general advice. You can take a relaxing bath with any of the herbs suggested above, if possible including *Lavender* as one of the ingredients. Or use one of the herbs that are rich in volatile oils (the best ones for headaches being *Lavender, Marjoram, Peppermint,* and *Rosemary*), which can be used in the form of oils or as strong infusions. They are either rubbed on the forehead and temples, or their vapor can be inhaled, both methods often easing pain surprisingly fast. Besides using herbs, relaxing techniques can also be helpful: a walk in the woods or a meditation or whatever helps you feel at ease.

The most common physical causes of headaches are digestive disorders such as indigestion and constipation, muscular and nervous tension, and menstrual problems.

For stomach-related headaches, the use of carminatives and bitters is indicated, with the following mixture often being helpful:

Balm	1 part
Lavender	1 part
Meadowsweet	1 part

This tea can be drunk whenever needed.

If this is needed often, the digestion and diet will need attention. Where chronic constipation is the problem, the advice given in the section on the digestive system should be followed.

Tension in the neck and shoulders, caused either by psychological stress or by postural problems (usually both together) will often bring on a headache. The use of nervine relaxants will ease this sort of headache, with *Valerian* often being the most effective.

Menstrual problems can also cause headaches and are best treated by correcting the hormonal balance, as described in the chapter on the reproductive system. However, for a short-term treatment, a tea of:

Skullcap	1 part
Valerian	1 part

is very helpful. A cup of this tea can be drunk whenever needed.

MIGRAINE

This distressing and intense headache is often accompanied by digestive disruptions like nausea and vomiting and by visual disturbances and photophobia. It can last for hours or days.

Like headaches, migraines can be triggered by a whole range of factors. Their treatment often involves both long-term attention to the cause and specific medications for an individual attack. To discover the underlying cause, it is sometimes necessary to seek expert advice, as self-diagnosis can be difficult.

The invaluable herb *Feverfew* must be mentioned here. While not quite the wonder remedy the media has led us to believe, the regular use of it either fresh or as a tablet or a tea will often clear the migraines after a month or so of treatment. If you have migraine, then plant *Feverfew* in your backyard!

A number of herbs will ease the pain of an attack, if they are taken at the first sign. These include *Black Willow, Jamaican Dogwood, Passion Flower, Valerian*, and *Wood Betony*.

If there are also digestive symptoms like nausea, vomiting, or acid ingestion, herbs like *Black Horehound, Chamomile, Golden Seal*, or *Meadowsweet* can be useful. Consult "The Herbal" section in order to decide which is the most appropriate herb or combination for the individual case concerned.

The underlying cause can be one single factor, but often a number of contributing elements play a part in bringing about a migraine. The elements are most often found in one of the following categories:

Diet: An allergic reaction to certain foods is the most common factor causing migraines. A comprehensive list of allergenic foods would include everything that can be eaten. However, the most common triggers are red meat, pork, chocolate, dairy products, coffee, strong tea, white sugar, yeast products, vitamin B supplements, pickles, acidic foods, animal fat, alcohol (especially red wine, sherry, port, etc.). Often the reaction is not triggered by a single allergenic food but by a number of reactions to different foods accumulating and reaching a critical threshold. If you suspect a single allergy or such an accumulation as the cause, fast for two days and gradually re-introduce different foods. If a migraine is set off by a specific item, you have identified a trigger and can avoid it in the future. To support your digestive system, a regular treatment with *Balmony, Golden Seal, Meadowsweet,* or *Wormwood* should be used for a number of months. After a while, fast again for two days, gradually re-introduce foods, and see if the reaction is still the same.

Stress: Stress leading to tension is another common and potent trigger for migraines. It is best approached through relaxation therapy and sometimes even necessitates some form of psychotherapy, Gestalt work, psychosynthesis, or other appropriate technique. Typical examples of people susceptible to stress-induced migraines are those unable to cope with responsibilities, leading to a constant state of frustration, or at the other extreme, those who are overly conscientious perfectionists. In both, the neurotic tension can lead to migraines. The appropriate herbs in such cases are nervine relaxants and tonics, like *Hops, Mistletoe, Oats, Skullcap,* or *Vervain*.

If instead the migraine is related to a debilitated state, nervine stimulants like *Damiana* or *Kola Nut* are appropriate.

One herb applicable in all cases of migraine caused by stress is *Ginseng*. It has to be taken for a number of weeks, though, before showing any clear effect.

Hormonal Problems: A common cause of migraines in women is hormonal problems associated with the onset of periods or possibly menopause. A long-term treatment, aiming at the balancing of the hormonal system with the aid of herbs like *Black Cohosh, Chasteberry, False Unicorn Root, Golden Ragwort (aka Life Root),* or *Wild Yam* may help. For more specific information, look under the section on the reproductive system.

Structural: A migraine can be brought about by structural problems in the neck or the spinal column, leading to muscular or nerve problems. A visit to a competent osteopath or chiropractor would be appropriate if any such problem is suspected.

Neuralgia

Neuralgia—or nerve pain—can range from excruciating pain that follows the length of a nerve to a local pain where the nerve reaches the skin. The pain can be caused by an infection or by an osteopathic problem, but most commonly it is due to a general debilitated condition, brought about by wrong diet, stress, and lack of rest.

To heal neuralgia, the underlying cause must be taken care of. If it is due to debility, the diet has to be improved and should include a lot of green vegetables and fruit with the addition of vitamin B-complex supplements for a while. Adequate rest and relaxation are also necessary.

Herbs like *Ginseng, Hops, Jamaican Dogwood, Pasqueflower, Passion Flower, St. John's Wort,* and *Valerian* are especially useful, and in addition to those used as teas, herbal preparations like *Rosemary* and *Lavender* liniments, and *St. John's Wort* oil, rubbed into the effected part, can ease the pain.

In any nervous condition, the liberal use of *Oats*—in the diet and perhaps as an infusion in the bath—is also strongly recommended. If it occurs in association with shingles, then take *Echinacea* and *Marigold* over a period of at least three months as well. This could be as a tea or tinctures.

MULTIPLE SCLEROSIS

Multiple sclerosis is a chronic degenerative disease of the nerve axons. Medicine has not clearly identified the cause; it has been suggested that viral or immunological actions play a part. From the viewpoint of holistic healing, it is clearly a disease arising when the inner harmony is out of balance, causing the degenerative changes. As such, the holistic approach will aim at restoring a balance. It is possible to improve multiple sclerosis considerably with the aid of appropriate herbs and with careful digestive control.

Detailed dietary advice can be found in any good cookbook on holistic nutrition; the main factors are the total elimination of dairy products and possibly of foods containing gluten. Further, saturated fats have to be kept to a minimum and need to be replaced by polyunsaturated ones, from vegetables.

With a disease like multiple sclerosis, it is particularly obvious that the symptoms are a manifestation of a long process of degeneration and that a holistic herbal treatment has to aim at strengthening and rebuilding the system. Thus, the treatment will vary with each individual and should be centered around the use of nervine tonics and stimulants and digestive tonics. The only herbal remedy to be recommended in all cases is the oil of *Evening Primrose*, which is rich in polyunsaturated fats and should be taken in capsules over a long period to enable the nerve sheaths to be rebuilt.

As multiple sclerosis is a very complex condition, it is best to seek professional help.

SHINGLES

Shingles are caused by a viral infection of the nerve ganglia, which can be extremely painful and long-lasting if not treated properly. The infection is usually accompanied by vesicles on the skin.

To treat shingles, it is necessary to strengthen the nerve cells with the aid of nervine tonics. Antimicrobials have to be used to aid the body in overcoming the infection, and anodynes in the form of nervine relaxants should be included to reduce the pain. A useful mixture is:

Echinacea	2 parts
Jamaican Dogwood	1 part
Oats	1 part
Passion Flower	1 part
St. John's Wort	1 part
Valerian	1 part

This tea should be drunk three times a day.

For a local treatment of the symptoms, regular herbal baths with the above herbs are recommended. The treatment has to be applied over a period of time and should pay attention to good nutrition, preferably one that is rich in vitamin B-complex supplements.

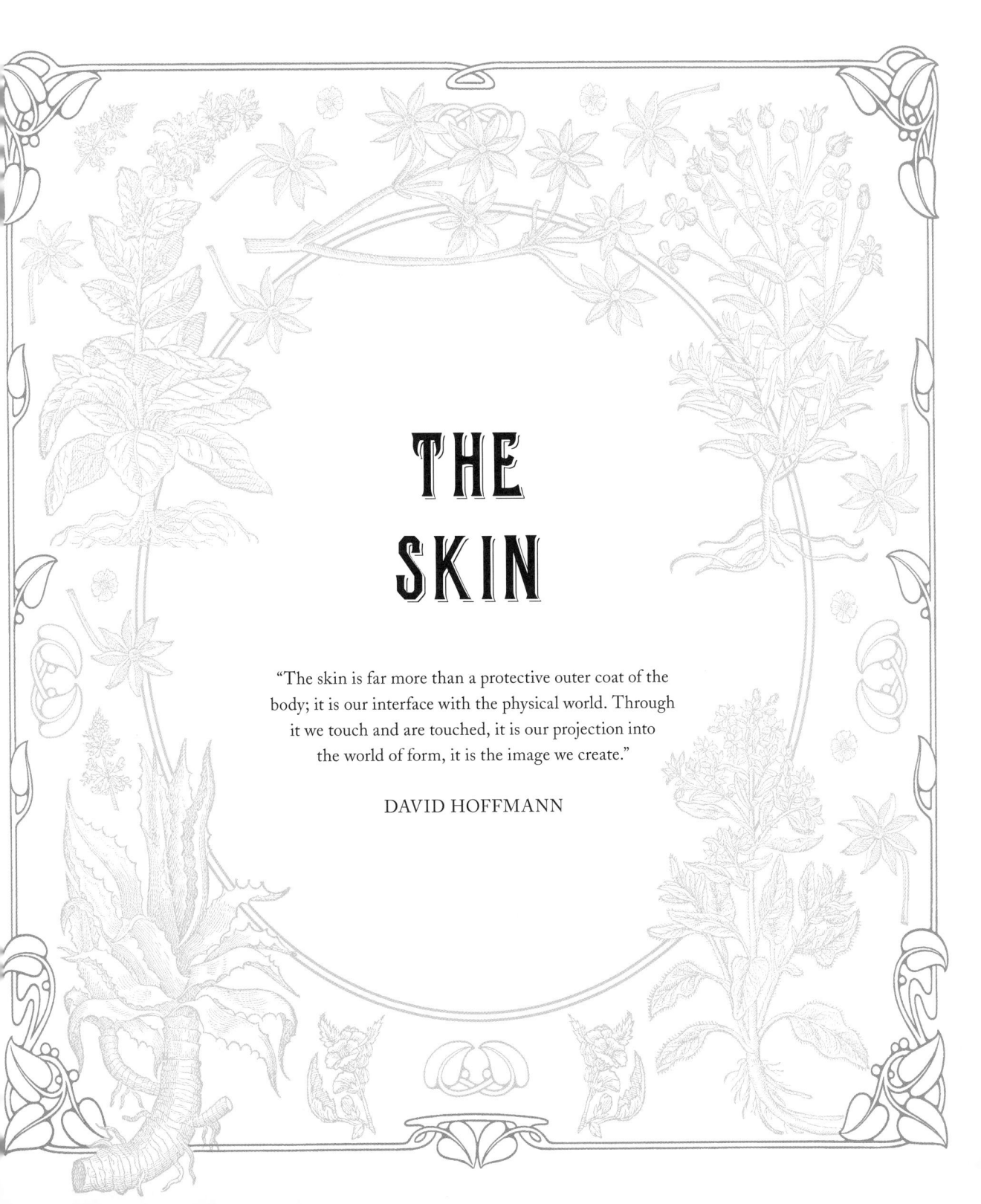

THE SKIN

"The skin is far more than a protective outer coat of the body; it is our interface with the physical world. Through it we touch and are touched, it is our projection into the world of form, it is the image we create."

DAVID HOFFMANN

The Skin

OUR SKIN HAS NUMEROUS FUNCTIONS. It is the primary protective organ of our body; without a complete and coherent skin, we would soon die of massive infection or of allergic shock, for the skin protects the body from injury, from light and chemicals, from extremes of temperature, and from invasion by microorganisms. Some of the protective functions are maintained through complex ecological processes, like protection against infections. Not only does the skin itself secrete antimicrobial substances, it also harbors a friendly natural community of bacteria. These resident bacteria protect the skin against the invasion of unfriendly microorganisms by maintaining an environment unfavorable to them. One of the potential problems of antibiotic therapy is the disruption of this friendly community, which opens the way for infections via the skin. Similarly, chemical deodorants and antiperspirants work partly by destroying the natural skin bacteria and thus disrupt this delicate balance.

The skin is also in many ways responsible for the maintenance of a stable and harmonious internal environment. On one hand, the skin protects us against the loss of water, salts, and organic substances from inside the body. On the other hand, it is one of the four main organs responsible for the excretion of waste products and water.

As the skin is responsible for the excretion of approximately a quarter of the body's waste products, any dysfunction of the skin in this field will put stress on the other three eliminative organs, namely the kidneys, the lungs, and the bowels, as they will have to deal with the extra burden. Thus a problem in the eliminative capacity of the skin can lead to secondary problems in the other organs and difficulties in those organs can conversely lead to difficulties with the skin. The skin also plays a part in temperature control, as its sweat glands can regulate the excretion of water.

It is through the skin that we have physical contact with our environment, as the whole area of the skin is rich in sensory nerve endings. In fact, it is worth noting that in the growing embryo the skin develops from the same source as the nervous tissue. This common origin points to the close relationship between skin and nervous system, a relationship that can be seen as a physical manifestation of the close connection between our inner being and the way it is reflected into the world. Thus, skin diseases will often be an outer reflection of internal problems and must be treated as such. Only rarely, as in bruises and wounds, can the skin be related to in isolation.

Herbs for the Skin

Even though skin problems may reflect a variety of internal conditions and all groups of herbs may play a role in its treatment, some groups are especially indicated. In particular, the vulneraries, the alteratives, the diaphoretics, the antimicrobials, and the nervines will be discussed.

VULNERARIES

Nature is rich in plants that promote the healing of fresh cuts and wounds, and this is to be expected if herbs are truly part of an ecological support system, integrated into and created by Gaia. As injuries of one sort or another are perhaps the most common physical problems, we find that every natural habitat is rich in those healing plants. The traditional knowledge of their use is reflected in their common names like *Woundwort*, *Boneset*, and *Self-Heal*.

Some of these herbs are astringents, and part of their efficiency is based upon their ability to arrest bleeding and to condense the tissue. The most common and useful vulneraries are *Aloe, Chickweed, Comfrey, Elderberry Flower* and *Berries, Geranium, Golden Seal, Horsetail, Irish Moss, Marigold Flowers, Marshmallow Root, Self-Heal, Slippery Elm, Witch Hazel,* and *Woundwort*. Some are applied externally, while others are used both externally and internally. Study them in "The Herbal" section to get to know them.

ALTERATIVES

Alteratives gradually alter and correct a "polluted" condition of the blood stream and restore a healthier functioning. The way the alteratives operate is poorly understood, but they certainly work and they are perhaps the herbs most often used in the context of skin conditions, the roots of which lie deep within the metabolism of the individual. They cleanse the whole of the body, but their activity is focused in different areas, some in the kidneys, some in the liver, etc., and they have to be chosen according to their specific indications.

Alteratives include *Blue Flag, Burdock, Cleavers, Figwort, Fumitory, Golden Seal, Mountain Grape, Nettles, Red Clover, Sarsaparilla, Sassafras, Thuja,* and *Yellow Dock*.

ANTIMICROBIALS

For some skin conditions, antimicrobials have to be used to rid the body of microorganisms that have invaded it or act on the skin. Herbs that help here include *Chickweed, Echinacea, Eucalyptus, Garlic, Marigold, Myrrh, Pasqueflower, Thuja, Thyme,* and *Wild Indigo*.

Patterns of Skin Disease

Orthodox medicine classifies the different skin diseases according to histological changes occurring in the skin tissue. This approach ignores to a large extent the idea that skin problems can be manifestations of internal problems and should be treated as such and not as local phenomena. Without limiting the holistic approach, we can categorize the areas that may lead to skin problems based on an identification of causes. Three areas can usefully be identified while recognizing that there is an overlap. There are internal causes, where the origins of a skin disease lie purely in internal disharmony, as in psoriasis or some eczemas; external causes, where the skin problem is the direct result of external influences, as with wounds, bruises, or sunburns; and internal reactions to external factors, where the skin problem is due to the body's inability to cope with an external factor, like in allergic eczema or skin infections due to bacteria or fungi.

Depending upon the type of cause, the healing approach will vary. With internal causes, the treatment has to aim within, for an external treatment like an ointment would be unable to touch the basic problem, whereas with external causes an ointment might be sufficient.

Internal Causes

Most of the intransigent and chronic skin conditions that affect humanity are the result of internal processes. As our skin is our interface with the world it is often the site to manifest disharmony in one's life. This disharmony can have physical and genetic roots; it can be focused in the liver, kidneys, circulation, or in other systems. The sources can be numerous, but the results may be the same. To treat effectively the conditions due to internal causes, the unique factors at work in a particular individual have to be identified.

Psoriasis

This is one of the most common skin problems to affect the Caucasian population, though it does occur throughout humanity. Up to 2% of people in the Western world suffer from psoriasis. It can be caused by a wide range of factors, often working together; therefore, the treatment will have to vary according to individual need. The root of the problem has to be identified, whether it is physical, psychological, or spiritual, and it must be remembered that the society we keep will also affect our inner harmony. In a condition like psoriasis, factors such as work-life and social expression should be re-evaluated.

While certain herbs are traditionally indicated for psoriasis, correct diagnosis and awareness of individual needs is important. Most of the herbs are alteratives and will be effective if used with other herbs and if the lifestyle is changed appropriately. They include *Burdock Root, Cleavers, Dandelion, Figwort, Mountain Grape, Red Clover, Sarsaparilla, Thuja*, and *Yellow Dock*.

Some of these are also hepatics, like *Dandelion* and *Yellow Dock*, while others are diuretics, like *Cleavers* or *Figwort*. Often the use of nervine tonics will be appropriate to strengthen the nerve response to stress and to the trials of life, particularly if there is any involvement of high blood pressure or of heart signs such as palpitations. *Lime Flowers* and *Motherwort* come to mind here, but *Mistletoe, Skullcap*, or *Valerian* can also be useful.

Taking all that has been said into account, a basic herbal approach that can be added to and modified includes equal parts of:

Burdock   *Cleavers*
Sarsaparilla *Yellow Dock*

This tea should be drunk three times daily. The treatment has to be continued over a long period of time, while attention should be given to a wholesome diet and to enough physical exercise.

Sunshine and seawater will often clear psoriasis, but this may not be permanent. Similarly, external remedies will ease irritations or help with the removal of scales, but will not give permanent relief. Ointments for this purpose can be made from *Chickweed, Comfrey,* or *Marshmallow*. Dr. Christopher also recommends an ointment made from *Balm of Gilead*.

ECZEMA

The term "eczema" covers a wide range of skin conditions, and even though orthodox medicine describes various forms, the differences are of no real importance as far as a holistic treatment is concerned.

As with psoriasis, it is necessary to search for the roots within. If an allergic reaction is involved, the allergen has to be identified and removed, as otherwise the body has no chance to heal itself or to take advantage of the herbal support that is given. If the allergy is due to something being touched, it can cause an eruption on the hands, the face, or the genitals. Often eczema is due to an allergic reaction to cow's milk, particularly if babies are bottle-fed with milk. Anyone with eczema should avoid milk and milk products, which can be replaced by goat's milk or soy milk products, if required.

The herbal remedies will be selected according to individual needs, but the digestive process should be examined and the use of bitters, carminatives, or laxatives considered. If the liver is suspected of impaired function, cholagogues or hepatics may be needed, and if the kidneys do not fulfill their vital responsibilities, diuretics will be indicated. Nervines may also be appropriate.

Traditionally, herbs like *Burdock Root, Figwort, Fumitory, Mountain Grape, Nettle, Pansy,* and *Red Clover* have a good reputation in the treatment of eczema as internal remedies.

A useful basic mixture can be made from equal parts of:

Figwort
Nettles
Red Clover

This tea should be drunk three times daily and is especially good for infantile eczema.

Initially the symptoms may apparently get worse, but this is nothing to worry about, as it will soon be followed by a marked improvement. We can use external remedies to reduce irritations and discomfort, but they will not heal unless used in conjunction with internal treatment. Herbs like *Burdock, Chickweed, Comfrey, Golden Seal, Marigold, Pansy,* or *Witch Hazel* can be used for compresses or ointments. For instance, a *Marigold* compress can be made by pouring 1 pint (0.5 liters) of boiling water on 2 tablespoons of dried flowers (or 3 of fresh flowers) and letting it stand until cool. Use this mixture to soak a compress, then place it on the affected area. Continually moisten the compress and leave it in place for one hour. Apply at least twice a day.

Burdock makes a very good and simple ointment. Express the sap of a fresh root and mix with Vaseline until it has the right consistency. It may be used on the irritated areas several times a day.

ACNE

This common problem of adolescence has two main underlying causes, a hormonal and a dietary one. The hormonal one is related to the level of male hormones and is most obvious during puberty, when profound body changes are inaugurated by various hormonal triggers. The prevalence of acne in young men during this time and in young women premenstrually illustrates this connection. The dietary factor is related to the state of the body's ability to metabolize fats and carbohydrates. If there is any metabolic problem or a preponderance of such food in the diet, acne may result or be aggravated. The herbal approach aims at supporting the metabolism of these foods and at helping lymphatic drainage and bodily elimination. Dietarily, the intake of fats, sugars, and carbohydrates must be drastically reduced, while more fruit and vegetables should be eaten. Alteratives such as *Cleavers, Figwort, Mountain Grape, Red Clover,* and *Yellow Dock* are especially useful, but lymphatics like *Echinacea* and *Pokeweed Root* and hepatics like *Blue Flag* and *Dandelion* should also be considered.

A mixture such as the following can be taken for a while:

Blue Flag	1 part
Cleavers	1 part
Echinacea	1 part
Figwort	1 part
Pokeweed Root	1 part

This tea should be drunk three times daily.

Externally, a lotion of equal parts or an infusion of *Chickweed*, *Marigold*, and distilled *Witch Hazel* may be useful, as may frequent washing with a pure soap.

INTERNAL REACTIONS TO EXTERNAL FACTORS

Sometimes the skin will show reactions to external factors, such as bacteria, that have led to internal processes, which reflect on the skin instead of manifesting internally. Usually these are reactions to microorganisms, which would not occur if the body's defense mechanisms were working normally and adequately. While the symptom on the skin should be attended to, the real problem lies in the weakened defense system, which should be toned and strengthened so that the body will rid itself of the infection.

There can be various reasons for the lowering of the body's resistance, but the treatment will always include the use of antimicrobials and alteratives and also aim for efficient elimination through the kidneys and bowel. Further, the general guidelines for the treatment of infections also hold true here. If antibiotics have been used recently, at least 0.04 ounces (1 gram) of vitamin C should be taken daily. Remember also that a person is being treated, not a disease. If something in life is getting you down, look at what needs to change so that a true healing can take place.

BOILS

The *staphylococcus pyogenes* bacteria, which are usually part of the surface ecology of the skin, only become a problem when the body is weakened and can then lead to boils. To effectively rid the body of boils, herbs have to be used both internally and externally. The body's innate vitality and resistance have to be brought to their peak, while at the same time aiding the body in dealing with the bacteria. This can best be achieved with a combination of antimicrobials and alteratives and possibly bitters. Three remedies that are considered specifics for boils are *Echinacea*, *Pasqueflower*, and *Wild Indigo*. They are best used in combinations that will aid the lymphatic system. A typical mixture would be:

Echinacea	2 parts
Wild Indigo	2 parts
Pasqueflower	1 part
Pokeweed Root	1 part

This tea should be drunk three times daily.

Externally, an ointment or a poultice should be used to draw pus from the boil. A poultice can be made from *Cabbage Leaf* or *Marshmallow Leaf,* while *Myrrh* or *Echinacea* will be useful to control the infection. A *Cabbage Leaf* poultice may be prepared by taking a few of the inner leaves of *White Cabbage*, washing them well, and drying them lightly. The large ribs can be removed. Tap the leaves with a rolling pin to soften them and place them on the affected area, holding them in place with a loose bandage. Leave for half an hour and then replace the old leaves with new ones.

IMPETIGO

Impetigo is a highly contagious infection that commonly occurs in children. Scrupulous hygiene is vital in its treatment, in conjunction with a diet rich in fruit, fresh green vegetables, and extra doses of vitamin C of about 0.1 ounce (2 grams) daily, together with raw *Garlic* as part of the diet. Herbally, the defense of the body has to be aided by the use of antimicrobials and supported by alteratives and tonics. Externally, a lotion of one or more herbs like *Echinacea, Marigold, Myrrh*, or *Wild Indigo* has to be used to combat the infection and to help rebuild the ecological barriers. A lotion will only be truly effective in conjunction with an internal treatment; the mixture given for boils should be used.

WARTS

The treatment of warts is surrounded by folklore and myth or associated with the drastic removal methods of conventional medicine. Warts are caused by viral infections, which can only occur if the "soil" is right, which indicates that a herbal treatment aims at creating a clean and sound inner environment. Diet and lifestyle should be wholesome and life-affirming, and herbs like *Cleavers, Garlic, Pokeweed Root, Prickly Ash*, or *Wormwood*, which are lymphatic cleansers and tonics, should be taken internally. Also take some vitamin C, about 0.1 ounce (2 grams) daily. For an external treatment and a quick removal of warts, *Greater Celandine* and *Thuja* are considered to be specifics. *Greater Celandine* is used by expressing the latex from fresh stems and applying it directly to the wart, whereas *Thuja* is made into a lotion or a tincture, which should be used often.

Vitamin E oil can also be applied to the wart or put on after the wart has been removed.

HERPES SIMPLEX

This very common viral infection, which is also known as cold sores, is a secondary manifestation of an initial infection with the herpes virus that usually occurs early in life. The infection often remains unnoticed, as the virus can reside latent within the body for the rest of the person's life, unless the resistance of the body is lowered. This reaction can be triggered by various factors, such as other infections (hence the name's association with colds), menstruation, or a bad diet. The treatment aims primarily at improving bodily health through a good diet, a high level of vitamin C (0.1–0.2 ounces/3–5 grams daily), and by supporting the body's eliminative processes. The treatment should be supported by an herbal mixture, which has to be taken for a period of time, such as:

Cleavers	2 parts
Echinacea	2 parts
Oats	1 part
Pokeweed Root	1 part

Drink this tea twice daily.

Externally, a lotion of *Echinacea* with or without *Myrrh* will prove useful.

RINGWORM

Ringworm is caused by a fungal infection of the skin, which can occur on various parts of the body and give rise to symptoms like athlete's foot. It commonly occurs between the toes, around the groin, or in circular patches anywhere on the body. It is made worse by sweating and by poor hygiene. The key to its effective removal lies in scrupulous hygiene and in making sure that some air can reach the affected parts. The herbal approach consists of internal and external remedies. Internally, a mixture that raises the body's resistance and increases lymphatic drainage should be used:

Echinacea	2 parts
Cleavers	1 part
Pokeweed Root	1 part
Wild Indigo	1 part
Yellow Dock	1 part

This tea should be drunk three times daily.

Externally, antifungal herbs like *Echinacea, Eucalyptus, Garlic, Golden Seal, Marigold, Myrrh,* or *Thuja* can be directly applied as lotions or as tinctures, with *Marigold* being by far the most effective, especially 50:50 with *Myrhh* as tincture applied, undiluted, three times a day.

LICE AND SCABIES

These infestations are described in the chapter on infections and infestations.

EXTERNAL CAUSES

Nature has supplied us with an abundant flora that will help heal the everyday traumas of living in the physical world, like wounds, bruises, burns, etc. I will only mention the most effective ones, the best of all being *Marigold*. The value of this exceptional herb cannot be exaggerated when it comes to treating skin problems like wounds, bruises, or burns. Its properties make it a healing plant that reduces soreness and inflammation, while also acting as an antimicrobial, which makes it a primary first-aid herb for any problem.

WOUNDS

Of the many vulnerary herbs, *Comfrey, Elderberry Flower, Golden Seal, Plantain,* and *St. John's Wort* are the most important, but in addition to the vulneraries it must be remembered that the first stage of wound healing lies in the clotting of blood, where the astringents can be useful. Of all these herbs, *Comfrey* has a deserved reputation as a potent healer of wounds, which is in part due to its content of allantoin in roots and leaves. This chemical stimulates cell division and so speeds up scar formation and total healing. As with the other herbs mentioned, it may be used in the form of a poultice, a compress, or as an ointment. If there is danger of an infection, an antimicrobial like *Echinacea* should also be added.

BRUISES

To help the body deal with bruises, sprains, and concussions, herbs like *Arnica, Daisy, Marigold, Witch Hazel,* or *Yarrow,* used as compresses, will be exceptionally effective. Of these, *Arnica** is the best and can produce astounding improvements in a very short time. To make a compress, it is very effective to use Arnica Tincture: if using dried *Arnica Flowers*, one part flowers should be mixed with 10 parts 70% alcohol. If fresh flowers are available, equal amounts of *Arnica* and alcohol can be used. Put the mixture for 2 weeks in a tightly sealed glass container, leave it in a warm place, and shake it every day. After two weeks, strain it through a muslin cloth and press out as much liquid as possible. This can be left for another two days to settle, when it can be filtered to obtain a clear liquid. To make a compress, mix 1 tablespoon of the tincture with 1 pint (0.5 liters) of water.

You can also make lotions, tinctures, compresses, or ointments from any of the other herbs mentioned above.

If bruising is a recurring problem without obvious external causes, increase the vitamin C foods in the diet. It may be necessary to investigate why the blood vessels rupture so readily. An infusion of *Horse Chestnut* and *Yarrow* drunk regularly for quite a while will help strengthen the blood vessel walls. Rutin and the other bioflavonoids will help, either as dietary supplements or in buckwheat. If this doesn't resolve the problem, see a practitioner in addition to these self-help measures. Move through your world more consciously, too!

BURNS

For minor burns and light sunburns, herbs can be very valuable, but any more severe burns must be treated with care. As a home treatment, perhaps the best plant to use is *Aloe*. It can be cultivated as a home plant and has succulent leaves rich in a healing gel that is best used fresh. The leaf should be opened, and its inside applied to the burn. Otherwise, *Marigold* or *St. John's Wort* will help. See the chapter on preparations for *St. John's Wort* oil. This is nature's answer for bad sunburn, and it will leave the skin in better shape than it started.

* Note that *Arnica* is never used on open wounds, but rather externally for bruises, with unbroken skin, or sprains and the like.

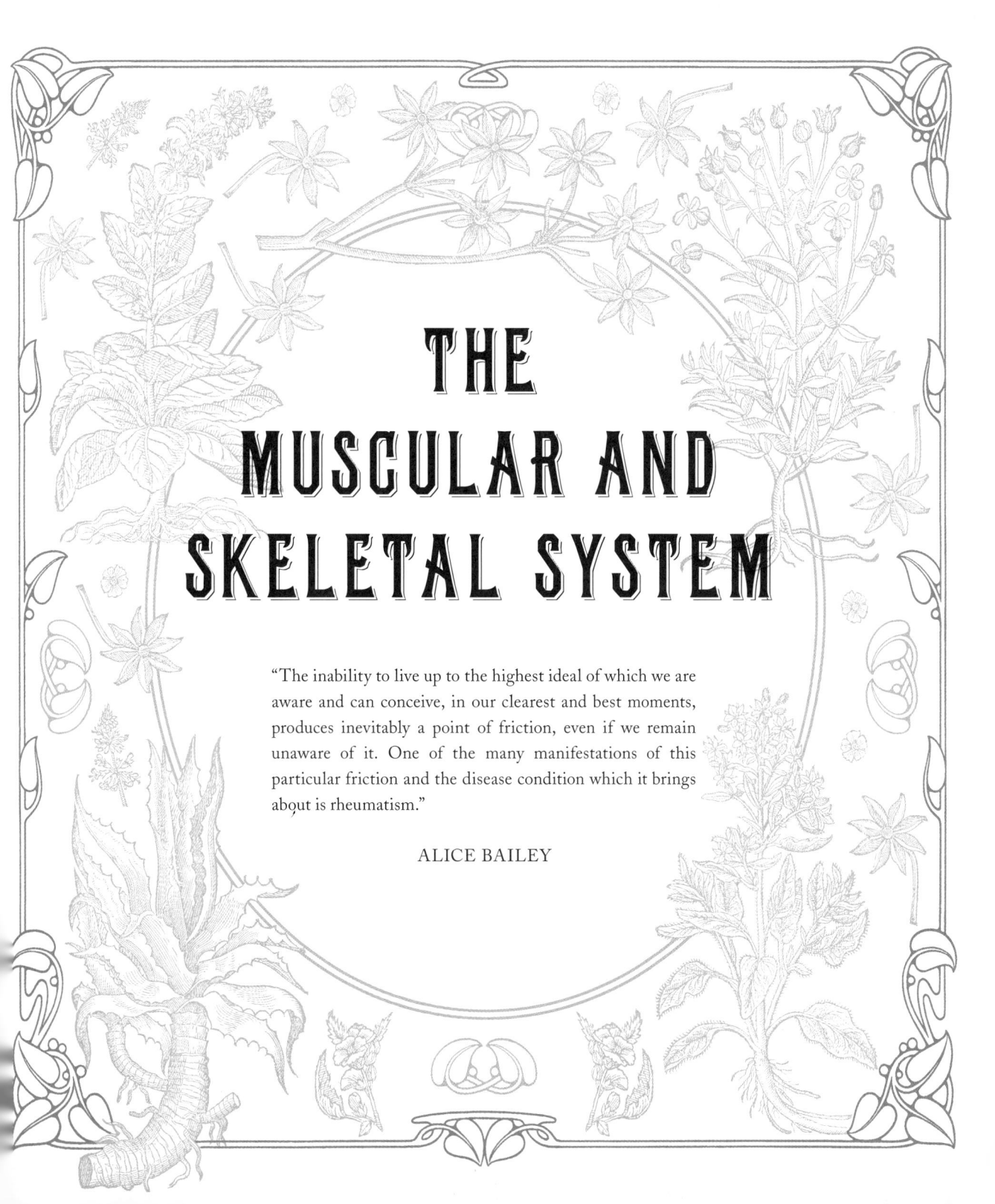

THE MUSCULAR AND SKELETAL SYSTEM

"The inability to live up to the highest ideal of which we are aware and can conceive, in our clearest and best moments, produces inevitably a point of friction, even if we remain unaware of it. One of the many manifestations of this particular friction and the disease condition which it brings about is rheumatism."

ALICE BAILEY

The Muscular and Skeletal System

OUR SKELETON, THE CONNECTIVE tissue, our muscles, and our joints hold us together, enable us to stand, to move, and give us our form. They are used—and misused—a lot and are the site of a lot of physical wear and tear. But the health of these tissues not only depends on the use to which they are put or the structure they are part of, but also to a large extent on the inner environment, on the state of our metabolism, on diet, and on lifestyle. Of course genetically based weaknesses can play a very important part as well, but if they are recognized, much can be done to keep them from manifesting as problems.

If problems are due to structural misalignments, a great deal can be done with the help of osteopathy or chiropractic. Sometimes the skeleton is so far out of normal alignment that proper neurological functions are impaired and the function of organs is disturbed or the harmony of the whole body is affected. Osteopathic or chiropractic techniques can help realign the body, as can methods of psychophysical adjustments like Rolfing, Alexander Technique, or Feldenkrais.

But a major source of conditions that plague this system is the systemic health of the body as a whole. Only as long as the inner environment and metabolism are in harmony is health and wholeness maintained. If our biochemical and metabolical processes are out of tune, one of the effects is that the body will be under much strain to remove waste and toxins. If this condition lasts for some years—which it often does unnoticed—toxins can build up in the connective tissue of the joints and sow the seeds for the development of rheumatism and arthritis, particularly if there is a genetic disposition in that direction. Of all the problems that can affect this system, it is in this area of chronic and degenerative ailments that herbal medicine has most to offer.

Herbs for the Muscular and Skeletal System

In this system, particularly in diseases like rheumatism or arthritis, the body has to be led back to a state of health and balance. To treat problems that manifest in the bones or muscles effectively, digestion and assimilation have to work well, as do the various aspects of elimination.

This should be kept in mind in choosing different kinds of herbs for particular needs.

ANTIRHEUMATICS

A vast array of herbs has the reputation of preventing, relieving, or curing rheumatic problems. I will give you a long—though far from complete—list of antirheumatics that includes a variety of herbs with different primary actions. They can be chosen according to the need of the whole body, as they include alteratives, anti-inflammatories, rubifacients, diuretics, stimulants, and digestives: *Angelica, Bearberry, Black Cohosh, Black Willow, Bladderwrack, Blue Flag, Buckbean, Boneset, Burdock, Cayenne, Celery Seed, Couch Grass, Dandelion, Devil's Claw, Ginger, Guaiacum, Juniper, Mountain Grape, Mustard, Nettles, Pokeweed Root, Prickly Ash, Ragwort, Sarsaparilla, White Poplar, Wild Yam, Wintergreen, Wormwood, Yarrow,* and *Yellow Dock.*

ALTERATIVES

Alteratives gradually cleanse and correct a "polluted" condition of the bloodstream and restore healthier functioning. The herbs work through different mechanisms, many of which are not yet understood, and they work in a range of conditions, including rheumatism. While most alteratives will help in problems of this system, *Black Cohosh, Buckbean, Celery Seed, Devil's Claw, Guiacum,* and *Sarsaparilla* are most widely used.

Most rheumatic and arthritic conditions are improved through the general revitalization and cleansing brought about by these herbs.

ANTI-INFLAMMATORIES

It is perhaps misleading to call these herbs anti-inflammatories, as in a holistic treatment we are not aiming at suppressing inflammations, which is usually part of a healthy body response. These herbs rather reduce inflammations by helping the body overcome the problem. These herbs can be helpful, particularly in rheumatic and arthritic conditions, where long-standing inflammations of joints and other tissues become self-defeating.

A good example is *Meadowsweet*; it is rich in natural aspirin, like substances that reduce swelling and pain, while it is also a diuretic and hepatic, thus aiding the body in cleaning and elimination and in time clearing the roots of the inflammation, which lie in an accumulation of waste and toxins.

The most effective anti-inflammatories are *Black Willow, Devil's Claw, Guaiacum, Meadowsweet, White Poplar,* and *Wild Yam.* Unlike drug anti-inflammatories, these herbs are safe in large doses, since they are in the dilute and balanced form designed by nature. A safe and effective dose of *Black Willow* could be 8 fluid ounces (250 milliliters) of tincture a week for some people.

THE MUSCULAR AND SKELETAL SYSTEM

RUBEFACIENTS

Rubefacients, when applied to the skin, stimulate circulation in that area. This increases the blood supply, which in turn relieves congestion and inflammation, thus making rubefacients particularly useful as the basis for liniments used in muscular rheumatism and similar conditions.

Most rubefacients are too strong to be used internally. Even on sensitive skin they should be used with care, and not at all when the skin is damaged. The particular way to use them will be described below; the most useful ones are *Cayenne, Ginger, Horseradish, Mustard, Peppermint Oil, Ragwort, Rosemary Oil*, and *Wintergreen*.

DIURETICS

Diuretics help the work of the kidneys and thus the elimination of metabolic waste and toxins, or the products of inflammation, which is essential, as these can lie at the root of many problems like arthritis or rheumatism. If there is any kidney problem, it must also be treated. To support the work of this vital organ generally, herbs like *Boneset, Celery, Juniper Berries*, or *Yarrow* can be used, and *Celery Seeds* are often considered specific for rheumatism.

CIRCULATORY STIMULANTS

Another way to cleanse the body of toxins is to stimulate the circulation, which increases blood flow to muscles and joints. This can be done without straining the heart by using herbs that stimulate the peripheral circulation, such as *Cayenne, Ginger, Pokeweed Root, Prickly Ash*, or *Rosemary*. Of course, if there is any circulatory or heart problem, this must be seen to as well.

PAIN-RELIEVERS

While the purist will never treat symptoms, the healer's art aims at relieving suffering. It may be necessary to use herbs that will reduce the often severe pain of conditions like rheumatism, which of course should only be given as part of a whole treatment of the cause. The anti-inflammatories will reduce pain to some degree, but the only effective way to reduce and eliminate pain is to clear the underlying problem. While this is being done, herbs such as *Guaiacum, Jamaican Dogwood, St. John's Wort*, or *Valerian* can help relieve the pain. They will be less effective if no other steps are taken.

DIGESTIVE TONICS

The digestive process has to work properly, as nutrients need to be properly absorbed to have the muscular and skeletal system work properly. The use of bitter tonics like *Gentian, Golden Seal, Wormwood*, or *Yarrow* may be useful.

If there is any appreciable degree of constipation or a buildup of fecal matter, the use of evacuants is called for, especially those that act by stimulating the liver, like *Boldo, Rhubarb Root*, or *Yellow Dock*.

Patterns of Muscular and Skeletal Disease

Rheumatism and Arthritis

We will not look into the differences between the various sorts of rheumatism and arthritis. It is arguable whether a differential diagnosis is necessary for a holistic treatment. What is necessary is to recognize the general and individual cause and the influences of the genetic framework. These conditions are a result of the body's inability to deal with pressures from the wrong diet and lifestyle or other stresses. The aim of the treatment will be to bring the individual to a state of health and vitality where the body can take care of the symptom, instead of attacking the symptom to attain the vitality.

An important insight into approaching these conditions is the idea of friction. The changes in the joints that occur in arthritis cause a rubbing together of bones in such a way as to cause friction, but there is often a long history of friction leading up to this physical change. It could be due to a particular physical job, as when farmers develop osteoarthritis in the shoulder on which they have carried hay bales for years, or it could be muscle tension binding joints too tightly together, which is usually due to a history of friction in life. The *Collins Dictionary* defines friction as "a resistance encountered when one body moves relative to another body with which it is in contact; . . . disagreement or conflict." When looking at the roots of rheumatic and arthritic problems, this definition covers it all, whether the two bodies are bones, people, or differing emotions and beliefs.

Conflicts, and the friction that ensues, can take many forms but the experience is fundamentally an inner one. For some, conflict is a state of mind, an attitude with which to relate to the world. Such conflict is really between inner aspects of the individual, a manifestation of psychological disharmony. This will externalise as conflict in relationships or lifestyle, but the roots are often deep in the psyche.

When trying to create the right environment within the body for healing to occur, as much attention has to go to emotional and mental harmony as to diet and herbal medicine. If the individual has an outlook on life that is tight, defensive, and lacking in vulnerability and openness, the rheumatism will be fed. If an inner process of relaxation is initiated that reduces emotional friction, allows a free interaction with people, and an opening up of emotions and beliefs, the stage will be set for the miracle of self-healing to occur, facilitated by the use of herbs.

One of the causes of rheumatism and arthritis is an accumulation of toxins or waste products in the affected tissue. A major contributing factor in the development of this condition is an inappropriate diet, either using foods that are wrong for your body or foods that are so devitalized and adulterated that they are detrimental anyway. As a general guideline, foods that cause the body to have an acidic reaction should be avoided, as should those that cause digestive problems or other adverse conditions, such as subtle allergic reactions. Instead of eating processed foods full of additives and preservatives, they should be fresh and untreated as much as possible.

Overt allergic reactions, or subtle ones like the minor digestive upsets of heartburn or wind, are often caused by gluten (mainly from wheat products) and by dairy products, which should both then be avoided. Acidic reactions are caused by meat (especially red meat), eggs, and dairy products; by such overtly acidic foods as vinegar and pickles; by refined carbohydrates and refined sugar; and by most spices. Foods rich in oxalic acid should also be shunned, like rhubarb, gooseberries, and black and red currants. Coffee, black tea, alcohol, anything made from black grapes, sugar, and salt should also be avoided for various reasons, as they all contribute to the accumulation of toxins and are detrimental to a cleansing process.

Instead, fruit (including citrus, which, in spite of their citric acid, appear to have an alkaline action on the metabolism) and vegetables should be eaten in abundance, particularly green and root vegetables, and at least 3 pints (1.5 liters) of fluid should be drunk daily to help flush the body. The fluid should preferably be water (but water low in mineral content) or water mixed with a little apple cider vinegar or apple juice. A vitamin C supplement of at least 500 milligrams daily is recommended. Fish and white meat may be eaten.

Through the use of appropriate herbs, and in combination with other techniques to support and aid the whole body, it is possible to cleanse the whole system and to remove the source of the rheumatic or arthritic development. Such a treatment takes time, as a degenerative process that took a long time to develop is not reversed in four weeks. But when the right treatment is used, it is not uncommon to hear comments like "I already feel better within myself" long before the actual symptoms of pain or stiffness are gone.

In addition to the general need for cleansing, each person has to be approached as a unique being. Does the digestive system need help in any way? Are the kidneys working well? Is there much stress in the person's life? Is the endocrine system working harmoniously? How is the diet?

With rheumatic and arthritic problems, more than with any other, it is essential to treat the whole being, otherwise healing will only be slight or temporary. But when the unique picture of the individual is taken into account, it is possible to open the gates for a quite miraculous healing to occur.

Having made that point quite clearly, here is a basic mixture for rheumatic and arthritic conditions:

Buckbean	2 parts
Black Cohosh	1 part
Celery Seed	1 part
Meadowsweet	1 part
Yarrow	1 part

This tea should be drunk three times a day for a long period of time.

This is just one possibility. The specifics should be selected in view of the particular individual, according to the suggestions given in the section on herbs for the system. If, for instance, a lot of inflammation or pain is involved, consider the anti-inflammatories and maybe the pain-relievers, and you might want to use *Black Willow*, *Guaiacum*, or *Wild Yam*.

If the person lacks sleep due to pain, it is necessary to do something about this, as much healing happens during sleep. A useful herbal combination to aid sleep and to reduce pain is:

Jamaican Dogwood	1 part
Valerian	1 part
Passion Flower	1 part

Drink this tea half an hour before going to bed. It is a safe mixture and may be used in stronger dosage than the normal 1 or 2 teaspoonfuls, if required.

In addition, external remedies can be used to ease pain and reduce inflammation, while at the same time stimulating circulation to the affected area to help in the elimination of toxins. While such treatment will not lead to a fundamental change by itself, it will help the whole process and ease discomfort. A very warming and stimulating liniment can be made by mixing equal parts of tincture of *Cayenne* and glycerine, which should be rubbed into the affected joints or muscles. Care must be taken not to use it on broken skin or to get it on the sensitive skin of the face. It won't do any harm but it may appear to "burn" until the volatile oil fades or is washed away. It is this same heat that relieves pain in cold, aching joints and stiff muscles.

If there is pain in the muscle tissue or any nerve pain, a liniment based on *St. John's Wort* oil can be most effective. You can prepare the oil yourself in late summer by picking fresh blossoms and putting them into oil: pick 4 ounces (100 grams) of fresh, just-opened blossoms and crush them in 1 tablespoon of olive or sunflower oil. Pour 1 pint (0.5 liters) of the same oil over the whole, mix it well, and put it into a clear glass container. Leave the container open in a warm place to ferment for three to five days, then seal the container well and place it in sunshine or put it in another warm place for three to six weeks, shaking it daily, until the oil has become bright red. After this time, press the mixture through a cloth and let the oil stand for a day to separate the oily from the watery part. Use the oily part only, which should be carefully poured off and stored in an airtight opaque container.

St. John's Wort oil may be rubbed on areas of rheumatic pain, and it can also be used for neuralgic or sciatic pains or on light burns.

We can also make other oils, either by making the base for them ourselves or by using a base with essential oils. If we use essential oils, we can add 0.1 fluid ounces (2–3 milliliters) of the oil to 1 fluid ounce (30 milliliters) of a base like almond, olive, or sunflower oil. Suitable oils are *Lavender, Marjoram, Peppermint*, and *Rosemary*, and they can also be mixed with each other.

Another simple but effective way of relieving pain and swelling is to alternate hot and cold fomentations of water. This first-aid technique can be used when oils and herbs are not at hand.

FIBROSITIS

The advice given for rheumatism and arthritis should be followed.

CRAMP

We have all experienced muscular cramps at one time or another, which are painful but nothing much to worry about. However, if it becomes an intransingent condition, it should be treated, not only to avoid the stressful symptom, but also because it suggests circulatory problems since it is a symptom of a lack of oxygen.

It is quite an easy matter to remove the problems herbally, if the treatment is continued for a period of time. A mixture of *Cramp Bark, Ginger,* and *Prickly Ash* may be used:

Cramp Bark	6 parts
Prickly Ash	2 parts
Ginger	1 part

Drink this decoction three times a day for a number of months.

BURSITIS

The bursae around the knee and elbow joints act as small, water-filled cushions between the larger tendons and bones. Inflammation of these sacs is called bursitis. When it occurs in the knees, it is often called housemaid's knee and tennis elbow when in that joint. The condition may be due to a hard knock or accident or to a slow change. When it is part of the gradual development of rheumatic tendencies, it should be treated as described in the section on rheumatism. When of short-term duration, it is best to help the tissues by using a compress on the affected area or a stimulating liniment (see the section on rheumatism and arthritis). Both will help reduce the inflammation and ease pain. However, if the problem continues, internal treatment as for rheumatism and arthritis should be started.

GOUT

This is a specific variety of joint problems due to a buildup of uric acid in the body that causes extremely painful inflammations. The body needs aid in elimination, especially from the kidneys. The use of diuretics as well as antirheumatic herbs will help. Herbs such as *Boneset, Celery, Queen Anne's Lace* (aka *Wild Carrot*), and *Yarrow* are especially useful out of all the diuretic available. The following mixture may prove useful:

Burdock Root	1 part
Celery Seed	1 part
Yarrow	1 part

Drink this infusion three times daily over a period of time. If there is much pain, *Thuja* an be included in the mixture.

Diet is paramount in treating and preventing the reoccurance of gout. A low-acid diet provides the basis with a strict avoidance of foods rich in purines that are metabolized in the body to uric acid. These foods include fish such as sardines, anchovies, fish roe, shellfish and crab, liver, kidney, sweetbreads, and beans. Coffee and tea should be left alone, and any overindulgence in general is out. Alcohol has to be totally avoided.

LUMBAGO

Lumbago is a general name for pain in the lower back and can be caused by a variety of conditions, ranging from kidney and reproductive system problems to rheumatism and back lesions. The root of the pain must be sought and the appropriate treatment used, whether it be herbs or osteopathy. A warming and stimulating liniment, as described for rheumatism and arthritis, will help. Hot compresses may also be considered for quick symptomatic relief while the cause is being investigated properly.

SCIATICA

This is strictly speaking a form of neuralgia characterized by intense pain and tenderness felt along the length of the sciatic nerve, the longest in the body, extending from the back of the thigh to the lower calf. The term is often used to describe pain that radiates from the hips to the thighs, which can be of many causes. There is often a misalignment of spine and hips involved, which in turn presses on the nerve and causes the pain. If this is the case, osteopathic or chiropractic therapy will be most appropriate. Where there is neuralgia or nerve pain, relaxing nervines and tonics will help (see the section on the nervous system). However, it is often found that abdominal congestion lies at the root of this painful problem. It is essential to ensure that the bowels are free of constipation and that the kidneys are working well. In the first place, an herb such as *Yellow Dock* is appropriate, but for the kidneys, *Bearberry* or *Dandelion* should be used. The general advice given in the section on rheumatism and arthritis is appropriate for sciatica. Massage of the lower back and legs may help a lot.

SPRAINS

Muscles can be pulled and ligaments and tendons sprained through accidents. Hot baths with a stimulating herb added can increase the circulation to the area involved, and so speed healing. *Rosemary* or *Thyme* make an excellent addition to a bath, whether for the whole body or a foot bath: 1–2 ounces (30–60 grams) of the dried herb is added to 1 pint (0.5 liters) of boiling water and infused. This infusion is added to the bath or used as a compress on the affected area. *Arnica* (unless the skin is broken) may be used as an excellent compress, as hot as can be borne. If the tincture is being used, add 1 teaspoonful to 1 pint (0.5 liters) of water and either soak the affected part in the hot solution for 15 minutes or soak a bandage or gauze in the solution and apply to the part. This should be repeated every four hours. When there has been a marked reduction in swelling and pain, the affected part should be bandaged and the bandage moistened with distilled *Witch Hazel*.

THE MUSCULAR AND SKELETAL SYSTEM

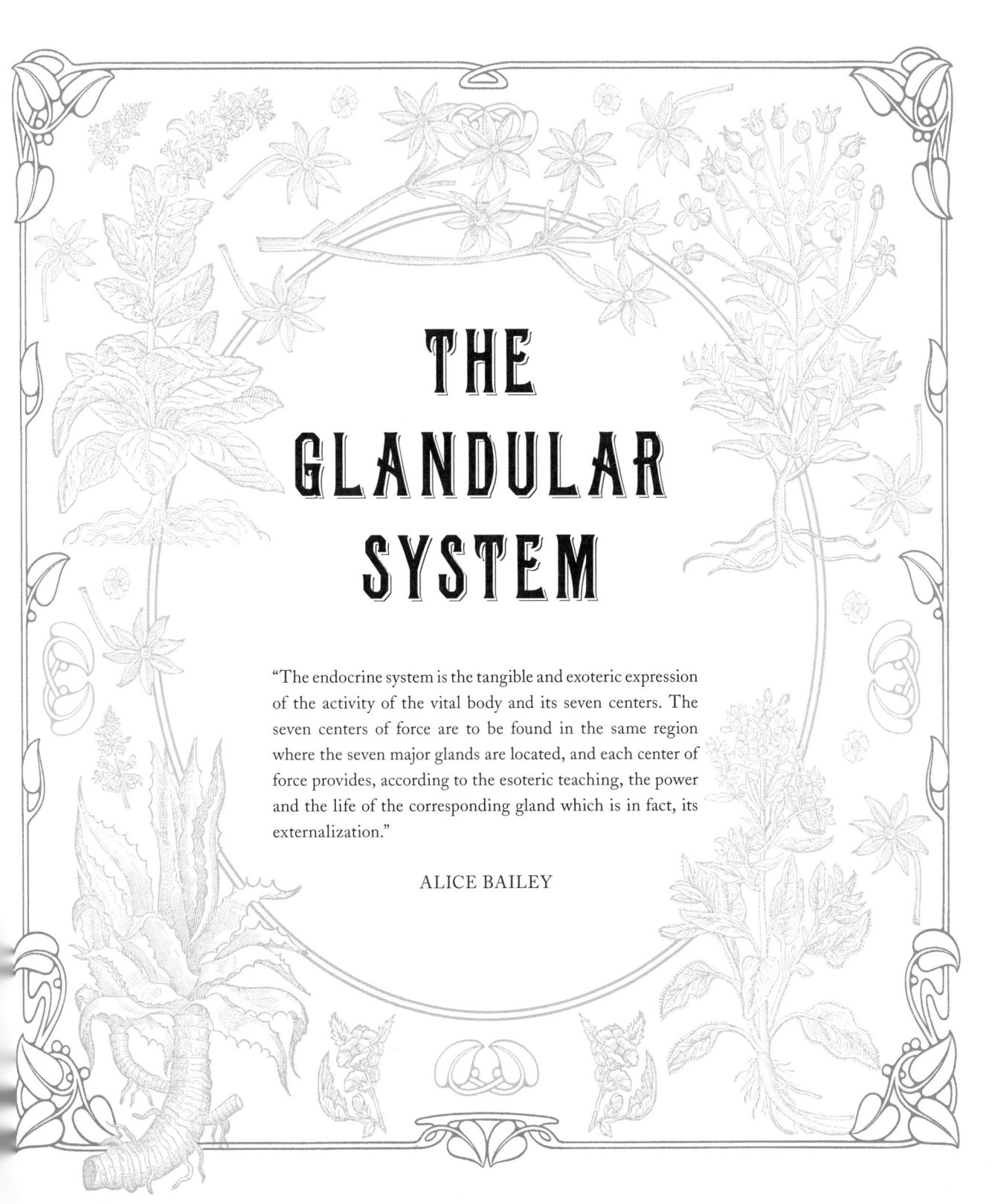

THE GLANDULAR SYSTEM

"The endocrine system is the tangible and exoteric expression of the activity of the vital body and its seven centers. The seven centers of force are to be found in the same region where the seven major glands are located, and each center of force provides, according to the esoteric teaching, the power and the life of the corresponding gland which is in fact, its externalization."

ALICE BAILEY

The Glandular System

It is in the complexities of our inner control systems that mind meets body most closely. If consciousness is seen as a faculty of the brain, then the partnership of nervous system and endocrine glands act as a bridge linking consciousness and body. We think and then act, imposing our will on the activities of muscles by means of nerves. If we are frightened, for instance, the hormone adrenaline (or epinephrine) will quicken the pulse as it goes to work.

Much of this is not under mental control, but occurs through the maintenance of the internal environment by nervous and hormonal action. The body's wisdom is demonstrated by the way in which it maintains this homeostasis and controls itself. Pervading every activity is the influence of the brain, the master control, with its servants the endocrine and nervous system.

The human body works efficiently only when the equilibrium within each organ, tissue, and cell is monitored and controlled in this way. Activity, growth, and repair of tissues need to be maintained, together with the supply of food and the removal of waste. The nervous system works in conjunction with the endocrine glands. These glands are situated in various parts of the body and are characterized by the fact that they release their hormones directly into the bloodstream. The hormones then travel to cells in all parts of the body. The membrane of each cell has receptors for one or more hormone, and the binding of a hormone to its specific receptor site starts particular changes in the internal metabolism of this "target" cell. The activity of hormones has been a focus of much exciting research and provides some astounding insights into the complexity and beauty of the human body.

To gain an overview, it will be helpful to examine the roles of the pituitary and hypothalamus glands in this introduction. The activity of these glands is constantly monitored and altered by the nervous, hormonal, and chemical information being fed to them. Hormone production is controlled in many cases by a negative feedback system in which overproduction of a hormone leads to a compensatory decrease in subsequent production until balance is restored. The pituitary gland has a central role in this process of maintaining harmony.

This gland is divided into two parts. The posterior part acts as a storage site for important hormones released by the hypothalamus, one of which has a role in inducing labor and starting milk production, and another promotes water retention to aid water conservation in the body. The anterior part produces hormones that direct the activity in other glands elsewhere in the body. In a small area of the forebrain, just above the pituitary, is the hypothalamus which is the main coordinating center between the endocrine and nervous systems. It functions as a monitor and regulator of the autonomic nervous system as well as the body's metabolism through eating, drinking, and temperature control and also monitors the menstrual cycle. The anterior pituitary responds to hormones secreted by the hypothalamus that either stimulate or inhibit the secretion of its own hormones. The precise details of balancing excess or underactive hormones is a beautifully integrated process, too complex to explore here. The hormones produced by this gland are responsible for influencing metabolic rate, affecting the development of bones and muscles, stimulating the production of milk by the breasts, and controlling hormone release by the ovaries and testes.

Health and the Glands

To be healthy is to have an integrated and smoothly functioning endocrine system. To ensure such health means living a truly whole lifestyle, with appropriate diet, life-affirming emotions and thinking, and a vital spiritual life. The endocrine system is a focus for such techniques as polarity therapy and energy balancing, for through this system the whole body can be healed, and if there is an endocrine imbalance, these therapies can be most effective in regaining harmony.

Endocrine problems have many causes, from external ones like stressful situations to internal ones like genetic disorders. The herbal approach is therefore broad, ensuring that the body becomes strong and vital, and at the same time using specific remedies for different glands.

Even in the absence of overt glandular illness, the endocrine system plays such a fundamental role in health and wholeness that any minor functional problem may lead to a general state of imbalance.

Herbs for the Glands

The group of herbs best indicated for endocrine treatment is the bitters. At first this might seem strange, as these herbs are often thought of as digestive tonics and stimulants. Their role in the glandular system is through a generalized reflex stimulation of the whole system. A stimulating action of this sort will promote right homeostatic function, reducing overactivity and increasing underactivity. This demonstrates how an herbal remedy can augment right action. Some specific agents have powerful effects, but most herbs help the whole body to heal and balance where appropriate.

In addition to the bitters, the alteratives are most useful in their action of cleansing and promoting proper blood functions. The best bitters for the glandular system include *Golden Seal*, *Mugwort*, *Rue*, *Wormwood*, and *Yarrow*. Useful alteratives are *Burdock*, *Cleavers*, *Dandelion*, *Echinacea*, *Red Clover*, *Sarsaparilla*, *Violet Leaves*, and *Yellow Dock*. There are also specific glandular agents like *Bladderwrack*, *Borage*, *Bugleweed*, *Ginseng*, *Goat's Rue*, *Licorice*, and *Wild Yam*. Since endocrine problems are so complex, herbs that are specific to another area, the kidney or liver for instance, may well be the ideal help to regain inner harmony. We must remember to view everything within the context of the whole.

Patterns of Disease of the Glandular System

The Pancreas

The pancreas is a large gland that is mainly concerned with secreting digestive enzymes to break down protein, fat, and carbohydrate in the duodenum and to neutralize the highly acidic juices from the stomach. However, scattered throughout the tissue of the pancreas there are groups of endocrine cells called Islets of Langerhans that produce two major hormones to control the handling of glucose and fatty acids in the body. When blood sugar rises, after a meal for instance, insulin is released that reduces glucose production by the liver and encourages its usage by the tissues of the body. The other hormone produced, glucagon, has the opposite effect to insulin in the liver and increases glucose production. If there is an imbalance in the amount of these hormones in the blood, either too high or too low of sugar levels will result.

Pancreatitis

Pancreatitis is a very painful inflammation of the pancreas and can show itself in acute or chronic attacks. There appears to be an "autodigestion" problem, where the powerful digestive enzymes produced by the pancreas start attacking the organ itself. Why this should be is uncertain, but a suggestion is that, since the pancreas and gallbladder share a common duct, there may be blockage caused by gallstones. In some cases, there is a connection with excessive alcohol intake. The herbal and dietary indications given in the section on the gallbladder should be observed. An herb that can be of specific help with this kind of pancreatic problem is *Fringe Tree Bark*.

Diabetes Mellitus

Diabetes mellitus is the most common of the endocrine disorders, affecting over 1% of people in the Western world. The basic problem in diabetes is that the level of glucose in the blood is higher than normal, while inside the cells it is low. The causes of this condition are complex, and it can result in a whole range of complications that occur primarily in the arteries and capillaries.

In most cases of diabetes, there is no clear initial trigger. The predisposing factor may be due to heredity, age, obesity, or stress. One of the bodily responses to stress is an increased activity of the adrenal glands, leading to an elevation of blood sugar levels. Severe stress does not actually cause diabetes, but it may unmask a latent form. Whatever the cause, the result will be a high blood glucose level with glucose-starved cells, leading to weight loss, thirst, an increase in the volume of urine passed, weakness, and eventually perhaps coma.

Diet is a major consideration in the treatment and control of diabetes. It is not simply a matter of avoiding foods rich in carbohydrate, but setting up an eating regime that avoids peaks of glucose entering the blood. But each diet must be tailor-made to the individual concerned.

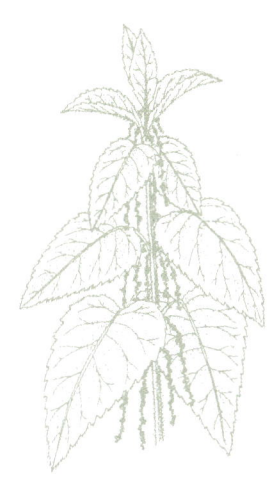

The roots of diabetes are complex, and treatment must get to these roots. Professional advice is definitely recommended. Herbs like *Fringe Tree Bark, Garlic, Ginseng, Goat's Rue, Jambul, Nettles,* and *Sweet Sumach* can be considered for diabetes, although treatment will vary with different conditions. It is now well established that many plants have a hypoglycaemic action—that is, they will lower blood sugar levels. There are records in all herbal traditions of the world mentioning such plants. Professor Farnsworth and his colleagues in America have done a screening of plants for this valuable property. Among those possessing the property are *Allspice, Artichoke, Banana, Barley, Bugleweed, Burdock, Cabbage, Carrot, Ginseng, Lettuce, Lily of the Valley, Nettles, Oats, Olive, Onion, Papaya, Pea, Spinach, Sunflower, Sweet Potato, Turnip,* and *Wormwood*. In this far from comprehensive list, we see that the realm of plants has much to offer for the treatment of blood sugar problems.

The Thyroid

The thyroid gland has an important role to play in the regulation of body metabolism. The two main thyroid hormones ensure that the appropriate metabolic rate of body biochemical activity is maintained. Problems may arise due to underactive or overactive states. The functioning of this gland affects the state of mind and mood but is also affected by it.

OVERACTIVE THYROID

When the gland is producing too much of these hormones, the body will burn up food much faster than normal and appetite will increase, but weight will be lost. There is a general overactivity with restlessness, anxiety, and tension. To treat this effectively involves the use of nervine relaxants to reduce excitability, digestive bitters, and a specific herb for this problem, which is *Bugleweed*.

These can relieve the symptoms quite effectively, but a longer term use of *Bugleweed* and other hormonal tonics is essential. A useful mixture would be:

Bugleweed	2 parts
Nettles	1 part
Valerian	1 part
Yarrow	1 part

This should be drunk three times a day over a period of time. Note that *Bugleweed* is a common name used for different plants in different places. This one is *Lycopus virginica*.

UNDERACTIVE THYROID

In this condition the opposite is occurring. The body's basic rate of activity lowers, weight is put on, lethargy and apathy are common, and there is a tendency to deep depression. The herbs that benefit here are the bitters, nervine tonics, and the specific thyroid agent, which in this case is *Bladderwrack*. An appropriate mixture is:

Bladderwrack	2 parts
Damiana (or Kola Nut)	1 part
Nettles	1 part
Oats	1 part
Wormwood	1 part

This should be drunk three times a day.

For thyroid conditions, a well-balanced and whole diet is essential to enable the body to deal effectively with the imbalance.

GOITER

This is a condition in which there is an enlargement of the thyroid gland, causing swelling around the front of the neck. It may be due to a variety of medical causes, the most common being either overactive or underactive thyroid glands, but it can also simply be due to a deficiency of the element iodine in the diet. As most of the bodily need for iodine is in the production of the thyroid hormones, any lack of this essential mineral will show in the thyroid gland. Until this nutritional connection was determined, goiter was a common occurrence in parts of the world where little natural iodine was present in the soil or water. Areas in Wales and the Alps affected people in this way. Iodine is often added to table salt, and in Tasmania it is even added to bread as a preventative measure. By far the richest plant source of iodine is seaweed, especially *Bladderwrack*.

THE ADRENAL GLANDS

The adrenal glands are found just above each of the kidneys. They consist of two distinct parts, the outer cortex and inner medulla. The adrenal cortex produces three groups of hormones in response to stimulation from pituitary hormones. One group acts to stimulate the retention of sodium in the body and the excretion of potassium. This hormone is thus intimately involved in the homeostatic maintenance of salt balance in the body. The second group affects glucose, amino acid, and fat metabolism. Of these groups, the steroid hormones help maintain a steady supply of essential building blocks and fuel to facilitate normal body repair and growth in all tissue. These hormones are involved in many bodily processes but also in the control of inflammation. It is this action that explains the use of synthetic steroid drugs by allopaths. They are very effective in the control of inflammation and such conditions as rheumatoid arthritis, but have very serious side effects. They are perhaps the most frightening source of illnesses caused by medical treatment. It is only occasionally that the risks of using such drugs are outweighed by the needs of the patient.

The third group of hormones produced in the adrenal cortex is the sex hormones, both androgens (the male hormones) and estrogens (the female ones). Both types are found in men and women, because it is the balance of them that is responsible for the biological differences between the sexes.

The adrenal medulla acts quite separately from the cortex, being the site of the production of adrenaline (epinephine) and norepinephrine. These hormones are responsible for the rapid bodily response to extreme stress, the so-called "fight or flight" effect. Stressful situations, such as emotional trauma, pain, extremes of temperature, or low blood sugar, will stimulate the hypothalamus to transmit a nerve impulse to the adrenal medulla. In response to this, adrenaline and norepinephrine are released into the bloodstream. Their combined action is to prepare the body for extreme activity by stimulating breathing, raising blood pressure, pulse rate, and heart output. Blood levels of glucose and fatty acids are also increased, liberating tissue food, enhancing muscle activity, and reducing blood supply to the intestines and skin so there is more blood available for the muscles.

This response will happen regardless of the details of stress involved. It is essential that when this response to a situation occurs, the energy released is used. If the response is inhibited, as it often is when triggered by emotional reactions, the body cannot simply forget the adrenaline. It reacts internally, as external expression is suppressed. Over a period of time this can lead to exhaustion and possibly lay the foundations for chronic disease anywhere in the body. It may take the form of overloading the pancreatic insulin supply because of the elevated blood sugar levels, which in turn may reveal an underlying tendency to diabetes.

With herbal medicine, there is the possibility of feeding and renewing the adrenal glands, promoting activity and reintegration in body function. In any case, where there has been an overexposure to stress leading to nervous exhaustion and debility, the herbs that aid adrenal function should be considered.

A number of plants are known to contain the natural precursors of the adrenal hormones (see the section on the chemistry of herbs for more details). The most important of these herbs are *Borage*, *Ginseng*, *Licorice*, and *Wild Yam*. The long-term use of these herbs can be highly beneficial for anyone in very stressful conditions, especially through regularly drinking *Borage* tea and taking *Ginseng*. If a person has been on steroid drug therapy, *Licorice* is indicated for revitalizing the adrenals. These hormone precursors are natural "building blocks" that the body can use while the gland is being restored to its natural function. These plant hormone precursors do not act like orthodox synthetic hormones, which usually come in an unnaturally concentrated form and, although doing the job for which they were designed, leave a trail of dangerous side effects in their wake.

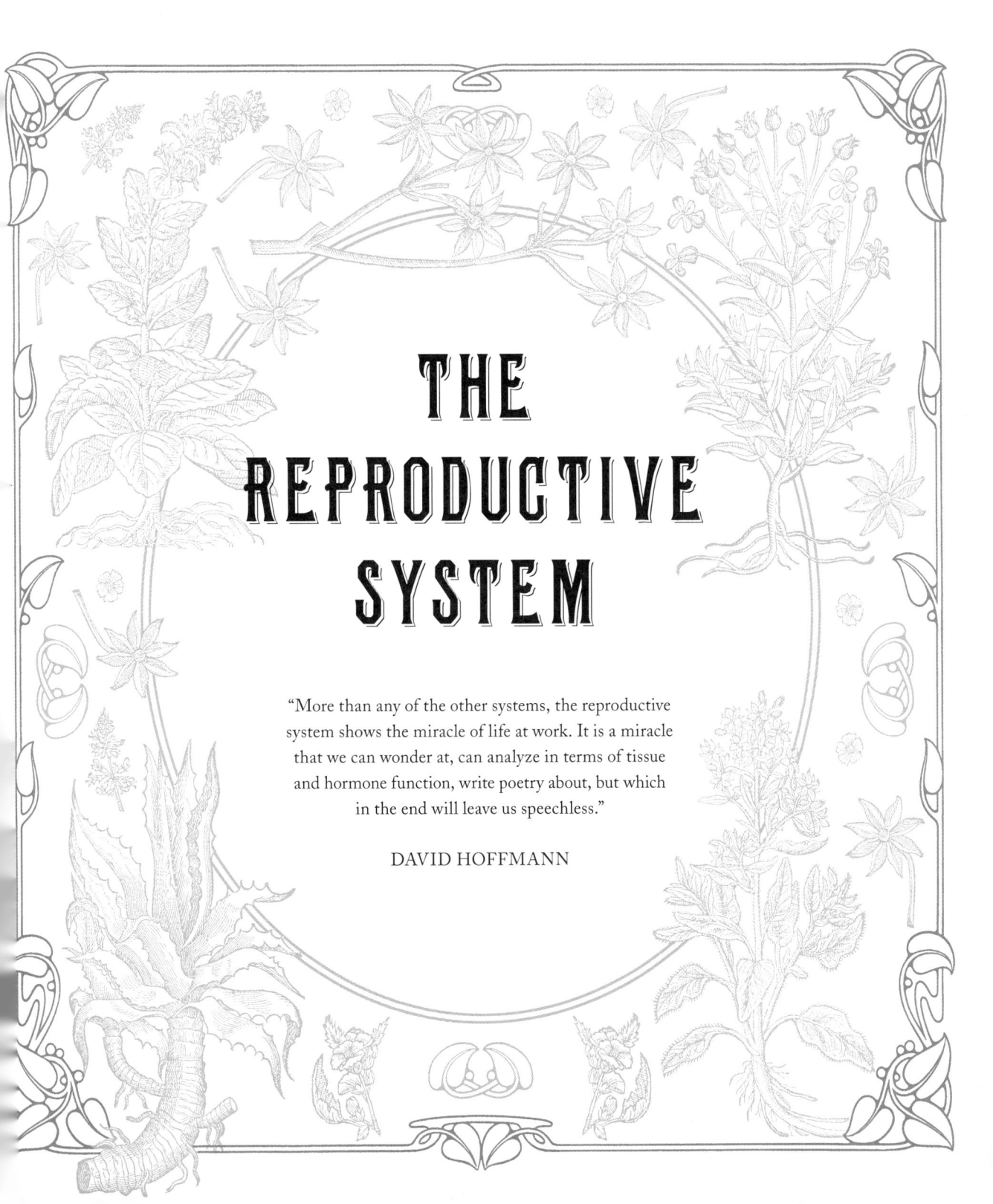

THE REPRODUCTIVE SYSTEM

"More than any of the other systems, the reproductive system shows the miracle of life at work. It is a miracle that we can wonder at, can analyze in terms of tissue and hormone function, write poetry about, but which in the end will leave us speechless."

DAVID HOFFMANN

The Reproductive System

THE FOCUS OF THIS CHAPTER IS primarily on the reproductive system of women, as this system is prone to some specific problems. By the nature of human anatomy, there is not the same degree of complexity of structure or function in the male reproductive system. The miracle of birth is a mystery inherent in the body form of a woman and less so for a man. The main physical problem that arises in men is associated with the prostate gland, and this is discussed in the chapter on the urinary system. Infections of the male reproductive system should be approached in the same way as described for infections of the female system.

For the reproductive system to be whole and functioning in a well-balanced and integrated way, body and spirit must be well and thriving as a whole. If the diet is deficient, menstrual problems or vaginal discharges may be generated. If one's way of living is not life-affirming, the system dedicated to the creation of new life will be adversely affected. For children to be born healthy and perfect, and for them to grow well, one's lifestyle during pregnancy has to be perfect! So it is best to check your health in general, but also check your relationships to the world—go for loving and nurturing emotional support. Check your thought life—do you think positively? What sort of books do you read, what movies do you watch, what kind of politics are you involved in? The energy within your body is affected by the energy around you but—more importantly—by the way you relate to it. Be at peace with your world and your relationships with it.[*]

---

[*] I would like to guide you to a book that is filled with deep wisdom, compassion, and humility, a book that every woman should have and every man should read: *Hygeia, a Woman's Herbal*, by Jeannine Parvati (Freestone Publishing, 2010).

Herbs for the Female Reproductive System

A great number of herbs benefit the female reproductive system. To help understand the herbal approach, we will, as usual, group them according to their actions.

Remarkably, many herbs for the female reproductive system, which cannot be duplicated by European remedies, have come to us from the cultures of the Native Americans. We can speculate that this may be due to the deep resonance that existed between these peoples and the Earth Mother, a resonance that manifested in physical terms, of deep healing and aid for women and for the birthing process.

Uterine Tonics

The uterine tonics have a specifically toning and strengthening action upon the whole system, both on the tissue of the organs and on their functioning. While each has its unique associated actions—which should be checked out to find the most appropriate ones—they all aid the whole reproductive system. Remedies like *Black Cohosh, Blue Cohosh, Chasteberry, False Unicorn Root, Golden Ragwort* (aka *Life Root*), *Motherwort, Raspberry*, and *Partridge Vine* (aka *Squaw Vine*) are used as healers in a holistic sense. They are often indicated when there is no obvious acute disease but where a weakness of the sexual organs has a detrimental effect on the whole body.

Emmenagogues

The emmenagogues stimulate and promote a normal menstrual flow. While most of the uterine tonics are also emmenagogues, which act through normalizing the system, there are many other emmenagogues that are not especially healing to the system as a whole. There are even emmenagogues that work by a stimulation that verges on irritation, which can be of benefit in some cases, but it is also the action of herbal abortifacients. A list of those herbs that have to be avoided during pregnancy is given later. The most useful emmenagogues, out of a potentially endless list, are *Blue Cohosh, False Unicorn Root, Golden Ragwort* (aka *Life Root*), *Motherwort, Parsley, Pennyroyal, Rue, Southernwood, Partridge Vine* (aka *Squaw Vine*), and *Yarrow*. The most appropriate one of these for use in specific treatment should be determined by considering their associated actions.

Hormonal Normalizers

The hormonal normalizers are an important group. They balance and normalize the functioning of the endocrine glands and so aid the proper functioning of the reproductive system. As they are discussed in detail in the chapter on the glandular system, I will only mention the most important one, *Chasteberry*. This valuable remedy normalizes estrogen and progesterone activity and thus finds use in all aspects of menstrual dysfunction and especially in conditions associated with menopause.

ALTERATIVES AND LYMPHATIC TONICS

As conditions of the reproductive system will affect the whole body and are affected by the condition of the whole body, it is often appropriate to use alteratives and lymphatic tonics like *Blue Flag, Burdock, Cleavers, Echinacea, Pokeweed Root,* or *Sarsaparilla*.

OTHERS

As there is often a buildup of water associated with conditions of the reproductive system, diuretics may need to be used, for their appropriate use will control this.

As the proper functioning of the digestive system is essential to health, the use of bitters can lend additional help.

NERVINES

The proper and healthy activity of the nerves is vital for the reproductive system to work correctly. Many of the emmenagogues have nervine activity, but in addition it is worth considering the relaxing herbs *Cramp Bark, Skullcap,* and *Valerian*. Nervine tonics such as *Damiana* and *Oats* will also be useful.

ASTRINGENTS

Astringents will often be used in the context of this system, and the following have a special affinity to it: *Bur Marigold, Geranium, Lady's Mantle, Periwinkle, Shepherd's Purse,* and *Trillium* (aka *Beth Root*). However, other astringents may also be of value and may be found in the general section on astringents.

DEMULCENTS

Demulcents are often used to provide a soothing and healing action on the system's mucous membranes. The urinary demulcents are often appropriate. A list of these includes *Bearberry, Blue Cohosh, Corn Silk, Golden Seal, Irish Moss,* and *Marshmallow*.

ANTISEPTICS

When a condition calls for the use of antiseptics, either one of the general ones or one of the urinary antiseptics can be used: *Bearberry, Couch Grass, Echinacea, Garlic, Juniper, Wild Indigo,* and *Yarrow*.

Patterns of Disease of the Female Reproductive System

We will consider the diseases of the reproductive system in four groups: those associated with the menstrual cycle, those with pregnancy and childbirth, those with menopause, and those associated with infections.

The Menstrual Cycle

To ensure a normal and easy menstrual cycle, any of the uterine tonics may be used regularly or perhaps just for the time leading up to the expected onset of the period. "Normal" is used here, recognizing that normalcy is relative and that each individual will have her own norm.

If problems like amenorrhea, menorrhagia, metrorrhagia, dysmenorrhea, or premenstrual syndrome occur, they can be treated herbally.

Amenorrhea

Amenorrhea is a condition in which there is an absence of menstruation. In adolescents, the first period cycle can be apparently delayed for various reasons, in which case the uterine tonics may help the body establish its natural rhythm. Perhaps the best herbs for this are *Blue Cohosh*, *Chasteberry*, *False Unicorn Root*, *Rue*, and *Southernwood*.

If menstruation is delayed or obstructed in adults, the uterine tonics will also help, especially where the cause lies primarily in a withdrawal from the contraceptive pill, with the need for the body to find its way back into its natural rhythm. A mixture of *Blue Cohosh*, *Chasteberry*, *False Unicorn Root*, and *Rue* will be very beneficial:

Chasteberry	2 parts
False Unicorn Root	2 parts
Blue Cohosh	1 part
Rue	1 part

This tea should be drunk three times a day.

An excellent old remedy for delayed periods is an infusion of equal parts of *Pennyroyal* and *Tansy*, which should be drunk three times a day until the period begins.

A word about pregnancy: Menstruation may be delayed because of conception. Check first whether the delay is due to a pregnancy, otherwise these herbs might act as abortifacients. The present Western herbal tradition does not have a safe and effective herbal abortifacient. Other traditions may. The emmenagogues are potentially dangerous if used to induce abortion. If you are pregnant and unhappy about it, go to a Family Planning Clinic. If you are not pregnant, these herbs are safe and healing when used as directed.

Menorrhagia

Occasionally your period flow will be stronger than normal, a condition called menorrhagia. This excessive flow can be normalized with the use of astringents, which will regulate it without inhibiting the natural process. If the excessive flow continues over a number of periods, it is advisable to consult a gynecologist to make sure it does not indicate a more severe problem.

While most astringents will help, those with a special affinity for the uterus and associated tissue are certainly the best. While they are listed above and should be studied to find the most applicable one, a treatment can be based on:

Geranium	1 part
Periwinkle	1 part
Trillium	
(aka *Beth Root*)	1 part

This tea should be drunk three times a day in the week leading up to a period and during the flow itself. If it is an ongoing problem, the tea should be drunk once or twice a day throughout the cycle.

METRORRHAGIA

Where bleeding occurs in the middle of the cycle—or, for that matter, at any unexpected time—the herbs recommended for menorrhagia will prove useful. However, it is important to establish the cause, which will often suggest the use of uterine tonics to help in a more fundamental way. Also, the use of *Chasteberry* is often indicated.

To balance the loss of additional blood during this time, a diet rich in natural iron is essential.

DYSMENORRHEA

Dysmenorrhea is a condition where the period is accompanied by cramping pains, which can be incapacitating in their intensity. Herbs like uterine tonics, antispasmodics, and nervines have a lot to offer in the relief of these pains. A mixture of *Black Haw Bark*, *Cramp Bark*, and *Pasqueflower* may be tried:

Black Haw Bark	2 parts
Cramp Bark	2 parts
Pasqueflower	1 part

This tea should be drunk three times daily when needed. Herbs like *Black Cohosh*, *False Unicorn Root*, and *Wild Yam* should be considered as well, depending on the condition. Consult "The Herbal" section to choose the most appropriate herb or combination for the individual case.

PREMENSTRUAL SYNDROME

In the days leading up to the onset of menstruation, tension and anxiety, agitation and depression can occasionally develop, sometimes together with a buildup of water in the body, a heightened sensitivity of the breasts, and a range of other symptoms. All of these are caused by the body's response to the hormonal changes at that time. An important question arises as to whether this is a "normal" response for that individual or compounded by psychological factors. Which comes first, the psychological condition or the hormonal problem?

Periods are a very special time in a woman's life. It is clearly a time when the magical quality of life is manifesting itself. Deep insights into the inner nature of a culture and its relationship to life can be found in examining whether it relates to menstruation as a magical time that is honored or an unclean time that is to be hidden. How a woman relates to the whole process of menstruation will deeply affect her body's response to it. Factors that may play a role in compounding premenstrual syndrome can be one's relationship to sexuality, the attitudes of relatives, childhood experiences, expectation of tension, or expectation of its interference with work and other activities. If the inner attitude to menstruation is blocked and congested, the experience of the period will reflect this. If the attitude—consciously or not—is clear, at ease, and flowing, the experience of menstruation will be the same.[*]

---

[*] To look deeper into the whole process of menstruation and the mental attitudes related to it, consult a book called *The Wise Wound, Menstruation and Everywoman*, by Penelope Shuttle and Peter Redgrove (Marion Boyars, 2005).

Taking all the above into account, herbs can do a lot to ease premenstrual syndrome. An infusion of equal parts of *Scullcap* and *Valerian* can be taken when and as often as needed. If there is associated cramping, *Cramp Bark* and *Pasqueflower* might be used, and if water retention also occurs, *Dandelion* can be added to the mixture.

THE PILL

While the need for effective contraception in our overcrowded world is undeniable, the extensive use of contraceptive pills—which are based on hormones—has also created problems in our society. On the physical level, the systemic impact of the pill poses important questions about the effect of its long-term use. The pill is a good example of the two-edged sword of technology, where the solution of one problem raises at least one new problem.

When you stop using the pill, the body and especially the hormonal balance take a while to regain their natural harmonic functions. Herbal remedies that act as endocrine balancers and uterine tonics can speed up the process:

Black Cohosh	1 part
Chasteberry	1 part
Licorice	1 part
Motherwort	1 part

Drink this tea three times a day for the first two weeks after coming off the pill, twice daily for the third week, and once a day for the fourth week.

In this mixture, *Licorice* will aid the adrenal glands, *Black Cohosh* and *Chasteberry* will tone the uterus and support the glands involved in the production of sex hormones, and *Motherwort*, while augmenting these actions, will also support the nervous system and allow an emotional balance to be regained.

PREGNANCY AND CHILDBIRTH

Pregnancy is a most special time, for mother and father as much as for the baby coming into life, a time to be treated with great respect and awe. For the baby, this time of peace and stillness, of security and wholeness, is dependent on the mother's lifestyle and that of those around her. What she eats and drinks will construct the child's body. The energies of her thoughts and feelings, and of the people around her, will color and influence the child. Be aware and take care!

While it is the mother who carries the child and directly experiences the miracle of gestation, we have all started our lives within the womb. Everybody involved should be wholly present in the process, with willingness, understanding, and love, which are essential to the well-being of the child. Loving consciousness is the key and the willingness to manifest that which is appropriate. This attitude is basic to all matters of wholeness. Herbal remedies or attention to diet are just parts of the process and will not be sufficient to ensure a natural birth and a healthy child.

While nature ensures that the placenta and other physical processes of mother and child will do the very best that can be done for the new being, much special care can be taken and herbs can be used to assist the process. Many excellent books on natural childbirth are now available and should be studied.* What is written here hopes to add to that knowledge.

---

*In particular I would like to refer you to an excellent book called *Spiritual Midwifery*, by Ina May Gaskin (The Book Publishing Company, 2002).

Nature offers an abundance of plants for all stages of the birthing process. Some may be used at specific times, and some throughout pregnancy, to ease, aid, and tone the tissue and to facilitate the birth itself. By far the best of these are *Partridge Vine* (aka *Squaw Vine*) and, *Raspberry Leaves* which may be taken individually or together. A cup per day should be taken for at least the last three months and better for the whole of the nine months—or at least as soon as you know you are pregnant. Apart from these two toners, it may be appropriate to use other herbs to augment health in general, ensuring that nutrition and bodily function are at their peak. A typical and usually appropriate example would be the use of *Nettles* as a source of iron.

HERBS TO BE AVOIDED DURING PREGNANCY

A number of herbs markedly stimulate the uterus; this is the basis of the action of some emmenagogues. Under most conditions this is of no consequence, but during pregnancy it is important that no externally produced stimulation or spasm occurs in the uterus, as this may trigger a miscarriage. The most common of these stimulating herbs are *Autumn Crocus, Barberry, Golden Seal, Juniper, Male Fern, Mandrake, Pennyroyal, Pokeweed Root, Rue, Sage, Southernwood, Tansy, Thuja*, and *Wormwood*. While these will not always act as abortifacients, it is well worth avoiding the risk of taking them, as their desired actions can be attained by other herbs.

THREATENED MISCARRIAGE

Occasionally, miscarriage is the body's natural response to certain situations. In such circumstances, no herbal remedies will oppose the body's purpose. However, miscarriage can also be threatened in cases of inadequate diet, stress, or trauma, and then herbs can provide that extra strength or vitality to avoid an unnecessary miscarriage. The body can use herbal aid to ensure that the baby thrives. While specific herbs may be appropriate, general uterine tonics like *Black Haw Bark, Blue Cohosh, Cramp Bark, False Unicorn Root*, or *True Unicorn Root* are indicated to protect against a threatened miscarriage. While all of these may be useful, a combination of toning, antispasmodic, and nervine relaxant actions can be especially effective:

Blue Cohosh	2 parts
False Unicorn Root	2 parts
Cramp Bark	1 part

Drink this tea three times daily.

If there is a considerable amount of stress involved, stronger nervines like *Skullcap* or *Valerian* may be considered as well.

MORNING SICKNESS

A common occurrence in the first few months of pregnancy is morning sickness, coming most frequently in the morning when the stomach is empty, although it can happen at other times. It seems to be the result of a number of factors acting together. Most important is the massive change in hormone levels that is going on, combined with low blood sugar and possibly low blood pressure. In more naturopathic terms, it can be seen as a cleansing of toxins from the system in preparation for pregnancy.

While it is best to avoid any medication during pregnancy, there are some specific and safe remedies that can be used if needed, such as *Black Horehound*, *Irish Moss*, and *Meadowsweet*. Gentle nervines that will help as well are *Chamomile*, *Hops*, and *Peppermint*. A useful mixture is:

Meadowsweet	2 parts
Black Horehound	1 part
Chamomile	1 part

This tea should be drunk three times a day or as needed. It will be needed less if the diet is nurturing, stress is avoided, and the woman respects body and spirit, self and child.

LABOR

If you drink a tea of *Partridge* (aka *Squaw Vine*) and *Raspberry Leaves* through at least the last three months of pregnancy, labor will probably be easy and not too prolonged. However, if labor should be protracted and if the strength of the uterus seems to be waning, herbs may be usefully employed to stimulate the uterus into contraction. By far the most useful and safe oxytocic herb in this case is *Golden Seal*. While it should not be used in pregnancy, during labor it may be used to support and strengthen the body's endeavors.

MILK PRODUCTION

You might find it difficult to either commence milk production or to maintain a high enough level of production when breast-feeding. Since it is best for the child to be on breast milk for as long as it is feasible, herbs that will help can be invaluable. For this, herbs like *Aniseed*, *Blessed Thistle*, *Caraway Seeds*, *Fennel Seeds*, *Fenugreek Seeds*, *Goat's Rue*, and *Vervain* are available, with *Goat's Rue* being perhaps the most powerful. It can safely be drunk three times a day as an infusion made from 1 or 2 tablespoons per cup of water.

The seeds I mentioned, which are rich in volatile oils, are also very effective and can be combined to make a very pleasant tea:

Caraway	2 parts
Fennel	1 part
Aniseed	1 part

or just

| *Fenugreek* | 2 parts |
| *Aniseed* | 1 part |

To make either of these teas, crush 2 tablespoons of the seeds and put them in a cup of cold water. Bring it to simmer and then remove it from the heat. Leave it to stand for 10 minutes, covered to reduce the loss of the volatile oils. Drink a cup of this tea three times a day.

If, for some reason, the milk flow needs to be stopped, the most effective herb is *Red Sage*, or—if not available—ordinary *Garden Sage*, made into an infusion and drunk three times daily until the desired result is obtained.

Menopause

Unfortunately, in our "civilized" society, menopause is approached with dread by many women, as it is feared as a time when their role as women becomes devalued. They are no longer sex objects, their role as mothers or potential mothers is reduced, the children have left home, and their traditional role as support for the husband in his struggle to earn money and establish himself has often been accomplished. As we tend to draw our identity from socially defined roles, indeed tend to become those identities, there seems to be not much left when those roles are gone. But we are not just socially defined roles!

Menopause can be a great gift in a woman's life, a liberation, an initiation. It presents an opportunity to re-evaluate one's purpose in life, perhaps to change one's life, to see change not as something to fear but as something to embrace as a friend and thus to move onward to greater fulfilment.

Apart from the psychological changes associated with menopause, it is also accompanied by hormonal changes that are physical manifestations of menopause and may lead to distressing symptoms. The most notable of these are the "hot flashes," brought about by rushes of hormones into the blood, for the gland system is adjusting to the new situation. As a combined effect of the physiological changes and the psychological impact of the new situation, there may be associated symptoms of "neurosis" or "depression." Disruptions due to the hormonal changes, problems related to the change in one's self-image, and the resistance to that change can all interact and lead to such psychological symptoms.

As this is a book about herbs, I shall limit my advice to herbal remedies. However, remember that there is much more going on than hormonal change and that a number of psychotherapeutic techniques are available to help you in this time of change.

A useful mixture—which will help the body balance and adapt to the changes, reducing the severity of hot flashes and their frequency quite quickly, too—should be taken for a few months until all symptoms are gone and the change is completed:

Chasteberry	2 parts
Wild Yam	2 parts
Black Cohosh	1 part
Golden Seal	1 part
Golden Ragwort (aka *Life Root*)	1 part
Oats	1 part
St. John's Wort	1 part

Drink this tea three times daily.

Use *Motherwort* in place of *St. John's Wort* if heart palpitations, high blood pressure, or tension are present.

This mixture will ease most of the associated problems and enable the body to establish a new level of hormonal function and integration. Remember that the body knows best. However, in cases of associated anxiety or depression, *Skullcap* or *Valerian* may also be added to the mixture.

INFECTIONS

The whole reproductive system is at least as open to infections as any other part of the body, and because it opens to the outside world, it also has distinct problems due to infections through contact. In some respect, the problems are similar to ear, nose, and throat, for here as well it is the mucous membranes that are open to the infection. Discharges of mucus are also common as responses to infections, or are due to the body's effort to get rid of excessive mucus accumulating elsewhere in the body.

To truly heal an infection of the vagina or of any other part of the system, remedies must be used that aid and clear the whole body. Douches or other local applications will at best only get rid of the symptoms for a while.

An appropriate treatment for vaginal infections involves the use of antimicrobials in association with herbs that clear the lymphatics, usually alteratives. To aid the healing of infected tissue, astringents will usually be indicated, especially in cases with mucus discharge. In addition, the whole picture has to be taken into account and the state of general health augmented with the addition of appropriate remedies. One common cause to bear in mind is the use of the pill or a recent withdrawal from it, for its use will often affect the ecology of the vaginal region. To illustrate this approach, the antimicrobials may include *Echinacea, Garlic*, or *Wild Indigo*, the lymphatics for this area should be *Cleavers* or *Pokeweed Root*, and out of the many astringents that can be applied, *False Unicorn Root, Geranium, Golden Ragwort* (aka *Life Root*), *Oak Bark, Periwinkle,* and *Trillium* (aka *Beth Root*) are the most frequently used. Most astringents will also prove effective as external applications in combination with a tea. A useful internal mixture would be:

Echinacea	2 parts
Geranium	2 parts
Periwinkle	2 parts
Trillium (aka *Beth Root*)	2 parts
Cleavers	1 part

This tea should be drunk three times daily.

The mixture may also be used as a douche, made in the same way as an infusion. It should be used three times a day also, to support the internal treatment, and has to be continued for a few days after the infection has cleared. In a similar way, yogurt may be used both internally and externally. This re-establishes the natural bacterial flora and so the regained ecology can look after itself. This is especially good when a problem follows the use of antibiotic drugs. The general guidelines on combating infection of course apply here. The diet should be rich in natural vitamins and minerals, especially from fruit and vegetable sources. Perhaps a vitamin C supplement is indicated, especially after antibiotic therapy. Abundant *Garlic* in the diet is advisable, preferably raw.

Herbs and Sexuality

Almost all cultural traditions in the world have favorite herbs that have the reputation of increasing libido and of reversing impotence. For one of them, *Damiana*, such a reputation was even carried into its botanical name, *Turnera aphrodisiaca*. Whether the aphrodisiacs work by directly stimulating a sexual urge is highly debatable. In my opinion, such an action does not exist. However, it is possible to enhance sexuality by using herbs if we look at it in holistic terms. If the body is full of vitality, is at ease, and the mind is poised and at peace, sex can be a powerful expression of that vitality. From this angle, herbs that will help us to be in such a space of ease and wholeness, will act in a roundabout way as aphrodisiacs. A few herbs like *Damiana, Ginseng*, and *Saw Palmetto* have a reputation as tonics for the reproductive glands and especially for the male system. They not only undoubtedly strengthen the system itself, but can also help move a person into a state of greater embodiment of their innate wholeness and vitality.

If sexual problems arise in connection with stress and tension, nervine relaxants and tonics like *Lime Blossom, Oats*, or *Skullcap* may be indicated.

If the general state of health is in any way below par, it should be aided by the appropriate remedies, with the bitter tonics often being helpful.

The old herbals are also rich in remedies that will reduce the sexual drive. Cures for nymphomania and masturbation abound! If it is appropriate to reduce the experience or expression of sexual energy, the combined use of nervine relaxants (to take off some of the energy) and of nervine tonics (to strengthen and support the system) can be indicated, with good herbs being *Passion Flower, Valerian*, or *Wild Lettuce. Hops* is especially good for men if there is a need to reduce sexual overexcitability.

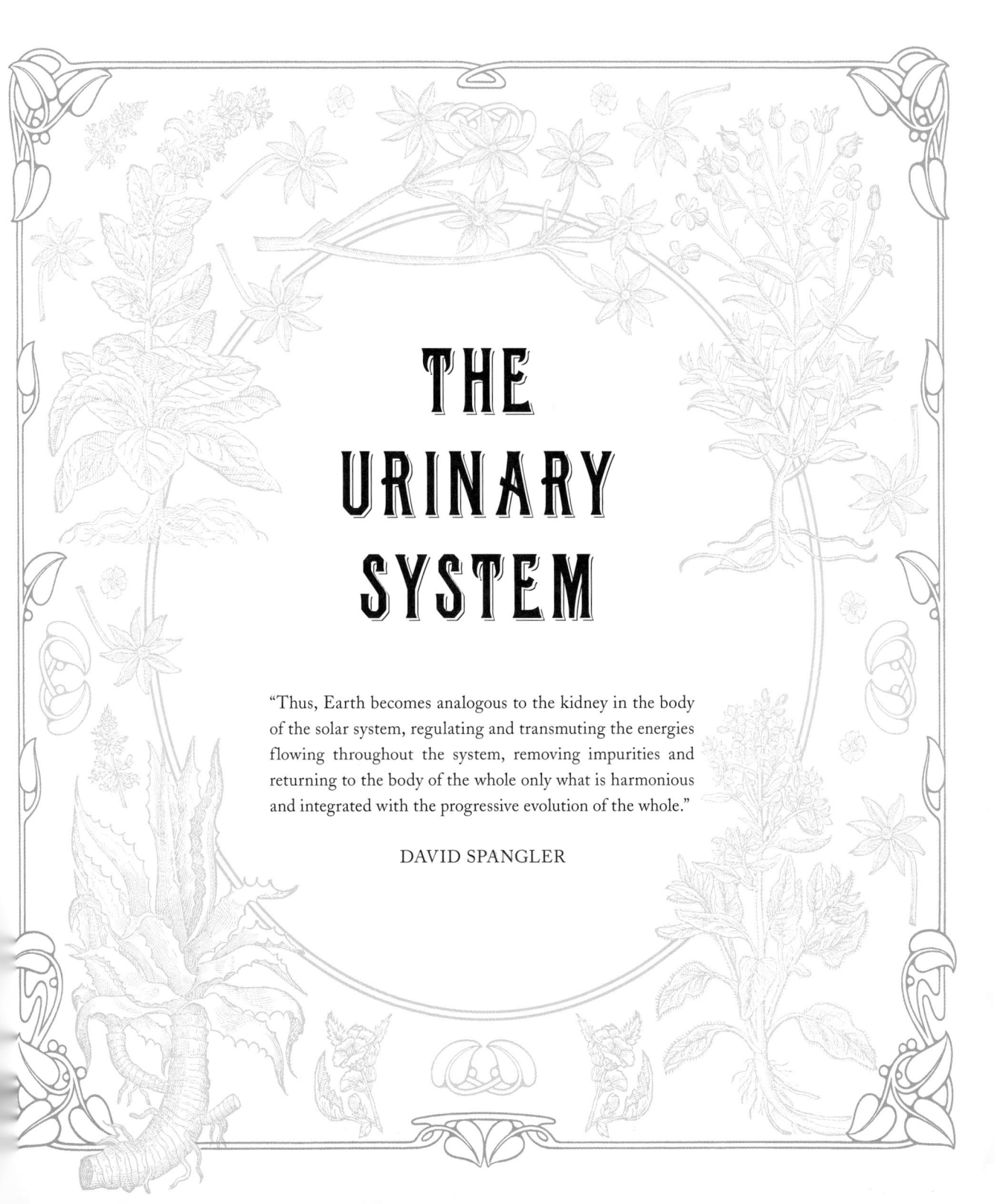

THE URINARY SYSTEM

"Thus, Earth becomes analogous to the kidney in the body of the solar system, regulating and transmuting the energies flowing throughout the system, removing impurities and returning to the body of the whole only what is harmonious and integrated with the progressive evolution of the whole."

DAVID SPANGLER

The Urinary System

With David Spangler's most eloquent description of the role our planet plays within its solar system, of its involvement in the purification of energies, we have a perfect description of the role the kidneys play within our body. Looking at such a pattern can provide insights into the resonance of being and meaning throughout creation, into the nature of the integration of wholes within greater wholes. Much that can be said about the relationship of the kidney to the body can also be said about the role of an individual or group within an ecosystem, about an ecosystem within the biosphere, about planets within the solar system, and so on outward. If we go inward, into our body and into the cell structure, we find similar patterns of relationships.

The kidney is primarily dedicated to the maintenance of a constant and healthy internal environment in the body. It is an organ of homeostasis. The inner architecture of the kidney and the way its amazing structure fulfills its complex functions is beyond the scope of this book. However, we should at least look at some of the things the kidney can do, to gain an understanding of how it works.

Its most important function is the regulation of the body's water content. Although the kidney is often described as excreting water, its duty is really more one of conserving it, for much of the water that passes through the kidney is reabsorbed. Only a comparatively small amount, which acts as a solvent for the waste materials, is actually passed on into the bladder. The kidney regulates the relative salt balance in the body, excreting excess amounts. Another important function of the kidney is the role it plays in the maintenance of the acid/alkali balance of the blood. It is also responsible for separating waste from useful substances. As the blood filters through the kidneys, many vital molecules such as glucose and amino acids leave the blood and enter the urine fraction. These important molecules are later reabsorbed, while waste products are excreted. The complexity of the kidney is partly due to this ability to differentiate between waste products and vital substances. The kidney is also involved in the production of the hormone renin, which is involved in the regulation of blood pressure via a complex pathway.

Herbs for the Urinary System

Considering the importance of the kidneys, it is not surprising that nature is abundant in herbs that can aid their functions. Looking at the role of the kidneys in a holistic context, it is obvious that the proper function of any part of the body is dependent on the effective elimination of waste products and toxins. As our diet tends to include unnatural and harmful chemicals, and as our lifestyle is largely out of harmony with our outer environment and the needs of the inner environment, the role of the kidneys becomes even more important. Herbs that aid the kidneys are not only useful for urinary problems but may be relevant to aid the body's cleansing mechanism in treating the whole body, no matter what the problem.

DIURETICS

In a strict sense, a diuretic is a plant that increases the excretion and flow of urine. However, the term tends to be used more generally for any herb that acts on the kidney or the bladder. The list of diuretics is enormous (as you can see in the section on the action of herbs), but perhaps the most effective and valuable diuretic recommended for general use is the root or leaf of *Dandelion*. Not only is it as effective as synthetic diuretics, it also contains a high percentage of potassium, an element that is often washed out of the body by the use of such synthetic diuretics. This has potentially dangerous consequences unless a potassium supplement is given to replace the loss. This process is not only avoided with *Dandelion*, but there is also an actual increase in the potassium level because of the high percentage it contains. *Dandelion* is also a liver tonic and a plant of many uses.

All the plants described throughout this chapter have diuretic properties, associated with other specific actions related to the urinary system. One more general diuretic worth mentioning here is *Cleavers*. Its simple diuretic action combined with alterative properties can safely benefit most conditions.

URINARY ANTISEPTICS

The antiseptic action of some diuretic herbs is usually due to a content of volatile oils or glycosides that are excreted through the kidney tubules, thus acting directly on the microbes. Typical examples are *Bearberry, Birch, Boldo, Buchu, Celery Seed, Couch Grass, Juniper,* and *Yarrow*. General antimicrobials such as *Echinacea* and *Wild Indigo Root* will also lend their properties to any diuretic. *Angelica Root* and *Goldenrod*, though primarily respiratory in their actions, are also urinary antiseptics. Usually the kidneys and bladder take care of themselves by flushing through the normal volume of urine. These herbs can aid that natural process when infections persist.

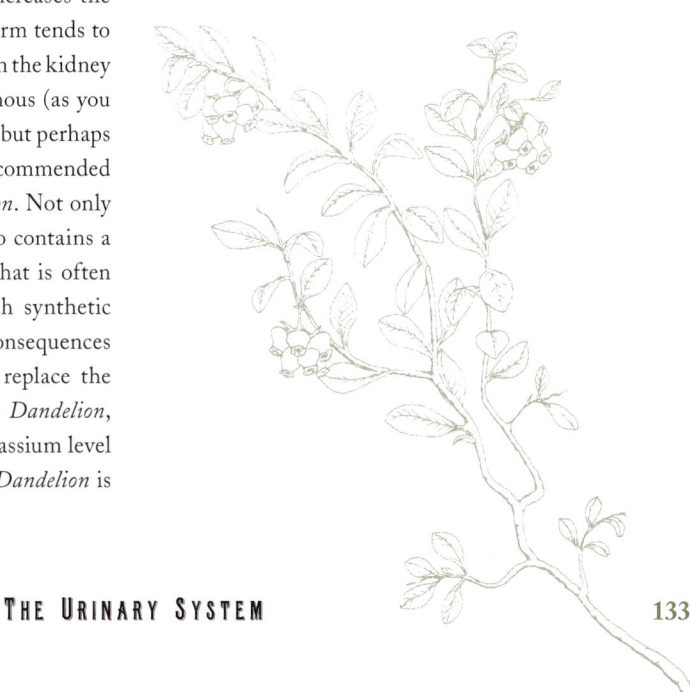

URINARY DEMULCENTS

In some conditions, the tissue of the urinary membranes needs to be soothed if it is irritated because of an infection or friction as from a kidney stone. Herbs such as *Corn Silk*, *Couch Grass*, or *Marshmallow Leaf* supply a demulcent action and can be used together with other urinary remedies.

URINARY ASTRINGENTS

While blood in the urine is a symptom that needs professional attention and diagnosis, it can be treated with the aid of astringents if it turns out to be caused by a minor problem. Astringents will stop hemorrhaging in the kidneys, bladder, urethra, or ureter and will also aid the healing of lesions. The best urinary astringents are *Bur Marigold*, *Horsetail*, *Plantain*, and *Trillium* (aka *Beth Root*). *Tormentil* is another good astringent that is mildly antiseptic and vulnerary at the same time.

ANTILITHICS

Another important property of some diuretics is their ability to prevent the formation or aid in the removal of calculi (stones or gravel) in the urinary system. There are many herbs with the reputation of being antilithics, but *Gravel Root*, *Hardhack* (aka *Stone Root*), *Hydrangea*, *Parsley Piert*, and *Pellitory* are perhaps the most effective ones. Names like *Gravel Root* and *Stone Root* show the medical preoccupation with kidney stones in the 18th and 19th centuries; bad diet probably led to an abundance of stones. Vegetables such as lovage, celery, asparagus, and artichoke are good preventatives of stone formation.

PATTERNS OF DISEASE OF THE URINARY SYSTEM

The urinary system, kidney, and bladder are prone to a range of problems that reflect those developing in the body as a whole. It is best to view urinary conditions as manifestations of systemic problems, which is really the way all specific diseases should be approached.

INFECTIONS

The urinary system is subject to a variety of infections. As with all infections anywhere in the body, these can only occur when the body's defenses are not functioning correctly. Low resistance may be caused by such things as inadequate diet or chronic constipation; another common cause is the use of antibiotics. When antibiotics are used—for the treatment of either urinary problems or others—they inflict a physiological shock upon the system and disturb our inner ecology. After their use, it is vital to help the body restrengthen its defense system, which may be done by eating live yogurt to renew the beneficial bacterial flora of the intestines and by taking additional vitamin C, but primarily by eating wholefoods, exercising, resting, and living the idea of well-being.

CYSTITIS

This infection of the bladder is characterized by a scalding pain experienced on passing water as well as by pain in the groin before, during, and just after urination. Cystitis may also be accompanied by an intense desire to pass water even though the bladder is empty. Herbs like *Bearberry*, *Buchu*, *Couch Grass*, *Juniper Berries*, and *Yarrow* may be used, with the precaution not to use

Juniper Berries if there is a tendency for an inflamed condition of the kidneys. While a hot tea of *Yarrow*, taken often, might solve the problem by itself, a mixture can also be used:

Bearberry	1 part
Couch Grass	1 part
Yarrow	1 part

The tea should be drunk hot every two hours as long as the cystitis is acute, then three times a day for a while to totally cure it. If the burning is very strong or if there is blood in the urine, a demulcent like *Corn Silk* may also be added.

The diet has to be low in acid-forming foods, as well as in sugar and artificial additives.

As a precaution, but also particularly in acute cases, the use of deodorant douches is to be strictly avoided as they disrupt the area's ecology and allow the wrong kind of microorganisms to thrive.

URETHRITIS

This infection of the urethra can be treated in the same way as cystitis, but it may be beneficial to increase the proportion of demulcent herbs in the mixture.

PROSTATITIS

When a man has an infection of the prostate gland, the symptoms may not be as localized as in the case of cystitis. Therefore, in addition to the urinary antiseptics used in cystitis, the systemic antimicrobial *Echinacea* can be added and the use of the gonad gland tonic *Saw Palmetto* should be considered. This is also used in the case of a swollen prostate gland, as discussed later. A useful mixture consists of:

Bearberry	1 part
Couch Grass	1 part
Echinacea	1 part
Horsetail	1 part
Hydrangea	1 part

This tea should be drunk three times daily.

PYELONEPHRITIS (PYELITIS)

Pyelonephritis is an infection located in the pelvis of the kidney. It may also affect other kidney tissue and can be accompanied by intense and incapacitating pain. It is advisable to seek professional help with this problem. The herbal approach is to treat the sufferer for systemic infection and fever, giving prominence to the urinary antiseptics such as *Bearberry, Buchu,* and *Pellitory,* which is sometimes considered to be a specific remedy for this problem.

KIDNEY PROBLEM

Herbal remedies have much to offer in the treatment of kidney problems, whether minor or major in nature. However, as this organ is so fundamental to health and life, any treatment of kidney disease should be undertaken by qualified and trained practitioners.

THE URINARY SYSTEM

WATER RETENTION

When the kidneys do not eliminate enough water, some of it collects in the body and is often retained, due to gravity, in the feet and lower legs. The cause for the retention must be sought, and it usually lies in the kidneys themselves or in the circulatory system. The basis of water retention can vary from premenstrual syndrome, through pregnancy to heart failure. It is impossible to give guidelines for differential diagnosis. Please get skilled advice before embarking on using herbs to remove the water. If the use of herbal diuretics produces little or no change within ten days, then definitely seek professional advice. Only when the basic cause is identified and treated can the water retention be truly stopped, but there are herbs that will remove the retained water. All of the diuretic herbs may be used, but the most effective ones are *Bearberry*, *Dandelion Leaf*, and *Yarrow*.

KIDNEY STONES

The formation of mineral deposits—stones or gravel—is a process that responds well to herbal treatment. Stones or gravel can be composed of the calcium salts of oxalic acid, uric acid, phosphates, or by combination with the amino acid cytisine. If the actual composition of the stone were known, a suitable diet could be adopted according to the type of deposit being formed, but as it is mostly unknown, general guidelines will have to suffice. A low-acid diet is indicated, totally avoiding foods high in oxalic acid such as rhubarb and spinach. It is important that anyone with stones or a tendency for their formation should drink a lot of water to ensure that the system is being flushed, which means that at least 6 pints (3 liters) of water should be drunk daily, preferably water low in mineral content. If there is a lot of sweating, it must also be compensated for.

To treat kidney stones herbally, antilithics are called for to dissolve the stones or aid their passing and to guard against any further deposits. Diuretic action is also needed to increase the amount of fluid going through the kidney and thus to flush out deposits. Fortunately, most antilithics are also diuretics. Herbs like *Gravel Root*, *Hardhack* (aka *Stone Root*), *Hydrangea*, *Parsley Piert*, *Pellitory* and *Queen Anne's Lace* (aka *Wild Carrot*) fall into this category. Urinary demulcents like *Corn Silk*, *Couch Grass*, and *Marshmallow Leaf* should also be considered to soothe the mucous membranes and to guard against any abrasion through friction. If there is any hint of an infection or even if there is only a tendency for one to develop, antimicrobials like *Bearberry*, *Echinacea*, or *Yarrow* should be used.

For a good general treatment of stones and gravel, a mixture can be used:

Corn Silk	1 part
Gravel Root	1 part
Hardhack	
(aka *Stone Root*)	1 part
Hydrangea	1 part

This tea should be drunk three times daily.

If you have a tendency to form kidney stones, you can also use this tea regularly once a day as a preventative measure.

RENAL COLIC

If a small stone moves into the ureter and gets stuck there, it may obstruct the flow of urine and cause renal colic, which can be extremely painful. The use of antispasmodic herbs like *Cramp Bark*, *Sea Holly*, or *Valerian* may help, but the attack will be relieved completely only when the blockage either moves or is passed altogether.

INCONTINENCE

Incontinence can be caused by a number of physical and psychological factors. As long as there is no organic defect or illness involved, it can be brought under control herbally, even where it is due to a loss of tone in the sphincter muscle of the bladder or to a general muscle or nervous debility. A good herbal mixture would be

Horsetail	2 parts
Agrimony	1 part
Sweet Sumach	1 part

Drink this tea three times a day.

Nighttime incontinence in children is often due to psychological factors that should be recognized and worked with if the herbs are not effective.

INFECTIONS AND INFESTATIONS

"The conflicts to which humanity is so often summoned lead—until understood and used as means to triumph and progress—to a condition of constant devitalization. Where this is present, resistance to disease fades out and practically all forms of ill health and bodily ills become possible. Diffusion of energy leads to a constant lessening of resistance. As a result you have debility, quick and bad reaction to the diseases indigenous in the planet itself, and a rapid taking on of infections and of contagious diseases."

ALICE BAILEY

Infections and Infestations

INFECTIONS—WHETHER OF BACTERIA, viruses, or fungi—will only occur when the body's defenses are weakened. Their natural strength can be diminished by many factors. Physical influences, such as an unhealthy diet, a drug therapy, or a pre-existing disease, can weaken the system. Emotional and mental factors are also crucial. Stress and tension can obviously reduce our energy to a level that allows infections to manifest, but "catching a cold" or getting other infections can also often be a signal to us, a message from our body asking us to stop and look at what we are doing.

To approach infectious diseases herbally we have to recognize that we do not "catch" them out of thin air but that we create the opportunity and the environment for the infection to thrive. It is not the bacteria's fault! To treat an infection in any real way we aim at restoring the normal resistance of the body, so a whole treatment ensuring health and vitality of all bodily systems is called for. In many cases, it is best to forget about the specific infection and to concentrate on supporting the body doing what it is designed to do—protect itself. This may take a few days and may even interfere with our all-important worldly commitments, but the need and the message are clear—it is time to give our body and our way of life some attention and care.

Infections often arise as part of an "epidemic." When there is a widespread disease attacking many people simultaneously in a community, it may be valid to consider the whole community as a multifaceted group being that acts in the same way as an individual. From this perspective, the cause of an epidemic is the same as the cause of an individual infection; it means that group resistance is down.

More people died in the influenza epidemic that followed the First World War than were killed in the war itself. This can be put down to problems of hygiene, sanitation, and nutrition following that tragic time, but it can also be seen as an outcome of deep communal wounds affecting the collective consciousness of humanity. It is not enough to be individually whole and healthy. The society we are part of must also radiate these qualities or we are part of an unhealthy system and so open to epidemics. These epidemics may be of influenza or AIDS, or of fear, alienation, and meaninglessness. Our health depends upon wholeness at all these levels.

Antibiotics

There are, no doubt, situations where it is strongly advisable to use drugs like antibiotics. They are an invaluable gift to humanity, saving lives and improving the quality of existence when they are used with discretion and where their use is appropriate. In cases such as meningitis and other potentially lethal infections, they have saved countless lives. Unfortunately, they are often used just because they are convenient and work fast, without paying too much attention to their overall effect and the consequences of their indiscriminate use.

When it is appropriate to resort to antibiotics, some steps can be taken to lessen their impact upon the system. One should take at least 0.07 ounces (2 grams) of vitamin C a day (until about a week after finishing with the antibiotics) and plenty of the vitamin B-complex. Both these vitamins help the body deal with stress—from the infection and from the antibiotics—and increase our natural resistance.

As some antibiotics destroy the natural bacterial flora of the intestines, live yogurt should be eaten in abundance to support this system against the chemical onslaught, as it helps balance the ecology of the gut.

While you take antibiotics, rest and be at ease, for you are under attack from powerful chemicals that should be treated with respect. However, be thankful that they are there to help you and express that gratitude to yourself in some meaningful way. To develop a sense of guilt about taking drugs—even though their use is appropriate—would only weaken you and block a deeper healing. When they must be taken, work with them, not against them.

Herbs can be used to help the antibiotic treatment. They can be used during the treatment to augment the action of the drugs and to aid the body and protect it against possible damage. The particular herbs will vary depending on the site of the infection and the person involved and should be chosen accordingly (see the rest of the chapter). Herbs can also be used after a drug therapy to tone the system with the aid of bitters and possibly nervine tonics. Cleansing the system with alteratives, diuretics, and lymphatic herbs is also important. While specific ones should be chosen according to individual needs, herbs like *Cleavers, Echinacea, Gentian, Golden Seal, Nettles, Oats,* and *Wormwood* are often indicated.

Herbs for Infections and Infestations

Herbs can be used in two ways for infections and infestations: through their antimicrobial action, they work directly against microbes and in addition they augment and vitalize the body's own defenses. Fortunately, in most cases they will be doing both at the same time. *Myrrh* is an example of an herb that combines direct toxic action on bacteria with the ability to stimulate our body's production of white corpuscles—the leucocytes—which are responsible for doing most of the defensive work in the body.

Other actions that are indicated are those that help eliminate toxins, like diaphoretics, laxatives, and diuretics. Any accumulation of waste material and toxins is a prime environment for microbes to breed in. Most herbs can play a role in treating infections or infestations, but here we will concentrate on the antimicrobials, diaphoretics, and anthelmintics.

Antimicrobials

Many plants have a direct toxic effect upon microbes. The first effective antibiotic drug, penicillin, was discovered in a plant, a fungus. Interestingly enough, an old Welsh remedy for festering sores is based upon moldy bread. For years this was mocked by the medical profession, until it became clear that there is a definite biochemical basis for this seemingly outlandish prescription, as the mold is caused by fungi.

Herbs work in complex ways that cannot always be explained—as not enough research has been done—and the processes whereby they deal with infections are numerous. The best antimicrobials that can be used safely to combat infections include *Echinacea, Eucalyptus, Garlic, Myrrh, Nasturtium, Thyme, Wild Indigo*, and *Wormwood*.

In the early part of the 20th century, the antiseptic power of some plant oils was compared with that of phenol, a commonly used chemical antiseptic, and it was found that many volatile oils are stronger than phenol, with *Thyme* oil being the strongest. The experiment looked at the antiseptic action on beef tea that had been infected with water from a sewage system and determined at what dilution (in parts per 1,000 parts) there was no more antiseptic action. *Thyme* oil proved to be eight times stronger than phenol. Further, while phenol damages tissue around the wound, the stronger plant oils like *Thyme* do not. Many other plants are also stronger than phenol:

Thyme	0.7	*Rosemary*	4.3
Sweet Orange	1.2	*Lavender*	5.0
Verbena	1.6	*Phenol*	5.6
Rose	1.8	*Fennel*	6.4
Clove	2.0	*Lemon*	7.0
Eucalytus	2.2	*Sassafras*	7.5
Peppermint	2.5	*Lime*	8.4
Orris	3.8	*Angelica*	10.0
Anise	4.3		

Garlic oil is another powerful antimicrobial worth mentioning. It was used during the First World War as an antiseptic dressing applied with *Sphagnum Moss* dressings.

DIAPHORETICS (FEBRIFUGES)

A diaphoretic is a remedy that induces the body to increase its amount of perspiration. This, in turn, increases elimination of toxins through the skin and helps cleanse the body. Diaphoretics are indicated in a wide range of conditions, but nowhere more than in the treatment of fevers and of infections affecting the whole system. Their use in influenza has already been discussed (in the section on ears, nose, throat, and eyes). With their strengthening and healing properties, they can often enable the body to rid itself of infections or fevers in an astoundingly short time. They speed up and augment the vital healing process without suppressing any part of it. They may be used individually or as part of a wider therapy. The most useful ones are *Angelica, Boneset, Catnip, Cayenne, Elderberry Flowers* (or *Berries*), *Ginger, Hyssop, Pennyroyal, Peppermint, Pleurisy Root, Thyme*, and *Yarrow*.

Treating Infections

With infections, it is particularly important to treat the underlying cause and not to suppress the symptoms. Fevers should not be viewed simply as a manifestation of disease that needs to be "cured" no matter what. The fever may be a symptom of the healing process itself, which should be supported, not suppressed. A basic mixture that helps the body work through the fever is as follows:

Boneset	2 parts
Yarrow	2 parts
Echinacea	1 part

Drink half a cup as hot as possible every two hours.

Echinacea is included to help the body deal with any microbes, but the simple use of diaphoretics like *Boneset* or *Yarrow* will often suffice. If the diaphoretic strength needs to be increased, add a pinch of *Cayenne*. If the glands are swollen, indicating lymphatic involvement, *Marigold* or *Cleavers* can be included. If the mucous membranes are involved, *Golden Seal* can be added as a useful general tonic and a specific help to the membranes. If there is much restlessness, nervine relaxants like *Chamomile* or *Skullcap* can be included. These mixtures can be used not only in fevers where the cause is not clear, but also in diseases such as chicken pox, measles, scarlet fever, or the like. This is because herbs do not merely halt the named disease but also bring balanced healing to a pattern of imbalance. Thus the same herbs and actions may suit a range of people with a range of infectious diseases. Where there is catarrhal involvement, as in measles, refer to the advice given in the chapter on ear, nose, throat, and eyes. If the skin is itching, the irritation may be eased by sponging the body with diluted, distilled *Witch Hazel*. In more intransigent viral infections such as glandular

ANTHELMINTICS (VERMIFUGES)

Anthelmintics rid the body of parasites and are used internally or externally. Some anthelmintics kill the parasite, others expel them from the body, and most of them are very powerful herbs, some even potentially toxic if taken in large doses. Great care should be taken not to overdose with them.

The British Medicine Act of 1968 restricts the sale or use by British herbalists of some of the more powerful plants. Unfortunately, among them are the more effective anthelmintics like *Kousso, Male Fern*, and *Santonica*. Limitations placed on the use of *Male Fern* are most regrettable, since it is very effective against tapeworm and not as potentially dangerous as *Kousso* or *Santonica*. These plants are still widely used by orthodox doctors and veterinarians. Other useful anthelmintics include *Garlic, Pomegranate, Pumpkin Seeds, Quassia, Southernwood, Tansy*, and *Wormwood*. In all cases, consult "The Herbal" section to find the most suitable herb or combination for the circumstances.

fever, a most beneficial mixture that can help even if the problem has turned into a low level, debilitating weakness that might go on for months, is as follows:

Echinacea	2 parts
Pokeweed Root	2 parts
Wild Indigo	2 parts
Wormwood	2 parts
Myrrh	1 part

The mixture should be drunk three times a day. If you do not like its unpleasant taste, you can mask it by the use of *Licorice*.

In any infection, the intake of vitamin C should be raised to at least 0.07 ounces (2 grams) daily, vitamin B-complex should be taken, and *Garlic* should be considered as an additional remedy, preferably eaten raw. A cleansing diet based on fruit and fruit juices should be the basis of nutrition. Sometimes fasting is advisable during an infection. It is best to continue with the medication for a short while after recovery.

Specific infections are dealt with in the sections on the body system in which they occur.

Treating Infestations

We live in a very close and ecological relationship with numerous organisms. They not only live around but also inside us and our interaction with them is, for the most part, symbiotic and mutually beneficial; we exist in homeostatic harmony. Many species of bacteria, for instance, defend our body against the invasion of unfriendly microbes or parasites, such as certain bacteria on the skin or in the intestines. However, this ecological harmony can easily be disrupted, thus opening the gates for the invasion of parasites. The best prevention of such an invasion lies in the maintenance of a natural and healthy outer and inner environment, in the maintenance of health and well-being, and in appropriate hygiene.

Intestinal worms

A number of animal species can become parasites in the human intestine. Each area on this planet with its own unique ecology has its local variety of parasites, and as we are truly part of our own environment, we sometimes harbor them. The most important intestinal parasites in Western societies are worms: roundworm, tapeworm, and threadworm.

Roundworm and tapeworm can be treated in basically the same fashion. The famous American herbalist Dr. Shook advises that, rather than fasting, we should eat foods that the worms do not like for a couple of days, thus weakening them before taking anthelmintics. Such foods are onions, garlic, pickles, and salty things. After eating these (together with your normal food) for some days, drink a strong cup of *Wormwood* tea in the morning and at night for three days. On the fourth day, drink a cup of *Senna* tea to cleanse the bowels of the dead parasites. *Licorice* can be added to the *Senna* tea to prevent griping pains that might occur, and, instead of *Wormwood*, any other anthelmintic may be used if it seems more appropriate. If tapeworm proves to be more tenacious, *Wormwood* might have to be used for a longer period or might have to be exchanged for the stronger *Pomegranate Seeds* or even *Male Fern* (keeping in mind the limitations on its use). As threadworms inhabit the rectum, a different approach is needed and enemas have to be used. The best herb to use is *Quassia*: pour a pint of boiling water onto an ounce of *Quassia* chips and let it infuse until it reaches body temperature, when it will be ready for use. Besides using this infusion for enemas, 2 teaspoonfuls of it, flavored with *Licorice* if necessary, should be taken before meals three times a day. Another traditional remedy is to insert a peeled clove of *Garlic* into the rectum at night, but make sure the first skin under the peel is unbroken, as otherwise it might be too strong and be irritating.

LICE AND FLEAS

It is possible to rid the body of lice and fleas by using herbal remedies, but only when we maintain a good diet and scrupulous hygiene at the same time. The whole environment of the parasite has to be taken care of, and the treatment has to be an ecological approach. If lifestyle is not attended to, herbs by themselves will not be powerful enough and the only effective way of ridding the body of the parasite will lie in the use of drugs.

Lice can be treated through the use of oils of *Aniseed*, *Sassafras*, or *Quassia*, with *Sassafras* oil being the most effective. For external use, mix one part of *Sassafras* oil with two parts of *Olive* oil, rub it into scalp and hair, and comb with a fine tooth comb to remove the dead lice and eggs. This process has to be repeated daily until the hair is completely cleared of lice and eggs.

SCABIES

This little animal can be very intransigent and must be treated with the greatest respect—and with rigorous hygiene. Bedding linen must be boiled after every use and in extreme cases has to be burned. As an external remedy, a strong decoction of *Tansy* should be applied liberally, either in the bath or sponged over the body often. Bitters and nervines should be taken internally for a few days after the last scabies appear to have gone. This helps the body return to a state of ease with itself. *Gentian* and *Skullcap* are ideal, but select the ones that are most appropriate to the individual involved.

INFECTIONS AND INFESTATIONS

CANCER

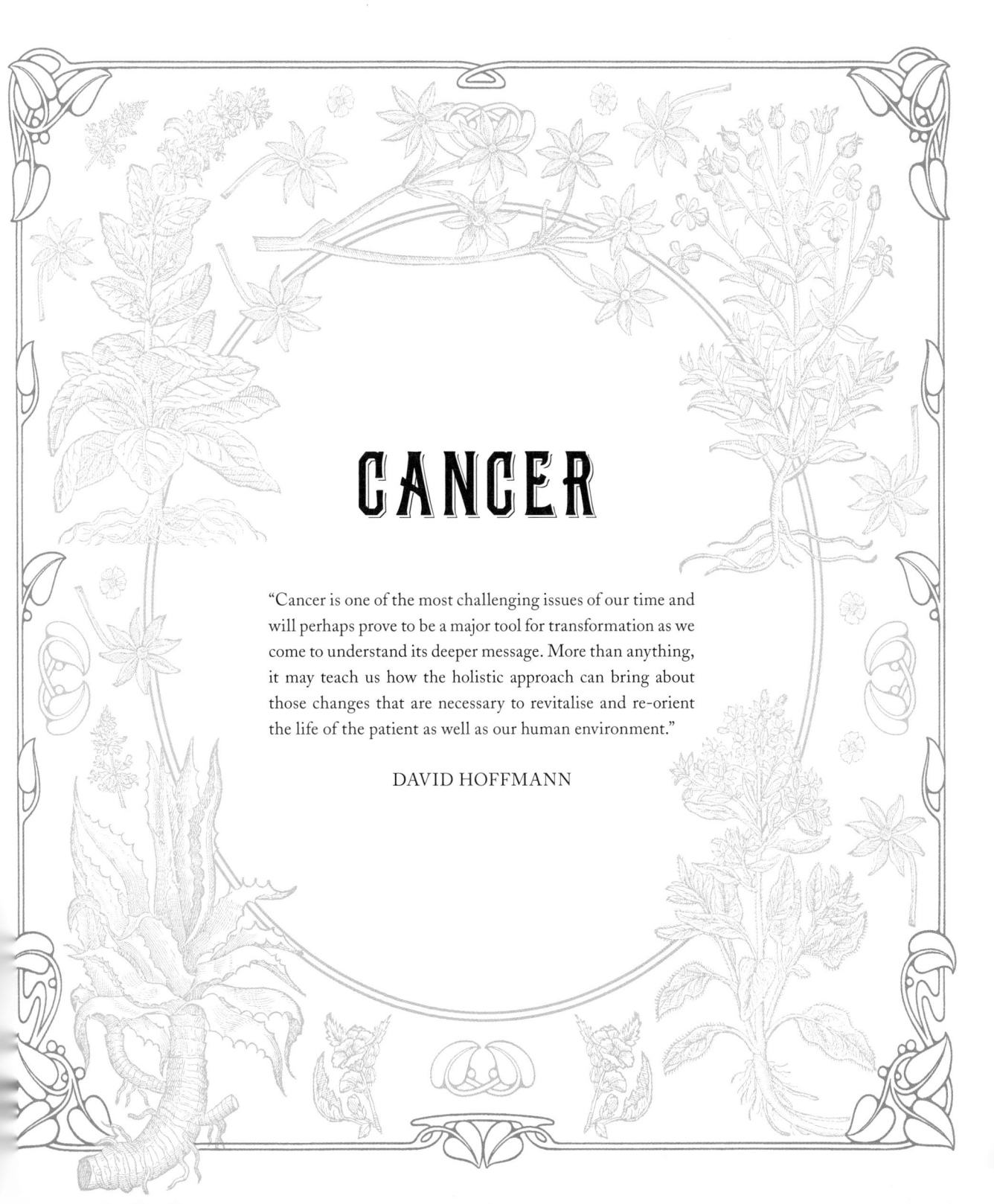

"Cancer is one of the most challenging issues of our time and will perhaps prove to be a major tool for transformation as we come to understand its deeper message. More than anything, it may teach us how the holistic approach can bring about those changes that are necessary to revitalise and re-orient the life of the patient as well as our human environment."

DAVID HOFFMANN

Cancer

THIS CONDITION, ABOVE ALL OTHERS, necessitates not only holistic therapy, but a clear holistic perception. It is becoming increasingly evident that cancer is the result of complex and multifactorial influences that are physical, physiological, psychological, social, and environmental in nature. It would be of little value to give herbal prescriptions to use in this or that cancer. What I hope to do is to share an approach to this condition, rather than give specific guidance. Each person is unique, not just a "cancer patient," and must of course be treated individually. Certain attitudes, however, can be shared. It must be stressed that qualified help is essential here, whether from an M.D., psychotherapist, or holistic healer, or all of these and more. A coordinated group of therapists working simultaneously with the person may be what it takes to facilitate remission to that point where self-healing takes over. This is an ideal point to consider the diagram of therapeutic ecology in the first chapter, in order to determine one's own initial steps of therapy. The first step is itself a healing, though cancer is a journey of many steps.

Much research and theorizing accompanies the enormous amount of attention given to cancer in our times. Theories range from viral causes, to environmental carcinogens, to psychological stress and spiritual imbalance. Many, possibly all, of these factors are involved in the generation of cancerous disorganization. Rather than draw specific conclusions about causation, I will suggest an approach that supports all aspects of the being during the profound process of cancer. From the holistic viewpoint, all of the causes must be acknowledged and worked with.

For the purpose of this book, we will focus upon three lines of approach: herbs, diet, and psychological reappraisal.

Herbs and Cancer

Many claims have been made for marked antineoplastic action in certain plants ("antineoplastic" is a term that means that some blocking or inhibiting effect is shown against neoplasm, or new growth). Every healing tradition in the world has plants that have a reputation for being anticancer herbs. A research project in the United States is monitoring every flowering plant in the world (it will take some time!) for cancer-inhibiting properties. Some of the "miracle drugs" used in the treatment of cancer by orthodox medicine were found in plants. The best example is the *Madagascan Periwinkle*, which is the source of the drugs vinblastine and vincristine that are used in leukemia.

This is an example of the way herbs may be used specifically or as sources of active ingredients. While not wanting to belittle the value of this approach, it is limited by the perception of cancer as a specific localized condition, which a specific drug (or herb) will counteract. It is far more appropriate to approach this condition as a manifestation of systemic disease and use such systemic treatments as are appropriate in aiding the body to regain control. Herbs can be most effective in supporting this sort of bodily transformation through their cleansing, strengthening, and healing properties. They work best when they are part of an approach to transformation—change in body, mind, and spirit—which is possibly the only effective context in which to treat cancer.

Using the whole-system approach, I recommend alternatives and specific antineoplastic herbs as the most relevant.

Alteratives

Through the cleansing and normalizing activity of the alteratives, herbs can support the process of the body ridding itself of cancerous growths. The remedies that work via the liver, augmenting its detoxifying activity, are especially useful. These include *Burdock, Blue Flag*, and *Yellow Dock*. The kidneys' important eliminative function is aided by *Cleavers* and *Dandelion*. Remedies that have a specific tonic and cleansing action on the lymphatic system are especially indicated in the herbal approach to cancer. Such herbs are *Cleavers, Echinacea*, and *Pokeweed Root*.

Antineoplastics

To aid the body in reasserting order and structured organization in the affected tissue, we use plants that appear to have a specific action in inhibiting and combating the development of tumors. Many claims are made for different plants, some justified, some wishful thinking. I could give a list culled from folklore and old herbals, but their efficacy is uncertain. Those we use in modern herbal therapeutics, in addition to those alteratives mentioned above, are *Guaiacum, Mistletoe, Red Clover*, and *Sweet Violet*. The way in which these herbs work has not been analyzed, but we know that they have a definite role to play in any herbal treatment of cancer.

In addition to specific antineoplastic plants, we should remember that, through aiding an organ or tissue with supportive and sustaining remedies, a renewal and release of "vital energy" will move the affected part of the body to heal itself of the cancer. It may in fact be appropriate to use plants that are specific for that organ or suggested by the general state of health that have "nothing" directly to do with cancer. For example, if there is a long history of lung infections, but the tumor is in the stomach, utilize tonics for both lungs and stomach. As explored throughout the book, healing comes from the life force of our own being and herbs can only facilitate this.

Nutrition and Cancer

Research has shown that at any one time in a healthy individual there can be up to 10,000 malignant cells in the body. They are inhibited from developing and killed by the body's superb defense mechanisms. This innate ability of the body is so effective that there must be a drastic disturbance in physical integration to allow malignancy to develop. There are a multitude of factors that may cause this breakdown of physical integrity. The subtle effects of negative emotion, mental problems, and social and personal interactions will be reviewed later, but first we will mention the undoubted impact on the body of negative factors in the environment, which are ingested through the foods we eat and our water and air.

Great concern is shown today about carcinogens (cancer-causing agents) in the environment. These are primarily products of human technology and as such tend to be alien to biological processes. While this concern is necessary and timely, it should be remembered that they act primarily by weakening the body's defense system, not always automatically causing cancer, but making it more likely, if other cofactors in our lives permit.

A list of identified carcinogens would be extremely long, but broad generalizations can be made. A good guideline is to avoid synthetic foods and additives, as human metabolism has not evolved to cope with many of these biochemical novelties. Pollutants of all sorts (and there are many) should be shunned. Fumes from cars, chimneys, industrial waste, and especially cigarette smoking are demonstrably dangerous. Coal tar products have a direct carcinogenic activity, so the drugs and food additives made from them are inadvisable. The most worrying potential danger is from radiation and radioactive substances such as plutonium. Without entering the economic argument for or against nuclear power, the potential health and environmental consequences concern us all. There is also the military use of nuclear weapons. Medical objections to such warfare are unassailable, but should it ever be put to the test in nuclear war, not only would there be few people left needing treatment for cancer, there would be even fewer plants left to treat them with. The extensive use of chemotherapy to suppress and relieve symptoms may well be another major contributing factor to the increase in degenerative illness, of which cancer is an example.

A dietary approach to the treatment of cancer can be suggested, but it should be subject to the care of a competent practitioner, as complications may develop. In the early stages, or if the tumor is small or very localized, a three- to five-day fast is advisable. If the condition is advanced, this should be reduced to a day, because of the problem of debility. During the fast, large amounts of fresh water should be drunk and purgatives taken as described in the section on constipation. This will cleanse the bowels and flush the kidneys, while the sweat glands can be aided by a visit to a sauna.

On completion of the fast, a diet of fruit and fruit juices should be commenced. Ideally, this should last for a week, but if debility is a problem it should be shortened. Grapes are perhaps the most appropriate fruit for this purpose. Buy organic if possible, or wash thoroughly, as pesticide residues are too untrustworthy to allow into the diet. The more primitive and simple the diet, the better. Once the fruit diet has ended, it is advisable that fruit should remain 50% of the total food intake. The rest of the diet should contain much raw vegetable produce. Potatoes or whole-grain rice should be the staple, and any oil used should be polyunsaturated, such as sunflower or safflower. Protein is important to help in the recovery of strength and should come from sources such as bean sprouts, fish, goat's milk, and the occasional egg. Meat is inadvisable, as are most dairy foods.

Psychological Factors and Cancer

Environmental and nutritional factors are without doubt important in the causation of cancer, but the individual's emotional state seems to be crucial as well. The holistic interpretation would be that psychological and physical states work together in the onset of the condition. It is becoming evident that emotional stress is implicated in two ways: in the suppression of the immune system and in the generation of hormonal imbalances that result in an increased production of malignant cells. These are ideal conditions for cancer to grow in. As already pointed out, there is a steady production of cancerous cells in the body that are normally destroyed by the body's defense system, the immune system. So when the immune system is not working, the production of malignant cells is increased just at the time when the body is least able to destroy them.

In the research that has been done on emotional and mental factors found in cancer patients, a common picture emerges. There has been crucial stress threatening some role or relationship central to the person's identity, or a situation has been set up from which there is apparently no escape. Such situations will characteristically generate feelings of despair, helplessness, and hopelessness. This despair may be internalized to such a degree that the person is unable to let others know that they feel hurt or angry. Because of this, serious illness, and even death, may become acceptable as a potential solution. This may not be conscious, of course, but can be present as a powerful unconscious thought form.

Perhaps the best example of an approach to the treatment of cancer where both physical and psychological components are recognized is in the work of Carl and Stephanie Simonton.[*] They see the first step in initiating the healing process as one of helping the individual become aware of a wider context to their illness, through an exploration of the psychological and social factors involved. Care is taken not to generate guilt, but to create a state of awareness from which the psychological impact upon the body can be reversed. To achieve this and then move beyond to transformation, the Simontons use counseling and psychotherapy as essential parts of their approach.

The inertia and blockage that is created by the accumulation of stressful events can only be effectively overcome through a change in belief system. In the Simontons' therapy, patients are shown that their situation seems hopeless only because they interpret it in ways that limit their response to it. The therapy thus involves a continual examination of belief system and world view.

Throughout all of this psychological work, an attitude of positivity is engendered that is crucial for the treatment. Studies have shown that the patient's response to treatment is more dependent upon attitude than on the severity of the disease. This attitudinal change has an effect upon the physical body in a similar but opposite way to stress. In other words, there is an augmenting of the immune system.

The approach of the Simontons and others involves physical therapy used in collaboration with the psychological work to help the body destroy cancer cells and to revitalize the immune system and health in general. Their approach here is allopathic, but herbal treatment and dietetics can be most appropriate, combined with regular physical exercise to reduce stress.

A powerful tool of theirs is to use visualization techniques in conjunction with relaxation exercises to make an image of the action of the immune system

---

[*] This is described by Carl and Stephanie Simonton in their book *Getting Well Again* (Bantam, 1992).

on the cancer. Because of the vital role visual imagery and symbolism plays in feedback from mind to body, this technique has proved to be an effective tool in strengthening the immune system. There is evidence that such a technique actually reduces and possibly eliminates malignant tissue.

What we have here is a multidimensional approach to the treatment of cancer that acknowledges and works with physical, emotional, mental, social, and spiritual aspects in an integrated and effective way. Inherent in this approach is the realization that treatment does not always lead to a "cure." Patients are made aware of the possibility that a point may come in the treatment where it is time for them to move consciously toward death. The issues are not avoided or disguised, but approached in a way that allows for a deep reappraisal of purpose and quality in the patient's life. This does, of course, bring to the fore some of the deepest questions of human existence. These issues are faced, and patients are aided in looking at their goals in life, their reasons for living, and in fact their relationships to the universe as a whole.

Cancer is one of the most challenging issues of our time and will perhaps prove to be a major tool for transformation as we come to understand its deeper message. More than anything, it may teach us how the holistic approach can bring about those changes that are necessary to revitalize and reorient the life of the patient, as well as our human environment.

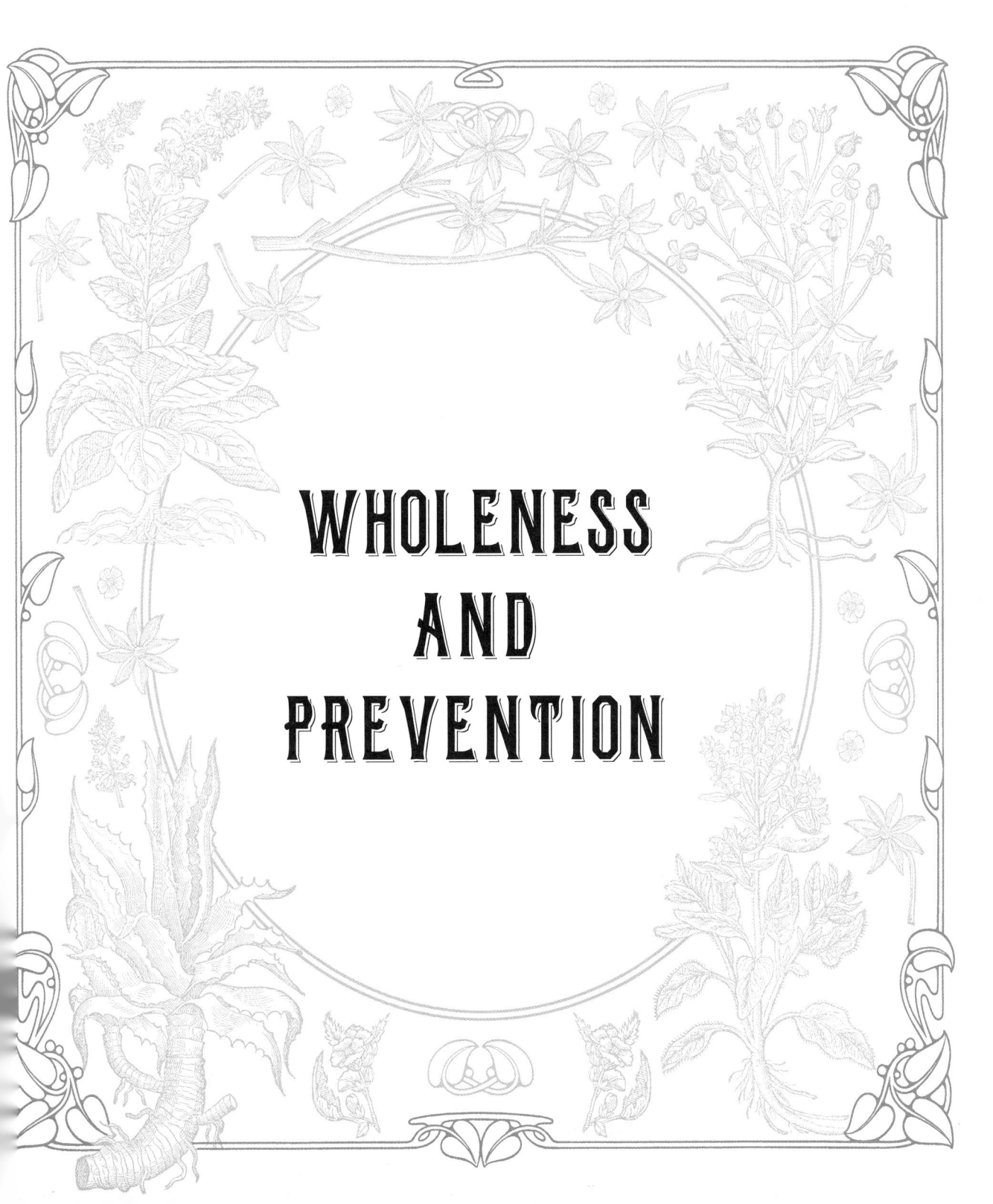

WHOLENESS AND PREVENTION

Wholeness and Prevention

So far in this book the attention has been on using herbal remedies for the safe alleviation of illness. Of course, this is not the only way to use these wonderful plants. Herbs can be used to support people's health and wholeness, helping them stay at their personal peak of vitality and prevent disease development.

Our evolution has placed us in the embrace of the natural world, and this world nurtures us in many ways. There is food that supplies nutritional needs (calories, proteins, and vitamins but also delicious tastes and aromas), as well as herbal "foods" that nurture our wholeness, integration, and well-being. These tonic remedies play a fundamental role in the maintenance of health and the prevention of disease. In this chapter, three aspects of this vast field will be considered:

—Prevention
—Detoxification and elimination
—Immune support

Herbal Preventative Medicine

Basic Ideas

Balance and harmony are the key to successful preventative medicine. There must be a clear and free flow of energy through the various aspects of the individual's life. Thus a range of issues must be addressed that go beyond the way herbal medicine can transform metabolic and physiological processes.

—*Nutrition* must be of a quality that enables the body to renew itself in a way that ensures health and wholeness. This can take many different forms, and the appropriate choice of diet will depend upon both the individual's specific health needs and his or her personal preferences (always very important!).
—*Structural factors* must be addressed, by skilled practitioners if this is indicated, but also through appropriate exercise, dance, or any enjoyable expression of bodily vitality.
—A conscious and free-flowing *emotional life* is fundamental to achieving any inner harmony. This does not mean that everyone must get involved in in-depth psychology, but that attention be given in the appropriate form for that individual's emotional needs.
—*Mental factors* are crucial as we are what we think! The Bible says that without vision, the people die. Without a personal vision, life becomes a slow process

of degeneration and decay. The emphasis must be on the personal aspect. Vision is different from taking on a dogmatic belief system. It is an expression of meaning in an individual's life and must come from their core.

—Some openness to *spirituality* in its various forms is vital. This may take the form of being uplifted by a sunset, being touched by poetry or art, belief in a religion, or simply a dogma-free joy in being alive.

HERBAL ACTIONS, TONICS, AND ALTERATIVES

The plant kingdom is an abundant and rich resource for anyone interested in prevention. The key is not so much in specific remedies but in an understanding of the role of herbal actions in maintaining health and correct physiological activity. With the insights that modern physiology provides about homeostasis, it is clear that herbs used in the right way will support the body's own process of maintaining a stable internal environment. A number of actions and herbal processes should be considered when formulating a program of preventative medicine:

—The concept of *system tonics* highlights the possibility of nourishing and toning the whole of a body system. This will aid both the structural form of the tissues and organs, as well as functional activity, without eliciting a specific physiological or biochemical response. Important system tonics are listed below.

—*Bitter tonics* as a group will have a generalized toning effect upon the body, as described in the chapter on the digestive system.

—*Immune support* will often be important. If immune-system issues are a factor in a preventative program, then apply the principles described below.

—*Cleansing and detoxification* can be gently facilitated through herbal support of the eliminatory systems of the body, described later in this chapter.

Do not worry that all of this might seem like adding procedure upon procedure. It will become apparent that there is much overlap between herbs common to these various procedures.

TONICS FOR THE SYSTEMS OF THE BODY

Tonics are herbs that strengthen and enliven either a specific organ, or system, or the whole body. They truly are gifts of Nature to a suffering humanity—whole plants that enliven whole human beings, gifts of the Mother Earth to her children. To ask how they work is to ask how life works. I would love to know the answer to that particular question!

A characteristic of tonic herbs is that they are all gentle remedies that have a mild yet profound effect upon the body. Not all herbal remedies are tonics, of course, with many having a powerful impact upon human physiology. These must be used with the greatest respect, their use being reserved for those times of illness where strong medicine is called for. Herbs can be divided in a number of different ways, but to highlight the role of tonics, consider this classification:

1. *Normalizers*—remedies that nurture and nourish the body in some way that supports inherent processes of growth, health, and renewal. These are the tonics and can be seen as herbal foods. *Nettles* are an excellent example.
2. *Effectors*—remedies that have an observable impact upon the body. The herbs used in the treatment of disease and pathology. These, in turn, can be divided into two groups depending upon how they work:
—*Whole plant actions*, where the effects are the result of the whole plant impacting the human body. An example would be antimicrobial remedy *Echinacea*.
—*Specific active chemicals*, where the effect is the result

of a chemical whose impact is so overpowering upon the human body that whole plant effects are not seen. The cardioactive herb *Foxglove* and the *Opium Poppy* are good examples. The value of tonic herbs lies in their normalizing, nurturing effects. Whenever possible, the herbalist will focus on the use of such remedies and will use an effector only if absolutely necessary. The chemically based effectors are hardly used at all. They are, however, the foundation of modern allopathic medicine.

The tonics can play a specific role in ensuring that individuals are at their own particular peak of health and vitality. The quality of such a state of well-being will vary from person to person, but everyone will sense an improvement in their general experience of life. Tonics may also be used specifically to ward off a known health problem or a family weakness.

Each system of the body has plants that are particularly suited to it, some of which are tonics. Here we shall see which remedies act as tonics for the major systems of the body. By the very nature of tonics, we can only talk in the most general terms when applying them to a specific system. They are usually interchangeable when it comes to their tonic action. However, always take into account the broader picture of a specific herb's range of actions, as it needs this breadth of vision to enable a coherent choice to be made.

— Infection: *Echinacea*, *Garlic*, and system-specific antimicrobials, such as *Bearberry* for the urinary system.
— Cardiovascular: *Garlic* and *Hawthorn*. The bioflavonoid containing herbs such as *Buckwheat*, *Ginkgo*, and *Lime Blossom* are especially useful for strengthening blood vessels.
— Respiratory: *Coltsfoot*, *Elecampane*, and *Mullein*.
— Digestive: No one herb will be an all-around tonic, as the system is so varied in its form and functions. The bitter tonics will often be helpful in preventative approaches in health. Examples are *Agrimony*, *Dandelion Root*, and *Gentian*. *Chamomile* is so generally helpful to the digestive process that it might be considered a general tonic here.
— Liver: Bitter tonics, especially *Milk Thistle*, are hepatics.
— Urinary: *Bearberry*, *Buchu*, and *Corn Silk* are very useful.
— Reproductive: For women, use *False Unicorn Root*, *Raspberry*, and other uterine tonics, while for men, use *Damiana*, *Sarsaparilla*, or *Saw Palmetto*.
— Nervous: *Mugwort*, *Oats*, *Skullcap*, *St. John's Wort*, and *Vervain* are all excellent tonic remedies. *Panax Ginseng* and *Siberian Ginseng* have a toning effect when the person is under stress because of their effect upon the adrenal glands.
— Musculoskeletal: *Buckbean*, *Celery Seed*, and *Nettles* will help prevent any systemic problems manifest as disease in this system. *Comfrey* and *Horsetail* will help strengthen the bones and connective tissue.
— The skin: *Cleavers*, *Nettles*, *Red Clover*, and most of the alterative remedies will help.

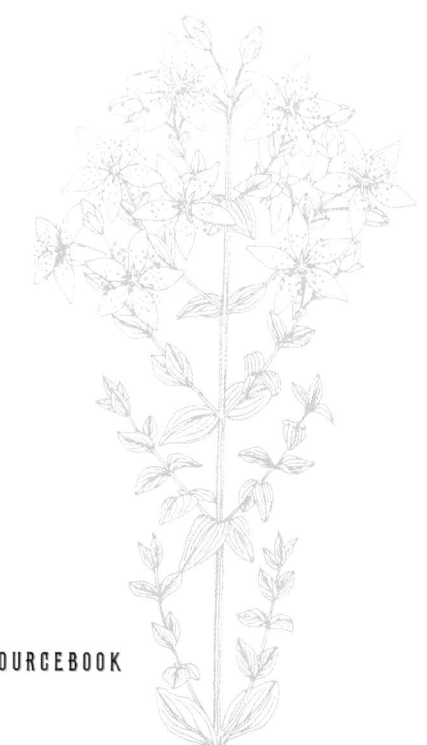

DETOXIFICATION AND ELIMINATIVE PROGRAMS

The herbal approach to detoxification is based upon the perception that the human body is a self-healing and homeostatic organism and that the therapist simply has to support normal processes. The body has a wonderfully effective and astoundingly complex mechanism for ridding the body of waste and poisons.

Using simple and safe herbs will support this natural process, as long as the eliminative processes are addressed as a whole, and not just the colon, as is often the case. This means that whenever such a program is undertaken, it is important to ensure that all organs of elimination are being helped at the same time. In addition, always help the specific area of the body that has been under most toxic pressure. Examples would be the lungs in a tobacco smoker or the liver in someone with alcohol-related problems. This process can be summarized as follows:

—Support for the whole process of elimination
—Specific support for overly taxed organs
—Alleviation of symptoms and addressing any pathologies that may also be present

HERBAL ACTIONS AND ELIMINATION

There are herbal actions whose physiological impact makes them especially indicated for the support of the different pathways of elimination in the body:

—For the digestive system and colon: laxative
—For the kidneys and urinary system: diuretic
—For the liver and blood: hepatic, alterative
—For the lymphatic system: alterative, lymphatic, tonic
—For skin: diaphoretic, alterative
—For the respiratory system: expectorant, anticatarrhal
—And for systemic support in general: tonic, alterative, adaptogen, antimicrobial

This does not specify which herb or even mention any remedy. There are potentially many appropriate plants that might be chosen. This diversity and abundance of healing plants is at once both the gift of herbalism and the frustration of the herb student!

SELECTION OF HERBS WITH THESE ACTIONS

There are many ways in which the medical herbalist would go about the task of selecting the appropriate remedy for any particular individual. However, there is a simple basic guideline to follow. Always use gentle remedies when stimulating elimination. If overly active plants are used, then the effect may be one of intense elimination. This can be unpleasant and uncomfortable and of no therapeutic benefit. "Purging and puking" is not a healing process, but rather the worst aspects of 19th-century "heroic" medicine.

Here are some suggestions for herbs that effectively supply the relevant actions while also being safe and mild. This is not a comprehensive list but simply examples to point the way.

—Laxative: *Dandelion Root, Yellow Dock*
—Diuretic: *Dandelion Leaf*
—Hepatic: *Beet* (as an example of a vegetable that will fulfill the same role), *Dandelion Root*
—Alterative: *Cleavers, Nettles*
—Lymphatic tonic: *Cleavers, Echinacea, Marigold*
—Diaphoretic: *Lime Blossom, Yarrow*
—Expectorant: *Coltsfoot, Mullein*
—Tonic: any tonic remedy that has an affinity for the parts of the body under pressure from toxic buildup

—Adaptogen: *Siberian Ginseng*
—Antimicrobial: *Echinacea, Garlic*

—Harmony not resistance
—Dynamic dance not barriers

AN HERBAL APPROACH TO THE IMMUNE SYSTEM

The immune system has become an increasingly crucial issue in recent years. Not only in medicine but in many aspects of our lives, having a grasp of the new concepts concerning human immunity has become essential in understanding our world and making personal choices. This is not only due to the AIDS epidemic, but also the statistical explosion of a whole range of autoimmune diseases.

To comprehend the possibilities of holistic approaches, it is important to have a grasp of the biological basis of immunity, but at least as important is a comprehension of the role it plays in human life. The wonderful (yet partial) understanding that immunology grants us illuminates the great complexity and ecological integration of the body, but there is much, much more involved. Herbal medicine is as limited as allopathic medicine if it is only used in a context of blood T and B cells without the benefit of a broader holistic context.

Some important insights arise when our immunity is placed in an ecological perspective and not simply a medical one. From such a perspective, it becomes evident that human immunity is a vital component of the interface between individuals and their world. Human activity is not simply that of resisting the "evil and dangerous" environment, rather it is a complex and beautiful dance of flowing to and fro within our world. All that follows is developed around the idea that the whole complex of immunity has the following characteristics:

This leads to some concepts and interpretations that raise exciting possibilities for the practitioners of holistic medicine, whether they be phytotherapist (the new buzz-word for herbalist!) or M.D.

—**Human immunity is ecology in action.** In other words, there is a relationship phenomenon in play. Not only must both sides of this relationship be identified and understood, but also the nature of their relationship clarified. This can prove extremely challenging, as it will be in dynamic flux at all times. As in all aspects of human life, relationships are complex, multifactorial phenomena that can rarely be taken at face value.

—**It is an ecological interface between inner and outer environments.** Such interfaces appear to be critical in the health and well-being of Gaia herself. The interface between desert and savanna, rainforest and mountains, woodland and grassland, agriculture and wilderness are places where much ecological interaction and integration take place. These transition zones facilitate the fine-tuning of biosphere health. Similarly, in human ecology the immune system is the interface where a complex of procedures and processes allows flow both in and out, resistance and embrace at the same time. To focus on one side of this profound dialogue is to miss the point and compromise the whole thing.

—**Immunity is an expression of homeostasis.** Homeostasis is the umbrella concept that describes the human body's wonderful physiological processes that maintain a stable internal environment. This inner homeostasis is a reflection of the planetary homeostasis that characterizes Gaia. It was the recognition of these planet-wide processes that led James Lovelock to propose the Gaia Hypothesis in the first place.

— **Immunity is an expression of relationship.** This is implicit in everything said so far, but carries the implication that the very nature of *relationship* plays a role in immune-system well-being. Thus the practitioner must explore patients' relationships with their world on all levels, from the food they eat, the people they love (or hate), to the way they relate to nature.

This all goes to emphasize that, as with all aspects of holistic healing, the approach to whole-body immunity must address all aspects of human life. As already described, these can be briefly seen as:

— *Bodily health and wholeness*, to ensure that the physical body has the correct nutrition and appropriate healing support for any ills it may be experiencing
— *Emotional well-being*, to ensure a well-rounded and nurturing feeling life, through both the joy and the pain of human life
— *Mental vision and perspective* to help create the mind-set within which individuals can find their place and make choices from that center, not from the stance of the victim
— *Spiritual openness and vitality* in whatever form that takes for the person involved

THE HERBAL POSSIBILITIES

There are many ways of using herbs to enhance immunological vitality. All the many diverse herbal traditions, with their unique cultural roots and expressions, have valuable insights into treatments and specific herbs for the system. This should come as no surprise after the ideas concerning the ecological nature of immunity described above. Herbal medicine is ecological medicine. It is based on an ecological relationship that has evolved through geological time, and so of course there will be remedies that directly address the ecological process of human immunity.

The herbal possibilities for immune-system support are a good example of where traditional knowledge is being confirmed by modern pharmacology. A growing number of remedies are being shown to have marked immunological effects in both the laboratory and the clinic. Some are stimulants to immunity, but most can best be described as modulators, that is they enable the body's natural responses to be more flexible in the face of disease. However, rather than focusing on the plant, we shall look at the whole treatment process. Looking for an herbal immunostimulant is simply "organic drug therapy," which is not the goal of the herbalist.

One approach is that based upon the work of the American herbalist Christopher Hobbs. His insightful synthesizing of Chinese and Western herbal modes has been an inspiration to this author and many other herbalists. It identifies three levels of herbal activity:

— Deep immune activation
— Surface immune activation
— "Adaptogens," or hormonal modulators

DEEP IMMUNE ACTIVATION

Increasing interest is being shown in plants that impact the immunological process within the tissue that mediates its work. They can be termed "deep immune activators." Chemical research points to constituents such as saponins and complex polysaccharides as key components in the immunological role played by such plants. However, please remember that herbs act as biological wholes, not simply vehicles for active ingredients. These immunomodulators, or adjuvants, have an effect upon the cellular foundations of the human immune response. They do not necessarily act as stimulants or inhibitors to the vastly complex processes of immunity, but rather "feed" the whole process in some, as yet unknown, way.

Important specific immunomodulators include:

—*Astragalus membranaceous*: diuretic, hypotensive, vasodilator, and tonic. The root is used in a decoction made with 0.2–0.3 ounces (6–9 grams).
—*Ligusticum wallichii*: tonic, antimicrobial, hypotensive, mild nervine. The root is used in a decoction made with 0.2–0.3 ounces (3–6 grams).
—*Lentinus edodes* (shiitake mushroom): this may be used as a food. It is interesting that a number of fungi are showing themselves to have a special role in immunity.
—*Schizandra chinensis*: tonic, for the central nervous system, uterine, and respiratory stimulant, antihepatotoxic. The berries are used in a decoction made with 0.2–0.3 ounces (6–9 grams).

At this early stage of research into plant immunomodulators, it may appear that they are all Chinese plants. While the Chinese *materia medica* is surprisingly rich in such remedies, their predominance in this field is simply an artifact of research. It is primarily Eastern scientists who are looking at "phytoimmunology" and so are focusing on their own herbs. If Western research attention were placed on our healing tonic remedies from an immunological perspective, I am sure that much of interest would result. Lack of research does not mean the herbs are no use. It simply means that no research has been done!

In addition to specific remedies for immunomodulation, support of bodily well-being through systemic support will help the immune system. Actions and processes to take into account include:

—Bitter tonics
—Alteratives and tonics
—Support of elimination and detoxification through using actions such as the hepatics, diuretics, diaphoretics, and pulmonaries described above

SURFACE IMMUNE ACTIVATION

This level of activity focuses on the resistance aspect of immunity. Surface immune activation addresses the need to help resist pathogenic microorganisms. There are many remedies known as antimicrobials. These are often plants that stimulate the activity and generation of white blood cells and thus also T cell populations. Important examples discussed in the chapter on infections and infestations are:

—*Echinacea*
—*Garlic*
—*Marigold*
—*Myrrh*
—*Thuja*
—*Wild Indigo*

"Adaptogens," or hormonal modulators
Remedies in this group work through a hormonal modulation of immune response.

1. True adaptogens working via the adrenals and the general adaptation syndrome:
—*Eleutherococcus senticosus*: Siberian Ginseng
—*Panax spp.*: Korean and American Ginseng
2. Herbs that affect the other endocrine glands, described in the chapter on the glandular system.

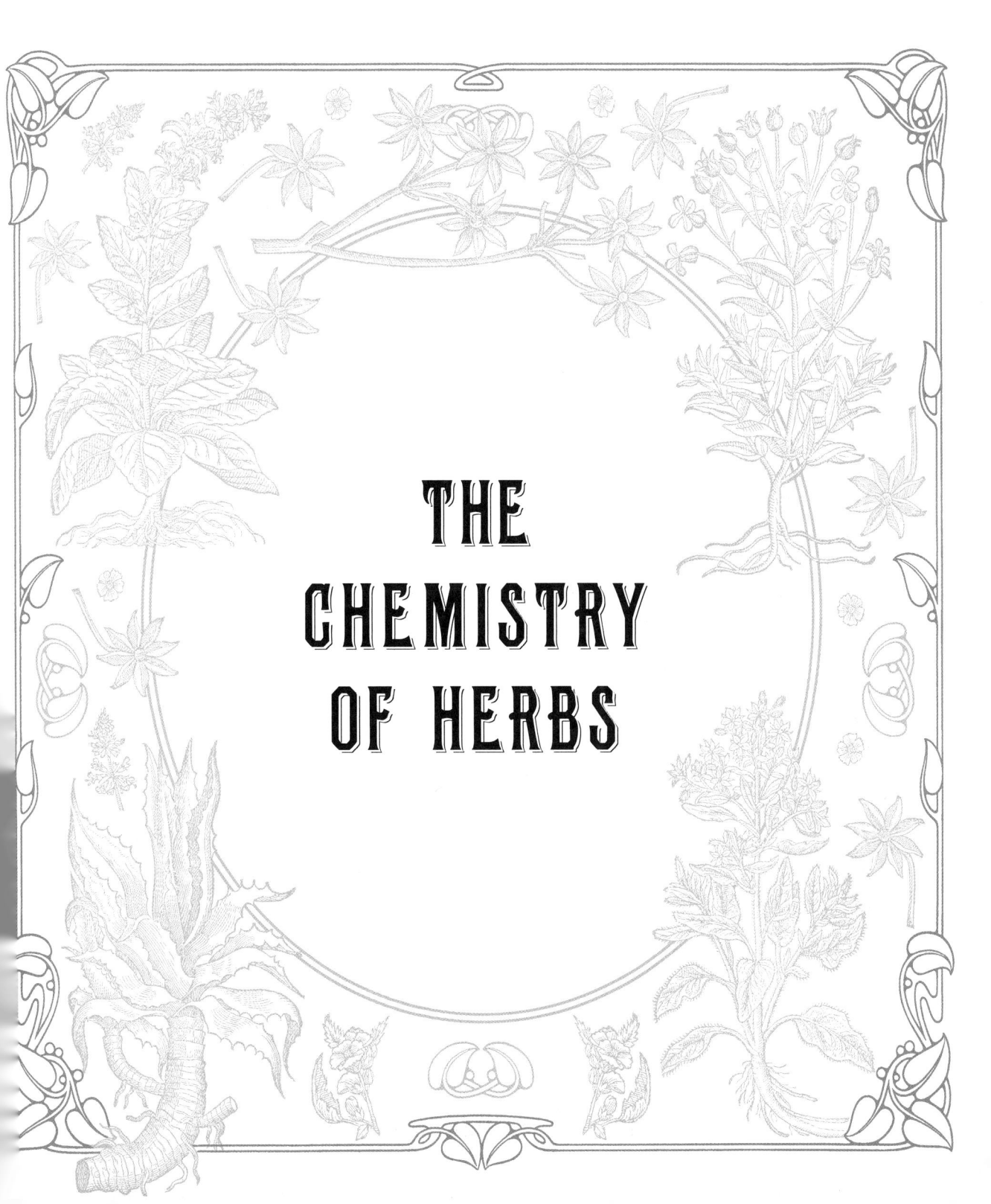

THE CHEMISTRY OF HERBS

The Chemistry of Herbs

In the previous chapters, we have seen how herbs fit into a holistic view of healing; we have noted that they are holistic agents as they work on many levels of the human being; and that even on the physical level—on the level of biochemistry—their actions are complex and synergistic. Despite the complexity, pharmacologists have undertaken a lot of research to find out what the constituents are and have classified these constituents according to their chemical groups. Even though this analytical approach to herbs is inherently limiting, it has produced a great deal of valuable information about some of the biochemical processes taking place; and it is well worth our having a closer look at their findings, as long as we do not lose contact with the overall picture.

In this chapter, we will look at plant pharmacology, briefly examining the various groupings that the numerous constituents have been divided into, looking at their function, and giving some examples of where they occur. Throughout the book, we are referring to these groupings and mentioning in particular, as far as they are known, the relevant constituents in "The Herbal" section. The groupings followed here are based on the structure of the constituents rather than on their function, which is dealt with in the chapter on the actions of herbs.

A knowledge of plant pharmacology is not essential to an herbalist, but is a great help in understanding the plant. In this chapter, a modicum of chemistry is assumed.[*]

Plants contain a vast range of chemicals, ranging from water and inorganic salts, sugars and carbohydrates, to highly complex proteins and alkaloids. We will focus here on the role these substances have to play, not in the plant itself, but in the body. We will mainly concentrate on the groups that act medicinally, though we shall look at some that are important nutrients and thus influence the body.

---

[*] The information presented here is largely drawn from material written by Simon Mills in his course on pharmacology for the National Institute of Medical Herbalists. For an in-depth examination of plant pharmacology and pharmacognosy (the study of the natural history, physical characteristics, and chemical properties of herbs), please consult: *Trease and Evans Pharmacognosy*, William C. Evans, Saunders, Ltd., 2009.

PLANT ACIDS

Weak organic acids are found throughout the plant kingdom. A typical example is the citric acid found in lemons.

The organic acids can be divided into those based on a carbon chain, and those containing a carbon ring in their structure, but they all have a -COOH group in common. The chain acids (or aliphatic acids) range from the simple formic acid we can feel in the sting of *Nettles* to the more complex ones like citric acid and valeric acid, the latter being the basis for a sedative used in allopathic medicine. The ring acids (aromatic acids) are an important pharmacological group. The simplest aromatic acid, benzoic acid, can be found in many resins and balsams, like *Balsam of Tolu, Gum Benzoin, Peru Balsam,* and also in *Cranberries*. It can be used as a lotion or an ointment, can be a beneficial inhalant for chronic bronchial problems, and has antiseptic, antipyretic, and diuretic actions. At one time, it could be found in every home in the form of Friar's Balsam.

Citric acid

Benzoic acid

Formic acid

Geraniol (molecular structure diagram)

ALCOHOLS

Alcohols are found in various forms in plants, often as constituents of volatile oils or as sterols, like the alcohol oil geraniol in *Attar of Rose* and menthol in *Peppermint* oil. Other common forms of alcohol are waxes, combinations of alcohols and fatty acids, which are found in plants in the coating of leaves and in other parts. The commonly used Carnauba Wax, for instance, is obtained from the palm *Copernicia cerifera*.

Menthol (molecular structure diagram)

VOLATILE OILS

Most of the volatile oils are based on simple molecules like isoprene or isopentane, which can combine in many different ways to form terpenes, containing multiples of the basic five-carbon molecules, sometimes with slight variations, making up the volatile oils.

We can find the volatile oils in the aromatic plants, such as *Peppermint* or *Thyme*, where different oils—sometimes up to 50 or more—combine to give the plant its particular smell. Depending on the combination of oils, the smell will vary and even be slightly different within the same species, depending on the concentrations of oils.

By extracting these oils, the so-called essential or aromatic oils are produced, which can be used therapeutically, but which also are used to a large extent for the production of perfumes.*

---

*The art of the perfumer is based upon the skilled combination of different oils. For more information, see the excellent series of books on perfumes: *Perfumes, Cosmetics* and *Soaps*, W. A. Poucher, Chapman & Hall Wiley, 1974.

The range of aromatic oils is very large, and they each have unique properties, but they also share some common actions worth mentioning.

All aromatic oils are antiseptics, good examples being *Eucalyptus* oil, *Garlic* oil, and *Thyme* oil. As the oils are very easily transported and distributed throughout the body, they act both locally and on the whole system. When they are taken internally or applied externally, they will soon show up in the urinary system, the lungs, and the bronchials, and in secretions like sweat, saliva, tears, or the vaginal fluids. They can even occur in mother's milk or travel through the placenta into the fetus. Besides their direct antiseptic action, they also stimulate the production of white blood cells, thereby augmenting the body's own natural defense system.

The volatile oils stimulate the tissue they come in contact with, either leading to slight "irritations" (as in the case of *Mustard* oil) or to a numbing (as with menthol and camphor). They aid digestion by stimulating the lining of the colon, which sets off a reflex that increases the flow of gastric juices and induces a feeling of hunger. Also, they can help to ease griping pains by relaxing the peristalsis in the lower part of the intestines.

The volatile oils also act on the central nervous system. Some will relax and sedate, like *Chamomile*, others will stimulate, like *Peppermint*, and all tend to induce a state of inner ease and well-being, thus reducing tension and depression. When aromatic oils are applied externally, part of their effect is due to their actions on the nose, as the olfactory nerves transmit the smell to the brain and trigger off a reaction there.

As volatile oils evaporate very easily, herbs containing these oils have to be stored carefully in well-sealed containers.

Isoprene

Isopentane

THE CHEMISTRY OF HERBS

CARBOHYDRATES

A great variety of carbohydrates can be found in plants, either in the form of sugars, such as glucose and fructose, or as starches, where they serve as the main energy store. They can also be in the more complex form of cellulose, which gives structural support to plants.

The large polysaccharides, like cellulose, can further bond with other chemicals and produce molecules like pectin, found, for instance, in apples, or seaweed gums like algin, agar, or carragum, found in *Irish Moss*. They are all very viscous and demulcent and are used to produce gels that are utilized in medicine and in food preparations.

Gums and mucilages, which are very complex carbohydrates, are contained in some excellent soothing and healing herbs, like the demulcents *Coltsfoot, Marshmallow,* and *Plantain*. Their action relaxes the lining of the gut, triggering a reflex that runs through the spinal nerves to areas related embryologically, like the lungs and the urinary system. In this way, the mucilages work in a twofold manner: they reduce irritation and inflammation in the whole of the alimentary canal, reduce the sensitivity to gastric acid, prevent diarrhea, and reduce the peristalsis; they also work via a reflex on the respiratory system, reducing tension and coughing and increasing the secretion of watery mucus.

Glucose

Fructose

PHENOLIC COMPOUNDS

Phenol is a basic building block of many important plant constituents. Phenolic compounds may be simple in structure or a complex combination of a range of basic molecules. One of the simple phenolics is salicylic acid, which is found often in combination with sugar, forming a glycoside, as in *Cramp Bark, Meadowsweet, Willow,* and *Wintergreen*. This chemical has antiseptic, pain-killing, and anti-inflammatory properties and is used by allopathic medicine in the form of acetylsalicylic acid, better known as aspirin.

Eugenol, the pain-killing oil found in *Cloves*, and thymol from oil of *Thyme* both have similar effects to salicylic acid. Part of the antiseptic action of *Bearberry* on the urinary system can be explained by the presence of the phenol hydroquinone.

Eugenol

Phenol

TANNINS

Tannins in herbs cause an astringent action. They act on proteins and some other chemicals and form a protective layer on the skin and the mucous membranes. Thus they can, for instance, bind the tissue of the gut and reduce diarrhea or internal bleeding. Externally, they are useful in the treatment of burns, for sealing wounds, and to reduce inflammation. Tannins help in infections of the eye (conjunctivitis), mouth, vagina, cervix, and rectum.

Salicyclic acid

Anthraquinone

THE CHEMISTRY OF HERBS

COUMARINS

The highly evocative smell of newly mowed hay has its basis in the coumarin group of chemicals. It is, of course, not just grass that contains these beautifully aromatic constituents; *Sweet Woodruff* is another example. Coumarin itself has limited effects on the body, but one of its metabolites, dicoumarol, is a powerful anticlotting agent. Allopathic medicine has used the coumarins as a basis for warfarin, an anticlotting drug used as a guard against thrombosis in small dosage and as a rat poison in large doses.

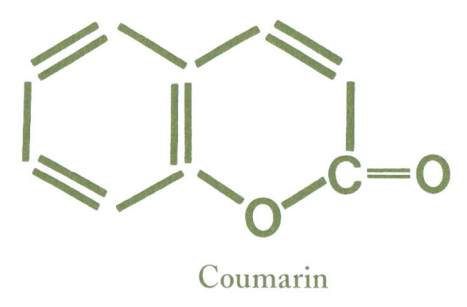

Coumarin

ANTHRAQUINONES

Plants containing anthraquinones are known to be effective purgatives, and they also happen to be good natural dyes. They appear usually in the form of glycosides (in a chemical combination with a sugar) and are found, for instance, in *Aloe, Buckthorn, Rhubarb, Senna,* and *Yellow Dock*. They work by gently stimulating the colon after about 8–12 hours of ingestion by stimulating the peristalsis of the intestines, but they can do this only when natural bile is present. As there may be a tendency to colic pains through an overstimulation of the colon wall, they are often given in combination with carminative herbs.

FLAVONES AND FLAVONOID GLYCOSIDES

One of the most common groups of plant constituents in herbs is the flavones and the flavonoid glycosides, and we will refer to them throughout "The Herbal" section. They are known to have a wide range of activities, from antispasmodic and diuretic to circulatory and cardiac stimulants. Some, for instance, like rutin, hesperidin, and the bioflavonoid vitamin P, reduce permeability and fragility of the capillaries and so help the body strengthen the circulatory system and lower the blood pressure. *Buckwheat* is a good example of a useful herb for such problems. The bioflavonoids are also essential for the complete absorption of vitamin C and occur in nature wherever vitamin C is present. Another flavonoid, present in *Milk Thistle*, is responsible for its action in aiding the liver.

Flavone

SAPONINS

The saponins have attracted the attention of pharmaceutical chemists, as they can be used in the synthesis of cortisone—a strong anti-inflammatory drug—and in the synthesis of sex hormones. While the saponins contained in herbs do not directly act in the same way, the body can use them as raw materials to build up appropriate chemicals. To show the similarity between a natural saponin and the more potent synthesized drugs, we can compare cortisone with diosgenin from *Wild Yam* and see that they are very similar.

Typical anti-inflammatory herbs that contain saponins include *Chickweed, Figwort, Golden Rod,* and *Wild Yam*.

Another important action of saponins is their expectorant action through the stimulation of a reflex of the upper digestive tract, which occurs in remedies such as *Daisy, Mullein, Primrose,* and *Violet*.

Diosgenin

Cortisone

CARDIAC GLYCOSIDES

Very similar to the saponins are the cardiac glycosides. These have been the object of intensive investigation ever since they were discovered in 1785 in *Foxglove*, when it was recognized by medicine that these glycosides can support the failing heart.

The cardiac glycosides are formed by a combination of a sugar and a steroidal agylcone. The main activity is defined by the shape and structure of the agylcone, but it is the sugar that determines the bioavailability of the active agylcone.

Many flowering plants contain cardiac glycosides. The best-known sources are *Foxglove, Lily of the Valley, Squill*, and the Strophanthus family. In herbal medicine, *Lily of the Valley* is preferred over *Foxglove*, as *Foxglove* is potentially poisonous, whereas *Lily of the Valley*, quite as effective, does not lead to a buildup of toxic components in the body.

Therapeutically, the cardiac glycosides have the incredible ability to increase the force and power of the heartbeat without increasing the amount of oxygen needed by the heart muscle. They can thus increase the efficiency of the heart and at the same time steady excess heartbeats without strain to the organ.

Digitoxigenin

BITTER PRINCIPLES

The bitter principles represent a grouping of chemicals that have an exceedingly bitter taste. Chemically, they show a wide diversity of structure, with most bitters belonging to the iridoids, some to the terpenes (see the section on volatile oils), and some to other groups.

The bitter principles have been shown to have valuable therapeutic effects. Through a reflex action via the taste buds, they stimulate the secretion of all the digestive juices and also stimulate the activity of the liver, aiding hepatic elimination. The value of these actions is explored in various sections of the book, particularly in the digestive system. Much pharmaceutical research is going on at the moment regarding these bitter principles, as they often show antibiotic, antifungal, and antitumor actions. Research from China suggests that the bitter principle in *Gossypium spp.* may have a role as a male contraceptive by reducing the level of sperm production.

The property of bitterness imparted to plants by these principles is usually part of the overall activity of the herb, and we find sedatives such as *Hops* and *Valerian*, cough remedies like *White Horehound*, anti-inflammatories such as *Buckbean* and *Devil's Claw*, and the vulnerary *Marigold*, all sharing this valuable action.

ALKALOIDS

The alkaloids are perhaps the most potent group of plant constituents that act upon the human body and mind. They include the hallucinogen mescaline at one extreme and the deadly poison brucine at the other. There are alkaloids that act on the liver, the nerves, the lungs, and the digestive system. Many of the most valued herbs contain these potent chemicals. However, within the plants themselves there appears to be no important function for them, apart from possibly being a store for excess nitrogen. Rather, they seem to be provided as a source of healing agents by Gaia for humanity and the animal realms through their interaction with the plant realm.

The alkaloids as a group are very diverse in structure. They have nitrogen in their structure, and all have a marked physiological activity. Chemically, they are divided into thirteen groups based upon their structure, and the activities they show are as diverse as these structures, which makes it almost impossible to say anything in general about them. As individual alkaloids come up in the course of the book, they are discussed whenever relevant.

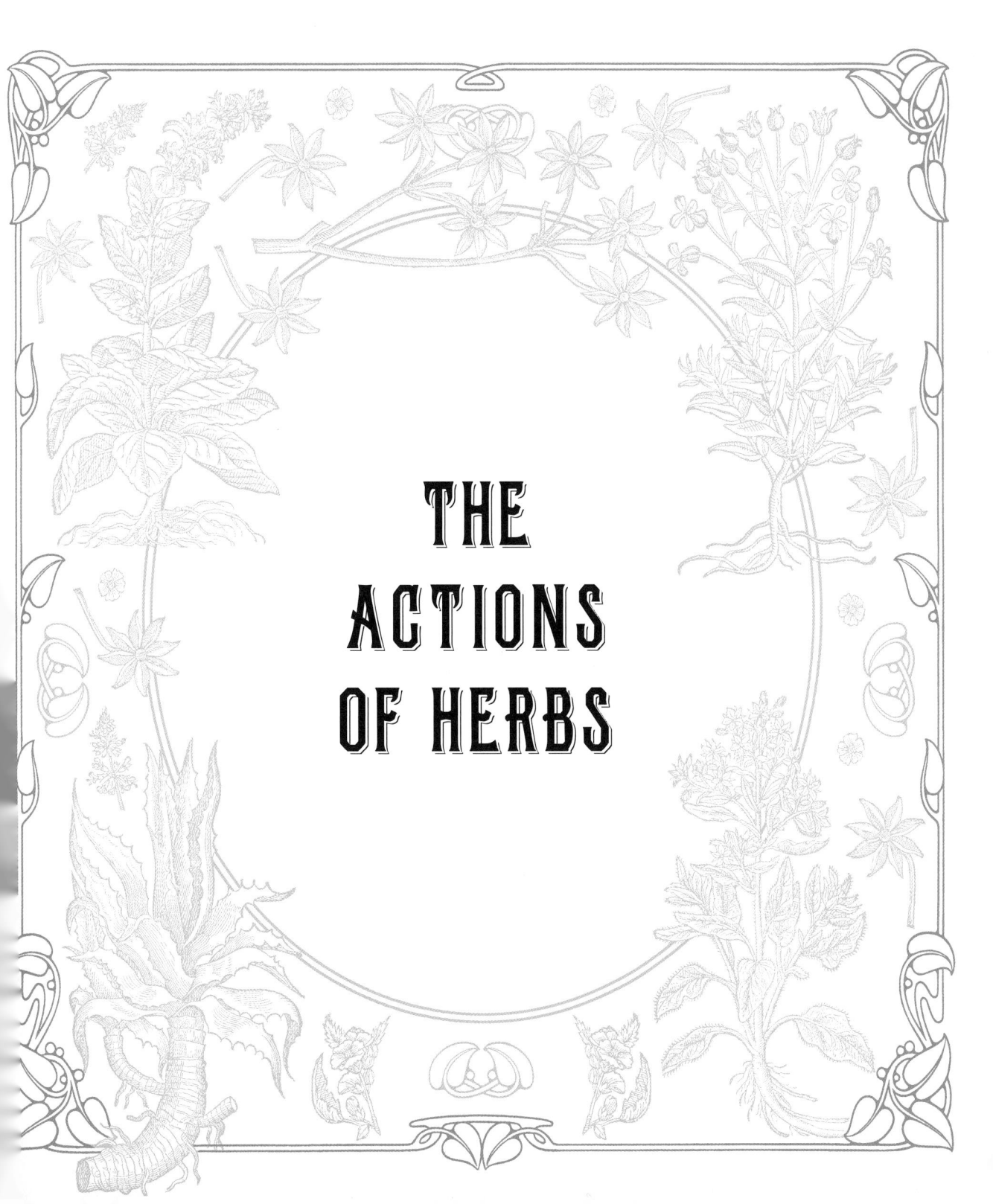

THE ACTIONS OF HERBS

The Actions of Herbs

A GREAT DEAL OF PHARMACEUTICAL research has gone into analyzing the active constituents of herbs to find out how and why they work. A much older approach is to categorize herbs by looking at what kinds of problems can be treated with their help. The understanding of actions and the way they may be used in combination is fundamental to a holistic approach.

In some cases, for instance, the action is due to a specific chemical or combination of chemicals present in the herb—the sedative *Valerian* is an example—or it may be due to a complex synergistic interaction between various constituents of the plant. However, it is best to view the actions as an attribute of the herb as a whole, and any understanding of its chemical basis as an aid in prescription.

To understand this approach, let us look at a couple of examples. *Peppermint*, for instance, is an anticatarrhal, an aromatic, an antimicrobial, a carminative, a diaphoretic, an emmenagogue, a febrifuge, a nervine, and a stimulant. *Boneset* is also an anticatarrhal, a diaphoretic, and a febrifuge, as well as being a bitter, a diuretic, an emetic, and a tonic, which *Peppermint* is not. If you needed an anticatarrhal that was at the same time a diuretic, you could use *Boneset*, and if a stimulating anticatarrhal was needed, you could use *Peppermint*. And the two could be combined for a wider effect.

Evidently, both herbs play a part in the treatment of a whole range of problems; they not only work on specifics but have a spectrum of actions, which really makes them into the holistic tools they are. Each herb has its own spectrum of actions, so it is important to take care in combining the herbs to cover a range of related problems and to treat the cause as well as the symptoms.

In this section a list of actions has been put together, and the most useful representatives in each category indicated. More information can be found in "The Herbal" section, where the actions of each herb are given. The more important of the herbs are underlined. They are in alphabetical order, not necessarily in order of importance.

ALTERATIVE

Alteratives are herbs that will gradually restore the proper function of the body and increase health and vitality. They were at one time known as "blood cleansers."

Bladderwrack Bloodroot Blue Flag Buckbean Burdock Cleavers Echinacea Figwort Fringe Tree Fumitory Garlic Guaiacum Golden Seal Mountain Grape Nettles Pasqueflower Pokeweed Root Queen's Delight Red Clover Sarsaparilla Sassafras Wild Indigo Yellow Dock

ANALGESIC, ANODYNE

Analgesics are herbs that reduce pain and are either applied externally or taken internally, depending on the case.

Figwort Hops Jamaican Dogwood Lady's Slipper Passion Flower Poppy Skullcap St. John's Wort Valerian

ANTHELMINTIC

Anthelmintics will destroy or expel worms from the digestive system. Unfortunately, many of the most effective anthelmintics are no longer available since the new Medicines Act was introduced, as they can be toxic in high dosage. Therefore, those are not listed here.

Aloe Garlic Pomegranate Rue Tansy Thuja Wormwood

ANTIBILIOUS

The antibilious herbs help the body remove excess bile and can thus aid in cases of biliary and jaundice conditions. Compare also cholagogues and hepatics.

Balmony Barberry Dandelion Fringe Tree Golden Seal Mugwort Vervain Wild Yam Wormwood

ANTICATARRHAL

The anticatarrhal herbs help the body remove excess catarrhal buildups, whether in the sinus area or other parts.

Bearberry Boneset Cayenne Coltsfoot Echinacea Elderberry Elecampane Eyebright Garlic Geranium Golden Rod Golden Seal Hyssop Iceland Moss Irish Moss Marshmallow Mullein Peppermint Sage Thyme Wild Indigo Yarrow

ANTI-EMETIC

The anti-emetics can reduce a feeling of nausea and can help relieve or prevent vomiting.

Balm Black Horehound Cayenne Cloves Dill Fennel Lavender Meadowsweet Peach Leaves

ANTI-INFLAMMATORY

The anti-inflammatory herbs help the body combat inflammations. Herbs mentioned under demulcents, emollients, and vulneraries will often act in this way, especially when they are applied externally.

Black Willow Buckbean Chamomile Devil's Claw Marigold St. John's Wort White Poplar Witch Hazel

ANTILITHIC

The antilithic herbs prevent the formation of stones or gravel in the urinary system and can help the body in their removal.

Bearberry Buchu Corn Silk Couch Grass Gravel Root Hardback (aka Stone Root) Hydrangea Parsley Piert Pellitory Sea Holly Wild Carrot

THE ACTIONS OF HERBS

ANTIMICROBIAL

The antimicrobial herbs can help the body destroy or resist pathogenic microorganisms.

Aniseed Balsam of Peru Bearberry Caraway Oil Cayenne <u>Clove</u> Coriander <u>Echinacea</u> Elecampane <u>Eucalyptus</u> Garlic Gentian Juniper Marigold <u>Myrrh</u> Olive Peppermint Plantain Rosemary Rue Sage Southernwood Thyme <u>Wild Indigo</u> Wild Marjoram <u>Wormwood</u>

ANTISPASMODIC

The antispasmodics can prevent or ease spasms or cramps in the body.

Black Cohosh <u>Black Haw</u> Chamomile <u>Cramp Bark</u> Eucalyptus <u>Lady's Slipper</u> Lime Blossom <u>Lobelia</u> Mistletoe <u>Motherwort</u> <u>Pasqueflower</u> <u>Skullcap</u> Skunk Cabbage Thyme <u>Valerian</u> Vervain Wild Lettuce <u>Wild Yam</u>

APERIENT

Aperient herbs are very mild laxatives. See "Laxative."

AROMATIC

The aromatic herbs have a strong and often pleasant odor and can stimulate the digestive system. They are often used to add aroma and taste to other medicines.

Angelica Aniseed Balm Basil Caraway Cardamom Celery Chamomile Cinnamon Cloves Coriander Dill Fennel Ginger Hyssop Meadowsweet Pennyroyal Peppermint Rosemary Valerian Wood Betony

ASTRINGENT

Astringents contract tissue by precipitating proteins and can thus reduce secretions and discharges. They contain tannins.

<u>Agrimony</u> Avens <u>Bayberry</u> Bearberry <u>Bistort</u> Black Catechu Bugleweed Elecampane Eyebright Geranium (aka Cranesbill) Golden Rod Ground Ivy Kola Nut Lesser Celandine (aka Pilewort) Lungwort Meadowsweet Mouse-Ear Mullein Oak Bark Periwinkle Plantain Ragwort Raspberry Red Sage Rhubarb Root Rosemary Slippery Elm St. John's Wort Tormentil <u>Trillium (aka Beth Root)</u> Wild Cherry Witch Hazel Yarrow

BITTER

Herbs that taste bitter act as stimulating tonics for the digestive system through a reflex via the taste buds.

<u>Barberry</u> Boneset <u>Centaury</u> Chamomile <u>Gentian</u> <u>Golden Seal</u> <u>Hops</u> <u>Rue</u> <u>Southernwood</u> <u>Tansy</u> White Horehound <u>Wormwood</u>

CARDIAC TONIC

Cardiac tonics affect the heart. Their specific function should be looked up in "The Herbal" section.

Broom Bugleweed Cayenne Hawthorn Lily of the Valley Motherwort Night-Blooming Cereus

CARMINATIVE

The carminatives are rich in volatile oils and, by their action, stimulate the peristalsis of the digestive system and relax the stomach, thereby supporting digestion and helping against gas in the digestive tract.

Angelica Aniseed Balm Caraway Cardamom Cayenne Chamomile Cinnamon Coriander Dill Fennel Galangal Garlic Ginger Hyssop Juniper Mustard Peppermint Sage Thyme Valerian

CHOLAGOGUE

The cholagogues stimulate the release and secretion of bile from the gallbladder, which can be a marked benefit in gallbladder problems. They also have a laxative effect on the digestive system, since the amount of bile in the duodenum increases when one takes them, and bile is our internally produced, all-natural laxative.

Balmony Barberry Black Root Blue Flag Boldo Dandelion Fringe Tree Fumitory Gentian Golden Seal Mountain Grape Wild Yam Winged Elm (aka Wahoo)

DEMULCENT

Demulcents are usually rich in mucilage and can soothe and protect irritated or inflamed internal tissue.

Coltsfoot Comfrey Corn Silk Couch Grass Flaxseed Irish Moss Licorice Lungwort Mallow Marshmallow Mullein Oatmeal Parsley Piert Slippery Elm

DIAPHORETIC

Diaphoretics aid the skin in the elimination of toxins and promote perspiration.

Angelica Bayberry Black Cohosh Boneset Buchu Cayenne Chamomile Elderberry Fennel Garlic Ginger Golden Rod Guaiacum Lime Blossom Peppermint Pleurisy Root Prickly Ash Thuja Thyme White Horebound Yarrow

DIURETIC

Diuretics increase the secretion and elimination of urine.

Agrimony Bearberry Blue Flag Boldo Boneset Borage Broom Buchu Bugleweed Burdock Celery Seed Cleavers Corn Silk Couch Grass Dandelion Elderberry Gravel Root Hardhack (aka Stone Root) Hawthorn Berries Juniper Kola Nut Lily of the Valley Lime Blossom Night-Blooming Cereus Parsley Parsley Piert Pellitory Pumpkin Seed Saw Palmetto Sea Holly Wild Carrot Yarrow

EMETIC

Emetics cause vomiting. Most of the herbs listed cause vomiting only when taken in high dosage, which can be found for each herb in "The Herbal" section description.

Balm Bloodroot Boneset Catnip Elderberry Flowers Ipecacuanba Lobelia Senega Squill

EMMENAGOGUE

Emmenagogues stimulate and normalize menstrual flow. The term is also often used in the wider context of remedies that act as tonics to the female reproductive system.

Black Cohosh Black Haw Blessed Thistle Blue Cohosh Carline Thistle Chamomile Chasteberry Cramp Bark False Unicorn Root Fenugreek Gentian Ginger Golden Seal Juniper Berry Lime Marigold Motherwort Mugwort Parsley Partridge Vine (aka Squaw Vine) Pasqueflower Pennyroyal Peppermint Raspberry Red Sage Rosemary Rue Shepherd's Purse Southernwood St. John's Wort Tansy Thyme Trillium (aka Beth Root) True Unicorn Root Valerian Vervain Wormwood Yarrow

EMOLLIENT

Emollients are applied to the skin to soften, soothe, or protect it and act externally in a manner similar to the way demulcents act internally.

Balm of Gilead Borage Chickweed Coltsfoot Comfrey Elecampane Fenugreek Flaxseed Licorice Mallow Marshmallow Mullein Plantain Quince Seed Rose Petals Slippery Elm

EXPECTORANT

The expectorants support the body in the removal of excess amounts of mucus from the respiratory system.

Aniseed Balm of Gilead Balsam of Peru Balsam of Tolu Bloodroot Coltsfoot Comfrey Elderberry Flower Elecampane Garlic Golden Seal Grindelia Hyssop Iceland Moss Irish Moss Licorice Lobelia Lungwort Marshmallow Mouse-Ear Mullein Pleurisy Root Senega Skunk Cabbage Squill Thuja Thyme Vervain White Horebound Wild Cherry

FEBRIFUGE, ANTIPYRETIC

The febrifuges help the body bring down fevers.

Angelica Balm Blessed Thistle Boneset Borage Cayenne Elderberry Flower Eucalyptus Hyssop Lobelia Marigold Pennyroyal Peppermint Peruvian Bark Plantain Pleurisy Root Prickly Ash Raspberry Red Sage Thyme Vervain

GALACTOGOGUE

The galactogogues can help the breast-feeding mother increase the flow of milk.

Aniseed Blessed Thistle Centaury Fennel Goat's Rue Raspberry Vervain

HEPATIC

The hepatics aid the liver. Their use tones and strengthens it and increases the flow of bile from the liver.

Agrimony Aloe Balm Balmony Barberry Black Root Blue Flag Boldo Buckbean Cascara Sagrada Celery Centaury Cleavers Dandelion Elecampane Fennel Fringe Tree Fumitory Gentian Golden Seal Horseradish Hyssop Mountain Grape Motherwort Prickly Ash Wild Indigo Wild Yam Winged Elm (aka Wahoo) Wormwood Yarrow Yellow Dock

HYPNOTIC

Hypnotics will induce sleep (not a hypnotic trance).

Hops Jamaican Dogwood Mistletoe Passion Flower Skullcap Valerian Wild Lettuce

LAXATIVE

The laxatives promote the evacuation of the bowels.

Balmony <u>Barberry</u> <u>Buckthorn</u> Burdock <u>Cascara Sagrada</u> Cleavers <u>Dandelion</u> Flaxseed Fringe Tree Mountain Grape Pellitory <u>Rhubarb Root</u> <u>Senna</u> Winged Elm (aka Wahoo) <u>Yellow Dock</u>

MUCILAGE

The mucilaginous herbs contain gelatinous constituents and will often be both demulcent and emollient.

Comfrey Fenugreek Flaxseed Iceland Moss Irish Moss Mallow Marshmallow Quince Seed Slippery Elm

NERVINE

The nervines have a beneficial effect on the nervous system and tone and strengthen it. Some act as stimulants, some as relaxants. Please refer to "The Herbal" section for more detailed information.

Balm Black Cohosh Black Haw Blue Cohosh Bugleweed Chamomile Cramp Bark Damiana Ginseng Hops Kola Nut Lady's Slipper Lavender Lemon Balm Lime Lobelia Mistletoe Motherwort Oats Pasqueflower Passion Flower Peppermint Red Clover Rosemary Skullcap Tansy Thyme Valerian Vervain Wild Lettuce Wormwood

OXYTOCIC

The oxytocics stimulate the contraction of the uterus and can thereby help in childbirth.

<u>Blue Cohosh</u> <u>Golden Seal</u> <u>Partridge Vine (aka Squaw Vine)</u> Rue Trillium (aka Beth Root)

PECTORAL

Pectorals have a general strengthening and healing effect on the respiratory system.

Angelica Aniseed Balm of Gilead Balsam of Peru Balsam of Tolu <u>Bloodroot</u> <u>Coltsfoot</u> <u>Comfrey</u> Elderberry <u>Elecampane</u> Garlic <u>Golden Seal</u> Hyssop Iceland Moss Irish Moss <u>Licorice</u> Lungwort Marshmallow Mouse-Ear <u>Mullein</u> Pleurisy Root Senega Skunk Cabbage Vervain White Horehound

RUBEFACIENT

When rubefacients are applied to the skin, they cause a gentle local irritation and stimulate the dilation of the capillaries, thus increasing circulation in the skin. The blood is drawn from deeper parts of the body into the skin and thus often internal pains are relieved.

<u>Cayenne</u> Cloves Garlic <u>Ginger</u> <u>Horseradish</u> Mustard Nettle Peppermint Oil Rosemary Oil Rue

SEDATIVE

The sedatives calm the nervous system and reduce stress and nervousness throughout the body. They can thus affect tissue of the body that has been irritated by nervous problems.

<u>Black Cohosh</u> Black Haw Bladderwrack Blue Cohosh Bloodroot Boldo <u>Bugleweed</u> Chamomile Cowslip Cramp Bark Hops <u>Jamaican Dogwood</u> <u>Lady's Slipper</u> Lobelia Motherwort <u>Pasqueflower</u> <u>Passion Flower</u> Red Clover Red Poppy Saw Palmetto <u>Skullcap</u> St. John's Wort <u>Valerian</u> Wild Cherry Wild Lettuce Wild Yam

SIALAGOGUE

The sialagogues stimulate the secretion of saliva from the salivary glands.

Bloodroot Blue Flag <u>Cayenne</u> <u>Centaury</u> <u>Gentian</u> Ginger Prickly Ash Senega

SOPORIFIC

The soporifics induce sleep; compare "Hypnotic."

STIMULANT

Stimulants quicken and enliven the physiological function of the body.

Angelica Balm of Gilead Balmony <u>Bayberry</u> Benzoin Bladderwrack Caraway Cardamom <u>Cayenne</u> Cinnamon Dandelion Eucalyptus Galangal Garlic Gentian Ginseng Gravel Root Ground Ivy <u>Horseradish</u> Juniper Marigold <u>Mustard</u> Pennyroyal Peppermint Prickly Ash Rosemary Rue Sage Southernwood <u>Tansy</u> White Horehound Wild Yam <u>Wormwood</u> Yarrow

STYPTIC

Styptics reduce or stop external bleeding by their astringency. See "Astringent."

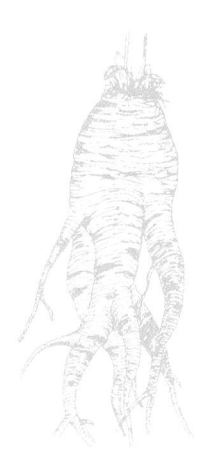

TONIC

The tonic herbs strengthen and enliven either specific organs or the whole body. This long list makes more sense when the section on tonics in each body system is revised.

Agrimony Angelica Aniseed Balm Balmony Bayberry Bearberry Bistort Black Cohosh Black Haw Black Root Boldo Boneset Buchu Buckbean Buckthorn Bugleweed Burdock Calumba Carline Thistle Cayenne Centaury Chamomile Cleavers Coltsfoot Comfrey Condurango Couch Grass Damiana Dandelion Echinacea Elecampane Eyebright False Unicorn Root Fringetree Fumitory Garlic Gentian Geranium (aka Cranesbill) Ginseng Golden Seal Gravel Root Grindelia Ground Ivy Hawthorn Horse Chestnut Hydrangea Hyssop Iceland Moss Lady's Slipper Licorice Lime Marigold Mistletoe Motherwort Mountain Grape Mugwort Mustard Myrrh Nettle Oats Parsley Partridge Vine (aka Squaw Vine) Periwinkle Pokeweed Root Raspberry Red Clover Rue Sarsaparilla Skullcap Tamarind Tansy Thyme Trillium (aka Beth Root) Vervain Virginia Snake Root Wild Yam Wood Betony Wormwood Yarrow Yellow Dock

VULNERARY

Vulneraries are applied externally and aid the body in the healing of wounds and cuts.

<u>Aloe</u> Arnica Bistort Black Willow Burdock <u>Chickweed</u> Cleavers <u>Comfrey</u> Daisy <u>Elderberry</u> Elecampane Fenugreek Flaxseed Garlic Geranium (aka Cranesbill) <u>Golden Seal</u> Horsetail Hyssop Irish Moss <u>Marigold</u> <u>Marshmallow</u> <u>Mullein</u> Myrrh <u>Plantain</u> Pokeweed Root Shepherd's Purse <u>Slippery Elm</u> <u>St. John's Wort</u> Thyme Witch Hazel <u>Wood Betony</u> Yarrow

THE COMPLETE HERBS SOURCEBOOK

THE PREPARATION OF HERBS

The Preparation of Herbs

THE PREPARATION OF HERBS

Part of the art of herbal medicine is knowing what techniques to use in preparing the remedies. Various methods of using plants have developed over the centuries to enable their healing properties to be released and become active. After the right choice of herbs has been made, the best way to prepare them must be selected.

No doubt the first way in which our ancestors used herbs was by eating the fresh plant. Since then, over the thousands of years during which herbs have been used, other methods of preparing them have been developed. With our modern knowledge of pharmacology, we can make conscious choices as to which process we use to release the biochemical constituents needed for healing without insulting the integrity of the plant by isolating fractions of the whole.

From what has been said so far in this book, it should be clear that the property of any herb is not just the sum of all the actions of various chemicals present. There is a synergy at work that acts to create a therapeutic whole that is more than the sum of its parts. If the method of preparation destroys or loses part of the whole, much of the healing power is lost. The preparation must be done carefully and consciously.

Methods of preparation are mentioned throughout the book, but they are not described in detail each time. In this section we will give a thorough explanation of methods; however, some of the examples used may require reference to other chapters for full understanding.

For clarity, we will divide the methods into those that are for use inside the body and those for external use.

Internal Remedies

From a holistic perspective, the best way of using herbs is to take them internally, since it is from within that healing takes place. The ways of preparing internal remedies are numerous, but with all of them it is essential to take care with the process to ensure you end up with what you want.

There are three basic kinds of preparations for taking internally:

1. Water-based
2. Alcohol-based
3. Fresh or dried herbs

Water-Based Preparations

There are two ways to prepare water-based extracts: infusions and decoctions. When the herb to be used contains any hard, woody material, decoctions are used; otherwise, infusions are used.

Infusion

If you know how to make tea, you know how to make an infusion. It is perhaps the most simple and common method of taking an herb, and fresh or dried herbs can be used to prepare it. However, where one part of dried herb is prescribed, it can be replaced by three parts of the fresh herb, the difference being due to the higher water content of the fresh herb. Therefore, if the instructions call for 1 teaspoonful of dried herb, it can be substituted by 3 teaspoonfuls of fresh herb.

To make an infusion:

1. Take a china or glass teapot that has been warmed and put 1 teaspoonful of the dried herb or herb mixture into it for each cup of tea.
2. Pour a cup of boiling water in for each teaspoonful of herb that is already in the pot and then put the lid on. Leave to steep for 10–15 minutes.

Infusions may be drunk hot—which is normally best for a medicinal herb tea—or cold, or have ice in them. They may be sweetened with *Licorice Root*, honey, or even brown sugar.

Herbal tea bags can be made by filling little muslin bags with herbal mixtures, taking care to remember how many teaspoonfuls have been put into each bag. They can be used in the same way as ordinary tea bags.

To make larger quantities to last for a while, the proportion should be 1 ounce (30 grams) of herb to 1 pint (0.5 liters) of water. The best way to store it is in a well-stoppered bottle in the refrigerator. However, the shelf life of such an infusion is not very long, as it is so full of life force that any microorganism that enters the infusion will multiply and thrive in it. If there is any sign of fermentation or spoiling, the infusion should be discarded. Whenever possible, infusions should be prepared when needed.

Infusions are most appropriate for plant parts such as leaves, flowers, or green stems, where the substances wanted are easily accessible. If we also want to infuse bark, root, seeds, or resin, it is best to powder them first to break down some of their cell walls and make them more accessible to the water. Seeds, for instance, like *Aniseed* and *Fennel*, should be slightly bruised before being used in an infusion to release the volatile oils from the cells. Any aromatic herb should be infused in a pot that has a well-sealing lid, to ensure that only a minimum of the volatile oil is lost through evaporation.

When we are working with herbs that are very sensitive to heat, either because they contain highly volatile oils or because their constituents break down at high temperature, we can also make a cold infusion. The proportion of herb to water is the same, but in this case the infusion should be left for six to twelve hours in a well-sealed earthenware pot. When the liquid is ready, strain and use it.

As an alternative, cold milk can also be used as a base for a cold infusion. Milk contains fats and oils that aid in the dissolution of the oily constituents of plants. These milk infusions can also be used for compresses and poultices, adding the soothing action of milk to that of the herbs. There is, however, one contraindication for the use of milk in an infusion: if there is any evidence of an internal reaction to milk in the form of oversensitivity or allergy, or if the skin becomes irritated when it is applied externally, then avoid such infusions.

The infusions made as directed will be the base for many other preparations described later.

Apart from the purely medicinal use of herbs with which this book is mostly concerned, herbs can make an exquisite addition to one's lifestyle and can open a whole world of subtle delights and pleasures. They are not only medicines or alternatives to coffee, but can in their own right make excellent teas. While each person will have their own favorite herbs, here is a list of some that make delicious teas, either singly or in combination. From this list you can select those you like the taste of most or those that also augment your health:

Flowers: *Chamomile, Elderberry Flower, Hibiscus, Lime Blossom, Red Clover*
Leaves: *Hyssop, Lemon Balm, Peppermint, Rosemary, Sage, Spearmint, Thyme, Vervain*
Berries: *Hawthorn, Rose Hips*
Seeds: *Aniseed, Caraway, Celery, Dill, Fennel*
Roots: *Licorice*

DECOCTION

Whenever the herb to be used is hard and woody, it is better to make a decoction rather than an infusion to ensure that the soluble contents of the herb actually reach the water. Roots, rhizomes, wood, bark, nuts, and some seeds are hard and their cell walls are very strong, so to ensure that the active constituents are transferred to the water, more heat is needed than for infusions and the herb has to be boiled in the water.

To make a decoction:

1. Put 1 teaspoonful of dried herb or 3 teaspoonfuls of fresh material for each cup of water into a pot or saucepan. Dried herbs should be powdered or broken into small pieces, while fresh material should be cut into small pieces. If large quantities are made, use 1 ounce (30 grams) of dried herb for each pint (0.5 liter) of water. (These are general guidelines; more specific dosages for each herb are given in "The Herbal" section.) The container should be glass, ceramic, or earthenware. If using metal, it should be enameled. Never use aluminum.
2. Add the appropriate amount of water to the herbs.
3. Bring to the boil and simmer for the time given for the mixture or specific herb, usually 10–15 minutes. If the herb contains volatile oils, put a lid on.
4. Strain the tea while still hot.

A decoction can be used in the same way as an infusion.

When preparing a mixture containing soft and woody herbs, it is best to prepare an infusion and a decoction separately to ensure that the more sensitive herbs are treated accordingly.

When using a woody herb that contains a lot of volatile oils, it is best to make sure that it is powdered as finely as possible and then used in an infusion, to ensure that the oils do not boil away.

ALCOHOL-BASED PREPARATIONS

In general, alcohol is a better solvent than water for the plant constituents. Mixtures of alcohol and water dissolve nearly all the relevant ingredients of an herb and at the same time act as a preservative. Alcohol preparations are called tinctures, an expression that is occasionally also used for preparations based on glycerine or vinegar, as described below.

The methods given here for the preparation of tinctures show a simple and general approach; when tinctures are prepared professionally according to descriptions in a pharmacopoeia, specific water/alcohol proportions are used for each herb, but for general use such details are unnecessary. For home use it is best to take an alcohol of at least 30% (60-proof)—vodka, for instance—as this is about the weakest alcohol/water mixture with a long-term preservative action.

To make an alcoholic tincture:

1. Put 4 ounces (120 grams) of finely chopped or ground dried herb into a container that can be tightly closed. If fresh herbs are used, twice the amount should be taken.
2. Pour 1 pint (0.5 liter) of 30% (60-proof) vodka on the herbs and close tightly.
3. Keep the container in a warm place for two weeks and shake it well twice every day.
4. After decanting the bulk of the liquid, pour the residue into a muslin cloth suspended in a bowl.
5. Wring out all the liquid. The residue makes excellent compost.
6. Pour the tincture into a dark bottle. It should be kept well stoppered.

As tinctures are much stronger, volume for volume, than infusions or decoctions, the dosage to be taken is much smaller, between five and fifteen drops, depending on the herb taken (see "The Herbal" section for details).

We can use tinctures in a variety of ways. They can be taken straight or mixed with a little water, or they can be added to a cup of hot water. If this is done, the alcohol will partly evaporate and leave most of the extract in the water, which with some herbs will make the water cloudy, as resins and other constituents not soluble in water will precipitate. Some drops of the tincture can be added to a bath or foot bath or used in a compressor mixed with oil and fat to make an ointment. Suppositories and lozenges can be made this way, too.

Another most pleasant way of making a kind of alcohol infusion is to infuse herbs in wine. Even though these wine-based preparations do not have the shelf life of tinctures and are not as concentrated, they can be very pleasant to take and most effective in some conditions. There is a long history of using wine in this way, and in fact most aperitifs and liqueurs were originally herbal remedies, based on herbs such as *Aniseed*, *Mugwort*, and *Wormwood* as aids to the digestive process.

In her book *Herbal Medicine*, Dian Dincin Buchman gives the following excellent recipe for a tonic wine with a very nice taste:

1 pint Madeira
1 sprig of *Wormwood*
1 sprig of *Rosemary*
1 small, bruised *Nutmeg*
1 inch of bruised *Ginger*
1 inch of bruised *Cinnamon Bark*
12 large organic raisins

"Pour off about an ounce of the wine. Place herbs in the wine. Cork the bottle tight. Place the bottle in a dark, cool place for a week or two. Strain off the herbs. Combine this medicated wine with a fresh bottle of Madeira and mix thoroughly. Sip a small amount whenever needed. It helps settle the stomach, gives energy and makes you feel better."

Just about any herbal wine can be made simply by steeping the herbs in a wine. Another commonly used kind is *Rosemary* wine:

1 bottle white wine
1 handful of fresh *Rosemary Leaves*

Steep the leaves for about a week in the wine and then filter off the herbs. You can use it whenever needed, and it will help to settle the digestion and act as a mild relaxing nervine.

You can also ferment the herbs themselves; after all, even grapes are herbs. All the aromatic herbs make exquisite wines, and *Dandelion* and *Elderberry* are especially useful as medicinal wines. To make a good *Dandelion* wine, you will need:

4 pints (2 liters) of *Dandelion Flowers*
1 tablespoon of bruised *Ginger Root*
the peel of 1 orange, finely cut
the peel of 1 lemon, finely cut
1.5 lb. (700 grams) of demerara sugar
the juice of 1 lemon
1 teaspoonful of wine yeast

Bring the 4 pints (2 liters) of water to the boil and then leave to cool. Separate the flowers of *Dandelion* from the bitter stalks and calyx and put them in a large bowl. Pour the cooled water over the flowers and leave for a day, stirring occasionally. Pour the whole into a large pot, add the *Ginger* and the rinds of orange and lemon, then boil for 30 minutes. Strain the liquid and pour it back into the rinsed bowl. Mix the sugar and the lemon juice into the bowl and allow the mixture to cool. Then cream the wine yeast with some of the liquid and add it to the bowl. Cover the bowl with a cloth and leave it to ferment in a warm place for two days, keeping a dish under the bowl to catch any liquid that may froth over the brim. After two days, pour the liquid into a cask that you have to bung with cotton wool to allow any gas to escape, or pour it into a jar that has an air lock (these bottles and air locks are commonly available from home-brewing suppliers or some larger health food stores). Leave the mixture in the cask until all the fermentation has ceased, when gas bubbles no longer form. Then close the cask tightly for about two months. Finally, siphon the clear liquid into bottles, which have to be kept for another six months before they are ready for drinking.

VINEGAR-BASED TINCTURE

Tinctures can also be made using vinegar, which contains acetic acid that acts as a solvent and preservative in a way similar to alcohol. Whenever you make a vinegar tincture, it is best to use apple cider vinegar, as it has in itself excellent health-augmenting properties. Synthetic chemical vinegar should not be used. The method is the same as for alcoholic tinctures and if you steep spices or aromatic herbs in vinegar, the resulting fragrant vinegar will be excellent for culinary use.

GLYCERINE-BASED TINCTURE

Tinctures based on glycerine have the advantage of being milder on the digestive tract than alcoholic tinctures, but they have the disadvantage of not dissolving resinous or oily materials quite as well. As a solvent, glycerine is generally better than water but not as good as alcohol.

To make a glycerine tincture, make up 1 pint (0.5 liter) of a mixture consisting of one part glycerine and one part water, add 4 ounces (110 grams) of the dried, ground herb and leave it in a well-stoppered container for two weeks, shaking it daily. After two weeks, strain and press or wring the residue as with alcoholic tinctures. For fresh herbs, due to their greater water content, put 80 ounces (220 grams) into a mixture of 75% glycerine/25% water.

SYRUP

In the case of fluid medicine—be it infusion, decoction, or tincture—that has a particularly unpleasant taste, it is sometimes advisable to mask the taste by combining the fluid with a sweetener. One way to do this is to use a syrup, which is the traditional way to make cough medicines more palatable for children, or any herbal preparation more "toothsome," as Culpepper used to call it.

A simple syrup base is made as follows: pour 1 pint (0.5 liter) of boiling water onto 2.5 pounds (1.1 kilograms) of sugar, place over heat, and stir until the sugar dissolves and the liquid begins to boil. Then take off the heat immediately.

This simple syrup can best be used together with a tincture: mix one part of the tincture with three parts of syrup and store for future use.

For use with an infusion or decoction, it is simpler to add the sugar directly to the liquid: for every pint (0.5 liter) of liquid add 0.75 pounds (350 grams) of sugar and heat gently until the sugar is dissolved. This again can be stored for future use and will keep quite well in a refrigerator.

Since too much sugar is not very healthy, syrups are best used for gargles and cough medicines only.

OXYMEL

When you have to take a particularly powerful-tasting herb, such as *Balm of Gilead*, *Garlic*, *Squill*, or the taste can best be covered by making an oxymel, which is made from five parts honey with one part vinegar. To make an oxymel base, put 1 pint (0.5 liter) of vinegar and 2 pounds (1 kilogram) of honey into a pot and boil until the liquid has the consistency of syrup.

Dr. Christopher gives the following recipe for the preparation of oxymel of *Garlic*: put 0.5 pint (250 milliliters) of vinegar into a vessel, boil in it 0.25 ounce (7 grams) of *Caraway Seeds* and the same quantity of *Fennel Seeds*. Add 1.5 ounce (40 grams) of fresh *Garlic Root* sliced, then press out the liquid and add 10 ounces (300 grams) of honey. Boil until it has the consistency of syrup.

This oxymel can either be used as a gargle or you can take about two tablespoons internally.

DRY PREPARATIONS

Sometimes it is more appropriate to take herbs in a dry form, with the advantage that you do not taste the herb and also that you can take in the whole herb, including the woody material. The main drawback lies in the fact that the dry herbs are unprocessed, and therefore the plant constituents are not always as readily available for easy absorption. In a process like infusion, heat and water help break down the walls of the plant cells and dissolve the constituents, something that is not always guaranteed during the digestive process in the stomach and small intestine. Also, when the constituents are already dissolved in liquid form, they are available a lot faster and begin their action sooner.

A second drawback for taking some of the herbs dry, as in capsules, lies in the very fact that you do not taste the herb. For various reasons—even though they taste unpleasant—the bitter herbs work much better when they are tasted, as their effectiveness depends on the neurological sensation of bitterness. When you put bitters into a capsule or a pill, their action may well be lost or diminished.

Taking all these considerations into account, there are still a number of ways to use herbs in dry form. The main thing we have to pay attention to is that the herbs should be powdered as finely as possible. This guarantees that the cell walls are largely broken down and helps in the digestion and absorption of the herb.

CAPSULES

The easiest way to use dry powdered herbs internally is to use gelatine capsules (which come in various sizes and can be obtained from most drugstores. Capsules not made of animal products are also produced. Ask in your area for suppliers). The size you need depends on the amount of herbs prescribed per dose and on the volume of the material. A capsule size 00, for instance, will hold about 0.02 ounces (0.5 grams) of finely powdered herb.

To fill a capsule is very easy:

1. Place the powdered herbs in a flat dish and take the halves of the capsule apart.
2. Move the halves of the capsules through the powder, filling them in the process.
3. Push the halves together.

PILLS

There are a number of ways to make pills, depending on the degree of technical skill you possess.

The simplest way to take an unpleasant remedy is to roll the powder into a small pill with fresh bread, which works most effectively with herbs such as *Cayenne* or *Golden Seal*. Instead of using bread, the powder can be combined with cream cheese.

You can make a more storable pill by making lozenges, which can be swallowed whole if you cut them to the appropriate size.

LOZENGES

The method of making lozenges is based on combining a powdered herb with sugar and a mucilage to produce the characteristic texture. Lozenges are the ideal preparation for remedies to help the mouth, throat, and upper respiratory tract, as this way they can work where they are most needed.

The mucilage may be obtained from *Comfrey Root*, *Marshmallow Root*, *Slippery Elm Bark*, or from one of the gums, such as *Acacia* or *Tragacanth*.

This is how to make lozenges using *Tragacanth*: Bring 1 pint (0.5 liter) of water to the boil and then mix it with 1 ounce (30 grams) of *Tragacanth*, which has been soaked in water for 24 hours and stirred as often as possible. Then beat the mixture to obtain a uniform consistency and afterward force the mixture through a muslin strainer. When the mucilage is ready, mix it with the powdered herb to form a paste and, if you feel you need to, add sugar for the taste. Roll the paste on a slab, preferably on marble, which has been spread with cornstarch or sugar to prevent the paste from sticking. Cut into any shape and size you like and leave the lozenges exposed to the air until dry. Then store them in an airtight container.

Instead of using dry herbs, you can also use essential oils. A good example would be *Peppermint Oil*. Mix 12 drops of pure *Peppermint Oil* with 2 ounces (60 grams) of sugar and then combine this with enough of the mucilage of *Tragacanth* to make a paste. Then proceed as above and store the product in an airtight container for later use.

External Remedies

As the body can absorb herbal compounds through the skin, a wide range of methods and formulations have been developed that take advantage of this fact. Douches and suppositories, though they might appear to be internal remedies, have traditionally been categorized as external remedies.

BATHS

The best and most pleasant way of absorbing herbal compounds through the skin is by bathing in a full-body bath with 1 pint (0.5 liter) of infusion or decoction added to the water. Alternatively, you can also take a foot or hand bath, in which case you would use the preparations in undiluted form.

Any herb that can be taken internally can also be used in a bath. Herbs can, of course, also be used to give the bath an excellent fragrance.

To give some idea of herbs that are particularly good to use: for a bath that is relaxing and at the same time exquisitely scented, infusions can be made of *Elderberry Flowers*, *Lavender Flowers*, *Lemon Balm*, or *Rosemary Leaves*. For a bath that will bring about a restful and healing sleep, add an infusion of either *Hops*, *Lime Blossom*, or *Valerian* to the bathwater. For children with sleep problems or when babies are teething, try either *Chamomile* or *Lime Blossom*, as the herbs mentioned above may be too strong. In feverish conditions or to help the circulation, stimulating and diaphoretic herbs can be used, like *Boneset*, *Cayenne*, *Ginger*, or *Yarrow*.

These are just some of the possibilities. Try out others for yourself. There are also ideas in books about aromatherapy, a healing system based on the external application of herbs in the form of essential oils. These oils can also be used in baths by putting a few drops of oil into the bathwater.

Instead of preparing an infusion of the herb beforehand, a handful of it can also be placed in a muslin bag, which is suspended from the hot water tap so that the water flows through it. In this way, a very fresh infusion can be made.

DOUCHES

Another method of using herbs externally is a douche, the application of herbs to the vagina, which is particularly indicated for local infections. Whenever possible, prepare a new infusion or decoction for each douche. Allow the tea to cool to a temperature that will be comfortable internally. Pour it into the container of a douche bag and insert the applicator vaginally. Allow the liquid to rinse the inside of the vagina. Note that the liquid will run out of the vagina, so it is easiest to douche sitting on the toilet. It is not necessary to actively hold in the liquid. In most conditions indicating a need for douching, it is advisable to use the tea undiluted for a number of days three times daily. If, however, a three- to seven-day course of douching (along with the appropriate internal herb remedies) has not noticeably improved a vaginal infection, see a qualified practitioner for a diagnosis.

OINTMENTS

Ointments or salves are semisolid preparations that can be applied to the skin. Depending on the purpose for which they are designed, there are innumerable ways of making ointments; they can vary in texture from very greasy ones to those made into a thick paste, depending on what base is used and on what compounds are mixed together.

Any herb can be used for making ointments, but *Arnica Flower* (note that *Arnica* us not advisable on open wounds), *Chickweed*, *Comfrey Root*, *Cucumber*, *Elderberry Flower*, *Eucalyptus*, *Golden Seal*, *Lady's Mantle*, *Marigold Flower*, *Marshmallow Root*, *Plantain*, *Slippery Elm Bark*, *Yarrow*, and *Woundwort* are particularly good for use in external healing mixtures. For the specific use of each herb, please refer to "The Herbal" section.

The simplest way to prepare an ointment is by using Vaseline or a similar petroleum jelly as a base. While this has the disadvantage of being an inorganic base, it also has a number of advantages. Vaseline is easy to handle, so a simple ointment can be made very quickly. Besides this, it has the advantage of not being absorbed itself by the skin, making it useful, for instance, as the base for the anticatarrhal balm described later. Here the Vaseline acts merely as a carrier for the volatile oils, which can thus evaporate and enter the nasal cavities without being absorbed through the skin.

The basic method for a Vaseline ointment is to simmer 2 tablespoons of an herb in 7 ounces (200 grams) of Vaseline for about 10 minutes. A single herb, a mixture, fresh or dried herbs, roots, leaves, or flowers can be used.

As an example, here is a recipe for a simple *Marigold* ointment, which is excellent for cuts, sores, and minor burns: Take 2 ounces (60 grams, or about a handful) of freshly picked *Marigold Flowers* and 7 ounces (200 grams) of Vaseline. Melt the Vaseline over low heat, add the *Marigold Flowers*, and bring the mixture to the boil. Simmer it very gently for about 10 minutes, stirring well. Then sift it through fine gauze and press out all the liquid from the flowers. Pour the liquid into a container and seal it after it has cooled.

In more traditional ointments, instead of using Vaseline, a combination of oils were used that act as a vehicle for the remedies and help them to be absorbed through the skin, plus hardening agents to create the texture desired. The following example is the prescription for a simple ointment from the *British Pharmacopoeia* from 1867 for "Unguentum Simplex":

White wax 2 ounces (60 grams)
Lard 3 ounces (90 grams)
Almond oil 3 fluid ounces (90 milliliters)

"Melt the wax and lard in the oil on a water bath, remove from heat when melted, add almond oil and stir until cool."

In this basic recipe, the lard and the almond oil facilitate the easy absorption of the herbal remedies through the skin. Instead of these carriers, we can use one or more of lanolin, cocoa butter, wheat germ oil, olive oil, and vitamin E. The wax thickens the final product, and for this effect we could also use lanolin, cocoa butter, or most ideally beeswax, depending on the consistency we want to achieve.

To make an herbal ointment from a simple base like the one described above involves a number of steps:

1. Make the appropriate water extract, either an infusion or decoction, and strain off the liquid to be used in step 4.
2. Measure out the fat and oil for the base.
3. Mix the fat and oil together.
4. Add the strained herbal extract and stir it into the base.
5. Simmer until the water has completely evaporated and the extract has become incorporated into the oil. Be careful not to overheat the mixture and watch particularly for the point when all the water has evaporated and the bubbling stops. If additional thickeners (like beeswax) need to be incorporated, they can be added at this point and melted with the base, heating slowly and stirring until completely blended.
6. If a perishable base is used (such as lard), a drop of tincture of *Benzoin* should be added for each ounce (30 grams) of base.
7. Pour the mixture into a container.

SUPPOSITORIES

Suppositories are designed to enable the insertion of remedies into the orifices of the body. While they can be shaped to be used in the nose or the ears, they are most commonly used for rectal or vaginal problems. They act as carriers for any herb that it is appropriate to use, and there are three general categories of these. Firstly, there are herbs acting to soothe the mucous membranes, reduce inflammations, and aid the healing process, such as the root and the leaf of *Comfrey*, the root of *Marshmallow* and of *Golden Seal*, and the bark of *Slippery Elm*.

Secondly, there are the astringent herbs that can help in the reduction of discharge or in the treatment of hemorrhoids, such as *Lesser Celandine (aka Pilewort)*, *Periwinkle*, *Witch Hazel*, and *Yellow Dock*.

And thirdly, there are remedies to stimulate the peristalsis of the intestines to overcome chronic constipation—in other words, the laxatives. It will often be appropriate in any of these three categories to include with the above one of the antimicrobial herbs.

As with ointments, we can choose from different bases, keeping in mind that it has to be firm enough to be inserted into the orifice, while at the same time being able to melt at body temperature once inserted, to liberate the herbs it contains. The herbs should be distributed uniformly in the base—particularly important when we are using a powdered herb, the easiest form for this. To prepare a suppository: Mix the finely powdered herb with a good base, preferably cocoa butter, and mold it in the way described below.

A more complex method has to be used when we want to avoid the introduction of powdered plant material into the body: The simplest form of preparing suppositories this way uses gelatin and glycerine—both animal products—and either an infusion, a decoction, or a tincture, in the following proportions:

Gelatin	10 parts
Water (or infusion, decoction, tincture)	40 parts
Glycerine	15 parts

The gelatin is soaked for a while in the water-based material and then dissolved with the aid of gentle heating. Then the glycerine is added and the whole mixture is heated on a water bath to evaporate the water, as the final consistency desired depends on how much water is removed. If it is removed completely, a very firm consistency will be achieved.

The easiest way to prepare a mold—for both kinds of bases—is to use tinfoil, which you can shape to the length and shape you need. The best shape is a torpedo-like, 1-inch- (2.5-cm-) long suppository. Pour the molten base into the mold and let it cool; you can then store the suppositories in the molds in a refrigerator for a while, though it is always preferable to make them when they are needed.

COMPRESSES

A compress or fomentation is an excellent way to apply a remedy to the skin to accelerate the healing process. To make a compress, use a clean cloth—made either of linen, gauze, a cotton ball, or cotton—and soak it in a hot infusion or decoction. Place this as hot as possible upon the affected area. As heat enhances the action of the herbs, either change the compress when it cools down or cover the cloth with plastic or waxed paper and place on it a hot water bottle, which you can change when it cools.

All the vulnerary herbs make good compresses, as do stimulants and diaphoretics in many situations.

POULTICES

The action of a poultice is very similar to that of a compress, but instead of using a liquid extract, the solid plant material is used for a poultice.

Either fresh or dried herbs can be used to make a poultice. With the fresh plant, you apply the bruised leaves or root material either directly to the skin or place it between thin gauze. Dried herbs must be made into a paste by adding either hot water or apple cider vinegar until the right consistency is obtained. To keep the poultice warm, you can use the same method as for the compress and place a hot water bottle on it.

When you are applying the herb directly to the skin, it is often helpful first to cover the skin with a small amount of oil, as this will protect it and make removal of the poultice easier.

Poultices can be made from warming and stimulating herbs, from vulneraries, astringents, and also from emollients, which are demulcents that are soothing and softening on the skin, such as *Comfrey Root*, *Flaxseed*, *Marshmallow Root*, *Oatmeal*, *Quince Seed*, and *Slippery Elm Bark*.

Poultices are often used to draw pus out of the skin, and there are a multitude of old recipes. Some of them use *Cabbage*, which is excellent; others use bread and milk; some even use soap or sugar. An old recipe for a *Flaxseed* meal poultice was as follows: "Mix a sufficient portion of the meal with hot water to make a mushy mass. Spread this with a tablespoon on a piece of thin flannel or old muslin. Then double in a half inch of the edge all round to keep the poultice from oozing out. When it is on, cover it at once with a piece of oiled silk, oiled paper, or thin rubber cloth, to keep the moisture in."

LINIMENTS

Liniments are specifically formulated to be easily absorbed through the skin, as they are used in massages that aim at the stimulation of muscles and ligaments. They must only be used externally, *never* internally. To carry the herbal components to the muscles and ligaments, liniments are usually made of a mixture of the herb with alcohol or occasionally with apple cider vinegar, sometimes with an addition of herbal oils. The main ingredient of a liniment is usually *Cayenne*, which may be combined with *Lobelia* or other remedies. The following liniment is described by Jethro Kloss (in *Back to Eden*): "Combine two ounces powdered *Myrrh*, one ounce powdered *Golden Seal*, one-half ounce *Cayenne Pepper*, one quart rubbing alcohol (70 percent): Mix together and let stand seven days; shake well every day, decant off, and bottle in corked bottles. If you do not have *Golden Seal*, make it without."

Another excellent liniment that warms and relaxes muscles at the same time is made with equal parts of *Cramp Bark* and *Lobelia*, plus a pinch of *Cayenne*. This is made into a tincture or liniment as described above.

OILS

As you can see in "The Herbal" section of the book, many herbs are rich in essential oils. There are herbs like *Peppermint*, where the oils are volatile, which makes the plant aromatic, and there are also those whose oils are not particularly aromatic, such as *St. John's Wort*.

Herbal oils can be used in two forms, depending on the mode of extraction. First of all there are the pure essential oils, which are extracted from the herb by a complex and careful process of distillation. Only an expert can make these at home. These oils are best obtained from specialist suppliers (see list in the section on suppliers), who distill them as the basis for aromatherapy and, as such, take care that they are as pure as possible.

The second way of extracting oils is much simpler and resembles the method of cold infusion. Instead of infusing the herb in water, it is put into an oil, whereby we obtain a solution of the essential oil in the oil base. The best oils to use are vegetable oils, such as olive, sunflower, or almond oil, but any good pressed vegetable oil can be used and these are preferable to mineral oils.

To make an herbal oil, first cut the herb finely, cover it with oil, and put in a clear glass container. Place this in the sun or leave in a warm place for two to three weeks, shaking the container daily. After that time, filter the liquid into a dark glass container and store the extracted oil.

A typical and very nice example of such an oil is *St. John's Wort* oil, which makes a very red oil that can be used externally for massages and to help sunburns and heal wounds. It can also be taken internally in very small doses to ease stomach pains. To make it, pick the flowers when they are just opened and crush them in a teaspoonful of olive oil. Cover them with more oil, mix well, and put in a glass container in the sun or a warm place for three to six weeks, at the end of which the oil will be bright red. Press the mixture through a cloth to remove all the oil and leave it to stand for a while, as there will be some water in the liquid that will settle on the bottom so that the oil can be decanted. Then store the oil in a well-sealed, dark container.

GATHERING HERBS

Gathering Herbs

THE GATHERING OF HERBS IS A delightful task. Whether harvesting a cultivated crop or searching out the plants in the wild, it is an opportunity to lovingly acknowledge and celebrate the abundance and wholeness of our planet. There are many details about times and processes of collecting and drying, but the heart of the matter is the consciousness that is brought to it by the collector. Collection can be a meditation, a ritual affirmation of our role as cocreators with nature.

Much research has gone into the effects of growth cycle, daily rhythms, and climate on the biochemical composition of medicinal plants. What this work shows us is that the old lore about the right times to pick each plant has a solid basis in plant chemistry. The active components are found at different levels at different times of the day, of the month, and of the growth cycle. However, some broad generalizations can usefully be made.

The level of active constituents is highest at the end of the period of most active growth. The plants should thus be gathered just before opening into blossom. A day without rain that has been sunny since daybreak is ideal for collecting. Though some leaves may dry quickly after rain, others, like the thick, furry ones of *Horehound*, retain the moisture, and if allowed to be massed before drying may easily develop mold and become rotten. Too much heat dries up the oil in the leaves. Only the best-shaped, greenest leaves should be gathered, and any that are withered, insect-bitten, or stained should be discarded. This applies also when the whole plant is gathered, for the leaves nearest the root may be imperfect.

Leaves and herbs should be cut with a sharp knife or pruning shears, for pulling them off by hand may easily damage the tender stems of plants, causing delay in new growth or the entry of fungus or insects into the damaged tissue.

Though many herbs grow along roadsides and in waste soil, pick only from those places free of excessive traffic. Also be sure to avoid fields sprayed with chemicals, as these will dry and infuse right along with your medicinal herb. Investigate fields, woodlands, and hedges surrounding organic farms, with the owner's permission, if unpolluted sources are otherwise rare in your area.

DRYING HERBS

Herbs should be dried by spreading them in loose, single layers on flat drying surfaces. Wire cooling racks from the kitchen may be especially useful surfaces, since these allow air circulation underneath and, hence, quicker drying. Time for drying depends on the herb and the environment, so check the herbs often and turn them as needed for even drying.

DRYING ROOTS

Roots are perhaps the most difficult part of herbs to dry, especially as they are usually very damp when dug up, since digging takes place in the autumn when the soil is likely to be muddy and sticky. Roots must not be dug for medicine while the leaves are still in full growth, as they have not achieved their maximum medicinal content, some of this still being retained in the part of the plant above ground.

When lifting, an effort must be made to get out the entire root, so a long spade or fork is needed. The root will come up with soil and mud adhering to it. A good deal of this can be scraped off, but the only efficient way to clean roots is by thorough washing. Scrubbing is usually necessary too. Top stems and rootlets should then be cut off, and large roots, such as those of *Burdock* and *Licorice*, may be sliced to hasten drying.

To dry, they should be spread out on shelves so they do not touch or should be tied singly on strings in a warm shed or greenhouse for about 10 days, being turned and inspected every day. When they have started to shrink well (roots loose about three quarters of their weight in drying), they can be finished by storing them above a stove or in a cool oven. This will probably take another ten days and is dependent on the moisture in the atmosphere. Roots are dry when they are brittle.

To dry bulbs and corms, tie them up in small bunches, like onions, in a shed. Keep constant watch to see that they are drying evenly.

STORING HERBS

As soon as it is dried, the herb, whether root or aerial part, should be placed immediately into a dry container. The material should be handled with great care, as it may be readily broken. Any herb that contains volatile oils should not be stored in ordinary plastic boxes or sacks, for these materials absorb the oils from the plant, which then evaporate from the external surface. Glazed ceramic, dark glass, or metal containers with tight-fitting lids are best for storage, away from direct sunlight or heat.

WHEN TO GATHER HERBS

In every season nature offers herbs, but naturally not everything is available at all times. To find out in which month an herb can be collected, refer to the calendar. It lists most of the herbs mentioned in the book, with the exception of those that are more difficult to find in Europe or the United States. When different parts of an herb are collected at different times, they are listed separately. The dates given refer to Middle and Northern Europe.

Month	Jan	Feb	Mar	Apr	May	Jun	Jul	Aug	Sep	Oct	Nov	Dec
Agrimony						•	•	•				
Angelica, leaves						•			•	•	•	
Aniseed							•	•	•			
Avens, aerial parts							•					
Avens, root				•	•							
Balm						•	•	•	•			
Balmony							•	•	•			
Barberry			•							•		
Bayberry			•									•
Birch, Silver				•	•	•	•					
Bistort						•	•	•	•			
Bittersweet									•	•		
Black Cohosh									•	•		
Black Haw									•	•		
Black Horehound							•					
Black Root									•	•		
Black Willow				•	•							

THE COMPLETE HERBS SOURCEBOOK

Month	Jan	Feb	Mar	Apr	May	Jun	Jul	Aug	Sep	Oct	Nov	Dec
Blessed Thistle, aerial parts						•	•	•				
Blessed Thistle, seeds									•	•		
Bloodroot					•	•			•	•		
Blue Cohosh									•	•		
Blue Flag									•	•		
Boldo		•	•	•	•	•	•	•	•	•	•	•
Boneset								•	•			
Borage					•	•	•	•	•			
Bouncing Bet (aka Soapwort), leaves									•	•		
Bouncing Bet (aka Soapwort), root and rhizome							•	•				
Broom Tops				•	•	•	•	•	•	•		
Buchu						•	•	•	•	•		
Buckbean					•	•	•					
Buckthorn									•	•		
Burdock									•	•		
Bur Marigold							•	•	•			
Butterbur, leaves			•	•	•	•	•	•				
Butterbur, rhizome					•	•	•	•				
Calamus									•	•		
Californian Poppy						•	•	•				
Caraway							•					
Carline Thistle									•	•		
Catnip						•	•	•	•			

GATHERING HERBS

Month	Jan	Feb	Mar	Apr	May	Jun	Jul	Aug	Sep	Oct	Nov	Dec
Celery						•	•	•	•			
Chamomile					•	•	•	•				
Chasteberry										•	•	
Chickweed	•	•	•	•	•	•	•	•	•	•	•	•
Cleavers			•	•	•							
Coltsfoot, flowers		•	•	•								
Coltsfoot, leaves					•	•						
Comfrey			•	•	•			•	•			
Coriander						•	•	•				
Couch Grass			•	•				•	•			
Cowslip, flowers			•	•	•							
Cowslip, root		•	•					•	•			
Cramp Bark				•	•							
Cudweed								•				
Daisy			•	•	•	•	•	•	•			
Dandelion, leaves	•	•	•	•	•	•	•	•	•	•	•	•
Dandelion, root						•	•	•				
Dill						•	•	•				
Echinacea									•	•		
Elderberry, bark and berries									•	•		
Elderberry, flowers					•	•	•	•				
Elecampane									•	•		
Ephedra									•	•	•	
Eyebright								•	•	•		

THE COMPLETE HERBS SOURCEBOOK

Month	Jan	Feb	Mar	Apr	May	Jun	Jul	Aug	Sep	Oct	Nov	Dec
False Unicorn Root									•	•		
Fennel								•	•	•		
Figwort					•	•	•					
Flax									•			
Fringe Tree Bark			•	•					•	•		
Fumitory						•	•	•				
Garlic									•			
Gentian									•	•		
Geranium (aka American Cranesbill)										•	•	
Goat's Rue							•	•				
Golden Ragwort (aka Life Root)						•	•					
Golden Rod							•	•	•	•		
Gravel Root									•	•		
Greater Celandine								•	•	•	•	
Ground Ivy					•	•	•					
Hardhack (aka Stone Root)									•	•		
Hawthorn Berries									•	•		
Hops								•	•			
Horse Chestnut									•	•		
Horseradish	•	•									•	•
Horsetail					•	•	•					
Hydrangea									•	•		
Hyssop							•					

Month	Jan	Feb	Mar	Apr	May	Jun	Jul	Aug	Sep	Oct	Nov	Dec
Iceland Moss					•	•	•	•	•			
Juniper Berries									•	•		
Lady's Mantle							•	•				
Lavender						•	•	•	•			
Lesser Celandine (aka Pilewort)					•	•						
Lily of the Valley					•	•						
Lime Blossom							•	•	•			
Lobelia								•	•			
Lungwort Herb			•	•	•	•	•	•	•			
Male Fern									•	•		
Mallow							•	•	•			
Marigold						•	•	•	•			
Marjoram, Wild							•	•	•			
Marshmallow, leaves					•	•	•					
Marshmallow, root									•	•		
Meadowsweet						•	•	•				
Mistletoe			•	•								
Motherwort						•	•	•	•			
Mountain Grape									•	•		
Mouse-Ear					•	•						
Mugwort							•	•	•			
Mullein, flowers							•	•	•			
Mullein, leaves							•	•				
Mustard							•	•				

THE COMPLETE HERBS SOURCEBOOK

Month	Jan	Feb	Mar	Apr	May	Jun	Jul	Aug	Sep	Oct	Nov	Dec
Nasturtium							•	•	•	•		
Nettle			•	•	•	•	•					
Oak Bark				•	•							
Oats								•				
Pansy			•	•	•	•	•	•				
Parsley Piert							•	•				
Partridge Vine (aka Squaw Vine)					•	•	•					
Pasqueflower				•	•							
Passion Flower					•	•	•					
Peach, bark				•	•							
Peach, leaves							•	•				
Pellitory							•	•	•			
Pennyroyal							•					
Periwinkle				•	•							
Pine, Scots		•	•	•								
Plantain							•	•	•			
Pleurisy Root				•	•							
Pokeweed Root		•	•							•	•	
Prickly Ash Bark									•	•		
Pumpkin									•	•		
Queen's Delight							•	•				
Quince									•	•		
Ragwort						•	•	•	•			
Raspberry					•	•	•	•	•	•	•	

GATHERING HERBS

Month	Jan	Feb	Mar	Apr	May	Jun	Jul	Aug	Sep	Oct	Nov	Dec
Red Clover						•	•	•	•	•		
Red Poppy							•	•				
Red Sage					•	•						
Rose Hips									•	•		
Rosemary						•	•	•	•			
Rue					•	•	•					
Self-Heal						•						
Senega									•	•		
Shepherd's Purse	•	•	•	•	•	•	•	•	•			
Silverweed						•						
Skullcap								•	•			
St. John's Wort								•	•	•		
Sundew							•	•				
Sweet Violet			•	•								
Tansy						•	•	•	•			
Thuja					•	•	•	•	•			
Thyme						•	•	•				
Tormentil									•	•		
Trillium (aka Beth Root)								•	•			
True Unicorn Root								•				
Valerian									•	•	•	
Vervain							•					
White Horehound							•	•	•			
White Poplar				•	•	•						
Wild Carrot, aerial parts						•	•	•				

Month	Jan	Feb	Mar	Apr	May	Jun	Jul	Aug	Sep	Oct	Nov	Dec
Wild Carrot, seeds								•	•			
Wild Cherry									•	•		
Wild Indigo									•	•		
Wild Lettuce						•	•					
Winged Elm (aka Wahoo)									•	•		
Wintergreen			•	•	•	•	•	•				
Witch Hazel				•	•	•	•	•				
Wood Sage				•	•	•	•	•				
Wormwood							•	•	•			
Yarrow						•	•	•	•			
Yellow Dock								•	•	•		

GATHERING HERBS

THE HERBAL

The Herbal

Details on each herb in the book are given in this chapter. The information is presented in the following form:

COMMON NAME OF THE HERB
Latin name of the herb
PLANT FAMILY

Common name: When another name for the plant is very common, it is given here.

Part used: The part of the plant that is used therapeutically.

Collection: When the part to be used is best collected and how it should be dried.

Constituents: A list of those chemical constituents that are most relevant for the medicinal action of the herb. For some plants, there is far more information available than for others, which reflects the amount of research done, not the importance of the plant.

Actions: A list of the most important actions shown by the herb. Please refer to the section on the actions of herbs (pages 174–180) for an explanation of the terms used.

Indications: Here the specific uses of the herb are discussed, as well as the conditions for which it should be used. Included is information on how the herb works within the body. If there are any contraindications, they are given here and again under **CAUTION**. In this chapter, each disease is written in *italics* for easy reference.

CAUTION: Lists contraindications. If there are any conditions when this herb should not be used, they are given here.

Combinations: A specific herb often combines well with other herbs in the treatment of certain conditions. Both the combinations and the relevant conditions are listed.

Preparation and dosage: Infusion or decoction: gives information on whether the plant is taken as an infusion or decoction, how much of the plant should be used per cup of water, and for how long it should be infused or simmered.

Tincture: This gives information on how much of the tincture should be taken and how often.

AGRIMONY
Agrimonia eupatoria
ROSACEAE

Part used: Dried aerial parts.
Collection: The whole of the plant above ground should be collected when the flowers are just blooming. It should be dried in the shade and not above 100°F (40°C).
Constituents: Tannins, glycosidal bitters, nicotinic acid, silicic acid, iron, vitamins B and K, essential oil.
Actions: Astringent, tonic, diuretic, vulnerary, cholagogue.

INDICATIONS:
The combination of astringency and of bitter tonic properties makes Agrimony a valuable remedy, particularly when an astringent action on the digestive system is needed, as its tonic action is due to the bitter stimulation of digestive and liver secretions. It is a specific in *childhood diarrhea*. Its properties give it a role in the treatment of *mucous colitis*. Agrimony is the herb of choice in *appendicitis*. It may be used in *indigestion*. There is a long tradition of its use as a *spring tonic*. It may be used in *urinary incontinence* and *cystitis*. As a gargle, it is beneficial in the relief of *sore throats* and *laryngitis*. As an ointment, it will aid the healing of *wounds* and *bruises*.

Combinations: It is often used with carminatives for digestive problems.

PREPARATION AND DOSAGE:
Infusion: pour a cup of boiling water onto 1–2 teaspoonfuls of the dried herb and leave to infuse for 10–15 minutes. This should be drunk three times a day. Tincture: take 1–3 milliliters of the tincture three times a day.

ALLSPICE
Pimento officinalis
MYRTACEAE

Part used: Fruit.
Actions: Carminative, digestive stimulant, aromatic.

INDICATIONS:
Allspice can be used freely wherever a pleasant carminative is called for. It will ease *flatulence* and *dyspeptic pain*.

ALOE
Aloe vera
LILIACEAE

Part used: Fresh or dehydrated juice from the leaves.
Constituents: Aloins, anthraquinones, resin.
Actions: Cathartic, vulnerary, emmenagogue, vermifuge. External demulcent, vulnerary.

> **INDICATIONS:**
> May be used internally where a powerful cathartic is needed. In a small dosage it increases the *menstrual flow*. Externally the juice is used fresh for *minor burns, sunburn, insect bites,* etc.

Combinations: If it is used internally to increase menstrual flow, it should be combined with carminatives to reduce griping.

> **CAUTION:**
> As Aloe stimulates uterine contractions, it should be avoided during pregnancy. As it is excreted in the mother's milk, it should be avoided during breast-feeding, or it may be purgative to the child.

PREPARATION AND DOSAGE:

For internal use, take 0.1–0.3 milliliters of the juice. For external use, put some of the fresh juice onto the afflicted area.

ANGELICA
Angelica archangelica
UMBELLIFERAE

Part used: Roots and leaves are used medicinally; the stems and seeds are used in confectionery.
Collection: The root is collected in the fall of its first year. If it is very thick, it can be cut longitudinally to speed its drying. The leaves should be collected in June.
Constituents: Essential oils, including phellandrene and pinene, angelica acid, coumarin compounds, bitter principle, tannins.
Actions: Carminative, antispasmodic, expectorant, diuretic, diaphoretic.

> **INDICATIONS:**
> This herb is a useful expectorant for *coughs, bronchitis,* and *pleurisy*, especially when they are accompanied by *fever, colds,* or *influenza*. The leaf can be used as a compress in *inflammations of the chest*. Its content of carminative essential oil explains its use easing *intestinal colic* and *flatulence*. As a digestive agent, it stimulates appetite and may be used in *anorexia nervosa*. It has been shown to help ease *rheumatic inflammations*. In *cystitis*, it acts as a urinary antiseptic.

Combinations: For *bronchial problems*, it combines well with Coltsfoot and White Horehound; for *indigestion, flatulence,* and *loss of appetite* with Chamomile.

PREPARATION AND DOSAGE:

Decoction: put a teaspoonful of the cut root in a cup of water, bring it to the boil, and simmer for two minutes. Take it off the heat and let it stand for 15 minutes. Take one cup three times a day.
Tincture: take 2–5 milliliters of the tincture three times a day.

ANISEED

Pimpinella anisum

UMBELLIFERAE

Part used: Dried fruit.
Collection: The ripe dry fruit should be gathered between July and September.
Constituents: Up to 6% volatile oils, which include anethole, 30% fatty oils, choline.
Actions: Expectorant, antispasmodic, carminative, parasiticide, aromatic.

INDICATIONS:

The volatile oil in Aniseed provides the basis for its internal use to ease *griping, intestinal colic,* and *flatulence*. It also has a marked expectorant and antispasmodic action and may be used in *bronchitis,* in *tracheitis* where there is persistent *irritable coughing,* and in *whooping cough*. Externally, the oil may be used in an ointment base for the treatment of *scabies*. The oil by itself will help in the control of *lice*.

Combinations: For *flatulent colic*, mix Aniseed with equal amounts of Fennel and Caraway. For *bronchitis*, it combines well with Coltsfoot, White Horehound, and Lobelia.

PREPARATION AND DOSAGE:

Infusion: the seeds should be gently crushed just before use to release the volatile oils. Pour one cup of boiling water over 1–2 teaspoonfuls of the seeds and let it stand covered for 5–10 minutes.

Take one cup three times daily. To treat *flatulence*, the tea should be drunk slowly before meals.

Oil: one drop of the oil may be taken internally by mixing it into half a teaspoonful of honey.

ARNICA

Arnica montana

COMPOSITAE

Part used: Flower heads.
Collection: The flowers are collected between June and August.
Constituents: Essential oils, sesquiterpene lactones, bitter glycosides, alkaloid, polyacetylenes, flavonoids, tannins.
Actions: Anti-inflammatory, vulnerary.

THE HERBAL

> **INDICATIONS:**
> While this herb should not be taken internally as it is potentially toxic, it provides us with one of the best remedies for external local healing and may be considered a specific when it comes to the treatment of *bruises* and *sprains*. The homeopathic preparation is entirely safe to take internally, especially when taken according to homeopathic directions. The herb itself, used externally, will help in the relief of *rheumatic pain* and the pain and inflammation of *phlebitis* and similar conditions. It may, in fact, be used wherever there is *pain* or *inflammation* on the skin, as long as the skin is not broken.

Combinations: For a lotion, it may be combined with distilled Witch Hazel.

> **CAUTION:**
> Do not use internally.

PREPARATION AND DOSAGE:

You can prepare your own tincture of this herb as follows: pour 1 pint (0.5 liter) of 70% alcohol over 2 ounces (50 grams) of freshly picked flowers. Seal it tightly in a clear glass container and let it stand for at least a week in the sun or in a warm place. Filter it and it is ready for use. To store it, put the tincture in a sealed container and keep it out of direct sunlight.

AVENS
Geum urbanum
ROSACEAE

Part used: Roots and aerial parts.
Collection: The roots are collected in the spring, when they are richest in volatile oils. The aerial parts are collected in July, when the flowers are at their best.
Constituents: Essential oils with gein and eugenol, tannins, bitter principle, flavone, resin, organic acids.
Actions: Astringent, styptic, diaphoretic, aromatic.

> **INDICATIONS:**
> Its strong astringency combined with its digestive properties give Avens its role in many intestinal troubles, as in *diarrhea*, *dysentry*, *mucous colitis*, and similar conditions. It may be used to settle *nausea* and to allay *vomiting*. Its astringency also explains its use in the treatment of *gingivitis* and *sore throats* as a mouthwash or gargle. It may also be used internally in *feverish colds* and in *catarrhs*. As a douche, Avens will be of value in *leukorrhea*.

Combinations: It is often combined with Agrimony in the treatment of digestive troubles, such as *colitis*.

PREPARATION AND DOSAGE:

Decoction: place 1 teaspoonful of the root in a cup of cold water, bring it to the boil, and let it simmer for five minutes. Take one cup three times daily.
Tincture: take 1–3ml of the tincture three times a day.

BALM

Melissa officinalis

LABIATAE

Part used: Dried aerial parts or fresh in season.
Collection: The leaves may be harvested two or three times a year between June and September. They are gathered by cutting off the young shoots when they are approximately 12 inches (30 centimeters) long. They should be dried in the shade at a temperature not above 95°F (35°C).
Constituents: Rich in essential oil containing citral, citronellal, geraniol, and linalol; bitter principles; flavones; resin.
Actions: Carminative, antispasmodic, anti-depressive, diaphoretic, hypotensive.

INDICATIONS:

Balm is an excellent carminative herb that relieves *spasms in the digestive tract* and is used in *flatulent dyspepsia*. Because of its antidepressive properties, it is primarily indicated where there is *dyspepsia* associated with *anxiety* or *depression*, as the gently sedative oils relieve *tension* and *stress reactions*, thus acting to lighten *depression*. Balm has a tonic effect on the heart and circulatory system causing mild vasodilation of the peripheral vessels, thus acting to lower *blood pressure*. It can be used in feverish conditions, such as *influenza*.

Combinations: In *digestive troubles*, it may be combined with Hops, Chamomile, or Meadowsweet. For *stress* and *tension*, it will combine with Lavender and Lime Blossom.

PREPARATION AND DOSAGE:

Infusion: pour a cup of boiling water onto 2–3 teaspoonfuls of the dried herb or four to six fresh leaves and leave to infuse for 10–15 minutes, well covered until drunk. A cup of this tea should be taken in the morning and the evening, or when needed.
Tincture: take 2–6 milliliters of the tincture three times a day.

BALM OF GILEAD
Populus gileadensis
SALICACEAE

Part used: Closed buds.
Constituents: Oleoresin, salicin.
Actions: Stimulating expectorant, antiseptic, anti-irritant, vulnerary.

> ### INDICATIONS:
> As it soothes, disinfects, and astringes the mucous membranes, Balm of Gilead is an excellent remedy for *sore throats, coughs,* and *laryngitis* and is, in fact, considered to be a specific for *laryngitis* that is accompanied by loss of voice. It may be used in *chronic bronchitis*. Externally, it can be used to ease inflammations due to *rheumatism* and *arthritis*, as well as for dry and scaly skin conditions, such as *psoriasis* and *dry eczema*.

Combinations: Coltsfoot, Red Sage, and White Horehound will combine well with it to enhance its actions on the respiratory system, while Chickweed will aid its strength in external applications.

PREPARATION AND DOSAGE:

Infusion: pour one cup of boiling water onto 2 teaspoonfuls of the bud and leave to infuse for 10–15 minutes. This should be drunk three times a day or more often until effective.
Tincture: take 1–2 milliliters of the tincture three times a day.

BALMONY
Chelone glabra
SCROPHULARIACEAE

Part used: Dried aerial parts.
Collection: The aerial parts are collected and dried during the flowering period between July and September.
Actions: Cholagogue, antiemetic, stimulant, laxative.

> ### INDICATIONS:
> Balmony is an excellent agent for *liver problems*. It acts as a tonic on the whole digestive and absorptive system. It has a stimulating effect on the secretion of digestive juices, and in this most natural way its laxative properties are produced. Balmony is used in *gallstones, inflammation of the gallbladder,* and in *jaundice*. It stimulates the *appetite*, eases *colic, dyspepsia,* and *biliousness*, and is helpful in *debility*. Externally, it has been used on *inflamed breasts, painful ulcers,* and *hemmorhoids*. It is considered a specific in gallstones that lead to *congestive jaundice*.

Combinations: For the relief of *constipation*, Balmony may be combined with Butternut. For *jaundice*, it will best be used with Golden Seal.

PREPARATION AND DOSAGE:

Infusion: pour a cup of boiling water onto 2 teaspoonfuls of the dried herb and let infuse for 10–15 minutes. This should be drunk three times a day.
Tincture: take 1–2 milliliters of the tincture three times a day.

BALSAM OF TOLU

Myroxylon toluifera

LEGUMINOSAE

Part used: Tolu is a balsam obtained by incision from the trunk of a large tree after it has been beaten and scorched. It originally came from Colombia and Venezuela.

Constituents: 80% resin, which is rich in cinnamic acid and benzoic acid, plus a little vanillin.

Actions: Antiseptic, expectorant.

INDICATIONS:
This balsam works mainly on the respiratory mucous membranes. It is often used as an expectorant in cough medicines in the form of a syrup or tincture.

PREPARATION AND DOSAGE:
This herb is rarely encountered by itself today. It may be used as an inhalant by putting about a teaspoonful of the Balsam into a steam bath. The internal dosage is ½–1 gram taken three times a day.

BARBERRY

Berberis vulgaris

BERBERIDACEAE

Part used: Bark of root or stem.

Collection: The roots should be unearthed in the spring (March) or the fall (November), and the stem bark should be collected at the same time. Pare off the bark from root and stem and dry in the shade.

Constituents: Alkaloids, including berberine, oxyancanthine, chelidonic acid, tannins.

Actions: Cholagogue, antiemetic, bitter tonic, laxative.

INDICATIONS:
Barberry is one of the best remedies for correcting liver function and promoting the flow of bile. It is indicated when there is an *inflammation of the gallbladder* or in the presence of *gallstones*. When *jaundice* occurs due to a congested state of the liver, Barberry is also indicated. As a bitter tonic with mild laxative effects, it is used with *weak* or *debilitated* people to strengthen and cleanse the system. An interesting action is its ability to reduce an *enlarged spleen*. It acts against *malaria* and is also effective in the treatment of *protozoal infection* due to *Leishmania spp*.

Combinations: In *gallbladder diseases*, it combines well with Fringe Tree Bark and Black Root.

CAUTION:
Avoid during pregnancy.

PREPARATION AND DOSAGE:
Decoction: put 1 teaspoonful of the bark into a cup of cold water and bring to the boil. Leave for 10–15 minutes. This should be drunk three times a day.

Tincture: take 2–4 milliliters of the tincture three times a day.

BAYBERRY
Myrica cerifera
MYRICACEAE

Part used: Bark of root.
Collection: The root should be unearthed in the spring or fall and its bark pared off and dried.
Constituents: Tannins, resin, volatile oil.
Actions: Astringent, circulatory stimulant, diaphoretic.

> ### INDICATIONS:
> As a circulatory stimulant, Bayberry plays a role in many conditions when they are approached in a holistic way. Due to its specific actions, it is a valuable astringent in *diarrhea* and *dysentry*. It is indicated in *mucous colitis*. As a gargle, it helps *sore throats*, and as a douche it helps in *leukorrhea*. It may be used in the treatment of *colds*.

Combinations: As a digestive astringent, it may be used with Comfrey Root and Agrimony.

PREPARATION AND DOSAGE:

Decoction: put 1 teaspoonful of the bark into a cup of cold water and bring to the boil. Leave for 10–15 minutes. This should be drunk three times a day.
Tincture: take 1–3 milliliters of the tincture three times a day.

BEARBERRY
Arctostaphylos uva-ursi
ERICACEAE

Part used: Leaves.
Collection: The evergreen leaves may be collected throughout the year, but preferably in the spring and summer.
Constituents: Glycosides, including arbutin and ericolin. 6% tannins, flavonoids, and resin.
Actions: Diuretic, astringent, antiseptic, demulcent.

> ### INDICATIONS:
> Bearberry has a specific antiseptic and astringent effect upon the membranes of the urinary system. It will generally soothe, tone, and strengthen them. It is specifically used where there is *gravel* or *ulceration in the kidney or bladder*. It may be used in the treatment of infections, such as *pyelitis* and *cystitis*, or as part of a holistic approach to more chronic kidney problems. It has a useful role to play in the treatment of *gravel* or a *calculus* in the kidney. With its high astringency, it is used in some forms of *bed-wetting*. As a douche, it may be helpful in *vaginal ulceration* and *infection*.

Combinations: Bearberry may be combined with Couch Grass and Yarrow for *urinary infections*.

PREPARATION AND DOSAGE:

Infusion: pour a cup of boiling water onto 1–2 teaspoonfuls of the dried leaves and let infuse for 10–15 minutes. This should be drunk three times a day.
Tincture: take 2–4 milliliters of the tincture three times a day.

BETONY
Betonica officinalis
LABIATAE

Part used: Dried aerial parts.
Collection: The aerial parts should be collected just before the flowers bloom. They should be dried carefully in the sun.
Constituents: Alkaloids, including betonicine, stachydrene, and trigonelline.
Actions: Sedative, nervine tonic, bitter.

> **INDICATIONS:**
> Betony feeds and strengthens the central nervous system and also has a sedative action. It finds use in *nervous debility* associated with *anxiety* and *tension*. It will ease *headaches* and *neuralgia* when they are of nervous origin.

Combinations: For the treatment of *nervous headache*, it combines well with Skullcap.

PREPARATION AND DOSAGE:

Infusion: pour a cup of boiling water onto 1–2 teaspoonfuls of the dried herb and leave to infuse for 10–15 minutes. This should be drunk three times a day.
Tincture: take 2–6 milliliters of the tincture three times a day.

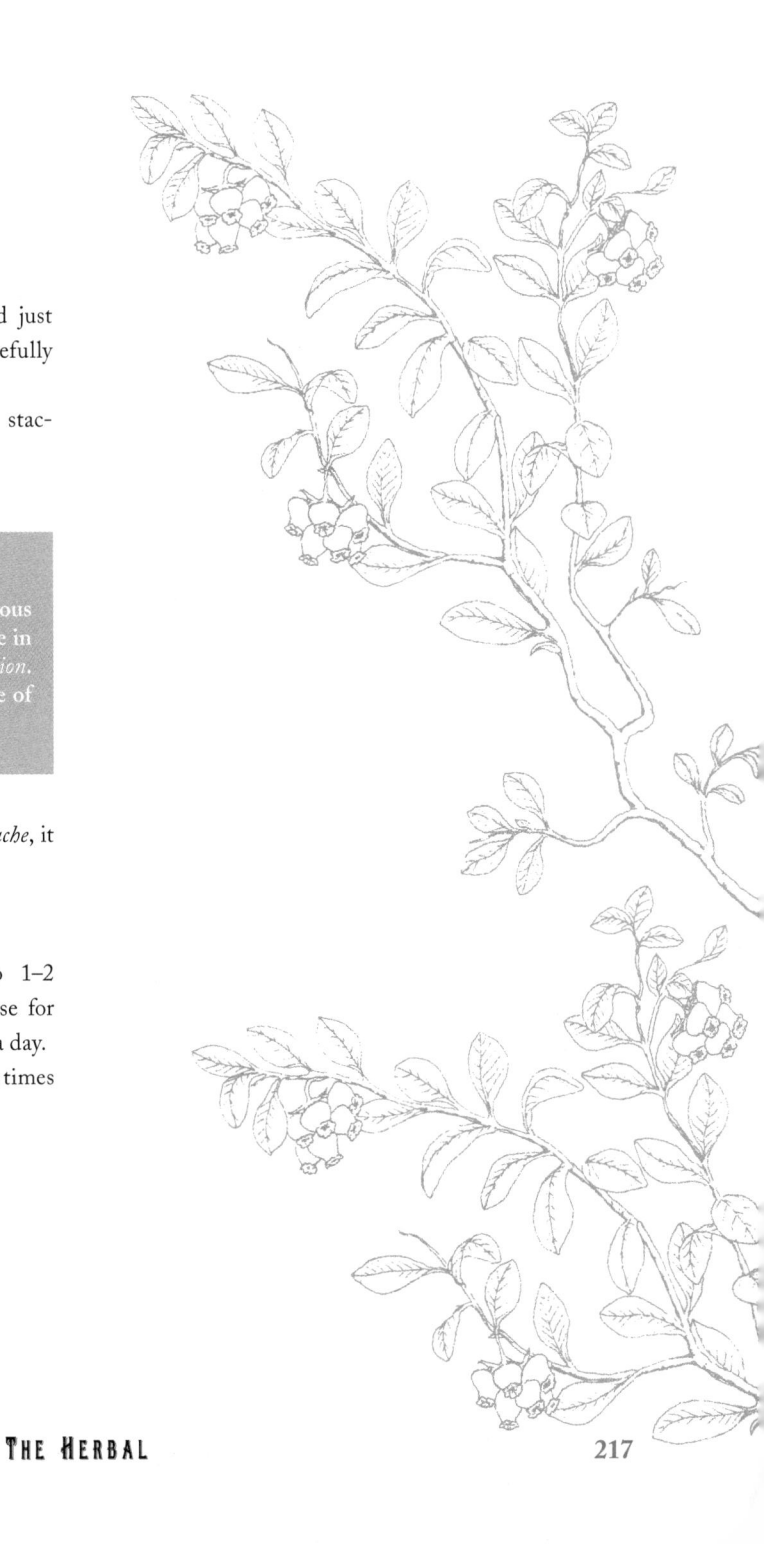

THE HERBAL

BIRCH (SILVER)
Betula pendula
BETULACEAE

Part used: Young leaves and bark.
Collection: The leaves are collected in the late spring or summer. When collecting the bark, it is important not to girdle or ringbark the tree—in other words, not to take off the bark all around the circumference; otherwise, the tree will die.
Constituents: Tannins, saponins, bitters, glycosides, essential oil, flavonoids.
Actions: Diuretic, antiseptic, tonic.

INDICATIONS:
Birch leaves act as an effective remedy for *cystitis* and other infections of the urinary system, as well as removing *excess water* from the body. Perhaps because of this cleansing diuretic activity, the plant has been used for *gout*, *rheumatism*, and mild *arthritic pain*. The bark will ease *muscle pain* if it is applied externally, putting the fresh, wet internal side of the bark against the skin.

Combinations: For *urinary infections*, it may be used with Bearberry, while for *rheumatic pain* it combines well with Black Willow.

PREPARATION AND DOSAGE:
Infusion: pour a cup of boiling water onto 1–2 teaspoonfuls of the dried leaves and let infuse for 10 minutes. This should be drunk three times a day.
Tincture: take 1–2 milliliters of the tincture three times a day.

BISTORT
Polygonum bistorta
POLYGONACEAE

Part used: Root and rhizome.
Collection: Roots and rhizomes are dug up in the fall from the moist pastures where Bistort thrives. The large roots should be cut longitudinally and dried in the sun.
Constituents: Between 15–20% tannins.
Actions: Astringent, anticatarrhal, demulcent, anti-inflammatory.

INDICATIONS:
Bistort is a powerful though soothing astringent that can be used widely, whenever astringency is needed, especially in *diarrhea* and *dysentery*. It is considered a specific in *childhood diarrhea*. It will add its astringency to any digestive remedy and may be used in *mucous colitis*. It can be used in *nasal catarrh* as an adjunct to other remedies. Externally it will make a useful mouthwash for *inflamed conditions of mouth or tongue*, as a gargle for *laryngitis* or *pharyngitis*, and as a douche for *leukorrhea*. It has been used as an ointment for *hemorrhoids* and *anal fissures*.

PREPARATION AND DOSAGE:
Decoction: pour a cup of water onto 1 teaspoonful of the dried herb, bring to the boil, and simmer for 10–15 minutes. This should be drunk three times a day. For external use, this tea can also be used as a mouthwash or gargle.
Tincture: take 2–4 milliliters of the tincture three times a day.

BITTERSWEET
Solanum dulcamara
SOLANACAEA

Part used: Leaves and stems.

> **CAUTION:**
> The berries are poisonous.

Collection: The stems are collected in September and October and the leaves in the summer.
Constituents: Dulcamarin, tannins, gum, 1% alkaloids, including solanidine.
Actions: Diuretic, alterative, antirheumatic, expectorant, mild sedative.

> **INDICATIONS:**
> The primary use of the stems of Bittersweet is in the treatment of skin and rheumatic complaints, possibly indicating a similarity of origin of these illnesses, both being the result of systemic factors. Bittersweet may be used in *psoriasis*, *eczema*, and *pityriasis*. Rheumatic and *arthritic inflammations* are eased, as well as gradually improved. It may be used for *diarrhea* and *dysentry*, *jaundice*, and *hepatic disease*. Ointments can be made from the stems and especially from the leaves and used for *eczema*, *psoriasis*, and *ulcers*.

> **CAUTION:**
> As the berries contain a much higher level of alkaloids, they may be poisonous and have to be avoided.

PREPARATION AND DOSAGE:
Infusion: pour a cup of boiling water onto 1 teaspoonful of the dried herb and leave to infuse for 10 minutes. This should be drunk twice daily.
Tincture: take 1–2 milliliters of the tincture three times a day.

BLACK CATECHU
Acacia catechu
LEGUMINOSAE

Part used: Dried extract prepared from the heartwood of the tree.
Constituents: 20–35% Catechutannic acid, acacatechin, quercitin.
Actions: Astringent, antiseptic.

> **INDICATIONS:**
> Black Catechu is a powerful astringent used in *chronic diarrhea*, *dysentery*, and *mucous colitis*. As a douche, it is used in *leukorrhea*. As a mouthwash or gargle, it is used in *gingivitis*, *stomatitis*, *pharyngitis*, and *laryngitis*.

Combinations: In conditions of the colon, it combines well with Calamus, Meadowsweet, Agrimony, and Peppermint. As a mouthwash, it combines well with Myrrh.

PREPARATION AND DOSAGE:
Infusion: pour a cup of boiling water onto 1 teaspoonful of the dried herb and leave to infuse for 10–15 minutes. This should be drunk three times a day.

BLACK COHOSH
Cimicifuga racemosa
RANUNCULACEAE

Part used: Root and rhizome; dried, not fresh.
Collection: The roots are unearthed with the rhizome in the fall after the fruit have ripened. They should be cut lengthwise and dried carefully.
Constituents: Resin, bitter glycosides, ranunculin (which changes to anemonin upon drying), salicylic acid, tannins, estrogenic principle.
Actions: Emmenagogue, antispasmodic, alterative, sedative.

> **INDICATIONS:**
> Black Cohosh is a most valuable herb that comes to us via the Native Americans. It has a most powerful action as a relaxant and a normalizer of the female reproductive system. It may be used beneficially in cases of *painful* or *delayed menstruation*. *Ovarian cramps* or *cramping pain* in the womb will be relieved by Black Cohosh. It has a normalizing action on the balance of female sex hormones and may safely be used to regain normal hormonal activity. It is very active in the treatment of rheumatic conditions of all kinds. It may be used in cases of *rheumatic pains*, but also in *rheumatoid arthritis, osteoarthritis*, and in *muscular* and *neurological pain*. It finds use in *sciatica* and *neuralgia*. As a relaxing nervine, it may be used in many situations where such an agent is needed. It will be useful in *labor* to aid uterine activity while allaying nervousness. Black Cohosh will reduce *spasm* and so aid in the treatment of pulmonary complaints such as *whooping cough*. It has been found beneficial in cases of *tinnitus*.

Combinations: For *uterine conditions*, combine with Blue Cohosh. For *rheumatic problems*, use with Buckbean.

PREPARATION AND DOSAGE:
Decoction: pour a cup of water onto ½–1 teaspoonfuls of the dried root and bring to the boil. Let it simmer for 10–15 minutes. This should be drunk three times a day.
Tincture: take 2–4 milliliters of the tincture three times a day.

BLACK HAW
Viburnum prunifolium
CAPRIFOLIACEAE

Part used: Dried bark of root, stem, or trunk.
Collection: The bark from the roots and the trunk is collected in the fall. The shrubs should be dug out and the bark stripped from roots and trunk. The bark from branches should be collected in the spring and summer. In both cases, the bark should be dried in the shade.
Constituents: Triterpenoids, coumarins, bitter principle, valerianic acid, salicosides, tannins.
Actions: Antispasmodic, sedative, hypotensive, astringent.

> **INDICATIONS:**
> Black Haw has a very similar use to Cramp Bark, to which it is closely related. It is a powerful relaxant of the uterus and is used for *dysmenorrhea (uterine cramps)* and *false labor pains*. It may be used in *threatened miscarriage* as well. Its relaxant and sedative actions explain its power in reducing *blood pressure*, which happens through a relaxation of the peripheral blood vessels. It may be used as an antispasmodic in the treatment of *asthma*.

Combinations: For *threatened miscarriage*, it will combine well with False Unicorn Root and Cramp Bark.

PREPARATION AND DOSAGE:

Decoction: put 2 teaspoonfuls of the dried bark in a cup of water, bring to the boil, and simmer for 10 minutes. This should be drunk three times a day.

Tincture: take 5–10 milliliters of the tincture three times a day.

Combinations: For the relief of *nausea* and *vomiting*, it may be combined with Meadowsweet and Chamomile.

PREPARATION AND DOSAGE:

Infusion: pour a cup of boiling water onto 1–2 teaspoonfuls of the dried herb and leave to infuse for 10–15 minutes. This should be drunk three times a day or as needed.

Tincture: take 1–2 milliliters of the tincture three times a day.

BLACK HOREHOUND
Ballota nigra
LABIATAE

Part used: Dried aerial parts.
Collection: The herb should be gathered just as it begins to bloom in July.
Constituents: Flavonoids.
Actions: Antiemetic, sedative, mild astringent, emmenagogue, expectorant.

INDICATIONS:
Black Horehound—which should not be confused with White Horehound—is an excellent remedy for the settling of *nausea* and *vomiting* where the cause lies within the nervous system rather than in the stomach. It may be used with safety in *motion sickness*, for example, where the *nausea* is triggered through the inner ear and the central nervous system. This herb will also be of value in helping the *vomiting of pregnancy* or *nausea* and *vomiting* due to nervousness. This remedy has a reputation as a normalizer of *menstrual function* and also as a mild expectorant.

THE HERBAL

BLACK ROOT
Leptandra virginica
SCROPHULARIACEAE

Part used: Rhizome and root.
Collection: This root, which was introduced to European herbalism via the Seneca Native Americans, should be dug up in the fall and stored for a year before use.
Constituents: Leptandrin, a bitter principle, glycosides, phytosterols, saponins, tannins, resin.
Actions: Cholagogue, mild cathartic, diaphoretic, antispasmodic.

INDICATIONS:
Black Root is used as a reliever of *liver congestion* and for an *inflamed gallbladder (cholecystitis)*. When *jaundice* is due to liver congestion, also use Black Root, as it will help whenever there is any sign of liver problems. *Chronic constipation* can often be due to a liver dysfunction, in which case this herb is also ideal.

Combinations: Black Root will combine well with Barberry and Dandelion.

PREPARATION AND DOSAGE:
Decoction: put 1–2 teaspoonfuls of the dried herb in a cup of cold water and bring to the boil. Simmer for 10 minutes. Take one cup three times a day.
Tincture: take 2–4 milliliters of the tincture three times a day.

BLACK WILLOW
Salix nigra
SALICACEAE

Part used: Bark.
Collection: The bark is collected in the spring, when new growth starts.
Constituents: Salicin, tannins.
Actions: Anti-inflammatory, antipyretic, analgesic, antiseptic, astringent.

INDICATIONS:
Black Willow is a safe natural source of aspirinlike chemicals, which helps explain its reputation in the treatment of *rheumatism* and *arthritis* where there is much associated pain and inflammation. It may be used as part of a wider treatment for any *connective tissue inflammation* anywhere in the body, but it is especially useful in *rheumatoid arthritis*. It may also be used in *fevers*, such as *influenza*.

Combinations: It may be used with Black Cohosh, Celery Seed, Guaiacum, and Buckbean in the treatment of rheumatoid arthritis.

PREPARATION AND DOSAGE:
Decoction: pour a cup of water onto 1–2 teaspoonfuls of the bark, bring to the boil, and simmer for 10 minutes. This should be drunk three times a day.
Tincture: take 2–4 milliliters of the tincture three times a day.

BLADDERWRACK
Fucus vesiculosus
FUCACEAE

Common name: Kelp.
Part used: The whole plant, which is a common seaweed.
Constituents: It is rich in algin and mannitol, carotene and zeaxanthin. Iodine and bromine are present.
Actions: Antihypothyroid, antirheumatic.

INDICATIONS:
Bladderwrack has proved most useful in the treatment of *underactive thyroid glands* and *goiter*. Through the regulation of thyroid function, there is an improvement in all the associated symptoms. Where *obesity* is associated with thyroid trouble, this herb may be very helpful in reducing the excess weight. It has a reputation for helping the relief of *rheumatism* and *rheumatoid arthritis*, both used internally and as an external application upon *inflamed joints*.

PREPARATION AND DOSAGE:
It may usefully be taken in tablet form as a dietary supplement or as an infusion by pouring a cup of boiling water onto 2–3 teaspoonfuls of the dried herb and leaving it to steep for 10 minutes. This should be drunk three times a day.

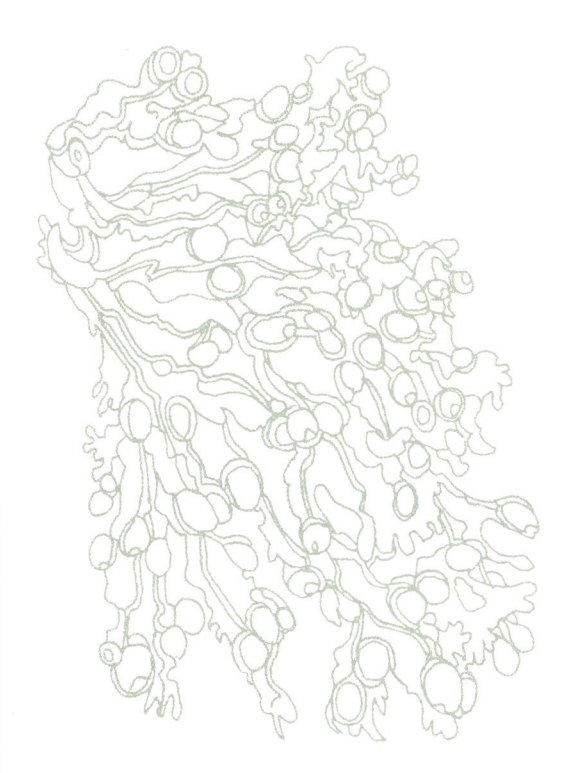

BLESSED THISTLE
Cnicus benedictus
COMPOSITAE

Part used: Dried aerial parts and seeds.
Collection: The leaves and flowering twigs should be gathered when blooming (June to August). Dry them in the shade and cut them up after drying. The seeds are collected in the fall when the plant has set seed.
Constituents: Bitter glycoside called cnicin; flavonoids, essential oil, mucilage.
Actions: Bitter tonic, astringent, diaphoretic, antibacterial, expectorant.

> **INDICATIONS:**
> Through its bitter properties, Blessed Thistle increases the flow of gastric and bile secretions. It may be used with benefit in *appetite loss (anorexia)*, *dyspepsia*, and *indigestion*, and it has a role in any disease of the digestive system that is accompanied by *wind* and *colic*. Because of its astringency, it may be used in *diarrhea* or *hemorrhage*. Externally, it is a vulnerary and antiseptic.

Combinations: In *indigestion* due to a sluggish state of the digestive system, it may be combined with Balmony and Kola Nut and in *diarrhea* with Meadowsweet and Tormentil.

PREPARATION AND DOSAGE:

Infusion: pour a cup of boiling water onto 1 teaspoonful of the dried herb and leave to infuse for 10–15 minutes. This should be drunk three times a day.

Tincture: take 1–2 milliliters of the tincture three times a day.

BLOODROOT
Sanguinaria canadensis
PAPAVERACEAE

Part used: Dried rhizome.
Collection: The rhizome is unearthed in the early summer (May to June) or in the fall, when the leaves have dried. It should be dried carefully in the shade.
Constituents: Alkaloids, including sanguinarine, chelerythrine, protopine, and homochelidine; red resin, citric acid, malic acids.
Actions: Expectorant, antispasmodic, emetic, cathartic, antiseptic, cardioactive, topical irritant.

> **INDICATIONS:**
> Bloodroot finds its main use in the treatment of *bronchitis* in any of its forms. While the stimulating properties show in its power as an emetic and expectorant, it demonstrates a relaxing action on the bronchial muscles. It thus has a role in the treatment of *asthma*, *croup*, and also *laryngitis*. It acts as a stimulant in cases of *deficient peripheral circulation*. It may be used as a snuff in the treatment of *nasal polypi*.

Combinations: May be combined with Lobelia in *bronchitic asthma*. In *pharyngitis*, it combines well with Red Sage and a pinch of Cayenne.

PREPARATION AND DOSAGE:

Decoction: put 1 teaspoonful of the rhizome in a cup of cold water, bring to the boil, and leave to infuse for 10 minutes. This should be drunk three times a day.

Tincture: take 2–4 milliliters of the tincture three times a day.

BLUE COHOSH
Caulophyllum thalictroides
BERBERIDACEAE

Part used: Rhizome and root.
Collection: The roots and rhizome are collected in the fall, as at the end of the growing season they are richest in natural chemicals.
Constituents: Steroidal saponins, alkaloids.
Actions: Uterine tonic, emmenagogue, antispasmodic, antirheumatic.

INDICATIONS:
Blue Cohosh is a plant that comes to us from the Native Americans, which shows in its other names of Partridge Vine (aka Squaw Vine) and Papoose Root. It is an excellent uterine tonic that may be used in any situation where there is a weakness or loss of tone. It may be used at any time during pregnancy if there is a threat of *miscarriage*. Similarly, because of its antispasmodic action, it will ease *false labor pains*. However, when labor does ensue, the use of Blue Cohosh just before birth will help ensure an easy delivery. In all these cases it is a safe herb to use. As an emmenagogue, it can be used to bring on a *delayed* or *suppressed menstruation* whilr ensuring that the pain that sometimes accompanies it is relieved. Blue Cohosh may be used in cases where an antispasmodic is needed such as in *colic*, *asthma*, or *nervous coughs*. It has a reputation for easing *rheumatic pain*.

Combinations: To strengthen the uterus, it may be used well with False Unicorn Root, Motherwort, and Yarrow.

PREPARATION AND DOSAGE:
Decoction: put 1 teaspoonful of the dried root in a cup of water, bring to the boil, and simmer for 10 minutes. This should be drunk three times a day.
Tincture: take 1–2 milliliters of the tincture three times a day.

BLUE FLAG
Iris versicolor
IRIDACEAE

Part used: Rhizome.
Collection: The rhizome is best collected in the fall.
Constituents: Oleoresin, salicylic acid, alkaloid, tannins.
Actions: Cholagogue, alterative, laxative, diuretic, anti-inflammatory.

INDICATIONS:
This useful remedy has a wide application in the treatment of skin diseases, apparently aiding the skin by working through the liver, the main detoxifying organ of the body. It may be used in skin eruptions, such as *eczema*, *pimples*, and *blemishes*. For the more chronic skin problems, such as *eczema* and *psoriasis*, it is valuable as part of a wider treatment. It may be used with value where there is *constipation* associated with *liver problems* or *biliousness*.

Combinations: Blue Flag combines well with Echinacea or Burdock and Yellow Dock.

PREPARATION AND DOSAGE:
Decoction: put ½–1 teaspoonful of the dried herb into a cup of water and bring to the boil. Let it simmer for 10–15 minutes. This should be drunk three times a day.
Tincture: take 2–4 milliliter of the tincture three times a day.

BOLDO
Peumus boldo
MONIMIACEAE

Part used: Dried leaves.
Collection: Gather the evergreen leaves at any time. Dry them carefully in shade not over 100ºF (40ºC).
Constituents: 2% volatile oils, the alkaloid boldine, glycosides, resins, and tannins.
Actions: Cholagogue, hepatic, diuretic, sedative.

> **INDICATIONS:**
> Boldo is a specific for *gallbladder problems* like *stones* or *inflammations*. It is also used when there is *visceral pain* due to other problems in liver or gallbladder. Boldo has mild urinary demulcent and antiseptic properties and so would be used in *cystitis*.

Combinations: When treating gallbladder or liver problems, it combines well with Fringe Tree Bark and Mountain Grape.

PREPARATION AND DOSAGE:
Infusion: pour a cup of boiling water onto 1 teaspoonful of the dried leaves and let infuse for 10–15 minutes. This should be drunk three times a day.
Tincture: take 1–2 milliliters of the tincture three times a day.

BONESET
Eupatorium perfoliatum
COMPOSITAE

Part used: Dried aerial parts.
Collection: Boneset should be collected as soon as the flowers open in August or September.
Constituents: A bitter glycoside called eupatorin, volatile oil, gallic acid, a glucosidal tannin.
Actions: Diaphoretic, aperient, tonic, antispasmodic, relaxes mucous membranes.

> **INDICATIONS:**
> Boneset is perhaps the best remedy for the relief of the associated symptoms that accompany *influenza*. It will speedily relieve the aches and pains, as well as aid the body in dealing with any *fever* that is present. Boneset may also be used to help clear the upper respiratory tract of *mucous congestion*. Its mild aperient activity will help clear the body of any buildup of waste and ease *constipation*. This remedy may safely be used in any *fever* and also as a general cleansing agent. It may provide symptomatic aid in the treatment of *muscular rheumatism*.

Combinations: In the treatment of *influenza*, it may be combined with Yarrow, Elderberry Flowers, Cayenne, or Ginger.

PREPARATION AND DOSAGE:
Infusion: pour a cup of boiling water onto 1–2 teaspoonfuls of the dried herb and leave to infuse for 10–15 minutes. This should be drunk as hot as possible. During fevers or the flu, it should be drunk every half hour.
Tincture: take 2–4 milliliters of the tincture three times a day.

BORAGE
Borago officinalis
BORAGINACEAE

Part used: Dried leaves.
Collection: The leaves should be gathered when the plant is coming into flower in the early summer. Strip each leaf off singly and reject any that are marked in any way. Do not collect when wet with rain or dew.
Constituents: Saponins, mucilage, tannins, essential oil.
Actions: Diaphoretic, expectorant, tonic, anti-inflammatory, galactogogue.

INDICATIONS:

Borage acts as a restorative agent on the adrenal cortex, which means that it will revive and renew the adrenal glands after a medical treatment with cortisone or steroids. There is a growing need for remedies that will aid this gland with the *stress* it is exposed to, both externally and internally. Borage may be used as a tonic for the adrenals over a period of time. It may be used during *fevers* and especially during *convalescence*. It has a reputation as an anti-inflammatory herb used in conditions such as *pleurisy*. The leaves and seeds stimulate the flow of milk in nursing mothers.

PREPARATION AND DOSAGE:

Infusion: pour a cup of boiling water onto 2 teaspoonfuls of the dried herb and leave to infuse for 10–15 minutes. This should be drunk three times a day.
Tincture: take 1–4 milliliters of the tincture three times a day.

THE HERBAL

BROOM TOPS
Sarothamnus scoparius
PAPILIONACEAE

Part used: Flowering tops.
Collection: May be gathered throughout the spring, summer, and fall. The tops may be dried in the sun or by heat.
Constituents: Alkaloids, including sparteine and cystisine; flavonoid glycosides; tannins; bitter principle; volatile oil.
Actions: Cardioactive diuretic, hypertensive, peripheral vasoconstrictor, astringent.

> **INDICATIONS:**
> Broom is a valuable remedy where there is a *weak heart* and *low blood pressure*. Since it is also a diuretic and produces peripheral constriction of the blood vessels while increasing the efficiency of each stroke of the heart, it can be used where *water retention* occurs due to heart weakness. Broom is used in cases of *overly profuse menstruation*.

Combinations: Broom can be combined with Lily of the Valley and Hawthorn Berries when treating the heart.

> **CAUTION:**
> Do not use Broom in pregnancy or hypertension.

PREPARATION AND DOSAGE:

Infusion: pour a cup of boiling water onto 1 teaspoonful of the dried herb and let infuse for 10–15 minutes. This should be drunk three times a day.
Tincture: take 1–2 milliliters of the tincture three times a day.

BOUNCING BET (AKA SOAPWORT)
Saponaria officinalis
CARYOPHYLLACEAE

Part used: Rhizome and roots, aerial parts to a lesser extent.
Collection: The root and rhizome is best dug up and dried between September and October. The leaves are collected between July and August.
Constituents: Saponins.
Actions: Expectorant, laxative, mild diuretic.

> **INDICATIONS:**
> Medicinally, Bouncing Bet can be used as an effective expectorant for use in *bronchitis* and *dry coughs*. It is also reported to have an effect upon *gallstones*. In higher doses, it is a powerful laxative, but it can cause stomach upsets. Externally, it may be used as a wash in skin problems such as *eczema*.

PREPARATION AND DOSAGE:

Decoction: the best way to make a decoction of this root is to soak 4 tablespoonfuls of the dried root (or 2 of the finely cut fresh root) in 2 pints (1 liter) of cold water for five hours. Bring this to the boil and simmer for 10 minutes. This should be drunk three to four times a day.
Tincture: take 1–2 milliliters of the tincture three times a day.

BUCHU
Agathosma betulina
RUTACEAE

Part used: Leaves.
Collection: The leaves should be collected during the flowering and fruiting stage.
Constituents: Up to 2.5% volatile oils, which contain diosphenol, limonene, and menthone.
Actions: Diuretic, urinary antiseptic.

INDICATIONS:
Buchu may be used in any infection of the genitourinary system, such as *cystitis*, *urethritis*, and *prostatitis*. Its healing and soothing properties indicate its use together with other relevant remedies in any condition of this system. It can be especially useful in *painful and burning urination*.

Combinations: In *cystitis*, it may be used with Yarrow or Couch Grass, in *burning urination* with Marshmallow or Corn Silk.

PREPARATION AND DOSAGE:
Infusion: pour a cup of boiling water onto 1–2 teaspoonfuls of the leaves and let infuse for 10 minutes. This should be drunk three times a day.
Tincture: take 2–4 milliliters of the tincture three times a day.

BUCKBEAN
Menyanthes trifoliata
MENYANTHACEAE

Common name: Buckbean or bogbean.
Part used: Leaves.
Collection: The leaves are best collected between May and July. They may be dried in the sun or under moderate heat.
Constituents: Bitter glycosides, alkaloids, saponin, essential oil, flavonoids, pectin.
Actions: Bitter, diuretic, cholagogue, antirheumatic.

INDICATIONS:
Buckbean is a most useful herb for the treatment of *rheumatism, arthritis,* and *rheumatoid arthritis*. It has a stimulating effect upon the walls of the colon, which will act as an aperient, but it should not be used to help *rheumatism* where there is any *colitis* or *diarrhea*. It has a marked stimulating action on the digestive juices and on bile flow and so will aid in *debilitated states* that are due to sluggish digestion, indigestion, and problems of the liver and gallbladder.

THE HERBAL

Combinations: For the treatment of *rheumatic conditions*, it will combine well with Black Cohosh and Celery Seed.

PREPARATION AND DOSAGE:

Infusion: pour a cup of boiling water onto 1–2 teaspoonfuls of the dried herb and leave to infuse for 10–15 minutes. This should be drunk three times a day.
Tincture: take 1–4 milliliters of the tincture three times a day.

BUCKTHORN
Rhamnus cathartica
RHAMNACEAE

Part used: Fresh or dried fruit.
Collection: The fruit should be collected in September and October.
Constituents: Anthraquinone derivates, including rhamnocarthrin; vitamin C.
Actions: Laxative, diuretic, alterative.

> ### INDICATIONS:
> Buckthorn is an effective and safe laxative.

PREPARATION AND DOSAGE:

Infusion: pour a cup of boiling water onto 2 teaspoonfuls of the fruit and leave to infuse for 10–15 minutes. This should be drunk in the morning or evening, as it takes about 12 hours to be effective. The seeds (about 10) may also be chewed before eating in the morning. If the dose is too high, Buckthorn might cause extreme diarrhea and possibly vomiting.
Tincture: take 1–2 milliliters of the tincture night and morning.

BUGLEWEED
Lycopus europaeus
LABIATAE

Common name: Water Horehound.
Part used: Aerial parts.
Collection: It should be collected just before the buds open.
Constituents: Flavone glycosides, volatile oil, tannins.
Actions: Cardioactive diuretic, peripheral vasoconstrictor, astringent, sedative, thyrocine antagonist, antitussive.

> ### INDICATIONS:
> Bugleweed is a specific for *overactive thyroid glands*, especially where the symptoms include tightness of breathing, palpitation, and shaking. It may safely be used where palpitations occur that are of nervous origin. Bugleweed will aid the *weak heart* where there is associated *buildup of water* in the body. As a sedative cough reliever, it will ease *irritating coughs*, especially when they are of nervous origin.

Combinations: Bugleweed may be used with nervines such as Skullcap or Valerian.

PREPARATION AND DOSAGE:

Infusion: pour a cup of boiling water onto 1 teaspoonful of the dried herb and let infuse for 10–15 minutes. This should be drunk three times a day.
Tincture: take 1–2 milliliters of the tincture three times a day.

BURDOCK
Arctium lappa
COMPOSITAE

Part used: Roots and rhizome.
Collection: The roots and rhizome should be unearthed in September or October.
Constituents: Flavonoid glycosides, bitter glycosides, alkaloid, antimicrobial substance, inulin.
Actions: Alterative, diuretic, bitter.

INDICATIONS:

Burdock is a most valuable remedy for the treatment of skin conditions that result in *dry and scaly skin*. It may be most effective for *psoriasis* if used over a long period of time. Similarly, all types of *eczema* (though primarily the dry kinds) may be treated effectively if Burdock is used over a period of time. It will be useful as part of a wider treatment for *rheumatic complaints*, especially where they are associated with *psoriasis*. Part of the action of this herb is through the bitter stimulation of the digestive juices and especially of bile secretion. Thus it will aid digestion and appetite. It has been used in *anorexia nervosa* and similar conditions, also to aid kidney function and to heal *cystitis*. In general, Burdock will move the body to a state of integration and health, removing such indicators of systemic imbalance as skin problems and *dandruff*. Externally, it may be used as a compress or poultice to speed up the healing of *wounds* and *ulcers*. *Eczema* and *psoriasis* may also be treated this way externally, but it must be remembered that such skin problems can only be healed from within and with the aid of internal remedies.

Combinations: For skin problems, combine with Yellow Dock, Red Clover, or Cleavers.

PREPARATION AND DOSAGE:

Decoction: put 1 teaspoonful of the root into a cup of water, bring to the boil, and simmer for 10–15 minutes. This should be drunk three times a day. For external use, see further information in the chapter on the skin.
Tincture: take 2–4 milliliters of the tincture three times a day.

BUR MARIGOLD
Bidens tripartita
COMPOSITAE

Part used: Aerial parts.
Collection: The whole of the plant above ground should be collected when in flower between July and September.
Actions: Astringent, diaphoretic, diuretic.

> ### INDICATIONS:
> Though little used today, Bur Marigold has a reputation as a valuable astringent used for *hemorrhage* wherever it occurs. It may be used for *fevers* and *water retention* when this is due to a problem in the kidneys. When the dried herb is burned, the flower heads give off a cedarlike smell that will act as an anti-insect incense.

PREPARATION AND DOSAGE:

Infusion: pour a cup of boiling water onto 1–2 teaspoonfuls of the dried herb and leave to infuse for 5–10 minutes. This should be drunk three times a day.
Tincture: take 1–2 milliliters of the tincture three times a day.

BUTTERBUR
Petasites hybridus
COMPOSITAE

Part used: Rhizome or leaves.
Collection: The rhizomes are collected in the summer, and the leaves throughout the growing season.
Constituents: Essential oil, mucilage, bitter glycosides, tannins.
Actions: Antispasmodic, diuretic, diaphoretic.

> ### INDICATIONS:
> Butterbur is a useful relaxant to muscles, used in conditions such as *intestinal colic, asthma,* or *dysmenorrhea (painful periods)*. It not only eases spasms in muscles, but has a pain relieving effect too. It can also be used for *fevers*. The fresh leaves can be used externally as a *wound* dressing.

PREPARATION AND DOSAGE:

Infusion: put 1 teaspoonful of the root in a cup of water, bring to the boil, and simmer for 10–15 minutes. This should be drunk three times a day.
Tincture: take 1–2 milliliters of the tincture three times a day.

CALAMUS

Acorus calamus

ARACEAE

Common name: Sweet Flag.

Part used: Dried rhizome.

Collection: The rhizome should be harvested between September and October. A hook may be needed to extract it from muddy soil. Free the rhizome from leaves and root and clean it thoroughly. Halve it along its length and dry it in the shade.

Constituents: Mucilage, up to 3% volatile oil, bitter principles, glycoside, tannins.

Actions: Carminative, demulcent, antispasmodic.

> **INDICATIONS:**
> Calamus combines demulcent effects of the mucilage with the carminative effect of the volatile oil and the stimulating effect of the bitters. It is thus an excellent tonic for the whole gastrointestinal tract. It may be used in *dyspepsia* of all kinds, in *gastritis* and *gastric ulcers*. It will stimulate a *flagging appetite* and help ease *exhaustion* and *weakness* when there is a digestive involvement. It may be considered a specific in *colic due to flatulence*.

Combinations: In *flatulent colic*, it combines well with Ginger and Wild Yam. In *gastric conditions*, it is best combined with Meadowsweet and Marshmallow.

PREPARATION AND DOSAGE:

Infusion: pour a cup of boiling water onto 2 teaspoonfuls of the dried herb and leave to infuse for 10–15 minutes. Drink a cup half an hour before meals.

Tincture: take 2–4 milliliters of the tincture three times a day.

CALIFORNIAN POPPY

Eschscholzia california

PAPAVERACEAE

Part used: Dried aerial parts.

Collection: The aerial parts are collected at the time of flowering, which is between June and September. They should be dried in the shade.

Constituents: Alkaloids similar to Opium Poppy; flavone glycosides.

Actions: Sedative, hypnotic, antispasmodic, anodyne.

> **INDICATIONS:**
> Californian Poppy has the reputation of being a nonaddictive alternative to the Opium Poppy, though it is less powerful. It has been used as a sedative and hypnotic for children, where there is *overexcitability* and *sleeplessness*. It can be used wherever an antispasmodic remedy is required. The Native Americans used it for *colic pains*, and it may be useful in the treatment of *gallbladder colic*.

THE HERBAL

PREPARATION AND DOSAGE:

Infusion: pour a cup of boiling water onto 1–2 teaspoonfuls of the dried herb and leave to infuse for 10 minutes. A cup should be drunk at night to promote restful sleep.

Tincture: take 1–4 milliliters of the tincture at night.

CALUMBA
Jateorhiza palmata
MENISPERMACEAE

Part used: Root.
Collection: This root is collected from a climbing plant indigenous to the forests of Mozambique and Madagascar.
Constituents: Alkaloids, including calumbamine, jateorrhizine, palmatine, and bitter glycosides.
Actions: Bitter tonic, digestive stimulant, sialagogue.

INDICATIONS:
Calumba is an excellent digestive remedy that tones the whole tract, stimulating it gently but having no astringent properties. It may be used whenever *debility* occurs that is connected with some digestive involvement.

PREPARATION AND DOSAGE:

Decoction: put 1–2 teaspoonfuls of the root in a cup of cold water and bring to the boil. Let it infuse for 10 minutes and drink a cup half an hour before meals.
Tincture: take 1–4 milliliters of the tincture three times a day.

CARAWAY
Carum carvi
UMBELLIFERAE

Part used: Seeds.
Collection: The flowering heads (umbels) are collected in July and left to ripen. The seeds are then easily collected as they can be shaken off.
Constituents: Up to 6% volatile oil, including carvone and limonene; fatty oil and tannins.
Actions: Carminative, antispasmodic, expectorant, emmenagogue, galactagogue, astringent, aromatic.

INDICATIONS:
Caraway is used as a calming herb to ease *flatulent dyspepsia* and *intestinal colic*, especially in children. It will stimulate the *appetite*. Its astringency will help in the treatment of *diarrhea* as well as in *laryngitis* as a gargle. It can be used in *bronchitis* and *bronchial asthma*. Its antispasmodic actions help in the relief of *period pains*. It has been used to increase *milk flow in nursing mothers*.

Combinations: For *flatulence* and *colic*, Caraway combines well with Chamomile and Calamus, in *diarrhea* with Agrimony and Bayberry, and in *bronchitis* with White Horehound.

PREPARATION AND DOSAGE:

Infusion: pour a cup of boiling water onto 1 teaspoonful of freshly crushed seeds and leave to infuse for 10–15 minutes. This should be drunk three times a day.
Tincture: take 1–4 milliliters of the tincture three times a day.

CARDAMOM

Elattaria cardamomum

ZINGIBERACEAE

Part used: Seeds.
Collection: The seeds are mainly obtained from commercial plants in Sri Lanka or Southern India, where the crop is gathered between October and December.
Constituents: Up to 4% volatile oil, including terpineol, cineole, limonene, sabinene, and pinene.
Actions: Carminative, sialagogue, orexigenic, aromatic.

> **INDICATIONS:**
> This valuable culinary herb may be used to treat *flatulent dyspepsia* and to relieve *griping pains*. It will stimulate the *appetite* and the *flow of saliva*. It is often used as a carminative flavoring agent when purgatives are given.

PREPARATION AND DOSAGE:

Infusion: pour a cup of boiling water onto 1 teaspoonful of the freshly crushed seeds and leave to infuse for 10–15 minutes. This should be drunk three times a day. If treating *flatulence* or *loss of appetite*, drink half an hour before meals.

CARLINE THISTLE

Carlina vulgaris

COMPOSITAE

Part used: Root.
Collection: The root of this perennial plant should be unearthed in the fall.
Constituents: Essential oil, sesquiterpene, tannins, inulin.
Actions: Diuretic, diaphoretic, vulnerary.

> **INDICATIONS:**
> This beautiful herb has been described as having properties similar to that of Elecampane. It has valuable antiseptic properties when used to aid *wound healing*. It may be used in any urinary problem, especially in infections such as *cystitis*.

PREPARATION AND DOSAGE:

Infusion: pour a cup of boiling water onto 1 teaspoonful of the dried leaves and let infuse for 10–15 minutes. This should be drunk three times a day.
Tincture: take 1–2 milliliters of the tincture three times a day.

THE HERBAL

CASCARA SAGRADA
Rhamnus purshiana
RHAMNACEAE

Part used: Dried bark.
Collection: The bark is stripped from the trunk of this Western American tree in the spring and summer and left to age for a few years. Due to indiscriminate cutting by white settlers during the 19th century, the number of wild trees has been greatly reduced.
Constituents: Anthraquinones, tannins, volatile oil.
Actions: Mild purgative, bitter tonic.

> **INDICATIONS:**
> Cascara Sagrada may be used in *chronic constipation*, as it encourages peristalsis and tones relaxed muscles of the digestive system.

Combinations: Cascara Sagrada should be combined with aromatics and carminatives—for instance, with Licorice.

PREPARATION AND DOSAGE:

Decoction: put 1–2 teaspoonfuls of the bark in a cup of water, bring to the boil, and leave to infuse for 10 minutes. This should be drunk at bedtime.
Tincture: take 1–2 milliliters of the tincture at bedtime.

CATNIP
Nepeta cataria
LABIATAE

Part used: Leaves and flowering tops.
Collection: The leaves and flowering tops are collected between June and September.
Constituents: Volatile oils, including citronellol, geraniol, and citral; bitter principle; tannins.
Actions: Carminative, antispasmodic, diaphoretic, sedative, astringent.

> **INDICATIONS:**
> Catnip is one of our traditional *cold* and *flu* remedies. It is a powerful diaphoretic used in any *feverish condition*, especially in *bronchitis*. As a carminative with antispasmodic properties, Catnip eases any *stomach upsets, dyspepsia, flatulence,* and *colic*. It is a perfect remedy for the treatment of *diarrhea* in children. Its sedative action on the nerves adds to its generally relaxing properties.

Combinations: May be used with Boneset, Elderberry, Yarrow, or Cayenne in *colds*.

PREPARATION AND DOSAGE:

Infusion: pour a cup of boiling water onto 2 teaspoonfuls of the dried herb and leave to infuse for 10–15 minutes. This should be drunk three times a day.
Tincture: take 2–4 milliliters of the tincture three times a day.

CAYENNE
Capsicum minimum
SOLANACEAE

Part used: Fruit.
Collection: The fruit should be harvested when fully ripe and dried in the shade.
Constituents: Capsaicin, carotenoids, flavonoids, essential oil, vitamin C.
Actions: Stimulant, carminative, tonic, sialagogue, rubefacient, antiseptic.

INDICATIONS:
Cayenne is the most useful of the systemic stimulants. It regulates the blood flow, equalizing and strengthening the heart, arteries, capillaries, and nerves. It is a general tonic and is specific for the circulatory and digestive system. It may be used in *flatulent dyspepsia* and *colic*. If there is insufficient peripheral circulation, leading to *cold hands and feet* and possibly *chilblains*, Cayenne may be used. It is used for treating *debility* and for warding off *colds*. Externally, it is used as a rubefacient in problems like *lumbago* and *rheumatic pains*. As an ointment, it helps unbroken *chilblains*, as long as it is used in moderation! As a gargle in *laryngitis*, it combines well with Myrrh. This combination is also a good antiseptic wash.

PREPARATION AND DOSAGE:
Infusion: pour a cup of boiling water onto ½–1 teaspoonful of Cayenne and leave to infuse for 10 minutes. A tablespoon of this infusion should be mixed with hot water and drunk when needed.
Tincture: take 0.25–1 milliliter of the tincture three times a day or when needed.

CELERY
Apium graveolens
UMBELLIFERAE

Part used: Dried ripe fruit.
Collection: The seeds should be collected when ripe in the fall.
Constituents: 2–3% volatile oil.
Actions: Antirheumatic, diuretic, carminative, sedative.

INDICATIONS:
Celery Seeds find their main use in the treatment of *rheumatism, arthritis*, and *gout*. They are especially useful in *rheumatoid arthritis* where there is an associated *mental depression*. Their diuretic action is obviously involved in rheumatic conditions, but they are also used as a urinary antiseptic, largely because of the volatile oil apiol.

Combinations: In *rheumatic conditions*, it combines well with Buckbean. They appear to work better in combination with Dandelion.

PREPARATION AND DOSAGE:
Infusion: pour a cup of boiling water onto 1–2 teaspoonfuls of freshly crushed seeds. Leave to infuse for 10–15 minutes. This should be drunk three times a day.
Tincture: take 2–4 milliliters of the tincture three times a day.

CENTAURY
Centaurium erythraea
GENTIANACEAE

Part used: Dried aerial parts.
Collection: The foliage should be collected at the time of flowering, which is from July to September. Dry it in the sun.
Constituents: Glycosidal bitter principles gentiopicrin and erythrocentaurine; nicotinic acid compounds; traces of essential oil; oleanolic acid and other acids; resin.
Actions: Bitter, aromatic, mild nervine, gastric stimulant.

> **INDICATIONS:**
> It may be used whenever a digestive and gastric stimulant is required. It is indicated primarily in *appetite loss (anorexia)* when it is associated with *liver weakness*. Centaury is a useful herb in *dyspepsia* and in any condition where a *sluggish digestion* is involved.

Combinations: In *dyspepsia*, it combines well with Meadowsweet, Marshmallow Root, and Chamomile. In *anorexia nervosa*, it is indicated with Burdock Root and Chamomile.

PREPARATION AND DOSAGE:

Infusion: pour a cup of boiling water onto 1 teaspoonful of the dried herb and leave to infuse for 5–10 minutes. Drink one cup half an hour before meals.
Tincture: take 1–2 milliliters of the tincture three times a day.

CHAMOMILE, GARDEN
Anthemus nobile
COMPOSITAE

and

CHAMOMILE, GERMAN
Matricaria chamomilla
COMPOSITAE

Part used: Flowers.
Collection: The flowers should be gathered between May and August when they are not wet with dew or rain. They should be dried with care at not too high a temperature.
Constituents: Volatile oil that includes chamazulene and isadol; mucilage; coumarin; flavone glycosides.
Actions: Antispasmodic, carminative, anti-inflammatory, analgesic, antiseptic, vulnerary.

> **INDICATIONS:**
> Chamomile is renowned for its medical and household uses. The apparently endless list of conditions it can help all fall into areas that the relaxing, carminative, and anti-inflammatory actions can aid. It is an excellent, gentle sedative, useful and safe for use with children. It will contribute its relaxing actions in any combination and is thus used

in *anxiety* and *insomnia*. *Indigestion* and *inflammations*, such as *gastritis*, are often eased with Chamomile. Similarly, it can be used as a mouthwash for inflammations of the mouth such as *gingivitis* and for bathing *inflamed and sore eyes*. As a gargle, it will help *sore throats*. As an inhalation over a steam bath, it will speed recovery from *nasal catarrh*. Externally, it will speed *wound* healing and reduce the swelling due to *inflammation*. As a carminative with relaxing properties, it will ease *flatulence* and *dyspeptic pain*.

PREPARATION AND DOSAGE:

Infusion: pour a cup of boiling water onto 2 teaspoonfuls of the dried leaves and let infuse for 5–10 minutes. For *digestive problems*, this tea should be drunk after meals. A stronger infusion should be used as a mouthwash for conditions such as *gingivitis*. Half a cup of flowers boiled in 4 pints (2 liters) of water make a steam bath. Cover your head with a towel and inhale the steam.

Tincture: take 2–4 milliliters of the tincture three times a day.

CHASTEBERRY
Vitex agnus-castus
VERBENACEAE

Part used: Fruit.
Collection: The very dark berries should be picked when ripe, which is between October and November. They may be dried in sun or shade.
Constituents: Iridoid glycosides which include aucbin and agnoside; flavonoids including casticin, isovitexin and orientin; essential oil.
Actions: Tonic for the reproductive organs.

INDICATIONS:

Chasteberry has the effect of stimulating and normalizing pituitary gland functions, especially its progesterone function. It may be called an amphoteric remedy, as it can produce apparently opposite effects, though, in truth, it is simply normalizing. It has for instance a reputation as both an aphrodisiac and an anaphrodisiac! It will always enable what is appropriate to occur. The greatest use of Chasteberry lies in normalizing the activity of female sex hormones, and it is thus indicated for *dysmenorrhea*, *premenstrual stress*, and other disorders related to hormone funtion. It is especially beneficial during *menopausal changes*. In a similar way, it may be used to aid the body to regain a natural balance after the use of the birth control pill.

PREPARATION AND DOSAGE:

Infusion: pour a cup of boiling water onto 1 teaspoonful of the ripe berries and leave to infuse for 10–15 minutes. This should be drunk three times a day.
Tincture: take 1–2 milliliters of the tincture three times a day.

CHICKWEED
Stellaria media
CARYOPHYLLACEAE

Part used: Dried aerial parts.
Collection: This very common weed of gardens and fields can be collected all year round, although it is not abundant during the winter.
Constituents: Saponins.
Actions: Antirheumatic, vulnerary, emollient.

> ### INDICATIONS:
> Chickweed finds its most common use as an external remedy for *cuts, wounds,* and especially for *itching* and *irritation*. If *eczema* or *psoriasis* causes this sort of irritation, Chickweed may be used with benefit. Internally, it has a reputation as a remedy for *rheumatism*.

Combinations: Chickweed makes an excellent ointment when combined with Marshmallow.

PREPARATION AND DOSAGE:
Infusion: pour a cup of boiling water onto 2 teaspoonfuls of the dried herb and leave to infuse for five minutes. This should be drunk three times a day. For external use, Chickweed may be made into an ointment or can be used as a poultice. To ease *itching*, a strong infusion of the fresh plant makes a useful addition to bathwater.

CINNAMON
Cinnamomum zeylanicum
LAURACEAE

Part used: Dried inner bark of the shoots.
Collection: The bark is collected commercially throughout the tropics.
Constituents: Volatile oils.
Actions: Carminative, astringent, aromatic, stimulant.

> ### INDICATIONS:
> Cinnamon is usually used as a carminative addition to other herbs. It relieves *nausea* and *vomiting*. Because of its mild astringency, it is used against *diarrhea*.

PREPARATION AND DOSAGE:
The bark, usually powdered, may be freely used in mixtures or by itself to flavor teas.

CLEAVERS
Galium aparine
RUBIACEAE

Common names: Goosegrass, Clives.
Part used: Dried aerial parts and the fresh expressed juice.
Collection: The plant should be gathered before flowering and dried in the shade.
Constituents: Glycoside asperuloside, gallotannic acid, citric acid.
Actions: Diuretic, alterative, anti-inflammatory, tonic, astringent, antineoplastic.

> **INDICATIONS:**
> Cleavers is a very valuable plant and is perhaps the best tonic to the lymphatic system available. As a lymphatic tonic with alterative and diuretic actions, it may be used in a wide range of problems where the lymphatic system is involved. Thus it would be used in *swollen glands (lymphadenitis)* anywhere in the body and especially in *tonsillitis* and in *adenoid trouble*. It is widely used in skin conditions, especially in the dry varieties such as *psoriasis*. It will be useful in the treatment of *cystitis* and other urinary conditions where there is pain and may be combined with demulcents for this. There is a long tradition for the use of Cleavers in the treatment of *ulcers* and *tumors*, which may be the result of the lymphatic drainage. Cleavers makes an excellent vegetable.

Combinations: For the lymphatic system, it will work well with Pokeweed Root, Echinacea, and Marigold. For skin conditions, it is best combined with Yellow Dock and Burdock.

PREPARATION AND DOSAGE:

Infusion: pour a cup of boiling water onto 2–3 teaspoonfuls of the dried herb and leave to infuse for 10–15 minutes. This should be drunk three times a day.

Tincture: take 2–4 milliliters of the tincture three times a day.

CLOVES
Eugenia caryophyllus
MYRTACEAE

Part used: Dried flowers and oil.
Collection: The flower buds are collected from this tree when their lower parts turn from green to purple. It grows all around the Indian Ocean.
Constituents: Up to 20% of volatile oil.
Actions: Stimulant, carminative, aromatic.

> **INDICATIONS:**
> Cloves may be used to allay *nausea, vomiting,* and *flatulence* and to stimulate the digestive system. It is a powerful local antiseptic and mild anesthetic, which may be used externally in *toothache*.

PREPARATION AND DOSAGE:

Cloves may be used as a spice in foods or in teas by putting some cloves into a cup with boiling water and infusing them for 10 minutes. For *toothache*, put a clove near the tooth and keep in the mouth. Alternatively pour some Clove oil on a cotton ball and put this near the tooth.

THE HERBAL

COLTSFOOT
Tussilago farfara
COMPOSITAE

Part used: Dried flowers and leaves.

Collection: The flowers should be gathered before they have fully bloomed (end of February to April) and dried carefully in the shade. The leaves are best collected between May and June. They should be chopped up before they are dried and stored. The fresh leaves can be used until the fall.

Constituents: Flowers: Mucin; flavonoids rutin and carotene; taraxanthin; arnidiol and faradiol; tannins; essential oil. Leaves: Mucin; abundant tannins; glycosidal bitter principle; inulin; sitosterol; zinc.

Actions: Expectorant, antitussive, demulcent, anti-catarrhal, diuretic.

INDICATIONS:
Coltsfoot combines a soothing expectorant effect with an antispasmodic action. There are useful levels of zinc in the leaves. This mineral has been shown to have marked anti-inflammatory effects. Coltsfoot may be used in *chronic or acute bronchitis, irritating coughs, whooping coughs,* **and** *asthma.* Its soothing expectorant action gives Coltsfoot a role in most respiratory conditions, including the chronic states of *emphysema.* As a mild diuretic it has been used in *cystitis.* The fresh bruised leaves can be applied to *boils, abscesses,* **and** *suppurating ulcers.*

Combinations: In the treatment of *coughs*, it may be used with White Horehound and Mullein.

PREPARATION AND DOSAGE:
Infusion: pour a cup of boiling water onto 1–2 teaspoonfuls of the dried flowers or leaves and let infuse for 10 minutes. This should be drunk three times a day, as hot as possible.

Tincture: take 2–4 milliliters of the tincture three times a day.

COMFREY
Symphytum officinale
BORAGINACEAE

Part used: Root and rhizome, leaf.

Collection: The roots should be unearthed in the spring or fall, when the allantoin levels are the highest. Split the roots down the middle and dry in moderate temperatures of about 100–140°F (40–60°C).

Constituents: Mucilage, gum, allantoin, tannins, alkaloids, resin, volatile oil.

Actions: Vulnerary, demulcent, astringent, expectorant.

INDICATIONS:

The impressive wound-healing properties of Comfrey are partially due to the presence of allantoin. This chemical stimulates cell proliferation and so augments wound healing both inside and out. The addition of much demulcent mucilage makes Comfrey a powerful healing agent in *gastric* and *duodenal ulcers*, *hiatus hernia*, and *ulcerative colitis*. Its astringency will help *hemorrhages* wherever they occur. It has been used with benefit in cases of *bronchitis* and *irritable cough*, where it will soothe and reduce irritation while helping expectoration. Comfrey may be used externally to speed wound healing and guard against scar tissue developing incorrectly. Care should be taken with very deep *wounds*, however, as the external application of Comfrey can lead to tissue forming over the wound before it has healed deeper down, possibly leading to abscesses. It may be used for any *external ulcer*, for *wounds* and *fractures* as a compress or poultice. It is excellent in *chronic varicose ulcers*. It has a reputed anticancer action.

Combinations: For *gastric ulcers* and *inflammations*, it combines well with Marshmallow and Meadowsweet. For chest and bronchial troubles, use it with Coltsfoot, White Horehound, or Elecampane.

PREPARATION AND DOSAGE:

Decoction: put 1–3 teaspoonfuls of the dried herb in a cup of water, bring to the boil, and let simmer for 10–15 minutes. This should be drunk three times a day. For external applications, see the chapter on the skin.
Tincture: take 2–4 milliliters of the tincture three times a day.

CONDURANGO
Marsdenia condurango
ASCLEPIADACEAE

Part used: Dried bark.
Constituents: Glycosides, resin, tannins, fixed oil.
Actions: Bitter, stomach sedative.

INDICATIONS:

This bitter may be used in a whole range of digestive and stomach problems. It is best known for its appetite-stimulating actions, common to all bitters. However, in addition it will relax the nerves of the stomach, making it of use in the settling of *indigestion* where this is affected by nervous tension and anxiety. The combination described in the chapter on the digestive system gives this herb a role in the treatment of *anorexia nervosa*.

Combinations: It will combine well with many bitters, carminatives, and nerviness, depending upon the specific condition and individual.

PREPARATION AND DOSAGE:

Infusion: pour a cup of boiling water onto 1–2 teaspoonfuls of the powdered bark and leave to infuse for 10–15 minutes. This should be drunk three times a day.
Tincture: take 1–2 milliliters of the tincture three times a day.

CORIANDER
Coriandrum sativum
UMBELLIFERAE

Part used: Ripe seeds.
Collection: The flowering heads (umbels) are collected in the late summer and left to ripen. The seeds are then easily collected as they can be shaken off.
Constituents: Essential oil, including coriandrol, fatty oil; tannins; sugar.
Actions: Carminative, aromatic.

INDICATIONS:
This exquisite spice is used medicinally as an herb that helps the digestive system get rid of *wind* and ease the *spasm pain (colic)* that sometimes accompanies it. It will also ease *diarrhea*, especially in children. It may be used as an equivalent to "gripe water," which is usually made from Dill Seeds. The oil acts as a stimulant to the stomach, increasing secretion of digestive juices and thus also stimulating the appetite.

PREPARATION AND DOSAGE:
Infusion: pour a cup of boiling water onto 1 teaspoonful of the bruised seeds and let infuse for five minutes in a closed pot. This should be drunk before meals.

CORN SILK
Zea mays
GRAMINACEAE

Part used: Stigmas from the female flowers of maize or corn. Fine soft threads 4–8 inches (10–20 centimeters) long.
Collection: The stigmas should be collected just before pollination occurs, the timing of which depends upon climate. It is best used fresh as some of the activity is lost with time.
Constituents: Saponins, a volatile alkaloid, sterols, allantoin, tannins.
Actions: Diuretic, demulcent, tonic.

INDICATIONS:
As a soothing diuretic, Corn Silk is helpful in any irritation of the urinary system. It is used for *renal problems in children* and as a urinary demulcent combined with other herbs in the treatment of *cystitis, urethritis, prostatitis*, and the like.

Combinations: With Couch Grass, Bearberry, or Yarrow in the treatment of *cystitis*.

PREPARATION AND DOSAGE:
Infusion: pour a cup of boiling water onto 2 teaspoonfuls of the fresh or dried herb and leave to infuse for 10–15 minutes. This should be drunk three times a day.
Tincture: take 3–6 milliliters of the tincture three times a day.

COUCH GRASS
Agropyron repens
GRAMINACEAE

Part used: Rhizome.
Collection: The rhizome should be unearthed in the spring or early fall. Wash it carefully and dry in sun or shade.
Constituents: Triticin, mucilage, silicic acid, potassium, inositol, mannitol, glycoside, an antimicrobial substance.
Actions: Diuretic, demulcent, antimicrobial.

INDICATIONS:
Couchgrass may be used in urinary infections, such as *cystitis*, *urethritis*, and *prostatitis*. Its demulcent properties soothe irritation and inflammation. It is of value in the treatment of *enlarged prostate glands*. It may also be used in *kidney stones* and *gravel*. As a tonic diuretic, Couch Grass has been used with other herbs in the treatment of *rheumatism*.

Combinations: For *cystitis*, *urethritis*, and *prostatitis*, it may be used with Buchu, Bearberry, or Yarrow. It can be combined with Hydrangea for *prostrate problems*.

PREPARATION AND DOSAGE:
Decoction: put 2 teaspoonfuls of the cut rhizome in a cup of water, bring to the boil, and let simmer for 10 minutes. This should be drunk three times a day.
Tincture: take 3–6 milliliters of the tincture three times a day.

COWSLIP
Primula veris
PRIMULACEAE

Part used: Yellow petals and the root.
Collection: The flower corollae should be gathered, without the green calyx, between March and May. Dry quickly in the shade. The roots should be unearthed either before Cowslip flowers or in the fall. Overcollecting has led to this plant becoming increasingly rare. Only pick if present in abundance and then only pick limited amounts.
Constituents: Up to 10% saponins; glycosides; essential oil; flavonoids.
Actions: Sedative, antispasmodic, expectorant.

INDICATIONS:
Cowslip is an excellent, generally applicable relaxing, sedative remedy. It will ease reactions to *stress* and *tension*, relaxing nervous excitement and facilitating restful sleep. It may be used with safety in *bronchitis*, *colds*, *chills*, and *coughs*. Try it in *nervous headaches* and *insomnia*.

Combinations: For *stress-related problems*, it may be used with any of the relaxing nervines such as Lime Blossom or Skullcap. For *coughs*, it may be used with Coltsfoot and Aniseed.

THE HERBAL

PREPARATION AND DOSAGE:

Infusion for petals: pour a cup of boiling water onto 2 teaspoonfuls of the petals and let infuse for 10–15 minutes. This should be drunk three times a day.

Decoction for root: put 1 teaspoonful of the root in a cup of water, bring to the boil, and simmer for five minutes. Take a cup three times a day.

Tincture: take 2–4 milliliters of the tincture three times a day.

Combinations: For the relief of *cramp*, it may be combined with Prickly Ash and Wild Yam. For *uterine* and *ovarian pains* or *threatened miscarriage*, it may be used with Black Haw and Valerian.

PREPARATION AND DOSAGE:

Decoction: put 2 teaspoonfuls of the dried bark into a cup of water and bring to the boil. Simmer gently for 10–15 minutes. This should be drunk hot three times a day.

Tincture: take 4–8 milliliters of the tincture three times a day.

CRAMP BARK
Viburnum opulus
CAPRIFOLIACEAE

Part used: Dried bark.
Collection: The bark is collected in April and May, cut into pieces, and dried.
Constituents: A bitter called viburnin, valerianic acid, salicosides, resin, tannins.
Actions: Antispasmodic, sedative, astringent.

> **INDICATIONS:**
> Cramp Bark shows by its name the richly deserved reputation it has as a relaxer of *muscular tension* and *spasm*. It has two main areas of use. Firstly in *muscular cramps* and secondly in *ovarian* and *uterine muscle problems*. Cramp Bark will relax the uterus and so relieve *painful cramps* associated with periods (*dysmenorrhea*). In a similar way it may be used to protect from *threatened miscarriage*. Its astringent action gives it a role in the treatment of *excessive blood loss in periods* and especially *bleeding associated with menopause*.

CUCUMBER
Cucumis sativa
CUCURBITACEAE

Part used: Whole fruit, seeds.
Actions: Demulcent, vulnerary, mild diuretic. Seeds: Anthelmintic.

> **INDICATIONS:**
> The seeds of the Cucumber are similar in effect to those of Pumpkin, as they also possess antitapeworm properties. The main use of Cucumber is as a cosmetic. The juice or fresh fruit is cooling, healing, and soothing to the skin.

PREPARATION AND DOSAGE:

For treating *tapeworm infestations*, take 2 ounces (60 grams) of ground seeds and mix them with sugar or honey. This should be taken while fasting and followed after two hours by a cathartic.

CUDWEED
Gnaphalium uliginosum
COMPOSITAE

Part used: Dried aerial parts.
Collection: The plant is collected in August when in flower and should be dried in the shade.
Constituents: Volatile oil.
Actions: Anticatarrhal, astringent, antiseptic, antitussive.

> ### INDICATIONS:
> Cudweed may be used in all cases of *upper respiratory catarrh* or inflammatory conditions, such as *laryngitis*, *tonsillitis*, or *quinsy*. For these last conditions, it may also be used as a gargle.

Combinations: For catarrh, it may be used with Golden Rod.

PREPARATION AND DOSAGE:

Infusion: pour a cup of boiling water onto 1–2 teaspoonfuls of the dried herb and leave to infuse for 10 minutes. This should be drunk three times a day.
Tincture: take 1–4 milliliters of the tincture three times a day.

DAISY
Bellis perenis
COMPOSITAE

Part used: Fresh or dried flower heads.
Collection: The flowers may be picked between March and October.
Constituents: Saponins, tannins, essential oil, flavones, bitter principle, mucilage.
Actions: Expectorant, astringent.

> ### INDICATIONS:
> Daisy, one of our most common plants, is useful for *coughs* and *catarrh*. For all conditions that manifest in these forms, Daisy may be used freely and safely. It has a reputation of value in *arthritis* and *rheumatism*, as well as in *liver* and *kidney problems*. Due to its astringency, it is also useful for *diarrhea*.

Combinations: For *respiratory catarrh*, it may be used with Golden Rod or Coltsfoot.

PREPARATION AND DOSAGE:

Infusion: pour a cup of boiling water onto 1 teaspoonful of the dried herb and leave to infuse for 10 minutes. This should be drunk three or four times a day.
Tincture: take 2–4 milliliters of the tincture three times a day.

THE Herbal

DAMIANA
Turnera aphrodisiaca
TURNERACEAE

Part used: Dried leaves and stems.
Collection: The leaves and stems are gathered at the time of flowering.
Constituents: Essential oil that includes pinene, cineol, cymol, arbutin, cymene, cadinene and copaenen; alkaloids, bitter; flavonoid; cyanogenic glycoside; tannins; resin.
Actions: Nerve tonic, antidepressant, urinary antiseptic, laxative.

INDICATIONS:
Damiana is an excellent strengthening remedy for the nervous system. It has an ancient reputation as an aphrodisiac. While this may or may not be true, it has a definite tonic action on the central nervous and the hormonal system. The pharmacology of the plant suggests that the alkaloids could have a testosterone-like action (testerone is a male hormone). As a useful antidepressant, Damiana is considered to be a specific in cases of *anxiety* and *depression* where there is a sexual factor. It may be used to strengthen the male sexual system.

Combinations: As a nerve tonic, it is often used with Oats. Depending on the situation, it combines well with Kola Nut or Skullcap.

PREPARATION AND DOSAGE:
Infusion: pour a cup of boiling water onto 1 teaspoonful of the dried leaves and let infuse for 10–15 minutes. This should be drunk three times a day.
Tincture: take 1–2 milliliters of the tincture three times a day.

DANDELION
Taraxacum officinale
COMPOSITAE

Part used: Root or leaf.
Collection: The roots are best collected between June and August when they are at their most bitter. Split longitudinally before drying. The leaves may be collected at any time.
Constituents: Glycosides, triterpenoids, choline, up to 5% potassium.
Actions: Diuretic, cholagogue, antirheumatic, laxative, tonic.

INDICATIONS:
Dandelion is a very powerful diuretic, its action comparable to that of the drug Frusemide. The usual effect of a drug stimulating the kidney function is a loss of vital potassium from the body, which aggravates any cardiovascular problem present. With Dandelion, however, we have one of the best natural sources of potassium. It thus makes an ideally balanced diuretic that may be used safely wherever such an action is needed, including in cases of *water retention due to heart problems*. As a cholagogue, it may be used in inflammation and congestion of liver and gallbladder. It is specific in cases of *congestive jaundice*. As part of a wider treatment for *muscular rheumatism*, it can be most effective. This herb is a most valuable general tonic and perhaps the best widely applicable diuretic and liver tonic.

Combinations: For *liver and gallbladder problems*, it may be used with Barberry or Balmony. For *water retention*, it may be used with Couch Grass or Yarrow.

PREPARATION AND DOSAGE:

Decoction: put 2–3 teaspoonfuls of the root into one cup of water, bring to the boil, and gently simmer for 10–15 minutes. This should be drunk three times a day. The leaves may be eaten raw in salads.

Tincture: take 5–10 milliliters of the tincture three times a day.

DEVIL'S CLAW
Harpagophytum procumbens
PEDALIACEAE

Part used: Rhizome.
Collection: This plant grows in Namibia in very arid conditions. The roots are collected at the end of the rainy season.
Constituents: Harpagoside, harpagide, procumbine.
Actions: Anti-inflammatory, anodyne, procumbine.

> **INDICATIONS:**
> This valuable plant has been found effective in the treatment of some cases of *arthritis*. This action appears to be due to the presence of a glycoside called harpagoside that reduces inflammation in the joints. Unfortunately, Devil's Claw is not always effective, but it is well worth considering in cases of *arthritis* where there is inflammation and pain. This plant also aids in *liver* and *gallbladder complaints*.

Combinations: It may be combined with Celery Seed, Buckbean, or Meadowsweet in the treatment of arthritis.

PREPARATION AND DOSAGE:

Decoction: put ½–1 teaspoonful of the rhizome into a cup of water, bring it to the boil, and simmer for 10–15 minutes. This should be drunk three times a day. It should be continued for at least one month.

Tincture: take 1–2 milliliters of the tincture three times a day.

THE HERBAL

DILL

Anethum graveolens

UMBELLIFERAE

Part used: Seeds.
Collection: The seeds should be collected when fully ripe, that is when they have turned brown. They should be spread out to dry, but not in artificial heat.
Constituents: 4% volatile oil, which includes carvone and limonene.
Actions: Carminative, aromatic, antispasmodic, galactogogue.

> **INDICATIONS:**
> Dill is an excellent remedy for *flatulence* and the *colic* that is sometimes associated with it. This is the herb of choice in the *colic of children*. It will stimulate the *flow of milk in nursing mothers*. Chewing the seeds will clear up *bad breath (halitosis)*.

PREPARATION AND DOSAGE:

Infusion: pour a cup of boiling water onto 1–2 teaspoonfuls of the gently crushed seeds and let infuse for 10–15 minutes. For the treatment of *flatulence*, take a cup before meals.
Tincture: take 1–2 milliliters of the tincture three times a day.

ECHINACEA

Echinacea angustifolia

COMPOSITAE

Part used: Cone flower.
Collection: The roots should be unearthed in the fall. It is suggested that the fresh extract is more effective than the dried root.
Constituents: Volatile oil, glycoside, echinaceine, phenolics.
Actions: Antimicrobial, alterative.

> **INDICATIONS:**
> Echinacea is the prime remedy to help the body rid itself of microbial infections. It is effective against both bacterial and viral attacks. It may be used in conditions such as *boils*, *septicemia*, and other infections of that sort. In conjunction with other herbs, it may be used for any infection anywhere in the body. For example, in combination with Yarrow or Bearberry, it will effectively stop *cystitis*. It is especially useful for infections of the upper respiratory tract, such as *laryngitis*, *tonsillitis*, and for *catarrhal conditions* of the nose and sinus. In general, it may be used widely and safely. The tincture or decoction may be used as a mouthwash in the treatment of *pyorrhea* and *gingivitis*. It may be used as an external lotion to help *septic sores* and *cuts*.

Combinations: This useful herb may be combined with many different plants.

PREPARATION AND DOSAGE:

Decoction: put 1–2 teaspoonfuls of the root in one cup of water and bring it slowly to the boil. Let it simmer for 10–15 minutes. This should be drunk three times a day.
Tincture: take 1–4 milliliters of the tincture three times a day.

ELDERBERRY
Sambucus nigra
CAPRIFOLIACEAE

Part used: Bark, flowers, berries, leaves.

Collection: The flowers are collected in the spring and early summer and dried as rapidly as possible in the shade. The bark and berries are best collected in August and September.

Constituents: Flowers: flavonoids, including rutin, isoquercitrine, and kampherol; the hydrocyanic glycoside sambunigrine; tannins; essential oil. Berries: invert sugar; fruit acids; tannin; vitamin C and P; anthrocyanic pigments; traces of essential oil.

Actions: Bark: purgative, emetic, diuretic.
Leaves: Externally emollient and vulnerary, internally as purgative, expectorant, diuretic and diaphoretic. Flowers: Diaphoretic, anticatarrhal. Berries: Diaphoretic, diuretic, laxative.

Combinations: For *colds* and *fevers*, it may be used with Peppermint, Yarrow, or Hyssop. For *influenza*, combine it with Boneset. For catarrhal states, mix it with Golden Rod.

INDICATIONS:
The Elderberry tree is a veritable medicine chest by itself. The leaves are used primarily for *bruises, sprains, wounds,* and *chilblains*. It has been reported that Elderberry Leaves may be useful in an ointment for *tumors*. Elderberry Flowers are ideal for the treatment of *colds* and *influenza*. They are indicated in any catarrhal inflammation of the upper respiratory tract such as *hay fever* and *sinusitis*. *Catarrhal deafness* responds well to Elderberry Flowers. Elderberries have similar properties to Elderberry Flowers with the addition of their usefulness in *rheumatism*.

PREPARATION AND DOSAGE:
Infusion: pour a cup of boiling water onto 2 teaspoonfuls of the dried or fresh blossoms and leave to infuse for 10 minutes. This should be drunk hot three times a day.

Juice: boil fresh berries in water for 2–3 minutes, then express the juice. To preserve, bring the juice to the boil with 1 part honey to 10 parts of juice. Take one glass diluted with hot water twice a day.

Ointment: take three parts of fresh Elderberry Leaves and heat them with six parts of melted Vaseline until the leaves are crisp. Strain and store.

Mrs. Grieves gives an excellent cooling and healing ointment: take 0.5 pound (220 grams) fresh Elderberry Leaves, 0.25 pound (110 grams) fresh Plantain Leaves, 2 ounces (60 grams) Ground Ivy, and 4 ounces (120 grams) fresh Wormwood. Cut into small pieces and heat in 4 pounds (1.8 kilograms) of Vaseline until the leaves are crisp. Strain and press out the ointment for storage.

Tincture: take 2–4 milliliters of the tincture (made from the flowers) three times a day.

ELECAMPANE
Inula helenium
COMPOSITAE

Part used: Rhizome.

Collection: The rhizome should be unearthed between September and October. The large pieces should be cut before drying in the sun or artifically at a temperature of 120–160ºF (50–70ºC).

Constituents: 40% inulin, essential oil called helenin, mucilage, triterpenes, bitter principle.

Actions: Expectorant, antitussive, diaphoretic, stomachic, antibacterial.

> ### INDICATIONS:
> Elecampane is a specific for *irritating bronchial coughs*, especially in children. It may be used wherever there is copious catarrh formed—for example, in *bronchitis* or *emphysema*. This remedy shows the complex and integrated ways in which herbs work. The mucilage has a relaxing effect accompanied by the stimulation of the essential oils. In this way, expectoration is accompanied by a soothing action that in this herb is combined with an antibacterial effect. It may be used in *asthma* and *bronchitic asthma*. Elecampane has been used in the treatment of *tuberculosis*. The bitter principle makes it useful also to stimulate digestion and appetite.

Combinations: Elecampane combines well with White Horehound, Coltsfoot, Pleurisy Root, and Yarrow for respiratory problems.

PREPARATION AND DOSAGE:

Infusion: pour a cup of cold water onto 1 teaspoonful of the shredded root. Let stand for 8–10 hours. Heat up and take very hot three times a day.

Tincture: take 1–2 milliliters of the tincture three times a day.

EPHEDRA
Ephedra sinica
EPHEDRACEAE

Common name: Ma Huang.
Part used: Aerial stems.
Collection: Gather the young branches in the fall before the first frost, as the alkaloid content is then highest. They may be dried in the sun.
Constituents: More than 1.25% alkaloids, which include ephedrine and norephedrine; tannins; saponin; flavone; essential oil.
Actions: Vasodilator, hypertensive, circulatory stimulant, anti-allergic.

> **INDICATIONS:**
> The alkaloids present in Ephedra have apparently opposite effects on the body. The overall action however is one of balance and benefit. It is used with great success in the treatment of *asthma* and associated conditions due to its power to relieve spasms in the bronchial tubes. It is thus used in *bronchial asthma, bronchitis,* and *whooping cough*. It also reduces allergic reactions, giving it a role in the treatment of *hay fever* and other allergies. It may be used in the treatment of *low blood pressure* and *circulatory insufficiency*.

PREPARATION AND DOSAGE:
Decoction: put 1–2 teaspoonfuls of the dried herb in one cup of water, bring it to the boil, and simmer for 10–15 minutes. This should be drunk three times a day.
Tincture: take 1–4 milliliters of the tincture three times a day.

EYEBRIGHT
Euphrasia officinalis
SCROPHULARIACEAE

Part used: Dried aerial parts.
Collection: Gather the whole plant while in bloom in the late summer or fall and dry it in an airy place.
Constituents: Glycosides, including aucubin, tannins, resins, volatile oil.
Actions: Anticatarrhal, astringent, anti-inflammatory.

> **INDICATIONS:**
> Eyebright is an excellent remedy for the problems of mucous membranes. The combination of anti-inflammatory and astringent properties makes it relevant in many conditions. Used internally, it is a powerful anticatarrhal and thus may be used in *nasal catarrh, sinusitis,* and other congestive states. It is best known for its use in conditions of the eye, where it is helpful in acute or chronic inflammations, stinging and weeping eyes, as well as oversensitivity to light. Used as a compress and taken internally, it is used in *conjunctivitis* and *blepharitis*.

Combinations: In catarrhal conditions, it combines well with Golden Rod, Elderberry Flower, or Golden Seal. In allergic conditions where the eyes are affected, it may be combined with Ephedra. As an eye lotion, it mixes with Golden Seal and distilled Witch Hazel.

PREPARATION AND DOSAGE:

Infusion: pour a cup of boiling water onto 1 teaspoonful of the dried herb and leave to infuse for 5–10 minutes. This should be drunk three times a day.

Compress: place a teaspoonful of the dried herb in 1 pint (0.5 liter) of water and boil for 10 minutes, then let cool slightly. Moisten a compress (cotton ball, gauze, or muslin) in the lukewarm liquid, wring out slightly, and place over the eyes. Leave the compress in place for 15 minutes. Repeat several times a day.

Tincture: take 1–4 milliliters of the tincture three times a day.

FALSE UNICORN ROOT

Chamaelirium luteum

LILIACEAE

Part used: Dried rhizome and root.
Collection: The underground parts are unearthed in the fall.
Constituents: Steroidal saponins, which include chamaelirin.
Actions: Uterine tonic, diuretic, anthelmintic, emetic, emmenagogue.

INDICATIONS:

This herb, which comes to us via the Native Americans, is one of the best tonics and strengtheners of the reproductive system that we have. Though primarily used for the female system, it can be equally beneficial for men. It is known to contain precursors of the estrogens (female hormones). However, it acts in an amphoteric way to normalize function. The body may use this herb to balance and tone, and thus it will aid in apparently opposite situations. While being of help in all uterine problems, it is specifically useful in *delayed* or *absent menstruation (amenorrhea)*. Where *ovarian pain* occurs, False Unicorn Root may be safely used. It is also indicated to prevent *threatened miscarriage* and ease *vomiting associated with pregnancy*. However, large doses will cause nausea and vomiting.

PREPARATION AND DOSAGE:

Decoction: put 1–2 teaspoonfuls of the root in a cup of water, bring to the boil, and simmer gently for 10–15 minutes. This should be drunk three times a day. For *threatened miscarriage*, it may be drunk copiously.

Tincture: take 2–4 milliliters of the tincture three times a day.

FENNEL
Foeniculum vulgare
UMBELLIFERAE

Part used: Seeds.
Collection: The seeds should be harvested when ripe and split in the fall. The brown umbel should be cut off. Comb the seeds to clean them. Dry slightly in the shade.
Constituents: Up to 6% volatile oil, which includes anethole and fenchone; fatty oil 10%.
Actions: Carminative, aromatic, antispasmodic, stimulant, galactogogue, rubefacient, expectorant.

INDICATIONS:
Fennel is an excellent stomach and intestinal remedy that relieves *flatulence* and *colic* while also stimulating the digestion and appetite. It is similar to Aniseed in its calming effect on *bronchitis* and *coughs*. It may be used to flavor cough remedies. Fennel will increase the *flow of milk in nursing mothers*. Externally, the oil eases *muscular* and *rheumatic pains*. The infusion may be used to treat *conjunctivitis* and *inflammation of the eyelids (blepharitis)* as a compress.

PREPARATION AND DOSAGE:
Infusion: pour a cup of boiling water onto 1–2 teaspoonfuls of slightly crushed seeds and leave to infuse for 10 minutes. This should be drunk three times a day. To ease *flatulence*, take a cup half an hour before meals.
Tincture: take 2–4 milliliters of the tincture three times a day.

FENUGREEK
Trigonella foenum-graecum
PAPILIONACEAE

Part used: Seeds.
Constituents: Steroidal saponins including diosgenin, alkaloid, 30% mucilage, bitter principle, volatile and fixed oil.
Actions: Expectorant, demulcent, tonic, galactogogue.

INDICATIONS:
Fenugreek is an herb that has an ancient history. It has great use in local healing and reducing inflammation for conditions such as *wounds, boils, sores, fistulas,* and *tumors*. It can be taken to help *bronchitis* and gargled to ease *sore throats*. Its bitterness explains its role in soothing disturbed digestion. It is a strong stimulator of milk production in mothers, for which it is perfectly safe, and has a reputation of stimulating development of the breasts.

PREPARATION AND DOSAGE:
Poultice: for external use, the seeds should be pulverized to make a poultice. Decoction: to increase milk production, gently simmer 1½ teaspoonfuls of the seeds in a cup of water for 10 minutes. Drink a cup three times a day. To make a more pleasant drink, add 1 teaspoonful of Aniseed to this mixture.
Tincture: take 1–2 milliliters of the tincture three times a day.

FEVERFEW
Tanacetum parthenium

Part used: Leaves.
Collection: The leaves may be picked throughout the spring and summer, although just before flowering is best.
Actions: Anti-inflammatory, vasodilatory, relaxant, digestive bitter, uterine stimulant.

INDICATIONS:
Feverfew has regained its deserved reputation as a primary remedy in the treatment of migraine headaches, especially those that are relieved by applying warmth to the head. It may also help arthritis when it is in the painfully active inflammatory stage. Dizziness and tinnitus may be eased, especially if it is used in conjunction with other remedies. Painful periods and sluggish menstrual flow will be relieved by Feverfew.

CAUTION:
Feverfew should not be used during pregnancy because of the stimulant action on the womb. The fresh leaves may cause mouth ulcers in sensitive people.

PREPARATION AND DOSAGE:
It is best to use the equivalent of one fresh leaf one to three times a day. It is best used fresh or frozen.

FIGWORT
Scrophularia nodosa
SCROPHULARIACEAE

Part used: Aerial parts.
Collection: The stalks and leaves are gathered during flowering between June and August.
Constituents: Saponins, cardioactive glycosides, flavonoids, resin, sugar, organic acids.
Actions: Alternative, diuretic, mild purgative, heart stimulant.

INDICATIONS:
Figwort acts in a broad way to help the body function well, bringing about a state of inner cleanliness. If may be used for eczema, psoriasis, and any skin condition where there is itching and irritation. Part of the cleansing occurs due to the purgative and diuretic actions. It may be used as a mild laxative in constipation. As a heart stimulant, Figwort should be avoided where there is any abnormally rapid heartbeat (tachycardia).

Combinations: It will combine well with Yellow Dock and Burdock Root in the treatment of skin problems.

CAUTION:
Avoid in case of abnormally rapid heartbeat (*tachycardia*).

PREPARATION AND DOSAGE:
Infusion: pour a cup of boiling water onto 1–3 teaspoonfuls of the dried leaves and let infuse for 10–15 minutes. This should be drunk three times a day.
Tincture: take 2–4 milliliters of the tincture three times a day.

FLAX
Linum usitatissimum
LINACEAE

Part used: Ripe seeds.
Collection: The seed pods are gathered when fully ripe in September.
Constituents: 30–40% of fixed oil, which includes linoleic, linolenic and oleic acids; mucilage; protein; the glycoside linamarin.
Actions: Demulcent, antitussive, laxative, emollient.

> **INDICATIONS:**
> Flax may be used in all pulmonary infections, especially in *bronchitis* with much catarrh formed. It is often used as a poultice in *pleurisy* and other pulmonary conditions. As a poultice, it can be used for *boils* and *carbuncles, shingles* and *psoriasis*. As a purgative, it relieves *constipation*.

Combinations: As a poultice for the chest, it combines well with Mustard. For *boils, swellings*, and *inflammations*, it combines with Marshmallow Root and Slippery Elm.

PREPARATION AND DOSAGE:

Infusion: pour a cup of boiling water onto 2–3 teaspoonfuls of the dried herb and leave to infuse for 10–15 minutes. This should be drunk morning and evening.
Poultice: For making a poultice, see the section on the preparation of herbs.
Tincture: take 2–6 milliliters of the tincture three times a day.

FRINGE TREE
Chionanthus virginicus
OLEACEAE

Part used: Root bark.
Collection: The roots are unearthed in the spring or fall. Wash carefully and peel the bark. They should be dried with care.
Constituents: Phyllyrin, a lignin glycoside, saponins.
Actions: Hepatic, cholagogue, alterative, diuretic, tonic, antenetic, laxative.

> **INDICATIONS:**
> This valuable herb may be safely used in all liver problems, especially when they have developed into *jaundice*. It is a specific for the treatment of *gallbladder inflammation* and a valuable part of treating *gallstones*. It is a remedy that will aid the liver in general, and as such it is often used as part of a wider treatment for the whole body. Through its action of releasing bile, it acts as a gentle and effective laxative.

Combinations: For the treatment of liver and gallbladder conditions, it may be used with Barberry, Winged Elm (aka Wahoo), or Wild Yam.

PREPARATION AND DOSAGE:

Infusion: pour a cup of boiling water onto 1–2 teaspoonfuls of the bark and leave to infuse for 10–15 minutes. This should be drunk three times a day.
Tincture: take 1–2 milliliters of the tincture three times a day.

FUMITORY
Fumaria officinalis
FUMARIACEAE

Part used: Aerial parts.
Collection: It should be collected when in flower, which is throughout the summer.
Constituents: Alkaloids, bitter principle, mucilage, fumaric acid, amino acids, resin.
Actions: Diuretic, laxative, alterative.

> ### INDICATIONS:
> Fumitory has a long history of use in the treatment of skin problems such as *eczema* and *acne*. Its action is probably due to a general cleansing mediated via the kidneys and liver. Fumitory may also be used as an eyewash to ease *conjunctivitis*.

Combinations: It may usefully be combined with Burdock, Cleavers, or Figwort.

PREPARATION AND DOSAGE:
Infusion: pour a cup of boiling water onto 1–2 teaspoonfuls of the dried herb and let infuse for 10–15 minutes. This may be drunk freely, but for skin problems it should be drunk at least three times a day.
Tincture: take 1–2 milliliters of the tincture three times a day.

GALANGAL
Alpinia officinarum
ZINGIBERACEAE

Part used: Rhizome.
Collection: This herb is cultivated in China, where the rhizomes are unearthed in the late summer and early fall, washed, cut into segments and dried.
Constituents: Volatile oil, acrid resin, galangol, kaempferol, galangin, alpinin.
Actions: Stimulant, carminative.

> ### INDICATIONS:
> Like many other valuable plants, Galangal is used little today. It provides us with a useful stimulating carminative that aids in *flatulence*, *dyspepsia*, and *nausea*, especially where due to a sluggish metabolism. It is reported to help in allaying seasickness. Mrs. Grieve tells us that the Arabs "use it to make their horses fiery."

PREPARATION AND DOSAGE:
Infusion: pour a cup of boiling water onto ½ teaspoonful of the powdered rhizome and leave to infuse for 10–15 minutes. This should be drunk three times a day.
Tincture: take 1–2 milliliters of the tincture three times a day.

GARLIC
Allium sativum
LILIACEAE

Part used: Bulb.
Collection: The bulb with its numerous cloves should be unearthed when the leaves begin to wither in September. They should be stored in a cool, dry place.
Constituents: Volatile oil, mucilage, glucokinins, germanium.
Actions: Antiseptic, antiviral, diaphoretic, cholagogue, hypotensive, antispasmodic.

INDICATIONS:
Garlic is among the few herbs that have a universal usage and recognition. Its daily usage aids and supports the body in ways that no other herb does. It is one of the most effective antimicrobial plants available, acting on bacteria, viruses, and alimentary parasites. The volatile oil is an effective agent, as it is largely excreted via the lungs. It is used in infections of this system such as *chronic bronchitis*, *respiratory catarrh*, *recurrent colds*, and *influenza*. It may be helpful in the treatment of *whooping cough* and as part of a broader approach to *bronchitic asthma*. In general it may be used as a preventative for most infectious conditions, digestive as well as respiratory. For the digestive tract, it has been found that Garlic will support the development of the natural bacterial flora while killing pathogenic organisms. In addition to these amazing properties, it will reduce *blood pressure* when taken over a period of time as well as reducing *blood cholesterol levels*. Garlic should be thought of as a basic food that will augment the body's health and protect it in general. It has been used externally for the treatment of *ringworm* and *threadworm*.

Combinations: For microbial infections, it will combine well with Echinacea.

PREPARATION AND DOSAGE:
A clove should be eaten three times a day. If the smell becomes a problem, use Garlic oil capsules; take three a day as a prophylactic or three times a day when an infection occurs.

GENTIAN ROOT
Gentiana lutea
GENTIANACEAE

Part used: Dried rhizome and root.
Collection: The underground parts are dug up in the fall, sliced, and dried slowly. It is during the drying process that the odor, color, and taste develop.
Constituents: Bitter principles, including gentiopicrin and amarogentine; pectin; tannins; mucilage; sugar.
Actions: Bitter, gastric stimulant, sialagogue, cholagogue.

INDICATIONS:
Gentian is an excellent bitter that, as do all bitters, stimulates the appetite and digestion via a general stimulation of the digestive juices. Thus it promotes the production of saliva, gastric juices, and bile. It also accelerates the emptying of the stomach. It is indicated wherever there is a *lack of appetite* and sluggishness of the digestive system. It may thus be used where the symptoms of sluggish digestion appear, these being *dyspepsia* and *flatulence*. Through the stimulation of the digestion it has a generally fortifying effect.

Combinations: Gentian is often used with other digestives such as Ginger and Cardamom.

PREPARATION AND DOSAGE:
Decoction: put ½ a teaspoonful of the shredded root in a cup of water and boil for five minutes. This should be drunk warm about 15–30 minutes before meals or at any time when acute stomach pains result from a feeling of fullness.
Tincture: take 1–4 milliliters of the tincture three times a day, according to the above guidelines.

GERANIUM (AKA AMERICAN CRANESBILL)
Geranium maculatum
GERANIACEAE

Part used: Rhizome.
Collection: The rhizome is unearthed in September and October, cut into pieces, and dried.

INDICATIONS:
Geranium, or American Cranesbill, is an effective astringent used in *diarrhea, dysentery,* and *hemorrhoids*. When bleeding accompanies *duodenal* or *gastric ulceration*, this remedy is used in combination with other relevant herbs. Where blood is lost in the feces, this herb will help, though careful diagnosis is vital. It may be used where *excessive blood loss during menstruation (menorrhagia)* or a *uterine hemorrhage (metrorrhagia)* occur. As a douche, it can be used in *leukorrhea*.

Constituents: 12–25% tannins, with the level being highest just before flowering.

Actions: Astringent, antihemorrhagic, anti-inflammatory, vulnerary.

Combinations: In *peptic ulcers*, it may be used with Meadowsweet, Comfrey, Marshmallow, or Agrimony. In *leukorrhea*, it can be combined with Trillium (aka Beth Root).

PREPARATION AND DOSAGE:

Decoction: put 1–2 teaspoonfuls of the rhizome in a cup of cold water and bring to the boil. Let simmer for 10–15 minutes. This should be drunk three times a day.

Tincture: take 2–4 milliliters of the tincture three times a day.

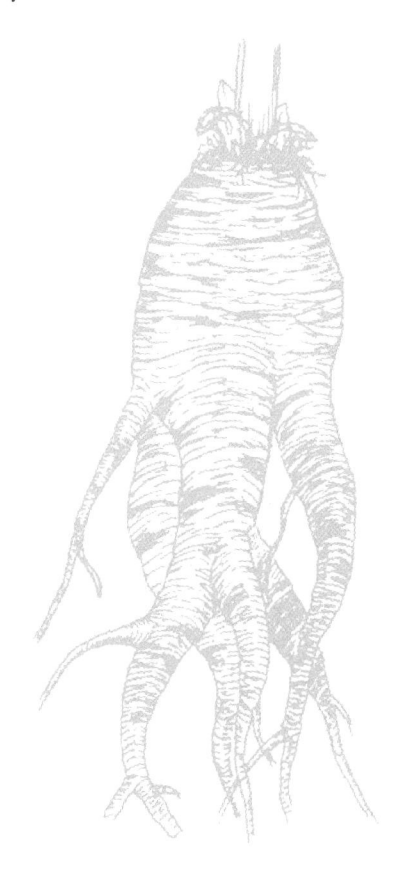

GINGER
Zingiber officinale
ZINGIBERACEAE

Part used: Rootstock.

Collection: The rootstock is dug up when the leaves have dried. The remains of the stem and root fibers should be removed. Wash thoroughly and dry in the sun.

Constituents: Rich in volatile oil, which includes zingiberene, zingiberole, phellandrene, borneol, cineole, citral; starch; mucilage; resin.

Actions: Stimulant, carminative, rubefacient, diaphoretic.

INDICATIONS:

Ginger may be used as a stimulant of the peripheral circulation in cases of *bad circulation*, *chilblains*, and *cramps*. In *feverish conditions*, Ginger acts as a useful diaphoretic, promoting perspiration. As a carminative, it promotes gastric secretion and is used in *dyspepsia*, *flatulence*, and *colic*. As a gargle, it may be effective in the relief of *sore throats*. Externally, it is the base of many *fibrositis* and *muscle sprain* treatments.

PREPARATION AND DOSAGE:

Infusion: pour a cup of boiling water onto 1 teaspoonful of the fresh root and let it infuse for five minutes. Drink whenever needed.

Decoction: if you are using the dried root in powdered or finely chopped form, make a decoction by putting 1½ teaspoonfuls to a cup of water. Bring it to the boil and simmer for 5–10 minutes. This can be drunk whenever needed.

Tincture: the tincture comes in two forms, weak Tincture B.P., which should be taken in a dose of 1.5–3 milliliters three times a day, and the Strong Tincture B.P., which should be taken in a dose of 0.25–0.5 milliliters three times a day.

GINSENG
Panax ginseng
ARALIACEAE

Part used: Root.
Collection: Ginseng is cultivated in China, Korea, and northeastern U.S.A.
Constituents: Steroidal glycosides called panaxosides; sterols; vitamins of D group.
Actions: Antidepressive, increases resistance and improves both physical and mental performance.

> ### INDICATIONS:
> Ginseng has an ancient history and as such has accumulated much folklore about its actions and uses. Many of the claims that surround it are inflated, but it is clear that this is a unique plant. It has the power to move a person to their physical peak, generally increasing vitality and physical performance. Specifically, it will raise *lowered blood pressure* to a normal level. It affects *depression*, especially where this is due to debility and exhaustion. It can be used in general for *exhaustion states* and *weakness*. It has a reputation as an aphrodisiac. Occasionally, the use of this herb may produce headaches.

PREPARATION AND DOSAGE:
The root is often chewed or a decoction may be made. Put ½ teaspoonful of the powdered root in a cup of water, bring to the boil, and simmer gently for 10 minutes. This should be drunk three times a day.

GOAT'S RUE
Galega officinalis
PAPILIONACEAE

Part used: Dried aerial parts.
Collection: The stalks with the leaves and flowers are gathered at the time of flowering, which is between July and August. Dry in the shade.
Constituents: Alkaloids, saponins, flavone glycosides, bitters, tannins.
Actions: Reduces blood sugar, galactogogue, diuretic, diaphoretic.

> ### INDICATIONS:
> Goat's Rue is one of many herbal remedies with the action of reducing blood sugar levels. Its use is thus indicated in the treatment of *diabetes mellitus*. This must not replace insulin therapy, however, and should occur under professional supervision. It is also a powerful galactogogue, stimulating the production and flow of milk. It has been shown to increase milk output by up to 50% in some cases. It may also stimulate the development of the mammary glands.

PREPARATION AND DOSAGE:
Infusion: pour a cup of boiling water onto 1 teaspoonful of the dried leaves and let infuse for 10–15 minutes. This should be drunk twice a day.
Tincture: take 1–2 milliliters of the tincture three times a day.

GOLDEN RAGWORT (AKA LIFE ROOT)
Senecio aureus

COMPOSITAE

Part used: Dried aerial parts.
Collection: The herb should be collected just before the small flowers open in the summer.
Constituents: Alkaloids, including senecifoline, senecine, resins.
Actions: Uterine tonic, diuretic, expectorant, emmenagogue.

INDICATIONS:
As a uterine tonic, Golden Ragwort (aka Life Root) may be used safely wherever strengthening and aid are called for. It is especially useful in cases of menopausal disturbances of any kind. Where there is *delayed* or *supressed menstruation*, Golden Ragwort (aka Life Root) may be used. For *leukorrhea*, it can be used as a douche. It also has a reputation as a general tonic for debilitated states and conditions such as *tuberculosis*.

Combinations: For menopausal problems, it may usefully be combined with St. John's Wort, Oats, or Pasqueflower.

PREPARATION AND DOSAGE:
Infusion: pour a cup of boiling water onto 1–3 teaspoonfuls of the dried herb and leave to infuse for 10–15 minutes. This should be drunk three times a day.
Tincture: take 1–4 milliliters of the tincture three times a day.

GOLDEN ROD
Solidago virgauria

COMPOSITAE

Part used: Dried aerial parts.
Collection: Gather stalks at the time of flowering, which is between July and October, preferably from plants not yet blooming. Dry in the shade or not above a temperature of 100°F (40°C).
Constituents: Saponins, essential oil, bitter principle, tannins, flavonoids.
Actions: Anticatarrhal, anti-inflammatory, antiseptic, diaphoretic, carminative, diuretic.

INDICATIONS:
Golden Rod is perhaps the first plant to think of for *upper respiratory catarrh*, whether acute or chronic. It may be used in combination with other herbs in the treatment of *influenza*. The carminative properties reveal a role in the treatment of *flatulent dyspepsia*. As an anti-inflammatory urinary antiseptic, Golden Rod may be used in *cystitis*, *urethritis*, and the like. It can be used to promote the healing of *wounds*. As a gargle, it can be used in *laryngitis* and *pharyngitis*.

Combinations: For *upper respiratory catarrh*, it may be used with Cudweed, Echinacea, Pokeweed Root, and Wild Indigo.

PREPARATION AND DOSAGE:
Infusion: pour a cup of boiling water onto 2–3 teaspoonfuls of the dried herb and leave to infuse for 10–15 minutes. This should be drunk three times a day.
Tincture: take 2–4 milliliters of the tincture three times a day.

GOLDEN SEAL
Hydrastis canadensis
RANUNCULACEAE

Part used: Root and rhizome.

Collection: Unearth root and rhizome from three-year-old plants in the fall, after the ripening of the seeds. Clean carefully and dry slowly in the air.

Constituents: 5% of the root consisits of the alkaloids hydrastine, berberine, and canadine; traces of essential oil; resin; fatty oil.

Actions: Tonic, astringent, anticatarrhal, laxative, muscular stimulant, oxytocic, bitter.

INDICATIONS:

Golden Seal is one of the most useful herbs available to us. It owes most of its specific uses to the powerful tonic qualities shown toward the mucous membranes of the body. It is thus of service in all digestive problems—for example, in *gastritis, septic ulceration,* and *colitis.* Its bitter stimulation gives it a role in *loss of appetite.* All catarrhal states benefit from Golden Seal, especially *upper respiratory tract catarrh.* The tonic and astringency contribute to its use in uterine conditions such as *menorrhagia (excessive menstruation)* and *hemorrhage.* With the additional stimulation of involuntary muscles, it is an excellent aid during *childbirth,* but for just this reason it should be avoided during pregnancy. Externally, it is used for the treatment of *eczema, ringworm, pruritis (itching), earache,* and *conjunctivitis.*

CAUTION:
As Golden Seal stimulates the involuntary muscles of the uterus, it should be avoided during pregnancy.

Combinations: In stomach conditions, it combines well with Meadowsweet and Chamomile. In *uterine hemorrhage,* it is best combined with Trillium (aka Beth Root). Externally as a wash for *irritation* and *itching,* it combines well with distilled Witch Hazel. As ear drops, it may be combined with Mullein.

PREPARATION AND DOSAGE:

Infusion: pour a cup of boiling water onto ½–1 teaspoonful of the powdered herb and leave to infuse for 10–15 minutes. This should be drunk three times a day.

Tincture: take 2–4 milliliters of the tincture three times a day.

GRAVEL ROOT
Eupatorium purpureum
COMPOSITAE

Part used: Rhizome and root.
Collection: The root and rhizome should be dug up in the fall after the plant has stopped flowering. Wash thoroughly, slice, and dry.
Constituents: Contains up to 0.07% of volatile oil; a yellow flavonoid called euparin; resin.
Actions: Diuretic, antilithic, antirheumatic.

> **INDICATIONS:**
> Gravel Root is used primarily for *kidney stones* or *gravel*. In urinary infections, such as *cystitis* and *urethritis*, it may be used with benefit, while it can also play a useful role in a systemic treatment of *rheumatism* and *gout*.

Combinations: For *kidney stones* or *gravel*, it combines well with Parsley Piert, Pellitory, or Hydrangea.

PREPARATION AND DOSAGE:

Decoction: put 1 teaspoonful of the herb in a cup of water, bring to the boil, and simmer for 10 minutes. This should be drunk three times a day.
Tincture: take 1–2 milliliters of the tincture three times a day.

GREATER CELANDINE
Chelidonium majus
PAPAVERACEAE

Part used: Roots or aerial parts.
Collection: The root should be unearthed in the late summer or fall and dried in the sun or shade. The foliage should be gathered at the time of flowering (May to June) and dried as quickly as possible in the shade.
Constituents: Root: Alkaloids, including chelidonine, chelerythine, coptisine, protopine; chelidonic acid; essential oil; saponin; yellow latex with carotenoid latex.

> **INDICATIONS:**
> At therapeutic doses, Greater Celandine is an excellent remedy for the treatment of *infections of the gallbladder* and *gallstones*. At higher doses, this plant is poisonous, causing powerful purging of the digestive tract. It may be used as an antispasmodic remedy in *stomach pain*. Externally, the orange latex from the stem may be used in the treatment of *verrucae*, *skin tumors*, and *tinea* (a fungal infection of the skin). It has been found that the alkaloid chelidonine inhibits mitosis.

Actions: Antispasmodic, cholagogue, anodyne, purgative, diuretic.

> **CAUTION:**
> Do not exceed the dose given below.

Combinations: In *gallbladder disease*, Greater Celandine combines well with Barberry and Dandelion.

PREPARATION AND DOSAGE:

Decoction: put 2 teaspoonfuls of the herb or 1 teaspoonful of the root in a cup of cold water, bring to the boil, and then remove from the heat. Let stand for 10 minutes. Take one cup twice a day.

NOTE: It is dangerous to exceed this dose.

Tincture: take 1–2 milliliters of the tincture three times a day.

PREPARATION AND DOSAGE:

Infusion: pour a cup of boiling water onto 1 teaspoonful of the dried herb and leave to infuse for 10–15 minutes. This should be drunk three times a day.

Tincture: take 1–2 milliliters of the tincture three times a day.

GRINDELIA

Grindelia camporum

COMPOSITAE

Part used: Dried aerial parts.

Collection: The aerial parts are collected before the flower buds open. They are dried as soon as possible in the sun.

Constituents: Saponins, volatile oil, bitter alkaloids, resin, tannins.

Actions: Antispasmodic, expectorant, hypotensive.

> **INDICATIONS:**
>
> Grindelia acts to relax smooth muscles and heart muscles. This helps explain its use in the treatment of *asthmatic* and *bronchial conditions*, especially where these are associated with a rapid heartbeat and nervous response. It may be used in *asthma*, *bronchitis*, *whooping cough*, and *upper respiratory catarrh*. Because of the relaxing effect on the heart and pulse rate, there may be a reduction in *blood pressure*. Externally, the lotion is used in the *dermatitis caused by poison ivy*.

Combinations: In the treatment of *asthmatic conditions*, it may be used with Lobelia and Pill-Bearing Spurge.

GROUND IVY

Nepeta hederacea

LABIATAE

Part used: Aerial parts.

Collection: The flowering stems should be collected between April and June.

Constituents: Bitter, tannins, volatile oil, resin, saponin.

Actions: Anticatarrhal, astringent, expectorant, diuretic, vulnerary.

> **INDICATIONS:**
>
> Ground Ivy may be used to treat *catarrhal conditions*, whether in the sinus region or in the chest. It will aid in the healing of *coughs* and *bronchitis*, but it works better if combined with other remedies. Where the catarrh has built up in the middle ear and is causing noises (tinnitus), Ground Ivy can prove most beneficial. The astringency of the herb helps in the treatment of *diarrhea* and *hemorrhoids*. It may also be used to treat *cystitis*.

Combinations: For *coughs*, it may be used with Coltsfoot, White Horehound, and Elecampane. For *sinus catarrh*, combine it with Golden Rod.

PREPARATION AND DOSAGE:

Infusion: pour a cup of boiling water onto 1 teaspoonful of the dried leaves and let infuse for 10–15 minutes. This should be drunk three times a day.

Tincture: take 1–4 milliliters of the tincture three times a day.

GUAIACUM
Guaiacum officinale

ZYGOPHYLLACEAE

Part used: Heartwood.
Collection: The resin of the wood exudes naturally and is often collected and used as such; otherwise the heartwood itself is cut into small chips. The tree is found in South America and the Caribbean.
Constituents: Resin acids, including guaiaconic, guaianetic, and guaiacic acid; saponins; polyterpenoid; vanillin.
Actions: Antirheumatic, anti-inflammatory, laxative, diaphoretic, diuretic.

> **INDICATIONS:**
> Guaiacum is a specific for *rheumatic complaints*. It is especially useful where there is much inflammation and pain present. It is thus used in *chronic rheumatism* and *rheumatoid arthritis*, particularly when an astringent is needed. It will aid in the treatment of *gout* and may be used as a preventative of recurrence in this disease.

Combinations: It may be used together with Buckbean, Meadowsweet, or Celery Seed.

PREPARATION AND DOSAGE:

Decoction: put 1 teaspoonful of the wood chips in a cup of water, bring to the boil, and simmer for 15–20 minutes. This should be drunk three times a day.

HARDHACK (AKA STONE ROOT)
Collinsonia canadensis

LABIATAE

Part used: Root and rhizome.
Collection: Roots and rhizome are unearthed in the fall.
Constituents: Saponins, resin, tannins, organic acid, alkaloid.
Actions: Antilithic, diuretic, diaphoretic.

> **INDICATIONS:**
> As its alternative name suggests, Stone Root finds its main use in the treatment and prevention of *stone and gravel in the urinary system and the gallbladder*. It can be used as a prophylactic but is also excellent when the body is in need of help in passing stones or gravel. It is also a strong diuretic.

Combinations: For urinary stone and gravel, it may be combined with Parsley Piert, Gravel Root, Pellitory, or Hydrangea.

PREPARATION AND DOSAGE:

Decoction: put 1–3 teaspoonfuls of the dried root in a cup of water, bring to the boil, and simmer for 10–15 minutes. This should be drunk three times a day.

Tincture: take 2–4 milliliters of the tincture three times a day.

THE HERBAL

HAWTHORN BERRIES
Crataegus oxyacanthoides
ROSACEAE

Part used: Ripe fruit.
Collection: The berries are collected in September and October.
Constituents: Saponins; glycosides; flavonoids; acids, including ascorbic acid; tannins.
Actions: Cardiac tonic, hypotensive.

INDICATIONS:
Hawthorn Berries provide us with one of the best tonic remedies for the heart and circulatory system. They act in a normalizing way upon the heart by either stimulating or depressing its activity depending upon the need. In other words, Hawthorn Berries will move the heart to normal function in a gentle way. As a long-term treatment, they may safely be used in *heart failure* or *weakness*. They can similarly be used in cases of *palpitations*. As a tonic for the circulatory system, they find their primary use in the treatment of *high blood pressure, arteriosclerosis*, and *angina pectoris*. While they can be very effective in the aiding of these conditions, qualified attention is essential.

Combinations: For the treatment of *high blood pressure* and the circulatory system, they can be combined with Lime Blossom, Mistletoe, and Yarrow.

PREPARATION AND DOSAGE:
Infusion: pour a cup of boiling water onto 2 teaspoonfuls of the berries and leave to infuse for 20 minutes. This should be drunk three times a day over a long period.
Tincture: take 2–4 milliliters of the tincture three times a day.

HOPS
Humulus lupulus
CANNABINACEAE

Part used: Flower inflorescence.
Collection: The Hops cones are gathered before they are fully ripe in August and September. They should be dried with care in the shade.
Constituents: Lupulin, bitters, resin, volatile oil, tannins, estrogenic substance.
Actions: Sedative, hypnotic, antiseptic, astringent.

INDICATIONS:
Hops is a remedy that has a marked relaxing effect upon the central nervous system. It is used extensively for the treatment of *insomnia*. It will ease *tension* and *anxiety* and may be used where this tension leads to *restlessness, headaches*, and possibly *indigestion*. As an astringent with these relaxing properties, it can be used in conditions such as *mucous colitis*. It should, however, be avoided where there is a marked degree of depression as this may be accentuated. Externally, the antiseptic action is utilised for the treatment of *ulcers*.

CAUTION:
Do not use in cases with marked depression.

Combinations: For *insomnia*, it can be combined with Valerian and Passion Flower.

PREPARATION AND DOSAGE:

Infusion: pour a cup of boiling water onto 1 teaspoonful of the dried flowers and let infuse for 10–15 minutes. A cup should be drunk at night to induce sleep. This dose may be strengthened if needed.

Tincture: take 1–4 milliliters of the tincture three times a day.

HORSE CHESTNUT
Aesculus hippocastanum
HIPPOCASTANACEAE

Part used: The fruit that is the Horse Chestnut itself.
Collection: The ripe chestnuts should be gathered as they fall from the trees in September and October.
Constituents: Saponins, tannins, flavones, starch, fatty oil, the glycosides aesculin and fraxin.
Actions: Astringent, circulatory tonic.

INDICATIONS:

The unique actions of Horse Chestnut are on the vessels of the circulatory system. It seems to increase the strength and tone of the veins in particular. It may be used internally to aid the body in the treatment of problems such as *phlebitis*, *inflammation in the veins*, *varicosity*, and *hemorrhoids*. Externally, it may be used as a lotion for the same conditions as well as for leg ulcers.

PREPARATION AND DOSAGE:

Infusion: pour a cup of boiling water onto 1–2 teaspoonfuls of the dried fruit and leave to infuse for 10–15 minutes. This should be drunk three times a day or used as a lotion.
Tincture: take 1–4 milliliters of the tincture three times a day.

HORSERADISH
Armoracia rusticana
CRUCIFERAE

Part used: Taproot.
Collection: The roots are collected in the winter and stored in sand.
Constituents: Essential oil that contains mustard oil glycosides; sinigrin.
Actions: Stimulant, carminative, rubefacient, mild laxative, diuretic.

INDICATIONS:

Horseradish is an old household remedy useful wherever a stimulating herb is called for. It can be used in *influenza* and *fevers* as a rough equivalent to Cayenne. It stimulates the digestive process while easing *wind* and *griping pains*. It has been used in cases of *urinary infection*. Externally, it has a stimulating action similar to Mustard Seed. It can be used for *rheumatism* and as a poultice in *bronchitis*.

PREPARATION AND DOSAGE:

The fresh root is often used as a vegetable.
Infusion: pour a cup of boiling water onto 1 teaspoonful of the powdered or chopped root. Leave to infuse for five minutes. This should be drunk three times a day or more often when being used to treat influenza or fevers.

HORSETAIL
Equisetum arvense
EQUISETACEAE

Part used: Dried aerial stems.
Collection: Collect in the early summer. Cut the plant just above the ground, hang in bundles, and dry in an airy place.
Constituents: Silicic acid (a source of silicon); saponin; flavone glycosides; organic acids; nicotine; palustrine.
Actions: Astringent, diuretic, vulnerary.

> **INDICATIONS:**
> Horsetail is an excellent astringent for the genitourinary system, reducing *hemorrhage* and healing *wounds*, thanks to the high silica content. While it acts as a mild diuretic, its toning and astringent actions make it invaluable in the treatment of *incontinence* and *bed-wetting* in children. It is considered a specific in cases of *inflammation or benign enlargement of the prostate gland*. Externally, it is a vulnerary (healing wounds). In some cases, it has been found to ease the pain of *rheumatism* and stimulate the healing of *chilblains*.

Combinations: Horsetail is often combined with Hydrangea in the treatment of *prostate troubles*.

PREPARATION AND DOSAGE:

Infusion: pour a cup of boiling water onto 2 teaspoonfuls of the dried plant and let infuse for 15–20 minutes. This should be drunk three times a day.
Bath: a useful bath can be made to help in *rheumatic pain* and *chilblains*. Allow 3.5 ounces (100 grams) of the herb to steep in hot water for an hour. Add this to the bath.
Tincture: take 2–4 milliliters of the tincture three times a day.

HYDRANGEA
Hydrangea arborescens
SAXIFRAGACEAE

Part used: Dried roots and rhizome.
Collection: The roots should be unearthed in the fall. Clean and slice while still fresh, as they become very hard on drying.
Constituents: Glycosides, saponins, resins.
Actions: Diuretic, antilithic.

> **INDICATIONS:**
> Hydrangea's greatest use is in the treatment of *inflamed* or *enlarged prostate glands*. It may also be used for *urinary stones* or *gravel* associated with infections such as *cystitis*.

Combinations: In *kidney stones*, it is often combined with Parsley Piert, Bearberry, and Gravel Root. In *prostate problems*, it combines well with Horsetail.

PREPARATION AND DOSAGE:

Decoction: put 2 teaspoonfuls of the root in a cup of water, bring to the boil, and simmer for 10–15 minutes. This should be drunk three times a day.
Tincture: take 2–4 milliliters of the tincture three times a day.

HYSSOP
Hyssopus officinalis
LABIATAE

Part used: Dried aerial parts.
Collection: The flowering tops of Hyssop should be collected in August and dried in the sun.
Constituents: Up to 1% volatile oil; flavonoid glycosides; diosmin; tannins.
Actions: Antispasmodic, expectorant, diaphoretic, sedative, carminative.

> ### INDICATIONS:
> Hyssop has an interesting range of uses that are largely attributable to the antispasmodic action of the volatile oil. It is used in *coughs*, *bronchitis*, and *chronic catarrh*. Its diaphoretic properties explain its use in the *common cold*. As a nervine, it may be used in *anxiety states*, *hysteria*, and *petit mal* (a form of epilepsy).

Combinations: It may be combined with White Horehound and Coltsfoot in the treatment of *coughs* and *bronchitis*. For the *common cold*, it may be mixed with Boneset, Elderberry Flower, and Peppermint.

PREPARATION AND DOSAGE:

Infusion: pour a cup of boiling water onto 1–2 teaspoonfuls of the dried herb and leave to infuse for 10–15 minutes. This should be drunk three times a day.
Tincture: take 1–4 milliliters of the tincture three times a day.

ICELAND MOSS
Cetraria islandica
PARMELIACEAE

Part used: The entire plant. It is a lichen.
Collection: The lichen may be gathered throughout the year, though between May and September is perhaps best. It should be freed from attached impurities and dried in the sun or the shade.
Constituents: Rich in mucilage; bitter fumaric acids; usnic acid; some iodine, traces of vitamin A.
Actions: Demulcent, anti-emetic, expectorant.

> ### INDICATIONS:
> As a soothing demulcent with its high mucilage content, Iceland Moss finds use in the treatment of *gastritis*, *vomiting*, and *dyspepsia*. It is often used in respiratory *catarrh* and *bronchitis*. It generally soothes the mucous membranes. In addition, its nourishing qualities contribute to the treatment of *cachexia*, a state of *malnourishment* and *debility*.

Combinations: For the treatment of *nausea* and *vomiting*, it can be combined with Black Horehound.

PREPARATION AND DOSAGE:

Decoction: put 1 teaspoonful of the shredded moss in a cup of cold water, boil for three minutes, and let stand for 10 minutes. A cup should be drunk morning and evening.
Tincture: take 1–2 milliliters of the tincture three times a day.

IPECACUANHA

Cephaelis ipecacuanha

RUBIACEAE

Part used: Root and rhizome.
Collection: The root of this small South American shrub is gathered throughout the year, although the native South Americans collect it when it is in flower during January and February.
Constituents: Alkaloids, including emetine and cephaeline; the glycosidal tannins ipecacuanhic acid and ipecacuanhin; ipecoside; starch; calcium oxalate.
Actions: Expectorant, emetic, sialagogue, antiprotozoal.

INDICATIONS:

Ipecacuanha is mainly used as an expectorant in *bronchitis* and conditions such as *whooping cough*. At higher doses it is a powerful emetic and as such is used in the treatment of *poisoning*. Care must be taken in the use of this herb. After an effective emetic dose has been given, large amounts of water should be taken as well. In the same way that Ipecacuanha helps expectoration through stimulation of mucous secretion and then its removal, it stimulates the production of saliva. It has been found effective in the treatment of *amebic dysentery*.

Combinations: In *bronchial conditions*, Ipecacuanha combines well with White Horehound, Coltsfoot, and Grindelia. In *amebic dysentery*, it may be used with Geranium (aka American Cranesbill) or Echinacea.

PREPARATION AND DOSAGE:

Infusion: as this is a very powerful herb, only a small amount should be used. Only 10–25 milligrams of the herb should be used for an infusion. Pour a cup of boiling water onto a small amount of the herb (equaling the size of a pea) and leave to infuse for five minutes. This can be drunk three times a day. If you need to use it as a powerful emetic, 1–2 grams should be used, which equals ¼–½ teaspoonful when used for an infusion.

IRISH MOSS

Chondrus crispus

RHODOPHYTA

Common name: Carragheen.
Part used: The dried thallus. It is a seaweed.
Collection: It is collected from the rocky coastlines of northwestern Europe, especially Ireland, all year round at low tide.
Constituents: Up to 80% mucilage; carrageenans; iodine; bromine; iron; other mineral salts; vitamin A and B 1.
Actions: Expectorant, demulcent.

INDICATIONS:

The mucilage present in this plant is used in large quantities by the food industry to make jellies or aspic and to be used as a smooth binder. This very property is the basis of its use in digestive conditions where a demulcent is called for, such as *gastritis* and *ulcers*. However, its main use is in respiratory problems such as *bronchitis*. It finds a use in cosmetics as a skin softener.

PREPARATION AND DOSAGE:

Infusion: pour a cup of boiling water onto 1–1½ teaspoonfuls of the dried herb and leave to infuse for 10 minutes. This should be drunk three times a day.
Tincture: take 1–2 milliliters of the tincture three times a day.

JAMAICAN DOGWOOD

Piscidia erythrina

LEGUMINOSAE

Part used: Stem bark.
Collection: The bark is collected in vertical strips from trees growing in the Caribbean, Mexico, and Texas.
Constituents: Glycosides, including piscidin, jamaicin, icthyone; flavonoids, including sumatrol, lisetin, piscerythrone, piscidine, rotenone; resin alkaloid.
Actions: Sedative, anodyne.

> ### INDICATIONS:
> Jamaican Dogwood is a powerful sedative, used in its West Indian homeland as a fish poison. While not being poisonous to humans, the given dosage level should not be exceeded. It is a powerful remedy for the treatment of painful conditions such as *neuralgia* and *migraine*. It can also be used in the relief of *ovarian* and *uterine pain*. Its main use is perhaps in *insomnia* where this is due to nervous tension or pain.

Combinations: For the easing of *insomnia*, it is best combined with Hops and Valerian. For *dysmenorrhea (painful periods)*, it may be used with Black Haw.

PREPARATION AND DOSAGE:

Decoction: put 1–2 teaspoonfuls of the root in a cup of water, bring to the boil, and simmer gently for 10–15 minutes. This should be drunk when needed.
Tincture: take 1–4 milliliters of the tincture three times a day.

JAMBUL

Syzygium cumini

MYRTACEAE

Part used: Dried fruit.
Collection: The fruit of this tree, which grows from India to Australia, is collected in the late summer.
Constituents: Volatile oil, fixed oil, resin containing ellagic acid, tannins.
Actions: Astringent, carminative, reputed hypoglycemic.

> ### INDICATIONS:
> Jambul may be used in *diarrhea* or in any condition where a mild and effective astringent is called for. Its carminative properties, due to the volatile oil, make it ideal for conditions where *diarrhea* is associated with *griping pain*. Jambul has been used in medicine for the treatment of *diabetes*.

PREPARATION AND DOSAGE:

Infusion: pour a cup of boiling water onto 1–2 teaspoonfuls of the seeds and leave to infuse for 10–15 minutes. This should be drunk three times a day.
Tincture: take 1–4 milliliters of the tincture three times a day.

JUNIPER BERRIES
Juniperus communis
CUPRESSACEAE

Part used: Dried ripe berries.

Collection: The ripe, unshriveled berries should be collected in the fall and dried slowly in the shade, to avoid losing the oil present.

Constituents: Rich in essential oil that contains monoterpenes and sesquiterpenes; invert sugar; flavone glycosides; resin; tannins; organic acids.

Actions: Diuretic, antiseptic, carminative, antirheumatic.

INDICATIONS:
Juniper Berries make an excellent antiseptic in conditions such as *cystitis*. The essential oil present is quite stimulating to the kidney nephrons, and so this herb should be avoided in kidney disease. The bitter action aids digestion and eases *flatulent colic*. It is used in *rheumatism* and *arthritis*. Externally, it eases *pain in the joints or muscles*.

CAUTION:
Due to its action on the kidneys, Juniper Berries should be avoided in any kidney disease.

It should also be avoided in pregnancy.

PREPARATION AND DOSAGE:
Infusion: Pour a cup of boiling water onto 1 teaspoonful of lightly crushed berries and leave to infuse for 20 minutes. A cup should be drunk night and morning. For the treatment of *chronic rheumatism*, this treatment should be continued for four to six weeks in the spring and fall.

KOLA NUT
Cola vera
STERCULIACEAE

Part used: Seed kernel.

Collection: The Kola tree grows in tropical Africa and is cultivated in South America. The seeds are collected when ripe and are initially white, turning the characteristic red upon drying.

INDICATIONS:
Kola Nut has a marked stimulating effect on the human consciousness. It can be used wherever there is a need for direct stimulation, which is less often than is usually thought. Through regaining proper health and therefore right functioning, the nervous system does not need such help. In the short term, it may be used in *nervous debility*, in states of *atony* and *weakness*. It can act as a specific in *nervous diarrhea*. It will aid in states of *depression* and may in some people give rise to euphoric states. In some varieties of *migraine*, it can help greatly. Through the stimulation it will be a valuable part of the treatment for *anorexia*. It can be viewed as specific in cases of *depression* associated with weakness and debility.

Constituents: Alkaloids that include more than 1.25% caffeine and theobromine; tannin; volatile oil.
Actions: Stimulant to central nervous system, anti-depressive, astringent, diuretic.
Combinations: Kola Nut will go well with Oats, Damiana, and Skullcap.

PREPARATION AND DOSAGE:

Decoction: put 1–2 teaspoonfuls of the powdered nuts in a cup of water, bring to the boil, and simmer gently for 10–15 minutes. This should be drunk when needed.
Tincture: take 1–4 milliliters of the tincture three times a day.

KOUSSO
Hagenia abyssinica
ROSACEAE

Part used: Flowers and unripe fruit.
Constituents: Volatile oil, bitter principle, koso-toxin.
Actions: Purgative, anthelmintic.

INDICATIONS:
Kousso is an effective treatment for tapeworm. Its action is due to a potent natural chemical that has led to its inclusion in the poisons list in Britain.

PREPARATION AND DOSAGE:

The dosage level given for this herb by Mrs. Grieve are 0.5 ounce (14 grams) of the herb to 1 pint (0.5 liter) of boiling water. This should be taken in 4 fluid ounce (110 milliliter) doses, repeated at two-hourly intervals.

LADY'S MANTLE
Alchemilla vulgaris
ROSACEAE

Part used: Leaves and flowering shoots.
Collection: The leaves and stems are collected between July and August.
Constituents: Tannins, bitter principle, traces of essential oil, salicylic acid.
Actions: Astringent, diuretic, anti-inflammatory, emmenagogue, vulnerary.

INDICATIONS:
This and other species of Alchemilla have been widely used in folk medicine throughout Europe. Lady's Mantle will help reduce *pains* associated with periods as well as ameliorating *excessive bleeding*. It also has a role to play in easing the changes of *menopause*. As an emmenagogue, it stimulates the proper menstrual flow if there is any resistance. Its astringency provides a role in the treatment of *diarrhea* and as a mouthwash for *sores* and *ulcers* and as a gargle for *laryngitis*.

PREPARATION AND DOSAGE:

Infusion: pour a cup of boiling water onto 2 teaspoonfuls of the dried herb and leave to infuse for 10–15 minutes. This should be drunk three times a day. To help *diarrhea* and as a mouthwash or lotion, a stronger dosage is made by boiling the herb for a few minutes to extract all the tannins.
Tincture: take 2–4 milliliters of the tincture three times a day.

LADY'S SLIPPER (AKA MOCCASIN FLOWER)

Cypripedium pubescens

ORCHIDACEAE

Part used: Root.
Collection: Lady's Slipper is an incredibly rare plant in the United Kingdom and United States and so should never be collected if found wild.
Constituents: Volatile oil, resins, glucosides, tannins.
Actions: Sedative, hypnotic, antispasmodic, nervine tonic.

INDICATIONS:

Lady's Slipper is one of the most widely applicable nervines that we posses in the *materia medica*. It may be used in all stress reactions, emotional tension, and anxiety states. It will help elevate the mood, especially where *depression* is present. It can help in easing *nervous pain*, though it is best used in combination with other herbs for this purpose. It is perhaps at its best when treating *anxiety* that is associated with *insomnia*.

Combinations: It combines well with Oats and Skullcap. For *nerve pain*, it may be used with Jamaican Dogwood, Passion Flower, and Valerian.

PREPARATION AND DOSAGE:

Infusion: pour a cup of boiling water onto 1–2 teaspoonfuls of the root and let infuse for 10–15 minutes. This should be drunk as required.
Tincture: take 1–4 milliliters of the tincture three times a day.

LAVENDER

Lavendula officinalis

LABIATAE

Part used: Flowers.
Collection: The flowers should be gathered just before opening between June and September. They should be dried gently at a temperature not above 95ºF (35ºC).
Constituents: The fresh flowers contain up to 0.5% of volatile oil, among other constituents, linalyl acetate, linalol, geraniol, cineole, limonene, and sesquiterpenes.
Actions: Carminative, antispasmodic, antidepressant, rubefacient.

INDICATIONS:

This beautiful herb has many uses, culinary, cosmetic, and medicinal. It is an effective herb for *headaches*, especially when they are related to stress. Lavender can be quite effective in the clearing of *depression*, especially if used in conjunction with other remedies. As a gentle strengthening tonic of the nervous system, it may be used in states of *nervous debility* and *exhaustion*. It can be used to soothe and promote natural sleep. Externally, the oil may be used as a stimulating liniment to help ease *rheumatism*.

Combinations: For *depression*, it will combine well with Rosemary, Kola Nut, or Skullcap. For *headaches*, it may be used with Lady's Slipper or Valerian.

PREPARATION AND DOSAGE:

Infusion: to take internally, pour a cup of boiling water onto 1 teaspoonful of the dried herb and leave to infuse for 10 minutes. This can be drunk three times a day.
External use: the oil should not be taken internally but can be inhaled, rubbed on the skin, or used in baths.

LESSER CELANDINE (AKA PILEWORT)

Ranunculus ficaria

RANUNCULACEAE

Common name: Lesser Celandine, Pilewort.
Part used: Root.
Collection: The root should be unearthed during May and June.
Constituents: Anemonin, protoanemonin, tannins.
Actions: Astringent.

INDICATIONS:

As one would expect from its other name, Pilewort is almost a specific for the treatment of *hemorrhoids*, or *piles*. For this end, it can be taken internally or made into a very effective ointment. It may also be used wherever an astringent is called for.

Combinations: Lesser Celandine (aka Pilewort) combines well with Plantain, Marigold, or Agrimony for the internal treatment of *hemorrhoids*.

PREPARATION AND DOSAGE:

Infusion: pour a cup of boiling water onto 1–2 teaspoonfuls of the dried herb and leave to infuse for 10 minutes. This should be drunk three times a day.
Ointment: The ointment is best made in Vaseline as described in the section on the preparation of herbs.
Tincture: take 2–4 milliliters of the tincture three times a day.

LICORICE

Glycyrrhiza glabra

LEGUMINOSAE

Part used: Dried root.
Collection: The roots are unearthed in the late fall. Clean thoroughly and dry.
Constituents: Glycosides called glycyrrhizin and glycyrrhizinic acid; saponins; flavonoids; bitter; volatile oil; coumarins; asparagine; estrogenic substances.
Actions: Expectorant, demulcent, anti-inflammatory, adrenal agent, antispasmodic, mild laxative.

THE HERBAL

INDICATIONS:

Licorice is one of a group of plants that have a marked effect upon the endocrine system. The glycosides present have a structure that is similar to the natural steroids of the body. The implications of this are discussed in the chapter on the glandular system. They explain the beneficial action that licorice has in the treatment of adrenal gland problems such as *Addison's disease*. It has a wide usage in bronchial problems such as *catarrh*, *bronchitis*, and *coughs* in general. Licorice is used in allopathic medicine as a treatment for *peptic ulceration*, a similar use to its herbal use in *gastritis* and *ulcers*. It can be used in the relief of *abdominal colic*.

Combinations: For bronchitic conditions, it is used with Coltsfoot or White Horehound. For gastric problems, it may be combined with Marshmallow, Comfrey, and Meadowsweet.

PREPARATION AND DOSAGE:

Decoction: put ½–1 teaspoonful of the root in a cup of water, bring to the boil, and simmer for 10–15 minutes. This should be drunk three times a day.

Tincture: take 1–3 milliliters of the tincture three times a day.

LILY OF THE VALLEY
Convallaria majalis

LILIACEAE

Part used: Dried leaves.
Collection: The leaves are gathered at the time of flowering in May and June.
Constituents: Cardiac glycosides, including convallatoxin and convallatoxol; saponins, including convallarin and convallaric acid; asparagin; flavonoids; essential oil with farnesol.
Actions: Cardioactive, diuretic.

INDICATIONS:

Lily of the Valley is perhaps the most valuable heart remedy that the medicinal herbalist uses today. The specifics of its mode of action are discussed in the chapter on herbal pharmacology, but it is well to remember that this herb has an action equivalent to Foxglove (*Digitalis*) without its potential toxic effects. Lily of the Valley may be used in the treatment of *heart failure* and *water retention (dropsy)* where this is associated with the heart. It will aid the body where there is difficulty with breathing due to congestive conditions of the heart.

Combinations: It combines well with Motherwort and Hawthorn.

PREPARATION AND DOSAGE:

Lily of the Valley should only be used under qualified supervision.

LIME BLOSSOM
Tilia europea
TILIACEAE

Common name: Linden.
Part used: Dried flowers.
Collection: The flowers should be gathered immediately after flowering in the midsummer. They should be collected on a dry day and dried carefully in the shade.
Constituents: Essential oil containing farnesol; mucilage; flavonoids; hesperidin; coumarin fraxoside; vanillin.
Actions: Nervine, antispasmodic, diaphoretic, diuretic, mild astringent.

INDICATIONS:
Lime Blossom is well known as a relaxing remedy for use in *nervous tension*. It has a reputation as a prophylactic against the development of *arteriosclerosis* and *hypertension*. It is considered to be a specific in the treatment of *raised blood pressure* associated with *arteriosclerosis* and *nervous tension*. Its relaxing action combined with a general effect upon the circulatory system give Lime Blossom a role in the treatment of some forms of *migraine*. The diaphoresis combined with the relaxation explain its value in *feverish colds* and *flu*.

Combinations: In *raised blood pressure*, it may be used with Hawthorn and Mistletoe, with Hops in *nervous tension*, and with Elderberry Flower in the *common cold*.

PREPARATION AND DOSAGE:
Infusion: pour a cup of boiling water onto 1 teaspoonful of the blossoms and leave to infuse for 10 minutes. This should be drunk three times a day. For a diaphoretic effect in fever, use 2–3 teaspoonfuls.
Tincture: take 1–2 milliliters of the tincture three times a day.

LOBELIA
Lobelia inflata
CAMPANULACEAE

Part used: Aerial parts.
Collection: The entire plant above ground should be collected at the end of the flowering time, between August and September. The seed pods should be collected as well.
Constituents: Alkaloids, including lobeline, lobelidine, lobelanine, isolobelanine; bitter glycosides; volatile oil; resin; gum.
Actions: Respiratory stimulant, anti-asthmatic, antispasmodic, expectorant, emetic.

INDICATIONS:
Lobelia is one of the most useful systemic relaxants available to us. It has a general depressant action on the central and autonomic nervous system and on neuromuscular action. It may be used in many conditions in combination with other herbs to further their effectiveness if relaxation is needed. Its primary specific use is in *bronchitic asthma* and *bronchitis*. An analysis of the action of the alkaloids present reveals apparently paradoxical effects. Lobeline is a powerful respiratory stimulant, while isolobelanine is an emetic and respiratory relaxant, which will stimulate catarrhal secretion and expectoration while relaxing the muscles of the respiratory system. The overall action is a truly holistic combination of stimulation and relaxation!

Combinations: It will combine well with Cayenne, Grindelia, Pill-Bearing Spurge, Sundew, and Ephedra in the treatment of *asthma*.

PREPARATION AND DOSAGE:

Infusion: pour a cup of boiling water onto ¼–½ teaspoonful of the dried leaves and let infuse for 10–15 minutes. This should be drunk three times a day.

Tincture: take ½–1 milliliters of the tincture three times a day.

LUNGWORT HERB
Pulmonaria officinalis
BORAGINACEAE

Part used: Leaves.
Collection: The leaves should be gathered during and after flowering, between March and September.
Constituents: Mucins, silicic acid, tannin, saponin, allantoin, quercetin, kaempferol, vitamin C.
Actions: Demulcent, expectorant, astringent, vulnerary.

INDICATIONS:

Lungwort has two broad areas of use. The one that provides its name is its use in the treatment of *coughs* and *bronchitis*, especially where associated with *upper respiratory catarrh*. The other broad area is that related to its astringency. This explains its use in the treating of *diarrhea*, especially in children, and in easing *hemorrhoids*. As with all plants, these two broad areas must be seen as part of the whole activity of the herb, acting as a unity. Externally, this plant may be used to heal *cuts* and *wounds*.

Combinations: For lung conditions, this herb may be used with White Horehound, Coltsfoot, or Lobelia.

PREPARATION AND DOSAGE:

Infusion: pour a cup of boiling water onto 1–2 teaspoonfuls of the dried herb and leave to infuse for 10–15 minutes. This should be drunk three times a day.

Tincture: take 1–4 milliliters of the tincture three times a day.

LUNGWORT MOSS
Lobaria pulmonaria
STICTACEAE

Part used: Dried lichen.
Collection: This lichen grows on Oak Bark and more rarely on heather stems or mossy rocks.
Constituents: A well-analyzed herb containing arabitol, gyrophoric acid, stictic acid, thelephoric acid, ergosterol, fugosterol; palmitic, oleic, and linoleic acids.
Actions: Expectorant, pulmonary demulcent.

> **INDICATIONS:**
> This lichen has properties that have been recognized in European herbal medicine for many generations. It may be safely used wherever a soothing expectorant is called for. It may be used in all varieties of *bronchitis* and especially where there is an *asthmatic* tendency. It may be used in children's *coughs* with much benefit.

Combinations: Lungwort Moss is often used in combination with Coltsfoot and White Horehound.

PREPARATION AND DOSAGE:
Infusion: pour a cup of boiling water onto 1 teaspoonful of the dried lichen and leave to infuse for 10 minutes. This should be drunk three times a day.
Tincture: take 1–2 milliliters of the tincture three times a day.

MALE FERN
Dryopteris filix-mas
POLYPODIACEAE

Part used: Rhizome freed of root.
Collection: The rhizome is unearthed in the fall.
Constituents: Filicin, filixid acid, tannin, phloroglucin derivatives, traces of essential oil.
Actions: Vermifuge.

> **INDICATIONS:**
> Male Fern is one of the most effective treatments for killing tapeworm. It is, however, potentially poisonous in overdose and should only be used under medical supervision.

MALLOW
Malva sylvestris
MALVACEAE

Part used: Flowers and leaves.
Collection: The flowers and leaves are collected and dried with care between July and September.
Constituents: Mucilage, essential oil, trace of tannin.
Actions: Demulcent, anti-inflammatory, expectorant, astringent.

INDICATIONS:
Mallow may be used in very similar ways to Marshmallow, to which it is generally inferior. Internally, it may be used to aid recovery from *gastritis* and *stomach ulcers*, *laryngitis* and *pharyngitis*, *upper respiratory catarrh*, and *bronchitis*. Externally, it may be used as an addition to bathwater or as a compress against *abscesses*, *boils*, and *minor burns*.

PREPARATION AND DOSAGE:
Infusion: for internal use, pour a cup of boiling water onto 2 teaspoonfuls of the dried herb and leave to infuse for 10–15 minutes. This should be drunk three times a day.
Compress: for external use, put 1 teaspoonful of the herb in a cup of water, bring to the boil, and simmer gently for 10–15 minutes. This decoction can be used for a compress.
Tincture: take 2–4 milliliters of the tincture three times a day.

MARIGOLD
Calendula officinalis
COMPOSITAE

Part used: Yellow petal (florets).
Collection: Either the whole flower tops or just the petals are collected between June and September. They should be dried with great care to ensure there is no discoloration.
Constituents: Saponins, carotenoids, bitter principle, essential oil, sterols, flavonoids, mucilage.
Actions: Anti-inflammatory, astringent, vulnerary, anti-fungal, cholagogue, emmenagogue.

INDICATIONS:

Marigold is one of the best herbs for treating local skin problems. It may be used safely wherever there is an *inflammation on the skin*, whether due to infection or physical damage. If may be used for any *external bleeding* or *wound, bruising,* or *strains*. It will also be of benefit in *slow-healing wounds* and *skin ulcers*. It is ideal for first-aid treatment of *minor burns* and *scalds*. Local treatments may be with a lotion, a poultice, or compress, whichever is most appropriate. Internally, it acts as a valuable herb for *digestive inflammations* or *ulcers*. Thus it may be used in the treatment of *gastric* and *duodenal ulcers*. As a cholagogue, it will aid in the relief of *gallbladder problems* and also through this process help in many of the vague digestive complaints that are called *indigestion*. Marigold has marked antifungal activity and may be used both internally and externally to combat such infections. As an emmenagogue, it has a reputation of helping *delayed menstruation* and *painful periods*. It is in general a normalizer of the menstrual process.

Combinations: For digestive problems, it may be used with Marshmallow Root and Geranium (aka American Cranesbill). As an external soothing application, it can be used with Slippery Elm and any other relevant remedy. A useful antiseptic lotion will be produced by combining it with Golden Seal and Myrrh.

PREPARATION AND DOSAGE:

Infusion: pour a cup of boiling water onto 1–2 teaspoonfuls of the florets and leave to infuse for 10–15 minutes. This should be drunk three times a day.
External use: see the directions in the chapter on the skin.
Tincture: take 1–4 milliliters of the tincture three times a day.

MARJORAM, WILD
Origanum vulgare
LABIATAE

Part used: Aerial parts.
Collection: The herb is gathered as soon as it flowers, avoiding the larger, thicker stalks.
Constituents: Essential oil with thymol, carvacrol; acids; tannins; bitter principle.
Actions: Stimulant, diaphoretic, antiseptic, expectorant, emmenagogue, rubefacient.

INDICATIONS:

Marjoram is a widely used herb in folk remedies and cooking. As a stimulating diaphoretic, it is often used in the treatment of *colds* and *flu*, its use here being similar to the use of Hyssop. The antiseptic properties give it a use in the treatment of mouth conditions as a mouthwash for *inflammations of the mouth and throat*. It may also be used externally for *infected cuts* and *wounds*. The infusion is used in *coughs* and *whooping cough*. *Headaches*, especially when due to tension, may be relieved by a tea of Marjoram or by rubbing the forehead and temples with the oil. The oil may also be used for rubbing into areas of *muscular* and *rheumatic pain*. A lotion may be made that will soothe *stings* and *bites*.

PREPARATION AND DOSAGE:

Infusion: for internal use, pour a cup of boiling water onto 1 teaspoonful of the herb and let infuse for 10–15 minutes. This should be drunk three times a day.
Mouthwash: this is made by pouring 1 pint (0.5 liter) of boiling water onto 2 tablespoonfuls of the herb. It is then left to stand in a covered container for 10 minutes. A gargle is made from this whenever needed by reheating it. Gargle for 5–10 minutes, three to four times a day.
Tincture: take 1–2 milliliters of the tincture three times a day.

MARSHMALLOW
Althaea officinalis
MALVACEAE

Part used: Root and leaf.

Collection: The leaves should be collected in the summer after flowering and the root is unearthed, in the late fall. It is cleaned of root fibers and cork and should be dried immediately.

Constituents: Root: 25–35% mucilage; tannins; pectin; asparagine. Leaf: Mucilage; traces of an essential oil.

Actions: Root: demulcent, diuretic, emollient, vulnerary. Leaf: Demulcent, expectorant, diuretic, emollient.

INDICATIONS:

The high mucilage content of Marshmallow makes it an excellent demulcent that can be used wherever such properties are called for. While having broadly similar effects, the root is used primarily for digestive problems and on the skin, while the leaf is used for the lungs and the urinary system. In all inflammations of the digestive tract, such as *inflammations of the mouth, gastritis, peptic ulcer, enteritis,* and *colitis,* the root is strongly advised. For *bronchitis, respiratory catarrh,* and *irritating coughs,* Marshmallow should be considered. In *urethritis* and *urinary gravel,* Marshmallow Leaf is very soothing. In fact, this herb is very soothing for any mucous membrane irritations anywhere. Externally, the root is indicated in *varicose veins* and *ulcers,* as well as *abscesses* and *boils.*

Combinations: In ulcerative conditions, internal or external, it may be used with Comfrey. For *bronchitis,* use with Licorice and White Horehound. It is often mixed with Slippery Elm to make ointments.

PREPARATION AND DOSAGE:

Decoction: the root should be made into a decoction by putting 1 teaspoonful of the chopped herb into a cup of water and boiling it gently for 10–15 minutes. This should be drunk three times a day.

Infusion: for an infusion of the leaf, pour boiling water onto 1–2 teaspoonfuls of the dried leaf and let infuse for 10 minutes. This should be drunk three times a day also.

Compress: a valuable compress or poultice can be made from this herb.

Tincture: take 1–4 milliliters of the tincture three times a day.

MEADOWSWEET
Filipendula ulmaria
ROSACEAE

Part used: Aerial parts.
Collection: The fully opened flowers and leaves are picked at the time of flowering, which is between June and August. They should be dried gently at a temperature not exceeding 100°F (40°C).
Constituents: Essential oil with salicylic acid compounds called spiraeine and gaultherin; salicylic acid; tannins, citric acid.
Actions: Antirheumatic, anti-inflammatory, stomachic, antacid, anti-emetic, astringent.

> **INDICATIONS:**
> Meadowsweet is one of the best digestive remedies available and as such will be indicated in most conditions, if they are approached holistically. It acts to protect and soothe the mucous membranes of the digestive tract, reducing *excess acidity* and easing *nausea*. It is used in the treatment of *heartburn, hyperacidity, gastritis,* and *peptic ulceration.* Its gentle astringency is useful in treating *diarrhea* in children. The presence of aspirinlike chemicals explains Meadowsweet's action in reducing *fever* and relieving the pain of *rheumatism* in muscles and joints.

PREPARATION AND DOSAGE:

Infusion: pour a cup of boiling water onto 1–2 teaspoonfuls of the dried herb and leave to infuse for 10–15 minutes. This should be drunk three times a day or as needed.
Tincture: take 1–4 milliliters of the tincture three times a day.

MILK THISTLE
Silybum marianum
COMPOSITAE

Part used: Seeds.
Collection: The mature achenes (seed heads) are cut and stored in a warm place. After a few days, tap the heads and collect the seeds.
Constituents: Flavones silybin, silydianin, and silychristin; essential oil; bitter principle; mucilage.
Actions: Cholagogue, galactogogue, demulcent.

> **INDICATIONS:**
> As the name of this herb shows, it is an excellent promoter of milk secretion and is perfectly safe to be used by all breast-feeding mothers. Milk Thistle can also be used to increase the secretion and flow of bile from the liver and gallbladder, and as such it may be used in all problems associated with the gallbladder.

PREPARATION AND DOSAGE:

Infusion: pour a cup of boiling water onto 1 teaspoonful of the dried leaves and let infuse for 10–15 minutes. This should be drunk three times a day.
Tincture: take 1–2 milliliters of the tincture three times a day.

MISTLETOE

Viscum alba

LORANTHACEAE

Part used: Dried leafy twigs.

Collection: The young leafy twigs should be collected in the spring.

> **CAUTION:**
> Do not use the Berries.

Constituents: Viscotoxin (a cardioactive polypeptide), triterpenoid saponins, choline, histamine, antitumor proteins.

Actions: Nervine, hypotensive, cardiac depressant, possibly antitumor.

> **INDICATIONS:**
> Mistletoe is an excellent relaxing nervine indicated in many cases. It will quiet, soothe, and tone the nervous system. This remedy acts directly on the vagus nerve to reduce heart rate while strengthening the wall of the peripheral capillaries. It will thus act to reduce blood pressure and ease *arteriosclerosis*. Where there is *nervous quickening of the heart (nervous tachycardia)*, it may be very helpful. *Headache* due to high blood pressure is relieved by it. It has been shown by current cancer research to have some antitumor activity.

Combinations: It combines well with Hawthorn Berries and Lime Blossom in the treatment of *raised blood pressure*.

PREPARATION AND DOSAGE:

Infusion: pour a cup of boiling water onto 1–2 teaspoonfuls of the dried herb and leave to infuse for 10–15 minutes. This should be drunk three times a day.

Tincture: take 1–4 milliliters of the tincture three times a day.

MOTHERWORT

Leonurus cardiaca

LABIATAE

Part used: Aerial parts.

Collection: The stalks should be gathered at the time of flowering, which is between June and September.

Constituents: Bitter glycosides, including leonurin and leonuridine; alkaloids, including leonuinine and stachydrene; volatile oil; tannins.

Actions: Sedative, emmenagogue, antispasmodic, cardiac tonic.

> **INDICATIONS:**
> The names of this plant show its range of uses. "Motherwort" shows its relevance to *menstrual and uterine conditions*, while *cardiaca* indicates its use in heart and circulation treatments. It is valuable in the stimulation of *delayed* or *suppressed menstruation*, especially where there is anxiety or tension involved. It is a useful relaxing tonic for aiding in *menopausal changes*. It may be used to ease *false labor pains*. It is an excellent tonic for the heart, strengthening without straining. It is a specific for *overly rapid heartbeat* where it is brought about by anxiety and other such causes. It may be used in all *heart conditions* that are associated with anxiety and tension.

PREPARATION AND DOSAGE:

Infusion: pour a cup of boiling water onto 1–2 teaspoonfuls of the dried herb and leave to infuse for

10–15 minutes. This should be drunk three times a day.
Tincture: take 1–4 milliliters of the tincture three times a day.

MOUNTAIN GRAPE
Berberis aquifolium
BERBERIDACEAE

Common name: Oregon Mountain Grape.
Part used: Rhizome and root.
Collection: The underground parts are collected in the fall, carefully cleaned, cut into slices, and dried.
Constituents: Alkaloids, including berberine, oxyacanthine, and berbamine.
Actions: Alterative, cholagogue, laxative, anti-emetic, anticatarrhal, tonic.

INDICATIONS:
Mountain Grape is similar in action to both Golden Seal and Barberry. It finds its main use in the treatment of chronic and scaly skin conditions such as *psorasis* and *eczema*. As skin problems of this sort are due to systemic causes within the body, the tonic activity of Mountain Grape on the liver and gallbladder may explain its potency. It can be used in *stomach and gallbladder conditions*, especially where there is associated *nausea* and *vomiting*. As a laxative, it may safely be used in *chronic constipation*.

Combinations: For skin problems, it will combine well with Burdock Root, Yellow Dock, and Cleavers. For gallbladder problems, it may be used with Black Root and Fringe Tree Bark.

PREPARATION AND DOSAGE:
Decoction: put 1–2 teaspoonfuls of the root in a cup of water, bring to the boil, and simmer for 10–15 minutes. This should be drunk three times a day.
Tincture: take 1–4 milliliters of the tincture three times a day.

MOUSE-EAR
Pilosella officinarum
COMPOSITAE

Common name: Hawkweed.
Part used: Aerial parts.
Collection: Mouse-Ear should be collected when in flower between May and June.
Constituents: The coumarin umbelliferone; flavones and flavonoids; caffeic acid; chlorogenic acid.
Actions: Antispasmodic, expectorant, anticatarrhal, astringent, sialagogue, vulnerary.

INDICATIONS:
Mouse-Ear, named after the shape of the leaf, is one of the ancient traditional herbs of England and Wales. It is used for *respiratory problems* where there is a lot of mucus being formed with soreness and possibly even the coughing of blood. It is considered a specific in cases of *whooping cough*. It may also be found beneficial in *bronchitis* or *bronchitic asthma*. Externally, it may be used as a poultice to aid *wound healing* or specifically to treat *hernias* and *fractures*.

Combinations: For *whooping cough*, it may be used with Sundew, White Horehound, Mullein, or Coltsfoot.

THE HERBAL

PREPARATION AND DOSAGE:
Infusion: pour a cup of boiling water onto 1–2 teaspoonfuls of the dried herb and leave to infuse for 10–15 minutes. This should be drunk three times a day.
Tincture: take 1–4 milliliters of the tincture three times a day.

> INDICATIONS:
> Mugwort can be used wherever a digestive stimulant is called for. It will aid the digestion through the bitter stimulation of the juices while also providing a carminative oil. It has a mildly nervine action in aiding *depression* and easing *tension*, which appears to be due to the volatile oil, so it is essential that this is not lost in preparation. Mugwort may also be used as an emmenagogue in the aiding of normal menstrual flow.

PREPARATION AND DOSAGE:
Infusion: pour a cup of boiling water onto 1–2 teaspoonfuls of the dried herb and leave to infuse for 10–15 minutes in a covered container. This should be drunk three times a day. Mugwort is used as a flavoring in a number of aperitif drinks—a pleasant way to take it!
Tincture: take 1–4 milliliters of the tincture three times a day.

MUGWORT
Artemisia vulgaris
COMPOSITAE

Part used: Leaves or root.
Collection: The leaves and flowering stalks should be gathered just at blossoming time, which is between July and September.
Constituents: Volatile oil containing cineole and thujone; a bitter principle, tannins, resin, inulin.
Actions: Bitter tonic, stimulant, nervine tonic, emmenagogue.

MULLEIN
Verbascum thapsus
SCROPHULARIACEAE

Part used: Dried leaves and flowers.
Collection: The leaves should be collected in the midsummer before they turn brown. Dry them in the shade. The flowers should be gathered between July and September during dry weather. They should be dried in the shade or with artificial heat not higher than 100°F (40°C). The flowers turn brown in the presence of moisture and become ineffective.
Constituents: Mucilage and gum; saponins; volatile oil; flavonoids, including hesperidin and verbascoside; glycosides, including aucubin.

Actions: Expectorant, demulcent, mild diuretic, mild sedative, vulnerary.

> ### INDICATIONS:
> Mullein is a very beneficial respiratory remedy useful in most conditions that affect this vital system. It is an ideal remedy for toning the mucous membranes of the respiratory system, reducing inflammation while stimulating fluid production and thus facilitating expectoration. It is considered a specific in *bronchitis* where there is a hard cough with soreness. Its anti-inflammatory and demulcent properties indicate its use in *inflammation of the trachea* and associated conditions. Externally, an extract made in olive oil is excellent in soothing and healing any inflamed surface.

Combinations: In *bronchitis*, it combines well with White Horehound, Coltsfoot, and Lobelia.

PREPARATION AND DOSAGE:

Infusion: pour a cup of boiling water onto 1–2 teaspoonfuls of the dried leaves or flowers and let infuse for 10–15 minutes. This should be drunk three times a day.

Tincture: take 1–4 milliliters of the tincture three times a day.

MUSTARD

Brassica alba and Brassica nigra

CRUCIFERAE

Part used: Seeds.
Collection: The ripe seed pods are collected in the late summer. Tap the seeds out and dry in a thin layer.
Constituents: Mucilage, fixed oil, volatile oil, sinigrin.
Actions: Rubefacient, irritant, stimulant, diuretic, emetic.

> ### INDICATIONS:
> This well-known spice has its main use in medicine as a stimulating external application. The rubefacient action causes a mild irritation to the skin, stimulating the circulation to that area and relieving *muscular and skeletal pain*. Its stimulating, diaphoretic action can be utilized in the way that Cayenne and Ginger are. For *feverishness, colds*, and *influenza*, Mustard may be taken as a tea or ground and sprinkled into a bath. The stimulation of circulation will aid *chilblains* as well as the conditions already mentioned. An infusion or poultice of Mustard will aid in cases of *bronchitis*.

THE HERBAL

PREPARATION AND DOSAGE:

Poultice: Mustard is most commonly used as a poultice, which can be made by mixing 4 ounces (100 grams) of freshly ground Mustard seeds with warm water (at about 110°F/45°C) to form a thick paste. This is spread on a piece of cloth the size of the body area that is to be covered. To stop the paste from sticking to the skin, lay a dampened gauze on the skin. Apply the cloth and remove after one minute. The skin may be reddened by this treatment, which can be eased by applying olive oil afterward.

Infusion: pour a cup of boiling water onto 1 teaspoonful of Mustard flour and leave to infuse for five minutes. This may be drunk three times a day.

Foot bath: make an infusion using 1 tablespoon of bruised seeds to 2 pints (1 liter) of boiling water.

MYRRH

Commiphora molmol

BURSERACEAE

Part used: Gum resin.

Collection: The gum resin is collected from the bushes that secrete it in the arid regions of East Africa and Arabia.

Constituents: Up to 17% essential oil, up to 40% resin, gums.

Actions: Antimicrobial, astringent, carminative, anti-catarrhal, expectorant, vulnerary.

Combinations: It will combine well with Echinacea for infections and as a mouthwash for *ulcers* and similar problems. For external use, it should be combined with distilled Witch Hazel.

INDICATIONS:

Myrrh is an effective antimicrobial agent that has been shown to work in two complementary ways. Primarily, it stimulates the production of white blood corpuscles (with their antipathogenic actions), and secondarily, it has a direct antimicrobial effect. Thus the herb will aid and support the natural process of defense, a vital activity, as so often today antibiotic drugs do this work for the body. Myrrh may be used in a wide range of conditions where an antimicrobial agent is needed. It finds specific use in the treatment of infections in the mouth such as *mouth ulcers, gingivitis, pyorrhea*, as well as the catarrhal problems of *pharyngitis* and *sinusitis*. It may also help with *laryngitis* and *respiratory complaints*. Systemically it is of value in the treatment of *boils* and similar conditions as well as *glandular fever* and *brucellosis*. It is often used as part of an approach to the treatment of the *common cold*. Externally, it will be healing and antiseptic for *wounds* and *abrasions*.

PREPARATION AND DOSAGE:

Infusion: as the resin only dissolves in water with difficulty, it should be powdered well to make an infusion. Pour a cup of boiling water onto 1–2 teaspoonfuls of the powder and leave to infuse for 10–15 minutes. This should be drunk three times a day.

Tincture: as the resin dissolves much more easily in alcohol, the tincture is preferable and easily obtainable. Take 1–4 milliliters of the tincture three times a day.

NASTURTIUM
Tropaeolum majus
TROPAEOLACEAE

Part used: Aerial parts.
Collection: The leaves and flowers should be collected between July and October.
Constituents: Glucosilinates, unknown antibacterial substance, vitamin C.
Actions: Antimicrobial.

> **INDICATIONS:**
> Nasturtium is quite a powerful antimicrobial, especially when used as a local remedy for the treatment of bacterial infection. Internally, it can be used with benefit in any bacterial infection but it is especially indicated for respiratory infections such as *bronchitis*. It has been found to be beneficial in *influenza* and the *common cold*. Some herbalists report it to be indicated in *infections of the female reproductive organs*.

PREPARATION AND DOSAGE:
Nasturtium is most effective when fresh. Use it externally as a poultice or compress. To make an infusion: pour a cup of boiling water onto 1–2 teaspoonfuls of the fresh leaves and let infuse for 10–15 minutes. This should be drunk three times a day.
Tincture: take 1–4 milliliters of the tincture three times a day.

NETTLE
Urtica dioica
URTICACEA

Part used: Aerial parts.
Collection: The herb should be collected when the flowers are in bloom.
Constituents: Histamine, formic acid, chlorophyll, glucoquinine, iron, vitamin C.
Actions: Astringent, diuretic, tonic.

> **INDICATIONS:**
> Nettles are one of the most widely applicable plants we have. They strengthen and support the whole body. They are beneficial in all the varieties of *eczema*, especially in *nervous eczema*. As an astringent, they may be used for *nosebleeds* or to relieve the symptoms wherever there is *hemorrhage* in the body—for example, in *uterine hemorrhage*.

Combinations: Nettles will combine well with Figwort and Burdock in the treatment of *eczema*.

PREPARATION AND DOSAGE:
Infusion: pour a cup of boiling water onto 1–3 teaspoonfuls of the dried herb and leave to infuse for 10–15 minutes. This should be drunk three times a day.
Tincture: take 1–4 milliliters of the tincture three times a day.

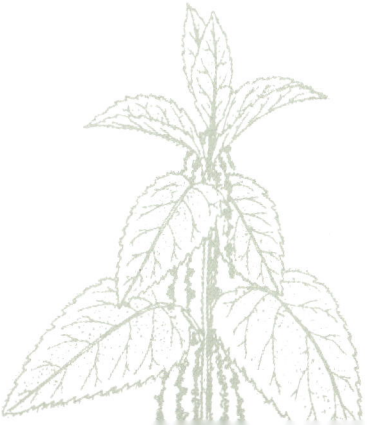

NIGHT-BLOOMING CEREUS

Selenicereus grandiflorus

CACTACEAE

Part used: Fresh stem.
Actions: Cardiac tonic, diuretic.

> **INDICATIONS:**
> This herb has an excellent reputation as a heart tonic, especially for problems related to *nerves* and *debility*. However, it is virtually unobtainable in Great Britain today, and in the United States, where it may be protected in the wild in certain desert areas, requiring a permit to collect it.

OAK BARK

Quercus robur

FAGACEAE

Part used: Bark.
Collection: The young bark is carefully pared from the trunk or from branches that are not more than 4 inches (10 centimeters) thick. Take care to only take off patches, never to take a whole ring around the trunk, which would kill the tree. The bark is collected in April or May. It must be smooth and free from blemishes.
Constituents: Up to 20% tannins, gallic acid, ellagitannin.
Actions: Astringent, anti-inflammatory, antiseptic.
Combinations: It is often given with Ginger before meals.

> **INDICATIONS:**
> Oak Bark may be used wherever an effective astringent is called for—for example, *diarrhea*, *dysentery*, or *hemorrhoids*. As a gargle, the decoction can be used in *tonsillitis*, *pharyngitis*, and *laryngitis*. It can be used as an enema for the treatment of *hemorrhoids* and as a douche for *leukorrhea*. It is primarily indicated for use in acute *diarrhea*, taken in frequent small doses.

PREPARATION AND DOSAGE:

Decoction: put 1 teaspoonful of the bark in a cup of water, bring to the boil, and simmer gently for 10–15 minutes. This can be drunk three times a day.
Tincture: take 1–2 milliliters of the tincture three times a day.

OATS

Avena sativa

GRAMINEAE

Part used: Seeds and whole plant.

Collection: The fruit and straw are gathered at harvest time, in August about four weeks after the rye harvest. The stalks are cut and bound together. Leave them upright to dry and then thresh out the fruit. The straw is just the crushed dry stalks.

Constituents: Seeds: 50% starch; alkaloids, including trigonelline and avenine; saponins; flavones; sterols; vitamin B. Plant straw: Rich in silicic acid; mucin; calcium.

Actions: Nervine tonic, antidepressant, nutritive, demulcent, vulnerary.

INDICATIONS:

Oats is one of the best remedies for "feeding" the nervous system, especially when under stress. It is considered a specific in cases of *nervous debility* and *exhaustion* when associated with *depression*. It may be used with most of the other nervines, both relaxant and stimulatory, to strengthen the whole of the nervous system. It is also used in *general debility*. The high levels of silicic acid in the straw will explain its use as a remedy for skin conditions, especially in external applications.

Combinations: For *depression*, it may be used with Skullcap and Lady's Slipper.

PREPARATION AND DOSAGE:

Oats may most conveniently be taken in the form of porridge or gruel.

Fluid extract: in liquid form it is most often given as a fluid extract. Take 3–5 milliliters three times a day.

Bath: a soothing bath for use in *neuralgia* and irritated skin conditions can be made: 1 pound (500 grams) of shredded straw is boiled in 4 pints (2 liters) of water for half an hour. The liquid is strained and added to the bath.

PANSY

Viola tricolor

VIOLACEAE

Common name: Heartsease.

Part used: Aerial parts.

Collection: The herb can be collected throughout its growing season from March to August.

Constituents: Salicylates, saponins, alkaloid, flavonoids, tannind, mucilage.

Actions: Expectorant, diuretic, anti-inflammatory, anti-rheumatic, laxative.

INDICATIONS:

Pansy is used mostly in three areas, the skin, lungs, and urinary system. It may be used in *eczema* and other skin problems where there is exudate (often called weeping) *eczema*. As an anti-inflammatory expectorant, it is used for *whooping cough* and acute *bronchitis* where it will soothe and help the body heal itself. For urinary problems, it will aid in the healing of *cystitis* and can be used to treat the symptoms of *frequent* and *painful urination*.

Combinations: For lung conditions, Pansy may be used with Coltsfoot. For skin problems, use it with Red Clover, Nettles, and Cleavers. For *cystitis*, combine it with Couchgrass and Buchu.

PREPARATION AND DOSAGE:

Infusion: pour a cup of boiling water onto 1–2 teaspoonfuls of the dried herb and leave to infuse for 10–15 minutes. This should be drunk three times a day.

Tincture: take 2–4 milliliters of the tincture three times a day.

PARSLEY
Petroselinum crispum
UMBELLIFERAE

Part used: Taproot, leaves, and seeds.
Collection: The root is collected in the fall from two-year-old plants. The leaves can be used any time during the growing season.
Constituents: Essential oil, including apiol and myristicin, vitamin C, glycoside apiin, starch.
Actions: Diuretic, expectorant, emmenagogue, carminative, supposed aphrodisiac.

INDICATIONS:

The fresh herb, so widely used in cookery, is one of our richest sources of vitamin C. Medicinally, Parsley has three main areas of usage. Firstly, it is an effective diuretic, helping the body get rid of excess water and so may be used wherever such an effect is desired. Remember, however, that the cause of the problem must be sought and treated—don't just treat symptoms. The second area of use is as an emmenagogue stimulating the menstrual process. It is advisable not to use Parsley in medicinal dosage during pregnancy as there may be excessive stimulation of the womb. The third use is as a carminative, easing *flatulence* and the *colic pains* that may accompany it.

CAUTION:
Do not use during *pregnancy* in medicinal dosage.

PREPARATION AND DOSAGE:

Infusion: pour a cup of boiling water onto 1–2 teaspoonfuls of the leaves or root and let infuse for 5–10 minutes in a closed container. This should be drunk three times a day.

Tincture: take 2–4 milliliters of the tincture three times a day.

PARSLEY PIERT
Aphanes arvensis
ROSACEAE

Part used: Aerial parts.
Collection: It should be collected in the summer when in flower.
Constituents: Tannins.
Actions: Diuretic, demulcent, antilithic.

INDICATIONS:

This delicate little plant is commonly used for the removal of *kidney* and *urinary stones* and *gravel*. Through its potent diuretic action associated with soothing demulcence of the urinary tract, it will help in all cases of *painful urination*. It may be used where there is *water retention*, especially where this is due to kidney or liver problems.

Combinations: It will combine well with Pellitory or Buchu in cases of *kidney stones* or *gravel*.

PREPARATION AND DOSAGE:

Infusion: pour a cup of boiling water onto 1–2 teaspoonfuls of the dried herb and leave to infuse for 10–15 minutes. This should be drunk three times a day.
Tincture: take 2–4 milliliters of the tincture three times a day.

PARTRIDGE VINE (AKA SQUAW VINE)
Mitchella repens

RUBIACEAE

Part used: Aerial parts.
Collection: Being an evergreen herb, it may be found all year round in the forest and woodland habitat it likes. It is best collected in flower between April and June.
Constituents: Saponins, mucilage.
Actions: Parturient, emmenagogue, diuretic, astringent, tonic.

INDICATIONS:
Partridge Vine (aka Squaw Vine) is one of the herbs brought to us via the Native Americans. It is among the best remedies for preparing the uterus and whole body for childbirth. For this purpose, it should be taken for some weeks before the child is due, thus ensuring a safe and wonderful birth for both of you. It may also be used for the relief of *painful periods (dysmenorrhea)*. As an astringent, it has been used in the treatment of *colitis*, especially if there is much mucus.

Combinations: As parturient to prepare for childbirth, it may be used with Raspberry Leaves. For *dysmenorrheal*, it could be combined with Cramp Bark and Pasqueflower.

PREPARATION AND DOSAGE:

Infusion: pour a cup of boiling water onto 1 teaspoonful of the herb and let infuse for 10–15 minutes. This should be drunk three times a day.
Tincture: take 1–2 milliliters of the tincture three times a day.

PASQUEFLOWER
Anemone pulsatilla

RANUNCULACEAE

Part used: Aerial parts.
Collection: The stalks should be gathered at the time of flowering, which is in March or April.
Constituents: Glycosides, saponins, tannins, resin.
Actions: Sedative, analgesic, antispasmodic, antibacterial.

INDICATIONS:
Pasqueflower is an excellent relaxing nervine for use in problems relating to nervous tension and spasm in the reproductive system. It may be used with safety in the relief of *painful periods (dysmenorrhea)*, *ovarian pain*, and *painful conditions of the testes*. It may be used to reduce *tension reactions* and *headaches* associated with them. It will help *insomnia* and general *overactivity*. The antibacterial actions give this herb a role in treating infections that affect the skin, especially *boils*. It is similarly useful in the treatment of *respiratory infections* and *asthma*. The oil or tincture will ease *earache*.

THE HERBAL

Combinations: For *painful periods*, it will combine well with Cramp Bark. For *skin conditions*, it combines with Echinancea.

> **CAUTION:**
> Do not use the fresh plant!

PREPARATION AND DOSAGE:
Infusion: pour a cup of boiling water onto ½–1 teaspoonful of the dried herb and leave to infuse for 10–15 minutes. This should be drunk three times a day or when needed.
Tincture: take 1–2 milliliters of the tincture three times a day.

PASSION FLOWER
Passiflora incarnata
PASSIFLORACEAE

Part used: Dried leaves.
Collection: If the foliage alone is to be collected, this should happen just before the flowers bloom, between May and July. The foliage may be collected with the fruit after flowering. It should be dried in the shade.
Constituents: Alkaloids, including harmine, harman, harmol, and passiflorine; flavone glycosides; sterols.
Actions: Sedative, hypnotic, antispasmodic, anodyne.
Combinations: For *insomnia*, it will combine well with Valerian, Hops, and Jamaican Dogwood.

> **INDICATIONS:**
> Passion Flower is the herb of choice for treating *intransigent insomnia*. It aids the transition into a restful sleep without any "narcotic" hangover. It may be used wherever an antispasmodic is required—for example, in *Parkinson's disease, seizures,* and *hysteria*. It can be very effective in nerve pain such as *neuralgia* and the viral infection of nerves called *shingles*. It may be used in *asthma* where there is much spasmodic activity, especially when there is associated tension.

PREPARATION AND DOSAGE:
Infusion: pour a cup of boiling water onto 1 teaspoonful of the dried herb and let infuse for 15 minutes. Drink a cup in the evening for sleeplessness and a cup twice a day for the easing of other conditions.
Tincture: take 1–4 milliliters of the tincture and use the same way as the infusion.

PEACH
Prunus persica
ROSACEAE

Part used: Leaves or bark.
Collection: The bark is collected in the spring by stripping it from young trees. The leaves are collected in June and July.
Actions: Demulcent, sedative, diuretic, expectorant.

> **INDICATIONS:**
> The leaves of this tree, which gives us that most pleasant fruit, the peach, provide a useful soothing demulcent to aid the digestive tract in conditions such as *gastritis*. It has a tradition of also being used in *whooping cough* and *bronchitis*.

PREPARATION AND DOSAGE:

Infusion: pour a cup of boiling water onto 1 teaspoonful of the bark or 2 teaspoonfuls of the leaves and let infuse for 10 minutes. This should be drunk three times a day.

PREPARATION AND DOSAGE:

Infusion: pour a cup of boiling water onto 1–2 teaspoonfuls of the dried herb and leave to infuse for 10–15 minutes. This should be drunk three times a day.
Tincture: take 2–4 milliliters of the tincture three times a day.

PELLITORY, OR PELLITORY OF THE WALL
Parietaria diffusa
URTICACEAE

Part used: Aerial parts.
Collection: The parts above ground are collected between June and September.
Constituents: Bitter principle, tannins.
Actions: Diuretic, demulcent.

INDICATIONS:
Pellitory may be used in the treatment of any inflammation of the urinary system and especially where soothing is needed. It may be used with benefit in *cystitis* and *pyelitis*. It is a good general diuretic which is used to relieve water retention where it is due to kidney-based causes. It has a valuable role to play in the treatment of *kidney stone* or *gravel*.

Combinations: It combines well with Parsley Piert, Buchu, Bearberry, or Juniper.

PENNYROYAL
Mentha pulegium
LABIATAE

Part used: Aerial parts.
Collection: The stems should be gathered just before flowering in July.
Constituents: Volatile oil, tannins, flavone glycosides.
Actions: Carminative, diaphoretic, stimulant, emmenagogue.

INDICATIONS:
With its richly aromatic volatile oil, Pennyroyal will ease *flatulence* and *abdominal colic* due to wind. It will relax *spasmodic pain* and ease *anxiety*. However, its main use is as an emmenagogue to stimulate the menstrual process and to strengthen uterine contractions. As it has been used in large doses as an abortifacient, it should be avoided during pregnancy. The oil should be avoided as it can act far too strongly.

CAUTION:
Avoid during pregnancy.

THE HERBAL

PREPARATION AND DOSAGE:
Infusion: pour a cup of boiling water onto 1–2 teaspoonfuls of the dried leaves and let infuse for 10–15 minutes. This should be drunk three times a day.
Tincture: take 1–2 milliliters of the tincture three times a day.

PENNYWORT
Umbilicus rupestris
CRASSULACEAE

Common name: Navelwort.
Part used: Fresh leaves.
Actions: Demulcent, anodyne.

INDICATIONS:
I have found Pennywort to be a specific in *earache*, while coming across no references to this in the herbal literature. The fresh leaves are pressed to extract the juice, which can be easily done in a metal sieve. The juice, abundant in the succulent leaves, is introduced into the ear and kept in place by a plug of a cotton ball. I have observed rapid and complete easing of the severe pain of earache in a very short time this way. This remedy may be safely used even with very young children. It is inadvisable if there is a suspicion of damage to the eardrum.

PEPPERMINT
Mentha piperita
LABIATAE

Part used: Aerial parts.
Collection: The aerial parts are collected just before the flowers open.
Constituents: Up to 2% volatile oil containing menthol, menthone, and jasmone; tannins, bitter principle.
Actions: Carminative, antispasmodic, aromatic, diaphoretic, anti-emetic, nervine, antiseptic, analgesic.

INDICATIONS:
Peppermint is one of the best carminative agents available. It has a relaxing effect on the visceral muscles, antiflatulent properties, and stimulates bile and digestive juice secretion, all of which help explain its value in relieving *intestinal colic, flatulent dyspepsia*, and other associated conditions. The volatile oil acts as a mild anesthetic to the stomach wall, which allays feelings of *nausea* and the desire to *vomit*. It helps relieve the *vomiting of pregnancy* and *travel sickness*. Peppermint plays a role in the treatment of *ulcerative colitis* and *Crohn's disease*. Peppermint is most valuable in the treatment of *fevers* and especially *colds* and *influenza*.

As an inhalant, it can be used as a temporary treatment for *nasal catarrh*. Where *migraine headaches* are associated with the digestion, this herb may be used. As a nervine it acts as a tonic, easing *anxiety, tension, hysteria*, etc. In *painful periods (dysmenorrhea)*, it relieves the pain and eases associated tension. Externally it may be used to relieve *itching* and *inflammations*.

Combinations: For *colds* and *influenza*, it may be used with Boneset, Elderberry Flowers, and Yarrow.

298   THE COMPLETE HERBS SOURCEBOOK

PREPARATION AND DOSAGE:

Infusion: pour a cup of boiling water onto a heaped teaspoonful of the dried herb and leave to infuse for 10 minutes. This may be drunk as often as desired.
Tincture: take 1–2 milliliters of the tincture three times a day.

PREPARATION AND DOSAGE:

Infusion: pour a cup of boiling water onto 1 teaspoonful of the dried herb and let infuse for 10–15 minutes. This should be drunk three times a day.
Tincture: take 1–2 milliliters of the tincture three times a day.

PERIWINKLE
Vinca major
APOCYNACEAE

Part used: Aerial parts.
Collection: This herb is collected in the spring.
Constituents: Alkaloids, tannins.
Actions: Astringent, sedative.

> **INDICATIONS:**
> Periwinkle is an excellent all-around astringent that may be used internally or externally. Its main use is in the treatment of *excessive menstrual flow*, either during the period itself (*menorrhagia*) or with blood loss between periods (*metrorrhagia*). It can be used in digestive problems such as *colitis* or *diarrhea*, where it will act to reduce the loss of fluid or blood while toning the membranes. It may also be used in cases of *nosebleed*, *bleeding gums*, *mouth ulcers*, or *sore throats*. It has a reputation for aiding in the treatment of *diabetes*.

Combinations: It will combine well with Geranium (aka Cranesbill) and Agrimony. For menstrual problems, it may be used with Trillium (aka Beth Root).

PERUVIAN BARK
Cinchona succiruba
RUBIACEAE

Part used: Bark.
Collection: The bark is collected by felling the six- to eight-year-old trees and then stripping the bark.
Constituents: Alkaloids, including quinine and quinidine; tannins; bitter principle.
Actions: Febrifuge, digestive bitter, anthelmintic, heart relaxant.

> **INDICATIONS:**
> Peruvian Bark is renowned as a treatment of feverish conditions and especially those that are periodic, such as *malaria*. It may be used in all *fevers*, but usually as part of a wider treatment. The bitter action gives this herb a role in the stimulation of the digestive system, aiding the whole process. It will stimulate the secretion of digestive juices and in this way act as a tonic. There is also a distinct action of quieting the heart, reducing *palpitations* and normalizing the function.

PREPARATION AND DOSAGE:

Infusion: pour a cup of boiling water onto 1 teaspoonful of the bark and leave to infuse for 30 minutes. This should be drunk three times a day.
Tincture: take 1–2 milliliters of the tincture three times a day.

PILL-BEARING SPURGE

Euphorbia pilulifera

EUPHORBIACEAE

Part used: Aerial parts.
Collection: Gather the aerial parts while Pill-Bearing Spurge is in flower.
Constituents: Glycoside, alkaloids, sterols, tannins, phorbic acid.
Actions: Anti-asthmatic, expectorant, antispasmodic.

> **INDICATIONS:**
> Pill-Bearing Spurge has a relaxing effect upon the smooth muscles of the lungs and acts with great benefit in conditions such as *asthma* and *bronchitis*. It will also relieve spasms in the larynx, helping *nervous coughs*. It will help relieve *upper respiratory catarrh*. This herb has a specific action of destroying the organisms that cause amoebic infections in the intestines.

Combinations: For the treatment of asthmatic conditions, it will combine well with Grindelia and Lobelia.

PREPARATION AND DOSAGE:

Infusion: pour a cup of boiling water onto ½–1 teaspoonful of the dried leaves and let infuse for 10–15 minutes. This should be drunk three times a day.
Tincture: take 1–2 milliliters of the tincture three times a day.

PINE, SCOTS

Pinus sylvestris

PINACEAE

Other species can be used, such as *Pinus pinaster*, *Pinus pinea*, and *Pinus nigra*.
Part used: Needles and young buds.
Collection: The needles and young buds are best collected with the twigs in the spring as young shoots.
Constituents: Tannins, resin, essential oil, terpenes, pinipricin.
Actions: Antiseptic, anticatarrhal, stimulant, tonic.

> **INDICATIONS:**
> The Scots Pine may be used in cases of *bronchitis*, *sinusitis*, or *upper respiratory catarrh*, both as an inhalant and internally. It may also be helpful in *asthma*. The stimulating action gives the herb a role in the internal treatment of *rheumatism* and *arthritis*. There is a tradition of adding a preparation of the twigs to bathwater to ease *fatigue*, *nervous debility*, and *sleeplessness*, as well as aiding the healing of *cuts* and soothing *skin irritations*.

PREPARATION AND DOSAGE:

Infusion: pour a cup of boiling water onto ½ teaspoonful of the twigs and leave to infuse for 10–15 minutes. This should be drunk three times a day.
Inhalant: bring 2–3 handfuls of the twigs to the boil in 4 pints (2 liters) of water, simmer for five minutes, and then use as an inhalant by covering the head with a towel and inhaling the steam for 15 minutes. Repeat often.
Bath: leave 3 handfuls of twigs to stand in 1.5 pints (750 milliliters) of water for half an hour, then bring to the boil, simmer for 10 minutes, strain, and add to the hot bath.
Tincture: take 1–2 milliliters of the tincture three times a day.

PREPARATION AND DOSAGE:

Infusion: pour a cup of boiling water onto 2 teaspoonfuls of the dried herb and leave to infuse for 10 minutes. This should be drunk three times a day.

Ointment: an ointment can be made that will aid the treatment of *hemorrhoids* and *cuts*.

Tincture: take 2–3 milliliters of the tincture three times a day.

PLEURISY ROOT
Asclepias tuberosa
ASCLEPIADACEAE

Part used: Rhizome.
Collection: The rhizome should be unearthed in March or April. Clean well and split up. Dry in shade or sun.
Constituents: Glycosides, including asclepiadin and possibly cardioactive glycosides; essential oil.
Actions: Diaphoretic, expectorant, antispasmodic, carminative.

> **INDICATIONS:**
> Pleurisy Root is effective against respiratory infections where it reduces inflammations and assists expectoration. It can be used in the treatment of *bronchitis* and other chest conditions. The addition of diaphoretic and antispasmodic powers will show why it is so highly valued in the treatment of *pleurisy* and *pneumonia*. It can be used in *influenza*.

Combinations: It will combine well with Cayenne, Lobelia, and Grindelia in the treatment of respiratory congestion.

PLANTAIN, GREATER
Plantago major
PLANTAGINACEAE

Part used: Leaves or aerial parts.
Collection: Gather during flowering throughout the summer. Dry as fast as possible, as the leaves will discolor if dried improperly.
Constituents: Glycosides, including aucubin, mucilage, chlorogenic acid, and ursolic acid; silicic acid.
Actions: Expectorant, demulcent, astringent, diuretic.

> **INDICATIONS:**
> Both the Greater Plantain and its close relative Ribwort Plantain have valuable healing properties. It acts as a gentle expectorant while also soothing inflamed and sore membranes, making it ideal for *coughs* and mild *bronchitis*. Its astringency aids in *diarrhea, hemorrhoids,* and also in *cystitis* where there is bleeding.

THE HERBAL

PREPARATION AND DOSAGE:

Infusion: pour a cup of boiling water onto ½–1 teaspoonful of the herb and let infuse for 10–15 minutes. This should be drunk three times a day.

Tincture: take 1–2 milliliters of the tincture three times a day.

POKEWEED ROOT (AKA POKE ROOT)
Phytolacca americana
PHYTOLACCACEAE

Part used: Root.
Collection: The root should be unearthed in the late fall or spring. Clean it and split lengthwise before drying.
Constituents: Tripterpenoid saponins, alkaloid, resins, phytolaccic acid, tannins, formic acid.
Actions: Antirheumatic, stimulant, anticatarrhal, purgative, emetic.

INDICATIONS:
Pokeweed Root has a wide range of uses and is a valuable addition to many holistic treatments. It may be seen primarily as a remedy for use in infections of the upper respiratory tract, removing catarrh and aiding the cleansing of the lymphatic glands. It may be used for *catarrh, tonsillitis, laryngitis, swollen glands (adenitis), mumps,* etc. It will be found of value in lymphatic problems elsewhere in the body and especially for *mastitis*, where it can be used internally and as a poultice. Pokeweed Root also has a use in *rheumatism*, especially where it is long standing. Care must be taken with this herb as in large dosage it is powerfully emetic and purgative. Externally as a lotion or ointment it may be used to rid the skin of *scabies* and other pests.

CAUTION:
In large dosage, Pokeweed Root is a powerful emetic and purgative.

Combinations: For lymphatic problems, it may be used with Cleavers or Blue Flag.

PREPARATION AND DOSAGE:

Decoction: only small amounts of this herb should be used. Put ¼–½ teaspoonful of the root in a cup of water, bring to the boil, and simmer gently for 10–15 minutes. This should be drunk three times a day.

Tincture: take ½–1 milliliters of the tincture three times a day.

POMEGRANATE
Punica granatum
LYTHRACEAE

Part used: Bark.
Constituents: Tannins, alkaloids.
Actions: Anthelmintic.

INDICATIONS:
Various parts of the Pomegranate can be used in medicine; however, the bark has marked antitapeworm activity. It can be rather strong and traumatic, associated as it often is with nausea and vomiting, since the treatment for tapeworm includes a regime of strict fasting followed by purging or enemas.

PREPARATION AND DOSAGE:

Decoction: Mrs. Grieve gives a dosage of 4 ounces (120 grams) of bark to 20 fluid ounces (600 milliliters) of water made into a decoction. Of this, 0.5 fluid ounce (15 milliliters) is taken. This should be drunk three times a day.

Tincture: take 2–4 milliliters of the tincture three times a day.

PRICKLY ASH
Zanthoxylum americanum
RUTACEAE

Part used: Bark and berries.
Collection: The berries are collected in the late summer, and the bark is stripped from the stems of this shrub in the spring.
Constituents: Alkaloids, volatile oil in the berries.
Actions: Stimulant (especially circulatory), tonic, alterative, carminative, diaphoretic.

> **INDICATIONS:**
> Prickly Ash may be used in a way that is similar to Cayenne, although it is slower in action. It is used in many chronic problems such as *rheumatism* and *skin diseases*. Any sign of poor circulation calls for the use of this herb, such as *chilblains, cramp in the legs, varicose veins,* and *varicose ulcers*. Externally, it may be used as a stimulation liniment for *rheumatism* and *fibrositis*. Due to its stimulating effect upon the lymphatic system, circulation and mucous membranes, it will have a role in the holistic treatment of many specific conditions.

PREPARATION AND DOSAGE:

Infusion: pour a cup of boiling water onto 1–2 teaspoonfuls of the bark and let infuse for 10–15 minutes.

PUMPKIN
Cucurbita pepo
CUCURBITACEAE

Part used: Seeds.
Collection: The seeds are removed from the pulp inside the pumpkin, which should be harvested in the late summer.
Constituents: Fatty oil, curcurbitin, albumin, lecithin, resin, phytosterin.
Actions: Anthelmintic.

> **INDICATIONS:**
> The seeds of this valuable vegetable have long been used as a remedy for worms and tapeworms. The effect appears to be a mechanical one. The seeds should be used when ripe and fresh.

PREPARATION AND DOSAGE:

Mrs. Grieve gives the following recipe: "A mixture is made by beating 2 ounces (60 grams) of the seeds with as much sugar and milk, or water, added to make a pint, and this mixture is taken fasting. In three doses, one every two hours, castor oil being taken a few hours after the last dose."

QUASSIA

Picrasma excelsor

SIMARUBACEAE

Part used: Chips or raspings of stem wood, free of bark.
Collection: Raspings of the wood are collected after felling the tree.
Constituents: Bitter glycosides, alkaloids.
Actions: Bitter tonic, sialagogue, anthelmintic.

INDICATIONS:

Quassia is an excellent remedy in dyspeptic conditions due to lack of tone. As with all bitters, it stimulates the production of saliva and digestive juices and so increases the appetite. It may safely be used in all cases of lack of appetite such as *anorexia nervosa* and digestive sluggishness. It is used in the expulsion of *threadworms* both as an enema and an infusion. Externally, as a lotion it may be used against *lice infestations*.

Combinations: In *dyspepsia*, it may be used with Meadowsweet, Marshmallow Root, and Hops.

PREPARATION AND DOSAGE:

Cold infusion: ½–1 teaspoonful of the wood is put in a cup of cold water and left to steep overnight. This should be drunk three times a day.
Enema: make a cold infusion with one part Quassia to 20 parts water.
Tincture: take ½–1 milliliters of the tincture three times a day.

QUEEN'S DELIGHT

Stillingia sylvatica

EUPHORBIACEAE

Part used: Root.
Collection: The root is unearthed after flowering has finished in July.
Constituents: Volatile oil, acrid resin, fixed oil, tannins.
Actions: Alterative, expectorant, diaphoretic, sialagogue.

INDICATIONS:

This North American herb finds use in the treatment of chronic skin conditions such as *eczema* and *psoriasis*. The treatment must be spread over a long period of time however. These skin conditions can be due to a whole range of contributing factors. Queen's Delight is most useful where there is lymphatic involvement. Another area of application is in *bronchitis* and *laryngitis*, especially where it is accompanied by loss of voice. As an astringent it may be used in a number of conditions, but especially for *hemorrhoids*.

Combinations: For the treatment of skin problems, it will combine well with Burdock, Yellow Dock, Cleavers, and Blue Flag.

PREPARATION AND DOSAGE:

Decoction: put ½–1 teaspoonful of the dried root in a cup of water, bring to the boil, and simmer gently for 10–15 minutes. This should be drunk three times a day.
Tincture: take 1–2 milliliters of the tincture three times a day.

QUINCE
Cydonia oblonga
ROSACEAE

Part used: Seeds.
Collection: The seeds are taken out of the Quince fruit, which is collected in the fall.
Constituents: Mucilage, tannins, fatty oil, pectin, amygdalin, vitamin C.
Actions: Astringent, anti-inflammatory, demulcent, laxative.

> **INDICATIONS:**
> Quince seeds can act as an effective and gentle laxative in cases of *constipation*, as well as a soothing astringent in conditions such as *gastritis* and *enteritis*. As a mouth wash they will ease *soreness* and *inflammation* in the mouth. They can also be used with good effect in *dry, irritating coughs* where an expectorant is called for. Externally, they may be applied to minor *burns*.

PREPARATION AND DOSAGE:

Infusion: the seeds should be soaked in water for 3–5 hours to get a solution of the slime from the outer coats of the seeds. This should be drunk as needed or three times a day.
Tincture: take 1–2 milliliters of the tincture three times a day or as needed.

RAGWORT
Senecio jacobaea
COMPOSITAE

Part used: Aerial parts.
Collection: This common plant is collected when in flower between June and September.
Constituents: Essential oil, rutin, an alkaloid, mucilage.
Actions: Rubefacient.

> **INDICATIONS:**
> Ragwort is potentially poisonous to the liver and must on no occasion be taken internally. As a liniment, it provides a stimulating and warming preparation used externally on *rheumatic muscles*.

PREPARATION AND DOSAGE:

Poultice: this herb may be made into a poultice according to the instruction in the chapter on the preparation of herbs.

> **CAUTION:**
> Never take this plant internally.

RASPBERRY
Rubus idaeus
ROSACEAE

Part used: Leaves and fruit.
Collection: The leaves may be collected throughout the growing season. Dry slowly in a well-ventilated area to ensure proper preservation of properties.
Constituents: Leaves: fruit sugar, volatile oil, pectin, citric acid, malic acid.
Actions: Astringent, tonic, refrigerant, parturient.

INDICATIONS:
Raspberry leaves have a long tradition of use in pregnancy to strengthen and tone the tissue of the womb, assisting contractions and checking any *hemorrhage* during labor. This action will occur if the herb is drunk regularly throughout pregnancy and also taken during labor. As an astringent, it may be used in a wide range of cases, including *diarrhea*, *leukorrhea*, and other loose conditions. It is valuable in the easing of mouth problems such as *mouth ulcers*, *bleeding gums*, and *inflammations*. As a gargle, it will help *sore throats*.

PREPARATION AND DOSAGE:
Infusion: pour a cup of boiling water onto 2 teaspoonfuls of the dried herb and let infuse for 10–15 minutes. This may be drunk freely.
Tincture: take 2–4 milliliters of the tincture three times a day.

RED CLOVER
Trifolium pratense
PAPILIONACEAE

Part used: Flower heads.
Collection: The flower heads are gathered between May and September.
Constituents: Phenolic glycosides, flavonoids, coumarins, cyanogenic glycosides.
Actions: Alterative, expectorant, antispasmodic.

INDICATIONS:
Red Clover is one of the most useful remedies for children with skin problems. It may be used with complete safety in any case of *childhood eczema*. It may also be of value in other chronic skin conditions such as *psoriasis*. While being most useful with children, it can also be of value for adults. The expectorant and antispasmodic action gives this remedy a role in the treatment of *coughs* and *bronchitis*, but especially in *whooping cough*. As an alterative it is indicated in a wide range of problems when approached in a holistic sense. There is some evidence to suggest an antineoplastic action in animals.

Combinations: For skin problems, it combines well with Yellow Dock and Nettles.

PREPARATION AND DOSAGE:
Infusion: pour a cup of boiling water onto 1–3 teaspoonfuls of the dried herb and leave to infuse for 10–15 minutes. This should be drunk three times a day.
Tincture: take 2–6 milliliters of the tincture three times a day.

RED POPPY

Papaver rhoeas

PAPAVERACEAE

Part used: Petals.
Collection: The petals should be collected on a dry morning after the dew has dried in the months of July and August. Dry carefully.
Constituents: Tannins, mucilage, traces of alkaloids.
Actions: Mild sedative, expectorant.

INDICATIONS:

This beautiful wayside herb does not have the potent activity of its relative, the Opium Poppy. It may be used to soothe *irritable coughs* and in cases of *respiratory catarrh*. The petals are often added to herbal teas and potpourris to add color.

PREPARATION AND DOSAGE:

Infusion: pour a cup of boiling water onto 1–2 teaspoonfuls of the dried petals and leave to infuse for 10–15 minutes. This should be drunk three times a day.
Tincture: take 2–4 milliliters of the tincture three times a day.

RED SAGE

Salvia officinalis

LABIATEAE

Part used: Leaves.
Collection: The leaves should be gathered shortly before or just at the beginning of flowering in dry, sunny weather in May or June. Dry in the shade or not above 95ºF (35ºC).
Constituents: Volatile oil, including 30% thujone, 5% cineole, linalol, borneol, camphor, salvene, and pinene; a bitter; tannins; triterpenoids; flavonoids; estrogenic substances; resin.
Actions: Carminative, spasmolytic, antiseptic, astringent, antihidrotic.

INDICATIONS:

Red Sage is the classic remedy for inflammations of the mouth, throat, and tonsils, its volatile oils soothing the mucous membranes. It may be used internally and as a mouthwash for *inflamed and bleeding gums (gingivitis), inflamed tongue (glossitis),* or *generalized mouth inflammation (stomatitis)*. It is an excellent remedy in *mouth ulcers (apthae)*. As a gargle, it will aid in the treatment of *laryngitis, pharyngitis, tonsillitis,* and *quinsy*. It is a valuable carminative used in *dyspepsia*. It reduces sweating when taken internally and may be used to reduce the production of breast milk. As a compress, it promotes the healing of *wounds*. Red Sage stimulates the muscles of the uterus and so should be avoided during pregnancy.

CAUTION:

Avoid during pregnancy.

Combinations: As a gargle for throat conditions, it combines well with Tormentil and Balm of Gilead. In *dyspepsia*, it can be combined with Meadowsweet and Chamomile.

PREPARATION AND DOSAGE:

Infusion: pour a cup of boiling water onto 1–2 teaspoonfuls of the leaves and let infuse for 10 minutes. This should be drunk three times a day.

Mouthwash: put 2 teaspoonfuls of the leaves in 1 pint (0.5 liter) of water, bring to the boil, and let stand, covered, for 15 minutes. Gargle deeply with the hot tea for 5–10 minutes several times a day.

Tincture: take 2–4 milliliters of the tincture three times a day.

RHATANY (AKA KRAMERIA)
Krameria triandra

KRAMERIACEAE

Part used: Root.
Collection: The root of this shrub is collected in Peru.

INDICATIONS:
Rhatany is a powerful astringent that was retained in the official pharmacopoeia until recently. It may be used wherever an astringent is indicated—for example, in *diarrhea, hemorrhoids, hemorrhages*, or as a styptic. Rhatany is often found in herbal toothpastes and powders, as it is especially good for *bleeding gums*. It can be used as a snuff with Bloodroot to treat *nasal polyps*.

Constituents: Up to 9% of a tannin called rhatanhiatannic acid.
Actions: Astringent.

PREPARATION AND DOSAGE:

Decoction: put 1–2 teaspoonfuls of the root in a cup of water, bring to the boil, and simmer gently for 10–15 minutes. This should be drunk three times a day.

Tincture: take 1–4 milliliters of the tincture three times a day.

RHUBARB ROOT
Rheum palmatum

POLYGONACEAE

Part used: Rhizome of *Rheum palmatum* and other species, not the garden rhubarb.
Collection: This root is collected in China and Turkey.
Constituents: Anthraquinones, tannins, bitter aromatic principle.
Actions: Bitter stomachic, mild purgative, astringent.

INDICATIONS:
Rhubarb Root has a purgative action for use in the treatment of *constipation*, but also has an astringent effect following this. It therefore has a truly cleansing action upon the gut, removing debris and then astringing with antiseptic properties as well.

NOTE:
Rhubarb Root may color the urine yellow or red.

Combinations: It should be combined with carminative herbs to relieve any griping that may occur.

PREPARATION AND DOSAGE:

Decoction: put ½-1 teaspoonful of the root in a cup of water, bring to the boil, and simmer gently for 10 minutes. This should be drunk morning and evening.
Tincture: take 1–2 milliliters of the tincture three times a day.

INDICATIONS:

Rose Hips provide one of the best natural and freely available sources of vitamin C. They may be used wherever this vitamin is required. They will help the body's defenses against infections and especially the development of *colds*. They make an excellent spring tonic and aid in *general debility* and *exhaustion*. They will help in cases of *constipation* and mild gallbladder problems as well as conditions of the kidney and bladder.

PREPARATION AND DOSAGE:

The decoction or syrup may be taken quite freely.
Decoction: put 2½ teaspoonfuls of the cut hips in a cup of water, bring to the boil, and simmer gently for 10 minutes.
Syrup: to make a syrup, follow the guidelines given in the chapter on the preparation of herbs. For this or any other culinary preparation, it is important to remove the seeds from the hips as well as the fine, brittle hairs found at one end.
Tincture: take 2–4 milliliters of the tincture three times a day.

ROSE HIPS

Rosa canina

ROSACEAE

Part used: The fruit (hips) and seeds of the Dog Rose.
Collection: The hips are collected in the fall.
Constituents: Vitamin C, tannins, pectin, carotene, fruit acids, fatty oil.
Actions: Nutrient, mild laxative, mild diuretic, mild astringent.

ROSEMARY

Rosmarinus officinalis

LABIATAE

Part used: Leaves and twigs.
Collection: The leaves may be gathered throughout the summer but are at their best during flowering time.
Constituents: 1% volatile oil, including borneol, linalol, camphene, cineole, and camphor; tannins; bitter principle; resins.

Actions: Carminative, aromatic, antispasmodic, antidepressive, antiseptic, rubefacient, parasiticide.

> ## INDICATIONS:
> Rosemary acts as a circulatory and nervine stimulant, which in addition to the toning and calming effect on digestion, makes it a remedy that is used where psychological tension is present. This may show for instance as *flatulent dyspepsia*, *headache*, or *depression* associated with debility. Externally, it may be used to ease *muscular pain*, *sciatica*, and *neuralgia*. It acts as a stimulant to the hair follicles and may be used in *premature baldness*. The oil is most effective here.

Combinations: For *depression*, it may be used with Skullcap, Kola Nut, and Oats.

PREPARATION AND DOSAGE:
Infusion: pour a cup of boiling water onto 1–2 teaspoonfuls of the dried herb and leave to infuse in a covered container for 10–15 minutes. This should be drunk three times a day.

Tincture: take 1–2 milliliters of the tincture three times a day.

RUE
Ruta graveolens
RUTACEAE

Part used: Dried aerial parts.
Collection: The herb should be collected before the flowers open in the summer and dried in the shade.
Constituents: Essential oil, rutin, furanocoumarins, alkaloids, tannins.
Actions: Antispasmodic, emmenagogue, antitussive, abortifacient.

> ## INDICATIONS:
> Rue is an herb with an ancient history. The genus name *Ruta* comes from the Greek word *reuo*, to set free, showing its reputation as a freer from disease. Its main use is the regulation of menstrual periods, where it is used to bring on *suppressed menses*. The oil of Rue is a powerful abortifacient; therefore, the plant is best avoided during pregnancy. The other area of usage is due to the plant's antispasmodic action. It may be used to relax smooth muscles, especially in the digestive system, where it will ease *griping* and *bowel tension*. The easing of spasm gives it a role in the stopping of *spasmodic coughs*. It also increases peripheral circulation and lowers *elevated blood pressure*. If the fresh leaf is chewed, it will relieve *tension headaches*, ease *palpitations*, and other anxiety problems.

Combinations: For use in the regulation of periods, it will combine well with False Unicorn Root and Golden Ragwort (aka Life Root).

PREPARATION AND DOSAGE:
Infusion: pour a cup of boiling water onto 1–2 teaspoonfuls of the dried herb and leave to infuse for 10–15 minutes. This should be drunk three times a day.
Tincture: take 1–4 milliliters of the tincture three times a day.

> **CAUTION:**
> Avoid during pregnancy.

SANTONICA

Artemisia cina

COMPOSITAE

Common name: Wormseed.
Part used: Seeds.
Collection: The seeds are collected in the fall in areas where they grow, which include most of Asia.
Constituents: Santonin, volatile oil, artemisin.
Actions: Anthelmintic.

INDICATIONS:
Santonica is one of the oldest worm remedies recorded. It proves most effective against roundworm and, to a lesser extent, threadworm. However, it will do nothing against tapeworm. Due to the potency and to a low level toxicity of santonin, this herb should only be used under medical supervision.

SARSAPARILLA

Smilax officinalis

LILIACEAE

Part used: Root and rhizome.
Collection: The roots and rhizome can be unearthed throughout the year.
Constituents: Sapogenins, glycosides, essential oil, resin.
Actions: Alterative, antirheumatic, diuretic, diaphoretic.
Combinations: For *psoriasis*, it will combine well with Burdock, Yellow Dock, and Cleavers.

INDICATIONS:
Sarsaparilla is a widely applicable alterative. It may be used to aid proper functioning of the body as a whole and in the correction of such diffuse systemic problems as skin and rheumatic conditions. It is particularly useful in scaling skin conditions such as *psoriasis*, especially where there is much irritation. As part of a wider treatment for *chronic rheumatism*, it should be considered and is especially useful for *rheumatoid arthritis*. It has been shown that Sarsaparilla contains chemicals with properties that aid testosterone activity in the body.

PREPARATION AND DOSAGE:
Decoction: put 1–2 teaspoonfuls of the root in a cup of water, bring to the boil, and simmer for 10–15 minutes. This should be drunk three times a day.
Tincture: take 1–2 milliliters of the tincture three times a day.

SASSAFRAS
Sassafras albidum
LAURACEAE

Part used: Root bark.
Collection: The root is unearthed to gather this herb, which grows over large areas of North America.
Constituents: Essential oil, including safrole; sesamin; tannins; resin.
Actions: Alterative, carminative, diaphoretic, diuretic.

> ### INDICATIONS:
> Sassafras is used primarily in skin problems such as *eczema* and *psoriasis*. As another aspect of its undoubted systemic activity, it may be used with benefit in the treatment of *rheumatism* and *gout*. As a diaphoretic, it may be used in *fevers* and systemic infections. The plant has a disinfectant action and makes a valuable mouthwash and dentifrice. It acts as a specific to combat *head lice* and other body infestations.

Combinations: For skin problems, it may be used with Burdock, Nettles, and Yellow Dock.

PREPARATION AND DOSAGE:
Infusion: pour a cup of boiling water onto 1–2 teaspoonfuls of the dried herb and leave to infuse for 10–15 minutes. This should be drunk three times a day.
Oil: The oil of Sassafras should be used for the external treatment of lice and never taken internally.
Tincture: take 1–2 milliliters of the tincture three times a day.

SAW PALMETTO BERRIES
Serenoa serrulata
PALMAE

Part used: Berries.
Collection: The berries of this impressive palm are gathered from September through until January.
Constituents: Volatile oil, steroids, dextrose, resins.
Actions: Diuretic, urinary antiseptic, endocrine agent.

> ### INDICATIONS:
> Saw Palmetto is an herb that acts to tone and strengthen the male reproductive system. It may be used with safety where a boost to the male sex hormones is required. It is a specific in cases of *enlarged prostate glands*. It will be of value in all *infections of the gastrourinary tract*.

Combinations: For debility associated with the reproductive system, it will combine well with Damiana and Kola Nut. For the treatment of *enlarged prostate glands*, it may be used with Horsetail and Hydrangea.

PREPARATION AND DOSAGE:
Decoction: put ½–1 teaspoonful of the berries in a cup of water, bring to the boil, and simmer gently for five minutes. This should be drunk three times a day.
Tincture: take 1–2 milliliters of the tincture three times a day.

SEA HOLLY
Eryngium maritimum
UMBELLIFERAE

Part used: Dried roots.
Collection: The roots are unearthed from their shoreline habitat at the end of the flowering time.
Actions: Diuretic, antilithic.

INDICATIONS:
This most impressive plant of sandy shores is used in a whole range of urinary conditions. It is a diuretic in the herbal sense that it has an affinity for the system rather than being a strong remover of water from the body. It has most use in *kidney stones* and *gravel*, especially if there is an associated restriction of urine flow. It will ease colic due to urinary problems as well as reducing *hemorrhage*. It can help in *cystitis*, *urethritis*, and *enlarged* and *inflamed prostate glands*.

PREPARATION AND DOSAGE:
Decoction: put 1–2 teaspoonfuls of the root in a cup of water, bring to the boil, and simmer for 10 minutes. This should be drunk three times a day.
Tincture: take 1–2 milliliters of the tincture three times a day.

SELF-HEAL
Prunella vulgaris
LABIATAE

Part used: Aerial parts.
Collection: The young shoots and leaves are collected in June before flowering.
Constituents: Volatile oil, bitter principle, tannins.
Actions: Astringent, vulnerary, tonic.

INDICATIONS:
As its name suggests, Self-Heal has a long tradition as a wound-healing herb. The fresh leaf may be used or a poultice or compress made to aid in the clean healing of *cuts* and *wounds*. As a gentle astringent, it is used internally for *diarrhea*, *hemorrhoids*, or mild *hemorrhages*. For *sore throats*, it may be used as a gargle, sweetened with honey. For *bleeding hemorrhoids*, it may be used as an ointment or lotion. Self-Heal may be used as a spring tonic or as a general tonic in convalescence.

PREPARATION AND DOSAGE:
Infusion: pour a cup of boiling water onto 1–2 teaspoonfuls of the dried herb and leave to infuse for 10 minutes. This should be drunk three times a day or used as a gargle or lotion.
Tincture: take 1–2 milliliters of the tincture three times a day.

SENEGA

Polygala senega

POLYGALACEAE

Common name: Snake Root.
Part used: Root and rhizome.
Collection: The roots and rhizome are collected in September and October.
Constituents: 5–6% saponins, fixed oil, mucilage, salicylic acid, resin.
Actions: Expectorant, diaphoretic, sialogogue, emetic.

INDICATIONS:

Senega comes to us from the Native Americans. It was used by the Seneca tribe for snake bites. It has excellent expectorant effects that may be utilized in the treatment of *bronchitic asthma*, especially where there is some difficulty with expectoration. It has a general power of stimulating secretion, including saliva. It may be used as a mouthwash and gargle in the treatment of *pharyngitis* and *laryngitis*. If too much is taken, it acts in a way that will irritate the lining of the gut and cause vomiting.

Combinations: For bronchitic conditions, it may be used with Bloodroot, White Horehound, Grindelia, or Pill-Bearing Spurge.

PREPARATION AND DOSAGE:

Infusion: pour a cup of boiling water onto ½–1 teaspoonful of the dried root and let infuse for 10–15 minutes. This should be drunk three times a day.
Tincture: take 1–2 milliliters of the tincture three times a day.

SENNA PODS

Cassia angustifolia and *Cassia senna*

LEGUMINOSAE

Part used: Dried fruit pods.
Collection: The pods are gathered during the winter in Egypt, Sudan, Jordan, and India.
Constituents: Anthraquinones.
Actions: Cathartic.

INDICATIONS:

Senna Pods are used as a powerful cathartic in the treatment of *constipation*. It is vital to recognize, however, that the constipation is a result of something else and not the initial cause and that this has to be sought and dealt with. See the chapter on the digestive system for more information.

Combinations: It is best to combine Senna Pods with aromatic, carminative herbs to increase palatability and reduce griping—for instance, by using Cardamom, Ginger, or Fennel.

PREPARATION AND DOSAGE:

Infusion: the dried pods should be steeped in warm water for 6–12 hours. If they are Alexandrian Senna Pods, use 3–6 in a cup of water; if they are Tinnevelly Senna, use 4–12 pods. These names are given to two different species when sold commercially.

Tincture: take 2–7 milliliters of the tincture three times a day.

SHEPHERD'S PURSE
Capsella bursa-pastoris
CRUCIFERAE

Part used: Aerial parts.
Collection: The herb can be collected from February until October.
Constituents: Tyramine, choline acetylcholine, tannins, essential oil, resin, saponins, flavonoids, diosmine, potassium.
Actions: Uterine stimulant, diuretic, astringent.

INDICATIONS:
This easily recognized plant may be used wherever a gentle diuretic is called for—for instance, in *water retention* due to kidney problems. As an astringent, it will prove effective in the treatment of *diarrhea, wounds, nosebleeds*, and other conditions. It has specific use in the stimulation of the menstrual process, while also being of use in the reduction of excess flow.

PREPARATION AND DOSAGE:

Infusion: pour a cup of boiling water onto 1–2 teaspoonfuls of the dried herb and leave to infuse for 10 minutes. If it is used for menstrual conditions, it should be drunk every 2–3 hours during and just before the period. Otherwise, drink it three times a day.

Tincture: take 1–2 milliliters of the tincture three times a day.

SIBERIAN GINSENG
Eleutherococcus senticosus

Part used: The root of a N.E. Asian shrub.
Constituents: The research so far indicates the pharmacologically important group to be triterpenoid saponins called eleutherosides.
Actions: Adaptogen, a circulatory stimulant, vasodilator.

INDICATIONS:
This herb may safely be used to increase stamina in the face of undue demands and stress. These may be physical or mental—they are one to the body. Thus it is used for *debility, exhaustion,* and *depression,* except where these are due to a specific medical reason that calls for defined treatment. It has a growing reputation for increasing all kinds of body resistance. However, the claims may be overenthusiastic. The claims for circulatory effects come from excellent Russian research, which has not yet been fully verified elsewhere.

Combinations: It is best used by itself, or with herbs that are specifically indicated for a person.

PREPARATION AND DOSAGE:
This herb is usually available as a tablet or powder, the dosage of which should be 0.2–1 gram three times a day over a period of time.

SILVERWEED
Potentilla anserina
ROSACEAE

Part used: Dried aerial parts.
Collection: Silverweed should be collected in June, with all discolored or insect-eaten leaves being rejected. It should be dried in the shade.
Constituents: Tannins, flavonoids, bitter principle, organic acids.
Actions: Astringent, anticatarrhal, diuretic, local anti-inflammatory.

INDICATIONS:
Silverweed is an effective anticatarrhal herb that may be used wherever there is an overproduction of mucus. It is known primarily for its astringent action. For *hemorrhoids,* it may be taken internally and also used as an effective compress. It is indicated in *diarrhea,* especially when accompanied by indigestion. Where inflammations of the mouth occur, such as *gingivitis* or *apthous ulcers,* a mouthwash of the infusion of Silverweed will be found effective. As a gargle, it will relieve *sore throats.*

PREPARATION AND DOSAGE:
Infusion: pour a cup of boiling water onto 2 teaspoonfuls of the dried herb and leave to infuse for 15 minutes. This should be drunk three times a day.
Compress: bring 1–2 tablespoonfuls of chopped Silverweed to the boil in 1 pint (0.5 liter) of water. Let stand for 20 minutes. Make a moist compress with the lukewarm liquid. Moisten again as soon as the compress begins to dry.
Tincture: take 2–4 milliliters of the tincture three times a day.

SKULLCAP
Scutellaria laterifolia
LABIATAE

Part used: Aerial parts.

Collection: The whole of the aerial parts should be collected late in the flowering period during August and September.

Constituents: Flavonoid glycoside, including scutellarin and scutellarein; trace of volatile oil; bitter.

Actions: Nervine tonic, sedative, antispasmodic.

> **INDICATIONS:**
> Skullcap is perhaps the most widely relevant nervine available to us in the *materia medica*. It relaxes states of *nervous tension* while at the same time renewing and revivifying the central nervous system. It has a specific use in the treatment of *seizure* and *hysterical states* as well as *epilepsy*. It may be used in all exhausted or depressed conditions. It can be used with complete safety in the easing of *premenstrual syndrome*.

Combinations: It combines well with Valerian.

PREPARATION AND DOSAGE:

Infusion: pour a cup of boiling water onto 1–2 teaspoonfuls of the dried herb and leave to infuse for 10–15 minutes. This should be drunk three times a day or when needed.

Tincture: take 2–4 milliliters of the tincture three times a day.

SKUNK CABBAGE
Symplocarpus foetidus
ARACEAE

Part used: Root and rhizome.

Collection: The underground parts should be unearthed in the fall or early spring. However, they should not be kept for more than one year as they deteriorate with age and drying.

Constituents: Volatile oil, resin, an acrid principle.

Actions: Antispasmodic, diaphoretic, expectorant.

> **INDICATIONS:**
> Skunk Cabbage may be used whenever there is a tense or spasmodic condition in the lungs. It will act to relax and ease *irritable coughs*. It may be used in *asthma*, *bronchitis*, and *whooping cough*. As a diaphoretic, it will aid the body during *fevers*.

Combinations: For the treatment of asthmatic conditions, it may be used with Grindelia, Pill-Bearing Spurge, and Lobelia.

PREPARATION AND DOSAGE:

Traditionally, Skunk Cabbage has been used as a powder mixed in honey, with one part Skunk Cabbage powder to eight parts honey. Of this, ½–1 teaspoonful would be taken three times a day. To make a tea, use ½ teaspoonful of the herb and make it into either an infusion or a decoction.

Tincture: take ½–1 milliliters of the tincture three times a day.

SLIPPERY ELM BARK

Ulmus fulva

ULMACEAE

Part used: Inner bark.
Collection: The bark is stripped from the trunk and large branches in the spring. In commercial use, this usually leads to the tree dying, as a large part of the bark is stripped. Ten-year-old bark is recommended.
Constituents: Mucilage, tannins.
Actions: Demulcent, emollient, nutrient, astringent.

INDICATIONS:

Slippery Elm Bark is a soothing nutritive demulcent that is perfectly suited for sensitive or inflamed mucous membrane linings in the digestive system. It may be used in *gastritis, gastric* or *duodenal ulcer, enteritis, colitis*, and the like. It is often used as a food during convalescence as it is gentle and easily assimilated. In *diarrhea*, it will soothe and astringe at the same time. Externally, it makes an excellent poultice for use in cases of *boils, abscesses,* or *ulcers*.

Combinations: For digestive problems, it may be used with Marshmallow.

PREPARATION AND DOSAGE:

Decoction: use one part of the powdered bark to eight parts of water. Mix the powder in a little water initially to ensure it will mix. Bring to the boil and simmer gently for 10–15 minutes. Drink half a cup three times a day.
Poultice: mix the coarse powdered bark with enough boiling water to make a paste.

SOUTHERNWOOD

Artemisia abrotanum

COMPOSITAE

Part used: Aerial parts.
Collection: It is best collected in midsummer, ideally with flowering tops. Dry it with care and ensure that not too much of the volatile oil is lost.
Constituents: Volatile oil.
Actions: Bitter, emmenagogue, anthelmintic, antiseptic.

INDICATIONS:

While having the general tonic action of bitters, Southernwood finds most use in aiding menstrual flow. It will act to initiate *delayed menstruation* (which has given rise to some pretty sexist names for the plant, such as Lad's Love). Its bitter stimulation also will help in removing *threadworm* in children.

Combinations: Southernwood combines well with False Unicorn Root for *delayed menstruation*.

PREPARATION AND DOSAGE:

Infusion: pour a cup of boiling water onto 1–2 teaspoonfuls of the dried herb and leave to infuse for 10–15 minutes in a closed container. This should be drunk three times a day. Mrs. Grieve recommends 1 teaspoonful of the powdered herb in treacle (you could use honey) morning and evening for worms in children.
Tincture: take 1–4 milliliters of the tincture three times a day.

SQUILL
Urginea maritima
LILIACEAE

Part used: Bulb.
Collection: The bulb should be collected soon after flowering.
Constituents: Cardiac glycoside, mucilage, tannins.
Actions: Expectorant, cathartic, emetic, cardioactive, diuretic.
Combinations: For *bronchitis*, it may be used with White Horehound and Coltsfoot and for *whooping cough* with Sundew.

INDICATIONS:

Squill is a powerful expectorant used in *chronic bronchitis*, especially where there is little sputum production, which causes a dry irritable cough. A more fluid mucus secretion is produced with Squill that, in turn, facilitates an easier expectoration. The mucilage content eases and relaxes the bronchiole passages, thereby balancing the stimulation of the glycosides. It may be used in *bronchial asthma* and *whooping cough*. It has a stimulating action on the heart and has been used for aiding *heart failure* and *water retention* when there is heart involvement.

PREPARATION AND DOSAGE:

Infusion: the dose is quite small, only 0.06–0.2 grams of the bulb. As this is a very small quantity, make 1 pint (0.5 liter) of the infusion at a time by pouring 1 pint (0.5 liter) of boiling water onto ½–1 teaspoonful of the bulb. Let infuse for 10–15 minutes. Store the liquid in a refrigerator and drink a cup three times a day.
Tincture: take ½–1 milliliters of the tincture three times a day.

St. John's Wort

Hypericum perforatum

HYPERICACEAE

Part used: Aerial parts.
Collection: The entire plant above ground should be collected when in flower and dried as quickly as possible.
Constituents: Glycosides, including rutin; volatile oil; tannins; resin; pectin.
Actions: Anti-inflammatory, astringent, vulnerary, sedative.

INDICATIONS:

Taken internally, St. John's Wort has a sedative and pain-reducing effect, which gives it a place in the treatment of *neuralgia*, *anxiety*, *tension*, and similar problems. It is especially regarded as an herb to use where there are menopausal changes triggering *irritability* and *anxiety*. It is recommended, however, that it be not used when there is marked depression. In addition to *neuralgic pain*, it will ease *fibrositis*, *sciatica*, and *rheumatic pain*. Externally, it is a valuable healing and anti-inflammatory remedy. As a lotion, it will speed the healing of *wounds* and *bruises*, *varicose veins*, and *mild burns*. The oil is especially useful for the healing of *sunburn*.

PREPARATION AND DOSAGE:

Infusion: pour a cup of boiling water onto 1–2 teaspoonfuls of the dried herb and leave to infuse for 10–15 minutes. This should be drunk three times a day.
External use: see the chapter on the skin.
Tincture: take 1–4 milliliters of the tincture three times a day.

SUNDEW
Drosera rotundifolia
DROSERACEAE

Part used: Entire plant.
Collection: The whole of the plant is gathered during the flowering period in July or August.
Constituents: Naphthaquinones, including plumbagin; flavonoids; tannins; citric and malic acid.
Actions: Antispasmodic, demulcent, expectorant.

INDICATIONS:
Sundew may be used with great benefit in *bronchitis* and *whooping cough*. The presence of plumbagin helps to explain this as it has been shown to be active against streptococcus, staphylococcus, and pneumococcus bacteria. Sundew will also help with infections in other parts of the respiratory tract. Its relaxing effect upon involuntary muscles helps in the relief of *asthma*. In addition to the pulmonary conditions, it has a long history in the treatment of *stomach ulcers*.

Combinations: In the treatment of *asthma*, Sundew may be used with Grindelia and Pill-Bearing Spurge.

PREPARATION AND DOSAGE:
Infusion: pour a cup of boiling water onto 1 teaspoonful of the dried herb and leave to infuse for 10–15 minutes. This should be drunk three times a day.
Tincture: take 1–2 milliliters of the tincture three times a day.

SWEET SUMACH
Rhus aromatica
ANACARDIACEAE

Part used: Root bark.
Constituents: Tannins.
Actions: Astringent.

INDICATIONS:
Sweet Sumach is a useful astringent that is especially indicated in the treatment of *urinary incontinence* for both the young and old alike. It may safely be used wherever an astringent is called for, such as in *diarrhea* or *hemorrhage*. This herb has a reputation for being able to reduce blood sugar. Its power in this direction is open to debate, however.

Combinations: For the control of *urinary incontinence*, it may be combined with Horsetail and Agrimony.

PREPARATION AND DOSAGE:
Decoction: put 1 teaspoonful of the root bark in a cup of water, bring to the boil, and simmer for 10 minutes. This should be drunk three times a day.
Tincture: take 1–2 milliliters of the tincture three times a day.

SWEET VIOLET
Viola odorata
VIOLACEAE

Part used: Leaves and flowers.
Collection: The leaves and flowers are gathered in the spring, in March and April. Dry with care.
Constituents: Saponins, menthyl salicylate, alkaloids, flavonoids, essential oil.
Actions: Expectorant, alterative, anti-inflammatory, diuretic, antineoplastic.

INDICATIONS:
Sweet Violet has a long history of use as a cough remedy and especially for the treatment of *bronchitis*. It may also be used to aid in the treatment of *upper respiratory catarrh*. With the combination of actions present, it has a use in skin conditions such as *eczema* and in a long-term approach to *rheumatism*. It may be used for *urinary infections*. Sweet Violet has a reputation as an anticancer herb; it definitely has a role in a holistic approach to the treatment of *cancer*.

PREPARATION AND DOSAGE:
Infusion: pour a cup of boiling water onto 1 teaspoonful of the herb and let infuse for 10–15 minutes. This should be drunk three times a day.
Tincture: take 1–2 milliliters of the tincture three times a day.

TANSY
Tanacetum vulgare
COMPOSITAE

Part used: Aerial parts.
Collection: The leaves and flowers are collected during the flowering time between June and September.
Constituents: Volatile oil containing thujone; bitter glycosides; sesquiterpene lactones; terpenoids; flavonoids; tannins.
Actions: Vermifuge, anthelmintic, digestive bitter, carminative, emmenagogue.

INDICATIONS:
Tansy is an effective remedy for use in ridding the digestive tract of infestations of worms. While it is quite safe for this, its continued use over a period of time should be avoided as some of the constituents of the oil are quite dangerous in large dosage. The herb is effective against *roundworm* and *threadworm* and may be used in children as an enema. As a bitter, it will stimulate the digestive process and ease *dyspepsia*, having all the actions of a bitter tonic. It may be used as an emmenagogue to stimulate menstruation, but must be avoided during pregnancy. Externally, a lotion will be useful in cases of *scabies*.

CAUTION:
Avoid during pregnancy.

Combinations: For intestinal worms, it may be used with Wormwood and a carminative such as Chamomile in conjunction with a purgative like Senna.

PREPARATION AND DOSAGE:

Infusion: pour a cup of boiling water onto 1 teaspoonful of the dried herb and leave to infuse for 10–15 minutes. This should be drunk twice a day.

Tincture: take 1–2 milliliters of the tincture three times a day.

THUJA
Thuja occidentalis
CUPRESSACEAE

Part used: Young twigs.
Collection: The twigs of this evergreen conifer can be gathered all year round, but are best during the summer.
Constituents: 1% volatile oil, including thujone; flavonoid glycoside; mucilage; tannins.
Actions: Expectorant, stimulant to smooth muscles, diuretic, astringent, alterative.

INDICATIONS:

Thuja's main action is due to its stimulating and alterative volatile oil. In *bronchial catarrh*, Thuja combines expectoration with a systemic stimulation beneficial if there is also *heart weakness*.

Thuja should be avoided where the *cough* is due to overstimulation, as in *dry, irritable coughs*. Thuja has a specific reflex action on the uterus and may help in *delayed menstruation*, but because of this action it should be avoided in pregnancy. Where *urinary incontinence* occurs due to loss of muscle tone, Thuja may be used. It has a role to play in the treatment of *psoriasis* and *rheumatism*. Externally, it may be used to treat *warts*. It is reported to counteract the ill effects of *smallpox vaccination*. A marked antifungal effect is found if used externally for *ringworm* and *thrush*.

CAUTION:
Avoid during pregnancy.

Combinations: When used in pulmonary conditions, it may be combined with Senega, Grindelia, or Lobelia.

PREPARATION AND DOSAGE:

Infusion: pour a cup of boiling water onto 1 teaspoonful of the dried herb and leave to infuse for 10–15 minutes. This should be drunk three times a day.

Tincture: take 1–2 milliliters of the tincture three times a day.

THYME
Thymus vulgaris
LABIATAE

Part used: Leaves and flowering tops.
Collection: The flowering branches should be collected between June and August on a dry, sunny day. The leaves are stripped off the dried branches.
Constituents: More than 1% volatile oil, which includes thymol, carvacrol, cymol, linalol, borneol; bitter principles; tannins; flavonoids; triterpenoids.
Actions: Carminative, antimicrobial, antispasmodic, expectorant, astringent, anthelmintic.

INDICATIONS:

With its high content of volatile oil, Thyme makes a good carminative for use in *dyspepsia* and *sluggish digestion*. This oil is also a strongly antiseptic substance, which explains many of Thyme's uses. It can be used externally as a lotion for *infected wounds*, but also internally for *respiratory* and *digestive infections*. It may be used as a gargle in *laryngitis* and *tonsillitis*, easing *sore throats* and soothing *irritable coughs*. It is an excellent cough remedy, producing expectoration and reducing unnecessary spasm. It may be used in *bronchitis, whooping cough,* and *asthma*. As a gentle astringent, it has found use in *childhood diarrhea* and *bed-wetting*.

Combinations: For asthmatic problems, it will combine well with Lobelia and Ephedra, adding its antimicrobial effect. For *whooping cough*, use it with Wild Cherry and Sundew.

PREPARATION AND DOSAGE:

Infusion: pour a cup of boiling water onto 2 teaspoonfuls of the dried herb and let infuse for 10 minutes. This should be drunk three times a day.

Tincture: take 2–4 milliliters of the tincture three times a day.

TORMENTIL
Potentilla tormentilla

ROSACEAE

Part used: Rhizome.
Collection: The rhizome is dug up in the fall, cut into small pieces, washed, and then dried.
Constituents: 15% tannins, glycosides, red coloring matter.
Actions: Astringent, vulnerary.

> ### INDICATIONS:
> Tormentil is a most useful astringent for use in cases of *diarrhea*, especially when it is acute or of nervous origin. It has often been used as part of the treatment of *colitis*, both the mucous and the ulcerative kind. Tormentil makes a good astringent gargle for the mucous membranes of the mouth and throat, where it may be used to help *laryngitis, pharyngitis, bleeding gums, mouth ulcers*, and the like. As a lotion, it is used externally to ease *hemorrhoids*. As an ointment, lotion, compress, or poultice, it will speed the healing of *wounds* and *cuts*.

PREPARATION AND DOSAGE:
Decoction: put 1–2 teaspoonfuls of the dried rhizome in a cup of water, bring to the boil, and simmer gently for 10–15 minutes. This should be drunk three times a day.
Tincture: take 2–4 milliliters of the tincture three times a day.

TRILLIUM (AKA BETH ROOT)
Trillium erectum

LILIACEAE

Part used: Dried rhizome or root.
Collection: The root and rhizome should be unearthed in the late summer or early fall.
Constituents: Steroidal saponins, steroidal glycosides, tannins, fixed oil.
Actions: Uterine tonic, astringent, expectorant.

> ### INDICATIONS:
> Trillium (aka Beth Root) is a plant that contains a natural precursor of the female sex hormones, which the body may use if it needs it or otherwise leave unused, an example of the normalizing power of some herbs. While this remedy is an excellent tonic for the uterus, its associated astringent power explains its use for *bleeding* and *hemorrhage*. It may be used where there is excessive blood flow during a period (*menorrhagia*) or where there is blood loss between periods (*metrorrhagia*). It is considered to be a specific for excessive blood loss associated with *menopausal changes*. It may be used in *leukorrhea* as a douche and as a poultice or ointment for the treatment of *external ulcers*. Its astringency can be utilized where there is *hemorrhage* anywhere in the body, as long as the cause of the blood loss is treated as well.

Combinations: For *excessive menstruation*, it may be combined with Periwinkle or Geranium (aka American Cranesbill).

PREPARATION AND DOSAGE:

Decoction: pour a cup of water onto 1–2 teaspoonfuls of the dried herb and simmer for 10 minutes. This should be drunk three times a day.

Tincture: take 1–4 milliliters of the tincture three times a day.

PREPARATION AND DOSAGE:

Decoction: put ½–1 teaspoonful of the root in a cup of water, bring to the boil, and simmer for 10 minutes. This should be drunk three times a day.

Infusion: pour a cup of boiling water onto 1–2 teaspoonfuls of the dried herb and leave to infuse for 10–15 minutes. This should be drunk three times a day.

Tincture: take 1–2 milliliters of the tincture three times a day.

TRUE UNICORN ROOT
Aletris farinosa
LILIACEAE

Part used: Rhizome and root.
Collection: The underground parts are unearthed at the end of flowering in August, washed and cut into pieces, and then dried.
Constituents: Bitter principle.
Actions: Bitter, antispasmodic, sedative.

INDICATIONS:

This herb should *not* be confused with False Unicorn Root *(Chamaelirium luteum)*. It is an excellent remedy for sluggish digestion, which may give rise to *dyspepsia*, *flatulence*, and *debility*. Its bitter nature will stimulate the digestive process, and so it often relieves *anorexia (appetite loss)*. Another name for True Unicorn Root is Colic Root, which shows its value in the treatment of *digestive colic*. As all these conditions often have a nervous involvement, this herb has been called a nervine. However, its benefit in *anxiety* is based on an easing of the physical aspects rather than on a direct relaxation of the nerves. It is reported to be of value in *threatened miscarriage*, but False Unicorn Root is preferable here.

VALERIAN
Valeriana officinalis
VALERIANACEAE

Part used: Rhizome and roots.
Collection: The roots are unearthed in the late fall. Clean thoroughly and dry in the shade.
Constituents: Volatile oil, including valerianic acid, isovalerianic acid, borneol, pinene, camphene; volatile alkaloids.
Actions: Sedative, hypnotic, antispasmodic, hypotensive, carminative.

INDICATIONS:

Valerian is one of the most useful relaxing nervines that is available to us. This fact is recognized by orthodox medicine as is shown by its inclusion in many pharmacopoeias as a sedative. It may safely be used to reduce tension and anxiety, overexcitability, and hysterical states. It is an effective aid in *insomnia*, producing a natural healing sleep. As an antispasmodic herb, it will aid in the relief of *cramp* and *intestinal colic* and will also be useful for the cramps and pain of periods. As a pain reliever, it is most indicated where that pain is associated with tension. Valerian can help in *migraine* and *rheumatic pain*.

Combinations: For the relief of *tension*, it will combine most effectively with Skullcap. For *insomnia*, it can be combined with Passion Flower and Hops. For the treatment of *cramps*, it will work well with Cramp Bark.

PREPARATION AND DOSAGE:

Infusion: pour a cup of boiling water onto 1–2 teaspoonfuls of the root and let infuse for 10–15 minutes. This should be drunk when needed.
Tincture: take 2–4 milliliters of the tincture three times a day.

VERVAIN
Verbena officinalis
LABIATAE

Part used: Aerial parts.
Collection: The herb should be collected just before the flowers open, usually in July. Dry quickly.
Constituents: Bitter glycosides called verbenalin; essential oil; mucilage; tannins.
Actions: Nervine tonic, sedative, antispasmodic, diaphoretic, possible galactagogue, hepatic.

Combinations: In the treatment of *depression*, it may be used with Skullcap, Oats, and Lady's Slipper.

> ## INDICATIONS:
> Vervain is an herb that will strengthen the nervous system while relaxing any tension and stress. It can be used to ease *depression* and *melancholia*, especially when this follows illness such as influenza. Vervain may be used to help in *seizure* and *hysteria*. As a diaphoretic, it can be used in the early stages of *fevers*. As a hepatic remedy, it will be found of help in *inflammation of the gallbladder* and *jaundice*. It may be used as a mouthwash against *caries* and *gum disease*.

PREPARATION AND DOSAGE:

Infusion: pour a cup of boiling water onto 1–3 teaspoonfuls of the dried herb and leave to infuse for 10–15 minutes. This should be drunk three times a day.

Tincture: take 2–4 milliliters of the tincture three times a day.

VIRGINIA SNAKEROOT

Aristolachia serpentaria

ARISTOLOCHIACEAE

Part used: Rhizome and root.

Collection: The underground parts are unearthed in the fall from woodlands throughout the eastern areas of North America.

Constituents: Aristolochic acid, essential oil, tannins, bitter principle.

Actions: Stimulant, digestive, tonic, diaphoretic.

> ## INDICATIONS:
> At one time, Virginia Snakeroot was considered one of the most important herbs to come to Europe from America, though today it is not widely used. Its name comes from its use in aiding the body to combat *nettle rash*, *poison ivy*, and some *snake bites*.
>
> This apparant anti-inflammatory action goes some way to explain its use in the treatment of *rheumatism* and *gout*. Its main use has been in the treatment of *dyspepsia, nausea, colic pains*, and similar digestive problems. It will stimulate the digestive system and aid its functions.

PREPARATION AND DOSAGE:

Infusion: pour a cup of boiling water onto 1 teaspoonful of the powdered root and leave to infuse for 10–15 minutes. This should be drunk three times a day.

Tincture: take 1–2 milliliters of the tincture three times a day.

WHITE HOREHOUND
Marrubium vulgare
LABIATAE

Part used: Dried leaves and flowering tops.
Collection: White Horehound is gathered while the herb is blossoming between June and September. It is dried in the shade at a temperature not greater than 95°F (35°C).
Constituents: Sesquiterpene bitters, including marrubin; essential oil; mucilage; tannins.
Actions: Expectorant, anti-spasmodic, bitter digestive, vulnerary.
Combinations: It combines well with Coltsfoot, Lobelia, and Mullein.

INDICATIONS:
White Horehound is a valuable plant in the treatment of *bronchitis* where there is a nonproductive cough. It combines the action of relaxing the smooth muscles of the bronchus while promoting mucus production and thus expectoration. It is used with benefit in the treatment of *whooping cough*. The bitter action stimulates the flow and secretion of bile from the gallbladder and thus aids digestion. White Horehound is used externally to promote the healing of *wounds*.

PREPARATION AND DOSAGE:
Infusion: pour a cup of boiling water onto ½–1 teaspoonful of the dried herb and leave to infuse for 10–15 minutes. This should be drunk three times a day.
Tincture: take 1–2 milliliters of the tincture three times a day.

WHITE POPLAR
Populus tremuloides
SALICACEAE

Part used: Bark.
Collection: The bark should be collected in the spring, taking care not to girdle or ringbark the tree and thus kill it.
Constituents: Glycosides, flavonoids, essential oil, tannins.
Actions: Anti-inflammatory, astringent, antiseptic, anodyne, cholagogue.
Combinations: In the treatment of *rheumatoid arthritis*, it may be used with Black Cohosh, Buckbean, and Celery. As a digestive stimulant, it can be used with Balmony and Golden Seal.

INDICATIONS:
White Poplar is an excellent remedy to use in the treatment of *arthritis* and *rheumatism* where there is much pain and swelling. Its use is quite similar to Black Willow. It is most effective when used in a broad therapeutic approach and not by itself. It is very helpful during the flare-ups of *rheumatoid arthritis*. As a cholagogue, it can be used to stimulate digestion and especially stomach and liver function, particularly where there is loss of appetite. In *feverish colds* and in infections such as *cystitis*, it may be considered. As an astringent, it can be used in the treatment of *diarrhea*.

PREPARATION AND DOSAGE:
Decoction: put 1–2 teaspoonfuls of the dried bark in a cup of water, bring to the boil and simmer for 10–15 minutes. This should be drunk three times a day. To stimulate appetite, drink 30 minutes before meals.
Tincture: take 2–4 milliliters of the tincture three times a day.

WILD CARROT
Daucus carrota
UMBELLIFERAE

Part used: Dried aerial parts and seeds.
Collection: The aerial parts of the herb should be collected between June and August when in flower or when seeding in August and September.
Constituents: Volatile oil, an alkaloid.
Actions: Diuretic, antilithic, carminative.

> ### INDICATIONS:
> The volatile oil that is present in Wild Carrot is an active urinary antiseptic, which helps explain its use in the treatment of such conditions as *cystitis* and *prostatitis*. It has been considered a specific in the treatment of *kidney stones* for a long time. In the treatment of *gout* and *rheumatism*, it is used in combination with other remedies to provide its cleansing diuretic action. The seeds can be used as a settling carminative agent for the relief of *flatulence* and *colic*.

Combinations: For urinary infections, it may be used with Yarrow and Bearberry. For *kidney stones*, use it with Hydrangea, Gravel Root, or Pellitory.

PREPARATION AND DOSAGE:

Infusion: pour a cup of boiling water onto 1 teaspoonful of the dried herb and let infuse for 10–15 minutes. This should be drunk three times a day. To prepare an infusion of the seeds, use $1/3$–1 teaspoonful to a cup of water.
Tincture: take 1–2 milliliters of the tincture three times a day.

WILD CHERRY BARK

Prunus serotina

ROSACEAE

Part used: Dried bark.
Collection: The bark is gathered from young plants in the fall, when it is most active. The outer bark is stripped off and the inner bark is carefully dried in the shade. It must be stored in an airtight container and protected from light.
Constituents: Cyanogenic glycosides, including prunasin; volatile oil; coumarins; gallitannins; resin.
Actions: Antitussive, expectorant, astringent, sedative, digestive bitter.

> ### INDICATIONS:
> Due to its powerful sedative action on the cough reflex, Wild Cherry Bark finds its main use in the treatment of *irritating coughs* and thus has a role in the treatment of *bronchitis* and *whooping cough*. It can be used with other herbs in the control of *asthma*. It must be remembered, however, that the inhibition of a cough does not equate with the healing of a chest infection, which will still need to be treated. It may also be used as a bitter where digestion is sluggish. The cold infusion of the bark may be helpful as a wash in cases of *inflammation of the eyes*.

PREPARATION AND DOSAGE:

Infusion: pour a cup of boiling water onto 1 teaspoonful of the dried bark and leave to infuse for 10–15 minutes. This should be drunk three times a day.
Tincture: take 1–2 milliliters of the tincture three times a day.

WILD INDIGO

Baptisia tinctoria

LEGUMINOSAE

Part used: Root.
Collection: The root is unearthed in the fall after flowering has stopped. Clean the root and cut, then dry well.
Constituents: Alkaloids, glycosides, oleoresin.
Actions: Antimicrobial, anticatarrhal, febrifuge.

> ### INDICATIONS:
> Wild Indigo is an herb to be considered wherever there is a focused infection. It is especially useful in the treatment of infections and catarrh in the ear, nose, and throat. It may be used for *laryngitis, tonsilitis, pharyngitis*, and catarrhal infections of the nose and sinus. Taken both internally and as a mouthwash, it will heal *mouth ulcers, gingivitis*, and help in the control of *pyorrhea*. Systemically, it may be helpful in the treatment of *enlarged and inflamed lymph glands (lymphadenitis)* and also to reduce *fevers*. Externally, an ointment will help *infected ulcers* and ease *sore nipples*. A douche of the decoction will help *leukorrhea*.

Combinations: For the treatment of infections, it may be used with Echinacea and Myrrh. For lymphatic problems, it can be combined with Cleavers and Pokeweed Root.

PREPARATION AND DOSAGE:

Decoction: put ½–1 teaspoonful of the root in a cup of water, bring to the boil, and simmer for 10–15 minutes. This should be drunk three times a day.
Tincture: take 1–2 milliliters of the tincture three times a day.

WILD LETTUCE
Lactuca virosa
COMPOSITAE

Part used: Dried leaves.
Collection: The leaves should be gathered in June and July.
Constituents: Latex containing lactucin, lactucone, lactupicrin, lactucic acid; alkaloids; triterpenes.
Actions: Sedative, anodyne, hypnotic.

INDICATIONS:
The latex of the Wild Lettuce was at one time sold as "Lettuce Opium," naming the use of this herb quite well! It is a valuable remedy for use in *insomnia, restlessness,* and *excitability* (especially in children) and other manifestations of an overactive nervous system. As an antispasmodic, it can be used as part of a holistic treatment of *whooping cough* and dry, irritated coughs in general. It will relieve *colic pains* in the guts and uterus and so may be used in *painful periods*. It will ease muscular pains related to *rheumatism*. It has been used as an anaphrodisiac.

Combinations: For *irritable coughs*, it may be used with Wild Cherry Bark. For *insomnia*, it combines with Valerian and Pasqueflower.

PREPARATION AND DOSAGE:
Infusion: pour a cup of boiling water onto 1–2 teaspoonfuls of the leaves and let infuse for 10–15 minutes. This should be drunk three times a day.
Tincture: take 2–4 milliliters of the tincture three times a day.

WILD YAM
Dioscorea villosa
DIOSCOREACEAE

Part used: Dried underground parts.
Collection: This tropical plant is uprooted in the fall, most stocks coming from West Africa.
Constituents: Steroidal saponins, including dioscine; phytosterols; alkaloids; tannina; much starch.
Actions: Antispasmodic, anti-inflammatory, anti-rheumatic, cholagogue.

INDICATIONS:
This valuable herb was at one time the sole source of the chemicals that were used as the raw materials for contraceptive hormone manufacture. In herbal medicine, Wild Yam is a valuable herb that can be used to relieve *intestinal colic*, to soothe *diverticulitis*, and to ease *dysmenorrhea* and *ovarian and uterine pains*. It is of great use in the treatment of *rheumatoid arthritis*, especially the acute phase where there is intense inflammation.

Combinations: To relieve *intestinal colic*, it may be combined with Calamus, Chamomile, and Ginger. For *rheumatoid arthritis*, it may be used with Black Cohosh.

PREPARATION AND DOSAGE:
Decoction: put 1–2 teaspoonfuls of the herb in a cup of water, bring to the boil, and simmer gently for 10–15 minutes. This should be drunk three times a day.
Tincture: take 2–4 milliliters of the tincture three times a day.

WINGED ELM (AKA WAHOO)

Euonymus atropurpureus

CELASTRACEAE

Part used: Root bark.

Collection: The bark is stripped off roots that have been unearthed in the fall. Stem bark can be used as a substitute.

Constituents: Euonymol, euonysterol, atropurpurol, dulcitol, citrullol, fatty acids.

Actions: Cholagogue, laxative, diuretic, circulatory stimulant.

INDICATIONS:

Winged Elm (aka Wahoo) is one of the primary liver herbs. It acts to remove congestion from the liver, allowing the free flow of bile and so helping the digestive process. It may be used in the treatment of *jaundice* and *gallbladder problems* such as *inflammation* and *pain* or *congestion due to stones*. It will relieve *constipation* where this is due to liver or gallbladder problems. Through its normalizing action upon the liver, it may help in a range of skin problems where there is a possible involvement of the liver.

PREPARATION AND DOSAGE:

Decoction: pour a cup of water onto ½–1 teaspoonful of the bark. Bring to the boil and let infuse for 10–15 minutes. This should be drunk three times a day.

Tincture: take 1–2 milliliters of the tincture three times a day.

WINTERGREEN
Gaultheria procumbens
ERICACEAE

Part used: Leaves.
Collection: The leaves can be gathered throughout the year, but the summer is preferable. Dry in the shade.
Constituents: Volatile oil, which is largely salicylate.
Actions: Anodyne, astringent, stimulant, diuretic, emmenagogue, galactogogue.

INDICATIONS:
Wintergreen is largely used for its oil, which is naturally rich in methyl salicylate. This chemical is the basis of the aspirin group and explains much of the activity of Wintergreen in reducing pain and inflammation in acute *rheumatism*. It is most commonly used externally as a liniment for the treatment of chronic forms of muscular and skeletal troubles like *lumbago* and *sciatica*. Internally, the plant has been used for its diuretic and emmenagogic activity. It is reported to be a galactogogue.

PREPARATION AND DOSAGE:
Infusion: pour a cup of boiling water onto 1 teaspoonful of the leaves and let infuse for 10–15 minutes. This should be drunk three times a day.
Liniments and poultice: see the section on the preparation of herbs for details.

WITCH HAZEL
Hamamelis virginiana
HAMAMELIADACEAE

Part used: Bark or leaves.
Collection: The leaves can be gathered throughout the summer and dried quickly to ensure that they do not become discolored. The bark is gathered in the spring after sprouting.
Constituents: Rich in tannins and gallic acid, bitters, traces of volatile oil.
Actions: Astringent.

INDICATIONS:
This herb can be found in most households in the form of distilled Witch Hazel. It is the most applicable and easy to use astringent for common usage. As with all astringents, this herb may be used wherever there has been bleeding, both internally or externally. It is especially useful in the easing of *hemorrhoids*. It has a deserved reputation in the treatment of *bruises* and *inflamed swellings*, also with *varicose veins*. Witch Hazel will control *diarrhea* and aid in the easing of *dysentry*.

Combinations: For the easing of *hemorrhoids*, it will combine well with Lesser Celandine (aka Pilewort).

PREPARATION AND DOSAGE:
Infusion: pour a cup of boiling water onto 1 teaspoonful of the dried leaves and let infuse for 10–15 minutes. This should be drunk three times a day.
Ointment: Witch Hazel can be made into an excellent ointment.
Tincture: take 1–2 milliliters of the tincture three times a day.

WOOD SAGE
Teucrium scorodonia
LABIATAE

Part used: Aerial parts.
Collection: The herb should be gathered when in flower throughout the summer.
Constituents: Essential oil, bitter principle, tannins, polyphenols, flavonoids, saponins.
Actions: Astringent, diaphoretic, carminative, vulnerary, antirheumatic, antimicrobial.

INDICATIONS:
Wood Sage may be used for all infections of the upper respiratory tract, especially for *colds* and *influenza*. It may be used as a diaphoretic in all *fevers*. It can prove beneficial in some cases of *rheumatism*. There is a marked stimulation of gastric juices, thereby aiding digestion and relieving *flatulent indigestion*. Externally, Wood Sage will speed the healing of *wounds*, *boils*, and *abscesses*.

Combinations: In the treatment of *colds* and *influenza*, it will combine well with Yarrow, Peppermint, and Elderberry Flower. Used as a poultice or ointment, it may be combined with Chickweed.

PREPARATION AND DOSAGE:
Infusion: pour a cup of boiling water onto 1–2 teaspoonfuls of the dried herb and leave to infuse for 10 minutes. This should be drunk three times a day.
Tincture: take 2–4 milliliters of the tincture three times a day.

WORMWOOD
Artemisia absinthum
COMPOSITAE

Part used: Leaves or flowering tops.
Collection: The leaves and flowering tops are gathered at the end of the flowering period between July and September.
Constituents: Rich in essential oils, including absinthol, thujyl, isovaleric acid; bitter sesquiterpenes; flavonoid glycosides.
Actions: Bitter tonic, carminative, anthelmintic, anti-inflammatory.

INDICATIONS:

Traditionally, Wormwood has been used in a wide range of conditions, most of which have been vindicated by analysis of the herb. It is primarily used as a bitter and therefore has the effect of stimulating and invigorating the whole of the digestive process. It may be used where there is *indigestion*, especially when due to a deficient quantity or quality of gastric juice. It is a powerful remedy in the treatment of *worm infestations*, especially *roundworm* and *pinworm*. It may also be used to help the body deal with *fever* and *infections*. Due to the general tonic action, it will be of benefit in many diverse conditions because it benefits the body in general.

PREPARATION AND DOSAGE:

Infusion: pour a cup of boiling water onto 1–2 teaspoonfuls of the dried herb and leave to infuse for 10–15 minutes. This should be drunk three times a day.

Pill: the powdered herb may be used to get rid of worms in the form of pills, thus avoiding the extreme, bitter taste.

Tincture: take 1–4 milliliters of the tincture three times a day.

WOUNDWORT
Stachys palustris
LABIATAE

Part used: Aerial parts.
Collection: The herb is collected in July when coming into flower.
Actions: Vulnerary, antiseptic, antispasmodic, astringent.

INDICATIONS:

As its name implies, Woundwort is renowned in folklore as a wound healer. Used as a vulnerary it is an equivalent of Comfrey in its effect on *wounds*. It may be used directly on the wound or as an ointment or compress. Internally, it will ease *cramps* and some *joint pains*, and also relieve *diarrhea* and *dysentry*.

PREPARATION AND DOSAGE:

Infusion: pour a cup of boiling water onto 1 teaspoonful of the dried herb and let infuse for 10–15 minutes. This should be drunk three times a day.

External use: follow the instructions given in the section on the preparation of herbs.

Tincture: take 1–2 milliliters of the tincture three times a day.

YARROW
Achillea millefolium

COMPOSITAE

Part used: Aerial parts.
Collection: The whole of the plant above ground should be gathered when in flower between June and September.
Constituents: Up to 0.5% volatile oil, flavonoids, tannins, a bitter alkaloid.
Actions: Diaphoretic, hypotensive, astringent, diuretic, antiseptic.

> ### INDICATIONS:
> Yarrow is one of the best diaphoretic herbs and is a standard remedy for aiding the body to deal with *fevers*. It lowers blood pressure due to a dilation of the peripheral vessels. It stimulates the digestion and tones the blood vessels. As a urinary antiseptic, it is indicated in infections such as *cystitis*. Used externally, it will aid in the healing of *wounds*. It is considered to be a specific in thrombotic conditions associated with high blood pressure.

Combinations: For *fevers*, it will combine well with Elderberry Flower, Peppermint, Boneset, and with Cayenne and Ginger. For *raised blood pressure*, it may be used with Hawthorn, Lime Blossom, and Mistletoe.

PREPARATION AND DOSAGE:
Infusion: pour a cup of boiling water onto 1–2 teaspoonfuls of the dried herb and leave to infuse for 10–15 minutes. This should be drunk hot three times a day. When feverish, it should be drunk hourly.
Tincture: take 2–4 milliliters of the tincture three times a day.

YELLOW DOCK
Rumex crispus

POLYGONACEAE

Part used: Root.
Collection: The roots should be unearthed in the late summer and fall, between August and October. Clean well and split lengthwise before drying.
Constituents: Anthraquinone glycosides, tannins.
Actions: Alterative, purgative, cholagogue.

> ### INDICATIONS:
> Yellow Dock is used extensively in the treatment of chronic skin complaints such as *psoriasis*. The anthraquinones present have a markedly cathartic action on the bowel, but in this herb they act in a mild way, possibly tempered by the tannin content. Thus it makes a valuable remedy for *constipation*, working as it does in a much wider way than simply stimulating the gut muscles. It promotes the flow of bile and has that somewhat obscure action of being a "blood cleanser." The action on the gallbladder gives it a role in the treatment of *jaundice* when this is due to congestion.

Combinations: It will combine well with Dandelion, Burdock, and Cleavers.

PREPARATION AND DOSAGE:
Decoction: put 1–2 teaspoonfuls of the root in a cup of water, bring to the boil, and simmer gently for 10–15 minutes. This should be drunk three times a day.
Tincture: take 1–4 milliliters of the tincture three times a day.

About the Author

While working in conservation and lecturing in ecology and the ecocrisis for the University of Wales, David Hoffmann became convinced that to heal the world, and to embrace planetary wholeness and responsibility for it with hope, he as an individual had to be whole within himself. This moved him to start exploring herbal medicine as a truly ecological healing for the body as well as the spirit. To this end he studied for four years with the National Institute of Medical Herbalists. He also cofounded a spiritual community in the Preseli Mountain area of West Wales. He has been practicing as a consultant medical herbalist for 35 years and has lectured widely on holistic herbalism, as well as personal and planetary transformation. He is active in the environmental movement, standing for U.K. Parliament in the 1983 election as a representative of the Ecology Party.

In 1987, he moved to California and has since become deeply involved in the herbal renaissance that is underway in North America. He was appointed to the post of Director of the California School of Herbal Studies, North America's premier center of herbal education, as well as being elected President of the American Herbalist Guild. He regularly teaches in Canada and the U.S.A. Hoffmann is the author of 17 books; his latest is a textbook on the science of herbal medicine and its therapeutic application in clinical practice, entitled *Medical Herbalism*, and published by Inner Traditions.

His commitment to herbalism is a reflection of a deep involvement in transformation—both personal and planetary.

Resources and Suppliers

In most cases it is preferable to use freshly picked, wild or cultivated herbs. Of course this is not always possible, so below is a list of highly reputable suppliers of herbs and herbal products.

Resources and Suppliers in the U.S.A.

American Herbalists Guild
14 Waverly Court
Asheville, NC 28805
Tel.: (617) 520-4372
ahgoffice@earthlink.net
www.americanherbalistsguild.com

American Botanical Council
PO Box 144345
Austin, TX 78714-4345
Tel.: (1-800) 373-7105
abc@herbalgram.org
www.herbalgram.org

HerbPharm
PO Box 116
Williams, OR 97544
Tel.: (1-800) 348-4372
HerbPharm@aol.com

Herbalist & Alchemist, Inc.
51 S. Wandling Ave.
Washington, NJ 07882
Tel.: (1-800) 611-8235
www.herbalist-alchemist.com

Gaia Herbs Inc.
108 Island Ford Road
Brevard, NC 28712
Tel.: (828) 884-4242
VOB@gaiaherbs.com
www.gaiaherbs.com

Eclectic Institute
36560 S.E. Industrial Way
Sandy, OR 97055
Tel.: (1-800) 859-4971
customerservice@eclectic-herb.com
www.eclecticherb.com

Resources and Suppliers in the U.K.

Leyland Mills
Leyland Mill Lane
Wigan WN1 2SB
Tel.: 01144 (0) 1942 405100

Phytoproducts, Ltd.
Park Works
Park Road
Mansfield Woodhouse
Notts NG19 8EF
Tel.: 01144 (0) 1623 644334

Arnold Pierce A., & Son
Herb, Spice Wholesalers
270 London Rd
Wallington SM6 7DJ
Tel.: 01144 (0) 20 8647 5330

Neal's Yard Remedies
15 Neal's Yard
Covent Garden
London WC2H 9DP
Tel.: 01144 (0) 20 7379 7222
www.nealsyardremedies.com
mail@nealsyardremedies.com

For Mail Order:

29 Dalton Street
Manchester M2 6DS
Tel.: 01144 (0) 161 831 7875
Fax: 01144 (0) 161 835 9322

Bibliography

Herbals

There are generally two types of books about herbs that are currently available. One type lists plants that are medicinally used and gives their properties. In order to use this type, the reader must have prior knowledge of the appropriate plant for a particular condition. The other type focuses on conditions and symptoms, giving herbs that will help to heal some. Though neither type is ideal, they can help a lot in the exploration of this fascinating field.

The list that follows is only a small selection of what is currently available. I have added commentary to some of these books. When looking for a book on herbs, it is best to go to a bookstore and browse.

Bove, Mary
An Encyclopedia of Natural Healing for Children and Infants. New Canaan, CT: Keats, 1996.

Chevallier, Andrew
The Encyclopedia of Medicinal Plants. New York, NY: DK Publishing, 1996.

Gladstar Rosemary
Family Herbal: A Guide to Living Life with Energy, Health, and Vitality. Pownal, VT: Storey Books, 2001.

Gladstar, Rosemary
Herbal Healing for Women. New York, NY: Simon & Schuster, 1993.

Grieve, Mrs. M.
A Modern Herbal. Dover Publications, 1931. By far the best source book on herbs, their origins, cultivation, medicinal use, and folklore. A must.

Hoffmann, David
Medical Herbalism: The Science and Practice of Herbal Medicine. Rochester, VT: Healing Arts Press, 2003.

Kloss, Jethro
Back to Eden. Beneficial Books, 1971. A classic of herbal and naturopathic medicine.

Lust, John
The Herb Book. Bantam Books, 1974. An American herbal that is a mine of information about the herbs covered, although it omits many British species.

McIntyre, Anne
The Complete Herbal Tutor: A Structured Course to Achieve Professional Expertise. Gaia Books, 2010.

McIntyre, Anne
The Complete Woman's Herbal. New York, NY: Henry Holt Company. pp. 166-170, 189; 1995.

Mills, Simon, and Bone, Kerry
Principles and Practice of Phytotherapy: Modern Herbal Medicine. Edinburgh, UK: Churchill Livingstone, 1999.

Potter's New Cyclopaedia of Botanical Drugs. Health

Science Press, 1975. This is one of the standard reference books, but it leaves a lot to be desired.

Wood, Matthew
The Earthwise Herbal: A Complete Guide to New World Medicinal Plants. Berkeley, CA: North Atlantic Books, 2009.

Pharmacognosy and Medicine

There is a wealth of information available about the constituents of plants and their use in medicine and pharmacology. The sources tend to be very esoteric academic tomes, but they are well worth exploring. There are a number of scientific journals that focus purely on plant medicines, such as *Lloydia, Plant Medica*, and the *Journal of Ethnobotany*. The following is a selection of books that cover the orthodox use of plants.

Barnes, J., Anderson, L. A., and Phillipson, J. D.
Herbal Medicines—A Guide for Health-care Professionals. London, England: The Pharmaceutical Press, 2002.

Bradley, P., ed.
British Herbal Compendium. Dorset, England: British Herbal Medicine Association. Vol. 2, 2006.

British Pharmaceutical Codex
Especially editions prior to 1949

United States Pharmacopoeia

Martindale
The Extra Pharmacopoeia
Pharmaceutical Press, 1989.

Trease & Evans
Pharmacognosy
Bailliere Tindall, 1989.

General

There are many books covering various aspects of holistic healing, the New Age, and herbalism in general. This is a token selection.

Bailey, Alice A.
Esoteric Healing. Lucis Press, 1953.

Bohm, David
Wholeness and the Implicate Order. Routledge & Kegan Paul, 1980.

Capra, Fritjof
The Tao of Physics. Fontana/Collins, 1975.

Capra, Fritjof
The Turning Point. Wildwood House, 1982. This is one of the most important books to be published in recent years. It is the clearest, most cogent exploration of the social, psychological, and spiritual transformation we are going through that I have come across. Capra's review of medicine has profound implications for herbal medicine.

Dossey, Larry
Space, Time and Medicine. Shambhala, 1982.

Gaskin, Ina M.
Spiritual Midwifery. The Book Publishing Company, 1980. This is an excellent book on natural childbirth.

Griggs, Barbara
Green Pharmacy. Norman & Hobhouse, 1981. A unique and insightful history of herbal medicine to the present day.

Grigson, Geoffrey
The Englishman's Flora. Paladin. An excellent book on the folklore of British plants.

Lovelock, J. E.
Gaia, A New Look at Life on Earth. Oxford University Press, 1979.

Poucher, W. A.
Perfumes, Cosmetics and Soaps. Chapman and Hall, HB, 1975; PB, 1978.

Schultes and Hoffmann
Plants of the Gods. Hutchinson. This book explores the use of hallucinogenic plants around the world. It is a testimony to the spiritual and ecological relationship between humanity and our planet.

Repertory

The repertory lists herbs that can be considered for specific diseases. Herbs that can be regarded as specifics are underlined.

ABSCESS

Blue Flag Cleavers Coltsfoot <u>Echinacea</u> Fenugreek <u>Garlic</u> Golden Seal Mallow <u>Marshmallow</u> <u>Myrrh</u> Pokeweed Root <u>Wild Indigo</u>

ACNE

<u>Blue Flag</u> <u>Cleavers</u> <u>Echinacea</u> Garlic <u>Pokeweed Root</u> <u>Wild Indigo</u>

ADENOIDS

<u>Cleavers</u> <u>Echinacea</u> Garlic <u>Golden Seal</u> <u>Marigold</u> <u>Pokeweed Root</u> <u>Wild Indigo</u>

AMENORRHEA

see "Menstruation (delayed)"

ANGINA PECTORIS

<u>Hawthorn</u> Motherwort

APPETITE LOSS

Balmony Blessed Thistle <u>Calamus</u> Calumba Caraway Cardamom <u>Centaury</u> Chamomile <u>Condurango</u> Galangal <u>Gentian</u> Golden Seal <u>Mugwort</u> Quassia Southernwood Tansy White Poplar <u>Wormwood</u>

ANXIETY

Balm Betony <u>Californian Poppy</u> <u>Chamomile</u> Cowslip Damiana Hops Hyssop Lime Blossom <u>Mistletoe</u> <u>Motherwort</u> Oats <u>Pasqueflower</u> Passion Flower Peppermint <u>St. John's Wort</u> <u>Skullcap</u> <u>Valerian</u> Vervain <u>Wild Lettuce</u>

APPENDICITIS

<u>Agrimony</u> Geranium (Cranesbill) Golden Seal Wild Yam

ARTERIOSCLEROSIS

Hawthorn <u>Lime Blossom</u> Mistletoe

ARTHRITIS

Birch Bittersweet <u>Black Cohosh</u> <u>Buckbean</u> <u>Celery Seed</u> Daisy <u>Guaiacum</u> Juniper Meadowsweet Pine <u>Prickly Ash</u> White Poplar Wintergreen Yarrow <u>Wild Yam</u>

ASTHMA

Balsam of Tolu Black Cohosh Black Haw Bloodroot Blue Cohosh Butterbur Coltsfoot <u>Elecampane</u> <u>Ephedra</u> <u>Grindelia</u> Lobelia Mullein Pasqueflower <u>Pill-Bearing Spurge</u> Senega <u>Sundew</u> <u>Wild Cherry</u>

347

BLOOD PRESSURE (HIGH)

Balm Black Haw Cramp Bark Garlic Hawthorn Lime Blossom Mistletoe Yarrow

BLOOD PRESSURE (LOW)

Broom Hawthorn

BOILS

Blue Flag Chickweed Cleavers Coltsfoot Comfrey Echinacea Fenugreek Figwort Flaxseed Garlic Mallow Marshmallow Myrrh Pasqueflower Pokeweed Root Plantain Wild Indigo

BRONCHITIS

Angelica Aniseed Balm of Gilead Balsam of Tolu Bloodroot Caraway Carline Thistle Coltsfoot Comfrey Cowslip Echinacea Elecampane Ephedra Fennel Fenugreek Flaxseed Garlic Grindelia Ground Ivy Horseradish Hyssop Iceland Moss Ipecacuanha Irish Moss Licorice Lobelia Mallow Marshmallow Mouse-Ear Mullein Nasturtium Pansy Pill-Bearing Spurge Pine Plantain Pleurisy Root Senega Bouncing Bet (Soapwort) Squill Sundew Sweet Violet Thyme White Horehound Wild Cherry

BRUISES

Arnica Chickweed Cucumber Elderberry Lady's Mantle Marigold St. John's Wort

BURNS

Aloe Chamomile Chickweed Comfrey Cucumber Elderberry Marigold Plantain Quince Seed St. John's Wort

CATARRH

Avens Balsam of Tolu Bistort Chamomile Coltsfoot Daisy Echinacea Elderberry Eyebright Fenugreek Garlic Golden Rod Golden Seal Grindelia Ground Ivy Hyssop Iceland Moss Mallow Mouse-Ear Mullein Myrrh Peppermint Pill-Bearing Spurge Pine Pokeweed Root Sweet Violet Wild Indigo

CHILBLAINS

Cayenne Ginger Horsetail Mustard Prickly Ash

CIRCULATION

Cayenne Ginger Horseradish Mustard Prickly Ash Rosemary

COLD

Angelica Avens Bayberry Catnip Cayenne Cowslip Echinacea Elderberry Eyebright Fenugreek Garlic Ginger Golden Rod Golden Seal Hyssop Lime Blossom Marjoram Peppermint Yarrow

COLIC

Allspice Angelica Aniseed Avens Balmony Blessed Thistle Blue Cohosh Boldo Butterbur Calamus Caraway Cardamom Catnip Cayenne Chamomile Cinnamon Condurango Coriander Cramp Bark Dill Fennel Gentian Ginger Horseradish Jambul Juniper Licorice Mugwort Pennyroyal Peppermint Rue Tormentil Valerian Wild Lettuce Wild Yam Wormwood

COLITIS

Agrimony Bayberry Bistort Black Catechu Comfrey Geranium (Cranesbill) Marshmallow Meadowsweet Oak Bark Tormentil

CONJUNCTIVITIS

Chamomile Eyebright Fennel Golden Seal Marigold

CONSTIPATION

Aloe Balmony Barberry Black Root Buckbean Boldo Buckthorn Butternut Cascara Sagrada Figwort Flaxseed Rhubarb Senna Winged Elm (Wahoo) Yellow Dock

COUGH

Angelica Aniseed Balm of Gilead Balsam of Tolu Caraway Carline Thistle Coltsfoot Comfrey Cowslip Daisy Elecampane Fennel Fenugreek Garlic Golden Seal Grindelia Ground Ivy Hyssop Licorice Mallow Marjoram Marshmallow Mouse-Ear Mullein Myrrh Pine Plantain Pleurisy Root Red Poppy Senega Bouncing Bet (Soapwort) Sundew Sweet Violet Thuja Thyme White Horehound Wild Lettuce

CRAMP

Black Cohosh Cayenne Cramp Bark Ginger Pasqueflower Skullcap Valerian Wild Lettuce Wild Yam Woundwort

CYSTITIS

Angelica Bearberry Benzoin Birch Boldo Buchu Carline Thistle Celery Seed Cleavers Coltsfoot Corn Silk Couch Grass Echinacea Golden Rod Gravel Root Ground Ivy Horsetail Hydrangea Juniper Pansy Pellitory Sea Holly Yarrow

DEBILITY

Agrimony Balmony Barberry Betony Blessed Thistle Calamus Cayenne Damiana Dandelion Ginger Golden Seal Kola Nut Golden Ragwort (Life Root) Mugwort Oats Rosemary True Unicorn Root White Poplar Wormwood

DEPRESSION

Balm Celery Chamomile Damiana Kola Nut Misteletoe Mugwort Oats Rosemary Skullcap Southernwood Valerian Vervain Wormwood

DIARRHEA

Agrimony Avens Bayberry Bistort Black Catechu Blessed Thistle Bur Marigold Caraway Catnip Cinnamon Comfrey Coriander Daisy Eyebright Geranium (Cranesbill) Ground Ivy Jambul Kola Nut Lady's Mantle Meadowsweet Oak Bark Plantain Rhatany Self-Heal Silverweed Tormentil

DIARRHEA (IN CHILDREN)

Geranium (Cranesbill) Lady's Mantle Meadowsweet

DIVERTICULITIS

Chamomile Comfrey Marshmallow Wild Yam

EARACHE (SEE ALSO "INFECTION")

Mullein Pasqueflower Pennywort

ECZEMA

Balm of Gilead Bittersweet Blue Flag Burdock Chickweed Cleavers Comfrey Figwort Golden Seal Mountain Grape Nettles Pansy Red Clover Sarsaparilla Sweet Violet Yellow Dock

EPILEPSY

Hyssop Passion Flower Skullcap Valerian

FEVER

Angelica <u>Boneset</u> *Borage Carline Thistle* <u>Catnip</u> <u>Cayenne</u> *Chamomile* <u>Ginger</u> *Horseradish Mustard Peppermint* <u>Peruvian Bark</u> <u>Pleurisy Root</u> *Vervain*

FIBROSITIS

<u>Cayenne</u> <u>Ginger</u> *Horseradish* <u>Pine</u> <u>Ragwort</u> *Rosemary St. John's Wort* <u>Wintergreen</u>

FLATULENCE

Allspice <u>Angelica</u> *Aniseed Balm Blessed Thistle* <u>Calamus</u> *Calumba* <u>Caraway</u> <u>Cardamom</u> *Catnip* <u>Cayenne</u> *Centaury Chamomile* <u>Cinnamon</u> *Cloves* <u>Condurango</u> <u>Coriander</u> *Fennel Galangal* <u>Gentian</u> <u>Ginger</u> *Horseradish Juniper Marjoram Mugwort Parsley Pennyroyal Peppermint Southernwood Thyme Valerian Wormwood*

FUNGUS INFECTION

Golden Seal Greater Celandine <u>Marigold</u> *Myrrh*

GALLBLADDER PROBLEMS

<u>Balmony</u> *Barberry* <u>Black Root</u> *Boldo Buckbean* <u>Dandelion</u> *Golden Seal Greater Celandine* <u>Fringe Tree Bark</u> *Marigold* <u>Milk Thistle</u> <u>Vervain</u> *Wild Yam* <u>Winged Elm (Wahoo)</u>

GASTRITIS

<u>Calamus</u> *Chamomile* <u>Comfrey</u> <u>Geranium (Cranesbill)</u> <u>Golden Seal</u> *Iceland Moss Irish Moss Licorice Mallow* <u>Marshmallow</u> <u>Meadowsweet</u> *Peach Leaves Quince* <u>Slippery Elm</u>

GINGIVITIS

Avens Bayberry <u>Bistory</u> *Black Catechu* <u>Echinacea</u> *Garlic* <u>Golden Seal</u> *Lady's Mantle* <u>Myrrh</u> <u>Oak Bark</u> <u>Pokeweed Root</u> *Red Sage* <u>Rhatany</u> *Self-Heal Silverweed Tormentil Vervain* <u>Wild Indigo</u>

GLANDS (SWOLLEN)

<u>Cleavers</u> *Echinacea Marigold* <u>Pokeweed Root</u> *Wild Indigo*

GLANDULAR FEVER

<u>Echinacea</u> *Eucalyptus Garlic* <u>Myrrh</u> <u>Pokeweed Root</u> *Wild Indigo* <u>Wormwood</u>

HALITOSIS

Dill Fennel

HAY FEVER

Elderberry <u>Ephedra</u> *Eyebright Garlic* <u>Golden Seal</u> *Peppermint*

HEADACHE

<u>Betony</u> *Chamomile Cowslip* <u>Feverfew</u> *Hops Marjoram Mistletoe Peppermint* <u>Rosemary</u> *Rue St. John's Wort Skullcap Valerian*

HEARTBURN

<u>Comfrey</u> *Iceland Moss Irish Moss Mallow* <u>Marshmallow</u> <u>Meadowsweet</u> *Slippery Elm*

HEMORRHOIDS

Balmony <u>Bistort</u> Comfrey Geranium (Cranesbill) Ground Ivy <u>Horse Chestnut</u> <u>Lesser Celandine (Pilewort)</u> <u>Lady's Mantle</u> Oak Bark Plantain Rhatany <u>Silverweed</u> <u>Tormentil</u>

HYPERSENSITIVITY

<u>Ephedra</u>

INCONTINENCE (URINARY)

Agrimony <u>Ephedra</u> Horsetail

INDIGESTION

Allspice Agrimony <u>Balm</u> Balmony Blessed Thistle Boldo <u>Calamus</u> Caraway Cardamom Catnip <u>Cayenne</u> <u>Centaury</u> <u>Chamomile</u> Cinnamon Cloves <u>Condurango</u> Dill <u>Fennel</u> Galangal Gentian Ginger Iceland Moss Marjoram Mugwort <u>Peppermint</u> Quassia Red Sage Rosemary Thyme True Unicorn Root <u>Valerian</u> Wild Lettuce <u>Wild Yam</u> Wormwood

INFECTION

Cayenne <u>Cleavers</u> Echinacea Fenugreek <u>Garlic</u> Ginger <u>Golden Seal</u> <u>Myrrh</u> Nasturtium Thyme <u>Wild Indigo</u> Wormwood

INFLUENZA

Angelica Balm <u>Boneset</u> Carline Thistle <u>Cayenne</u> <u>Echinacea</u> Elderberry <u>Garlic</u> Ginger <u>Golden Seal</u> Horseradish Lime Blossom Marjoram Mustard Myrrh Nasturtium Peppermint <u>Pleurisy Root</u> White Poplar Yarrow

INSOMNIA

<u>Californian Poppy</u> Chamomile Cowslip <u>Hops</u> <u>Jamaican Dogwood</u> Lime Blossom Pasqueflower <u>Passion Flower</u> Skullcap <u>Valerian</u> <u>Wild Lettuce</u>

ITCHING

Chamomile <u>Chickweed</u> Cleavers Cucumber <u>Golden Seal</u> <u>Marigold</u> Peppermint St. John's Wort

JAUNDICE

<u>Balmony</u> <u>Barberry</u> Bittersweet <u>Black Root</u> Centaury <u>Dandelion</u> Golden Seal Mountain Grape <u>Vervain</u> Wild Yam <u>Winged Elm (Wahoo)</u> <u>Yellow Dock</u>

KIDNEY STONES

<u>Bearberry</u> <u>Corn Silk</u> <u>Couch Grass</u> Dandelion <u>Gravel Root</u> <u>Hardhack (Stone Root)</u> <u>Hydrangea</u> <u>Pellitory</u> Sea Holly Wild Carrot Yarrow

LABOR PAINS (FALSE)

<u>Black Cohosh</u> Blue Cohosh <u>Cramp Bark</u> <u>Motherwort</u> Valerian Wild Lettuce <u>Wild Yam</u>

LARYNGITIS

Agrimony <u>Balm of Gilead</u> Bayberry Bistort Black Catechu <u>Bloodroot</u> Caraway Cayenne Chamomile <u>Echinacea</u> Fenugreek Golden Rod <u>Golden Seal</u> Lady's Mantle Mallow <u>Myrrh</u> <u>Oak Bark</u> Pokeweed Root <u>Red Sage</u> <u>Thyme</u> Tormentil Wild Indigo

LEUKRRHEA

Avens <u>Bayberry</u> Bearberry <u>Trillium (Beth Root)</u> Bistort Black Catechu <u>Geranium (Cranesbill)</u> <u>Golden Seal</u> Ground Ivy <u>Lady's Mantle</u> <u>Golden Ragwort (Life Root)</u> <u>Myrrh</u> <u>Nasturtium</u> Oak Bark <u>Wild Indigo</u>

LIVER TONIC

<u>Balmony</u> <u>Black Root</u> <u>Blue Flag</u> Buckbean Burdock <u>Centaury</u> <u>Dandelion</u> Garlic Golden Seal Mountain Grape Wild Yam <u>Winged Elm (Wahoo)</u> <u>Yellow Dock</u>

LUMBAGO

<u>Cayenne</u> <u>Mustard</u> <u>Ragwort</u> <u>Wintergreen</u>

MENOPAUSE

<u>Black Cohosh</u> <u>Chasteberry</u> <u>False Unicorn Root</u> <u>Golden Ragwort (Life Root)</u> <u>Golden Seal</u> <u>St. John's Wort</u> <u>Trillium (Beth Root)</u>

MENSTRUATION (DELAYED)

<u>Blue Cohosh</u> <u>Chasteberry</u> <u>False Unicorn Root</u> <u>Golden Ragwort (Life Root)</u> Marigold Motherwort Mugwort <u>Parsley</u> <u>Pennyroyal</u> <u>Rue</u> <u>Southernwood</u> <u>Tansy</u> Thuja <u>Wormwood</u> Yarrow

MENSTRUATION (EXCESSIVE)

<u>Geranium (Cranesbill)</u> Golden Seal Lady's Mantle <u>Periwinkle</u> <u>Trillium (Beth Root)</u>

MENSTRUATION (PAINFUL)

<u>Black Cohosh</u> <u>Black Haw</u> Blue Cohosh Butterbur Caraway Chasteberry <u>Cramp Bark</u> False Unicorn Root <u>Jamaican Dogwood</u> Marigold Partridge Vine (Squaw Vine) <u>Pasqueflower</u> <u>St. John's Wort</u> <u>Skullcap</u> <u>Valerian</u> <u>Wild Lettuce</u> Wild Yam

METRORRHAGIA

<u>Geranium (Cranesbill)</u> <u>Golden Seal</u> Lady's Mantle <u>Periwinkle</u> <u>Trillium (Beth Root)</u>

MIGRAINE

<u>Feverfew</u> Jamaican Dogwood Kola Nut Mistletoe Peppermint Skullcap Wormwood

MILK STIMULATION (BREAST)

Borage Caraway Dill Fennel Fenugreek <u>Goat's Rue</u> <u>Milk Thistle</u>

MISCARRIAGE (THREATENED)

Black Haw <u>Blue Cohosh</u> Cramp Bark <u>False Unicorn Root</u>

MOUTH ULCERS

Bistort Chamomile Lady's Mantle <u>Myrrh</u> Oak Bark <u>Red Sage</u>

NAUSEA

Avens <u>Black Horehound</u> Cayenne <u>Chamomile</u> Cinnamon Cloves Fennel Galangal Marshmallow <u>Meadowsweet</u> <u>Peppermint</u>

NEURALGIA

<u>Betony</u> <u>Black Cohosh</u> Hops <u>Jamaican Dogwood</u> <u>Mistletoe</u> Pasqueflower <u>Passion Flower</u> Rosemary <u>St. John's Wort</u> <u>Skullcap</u> <u>Valerian</u>

NOSEBLEED

<u>Lady's Mantle</u> Marigold Tormentil <u>Witch Hazel</u>

OVARIAN PAIN

<u>Jamaican Dogwood</u> <u>Pasqueflower</u> Passion Flower St. John's Wort Skullcap <u>Valerian</u> Wild Yam

PAIN

<u>Black Cohosh</u> <u>Black Willow</u> Cramp Bark Guaiacum Hops <u>Jamaican Dogwood</u> Rosemary Skullcap <u>Valerian</u> <u>Wild Lettuce</u>

PALPITATIONS

<u>Motherwort</u> Skullcap Valerian

PHLEBITIS

<u>Hawthorn</u> <u>Horse Chestnut</u> Lime Mistletoe

PIMPLES

<u>Blue Flag</u> <u>Cleavers</u> <u>Echinacea</u> <u>Figwort</u> <u>Garlic</u> <u>Pokeweed Root</u>

PREGNANCY TONIC

Partridge Vine (Squaw Vine) <u>Raspberry Leaves</u>

PREGNANCY (VOMITING)

<u>Black Horehound</u> Blue Cohosh <u>False Unicorn Root</u> <u>Meadowsweet</u> Peppermint

PREMENSTRUAL SYNDROME

<u>Chasteberry</u> Lime Blossom Pasqueflower <u>Skullcap</u> <u>Valerian</u>

PROSTATE

Corn Silk Couch Grass <u>Damiana</u> <u>Horsetail</u> <u>Hydrangea</u> <u>Saw Palmetto</u> Sea Holly

PSORIASIS

Balm of Gilead <u>Blue Flag</u> <u>Burdock</u> Chickweed <u>Cleavers</u> <u>Figwort</u> Flaxseed <u>Mountain Grape</u> <u>Red Clover</u> <u>Sarsaparilla</u> Sassafras Thuja <u>Yellow Dock</u>

RHEUMATISM

<u>Angelica</u> Arnica Birch Bittersweet <u>Black Cohosh</u> Blue Cohosh <u>Buckbean</u> Burdock Cayenne <u>Celery Seed</u> Couch Grass Daisy Dandelion Elderberry Fennel Gravel Root <u>Guaiacum</u> Horseradish Horsetail Juniper <u>Meadowsweet</u> Mustard Pine Pokeweed Root <u>Prickly Ash</u> Ragwort St. John's Wort Sarsaparilla Sassafras Thuja <u>White Poplar</u> Wild Carrot <u>Wild Lettuce</u> <u>Wild Yam</u> <u>Wintergreen</u> <u>Yarrow</u>

SCIATICA

<u>Black Cohosh</u> <u>Jamaican Dogwood</u> <u>St. John's Wort</u> Yarrow

SHINGLES

Flaxseed Hops <u>Jamaican Dogwood</u> <u>Mistletoe</u> <u>Passion Flower</u> <u>St. John's Wort</u> Skullcap Valerian Wild Lettuce Wild Yam

SINUSITIS

Chamomile <u>Elderberry</u> <u>Eucalyptus</u> <u>Eyebright</u> <u>Garlic</u> <u>Golden Rod</u> <u>Golden Seal</u> Myrrh Peppermint <u>Pine</u> <u>Pokeweed Root</u> Thyme <u>Wild Indigo</u> Yarrow

SORE THROAT

Agrimony <u>Balm of Gilead</u> Bayberry Cayenne Chamomile <u>Echinacea</u> <u>Garlic</u> Ginger Golden Rod <u>Golden Seal</u> Myrrh <u>Oak Bark</u> Pokeweed Root Silverweed Thyme

STRESS

Balm Betony Borage Chamomile Cowslip <u>Damiana</u> Hops <u>Lime Blossom</u> <u>Mistletoe</u> Oats Pasqueflower Passion Flower <u>St. John's Wort</u> <u>Skullcap</u> Valerian Wild Lettuce Wormwood

SUNBURN

<u>Aloe</u> Eyebright <u>Marigold</u> St. John's Wort

TENSION

Balm <u>Betony</u> Californian Poppy <u>Cowslip</u> Damiana Hops <u>Jamaican Dogwood</u> <u>Lime Blossom</u> Mistletoe <u>Motherwort</u> <u>Pasqueflower</u> <u>Passion Flower</u> Peppermint <u>St. John's Wort</u> Skullcap <u>Valerian</u> Vervain <u>Wild Lettuce</u>

TINNITUS

<u>Black Cohosh</u> Golden Rod <u>Golden Seal</u> Ground Ivy

TONSILLITIS

<u>Cleavers</u> <u>Echinacea</u> <u>Garlic</u> <u>Golden Seal</u> <u>Myrrh</u> <u>Pokeweed Root</u> <u>Red Sage</u> Thyme Wild Indigo

TOOTHACHE

<u>Cloves</u>

TRAVEL SICKNESS

<u>Black Horehound</u> Galangal Peppermint

TUMORS

Cleavers Comfrey Elder Fenugreek Greater Celandine Red Clover Sweet Violet Thuja

ULCERS (MOUTH)

see "Mouth ulcers"

ULCERS (PEPTIC)

Calamus <u>Comfrey</u> <u>Geranium (Cranesbill)</u> Golden Seal Irish Moss Licorice Mallow <u>Marshmallow</u> <u>Meadowsweet</u> <u>Slippery Elm</u>

ULCERS (SKIN)

<u>Chickweed</u> <u>Comfrey</u> Echinacea <u>Golden Seal</u> <u>Marigold</u> Marshmallow

VARICOSE ULCERS

Comfrey <u>Golden Seal</u> <u>Horse Chestnut</u> <u>Marigold</u> Marshmallow

VARICOSE VEINS

Hawthorn <u>Horse Chestnut</u> Lime Blossom St. John's Wort Witch Hazel

VOMITING

<u>Black Horehound</u> Cinnamon Cloves Comfrey False Unicorn Root Iceland Moss <u>Meadowsweet</u> Peppermint Rosemary

WARTS

<u>Greater Celandine</u> Thuja

WATER RETENTION

<u>Bearberry</u> Birch <u>Broom Tops</u> <u>Buchu</u> Bur Marigold Carline Thistle Celery Seed Corn Silk <u>Dandelion</u> <u>Gravel Root</u> Hardhack (Stone Root) Horsetail <u>Juniper Berries</u> Parsley <u>Pellitory</u> Sea Holly <u>Wild Carrot</u> Yarrow

WHOOPING COUGH

Black Cohosh <u>Coltsfoot</u> Ephedra Garlic <u>Grindelia</u> <u>Lobelia</u> <u>Mouse-Ear</u> Mullein Pansy Red Clover Sundew Wild Cherry

WORMS

Cucumber Garlic Kousso Male Fern Pomegranate Pumpkin Quassia Santonica Tansy Wormwood

WOUNDS

Carline Thistle Chamomile <u>Chickweed</u> <u>Comfrey</u> <u>Elderberry</u> Fenugreek Garlic <u>Golden Seal</u> Horsetail Lady's Mantle <u>Marigold</u> Marshmallow Mouse-Ear <u>Plantain</u> Red Sage <u>St. John's Wort</u> <u>Self-Heal</u> Tormentil <u>Woundwort</u>

Index

GUIDE TO INDEXES

For reader convenience, there are three indexes included.

The first is a General Index, which includes English and botanical herb names.

To make it easy to find specific herbs, the second listing is an Index of English Names for herbs.

Third, there is an Index of Botanical Names, listing the herbs by their Latin names. Certain page numbers are set in bolder type to indicate wider discussion of the issue (i.e. "adrenal glands 94, 95, **96**, 185").

Where an herb is discussed in depth, the page number is indicated in bold. Likewise, where a disease or other important topic is discussed in depth, the pages are given in bold type.

General Index

A

Abdominal pain 63, 69, 70
Abortifacient 121, 123, 126, 297, 310
Abortion 121, 123, 126, 297, 310
Abscess 51, 64, **65**, 242, 243, 282, 284, 318, 335, **347**
Acacia catechu (*Black Catechu*) 176, **219**
Acerola berries 53
Achillea millefolium (*Yarrow*) 13, 33, 34, 37, 38, 39, 51, 53, 99, 103, 104, 106, 108, 113, 115, 121, 122, 133, 134–5, 136, 142, 143, 157, 175, 176, 177, 178, 180, 189, 205, 216, 225, 226, 229, 236, 244, 245, 248, 250, 251, 252, 268, 298, 330, 335, **337**
Acidity 66, 67, 68, 105, 114, 285

Acids, plant 163
Acne **96**, 258, **347**
Acorus calamus (*Calamus*) 61, 67, 71, 199, 219, **233**, 234, 332
Acupuncture 22, 25
Adaptogen 82, 157, 158, 159, 160, 316
Addison's disease 278
Additives, food 40, 59, 72, 84–5, 105, 135, 150
Adenitis 302
Adenoid problems 241, **347**
Adrenal glands 8, 114, **116–17**, 125, 156, 227, 278
Adrenalin 112, 116, 117
Aesculus hippocastanum (*Horse Chestnut*) 33, 39, 99, 180, 201, **269**

Agathosma betulina (*Buchu*) 12, 133, 134, 135, 156, 175, 177, 180, 199, **229**, 245, 293, 294, 297

Agrimonia eupatoria (*Agrimony*) 55, 61, 70, 71, 78, 137, 156, 176, 177, 178, 180, 198, **209**, 212, 216, 219, 234, 261, 277, 299, 321

Agrimony (Agimonia eupatoria) 55, 61, 70, 71, 78, 137, 156, 176, 177, 178, 180, 198, **209**, 212, 216, 219, 234, 261, 277, 299, 321

Agropyron repens (*Couch Grass*) 103, 122, 133, 134, 135, 136, 175, 177, 180, 200, 216, 229, 244, **245**, 248, 293

AIDS 158

Air 42

Alchemilla vulgaris (*Lady's Mantle*) 63, 122, 189, 202, **275**

Alcohol 31, 38, 40, 59, 65, 66, 67, 68, 71, 73, 88, 99, 105, 108, 114, 157, **164**

Alcoholic tincture **185–7**

Aletris farinosa (*True Unicorn Root*) 126, 278, 204, **326**

Alfalfa 64

Alkaloid 21, 22, 74, 162, **171**

Allantoin 99, 242–3

Allergy 35, 36–7, 48, 50, 52, 54, 66, 69–70, 71, 86, 88, 92, 94, 95, 105, 184, 253

Allium sativum (*Garlic*) 36, 37, 38, 47, 51, 52, 54, 71, 93, 97, 98, 115, 122, 129, 142, 143, 144, 145, 156, 158, 160, 165, 175, 176, 177, 178, 179, 180, 187, 201, **259**

Allopathic medicine 20, 21, 22, 24, 76, 116, 151, 156, 158, 163, 167, 168, 278

Almond oil 51, 190, 193

Allspice (Pimenta officinalis) 115, **209**

Aloe (Aloe vera) 60, 93, 99, 168, 175, 178, 180, **210**

Aloe vera (*Aloe*) 60, 93, 99, 168, 175, 178, 180, **210**

Alpina officinarum (*Galangal*) 177, 180, **258–9**

Alteratives 39, 51, 55, 64, 68, 71, 84, **93**, 94, 96, 97, **103**, 113, 122, 129, 133, 141, **149**, 155, 156, 157, 160, **175**, 219, 241, 306, 311, 323

Althea officinalis (*Marshmallow*) 8, 13, 39, 45, 46, 51, 54, 61, 63, 64, 67, 68, 70, 71, 74, 93, 95, 97, 122, 134, 136, 166, 175, 177, 178, 179, 180, 188, 189, 191, 192, 202, 229, 233, 238, 240, 253, 257, 261, 278, 282, 283, **284**, 304, 318

Amenorrhea **123**, 254, **347**

American Cranesbill see *Cranesbill, American* or *Geranium*

Amoebic dysentry 272, 300

Amphetamine 22

Amphoteric 33, **44–5**, 239, 254

Analgesic 64, **175**, 222, 238, 295, 298

Anemia 69

Anemone pulsatilla (*Pasqueflower*) 77, 88, 93, 97, 124, 125, 175, 176, 178, 179, 203, 263, **295–6**, 332

Anethum graveolens (*Dill*) 175, 176, 177, 184, 200, 244, **250**

Angelica (Angelica archangelica) 44, 46, 61, 103, 133, 142, 176, 177, 178, 179, 180, 198, **210**

Angelica archangelica (*Angelica*) 44, 46, 61, 103, 133, 142, 176, 177, 178, 179, 180, 198, **210**

Angina 33, 36, **347**

Angina pectoris 268

Aniseed (Pimpinella anisum) 13, 44, 46, 47, 48, 61, 66, 127, 145, 176, 177, 178, 179, 180, 183, 184, 185, 198, **211**, 245, 255

Anodyne 86, 89, **175**, 233, 249, 265, 273, 296, 298, 329, 334

Anorexia **63–4**, 210, 224, 231, 238, 243, 274, 304, 326

Anorexia nervosa **63–4**, 210, 224, 231, 238, 243, 304

Anthelmintic 61, 141, **143**, 144, 145, **175**, 246, 254, 275, 299, 302, 303, 304, 311, 318, 322, 324, 335

Anthemis nobile (*Chamomile, Garden*) 13, 51, 53, 61, 64, 66, 69, 70, 71, 77, 86, 87, 127, 143, 156, 165, 175, 176, 177, 178, 179, 180, 184, 189, 200, 210, 213, 221, 234, **238**, 264, 308, 322, 332

Anthraquinones 167, **168**, 210, 230, 236, 308, 314, 337

Antibiotic 43, 45, 54, 65, 92, 96, 129, 134, **141–2**, 171, 290

Anticatarrhal 51, 52, 53, 54, 157, 174, **175**, 190, 218, 242, 247, 251, 253, 263, 264, 266, 287, 290, 300, 302, 316, 331

Anti-inflammatory 70, 71, **103**, 106, 167, 169, 171, **175**, 211, 222, 227, 238, 240, 242, 249, 253, 256, 261, 263, 267, 275, 277, 282, 285, 292, 293, 305, 320, 322, 328, 329, 332

Antilithic **134**, 136, **175**, 265, 267, 270, 294, 313, 330

Antimicrobial 40, 47, 51, 52, 54, 55, 56, **61–2**, 64, 71, 89, 92, **93**, 96, 97, 99, 129, 133, 135, 136, **141–2**, 155, 156, 157, 158, 160, 174, **176**, 191, 231, 245, 250, 259, 290, 291, 324, 331, 335

Antineoplastic **149**

Antirheumatic 103, 108, 219, 223, 225, 229, 237, 240, 248, 265, 267, 274, 285, 293, 302, 311, 332, 335

Antispasmodic **61**, 63, 77, 83, 124, 136, 137, 168, **176**, 210, 211, 213, 220, 222, 224, 225, 226, 232, 233, 234, 236, 238, 242, 245, 246, 250, 255, 259, 265, 266, 271, 276, 277, 279, 286, 287, 295, 296, 298, 300, 301, 306, 310, 317, 321, 324, 326

Anus 72

Anxiety 34, 35–6, 37, 48, 59, 65, 66, 71, 77, 78, **83**, 85, 115, 124, 128, 213, 217, 239, 243, 248, 268, 271, 276, 286, 297, 298, 310, 320, 326, 327, **347**

Aorta 38

Apathy 79, 116

Aphanes arvensis (*Parsley Piert*) 134, 136, 175, 177, 203, 265, 267, 270, **294–5**

Aphrodisiac 130, 239, 248, 262, 294, 332

Apium graveolens (*Celery*) 12, 13, 103, 104, 106, 108, 133, 134, 156, 176, 177, 178, 184, 200, 222, 230, **237**, 249, 267, 329

Appendicitis **70**, 209, **347**

Appendix 70

Appetite 60, 62, **63**, 115, 210, 214, 224, 231, 233, 234, 235, 238, 243, 244, 252, 255, 260, 264, 304, 326, 329, **347**

Apple cider vinegar 106, 186, 192

Apprehension 78

Apthea see mouth ulcer

Arctium lappa (*Burdock*) 13, 93, **94–6**, 103, 108, 113, 115, 122, 149, 175, 177, 179, 180, 197, 199, 225, 231, 238, 241, 256, 258, 287, 291, 304, 311, 312, 337

Arctostaphylos uva ursi (*Bearberry*) 103, 109, 122, 133, 134, 135, 136, 156, 167, 175, 176, 177, 180, **216**, 218, 244, 245, 250, 270, 297, 330

Armoracia rusticana (*Horseradish*) 64, 104, 178, 179, 180, 201, **269**

Aristolachia serpentaria (*Virginia Snakeroot*) 180, **328**

Arnica (Arnica montana) 13, 38, 99, 109, 180, 189, **211–12**

Arnica montana (*Arnica*) 13, 38, 99, 109, 180, 189, **211–12**

Arnica tincture 99

Aromatic oils 164–5, **176**

Artemisia abrotanum (*Southernwood*) 121, 123, 126, 143, 176, 178, 180, **318**

Artemisia absinthum (*Wormwood*) 13, 37, 60, 62, 63, 66, 73, 86, 88, 97, 103, 104, 113, 115, 116, 126, 141, 142, 143, 144, 145, 175, 176, 178, 179, 180, 185, 205, 251, 322, **335–6**

Artemisia vulgaris (*Mugwort*) 113, 156, 175, 178, 180, 185, 202, **288**

Arteriosclerosis **38**, 268, 279, 286, **347**

Artery 38

Arthritis 12, 102–4, **105–7**, 108, 109, 116, 214, 218, 219, 220, 222, 223, 229, 237, 247, 249, 256, 267, 274, 300, 311, 329, 332, **347**

Asclepias tuberosa (*Pleurisy Root*) 45, 47, 142, 177, 178, 179, 203, 210, 227, 252, 257, 301

Aspirin 22, 65, 103, 167, 222, 285, 334

Assimilation 58, 59, 102, 318

Asthma 22, **48**, 80, 84, 220, 224, 225, 232, 234, 242, 252, 253, 259, 266, 279, 281, 287, 295, 296, 300, 314, 317, 319, 321, 324, 331, **347**

Astragalus membranaceous 160

Astringent 51, 52, 54, 55, 60, 61, 63, 68, 70, 71, 72, 93, 99, **122**, 123, 129, 134, 167, **176**, 180, 191, 192

Atheroma 36, 38

Athlete's foot 98

Atony 274

INDEX 359

Autonomic nervous system 59, 112, 279
Autumn crocus 126
Avena sativa (*Oats*) 37, 61, 77, 82, 85, 88, 89, 98, 115, 116, 122, 128, 130, 141, 156, 179, 180, 203, 248, 263, 275, 276, **293**, 310, 328
Avens (Geum urbanum) 176, 198, **212**
Awareness 8, 10, 16, 17, 23, 50, 58, 151

B

B cells 158
Bach Flower Remedies 25, 27, **78–9**
Bacteria 43, 45, 47, 50, 52, 54, 70, 92, 94, 96, 97, 129, 134, 140, 141, 144
Bad circulation 30–1
Bailey, Alice 16, 29, 41, 57, 75, 101, 111, 139
Baldness 310
Ballota nigra (*Black Horehound*) 87, 127, 175, 198, **220–1**, 271
Balm (Melissa officinalis) 34, 35, 51, 61, 66, 69, 86, 87, 175, 176, 177, 178, 179, 180, 198, **213**
Balm of Gilead (Populus gileadensis) 51, 55, 95, 178, 179, 180, 187, **214**, 308
Balmony (Chelone glabra) 60, 73, 74, 88, 175, 177, 178, 179, 180, 198, **214**, 224, 248, 329
Balsam of Peru (Myroxylon pereirae) 176, 178, 179
Balsam of Tolu (Myroxylon toluifera) 163, 178, 179, **215**
Baptisia tinctoria (*Wild Indigo*) 51, 52, 93, 97, 98, 122, 129, 133, 142, 144, 160, 175, 176, 178, 205, 263, 331
Barberry (Berberis vulgaris) 60, 62, 72, 73, 74, 126, 175, 176, 177, 178, 179, 198, **215**
Bath **189**
Bayberry (Myrica cerifera) 61, 63, 70, 71, 176, 177, 180, 198, **216**
Bearberry (Arctostaphylos uva ursi) 103, 109, 122, 133, 134, 135, 136, 156, 167, 175, 176, 177, 180, **216**, 218, 244, 245, 250, 270, 297, 330
Bed-wetting 216, 270, 324
Beet 157
Bellis perenis (*Daisy*) 44, 99, 169, 180, 200, **247**
Benzoic acid 84, 163, 215
Benzoin 180, 190
Berberis aquilfolium (*Mountain Grape*) 74, 93, 94, 95, 96, 103, 175, 177, 178, 179, 180, 202, 226, **287**
Berberis vulgaris (*Barberry*) 60, 62, 72, 73, 74, 126, 175, 176, 177, 178, 179, 198, **215**
Beth Root (Trillium erectum) 122, 124, 129, 134, 176, 178, 179, 180, 204, 261, 264, 299, **325–6**
Betonica officinalis (*Betony*) **217**
Betony (Betonica officinalis) **217**
Betula pendula (*Birch, silver*) 198, **218**
Bible, The 154
Bidens tripartita (*Bur Marigold*) 122, 134, 199, 232
Bile 60, 72, 73, 168, 175, 177, 178, 215, 224, 229, 231, 257, 260, 285, 298, 329, 333, 337
Biochemistry **162–71**
Bioflavonoids 53, 99, 156, 168
Birch, silver (Betula pendula) 198, **218**
Birth 120, 121, 123, 125–7, 179, 225, 239, 264, 295
Birth control pill **125**, 239
Bistort (Polygonum bistorta) 176, 180, 198, **218**
Bitter 37, 44, 51, 53, 59, 60, 66, 73, 87, 95, 97, 113, 115, 116, 122, 141, 145, 171, **176**, 187, 198, 209, 218, 219, 233, 243, 260, 262, 268, 304, 318, 329, 334
Bitter tonics 85, 104, 130, 155, 156, 160, 209, 215, 223, 234, 236, 288, 304, 322, 335
Bittersweet (Solanum duleamara) 44, 198, **219**
Black Catechu (Acacia catechu) 176, **219**
Black Cohosh (Cimifuga racemosa) 52, 77, 88, 103, 106, 121, 125, 128, 176, 177, 178, 179, 180, 198, **220**, 222, 230, 329, 332
Black Haw (Viburnum prunifolium) 77, 124, 126, 176, 178, 179, 180, 198, **220–1**, 246, 273

Black Horebound (Ballota nigra) 87, 127, 175, 198, **221**, 271

Black Root (Leptandra virginica) 60, 73, 177, 178, 180, 198, 215, **222**, 287

Black Willow (Salix nigra) 13, 22, 87, 103, 106, 175, 180, 198, 218, **222**, 329

Bladder 132, 133, 134, 137

Bladderwrack (Fucus vesiculosus) 103, 113, 116, 175, 179, 180, **223**

Bleeding see hemorrhage

Blepharitis 253, 255

Blessed Thistle (Cnicus benedictus) 127, 178, 199, **223–4**

Blood 29, 30, 31, 32, 33, 35, 36–7, 68, 72, 73, 93, 94, 99, 104, 113, 114, 115, 116, 117

Blood pressure 33, 35, 36–7, 38, 55, 80, 94, 117, 127, 128, 132, 168, 213, 220, 228, 253, 259, 262, 266, 268, 279, **348**

Bloodroot (Sanguinaria canadensis) 45, 46, 48, 54, 175, 177, 178, 179, 180, 199, **224**, 308, 314

Blood sugar 23, 72, 114, 115, 116, 117, 127, 262, 321

Blood vessel 30, 31, 33, 36, 37, 39, 99, 156, 220, 228, 337

Blue Cohosh (Caulophyllum thalictroides) 121, 122, 123, 126, 178, 179, 199, 220, **225**

Blue Flag (Iris versicolor) 51, 56, 60, 65, 73, 93, 96, 103, 122, 149, 175, 177, 178, 180, 199, **225**, 302, 304

Bodywork 25, 36

Bogbean (Menyanthes trifoliata) see Buckbean

Bohm, David 18

Boils 52, **97**, 242, 250, 255, 257, 282, 284, 290, 295, 318, 335, **348**

Boldo (Peumus boldo) 60, 62, 63, 73, 74, 104, 133, 177, 178, 179, 180, 199, **226**

Boneset (Eupatorium perfoliatum) 13, 47, 51, 53, 93, 103, 104, 108, 142, 143, 174, 175, 176, 177, 178, 180, 189, 199, **226**, 236, 251, 271, 298, 337

Borage (Borago officinalis) 113, 117, 177, 178, 199, **227**

Borago officinalis (*Borage*) 113, 117, 177, 178, 199, **227**

Brain 38, 42, 112

Brassica alba (*Mustard*) 47, 103, 104, 165, 177, 179, 180, 202, 257, 269, **289–90**

Brassica nigra (*Mustard*) 47, 103, 104, 165, 177, 179, 180, 202, 257, 269, **289–90**

Breasts 113, 214, 255

Breast inflammation 210

Breastfeeding 128, 178, 285

Breath 250

Breathing 42, 43, 48

Bronchials 45–8, 50, 60, 163, 165, 210, 224, 234, 243, 252, 253, 266, 272, 278, 319

Bronchiectasis 47

Bronchitis 43, **46–7**, 210, 211, 214, 224, 228, 234, 236, 242, 243, 245, 252, 253, 255, 257, 259, 266, 269, 271, 272, 278, 279, 280, 281, 282, 284, 287, 289, 291, 293, 296, 300, 301, 304, 306, 317, 319, 321, 322, 324, 329, 331, **348**

Broom (Sarothamnus scoparius) 32, 33, 34, 35, 37, 176, 177, 199, **228**

Brucellosis 290

Bruises 92, 94, **99**, 183, 209, 212, 251, 320, 334, **348**

Buchmann, Dian D. 185

Buchu (Agathosma betulina) 12, 133, 134, 135, 156, 175, 177, 180, 199, **229**, 245, 293, 294, 297

Buckbean (Menyanthes trifoliata) 103, 106, 156, 171, 175, 178, 180, 199, 220, 222, **229**, 237, 249, 267, 329

Buckthorn (Rhamnus cathartica) 60, 168, 179, 180, 199, **230**

Buckwheat (Fagopyrum esculentum) 33, 37, 39, 99, 156, 168

Bugleweed (Lycopus europaeus) 32, 33, 35, 113, 115, 176, 177, 179, 180, **230**

Burdock (Arctium lappa) 13, 93, 94–6, 103, 108, 113, 115, 122, 149, 175, 177, 179, 180, 197, 199, 225, **231**, 238, 241, 256, 258, 287, 291, 304, 311, 312, 337

Burn 94, **99**, 167, 190, 193, 210, 282, 283, 305, 320, **348**

Bur Marigold (Bidens tripartita) 122, 134, 199, **232**
Bursa 108
Bursitis **108**
Butterbur (Petasites hybridicus) 199, **232**

C

Cabbage 97, 115
Cabbage leaf poultice 97
Cachexia 271
Calamus (Acorus calamus) 61, 67, 71, 199, 219, **233**, 234, 332
Calcium 38
Calendula officinalis (*Marigold*) 13, 38, 39, 40, 55, 56, 88, 93, 95, 96, 97, 98, 99, 122, 134, 143, 157, 160, 171, 175, 176, 178, 180, 189, 190, 199, 202, 232, 241, 277, **282–3**
California Poppy (Eschscholzia californica) 77, 85, 199, **233–4**
Calumba (Jateorrhiza palmata) 72, 180, **234**
Cancer 43, 45, **147–52**, 286, 322
Capsella bursa-pastoris (*Shepherd's Purse*) 71, 122, 178, 180, 204, **315**
Capsicum minimum (*Cayenne*) 13, 33, 39, 47, 60, 61, 86, 103, 104, 107, 142, 143, 175, 176, 177, 178, 179, 180, 188, 189, 192, 224, 226, 236, 237, 269, 279, 289, 301, 303, 337
Caraway (Carum carvi) 61, 63, 127, 176, 177, 180, 184, 187, 199, 211, **234**
Cardamom (Elattaria cardamonum) 61, 66, 70, 176, 177, 180, **235**, 260, 315
Carbohydrates 36, **166**
Carbon dioxide 42
Carbuncle 257
Carcinogen 148, 150
Cardiac glycoside 32, **170**

Cardiac problem 30, 32, 46
Cardiovascular 31, 33, 34, 36, 38, 156, 248
Carlina vulgaris (*Carline Thistle*) 180, 199, **235**
Carminatives 61, 63, 66, 70, 72, 87, 95, 168, 174, **177**
Carum carvi (*Caraway*) 61, 63, 127, 176, 177, 180, 184, 187, 199, 211, **234**
Cascara Sagrada (Rhamnus purshianus) 60, 62, 178, 179, **236**
Cassia angustifolia (*Senna*) 13, 60, 72, 144, 168, 179, **314–15**, 322
Cassia senna (*Senna*) 13, 60, 72, 144, 168, 179, **314–15**, 322
Catarrh 45, 50, **52–3**, 143, 157, 174, 175, 190, 212, 218, 239, 242, 247, 250, 251, 252, 253, 257, 259, 263, 264, 266, 271, 278, 279, 280, 282, 284, 287, 290, 298, 300, 302, 307, 316, 322, 323, 331, **348**
Catnip (Nepeta cataria) 142, 177, 199, **236**
Caulophyllum thalictroides (*Blue Cohosh*) 121, 122, 123, 126, 178, 179, 199, 220, **225**
Cayenne (Capsicum minimum) 13, 33, 39, 47, 60, 61, 86, 103, 104, 107, 142, 143, 175, 176, 177, 178, 179, 180, 188, 189, 192, 224, 226, 236, 237, 269, 279, 289, 301, 303, 337
Cayenne liniment 107
Celandine, Greater see *Greater Celandine*
Celery (Apium graveolens) 12, 13, 103, 104, 106, 108, 133, 134, 156, 176, 177, 178, 184, 200, 222, 230, **237**, 249, 267, 329
Celiac disease 69, 70
Centaurium erythraea (*Centaury*) 60, 78, 85, 176, 178, 180, **238**
Centaury (Erythraea centaurium) 60, 78, 85, 176, 178, 180, **238**
Central nervous system 160, 165
Cephaelis ipecacuanha (*Ipecacuanha*) 61, 177, **272**, **348**
Cetraria islandica (*Iceland Moss*) 61, 175, 178, 179, 180, 202, **271**
Chamaelirium luteum (*False Unicorn Root*) 13, 25, 88,

121, 123, 124, 126, 129, 156, 178, 180, 201, 221, 225, **254**, 310, 318, 326

Chamomile (Matricaria chamomilla) 13, 51, 53, 61, 64, 66, 69, 70, 71, 77, 86, 87, 127, 143, 156, 165, 175, 176, 177, 178, 179, 180, 184, 189, 200, 210, 213, 221, 234, 238, 239, 264, 308, 322, 332

Chardin, Teilhard de 17

Chasteberry (Vitex agnus-castus) 88, 121, 123, 124, 125, 128, 178, 200, **239**

Chelidonium majus (*Greater Celandine*) 97, 201, **265–6**

Chelone glabra (*Balmony*) 60, 73, 74, 88, 175, 177, 178, 179, 180, 198, **214**, 224, 248, 329

Chemotherapy 22, 23, 24, 25, 150

Chickenpox 143

Chickweed (Stellaria media) 13, 93, 95, 96, 169, 178, 180, 189, 200, 214, **240**, 335

Chilblain 39, 237, 251, 261, 270, 289, 303, **348**

Childbirth 125–7, 179, 264, 295

Childhood asthma 48

Childhood diarrhea 63, 209, 218, 324

Childhood eczema 306, 312

Chionanthus virginicus (*Fringetree*) 60, 73, 74, 114, 115, 175, 177, 178, 179, 180, 201, 215, 226, **257**, 287

Chiropractic 25

Cholagogues 95, **177**

Cholecystitis 222

Cholesterol 31, 36, 38, 72, 259

Chrondrus crispus (*Irish Moss*) 61, 66, 93, 122, 127, 166, 175, 177, 178, 179, 180, **272**

Christopher, Dr. 95, 187

Cilantro see *Coriander*

Cilia 50

Cimifuga racemosa (*Black Cohosh*) 52, 77, 88, 103, 106, 121, 125, 128, 176, 177, 178, 179, 180, 198, **220**, 222, 230, 329, 332

Cinchona succiruba (*Peruvian Bark*) 178, **299**

Cinnamon (Cinnamonum zeylandica) 64, 176, 177, 180, 185, **240**

Cinnamonum zeylandica (*Cinnamon*) 64, 176, 177, 180, 185, **240**

Circulation 24–31, 35, 36, 78, 183, 198, 203, 206

Circulatory system 12, 21, 23, **29–40**, 42, 43, 44, 56, 80, 94, **104**, 107, 109, 136, 168, 179, 189, 213, 216, 237, 268, 269, 279, 289, 303, 310, 316, **348**

Citric acid 106, 133

Cleansing 40, 133

Cleavers (Galium aparine) 13, 40, 47, 51, 55, 56, 65, 93, 94, 95, 96, 97, 98, 113, 122, 129, 133, 141, 143, 149, 156, 157, 175, 177, 178, 179, 180, 200, 231, **240–1**, 258, 287, 293, 302, 304, 311, 331, 337

Cloves (Eugenia caryphyllus) 64, 167, 175, 176, 179, **241**

Cnicus benedictus (*Blessed Thistle*) 127, 178, 199, **223–4**

Cola vera (*Kola Nut*) 37, 78, 85, 88, 116, 176, 177, 179, 224, 248, **274–5**, 276, 310, 312

Cold 52, **53**, 98, 210, 212, 216, 236, 237, 245, 251, 259, 279, 283, 289, 298, 309, 329, 335, **348**

Cold infusion 67, 184, 193, 304, 331

Cold sore 98

Colic 61, 62, 63, 137, 168, 210, 211, 214, 224, 225, 232, 233, 234, 236, 237, 244, 250, 255, 261, 274, 278, 294, 297, 298, 313, 326, 327, 328, 330, 332, **348**

Colic Root see *True Unicorn Root*

Colitis **70–1**, 209, 212, 216, 218, 219, 229, 243, 264, 268, 284, 295, 298, 299, 318, 325, **348**

Collinsonia canadensis (*Stone Root*) 134, 136, 175, 177, 201, **267**

Colon 70

Coltsfoot (Tussilago farfara) 13, 44, 45, 46, 47, 48, 156, 157, 166, 175, 177, 178, 179, 180, 200, 210, 211, 214, **242**, 243, 245, 247, 252, 266, 271, 272, 278, 280, 281, 287, 289, 293, 319, 329

Coma 114

Comfrey (Symphytum officinale) 8, 13, 38, 39, 45, 46, 47, 48, 61, 63, 67, 68, 70, 71, 93, 95, 99, 156, 177, 178, 179, 180, 188, 189, 191, 192, 200, 216, **242–3**, 261, 278, 284, 336

Commiphora molmol (*Myrrh*) 55, 62, 64, 65, 93, 97, 98, 141, 142, 144, 160, 176, 180, 192, 219, 237, 283, **290**, 331

Compress 38, 39, 47, 56, 95, 99, 108, 109, 184, 195, **191**, 192, 210, 231, 243, 253, 254, 255, 282, 283, 284, 291, 307, 313, 316, 325, 336

Concussion 99

Condurango (Marsdenia condurango) 64, 180, **243**

Congestion 30, **45**, 48, 52, 54, 73, 104, 109, 222, 226, 248, 301, 333, 337

Conjunctivitis 56, 58, 77, 95, 97, 112, 151, 167, 250, 253, 255, 256, 258, 264, 276, 322, **349**

Consciousness 16–22, 31, 112, 125, 140, 196, 274

Constipation 12, 36, 39, **62–3**, 70, 72, 87, 104, 109, 134, 150, 191, 214, 222, 225, 226, 236, 256, 257, 287, 305, 308, 309, 314, 333, 337, **349**

Contraception 123, 125, 171, 332

Convallaria majalis (*Lily of the Valley*) 23, 32, 33, 34, 35, 36, 115, 170, 176, 177, 202, 228, **278**

Convalescence 227, 313, 318

Coriander (Coriandrum sativum) 61, 176, 177, 200, **244**

Coriandrum sativum (*Coriander*) 61, 176, 177, 200, **244**

Corn Silk (Zea mays) 122, 134, 135, 136, 156, 175, 177, 229, **244**

Coronary arteries 36

Coronary circulation 33, 80

Cortisone 169, 170, 227

Couch Grass (Agropyron repens) 103, 122, 133, 134, 135, 136, 175, 177, 180, 200, 216, 229, 244, **245**, 248, 293

Cough **46**, 47, 80, 166, 171, 187, 210, 211, 214, 215, 220, 225, 228, 230, 242, 243, 245, 247, 252, 253, 255, 259, 266, 271, 272, 278, 280, 281, 283, 284, 287, 289, 293, 296, 300, 301, 305, 306, 307, 310, 317, 319, 321, 322, 323, 324, 329, 331, 332, **349**

Coumarin 168

Cowslip (Primula veris) 44, 179, 200, **245–6**

Cramp 37, 77, 81, **107–8**, 124, 125, 176, 220, 246, 261, 303, 327, 336, **349**

Cramp Bark (Viburnum opulus) 37, 77, 108, 122, 124, 125, 126, 136, 167, 176, 178, 179, 192, 200, 220, 221, **246**, 295, 296, 327

Cranesbill, American (Geranium maculatum) 176, 180, 201, **260–1**, 272, 283, 299, 325

Crataegus oxyacanthoides (*Hawthorn Berries*) 12, 33, 35, 36, 37, 38, 39, 177, 180, 184, 201, 228, **268**, 286

Crohn's disease 70, 298

Croup 224

Cucumber (Cucumis sativa) 189, **246**

Cucumis sativa (*Cucumber*) 189, **246**

Cucurbita pepo (*Pumpkin*) 143, 177, 203, 246, **303**

Cudweed (Gnaphalium uliginosum) 200, **247**, 263

Cydonia oblonga (*Quince*) 61, 178, 179, 192, 203, **305**

Cypripedium pubescens (*Lady's Slipper*) 77, 83, 85, 86, 175, 176, 179, 180, **276**, 293, 328

Cystitis **134–5**, 209, 210, 216, 218, 222, 226, 229, 231, 235, 241, 242, 244, 245, 250, 263, 265, 266, 270, 274, 293, 297, 301, 313, 319, 330, 337, **349**

D

Dairy products 31, 37, 46, 48, 88, 89, 105

Daisy (Bellis perennis) 44, 99, 169, 180, 200, **247**

Damiana (Turnera aphrodisiaca) 77, 85, 88, 116, 122, 130, 156, 179, 180, **248**, 275, 312

Dandelion (Taraxacum officinalis) 13, 33, 34, 35, 39, 60, 63, 72, 73, 74, 85, 94, 96, 103, 109, 113, 125, 133, 136, 149, 156, 157, 175, 177, 178, 179, 180, 186, 200, 222, 237, **248–9**, 265, 337

Dandruff 231

Daucus carrota (*Wild Carrot*) 108, 136, 175, 177, 204, 205, **330**

Deafness **52**, 251

Death 151, 152

Debility 37, 68, 77, 85, 88, 117, 137, 150, 214, 217, 234, 237, 262, 271, 274, 276, 292, 293, 300, 309, 310, 312, 316, 326, **349**

Decoction 183, **184**

Deep immune activation **159–60**

Defense system 3, 165

Deficiency 68, 69

Degeneration 102, 106, 155

Demulcents 44, 45, 46, 47, 54, 55, 61, **122**, **177**

Depression 70, 77, **85**, 116, 124, 128, 165, 213, 237, 248, 262, 268, 274, 276, 288, 293, 310, 316, 320, 328, **349**

Dermatitis 266

Despondency and despair 78

Detoxification 72, 154, 155, **157–8**, 160

Devil's Claw (Harpagophytum procumbens) 103, 171, 175, **249**

Diabetes mellitus **114–15**, 117, 262, 273, 299

Diaphoretic 33, 47, 53, 93, 141, **142**, 145, 157, 160, 174, **177**, 189, 191

Diarrhea 62, **63**, 70, 166, 167, 209, 212, 216, 218, 219, 224, 229, 230, 234, 236, 240, 244, 247, 260, 266, 273, 274, 275, 280, 285, 292, 299, 301, 306, 308, 313, 315, 316, 318, 321, 324, 325, 329, 334, 336, **349**

Diet 8, 21, 31, 36, 38, 39, 40, 43, 45, 46, 48, 52, 53, 54, 59, 62, 64, 66, 67, 68, 69, 70, 71, 72, 73, 74, 76, 83, 84, 86, 87, 88, 89, 95, 96, 97, 98, 99, 102, 105, 106, 108, 113, 114, 116, 120, 124, 125, 126, 127, 129, 133, 134, 135, 136, 140, 144, 145, 148, 150, 151

Digestion 12, 36, 37, 43, 44, 54, **57–74**, 78, 80, 86, 87, 88, 89, 95, 102, 103, 104, 105, 106, 113, 114, 115, 122, 155, 156, 157, 165, 169, 171, 175, 176, 177, 185, 186, 187, 188, 209, 210, 212, 214, 216, 218, 224, 229, 231, 234, 236, 237, 238, 239, 241, 243, 244, 252, 255, 256, 259, 260, 264, 265, 268, 269, 272, 274, 283, 284, 285, 288, 298, 299, 304, 310, 314, 316, 318, 322, 324, 326, 328, 329, 331, 333, 335, 336, 337

Digestive bitter 115

Digestive juice 58, 60, 72, 171, 214, 229, 231, 244, 248, 260, 298, 299, 304

Digestive stimulant 60, 63, 209, 234, 288, 329

Digestive system 12, 36, 43, 44, **57–74**, 80, 87, 88, 106, 122, 155, 157, 171, 175, 176, 177, 209, 224, 236, 237, 243, 244, 260, 299, 310, 314, 318, 328

Dill (Anethum graveolens) 175, 176, 177, 184, 200, 244, **250**

Dioscorea villosa (*Wild Yam*) 22, 60, 63, 69, 70, 71, 73, 88, 103, 106, 113, 117, 124, 128, 169, 175, 176, 177, 178, 179, 180, 233, 246, 257, **332**

Diuretic **33–4**, 37, 39, 53, 94, 95, 103, **104**, 108, 122, **133**, 134, 136, 141, 157, 160, 163, 168, 174, **177**, 209, 210, 216, 218, 219, 225, 226, 228, 229, 230, 231, 232, 235, 237, 240, 241, 242, 244, 245, 246, 248, 251, 254, 256, 257, 258, 262, 263, 265, 267, 269, 270, 274, 275, 278, 279, 284, 289, 291, 292, 293, 294, 295, 296, 297, 301, 309, 311, 312, 313, 315, 316, 319, 322, 323, 330, 333, 334, 337

Diverticulitis **71–2**, 332, **349**

Dizziness 256

Douche 129, 135, **189**, 212, 216, 218, 219, 260, 263, 292, 325, 331

Dropsy see Water retention

Drosera rotundifolia (*Sundew*) 44, 47, 48, 204, 279, 287, 319, **321**, 324

Dryopteris filix–mas (*Male Fern*) 126, 143, 145, 202, **281**

Duodenal ulcer 59, 67, **68–9**, 71, 243, 260, 283, 318

Duodenum 59, 60, 68, 72, 114, 177

Dysentry 212, 216, 218, 219, 272, 334, 336

Dysmenorrhea 123, **124**, 220, 232, 239, 246, 273, 295, 298, 332

Dyspepsia 66, 80, 209, 213, 214, 224, 233, 234, 235, 236, 237, 238, 239, 258, 260, 261, 263, 271, 298, 304, 307, 308, 310, 322, 324, 326, 328

Dyspeptic pain 209, 239

E

E numbers (food additives) 84–5
Earache **51**, 264, 295, 298, **349**
Ears **50–2**, 241
Earth 10, 15, 17–20, 23, 25, 121
Echinacea (Echinacea angustifolia) 13, 39, 40, 47, 51, 52, 54, 55, 56, 62, 64, 65, 68, 70, 71, 88, 89, 93, 96, 97, 98, 99, 113, 122, 129, 133, 135, 136, 141, 142, 143, 144, 149, 155, 156, 157, 158, 160, 175, 176, 180, 200, 225, 241, **250**, 259, 263, 272, 290, 296, 331
Echinacea angustifolia (*Echinacea*) 13, 39, 40, 47, 51, 52, 54, 55, 56, 62, 64, 65, 68, 70, 71, 88, 89, 93, 96, 97, 98, 99, 113, 122, 129, 133, 135, 136, 141, 142, 143, 144, 149, 155, 156, 157, 158, 160, 175, 176, 180, 200, 225, 241, **250**, 259, 263, 272, 290, 296, 331
Ecology 16, **20–1**, 22, 23, 24, 42, 43
Ecosystem 19, 20, **21–2**
Eczema 48, 55, 84, 94, **95–6**, 214, 219, 225, 228, 231, 240, 256, 258, 264, 287, 291, 293, 306, 312, 322, **349**
Effectors 155, 156
Elattaria cardamonum (*Cardamom*) 61, 66, 70, 176, 177, 180, **235**, 260, 315
Elderberry (Sambucus nigra) 13, 51, 52, 53, 54, 86, 93, 99, 142, 175, 177, 178, 179, 180, 184, 186, 189, 200, 226, 236, **251**, 253, 271, 279, 298, 335, 337
Elecampane (Iluna helenium) 44, 46, 48, 156, 175, 176, 178, 179, 180, 200, 235, 243, **252**, 266
Eleutherococcus senticosus (*Siberian Ginseng*) 82, 156, 158, 160, **316**
Elimination 43, 47, 57, 59, 89, 96, 102, 103, 104, 107, 108, 133, 152, 154, 157, 160, 171, 177
Emetic **61**, 177
Emmenagogue **121**, 122, 123, 126, 174, **178**, 210, 220, 221, 225, 234, 254, 263, 275, 282, 283, 286, 288, 294, 295, 297, 310, 318, 322, 344
Emotional life 154, 159

Emotional tension 31, 276
Emphysema 47, 242, 252
Endocrine system 72, 80, 106, 111, 112, 113, 114, 121, 125, 278, 312
Enema 145
Enteric brain 58
Enteritis **69**, 284, 305, 315
Environment 8, 9, 17, 20, 23, 24, 27, 31, 43, 44
Ephedra (Ephedra sinica) 22, 44, 48, 54, 200, **253**, 279, 324
Ephedra sinica (*Ephedra*) 22, 44, 48, 54, 200, **253**, 279, 324
Ephedrine 22
Epidemic 140
Epilepsy 271, 317, **349**
Equilibrium 112
Equisetum arvense (*Horsetail*) 93, 134, 135, 137, 156, 180, 201, **270**, 312, 321
Eryngium maritimum (*Sea Holly*) 137, 175, 177, **313**
Eschscholzia california (*California Poppy*) 77, 85, 199, **233–4**
Essential hypertension 36
Essential oil 107, 188, 189, 192, 193
Estrogen 72, 116, 121
Eucalyptus (Eucalyptus globulus) 47, 51, 52, 53, 64, 93, 98, 142, 165, 176, 178, 180, 189
Eugenia caryphyllus (*Cloves*) 64, 167, 175, 176, 179, **241**
Eugenol 64, 167
Euonymus atropurpureus (*Winged Elm*, or *Wahoo*) 60, 73, 74, 177, 178, 179, 205, 257, **333**
Eupatorium perfoliatum (*Boneset*) 13, 47, 51, 53, 93, 103, 104, 108, 142, 143, 174, 175, 176, 177, 178, 180, 189, 199, **226**, 236, 251, 271, 298, 337
Eupatorium purpureum (*Gravel Root*) 134, 136, 175, 177, 180, 201, **265**, 267, 270, 330
Euphorbia pilulifera (*Pill–Bearing Spurge*) 44, 48, 266, 279, **300**, 314, 317, 321
Euphrasia officinalis (*Eyebright*) 51, 52, 54, 56, 175, 176, 180, 200, **253–4**
Eustachian tube 51

Evacuant 60, 62, 104, 179
Evening Primrose (Oenothera biennis) 89
Evolution 17, 19, 20, 43, 154
Exercise 31, 36, 38, 39, 43
Exertion 35
Exhaustion 31, 37, 48, 79, 117, 233, 262, 276, 293, 309, 316
Expectoration 44, 46, 48, 157, 169, **178**
Eyeball 56
Eyebright (Euphrasia officinalis) 51, 52, 54, 56, 175, 176, 180, 200, **253–4**
Eyes **56**
Eyewash 56, 258

F

False Unicorn Root (Chamaelirium luteum) 13, 25, 88, 121, 123, 124, 126, 129, 156, 178, 180, 201, 221, 225, **254**, 310, 318, 326
Fasting 144
Fat 30, 31, 36, 38
Fatigue 300
Fatty deposits 36, 37
Fear 5, 48, 59, 78, 79, 82
Febrifuges 142, **178**
Fennel (Foeniculum vulgare) 61, 63, 66, 127, 142, 175, 176, 177, 178, 183, 184, 187, 201, 211, **255**, 315
Fenugreek (Trigonella foenum–graecum) 127, 178, 179, 180, **255**
Ferguson, Marilyn 19
Fever 47, 53, 54, 80, 87, 135, 142, 143, 144, 178, 189, 210, 212, 213, 222, 226, 227, 232, 236, 251, 253., 256, 261, 269, 278, 285, 289, 290, 298, 299, 312, 317, 328, 329, 331, 335, 336, 337, **350**
Feverfew 87, **256**
Fibrositis **107**, 261, 303, 320

Figwort (Scrophularia nodosa) 32, 33, 93, 94, 95, 96, 175, 201, **256**, 258, 291
Filipendula ulmaria (*Meadowsweet*) 8, 12, 13, 22, 61, 63, 66, 67, 70, 73, 87, 88, 103, 106, 127, 167, 175, 176, 202, 213, 219, 221, 224, 233, 238, 243, 249, 261, 264, 267, 278, **285**, 304, 308
Fistula 255
Flatulence 63, 66, 72, 80, 209, 210, 211, 213, 233, 234, 235, 236, 237, 239, 241, 250, 255, 258, 260, 261, 263, 274, 294, 297, 298, 310, 326, 330, 335, **350**
Flavone **168**
Flax (Linum usitatissimum) 44, 45, 46, 47, 177, 178, 179, 180, 192, 201, **257**
Fleas **145**
Flower essences (Bach) 25, 27, 78–9
Flu see influenza
Foeniculum vulgare (*Fennel*) 61, 63, 66, 127, 142, 175, 176, 177, 178, 183, 184, 187, 201, 211, **255**, 315
Food additives 84, 150
Foxglove (Digitalis purpurea) 23, 32, 156, 170, 278
Fracture 243, 287
Fringetree (Chionanthus virginicus) 60, 73, 74, 114, 115, 175, 177, 178, 179, 180, 201, 215, 226, **257**, 287
Fructose 166
Fucus vesiculosus (*Bladderwrack*) 103, 113, 116, 175, 179, 180, **223**
Fumaria officinalis (*Fumitory*) 93, 95, 175, 177, 178, 180, 201, **258**
Fumitory (Fumaria officinalis) 93, 95, 175, 177, 178, 180, 201, **258**
Fungal infection 98, 171, 265, 282, 283, 323

G

Gaia 10, **17–20**, 21, 22, 23, 24, 27, 93, 158, 171
Galangal (Alpinia officinarum) 177, 180, **258–9**

Galega officinalis (*Goat's Rue*) 113, 115, 127, 178, 201, **262**
Galium aparine (*Cleavers*) 13, 40, 47, 51, 55, 56, 65, 93, 94, 95, 96, 97, 98, 113, 122, 129, 133, 141, 143, 149, 156, 157, 175, 177, 178, 179, 180, 200, 231, **240–1**, 258, 287, 293, 302, 304, 311, 331, 337
Gallbladder 59, 62, **72–3**, **74**, 114, 177, 214, 215, 222, 226, 229, 233, 248, 249, 257, 265, 267, 283, 285, 287, 309, 328, 329, 333, 337, **350**
Gallbladder colic 233
Gallbladder inflammation 74, 214, 215, 257, 265, 328
Gallstones **74**, 114, 214, 215, 228, 265
Gargle 55, 56, 187, 209, 212, 216, 218, 219, 234, 239, 247, 255, 261, 263, 275, 283, 292, 306, 307, 308, 313, 314, 316, 324, 325
Garlic (*Allium sativum*) 36, 37, 38, 47, 51, 52, 54, 71, 93, 97, 98, 115, 122, 129, 142, 143, 144, 145, 156, 158, 160, 165, 175, 176, 177, 178, 179, 180, 187, 201, **259**
Gastric ulcer 59, **67–8**, 233, 243, 260
Gastritis **66–7**, 233, 239, 264, 271, 272, 278, 282, 284, 285, 296, 305, 318
Gaultheria procumbens (*Wintergreen*) 103, 104, 167, 205, **334**
Gentian (*Gentiana lutea*) 37, 60, 63, 64, 66, 73, 79, 104, 141, 145, 156, 176, 177, 178, 180, 201, 238, **260**
Gentiana lutea (*Gentian*) 37, 60, 63, 64, 66, 73, 79, 104, 141, 145, 156, 176, 177, 178, 180, 201, 238, **260**
Geraniol 164
Geranium maculatum (*Cranesbill, American*) 176, 180, 201, **260–1**, 272, 283, 299, 325
Gestation 125–7
Geum urbanum (*Avens*) 176, 198, **212**
Ginger (*Zingiber officinale*) 33, 39, 60, 61, 62, 63, 72, 103, 104, 108, 142, 176, 177, 178, 179, 180, 185, 186, 189, 226, 233, 260, **261**, 289, 292, 315, 332, 337
Gingivitis **64–5**, 212, 219, 239, 250, 290, 307, 316, 331
Ginkgo 156

Ginseng (*Panax ginseng*) 37, 85, 88, 113, 115, 117, 130, 179, 180, **262**
Ginseng, Siberian (*Eleutherococcus senticosus*) 82, 156, 158, 160, **316**
Glands 40, 47, 55, 56, 92, 112–17, 121, 125, 130, 143, 150, 156, 160, 180, 223, 227, 230, 241, 245, 262, 270, 302, 312, 313, 331, **350**
Glandular fever 290, **350**
Glandular system 80, **111–17**, 121, 160, 278
Glossitis 307
Glucagon 114
Glucose 114, 116, 117, 132, 166
Gluten 46, 66, 69, 89, 105
Glycerine tincture **186–7**
Glycoside 21
Glycyrrhiza glabra (*Licorice*) 45, 46, 47, 48, 53, 55, 60, 62, 64, 113, 117, 125, 144, 145, 177, 178, 179, 180, 183, 184, 197, 236, **277–8**, 284
Gnaphalium uliginosum (*Cudweed*) 200, **247**, 263
Goat's Rue (*Galega officinale*) 113, 115, 127, 178, 201, **262**
Goiter **116**, 223
Golden Ragwort or *Life Root* (*Senecia aurens*) 88, 121, 128, 129, 201, **263**, 310
Golden Rod (*Solidago virgauria*) 51, 52, 54, 169, 175, 176, 177, 201, 247, 251, 253, **263**, 266
Golden Seal (*Hydrastis canadensis*) 8, 40, 51, 52, 54, 55, 56, 60, 66, 67–8, 70, 72, 73, 74, 87, 88, 93, 95, 98, 99, 104, 113, 122, 126, 127, 128, 141, 143, 175, 176, 177, 178, 179, 180, 188, 189, 191, 192, 214, 253, **264**, 283, 287, 329
Gonad gland 135
Gout **108**, 218, 237, 265, 267, 312, 328, 330
Gravel 134, 136, 175, 177, 180, 201, 216, 246, 265, 267, 270, 284, 294, 297, 313
Gravel Root (*Eupatorium purpureum*) 134, 136, 175, 177, 180, 201, **265**, 267, 270, 330
Greater Celandine (*Chelidonium majus*) 97, 201, **265–6**

Grindelia (Grindelia camporum) 44, 48, 178, 180, **266**, 272, 279, 300, 301, 314, 317, 321, 323

Grindelia camporum (*Grindelia*) 44, 48, 178, 180, **266**, 272, 279, 300, 301, 314, 317, 321, 323

Griping pain 63, 124, 145, 165, 220, 235, 269, 273

Ground Ivy (Nepeta hederacea) 86, 176, 180, 201, 251, **266–7**

Guaiacum (Guaiacum officinale) 103, 104, 106, 149, 175, 177, 222, **267**

Guaiacum officinale (*Guaiacum*) 103, 104, 106, 149, 175, 177, 222, **267**

Gums 64, 65, 166, 188, 290, 299, 306, 307, 308, 325

H

Hagenia abyssinica (*Kousso*) 143, **275**

Halitosis 250

Hamamelis virginiana (*Witch Hazel*) 13, 39, 55, 64, 72, 93, 95, 96, 99, 109, 143, 175, 176, 180, 191, 205, 212, 253, 264, 290, **334**

Harpagophytum procumbens (*Devil's Claw*) 103, 171, 175, **249**

Hawthorn Berries (Crataegus oxyacanthoides) 12, 33, 35, 36, 37, 38, 39, 177, 180, 184, 201, 228, **268**, 286

Hay fever **54**, 80, 251, 253

Headache 37, 62, **86–7**, 217, 245, 256, 262, 268, 276, 283, 286, 295, 298, 310

Healer 16, 24, 45, 76, 104, 121, 148

Healing 22–3

Hearing 52

Heart 30, 31, **32–7**, 38, 39, 42, 46, 48, 66, 94, 104, 105, 117, 128, 136, 170, 176

Heartbeat 31, 33, 35, 36, 170

Heartburn 66, 205, 285, **350**

Heart tonic **32–3**, 292

Hemorrhage 224, 232, 243, 260, 264, 270, 291, 306, 308, 313, 321, 325

Hemorrhoids **72**, 191, 214, 218, 260, 266, 269, 277, 280, 292, 301, 304, 308, 313, 316, 334

Hepatics **60**, 72, 73, 94, 95, 96, 156, 160, 175, **178**

Hernia 243, 287

Herpes simplex 55, **98**

Hiatus hernia 243

High blood pressure **36–7**, 38, 55, 80, 94, 114, 128, 268, 286, 337

Hobbs, Christopher 159

Holstic herbalism 8–10, 16, 89

Hologram 18

Homeostasis 17, 21, **23–4**, 82, 112, 113, 116, 132, 144, 155, 157, 158

Hops (Humulus lupulus) 34, 48, 61, 65, 66, 68, 70, 777, 85, 88, 127, 130, 171, 175, 176, 178, 179, 189, 201, 213, **268–9**, 273, 279, 296, 304, 327

Hormonal modulators 159, 160

Hormonal normalizer **121**

Hormones 24, 58, 72, 96, 112–13, 114, 115, 116, 117, 125, 128, 169, 220, 239, 254, 312, 325

Horse Chestnut (Aesculus hippocastanum) 33, 39, 99, 180, 201, **269**

Horseradish (Armoracia rusticana) 64, 104, 178, 179, 180, 201, **269**

Horsetail (Equisetum arvense) 93, 134, 135, 137, 156, 180, 201, **270**, 312, 321

Hot flashes 128

Housemaid's knee 108

Humulus lupulus (*Hops*) 34, 48, 61, 65, 66, 68, 70, 777, 85, 88, 127, 130, 171, 175, 176, 178, 179, 189, 201, 213, **268–9**, 273, 279, 296, 304, 327

Hydrangea (Hydrangea aborescens) 134, 135, 136, 175, 180, 201, 245, 265, 267, **270**, 312, 330

Hydrangea aborescens (*Hydrangea*) 134, 135, 136, 175, 180, 201, 245, 265, 267, **270**, 312, 330

Hydrastis canadensis (*Golden Seal*) 8, 40, 51, 52, 54, 55, 56, 60, 66, **67–8**, 70, 72, 73, 74, 87, 88, 93, 95, 98, 99, 104, 113, 122, 126, 127, 128, 141, 143, 175, 176, 177,

178, 179, 180, 188, 189, 191, 192, 214, 253, **264**, 283, 287, 329
Hygiene 64, 97, 98, 140, 144, 145
Hyperacidity 285
Hyperactivity 48, **83–5**
Hypericum perforatum (*St. John's Wort*) 77, 88, 89, 99, 104, 107, 128, 156, 175, 176, 178, 179, 180, 192, 193, 204, 263, **320**
Hypertension 36, 48, 228, 253, 279
Hypnotic 85, **178**, 180, 223, 268, 276, 296, 327, 332
Hypoglycaemia 115, 273
Hypotensive 160
Hypothalamus 112–13, 116–17
Hyssop (Hyssopus officinalis) 44, 46, 47, 51, 77, 142, 175, 176, 177, 178, 179, 180, 184, 201, 251, **271**, 283
Hyssopus officinalis (*Hyssop*) 44, 46, 47, 51, 77, 142, 175, 176, 177, 178, 179, 180, 184, 201, 251, **271**, 283
Hysteria 271, 296, 298, 328

I

Iceland Moss (Cetraria islandica) 61, 175, 178, 179, 180, 202, **271**
Ileitis 69
Immune system 151, 152, 154, **158–60**
Immunization 43
Immunological reaction 54, 159–60
Impetigo 80, **97**
Incontinence **137**, 209, 270, 321, 323, **351**
Indecision 78, 79
Indian, North American see Native American
Indigestion 58, **66**, 87, 209, 210, 224, 229, 239, 243, 268, 283, 316, 335, 336
Infection 39, 43, 45, 46, 47, 50, 51, 52, 53, 54, 55, 56, 61, 63, 64, 65, 66, 70, 73, 88, 89, 92, 94, 96, 97, 98, 99, 120, 123, **129**, 133, 134, 135, 136, **140–4**, 149, 156, 160, 167, 189, 214, 215, 216, 218, 229, 235, 245, 250, 257, 259, 265, 269, 270, 283, 290, 291, 295, 296, 301, 302, 309, 312, 321, 322, 324, 329, 330, 331, 335, 336, 336, 349, 350, **351**
Infestation 61, 98, 140, **141–5**, 160, 246, 304, 312, 322, 336
Inflammation 166, 167, 169, 171, 175, 210, 211, 212, 214, 215, 218, 219, 222, 225, 226, 227, 238, 239, 240, 242, 243, 245, 247, 248, 249, 251, 253, 255, 256, 257, 261, 263, 267, 269, 270, 275, 282, 283, 284, 285, 289, 292, 293, 297, 298, 301, 305, 306, 307, 316, 320, 322, 328, 329, 331, 332, 333, 334, 335
Influenza **53–4**, 643, 65, 140, 210, 213, 222, 226, 251, 259, 269, 281, 291, 298, 301, 328, 335, **351**
Infusion **183–4**
Inhalation 47, 53, 54, 81
Insect bites 196
Insomnia **85–6**, 239, 245, 268, 269, 273, 276, 295, 296, 327, 332
Insulin 59, 114, 117
Intestinal colic 210, 211, 232, 234, 298, 327, 332
Intestinal wall 58, 62
Intestinal worms **144–5**, 322
Inula helenium (*Elecampane*) 44, 46, 48, 156, 175, 176, 178, 179, 180, 200, 235, 243, **252**, 266
Iodine 116
Ipecacuanha (Cephaelis ipecacuanha) 61, 177, **272**, 348
Irish Moss (Chondrus crispus) 61, 66, 93, 122, 127, 166, 175, 177, 178, 179, 180, **272**
Iris versicolor (*Blue Flag*) 51, 56, 60, 65, 73, 93, 96, 103, 122, 149, 175, 177, 178, 180, 199, **225**, 302, 304

J

Jamaican Dogwood (Piscidia erythrina) 77, 85, 86, 87, 88, 89, 104, 106, 175, 178, 179, **273**, 276, 296
Jambul (Syzygium cumini) 115, **273**

370   THE COMPLETE HERBS SOURCEBOOK

Jateorrhiza palmata (*Calumba*) 72, 180, **234**
Jaundice 62, **73**, 175, 214, 215, 219, 222, 248, 257, 328, 333, 337, **351**
Jejuvinitis 69
Jogging 25
Juniper Berries (Juniperus communis) 103, 104, 122, 126, 133, 134, 135, 176, 177, 178, 180, 202, **274**, 297
Juniperus communis (*Juniper Berries*) 103, 104, 122, 126, 133, 134, 135, 176, 177, 178, 180, 202, **274**, 297

K

Kelp see *Bladderwrack*
Kidney 33, 37, 43, 73, 92, 93, 94, 95, 96, 104, 106, 108, 109, 113, 116, 132–7, 149, 150, 157, 216, 231, 232, 245, 247, 248, 258, 265, 270, 274, 294, 297, 309, 313, 315, 330
Kidney stones 134, **136–7**, 245, 265, 270, 294, 297, 313, 330, **351**
Kloss, Jethro 192
Koestler, Arthur 18
Kola Nut (Cola vera) 37, 78, 85, 88, 116, 176, 177, 179, 224, 248, **274–5**, 276, 310, 312
Kousso (Hagenia abyssinica) 143, **275**
Krameria triandra (*Rhatany*) 54, **308**

L

Labor 112, 127, 151, 306
Labor pains, false 220, 225, 286
Lactuca virosa (*Wild Lettuce*) 44, 46, 65, 130, 176, 178, 179, 205, **332**
Lady's Mantle (Alchemilla vulgaris) 63, 122, 189, 202, **275**
Lady's Slipper (Cypripedium pubescens) 77, 83, 85, 86, 175, 176, 179, 180, **276**, 293, 328

Langerhans, Islets of 114
Large intestine **70–2**
Laryngitis 55, **56**, 209, 214, 218, 219, 224, 234, 237, 247, 250, 263, 275, 282, 290, 292, 302, 304, 307, 314, 324, 325, 331, **351**
Lavender (Lavendula officinalis) 66, 69, 77, 85, 86, 87, 88, 107, 142, 175, 179, 189, 202, 213, **276**
Lavendula officinalis (*Lavender*) 66, 69, 77, 85, 86, 87, 88, 107, 142, 175, 179, 189, 202, 213, **276**
Laxatives **60**, 62, 70, 72, 95, 141, 157, 176, 177, **179**, 191
Lentinus edodes 160
Leonurus cardiaca (*Motherwort*) 32, 33, 34, 35, 36, 46, 48, 77, 94, 121, 125, 128, 176, 178, 179, 180, 202, 225, 278, **286–7**
Leptandra virginica (*Black Root*) 60, 73, 177, 178, 180, 198, 215, **222**, 287
Lesser Celandine (Ranunculus ficaria) 61, 72, 176, 191, 202, **277**, 334
Lethargy 116
Lettuce 115
Leucocytes 141
Leukemia 149
Leukorrhea 212, 216, 218, 219, 260, 261, 263, 292, 306, 325, 331
Lice **98**, **145**, 211, 304, 312
Licorice (Glycyrrhiza glabra) 45, 46, 47, 48, 53, 55, 60, 62, 64, 113, 117, 125, 144, 145, 177, 178, 179, 180, 183, 184, 197, 236, **277–8**, 284
Life force 16, 23, 78, 149, 183
Lifestyle 11, 21, 27, 34, 38, 43, 48, 52, 54, 59, 61, 66, 69, 76, 94, 97, 102, 105, 113, 120, 125, 133, 145, 184
Life Root see *Golden Ragwort*
Ligaments 89
Ligusticum wallichii 160
Lily of the Valley (Convallaria majalis) 23, 32, 33, 34, 35, 36, 115, 170, 176, 177, 202, 228, **278**

Lime Blossom (Tilia europaea) 33, 35, 36, 37, 38, 48, 69, 71, 77, 83, 85, 86, 130, 156, 157, 176, 177, 184, 189, 202, 245, 268, **279**, 286, 337

Liniment 88, 104, 107, 108, 109, **192**, 276, 303, 305, 334

Linum usitatissimum (*Flax*) 44, 45, 46, 47, 177, 178, 179, 180, 192, 201, **257**

Liver 59, 60, 62, 63, 71, **72–3**, 93, 94, 95, 104, 108, 113, 114, 133, 149, 156, 157, 168, 171, 178, 209, 214, 215, 22, 225, 226, 229, 238, 247, 248, 249, 257, 258, 285, 287, 294, 305, 329, 333

Lobaria pulmonaria (*Lungwort Moss*) 45, **281**

Lobelia (Lobelia inflata) 45, 46, 48, 51, 61, 176, 177, 178, 179, 192, 202, 211, 224, 266, **279–80**, 289, 300, 301, 317, 323, 324, 329

Lobelia inflata (*Lobelia*) 45, 46, 48, 51, 61, 176, 177, 178, 179, 192, 202, 211, 224, 266, **279–80**, 289, 300, 301, 317, 323, 324, 329

Loneliness 78

Lotion 38, 39, 96, 97, 98, 99, 163

Lovelock, James 158

Low blood pressure **37**, 228, 253

Lozenges **188**

Lumbago **109**, 237, 334, **352**

Lungs 42–3, 44, 45, 46, 47, 55, 92, 149, 157, 165, 166, 171, 259, 280, 284, 293, 300, 317

Lungwort Herb (Pulmonaria officinalis) 45, 176, 177, 178, 179, 203, **280**

Lungwort Moss (Lobaria pulmonaria) 45, **281**

Lycopus europaeus (*Bugleweed*) 32, 33, 35, 113, 115, 176, 177, 179, 180, **230**

Lymphadenitis 56, 241, 331

Lymphatic cleansers 40, 64, 97

Lymphatic glands 40, 55, 302

Lymphatic system **40**, 47, 51, 52, 97, 149, 157, 241, 303

M

Ma Huang see *Ephedra*

Malabsorption 58, 68, **69–70**

Malaria 215, 299

Male Fern (Dryopteris filix–mas) 126, 143, 145, 202, **281**

Malignancy 150, 151, 152

Mallow (Malva sylvestris) 46, 178, 202, **282**

Malnutrition 69

Malva sytlvestris (Mallow) 46, 178, 202, **282**

Marigold (Calendula officinalis) 13, 38, 39, 40, 55, 56, 88, 93, 95, 96, 97, 98, 99, 122, 134, 143, 157, 160, 171, 175, 176, 178, 180, 189, 190, 199, 202, 232, 241, 277, **282–3**

Marigold compress 95

Marigold ointment 190

Marjoram, Wild (Origanum vulgare) 86, 107, 176, 202, **283**

Marrubium vulgare (*White Horehound*) 44, 45, 47, 60, 171, 176, 177, 178, 179, 180, 204, 210, 211, 214, 221, 234, 242, 243, 252, 266, 271, 272, 278, 280, 281, 284, 287, 289, 314, 319, **329**

Marsdenia condurango (*Condurango*) 64, 180, **243**

Marshmallow (Althea officinalis) 8, 13, 39, 45, 46, 51, 54, 61, 63, 64, 67, 68, 70, 71, 74, 93, 95, 97, 122, 134, 136, 166, 175, 177, 178, 179, 180, 188, 189, 191, 192, 202, 229, 233, 238, 240, 253, 257, 261, 278, 282, 283, **284**, 304, 318

Massage 25, 36, 109, 192, 193

Mastitis 302

Mastoiditis **51–2**

Masturbation 130

Matricaria chamomilla (*Chamomile, German*) 13, 51, 53, 61, 64, 66, 69, 70, 71, 77, 86, 87, 127, 143, 156, 165, 175, 176, 177, 178, 179, 180, 184, 189, 200, 210, 213, 221, 234, **238–9**, 239, 264, 308, 322, 332

Meadowsweet (Filipendula ulmaria) 8, 12, 13, 22, 61, 63, 66, 67, 70, 73, 87, 88, 103, 106, 127, 167, 175, 176,

202, 213, 219, 221, 224, 233, 238, 243, 249, 261, 264, 267, 278, **285**, 304, 308

Measles 143

Meditation 21, 25, 26, 27, 62, 80, 86, 196

Medulla oblongata 42

Melancholia 328

Melissa officinalis (*Balm*) 34, 35, 51, 61, 66, 69, 86, 87, 175, 176, 177, 178, 179, 180, 198, **213**

Meningitis 141

Menopause 35, 79, 88, 121, 123, **128**, 239, 246, 263, 275, 286, 320, 325

Menorrhagia **123–4**, 220, 232, 239, 246, 254, 260, 264, 273, 295, 298, 299, 325, 332, **347**

Menstrual problems 87, 120, 121, **123–5**, 178, 210, 221, 239, 256, 275, 299

Menstruation 80, 98, **123–5**, 220, 225, 228, 254, 260, 263, 264, 283, 286, 318, 322, 323, 325, **352**

Mentha piperita (*Peppermint*) 13, 51, 52, 53, 61, 64, 66, 78, 86, 104, 107, 127, 142, 164, 165, 174, 175, 176, 177, 178, 179, 180, 184, 188, 192, 219, 251, 271, **298–9**, 335, 337

Mentha pulegium (*Pennyroyal*) 121, 123, 126, 142, 176, 178, 180, 203, **297–8**

Menthol 164, 165

Menyanthes trifoliata (*Buckbean*) 103, 106, 156, 171, 175, 178, 180, 199, 220, 222, **229**, 237, 249, 267, 329

Metabolism 21, 72, 93, 96, 102, 106, 112, 115, 116, 150

Metrorrhagia 123, **124**, 299, 325, **352**

Migraine **87–8**, 256, 273, 274, 279, 298, 327

Middle ear 51–2, 266

Milk, mother's **127**, 165, 210, 227, 250, 255

Milk Thistle (Silybum marianum) 156, 168, **285**

Mineral deficiency 69

Miscarriage 126, 220, 221, 225, 246, 254, 326

Mistletoe (Viscum alba) 33, 35, 36, 37, 38, 61, 77, 83, 88, 94, 149, 176, 178, 179, 180, 202, 268, 279, **286**, 337

Mitchella repens (*Partridge Vine*) 121, 126, 178, 179, 180, 203, 225, **295**

Morning sickness **127**

Motherwort (Leonurus cardiaca) 32, 33, 34, 35, 36, 46, 48, 77, 94, 121, 125, 128, 176, 178, 179, 180, 202, 225, 278, **286–7**

Motion sickness 221

Mountain Grape (Berberis aquifolium) 74, 93, 94, 95, 96, 103, 175, 177, 178, 179, 180, 202, 226, **287**

Mouse–Ear (Pilosella officinarum) 46, 47, 48, 176, 178, 179, 202, **287–8**

Mouth 64–**5**, 200, 218, 239, 241, 250, 256, 275, 283, 284, 290, 299, 305, 306, 307, 316, 325, 328, 331, **352**, 354

Mouth ulcer 64, **65**, 256, 290, 299, 306, 307, 325, 331, **352**

Mouthwash 56, 65, 212, 218, 219, 239, 250, 275, 283, 290, 307, 308, 312, 314, 316, 328, 331

Mucous colitis 209, 212, 216, 218, 219, 268

Mucous membranes 44, 45, 50, 51, 52, 53, 54, 67, 68, 70, 122, 129, 136, 143, 167, 191, 214, 215, 226, 253, 264, 271, 284, 285, 289, 303, 207, 218, 325

Mucus 44, 45, 46, 50, 52, 53, 54, 129, 166, 178, 287, 295, 316, 319, 326

Mugwort (Artemisia vulgaris) 113, 156, 175, 178, 180, 185, 202, **288**

Mullein (Verbascum thapsus) 12, 45, 46, 47, 51, 156, 157, 169, 175, 176, 177, 178, 179, 180, 202, 242, 264, 287, **289–90**, 329

Multiple sclerosis 86, **89**

Mumps 302

Muscle pain 218, 220, 246, 255, 283, 289, 310, 332

Muscle tension 83, 87, 105, 220, 246, 255

Muscular system 12, 88, **102–9**

Mustard (Brassica alba or nigra) 47, 103, 104, 165, 177, 179, 180, 202, 257, 269, **289–90**

Myrica cerifera (*Bayberry*) 61, 63, 70, 71, 176, 177, 180, 198, **216**

INDEX 373

Myroxylon toluifera (*Balsam of Tolu*) 163, 178, 179, **215**
Myrrh (Commiphora molmol) 55, 62, 64, 65, 93, 97, 98, 141, 142, 144, 160, 176, 180, 192, 219, 237, 283, **290**, 331
Mysticism 9, 16, 17, 18

N

Nasal catarrh 52, 53, 218, 239, 253, 298
Nasal polypi **54–5**, 224, 308
Nasturtium (Tropaeolum majus) 142, 203, **291**
Native American 22, 121, 220, 222, 225, 233, 254, 295, 314
Nausea 70, 87, 212, 221, 240, 241, 254, 258, 271, 285, 287, 298, 302, 328, **352**
Navelwort see *Pennywort*
Neoplasm 149
Nepeta cataria (*Catnip*) 142, 177, 199, **236**
Nepeta hederacea (*Catnip*) 142, 177, 199, **236**
Nepeta hederacea (*Ground Ivy*) 86, 176, 180, 201, 251, **266–7**
Nervine relaxants 46, 66, **77**, 83, 84, 85, 86, 87, 88, 89, 115, 126, 130, 143
Nervines **34**, 48, 61, 64, 65, 69, 70, 71, 74, 77, 80, 93, 95, 109, 122, 124, 126, 127, 145, **179**, 230, 243, 245, 276, 293, 327
Nervine stimulants **78**
Nervous debility 77, 137, 217, 274, 276, 293, 300
Nervous exhaustion 37, 117
Nervous system 12, 35, 36, 48, 58, 59, 74, **75–89**, 92, 109, 112, 125, 160, 165, 179, 217, 221, 248, 268, 274, 275, 276, 279, 286, 293, 317, 328, 332
Nervous tachycardia 35
Nervous tension see tension
Nettle (Urtica dioica) 12, 13, 61, 93, 95, 103, 115, 116, 126, 141, 155, 156, 157, 163, 175, 179, 180, 203, **291**, 293, 306, 312, 328
Nettle rash 328
Neuralgia **88**, 107, 109, 217, 220, 273, 293, 296, 310, 320, **352**
Neurological diseases **86–9**, 220
New age 16
Night-Blooming Cereus (Selenicereus grandiflorus) 32, 33, 176, 177, **292**
Normalizers 121, 155
Nose 50, **52–5**
Nosebleed **55**, 291, 299, 315, **353**
Nutrition 150, 154
Nymphomania 130

O

Oak Bark (Quercus robur) 61, 63, 71, 129, 176, 203, 281, **292**
Oats (Avena sativa) 37, 61, 77, 82, 85, 88, 89, 98, 115, 116, 122, 128, 130, 141, 156, 179, 180, 203, 248, 263, 275, 276, **293**, 310, 328
Obesity 33, 66, 114, 223
Ointment 13, 39, 72, 94, 95, 96, 97, 99, 163, 185, **189–90**
Opium 156, 233, 307, 332
Organic acid 163
Origanum vulgare (*Marjoram, Wild*) 86, 107, 176, 202, 283
Osteopathy 25, 48, 88, 102, 109
Ovarian cramp 220, 246, 254, 273, 295, 332, **353**
Overactive thyroid **115**, 230
Oversensitivity 78, 184, 253
Oxalic acid 105, 136
Oxygen 32, 35, 36, 38, 42, 43, 107, 170
Oxymel 187

P

Palpitation 94, 128, 230, 268, 299, 310, **353**
Panax ginseng (*Ginseng*) 37, 85, 88, 113, 115, 117, 130, 179, 180, **262**
Pancreas **114**
Pancreatitis **114**
Pansy (Viola tricolor) 95, 203, **293–4**
Papaver rhoeas (*Red Poppy*) 46, 179, 204, **307**
Papaya 115
Paradigm shift 19
Parasites 143–5
Paritaria diffusa (*Pellitory*) 134, 135, 136, 175, 177, 179, 203, 265, 267, 294, **297**, 330
Parkinson's disease 296
Parsley (Petroselinum crispum) 121, 134, 136, 175, 177, 178, 180, 203, 265, 267, 270, **294**, 297
Parsley Piert (Aphanes arvensis) 134, 136, 175, 177, 203, 265, 267, 270, **294–5**
Partridge Vine (Mitchella repens) 121, 126, 178, 179, 180, 203, 225, **295**
Pasqueflower (Anemone pulsatilla) 77, 88, 93, 97, 124, 125, 175, 176, 178, 179, 203, 263, **295–6**, 332
Passiflora incarnata (*Passion Flower*) 35, 77, 85, 86, 87, 88, 89, 106, 130, 175, 178, 179, 203, 269, 276, **296**, 327
Passion Flower (Passiflora incarnata) 35, 77, 85, 86, 87, 88, 89, 106, 130, 175, 178, 179, 203, 269, 276, **296**, 327
Peach (Prunus persica) 203, **296–7**
Penicillin 141
Pellitory of the Wall see *Pellitory*
Pennyroyal (Mentha pulegium) 121, 123, 126, 142, 176, 178, 180, 203, **297–8**
Pennywort (Umbilicus rupestris) 51, **298**
Peppermint (Mentha piperata) 13, 51, 52, 53, 61, 64, 66, 78, 86, 104, 107, 127, 142, 164, 165, 174, 175, 176, 177, 178, 179, 180, 184, 188, 192, 219, 251, 271, **298–9**, 335, 337
Peptic ulcer 80, 261, 278, 284, 285
Period/period pain 88, 123, 124, 232, 234, 246, 256, 273, 275, 283, 295, 296, 298, 299, 304, 310, 325, 327, 332
Peripheral blood vessels 32, 36, 37, 220
Peristalis 61, 62, 165, 166, 168, 177, 191, 236
Peritonitis 70
Periwinkle (Vinca major) 71, 72, 122, 124, 129, 149, 176, 180, 191, 203, 299, 325
Peruvian Bark (Cinchona succiruba) 178, **299**
Petasites hybridus (Butterbur) 199, **232**
Petit mal 271
Petroselinum crispum (*Parsley*) 121, 134, 136, 175, 177, 178, 180, 203, 265, 267, 270, **294**, 297
Peumus boldo (*Boldo*) 60, 62, 63, 73, 74, 104, 133, 177, 178, 179, 180, 199, **226**
Pharmacology 159
Pharyngitis 55, 218, 219, 224, 263, 282, 290, 292, 307, 314, 325, 331
Phenol 142, **167**
Phlebitis 38, 212, 269, **353**
Photophobia 87
Phytolacca americana (*Pokeroot*) 40, 47, 51, 52, 55, 56, 65, 92, 96, 97, 98, 103, 104, 122, 126, 129, 144, 149, 175, 180, 203, 241, 263, **302**
Picrasma excelsor (*Quassia*) 143, 145, **304**
Piles (see also hemorrhoids) 72, 277
Pilewort see *Lesser Celandine*
Pill 123, 125
Pill–Bearing Spurge (Euphorbia pilulifera) 44, 48, 266, 279, **300**, 314, 317, 321
Pilosella officinarum (*Mouse–Ear*) 46, 47, 48, 176, 178, 179, 202, **287–8**
Pimento officinalis (*Allspice*) 115, **209**
Pimpinella anisum (*Aniseed*) 13, 44, 46, 47, 48, 61, 66, 127, 145, 176, 177, 178, 179, 180, 183, 184, 185, 198, **211**, 245, 255

Pine, Scots (Pinus sylvestris) **300**
Pinus nigra see pinus sylvestris
Pinus pinaster see pinus sylvestris
Pinus pinea see pinus sylvestris
Pinus sylvestris (Pine, Scots) **300**
Pinworm 336
Piscidia erythrina (*Jamaican Dogwood*) 77, 85, 86, 87, 88, 89, 104, 106, 175, 178, 179, 273, 276, 296
Pituitary gland 82, 112–13, 116, 239
Placenta 125, 165
Planetary consciousness 16, 17, 19
Plantago major (*Plantain, Greater*) 44, 99, 134, 166, 176, 178, 180, 189, 203, 251, 277, **301**
Plantain, Greater (Plantago major) 44, 99, 134, 166, 176, 178, 180, 189, 203, 251, 277, **301**
Pleurisy **47**, 210, 227, 257, 301
Pleurisy Root (Asclepias tuberosa) 45, 47, 142, 177, 178, 179, 203, 210, 227, 252, 257, **301–2**
Pneumococcus 321
Pneumonia 47, 301
Poison 63, 157
Poisoning 32, 33, 61, 72, 170, 171, 219
Poison ivy 266, 328
Pokeroot (Phytolacca americana) 40, 47, 51, 52, 55, 56, 65, 92, 96, 97, 98, 103, 104, 122, 126, 129, 144, 149, 175, 180, 203, 241, 263, **302**
Pollution 84, 86
Polygale senega (*Senega*) 44, 46, 48, 61, 204, **314**
Polygonum bistorta (*Bistort*) 176, 180, 198, **218**
Polypi see nasal polypi
Polysaccharides 159, 166
Pomegranate (Punica granatum) 143, 145, 175, **302–3**
Populus gileadensis (*Balm of Gilead*) 51, 55, 95, 178, 179, 180, 187, **214**, 308
Populus tremuloides (*White Poplar*) 103, 175, 204, **329**
Potassium 34, 35, 116, 133
Potentilla anserina (*Silverweed*) 51, 204, **316**

Potentilla tormentilla (*Tormentil*) 61, 72, 134, 176, 204, 224, 308, **325**
Poultice 38, 39, 47, 97, 99, 184, **192**
Pregnancy 120, 121, 123, **125–7**, 136
Premenstrual syndrome **83**, 96, 123, **124–5**, 136, 239, 317, **353**
Prevention 9, 30–1, 36, 38, 42–3, 59, **154–60**
Prickly Ash (Zanthoxylum americanum) 39, 97, 103, 104, 108, 177, 178, 180, 203, 246, **303**
Primula veris (*Cowslip*) 44, 179, 200, **245–6**
Progesterone 121, 239
Prostate gland 120, 135, 245, 270, 312, 313
Prostatitis **135**, 229, 244, 245, 330
Protozoal infection 215
Prunella vulgaris (*Self–Heal*) 93, **313**
Prunus persica (*Peach*) 203, **296–7**
Prunus serotina (*Wild Cherry Bark*) 44, 48, 176, 178, 179, 205, **331**, 332
Psoriasis **94–5**, 215, 219, 225, 231, 240, 241, 256, 257, 304, 306, 311, 312, 323, 337
Psychosomatic 80
Psychological disease **82–6**
Psychotherapy 88, 128, 151–2
Pulmonaria officinalis (*Lungwort*) 45, 176, 177, 178, 179, 203, 280
Pulmonary infection 46, 257
Pumpkin (Cucurbita pepo) 143, 177, 203, 246, **303**
Punica granatum (*Pomegranate*) 143, 145, 175, **302–3**
Purgative 60, 62
Purines 108
Pus 97
Pyelitis **135**, 216, 297
Pyelonephritis **135**
Pyloric sphincter 68
Pyorrhea **64–5**, 250, 290, 331

Q

Quassia (Picrasma excelsor) 143, 145, **304**
Queen's Delight (Stillingia sylvatica) 175, 203, **304**
Quercus robur (*Oak Bark*) 61, 63, 71, 129, 176, 203, 281, **292**
Quince (Cydonia oblonga) 61, 178, 179, 192, 203, **305**
Quinsy 247, 307

R

Racing of the heart 35
Ragwort (Senecio jacobaea) 103, 176, **305**
Ranunculus ficaria (*Lesser Celandine*) 61, 72, 176, 191, 202, **277**, 334
Raspberry (Rubus idaeus) 55, 71, 121, 126, 127, 156, 176, 178, 180, 203, 295, **306**
Rectum 58, 62, 72, 145, 167
Red Clover (Trifolium pratense) 84, 86, 93, 94, 95, 96, 113, 149, 156, 175, 179, 180, 184, 204, **306**
Red Poppy (Papaver rhoeas) 46, 179, 204, **307**
Red Sage (Salvia officinalis) 55, 56, 65, 127, 176, 178, 204, **307–8**
Regeneration 26
Relationship 158–9
Relaxant 33, 44, 46, 61
Relaxation 31, 36, 48, 62, 69, 77, **80–2**, 85, 88, 105, 151
Renal colic **137**
Reproduction system 80, 83, 87, 88, 109, **119–30**, 156, 178
Rescue Remedy 79
Resistant bacteria 43
Respiration **42–8**, 50
Respiratory demulcents **45**, 47
Respiratory relaxants **44**, 46
Respiratory stimulants 44
Respiratory system **41–8**, 52, 54, 80, 157, 166, 178, 179
Rhamnus cathartica (*Buckthorn*) 60, 168, 179, 180, 199, **230**
Rhamnus purshiana (*Cascara sagrada*) 60, 62, 178, 179, **236**
Rhatany (Krameria triandra) 54, **308**
Rheumatism 102, 103, 104, **105–6**, 107, 108, 109, 116, 210, 212, 214, 218, 219, 220, 220, 223, 225, 226, 229, 230, 231, 237, 240, 245, 247, 248, 251, 255, 265, 267, 269, 270, 274, 286, 283, 285, 293, 300, 302, 303, 305, 311, 312, 320, 322, 323, 327, 328, 329, 330, 332, 334, 335, **353**
Rheum palmatum (*Rhubarb Root*) 60, 62, 72, 104, 176, 179, **308–9**
Rhinitis 54
Rhubarb Root (*Rheum palmatum*) 60, 62, 72, 104, 176, 179, **308–9**
Rhus aromatica (*Sweet Sumach*) 115, 137, **321**
Ringworm **98**, 259, 264, 323
Rosa canina (*Rose Hips*) 184, 204, **309**
Rose Hips (Rosa canina) 184, 204, **309**
Rosmarinus officinalis (*Rosemary*) 66, 77, 85, 86, 88, 104, 107, 109, 142, 176, 178, 179, 180, 184, 185, 186, 189, 204, 276, **309–10**
Rosemary (Rosmarinus officinalis) 66, 77, 85, 86, 88, 104, 107, 109, 142, 176, 178, 179, 180, 184, 185, 186, 189, 204, 276, **309–10**
Rosemary wine 186
Roughage 59, 62, 67, 72
Roundworm 144, 311, 322, 336
Rubefacients **104**, 179
Rubus idaeus (*Raspberry*) 55, 71, 121, 126, 127, 156, 176, 178, 180, 203, 295, **306**
Rue (Ruta graveolens) 86, 113, 115, 121, 123, 126, 127, 175, 176, 178, 179, 180, 201, 204, **310**
Rumex crispus (*Yellow Dock*) 12, 60, 72, 73, 93, 94, 95,

INDEX   377

96, 98, 103, 104, 109, 113, 149, 157, 168, 175, 178, 179, 180, 191, 205, 225, 231, 241, 256, 287, 304, 306, 311, 312, 337
Ruta graveolens (Rue) 86, 113, 115, 121, 123, 126, 127, 175, 176, 178, 179, 180, 201, 204, **310**

S

Sage see *Red Sage*
Salicylic acid 167
Saliva 60, 64, 165, 180, 235, 260, 272, 304, 314
Salix nigra (*Black Willow*) 13, 22, 87, 103, 106, 175, 180, 198, 218, **222**, 329
Salve 189–90
Salvia officinalis (*Red Sage*) 55, 56, 65, 127, 176, 178, 204, **307–8**
Sambucus nigra (*Elder*) 13, 51, 52, 53, 54, 86, 93, 99, 142, 175, 177, 178, 179, 180, 184, 186, 189, 200, 226, 236, **251**, 253, 271, 279, 298, 335, 337
Sanguinaria canadensis (*Bloodroot*) 45, 46, 48, 54, 175, 177, 178, 179, 180, 199, **224**, 308, 314
Santonica (Artemisia cina) 143, **311**
Saponaria officinalis (*Soapwort*) 44, **228**
Saponins 159, **169**
Sarsaparilla (Smilax utilis) 93, 94, 95, 103, 113, 122, 156, 175, 180, **311**
Sassafras (Sassafras albidum) 93, 142, 145, 175, **312**
Sassafras albidum (Sassafras) 93, 142, 145, 175, **312**
Saturated fat 31
Saw Palmetto Berries (Serenoa serrulata) 130, 135, 156, 177, 179, **312**
Scabies 98, **145**, 211, 302, 322
Scales 95
Scarlet fever 143
Schizandra chinensis 160
Sciatica 107, **109**

Scrophularia nodosa (*Figwort*) 32, 33, 93, 94, 95, 96, 175, 201, **256**, 258, 291
Scrutellaria laterifolia (*Skullcap*) 12, 13, 34, 35, 37, 48, 53, 61, 64, 69, 72, 77, 82, 83, 85, 86, 87, 88, 94, 122, 126, 128, 130, 143, 145, 156, 175, 176, 178, 179, 180, 204, 217, 230, 245, 248, 275, 276, 293, 310, **317**, 327, 328
Sea Holly (Eryngium maritimum) 137, 175, 177, **313**
Seizure 296, 317, 328
Selenicereus grandiflorus (*Night–Blooming Cereus*) 32, 33, 176, 177, **292**
Self–Heal (Prunella vulgaris) 93, **313**
Self healing 24–7
Senecio aureus (*Golden Ragwort*) 88, 121, 128, 129, 201, **263**, 310
Senecio jacobaea (*Ragwort*) 103, 176, **305**
Senega (Polygale senega) 44, 46, 48, 61, 204, **314**
Senna (Cassia angustifolia) 13, 60, 72, 144, 168, 179, **314–15**, 322
Septicemia 250
Serenoa serrulata (*Saw Palmetto Berries*) 130, 135, 156, 177, 179, **312**
Sexual excitement 35
Sexuality 124, **130**
Sexual organs 121
Shepherd's Purse (Capsella bursa–pastoris) 71, 122, 178, 180, 204, **315**
Shiitake mushroom 160
Shingles 88, **89**, 257, 296
Shock 77, 92, 134
Shook, Dr. 144
Sialagogues **60, 180**
Siberian Ginseng (Eleutherococcus senticosus) 82, 156, 158, 160, **316**
Silica 270
Silverweed (Potentilla anserina) 51, 204, **316**
Silybum marianum (*Milk Thistle*) 156, 168, **285**
Simonton 151
Sinus congestion 45

378 THE COMPLETE HERBS SOURCEBOOK

Sinusitis **54**, 251, 253, 290, 300
Skeletal system **102–9**
Skin 33, 43, 47, 52, 55, 58, 73, 80, 86, 88, 89, **91–9**, 104, 107, 109, 117, 142, 143, 144, 145, 156, 157, 167, 177, 178, 179, 184, 189, 190, 191, 192, 212, 214, 218, 219, 225, 228, 231, 241, 243, 246, 256, 258, 265, 272, 276, 283, 284, 287, 289, 290, 293, 295, 296, 300, 302, 303, 304, 306, 311, 312, 320, 322, 333, 337
Skullcap (Scutellaria laterifolia) 12, 13, 34, 35, 37, 48, 53, 61, 64, 69, 72, 77, 82, 83, 85, 86, 87, 88, 94, 122, 126, 128, 130, 143, 145, 156, 175, 176, 178, 179, 180, 204, 217, 230, 245, 248, 275, 276, 293, 310, **317**, 327, 328
Skunk Cabbage (Symplocarpus foetidus) 176, 178, 179, **317**
Sleep 85–6
Sleeplessness (see also insomnia) 85–6, 106, 180, 189, 233, 296, 300
Slippery Elm (Ulmus fulva) 61, 67, 69, 70, 71, 72, 93, 176, 177, 178, 179, 180, 188, 189, 191, 192, 257, 283, 284, **318**
Small intestine **68–70**
Smoking 31, 43, 68, 150
Snake bite 314, 328
Snuff 54–5, 224, 308
Soapwort (Saponaria officinalis), 44, **228**
Sodium 116
Solanum dulcamara (*Bittersweet*) 44, 198, **219**
Solidago virgauria (*Golden Rod*) 51, 52, 54, 169, 175, 176, 177, 201, 247, 251, 253, **263**, 266
Somatopsychic 80
Sore throat 209, 212, 214, 216, 239, 255, 261, 299, 306, 313, 316, 324
Sorothamnus scoparius (*Broom*) 32, 33, 34, 35, 37, 176, 177, 199, **228**
Soul 80
Southernwood (Artemisia abrontanum) 121, 123, 126, 143, 176, 178, 180, **318**
Spasm 45, 47, **48**, 61, 63, 77, 83, 124, 126, 137, 168, 176
Spirituality 18, 20, 26, 155

Spleen 215
Sputum 46, 48, 319
Sprain 99, **109**, 251, 261
Spring tonic 73, 209, 309, 313
Squaw Root see *Blue Cohosh*
Squaw Vine see *Partridge Vine*
Squill (Urginea maritima) 32, 44, 170, 177, 178, 187, **319**
Stachys palustris (*Woundwort*) 93, 189–90, **336**
Steam inhalation 53, 54
Stellaria media (*Chickweed*) 13, 93, 95, 96, 169, 178, 180, 189, 200, 214, **240**, 335
Steroids 72
Stillingia sylvatica (*Queen's Delight*) 175, 203, **304**
Sting 283
St. John's Wort (Hypericum perforatum) 77, 88, 89, 99, 104, 107, 128, 156, 175, 176, 178, 179, 180, 192, 193, 204, 263, **320**
St. John's Wort liniment 128
Stomach 8, 50, 55, 59, 61, 63, **65–8**, 73, 81, 87
Stomach pain 193, 260, 265
Stomach ulcer 8, 63, 282, 321
Stomatitis 219, 307
Stone Root (Collinsonia canadensis) 134, 136, 175, 177, 201, **267**
Streptococcus 321
Stress 31, 34, 35, 36, 37, 38, 48, 52, 53, 54, 59, 60, 63, 64, 65, 66, 67, 68, 69, 71, 72, 74, 77, 79, **82**, 83, 84, 85, 86, 87, 88, 92, 94, 105, 106, 107, 113, 114, 116, 117, 126, 127, 130, 140, 141, 148, 151, 156, 179, 213, 227, 239, 245, 276, 293, 316, 328
Styes 56
Sunburn 94, 99, 193, 310, 320
Sundew (Drosera rotundifolia) 44, 47, 48, 204, 279, 287, 319, **321**, 324
Suppositories 185, 189, **191**
Surface immune activation 159, **160**
Sweet Flag see *Calamus*
Sweet Sumach (Rhus aromatica) 115, 137, **321**

Sweet Violet (Viola odorata) 149, 204, **322**
Swollen glands 40, 47, 56, 241, 302
Symphytum officinale (*Comfrey*) 8, 13, 38, 39, 45, 46, 47, 48, 61, 63, 67, 68, 70, 71, 93, 95, 99, 156, 177, 178, 179, 180, 188, 189, 191, 192, 200, 216, **242–3**, 261, 278, 284, 336
Symplocarpus foetidus (*Skunk Cabbage*) 176, 178, 179, **317**
Synergy 20, 23
Syrup **187**
Syzygium cumini (*Jambul*) 115, **273**

T

T cells 160
Tachycardia 35, 256, 286
Tanacetum parthenium (*Feverfew*) 87, **256**
Tanacetum vulgare (*Tansy*) 86, 123, 126, 143, 145, 175, 176, 178, 179, 180, 204, **322–3**
Tannins **167**
Tansy (Tanacetum vulgare) 86, 123, 126, 143, 145, 175, 176, 178, 179, 180, 204, **322–3**
Tapeworm 143, 144, 145, 246, 275, 281, 302, 303, 311
Taraxacum officinale (*Dandelion*) 13, 33, 34, 35, 39, 60, 63, 72, 73, 74, 85, 94, 96, 103, 109, 113, 125, 133, 136, 149, 156, 157, 175, 177, 178, 179, 180, 186, 200, 222, 237, **248–9**, 265, 337
Teabags 183
Tearglands 56
Teeth 64
Tendon 108, 109
Tennis elbow 108
Tension 31, 35, 36, 37, 44, 48, 58, 61, 65, 66, 68, 69, 77, 78, 81, 82, 83, 86, 87, 88, 105, 115, 124, 128, 130, 140, 165, 166, 213, 217, 228, 243, 245, 246, 268, 273, 276, 279, 283, 286, 288, 295, 296, 298, 310, 317, 320, 327, 328, **354**

Testes, painful 295
Teucrium sorodonia (*Wood Sage*) **335**
Therapeutic ecology 24
Threadworm 144, 145, 259, 304, 311, 318, 322
Threatened miscarriage **126**, 220, 221, 246, 254, 326
Throat 40, 45, 50, 51, **55–6**, 129, 142, 143, 188, 209, 212, 214, 216, 239, 255, 261, 295, 306, 307, 308, 313, 316, 324, 325, 331, **354**
Thrombosis **38**, 168
Thrush 323
Thuja (Thuja occidentalis) 44, 55, 93, 94, 97, 98, 108, 126, 160, 175, 177, 178, 204, **323–4**
Thuja occidentalis (*Thuja*) 44, 55, 93, 94, 97, 98, 108, 126, 160, 175, 177, 178, 204, **323–4**
Thyme (Thymus vulgaris) 44, 46, 47, 61, 62, 86, 93, 109, 142, 164, 165, 167, 175, 176, 177, 178, 179, 180, 184, 204, **324**
Thymus vulgaris (*Thyme*) 44, 46, 47, 61, 62, 86, 93, 109, 142, 164, 165, 167, 175, 176, 177, 178, 179, 180, 184, 204, **324**
Thyroid 80, **115–16**, 223, 230
Tilia europea (*Lime Blossom*) 33, 35, 36, 37, 38, 48, 69, 71, 77, 83, 85, 86, 130, 156, 157, 176, 177, 184, 189, 202, 245, 268, **279**, 286, 337
Tincture 185–7
Tinea 265
Tinnitus **52**, 220, 256, 266, **354**
Tobacco 31, 38, 43, 52, 59, 67, 68, 157
Tongue, inflamed 307
Tonic herbs 155, 156, **180**
Tonsillitis **55–6**, 241, 247, 250, 292, 302, 307, 324, 331, **354**
Toothache 64, 241
Toothbrush 64
Toothpaste 64
Tormentil (Potentilla tormentilla) 61, 72, 134, 176, 204, 224, 308, **325**
Toxins 52, 68, 102, 103, 104, 105, 106, 107, 127, 133, 141, 142, 177

380   THE COMPLETE HERBS SOURCEBOOK

Tracheitis 211, 289
Tragacanth 188
Tranquilizer 77
Travel sickness 298, **354**
Trifolium pratense (*Red Clover*) 84, 86, 93, 94, 95, 96, 113, 149, 156, 175, 179, 180, 184, 204, **306**
Trigonella foenum–graecum (*Fenugreek*) 127, 178, 179, 180, **255**
Trillium (*Beth Root*) 122, 124, 129, 134, 176, 178, 179, 180, 204, 261, 264, 299, **325–6**
Tropaeolum majus (*Nasturtium*) 142, 203, **291**
*True Unicorn Root (*Aletris farinosa) 126, 278, 204, **326**
Tuberculosis 252, 263
Tubules 133
Tumor 149, 150, 171, 241, 251, 255, 265
Turkey Rhubarb Root see *Rhubarb Root*
Turnera aphrodisiaca (*Damiana*) 77, 85, 88, 116, 122, 130, 156, 179, 180, **248**, 275, 312
Tussilago farfara (*Coltsfoot*) 13, 44, 45, 46, 47, 48, 156, 157, 166, 175, 177, 178, 179, 180, 200, 210, 211, 214, **242**, 243, 245, 247, 252, 266, 271, 272, 278, 280, 281, 287, 289, 293, 319, 329

U

Ulcer 8, 39, 59, 63, 64, 65, 67–9, 71, 80, 214, 216, 219, 231, 233, 241, 242, 243, 256, 260, 261, 264, 268, 269, 272, 275, 278, 282, 283, 284, 285, 290, 298, 299, 303, 306, 307, 316, 318, 321, 325, 331, **352**
Ulmus fulva (*Slippery Elm Bark*) 61, 67, 69, 70, 71, 72, 93, 176, 177, 178, 179, 187, 188, 189, 191, 192, 257, 283, 284, **318**
Umbilicus rupestris (*Pennywort*) 51, **298**
Underactive thyroid **116**, 223
Unsaturated fat 31
Urethra 134, 135

Urethritis **135**, 229, 244, 245, 263, 265, 284, 313
Urginea maritima (*Squill*) 32, 44, 170, 177, 178, 187, **319**
Uric acid 108, 136
Urinary antiseptic **133**
Urinary astringents **134**
Urinary bladder **133–6**
Urinary demulcents **134**
Urinary gravel 134, 136, 216, 245, 265, 267, 270, 284, 294, 297, 313
Urinary incontinence **137**, 209, 321, 351
Urinary infection 216, 218, 245, 265, 269, 322, 330
Urinary system 12, 120, **131–7**, 156, 157, 165, 166, 167, 175, 216, 218, 244, 267, 284, 293, 297
Urination, painful 293
Urine 133–6
Urtica dioica (*Nettle*) 12, 13, 61, 93, 95, 103, 115, 116, 126, 141, 155, 156, 157, 163, 175, 179, 180, 203, **291**, 293, 306, 312, 328
Uterine tonics **121**, 123, 124, 125, 126, 156, 225, 254, 263, 325
Uterus 124, 125, 126, 127, 179, 220, 225, 246, 264, 295, 307, 323, 325, 332
Uva Ursi see *Bearberry*

V

Vaccination 323
Vagina 120, 129
Vaginal infection **129**, 167, 189
Valerian (Valeriana officinalis) 13, 34, 35, 37, 48, 61, 63, 65, 66, 67, 68, 69, 71, 74, 77, 83, 85, 86, 87, 88, 89, 94, 104, 106, 115, 122, 125, 126, 128, 130, 137, 171, 174, 175, 176, 177, 178, 179, 189, 204, 220, 230, 246, 269, 273, 276, 296, 317, **327**, 332
Valeriana officinalis (*Valerian*) 13, 34, 35, 37, 48, 61, 63, 65, 66, 67, 68, 69, 71, 74, 77, 83, 85, 86, 87, 88, 89, 94,

104, 106, 115, 122, 125, 126, 128, 130, 137, 171, 174, 175, 176, 177, 178, 179, 189, 204, 220, 230, 246, 269, 273, 276, 296, 317, **327**, 332
Valeric acid 163
Vaginal ulceration 216
Vagus nerve 286
Varicose ulcer **39**, 243, 303, **354**
Varicose veins **38–9**, 284, 303, 320, 334, **354**
Vasodilation 160, 213, 253, 256, 316
Veins 38–9
Venous system 33
Verbascum thapsus (*Mullein*) 12, 45, 46, 47, 51, 156, 157, 169, 175, 176, 177, 178, 179, 180, 202, 242, 264, 287, **289–90**, 329
Verbena officinalis (*Vervain*) 53–4, 60, 73, 77, 79, 85, 88, 127, 156, 175, 176, 177, 178, 179, 180, 184, 204, **327–8**
Vermifuges 143
Vervain (*Verbena officinalis*) 53–4, 60, 73, 77, 79, 85, 88, 127, 156, 175, 176, 177, 178, 179, 180, 184, 204, **327–8**
Viburnum opulus (*Cramp Bark*) 37, 77, 108, 122, 124, 125, 126, 136, 167, 176, 178, 179, 192, 200, 220, 221, **246**, 295, 296, 327
Viburnum prunifolium (*Black Haw*) 77, 124, 126, 176, 178, 179, 180, 198, **220–1**, 246, 273
Vinblastine 149
Vinca major (*Periwinkle*) 71, 72, 122, 124, 129, 149, 176, 180, 191, 203, 299, 325
Vincristine 149
Vinegar tincture **186**
Viola odorata (*Sweet Violet*) 149, 204, **322**
Viola tricolor (*Pansy*) 95, 203, **293–4**
Virginia Snakeroot (Aristolachia serpentaria) 180, **328**
Viscum alba (*Mistletoe*) 33, 35, 36, 37, 38, 61, 77, 83, 88, 94, 149, 176, 178, 179, 180, 202, 268, 279, **286**, 337
Vitamin A 72
Vitamin B complex 39, 65, 82, 85, 88, 89, 141, 144

Vitamin C 53, 54, 65, 82, 96, 97, 98, 99, 106, 129, 134, 141, 144, 168, 230, 237, 251, 280, 291, 294, 305, 309
Vitamin D 72
Vitamin deficiency 69
Vitamin E 97, 190
Vitamin K 72
Vitamin P 168
Vitamins 53–4
Vitex agnus–castus (*Chasteberry*) 88, 121, 123, 124, 125, 128, 178, 200, **239**
Volatile oils 47, 51, 52, 53, 61, 78, 86, 107, 127, 133, 142, **164–5**, 171, 177, 183–4, 190, 197
Vomiting 47, 61, 62, 70, 87, 175, 177, 212, 221, 230, 240, 241, 254, 271, 287, 298, 302, 314, 353, **354**

W

Wahoo see *Winged Elm*
Warts **97**, 323, **354**
Water retention 35, 37, 39, 112, 125, 126, **136**, 228, 232, 248, 278, 294, 297, 315, 319, **355**
Wax 52
Weight, gain of 116
Weight, loss of 69, 114, 115, 223
White Horehound (Marrubium vulgare) 44, 45, 47, 60, 171, 176, 177, 178, 179, 180, 204, 210, 211, 214, 221, 234, 242, 243, 252, 266, 271, 272, 278, 280, 281, 284, 287, 289, 314, 319, **329**
White Poplar (Populus tremuloides) 103, 175, 204, **329**
Whooping cough **47–8**, 211, 220, 242, 253, 259, 266, 272, 283, 287, 293, 296, 306, 317, 319, 321, 324, 329, 331, 332
Wild Carrot (Daucus carrot) 108, 136, 175, 177, 204, 205, **330**
Wild Cherry Bark (Prunus serotina) 44, 48, 176, 178, 179, 205, **331**, 332

Wild Indigo (Baptisia tinctoria) 51, 52, 93, 97, 98, 122, 129, 133, 142, 144, 160, 175, 176, 178, 205, 263, 331

Wild Lettuce (Lactuca virosa) 44, 46, 65, 130, 176, 178, 179, 205, **332**

Wild Yam (Dioscorea villosa) 22, 60, 63, 69, 70, 71, 73, 88, 103, 106, 113, 117, 124, 128, 169, 175, 176, 177, 178, 179, 180, 233, 246, 257, **332**

Wine 185–6

Winged Elm (Euonymus atropurpureus) 60, 73, 74, 177, 178, 179, 205, 257, **333**

Wintergreen (Gaulteria procumbens) 103, 104, 167, 205, **334**

Witch Hazel (Hamamelis virginiana) 13, 39, 55, 64, 72, 93, 95, 96, 99, 109, 143, 175, 176, 180, 191, 205, 212, 253, 264, 290, **334**

Womb 125, 220, 256, 294, 306

Wood Betony 37, 77, 86, 87, 176, 180

Wood Sage (Teucrium scorodonia) **335**

Worms 61, 144, 145, 175, 303, 304, 311, 318, 322, 336

Wormwood (Artemisia absinthum) 13, 37, 60, 62, 63, 66, 73, 86, 88, 97, 103, 104, 113, 115, 116, 126, 141, 142, 143, 144, 145, 175, 176, 178, 179, 180, 185, 205, 251, 322, **335–6**

Wound 92, 93, 94, **99**, 124, 140, 142, 167, 180, 189, 193, 209, 231, 232, 235, 239, 240, 243, 251, 255, 263, 270, 280, 283, 287, 290, 307, 313, 315, 320, 324, 325, 329, 335, 336, 337, **355**

Woundwort (Stachys palustris) 93, 189–90, **336**

Y

Yarrow (Achilliea millefolium) 13, 33, 34, 37, 38, 39, 51, 53, 99, 103, 104, 106, 108, 113, 115, 121, 122, 133, 134–5, 136, 142, 143, 157, 175, 176, 177, 178, 180, 189, 205, 216, 225, 226, 229, 236, 244, 245, 248, 250, 251, 252, 268, 298, 330, 335, **337**

Yellow Dock (Rumex crispus) 12, 60, 72, 73, 93, 94, 95, 96, 98, 103, 104, 109, 113, 149, 157, 168, 175, 178, 179, 180, 191, 205, 225, 231, 241, 256, 287, 304, 306, 311, 312, **337**

Yoga 25

Yogurt 46, 55, 129, 134, 141

Young, J. Z. 24

Z

Zanthoxylum americanum (*Prickly Ash Bark*) 39, 97, 103, 104, 108, 177, 178, 180, 203, 246, **303**

Zea mays (*Corn Silk*) 122, 134, 135, 136, 156, 175, 177, 229, **244**

Zinc 242

Zingiber officinale (*Ginger*) 33, 39, 60, 61, 62, 63, 72, 103, 104, 108, 142, 176, 177, 178, 179, 180, 185, 186, 189, 226, 233, 260, **261**, 289, 292, 315, 332, 337

The Index of English Names

A

Acerola Berries 53
Agrimony (Agrimonia eupatoria) 55, 61, 70, 71, 78, 137, 156, 176, 177, 178, 180, 198, **209**, 212, 216, 219, 234, 261, 277, 299, 321
Allspice (Pimenta officinalis) 115, **209**
Aloe (Aloe vera) 60, 93, 99, 168, 175, 178, 180, **210**
American Cranesbill see *Cranesbill, American* or *Geranium*
Angelica (Angelica archangelica) 44, 46, 61, 103, 133, 142, 176, 177, 178, 179, 180, 198, **210**
Aniseed (Pimpinella anisum) 13, 44, 46, 47, 48, 61, 66, 127, 145, 176, 177, 178, 179, 180, 183, 184, 185, 198, **211**, 245, 255
Arnica (Arnica montana) 13, 38, 99, 109, 180, 189, **211–12**
Avens (Geum urbanum) 176, 198, **212**

B

Balm (Melissa officinalis) 34, 35, 51, 61, 66, 69, 86, 87, 175, 176, 177, 178, 179, 180, 198, **213**
Balm of Gilead (Populus gileadensis) 51, 55, 95, 178, 179, 180, 187, **214**, 308
Balmony (Chelone glabra) 60, 73, 74, 88, 175, 177, 178, 179, 180, 198, **214**, 224, 248, 329
Balsam of Peru (Myroxylon pereirae) 176, 178, 179
Balsam of Tolu (Myroxylon toluifera) 163, 178, 179, **215**
Barberry (Berberis vulgaris) 60, 62, 72, 73, 74, 126, 175, 176, 177, 178, 179, 198, **215**

Bayberry (Myrica cerifera) 61, 63, 70, 71, 176, 177, 180, 198, **216**
Bearberry (Arctostaphylos uva ursi) 103, 109, 122, 133, 134, 135, 136, 156, 167, 175, 176, 177, 180, **216**, 218, 244, 245, 250, 270, 297, 330
Betony (Betonica officinalis) **217**
Birch, silver (Betula pendula) 198, **218**
Bistort (Polygonum bistorta) 176, 180, 198, **218**
Bittersweet (Solanum duleamara) 44, 198, **219**
Black Catechu (Acacia catechu) 176, **219**
Black Cohosh (Cimifuga racemosa) 52, 77, 88, 103, 106, 121, 125, 128, 176, 177, 178, 179, 180, 198, **220**, 222, 230, 329, 332
Black Haw (Viburnum prunifolium) 77, 124, 126, 176, 178, 179, 180, 198, **220–1**, 246, 273
Black Horebound (Ballota nigra) 87, 127, 175, 198, **221**, 271
Black Root (Leptandra virginica) 60, 73, 177, 178, 180, 198, 215, **222**, 287
Black Willow (Salix nigra) 13, 22, 87, 103, 106, 175, 180, 198, 218, **222**, 329
Bladderwrack (Fucus vesiculosus) 103, 113, 116, 175, 179, 180, **223**
Blessed Thistle (Cnicus benedictus) 127, 178, 199, **223–4**
Bloodroot (Sanguinaria canadensis) 45, 46, 48, 54, 175, 177, 178, 179, 180, 199, **224**, 308, 314
Blue Cohosh (Caulophyllum thalictroides) 121, 122, 123, 126, 178, 179, 199, 220, **225**
Blue Flag (Iris versicolor) 51, 56, 60, 65, 73, 93, 96, 103, 122, 149, 175, 177, 178, 180, 199, **225**, 302, 304
Bogbean (Menyanthes trifoliata) see *Buckbean*

385

Boldo (Peumus boldo) 60, 62, 63, 73, 74, 104, 133, 177, 178, 179, 180, 199, **226**

Boneset (Eupatorium perfoliatum) 13, 47, 51, 53, 93, 103, 104, 108, 142, 143, 174, 175, 176, 177, 178, 180, 189, 199, **226**, 236, 251, 271, 298, 337

Borage (Borago officinalis) 113, 117, 177, 178, 199, **227**

Broom (Sarothamnus scoparius) 32, 33, 34, 35, 37, 176, 177, 199, **228**

Buchu (Agathosma betulina) 12, 133, 134, 135, 156, 175, 177, 180, 199, **229**, 245, 293, 294, 297

Buckbean (Menyanthes trifoliata) 103, 106, 156, 171, 175, 178, 180, 199, 220, 222, **229**, 237, 249, 267, 329

Buckthorn (Rhamnus cathartica) 60, 168, 179, 180, 199, **230**

Buckwheat (Fagopyrum esculentum) 33, 37, 39, 99, 156, 168

Bugleweed (Lycopus europaeus) 32, 33, 35, 113, 115, 176, 177, 179, 180, **230**

Burdock (Arctium lappa) 13, 93, 94–6, 103, 108, 113, 115, 122, 149, 175, 177, 179, 180, 197, 199, 225, **231**, 238, 241, 256, 258, 287, 291, 304, 311, 312, 337

Bur Marigold (Bidens tripartita) 122, 134, 199, **232**

Butterbur (Petasites hybridicus) 199, **232**

C

Calamus (Acorus calamus) 61, 67, 71, 199, 219, **233**, 234, 332

California Poppy (Eschscholzia californica) 77, 85, 199, **233–4**

Calumba (Jateorrhiza palmata) 72, 180, **234**

Caraway (Carum carvi) 61, 63, 127, 176, 177, 180, 184, 187, 199, 211, **234**

Cardamom (Elattaria cardamonum) 61, 66, 70, 176, 177, 180, **235**, 260, 315

Cascara Sagrada (Rhamnus purshianus) 60, 62, 178, 179, **236**

Catnip (Nepeta cataria) 142, 177, 199, **236**

Cayenne (Capsicum minimum) 13, 33, 39, 47, 60, 61, 86, 103, 104, 107, 142, 143, 175, 176, 177, 178, 179, 180, 188, 189, 192, 224, 226, 236, 237, 269, 279, 289, 301, 303, 337

Cayenne liniment 107

Celandine, Greater see *Greater Celandine*

Celery (Apium graveolens) 12, 13, 103, 104, 106, 108, 133, 134, 156, 176, 177, 178, 184, 200, 222, 230, **237**, 249, 267, 329

Centaury (Erythraea centaurium) 60, 78, 85, 176, 178, 180, **238**

Chamomile (Matricaria chamomilla) 13, 51, 53, 61, 64, 66, 69, 70, 71, 77, 86, 87, 127, 143, 156, 165, 175, 176, 177, 178, 179, 180, 184, 189, 200, 210, 213, 221, 234, 238, 239, 264, 308, 322, 332

Chasteberry (Vitex agnus–castus) 88, 121, 123, 124, 125, 128, 178, 200, **239**

Chickweed (Stellaria media) 13, 93, 95, 96, 169, 178, 180, 189, 200, 214, **240**, 335

Cilantro see *Coriander*

Cinnamon (Cinnamonum zeylandica) 64, 176, 177, 180, 185, **240**

Cleavers (Galium aparine) 13, 40, 47, 51, 55, 56, 65, 93, 94, 95, 96, 97, 98, 113, 122, 129, 133, 141, 143, 149, 156, 157, 175, 177, 178, 179, 180, 200, 231, **240–1**, 258, 287, 293, 302, 304, 311, 331, 337

Cloves (Eugenia caryphyllus) 64, 167, 175, 176, 179, **241**

Colic Root see *True Unicorn Root*

Coltsfoot (Tussilago farfara) 13, 44, 45, 46, 47, 48, 156, 157, 166, 175, 177, 178, 179, 180, 200, 210, 211, 214, **242**, 243, 245, 247, 252, 266, 271, 272, 278, 280, 281, 287, 289, 293, 319, 329

Comfrey (Symphytum officinale) 8, 13, 38, 39, 45, 46, 47, 48, 61, 63, 67, 68, 70, 71, 93, 95, 99, 156, 177, 178, 179, 180, 188, 189, 191, 192, 200, 216, **242–3**, 261, 278, 284, 336

Condurango (Marsdenia condurango) 64, 180, **243**

Coriander (Coriandrum sativum) 61, 176, 177, 200, **244**

Corn Silk (Zea mays) 122, 134, 135, 136, 156, 175, 177, 229, **244**

Couch Grass (Agropyron repens) 103, 122, 133, 134, 135, 136, 175, 177, 180, 200, 216, 229, 244, **245**, 248, 293

Cowslip (Primula veris) 44, 179, 200, **245–6**

Cramp Bark (Viburnum opulus) 37, 77, 108, 122, 124, 125, 126, 136, 167, 176, 178, 179, 192, 200, 220, 221, **246**, 295, 296, 327

Cranesbill, American (Geranium maculatum) 176, 180, 201, **260–1**, 272, 283, 299, 325

Cucumber (Cucumis sativa) 189, **246**

Cudweed (Gnaphalium uliginosum) 200, **247**, 263

D

Daisy (Bellis perennis) 44, 99, 169, 180, 200, **247**

Damiana (Turnera aphrodisiaca) 77, 85, 88, 116, 122, 130, 156, 179, 180, **248**, 275, 312

Dandelion (Taraxacum officinalis) 13, 33, 34, 35, 39, 60, 63, 72, 73, 74, 85, 94, 96, 103, 109, 113, 125, 133, 136, 149, 156, 157, 175, 177, 178, 179, 180, 186, 200, 222, 237, **248–9**, 265, 337

Devil's Claw (Harpagophytum procumbens) 103, 171, 175, **249**

Dill (Anethum graveolens) 175, 176, 177, 184, 200, 244, **250**

E

Echinacea (Echinacea angustifolia) 13, 39, 40, 47, 51, 52, 54, 55, 56, 62, 64, 65, 68, 70, 71, 88, 89, 93, 96, 97, 98, 99, 113, 122, 129, 133, 135, 136, 141, 142, 143, 144, 149, 155, 156, 157, 158, 160, 175, 176, 180, 200, 225, 241, **250**, 259, 263, 272, 290, 296, 331

Elder (Sambucus nigra) 13, 51, 52, 53, 54, 86, 93, 99, 142, 175, 177, 178, 179, 180, 184, 186, 189, 200, 226, 236, **251**, 253, 271, 279, 298, 335, 337

Elecampane (Iluna helenium) 44, 46, 48, 156, 175, 176, 178, 179, 180, 200, 235, 243, **252**, 266

Ephedra (Ephedra sinica) 22, 44, 48, 54, 200, **253**, 279, 324

Eucalyptus (Eucalyptus globulus) 47, 51, 52, 53, 64, 93, 98, 142, 165, 176, 178, 180, 189

Evening Primrose (Oenothera biennis) 89

Eyebright (Euphrasia officinalis) 51, 52, 54, 56, 175, 176, 180, 200, **253–4**

F

False Unicorn Root (Chamaelirium luteum) 13, 25, 88, 121, 123, 124, 126, 129, 156, 178, 180, 201, 221, 225, **254**, 310, 318, 326

Fennel (Foeniculum vulgare) 61, 63, 66, 127, 142, 175, 176, 177, 178, 183, 184, 187, 201, 211, **255**, 315

Fenugreek (Trigonella foenum–graecum) 127, 178, 179, 180, **255**

Feverfew (Tanacetum parthenium) 87, **256**

Figwort (Scrophularia nodosa) 32, 33, 93, 94, 95, 96, 175, 201, **256**, 258, 291

Flax (Linum usitatissimum) 44, 45, 46, 47, 177, 178, 179, 180, 192, 201, **257**

Foxglove (Digitalis purpurea) 23, 32, 156, 170, 278

Fringetree (Chionanthus virginicus) 60, 73, 74, 114, 115, 175, 177, 178, 179, 180, 201, 215, 226, **257**, 287

Fumitory (Fumaria officinalis) 93, 95, 175, 177, 178, 180, 201, **258**

G

Galangal (Alpinia officinarum) 177, 180, **258–9**

Garlic (Allium sativum) 36, 37, 38, 47, 51, 52, 54, 71, 93,

97, 98, 115, 122, 129, 142, 143, 144, 145, 156, 158, 160, 165, 175, 176, 177, 178, 179, 180, 187, 201, **259**
Gentian (Gentiana lutea) 37, 60, 63, 64, 66, 73, 79, 104, 141, 145, 156, 176, 177, 178, 180, 201, 238, **260**
Geranium (Geranium maculatum) 61, 63, 68, 71, 93, 122, 124, 129, 175, 176, 180, 201, **260–1**, 272, 283, 299, 325
Ginger (Zingiber officinale) 33, 39, 60, 61, 62, 63, 72, 103, 104, 108, 142, 176, 177, 178, 179, 180, 185, 186, 189, 226, 233, 260, **261**, 289, 292, 315, 332, 337
Ginseng (Panax ginseng) 37, 85, 88, 113, 115, 117, 130, 179, 180, **262**
Golden Ragwort (Senecia aureus) 88, 121, 128, 129, 201, **263**, 310
Goat's Rue (Galega officinale) 113, 115, 127, 178, 201, **262**
Golden Rod (Solidago virgauria) 51, 52, 54, 169, 175, 176, 177, 201, 247, 251, 253, **263**, 266
Golden Seal (Hydrastis canadensis) 8, 40, 51, 52, 54, 55, 56, 60, 66, 67–8, 70, 72, 73, 74, 87, 88, 93, 95, 98, 99, 104, 113, 122, 126, 127, 128, 141, 143, 175, 176, 177, 178, 179, 180, 188, 189, 191, 192, 214, 253, **264**, 283, 287, 329
Gravel Root (Eupatorium purpureum) 134, 136, 175, 177, 180, 201, **265**, 267, 270, 330
Greater Celandine (Chelidonium majus) 97, 201, **265–6**
Grindelia (Grindelia camporum) 44, 48, 178, 180, **266**, 272, 279, 300, 301, 314, 317, 321, 323
Ground Ivy (Nepeta hederacea) 86, 176, 180, 201, 251, **266–7**
Guaiacum (Guaiacum officinale) 103, 104, 106, 149, 175, 177, 222, **267**

H

Hawthorn Berries (Crataegus oxyacanthoides) 12, 33, 35, 36, 37, 38, 39, 177, 180, 184, 201, 228, **268**, 286

Hops (Humulus lupulus) 34, 48, 61, 65, 66, 68, 70, 77, 85, 88, 127, 130, 171, 175, 176, 178, 179, 189, 201, 213, **268–9**, 273, 279, 296, 304, 327
Horse Chestnut (Aesculus hippocastanum) 33, 39, 99, 180, 201, **269**
Horseradish (Armoracia rusticana) 64, 104, 178, 179, 180, 201, **269**
Horsetail (Equisetum arvense) 93, 134, 135, 137, 156, 180, 201, **270**, 312, 321
Hydrangea (Hydrangea aborescens) 134, 135, 136, 175, 180, 201, 245, 265, 267, **270**, 312, 330
Hyssop (Hyssopus officinalis) 44, 46, 47, 51, 77, 142, 175, 176, 177, 178, 179, 180, 184, 201, 251, **271**, 283

I

Iceland Moss (Cetraria islandica) 61, 175, 178, 179, 180, 202, **271**
Ipecacuanha (Cephaclis ipecacuanha) 61, 177, **272**, **348**
Irish Moss (Chondrus crispus) 61, 66, 93, 122, 127, 166, 175, 177, 178, 179, 180, **272**

J

Jamaican Dogwood (Piscidia erythrina) 77, 85, 86, 87, 88, 89, 104, 106, 175, 178, 179, **273**, 276, 296
Jambul (Syzygium cumini) 115, **273**
Juniper Berries (Juniperus communis) 103, 104, 122, 126, 133, 134, 135, 176, 177, 178, 180, 202, **274**, 297

K

Kelp see *Bladderwrack*
Kola Nut (Cola vera) 37, 78, 85, 88, 116, 176, 177, 179, 224, 248, **274–5**, 276, 310, 312
Kousso (Hagenia abyssinica) 143, **275**

L

Lady's Mantle (Alchemilla vulgaris) 63, 122, 189, 202, **275**
Lady's Slipper (Cypripedium pubescens) 77, 83, 85, 86, 175, 176, 179, 180, **276**, 293, 328
Lavender (Lavendula officinalis) 66, 69, 77, 85, 86, 87, 88, 107, 142, 175, 179, 189, 202, 213, **276**
Lesser Celandine (Ranunculus ficaria) 61, 72, 176, 191, 202, **277**, 334
Licorice (Glycyrrhiza glabra) 45, 46, 47, 48, 53, 55, 60, 62, 64, 113, 117, 125, 144, 145, 177, 178, 179, 180, 183, 184, 197, 236, **277–8**, 284
Life Root see *Golden Ragwort* (Senecia aureus) 88, 121, 128, 129, 201, **263**, 310
Lily of the Valley (Convallaria majalis) 23, 32, 33, 34, 35, 36, 115, 170, 176, 177, 202, 228, **278**
Lime Blossom (Tilia europaea) 33, 35, 36, 37, 38, 48, 69, 71, 77, 83, 85, 86, 130, 156, 157, 176, 177, 184, 189, 202, 245, 268, **279**, 286, 337
Lobelia (Lobelia inflata) 45, 46, 48, 51, 61, 176, 177, 178, 179, 192, 202, 211, 224, 266, **279–80**, 289, 300, 301, 317, 323, 324, 329
Lungwort Herb (Pulmonaria officinalis) 45, 176, 177, 178, 179, 203, **280**
Lungwort Moss (Lobaria pulmonaria) 45, **281**

M

Ma Huang see *Ephedra*
Male Fern (Dryopteris filix–mas) 126, 143, 145, 202, **281**
Mallow (Malva sylvestris) 46, 178, 202, **282**
Marigold (Calendula officinalis) 13, 38, 39, 40, 55, 56, 88, 93, 95, 96, 97, 98, 99, 122, 134, 143, 157, 160, 171, 175, 176, 178, 180, 189, 190, 199, 202, 232, 241, 277, **282–3**
Marigold compress 95

Marigold ointment 190
Marjoram, Wild (Origanum vulgare) 86, 107, 176, 202, **283**
Marshmallow (Althea officinalis) 8, 13, 39, 45, 46, 51, 54, 61, 63, 64, 67, 68, 70, 71, 74, 93, 95, 97, 122, 134, 136, 166, 175, 177, 178, 179, 180, 188, 189, 191, 192, 202, 229, 233, 238, 240, 253, 257, 261, 278, 282, 283, **284**, 304, 318
Meadowsweet (Filipendula ulmaria) 8, 12, 13, 22, 61, 63, 66, 67, 70, 73, 87, 88, 103, 106, 127, 167, 175, 176, 202, 213, 219, 221, 224, 233, 238, 243, 249, 261, 264, 267, 278, **285**, 304, 308
Milk Thistle (Silybum marianum) 156, 168, **285**
Mistletoe (Viscum alba) 33, 35, 36, 37, 38, 61, 77, 83, 88, 94, 149, 176, 178, 179, 180, 202, 268, 279, **286**, 337
Motherwort (Leonurus cardiaca) 32, 33, 34, 35, 36, 46, 48, 77, 94, 121, 125, 128, 176, 178, 179, 180, 202, 225, 278, **286–7**
Mountain Grape (Berberis aquifolium) 74, 93, 94, 95, 96, 103, 175, 177, 178, 179, 180, 202, 226, **287**
Mouse–Ear (Pilosella officinarum) 46, 47, 48, 176, 178, 179, 202, **287**
Mugwort (Artemisia vulgaris) 113, 156, 175, 178, 180, 185, 202, **288**
Mullein (Verbascum thapsus) 12, 45, 46, 47, 51, 156, 157, 169, 175, 176, 177, 178, 179, 180, 202, 242, 264, 287, **289–90**, 329
Mustard (Brassica alba or nigra) 47, 103, 104, 165, 177, 179, 180, 202, 257, 269, **289–90**
Myrrh (Commiphora molmol) 55, 62, 64, 65, 93, 97, 98, 141, 142, 144, 160, 176, 180, 192, 219, 237, 283, **290**, 331

N

Nasturtium (Tropaeolum majus) 142, 203, **291**
Navelwort see *Pennywort*

Nettle (Urtica dioica) 12, 13, 61, 93, 95, 103, 115, 116, 126, 141, 155, 156, 157, 163, 175, 179, 180, 203, **291**, 293, 306, 312, 328

Night–Blooming Cereus (Selenicereus grandiflorus) 32, 33, 176, 177, **292**

O

Oak Bark (Quercus robur) 61, 63, 71, 129, 176, 203, 281, **292**

Oats (Avena sativa) 37, 61, 77, 82, 85, 88, 89, 98, 115, 116, 122, 128, 130, 141, 156, 179, 180, 203, 248, 263, 275, 276, **293**, 310, 328

P

Pansy (Viola tricolor) 95, 203, **293–4**

Parsley (Petroselinum crispum) 121, 134, 136, 175, 177, 178, 180, 203, 265, 267, 270, **294**, 297

Parsley Piert (Aphanes arvensis) 134, 136, 175, 177, 203, 265, 267, 270, **294–5**

Partridge Vine (Mitchella repens) 121, 126, 178, 179, 180, 203, 225, **295**

Pasqueflower (Anemone pulsatilla) 77, 88, 93, 97, 124, 125, 175, 176, 178, 179, 203, 263, **295–6**, 332

Passion Flower (Passiflora incarnata) 35, 77, 85, 86, 87, 88, 89, 106, 130, 175, 178, 179, 203, 269, 276, **296**, 327

Peach (Prunus persica) 203, **296–7**

Pellitory (Parietaria diffusa) 134, 135, 136, 175, 177, 179, 203, 265, 267, 294, 297, 330

Pellitory of the Wall see *Pellitory*

Pennyroyal (Mentha pulegium) 121, 123, 126, 142, 176, 178, 180, 203, **297–8**

Pennywort (Umbilicus rupestris) 51, **298**

Peppermint (Mentha piperata) 13, 51, 52, 53, 61, 64, 66, 78, 86, 104, 107, 127, 142, 164, 165, 174, 175, 176, 177, 178, 179, 180, 184, 188, 192, 219, 251, 271, **298–9**, 335, 337

Periwinkle (Vinca major) 71, 72, 122, 124, 129, 149, 176, 180, 191, 203, 299, 325

Peruvian Bark (Cinchona succiruba) 178, **299**

Pilewort see *Lesser Celandine*

Pill–Bearing Spurge (Euphorbia pilulifera) 44, 48, 266, 279, **300**, 314, 317, 321

Pine, Scots (Pinus sylvestris) **300**

Plantain, Greater (Plantago major) 44, 99, 134, 166, 176, 178, 180, 189, 203, 251, 277, **301**

Pleurisy Root (Asclepias tuberosa) 45, 47, 142, 177, 178, 179, 203, 210, 227, 252, 257, **301–2**

Pokeroot (Phytolacca americana) 40, 47, 51, 52, 55, 56, 65, 92, 96, 97, 98, 103, 104, 122, 126, 129, 144, 149, 175, 180, 203, 241, 263, **302**

Pomegranate (Punica granatum) 143, 145, 175, **302–3**

Prickly Ash (Zanthoxylum americanum) 39, 97, 103, 104, 108, 177, 178, 180, 203, 246, **303**

Pumpkin (Cucurbita pepo) 143, 177, 203, 246, **303**

Q

Quassia (Picrasma excelsor) 143, 145, **304**

Queen's Delight (Stillingia sylvatica) 175, 203, **304**

Quince (Cydonia oblonga) 61, 178, 179, 192, 203, **305**

R

Ragwort (Senico jacobaea) 103, 176, **305**

Raspberry (Rubus idaeus) 55, 71, 121, 126, 127, 156, 176, 178, 180, 203, 295, **306**

Red Clover (Trifolium pratense) 84, 86, 93, 94, 95, 96, 113, 149, 156, 175, 179, 180, 184, 204, **306**

Red Poppy (Papaver rhoeas) 46, 179, 204, **307**

Red Sage (Salvia officinalis) 55, 56, 65, 127, 176, 178, 204, **307–8**

Rhatany (Krameria triandra) 54, **308**

Rhubarb Root (Rheum palmatum) 60, 62, 72, 104, 176, 179, **308–9**

Rose Hips (Rosa canina) 184, 204, **309**

Rosemary (Rosmarinus officinalis) 66, 77, 85, 86, 88, 104, 107, 109, 142, 176, 178, 179, 180, 184, 185, 186, 189, 204, 276, **309–10**

Rue (Ruta graveolens) 86, 113, 115, 121, 123, 126, 127, 175, 176, 178, 179, 180, 201, 204, **310**

S

Sage see *Red Sage*

Santonica (Artemisia cina) 143, **311**

Sarsaparilla (Smilax utilis) 93, 94, 95, 103, 113, 122, 156, 175, 180, **311**

Sassafras (Sassafras albidum) 93, 142, 145, 175, **312**

Saw Palmetto Berries (Serenoa serrulata) 130, 135, 156, 177, 179, **312**

Sea Holly (Eryngium maritimum) 137, 175, 177, **313**

Self-Heal (Prunella vulgaris) 93, **313**

Senega (Polygale senega) 44, 46, 48, 61, 204, **314**

Senna (Cassia angustifolia) 13, 60, 72, 144, 168, 179, **314–15**, 322

Shepherd's Purse (Capsella bursa-pastoris) 71, 122, 178, 180, 204, **315**

Siberian Ginseng (Eleutherococcus senticosus) 82, 156, 158, 160, **316**

Silverweed (Potentilla anserina) 51, 204, **316**

Skullcap (Scutellaria laterifolia) 12, 13, 34, 35, 37, 48, 53, 61, 64, 69, 72, 77, 82, 83, 85, 86, 87, 88, 94, 122, 126, 128, 130, 143, 145, 156, 175, 176, 178, 179, 180, 204, 217, 230, 245, 248, 275, 276, 293, 310, **317**, 327, 328

Skunk Cabbage (Symplocarpus foetidus) 176, 178, 179, **317**

Slippery Elm (Ulmus fulva) 61, 67, 69, 70, 71, 72, 93, 176, 177, 178, 179, 180, 188, 189, 191, 192, 257, 283, 284, **318**

Soapwort (Saponaria officinalis), 44, **228**

Southernwood (Artemisia abrotanum) 121, 123, 126, 143, 176, 178, 180, **318**

Squaw Root see *Blue Cohosh*

Squaw Vine see *Partridge Vine*

Squill (Urginea maritima) 32, 44, 170, 177, 178, 187, **319**

St. John's Wort (Hypericum perforatum) 77, 88, 89, 99, 104, 107, 128, 156, 175, 176, 178, 179, 180, 192, 193, 204, 263, **320**

Stone Root (Collinsonia canadensis) 134, 136, 175, 177, 201, **267**

Sundew (Drosera rotundifolia) 44, 47, 48, 204, 279, 287, 319, **321**, 324

Sweet Flag see *Calamus*

Sweet Sumach (Rhus aromatica) 115, 137, **321**

Sweet Violet (Viola odorata) 149, 204, **322**

T

Tansy (Tanacetum vulgare) 86, 123, 126, 143, 145, 175, 176, 178, 179, 180, 204, **322–3**

Thuja (Thuja occidentalis) 44, 55, 93, 94, 97, 98, 108, 126, 160, 175, 177, 178, 204, **323–4**

Thyme (Thymus vulgaris) 44, 46, 47, 61, 62, 86, 93, 109, 142, 164, 165, 167, 175, 176, 177, 178, 179, 180, 184, 204, **324**

Tormentil (Potentilla tormentilla) 61, 72, 134, 176, 204, 224, 308, **325**

Trillium (Trillium erectum) 122, 124, 129, 134, 176, 178, 179, 180, 204, 261, 264, 299, **325–6**

True Unicorn Root (Aletris farinosa) 126, 278, 204, **326**
Turkey Rhubarb Root see *Rhubarb Root*

U

Uva Ursi see *Bearberry*

V

Valerian (Valeriana officinalis) 13, 34, 35, 37, 48, 61, 63, 65, 66, 67, 68, 69, 71, 74, 77, 83, 85, 86, 87, 88, 89, 94, 104, 106, 115, 122, 125, 126, 128, 130, 137, 171, 174, 175, 176, 177, 178, 179, 189, 204, 220, 230, 246, 269, 273, 276, 296, 317, **327**, 332
Vervain (Verbena officinalis) 53–4, 60, 73, 77, 79, 85, 88, 127, 156, 175, 176, 177, 178, 179, 180, 184, 204, **327–8**
Virginia Snakeroot (Aristolachia serpentaria) 180, **328**

W

Wahoo see *Winged Elm*
White Horebound (Marrubium vulgare) 44, 45, 47, 60, 171, 176, 177, 178, 179, 180, 204, 210, 211, 214, 221, 234, 242, 243, 252, 266, 271, 272, 278, 280, 281, 284, 287, 289, 314, 319, **329**
White Poplar (Populus tremuloides) 103, 175, 204, **329**
Wild Carrot (Daucus carrota) 108, 136, 175, 177, 204, 205, **330**
Wild Cherry Bark (Prunus serotina) 44, 48, 176, 178, 179, 205, **331**, 332

Wild Indigo (Baptisia tinctoria) 51, 52, 93, 97, 98, 122, 129, 133, 142, 144, 160, 175, 176, 178, 205, 263, 331
Wild Lettuce (Lactuca virosa) 44, 46, 65, 130, 176, 178, 179, 205, **332**
Wild Yam (Dioscorea villosa) 22, 60, 63, 69, 70, 71, 73, 88, 103, 106, 113, 117, 124, 128, 169, 175, 176, 177, 178, 179, 180, 233, 246, 257, **332**
Winged Elm (Euonymus atropurpureus) 60, 73, 74, 177, 178, 179, 205, 257, **333**
Wintergreen (Gaulteria procumbens) 103, 104, 167, 205, **334**
Witch Hazel (Hamamelis virginiana) 13, 39, 55, 64, 72, 93, 95, 96, 99, 109, 143, 175, 176, 180, 191, 205, 212, 253, 264, 290, **334**
Wood Betony 37, 77, 86, 87, 176, 180
Wood Sage (Teucrium scorodonia) **335**
Wormwood (Artemisia absinthum) 13, 37, 60, 62, 63, 66, 73, 86, 88, 97, 103, 104, 113, 115, 116, 126, 141, 142, 143, 144, 145, 175, 176, 178, 179, 180, 185, 205, 251, 322, **335–6**
Woundwort (Stachys palustris) 93, 189–90, **336**

Y

Yarrow (Achillea millefolium) 13, 33, 34, 37, 38, 39, 51, 53, 99, 103, 104, 106, 108, 113, 115, 121, 122, 133, 134–5, 136, 142, 143, 157, 175, 176, 177, 178, 180, 189, 205, 216, 225, 226, 229, 236, 244, 245, 248, 250, 251, 252, 268, 298, 330, 335, **337**
Yellow Dock (Rumex crispus) 12, 60, 72, 73, 93, 94, 95, 96, 98, 103, 104, 109, 113, 149, 157, 168, 175, 178, 179, 180, 191, 205, 225, 231, 241, 256, 287, 304, 306, 311, 312, **337**

The Index of Botanical Names

A

Acacia catechu (*Black Catechu*) 176, **219**
Achillea millefolium (*Yarrow*) 13, 33, 34, 37, 38, 39, 51, 53, 99, 103, 104, 106, 108, 113, 115, 121, 122, 133, 134–5, 136, 142, 143, 157, 175, 176, 177, 178, 180, 189, 205, 216, 225, 226, 229, 236, 244, 245, 248, 250, 251, 252, 268, 298, 330, 335, **337**
Acorus calamus (*Calamus*) 61, 67, 71, 199, 219, **233**, 234, 332
Aesculus hippocastanum (*Horse Chestnut*) 33, 39, 99, 180, 201, **269**
Agathosma betulina (*Buchu*) 12, 133, 134, 135, 156, 175, 177, 180, 199, **229**, 245, 293, 294, 297
Agrimonia eupatoria (*Agrimony*) 55, 61, 70, 71, 78, 137, 156, 176, 177, 178, 180, 198, **209**, 212, 216, 219, 234, 261, 277, 299, 321
Agropyron repens (*Couch Grass*) 103, 122, 133, 134, 135, 136, 175, 177, 180, 200, 216, 229, 244, **245**, 248, 293
Alchemilla vulgaris (*Lady's Mantle*) 63, 122, 189, 202, **275**
Aletris farinosa (*True Unicorn Root*) 126, 278, 204, **326**
Allium sativum (*Garlic*) 36, 37, 38, 47, 51, 52, 54, 71, 93, 97, 98, 115, 122, 129, 142, 143, 144, 145, 156, 158, 160, 165, 175, 176, 177, 178, 179, 180, 187, 201, **259**
Aloe vera (*Aloe*) 60, 93, 99, 168, 175, 178, 180, **210**
Alpina officinarum (*Galangal*) 177, 180, **258–9**
Althea officinalis (*Marshmallow*) 8, 13, 39, 45, 46, 51, 54, 61, 63, 64, 67, 68, 70, 71, 74, 93, 95, 97, 122, 134, 136, 166, 175, 177, 178, 179, 180, 188, 189, 191, 192, 202, 229, 233, 238, 240, 253, 257, 261, 278, 282, 283, **284**, 304, 318
Anemone pulsatilla (*Pasqueflower*) 77, 88, 93, 97, 124, 125, 175, 176, 178, 179, 203, 263, **295–6**, 332
Anethum graveolens (*Dill*) 175, 176, 177, 184, 200, 244, **250**
Angelica archangelica (*Angelica*) 44, 46, 61, 103, 133, 142, 176, 177, 178, 179, 180, 198, **210**
Anthemis nobile (*Chamomile, Garden*) 13, 51, 53, 61, 64, 66, 69, 70, 71, 77, 86, 87, 127, 143, 156, 165, 175, 176, 177, 178, 179, 180, 184, 189, 200, 210, 213, 221, 234, **238**, 264, 308, 322, 332
Aphanes arvensis (*Parsley Piert*) 134, 136, 175, 177, 203, 265, 267, 270, **294–5**
Apium graveolens (*Celery*) 12, 13, 103, 104, 106, 108, 133, 134, 156, 176, 177, 178, 184, 200, 222, 230, **237**, 249, 267, 329
Arctium lappa (*Burdock*) 13, 93, 94–6, 103, 108, 113, 115, 122, 149, 175, 177, 179, 180, 197, 199, 225, **231**, 238, 241, 256, 258, 287, 291, 304, 311, 312, 337
Arctostaphylos uva ursi (*Bearberry*) 103, 109, 122, 133, 134, 135, 136, 156, 167, 175, 176, 177, 180, **216**, 218, 244, 245, 250, 270, 297, 330
Armoracia rusticana (*Horseradish*) 64, 104, 178, 179, 180, 201, **269**
Arnica montana (*Arnica*) 13, 38, 99, 109, 180, 189, **211–12**
Artemisia abrotanum (*Southernwood*) 121, 123, 126, 143, 176, 178, 180, **318**

Artemisia absinthum (*Wormwood*) 13, 37, 60, 62, 63, 66, 73, 86, 88, 97, 103, 104, 113, 115, 116, 126, 141, 142, 143, 144, 145, 175, 176, 178, 179, 180, 185, 205, 251, 322, **335–6**

Artemisia vulgaris (*Mugwort*) 113, 156, 175, 178, 180, 185, 202, **288**

Asclepias tuberosa (*Pleurisy Root*) 45, 47, 142, 177, 178, 179, 203, 210, 227, 252, 257, 301

Avena sativa (*Oats*) 37, 61, 77, 82, 85, 88, 89, 98, 115, 116, 122, 128, 130, 141, 156, 179, 180, 203, 248, 263, 275, 276, **293**, 310, 328

B

Ballota nigra (*Black Horehound*) 87, 127, 175, 198, **221**, 271

Baptisia tinctoria (*Wild Indigo*) 51, 52, 93, 97, 98, 122, 129, 133, 142, 144, 160, 175, 176, 178, 205, 263, 331

Bellis perenis (*Daisy*) 44, 99, 169, 180, 200, **247**

Berberis aquifolium (*Mountain Grape*) 74, 93, 94, 95, 96, 103, 175, 177, 178, 179, 180, 202, 226, **287**

Berberis vulgaris (*Barberry*) 60, 62, 72, 73, 74, 126, 175, 176, 177, 178, 179, 198, **215**

Betonica officinalis (*Betony*) **217**

Betula pendula (*Birch, Silver*) 198, **218**

Bidens tripartita (*Bur Marigold*) 122, 134, 199, **232**

Borago officinalis (*Borage*) 113, 117, 177, 178, 199, **227**

Brassica alba (*Mustard*) 47, 103, 104, 165, 177, 179, 180, 202, 257, 269, **289–90**

Brassica nigra (*Mustard*) 47, 103, 104, 165, 177, 179, 180, 202, 257, 269, **289–90**

C

Calendula officinalis (*Marigold*) 13, 38, 39, 40, 55, 56, 88, 93, 95, 96, 97, 98, 99, 122, 134, 143, 157, 160, 171, 175, 176, 178, 180, 189, 190, 199, 202, 232, 241, 277, **282–3**

Capsella bursa–pastoris (*Shepherd's Purse*) 71, 122, 178, 180, 204, **315**

Capsicum minimum (*Cayenne*) 13, 33, 39, 47, 60, 61, 86, 103, 104, 107, 142, 143, 175, 176, 177, 178, 179, 180, 188, 189, 192, 224, 226, 236, 237, 269, 279, 289, 301, 303, 337

Carlina vulgaris (*Carline Thistle*) 180, 199, **235**

Carum carvi (*Caraway*) 61, 63, 127, 176, 177, 180, 184, 187, 199, 211, **234**

Cassia angustifolia (*Senna*) 13, 60, 72, 144, 168, 179, **314–15**, 322

Cassia senna (*Senna*) 13, 60, 72, 144, 168, 179, **314–15**, 322

Caulophyllum thalictroides (*Blue Cohosh*) 121, 122, 123, 126, 178, 179, 199, 220, **225**

Centaurium erythraea (*Centaury*) 60, 78, 85, 176, 178, 180, **238**

Cephaelis ipecacuanha (*Ipecacuanha*) 61, 177, **272**, 348

Cetraria islandica (*Iceland Moss*) 61, 175, 178, 179, 180, 202, **271**

Chamaelirium luteum (*False Unicorn Root*) 13, 25, 88, 121, 123, 124, 126, 129, 156, 178, 180, 201, 221, 225, **254**, 310, 318, 326

Chelidonium majus (*Greater Celandine*) 97, 201, **265–6**

Chelone glabra (*Balmony*) 60, 73, 74, 88, 175, 177, 178, 179, 180, 198, **214**, 224, 248, 329

Chionanthus virginicus (*Fringetree*) 60, 73, 74, 114, 115, 175, 177, 178, 179, 180, 201, 215, 226, **257**, 287

Chondrus crispus (*Irish Moss*) 61, 66, 93, 122, 127, 166, 175, 177, 178, 179, 180, **272**

Cimifuga racemosa (*Black Cohosh*) 52, 77, 88, 103, 106, 121, 125, 128, 176, 177, 178, 179, 180, 198, **220**, 222, 230, 329, 332

Cinchona succiruba (*Peruvian Bark*) 178, **299**

Cinnamonum zeylandica (*Cinnamon*) 64, 176, 177, 180, 185, **240**

Cnicus benedictus (*Blessed Thistle*) 127, 178, 199, **223–4**

Cola vera (*Kola Nut*) 37, 78, 85, 88, 116, 176, 177, 179, 224, 248, **274–5**, 276, 310, 312

Collinsonia canadensis (*Stone Root*) 134, 136, 175, 177, 201, **267**

Commiphora molmol (*Myrrh*) 55, 62, 64, 65, 93, 97, 98, 141, 142, 144, 160, 176, 180, 192, 219, 237, 283, **290**, 331

Convallaria majalis (*Lily of the Valley*) 23, 32, 33, 34, 35, 36, 115, 170, 176, 177, 202, 228, **278**

Coriandrum sativum (*Coriander* or *Cilantro*) 61, 176, 177, 200, **244**

Crataegus oxyacanthoides (*Hawthorn Berries*) 12, 33, 35, 36, 37, 38, 39, 177, 180, 184, 201, 228, **268**, 286

Cucumis sativa (*Cucumber*) 189, **246**

Cucurbita pepo (*Pumpkin*) 143, 177, 203, 246, **303**

Cydonia oblonga (*Quince*) 61, 178, 179, 192, 203, **305**

Cypripedium pubescens (*Lady's Slipper*) 77, 83, 85, 86, 175, 176, 179, 180, **276**, 293, 328

D

Daucus carrota (*Wild Carrot*) 108, 136, 175, 177, 204, 205, **330**

Digitalis purpurea 23, 32, 156, 170, 278

Drosera rotundifolia (*Sundew*) 44, 47, 48, 204, 279, 287, 319, **321**, 324

Dryopteris filix–mas (*Male Fern*) 126, 143, 145, 202, **281**

E

Echinacea angustifolia (*Echinacea*) 13, 39, 40, 47, 51, 52, 54, 55, 56, 62, 64, 65, 68, 70, 71, 88, 89, 93, 96, 97, 98, 99, 113, 122, 129, 133, 135, 136, 141, 142, 143, 144, 149, 155, 156, 157, 158, 160, 175, 176, 180, 200, 225, 241, **250**, 259, 263, 272, 290, 296, 331

Elattaria cardamonum (*Cardamom*) 61, 66, 70, 176, 177, 180, **235**, 260, 315

Eleutherococcus senticosus (*Siberian Ginseng*) 82, 156, 158, 160, **316**

Ephedra sinica (*Ephedra*) 22, 44, 48, 54, 200, **253**, 279, 324

Equisetum arvense (*Horsetail*) 93, 134, 135, 137, 156, 180, 201, **270**, 312, 321

Eryngium maritimum (*Sea Holly*) 137, 175, 177, **313**

Eschscholzia california (*California Poppy*) 77, 85, 199, **233–4**

Eugenia caryphyllus (*Cloves*) 64, 167, 175, 176, 179, **241**

Euonymus atropurpureus (*Winged Elm*) 60, 73, 74, 177, 178, 179, 205, 257, **333**

Eupatorium perfoliatum (*Boneset*) 13, 47, 51, 53, 93, 103, 104, 108, 142, 143, 174, 175, 176, 177, 178, 180, 189, 199, **226**, 236, 251, 271, 298, 337

Eupatorium purpureum (*Gravel Root*) 134, 136, 175, 177, 180, 201, **265**, 267, 270, 330

Euphorbia pilulifera (*Pill–Bearing Spurge*) 44, 48, 266, 279, **300**, 314, 317, 321

Euphrasia officinalis (*Eyebright*) 51, 52, 54, 56, 175, 176, 180, 200, **253–4**

F

Fagopyrum esculentum 33, 37, 39, 99, 156, 168

Filipendula ulmaria (*Meadowsweet*) 8, 12, 13, 22, 61, 63, 66, 67, 70, 73, 87, 88, 103, 106, 127, 167, 175, 176, 202, 213, 219, 221, 224, 233, 238, 243, 249, 261, 264, 267, 278, **285**, 304, 308

Foeniculum vulgare (*Fennel*) 61, 63, 66, 127, 142, 175, 176, 177, 178, 183, 184, 187, 201, 211, **255**, 315

Fucus vesiculosus (*Bladderwrack*) 103, 113, 116, 175, 179, 180, **223**

Fumaria officinalis (*Fumitory*) 93, 95, 175, 177, 178, 180, 201, **258**

G

Galega officinalis (*Goat's Rue*) 113, 115, 127, 178, 201, **262**

Galium aparine (*Cleavers*) 13, 40, 47, 51, 55, 56, 65, 93, 94, 95, 96, 97, 98, 113, 122, 129, 133, 141, 143, 149, 156, 157, 175, 177, 178, 179, 180, 200, 231, **240–1**, 258, 287, 293, 302, 304, 311, 331, 337

Gaulteria procumbens (*Wintergreen*) 103, 104, 167, 205, **334**

Gentiana lutea (*Gentian*) 37, 60, 63, 64, 66, 73, 79, 104, 141, 145, 156, 176, 177, 178, 180, 201, 238, **260**

Geranium maculatu n (*Cranesbill, American* or *Geranium*) 176, 180, 201, **260–1**, 272, 283, 299, 325

Geum urbanum (*Avens*) 176, 198, **212**

Glycyrrhiza glabra (*Licorice*) 45, 46, 47, 48, 53, 55, 60, 62, 64, 113, 117, 125, 144, 145, 177, 178, 179, 180, 183, 184, 197, 236, **277–8**, 284

Gnaphalium uliginosum (*Cudweed*) 200, **247**, 263

Grindelia camporum (*Grindelia*) 44, 48, 178, 180, **266**, 272, 279, 300, 301, 314, 317, 321, 323

Guaiacum officinale (*Guaiacum*) 103, 104, 106, 149, 175, 177, 222, **267**

H

Hagenia abyssinica (*Kousso*) 143, **275**

Hamamelis virginiana (*Witch Hazel*) 13, 39, 55, 64, 72, 93, 95, 96, 99, 109, 143, 175, 176, 180, 191, 205, 212, 253, 264, 290, **334**

Harpagophytum procumbens (*Devil's Claw*) 103, 171, 175, **249**

Humulus lupulus (*Hops*) 34, 48, 61, 65, 66, 68, 70, 777, 85, 88, 127, 130, 171, 175, 176, 178, 179, 189, 201, 213, **268–9**, 273, 279, 296, 304, 327

Hydrangea aborescens (*Hydrangea*) 134, 135, 136, 175, 180, 201, 245, 265, 267, **270**, 312, 330

Hydrastis canadensis (*Golden Seal*) 8, 40, 51, 52, 54, 55, 56, 60, 66, 67–8, 70, 72, 73, 74, 87, 88, 93, 95, 98, 99, 104, 113, 122, 126, 127, 128, 141, 143, 175, 176, 177, 178, 179, 180, 188, 189, 191, 192, 214, 253, **264**, 283, 287, 329

Hypericum perforatum (*St. John's Wort*) 77, 88, 89, 99, 104, 107, 128, 156, 175, 176, 178, 179, 180, 192, 193, 204, 263, **320**

Hyssopus officinalis (*Hyssop*) 44, 46, 47, 51, 77, 142, 175, 176, 177, 178, 179, 180, 184, 201, 251, **271**, 283

I

Inula helenium (*Elecampane*) 44, 46, 48, 156, 175, 176, 178, 179, 180, 200, 235, 243, **252**, 266

Iris versicolor (*Blue Flag*) 51, 56, 60, 65, 73, 93, 96, 103, 122, 149, 175, 177, 178, 180, 199, **225**, 302, 304

J

Jateorrhiza palmata (*Calumba*) 72, 180, **234**

Juniperus communis (*Juniper Berries*) 103, 104, 122, 126, 133, 134, 135, 176, 177, 178, 180, 202, **274**, 297

K

Krameria triandra (*Rhatany*) 54, **308**

L

Lactuca virosa (*Wild Lettuce*) 44, 46, 65, 130, 176, 178, 179, 205, **332**

Lavendula officinalis (*Lavender*) 66, 69, 77, 85, 86, 87, 88, 107, 142, 175, 179, 189, 202, 213, **276**

Leonurus cardiaca (*Motherwort*) 32, 33, 34, 35, 36, 46, 48, 77, 94, 121, 125, 128, 176, 178, 179, 180, 202, 225, 278, **286–7**

Leptandra virginica (*Black Root*) 60, 73, 177, 178, 180, 198, 215, **222**, 287

Linum usitatissimum (*Flax*) 44, 45, 46, 47, 177, 178, 179, 180, 192, 201, **257**

Lobaria pulmonaria (*Lungwort Moss*) 45, **281**

Lobelia inflata (*Lobelia*) 45, 46, 48, 51, 61, 176, 177, 178, 179, 192, 202, 211, 224, 266, **279–80**, 289, 300, 301, 317, 323, 324, 329

Lycopus europaeus (*Bugleweed*) 32, 33, 35, 113, 115, 176, 177, 179, 180, **230**

M

Malva sylvestris (*Mallow*) 46, 178, 202, **282**

Marrubium vulgare (*White Horehound*) 44, 45, 47, 60, 171, 176, 177, 178, 179, 180, 204, 210, 211, 214, 221, 234, 242, 243, 252, 266, 271, 272, 278, 280, 281, 284, 287, 289, 314, 319, **329**

Marsdenia condurango (*Condurango*) 64, 180, **243**

Matricaria chamomilla (*Chamomile, German*) 13, 51, 53, 61, 64, 66, 69, 70, 71, 77, 86, 87, 127, 143, 156, 165, 175, 176, 177, 178, 179, 180, 184, 189, 200, 210, 213, 221, 234, **238–9**, 239, 264, 308, 322, 332

Melissa officinalis (*Balm*) 34, 35, 51, 61, 66, 69, 86, 87, 175, 176, 177, 178, 179, 180, 198, **213**

Mentha piperita (*Peppermint*) 13, 51, 52, 53, 61, 64, 66, 78, 86, 104, 107, 127, 142, 164, 165, 174, 175, 176, 177, 178, 179, 180, 184, 188, 192, 219, 251, 271, **298–9**, 335, 337

Mentha pulegium (*Pennyroyal*) 121, 123, 126, 142, 176, 178, 180, 203, **297–8**

Menyanthes trifoliata (*Buckbean*) 103, 106, 156, 171, 175, 178, 180, 199, 220, 222, **229**, 237, 249, 267, 329

Mitchella repens (*Partridge vine*) 121, 126, 178, 179, 180, 203, 225, **295**

Myrica cerifera (*Bayberry*) 61, 63, 70, 71, 176, 177, 180, 198, **216**

Myroxylon toluifera (*Balsam of Tolu*) 163, 178, 179, **215**

N

Nepeta cataria (*Catnip*) 142, 177, 199, **236**

Nepeta hederacea (*Ground Ivy*) 86, 176, 180, 201, 251, **266–7**

O

Origanum vulgare (*Marjoram, Wild*) 86, 107, 176, 202, 283

P

Panax ginseng (*Ginseng*) 37, 85, 88, 113, 115, 117, 130, 179, 180, **262**

Papaver rhoeas (*Red Poppy*) 46, 179, 204, **307**

Parietaria diffusa (*Pellitory*) 134, 135, 136, 175, 177, 179, 203, 265, 267, 294, 297, 330

Passiflora incarnata (*Passion Flower*) 35, 77, 85, 86, 87, 88, 89, 106, 130, 175, 178, 179, 203, 269, 276, **296**, 327

Petasites hybridus (*Butterbur*) 199, **232**

Petroselinum crispum (*Parsley*) 121, 134, 136, 175, 177, 178, 180, 203, 265, 267, 270, **294**

Peumus boldo (*Boldo*) 60, 62, 63, 73, 74, 104, 133, 177, 178, 179, 180, 199, **226**

Phytolacca americana (*Pokeroot*) 40, 47, 51, 52, 55, 56, 65, 92, 96, 97, 98, 103, 104, 122, 126, 129, 144, 149, 175, 180, 203, 241, 263, **302**

Picrasma excelsor (*Quassia*) 143, 145, **304**

Pilosella officinarum (*Mouse–Ear*) 46, 47, 48, 176, 178, 179, 202, **287–8**

Pimento officinalis (*Allspice*) 115, **209**

Pimpinella anisum (*Aniseed*) 13, 44, 46, 47, 48, 61, 66, 127, 145, 176, 177, 178, 179, 180, 183, 184, 185, 198, **211**, 245, 255

Pinus nigra see pinus sylvestris

Pinus pinaster see pinus sylvestris

Pinus pinea see pinus sylvestris

Pinus sylvestris (*Pine, Scots*) **300**

Piscidia erythrina (*Jamaican Dogwood*) 77, 85, 86, 87, 88, 89, 104, 106, 175, 178, 179, **273**, 276, 296

Plantago major (*Plantain, Greater*) 44, 99, 134, 166, 176, 178, 180, 189, 203, 251, 277, **301**

Polygale senega (*Senega*) 44, 46, 48, 61, 204, **314**

Polygonum bistorta (*Bistort*) 176, 180, 198, **218**

Populus gileadensis (*Balm of Gilead*) 51, 55, 95, 178, 179, 180, 187, **214**, 308

Populus tremuloides (*White Poplar*) 103, 175, 204, **329**

Potentilla anserina (*Silverweed*) 51, 204, **316**

Potentilla tormentilla (*Tormentil*) 61, 72, 134, 176, 204, 224, 308, 325

Primula veris (*Cowslip*) 44, 179, 200, **245–6**

Prunella vulgaris (*Self–Heal*) 93, **313**

Prunus persica (*Peach*) 203, **296–7**

Prunus serotina (*Wild Cherry Bark*) 44, 48, 176, 178, 179, 205, **331**, 332

Pulmonaria officinalis (*Lungwort Herb*) 45, 176, 177, 178, 179, 203, **280**

Punica granatum (*Pomegranate*) 143, 145, 175, **302–3**

Q

Quercus robur (*Oak Bark*) 61, 63, 71, 129, 176, 203, 281, **292**

R

Ranunculus ficaria (*Lesser Celandine*) 61, 72, 176, 191, 202, **277**, 334

Rhamnus cathartica (*Buckthorn*) 60, 168, 179, 180, 199, **230**

Rhamnus purshiana (*Cascara sagrada*) 60, 62, 178, 179, **236**

Rheum palmatum (*Rhubarb Root*) 60, 62, 72, 104, 176, 179, **308–9**

Rhus aromatica (*Sweet Sumach*) 115, 137, **321**

Rosa canina (*Rose Hips*) 184, 204, **309**

Rosmarinus officinalis (*Rosemary*) 66, 77, 85, 86, 88, 104, 107, 109, 142, 176, 178, 179, 180, 184, 185, 186, 189, 204, 276, **309–10**

Rubus idaeus (*Raspberry*) 55, 71, 121, 126, 127, 156, 176, 178, 180, 203, 295, 306

Rumex crispus (*Yellow Dock*) 12, 60, 72, 73, 93, 94, 95, 96, 98, 103, 104, 109, 113, 149, 157, 168, 175, 178, 179, 180, 191, 205, 225, 231, 241, 256, 287, 304, 306, 311, 312, 337

Ruta graveolens (*Rue*) 86, 113, 115, 121, 123, 126, 127, 175, 176, 178, 179, 180, 201, 204, **310**

S

Salix nigra (*Black Willow*) 13, 22, 87, 103, 106, 175, 180, 198, 218, **222**, 329

Salvia officinalis (*Red Sage*) 55, 56, 65, 127, 176, 178, 204, **307–8**

Sambucus nigra (*Elder*) 13, 51, 52, 53, 54, 86, 93, 99, 142, 175, 177, 178, 179, 180, 184, 186, 189, 200, 226, 236, **251**, 253, 271, 279, 298, 335, 337

Sanguinaria canadensis (*Bloodroot*) 45, 46, 48, 54, 175, 177, 178, 179, 180, 199, **224**, 308, 314

Saponaria officinalis (*Soapwort*) 44, **228**

Sassafras albidum (*Sassafras*) 93, 142, 145, 175, **312**

Scrophularia nodosa (*Figwort*) 32, 33, 93, 94, 95, 96, 175, 201, **256**, 258, 291

Scrutellaria laterifolia (*Skullcap*) 12, 13, 34, 35, 37, 48, 53, 61, 64, 69, 72, 77, 82, 83, 85, 86, 87, 88, 94, 122, 126, 128, 130, 143, 145, 156, 175, 176, 178, 179, 180, 204, 217, 230, 245, 248, 275, 276, 293, 310, **317**, 327, 328

Selenicereus grandiflorus (*Night-Blooming Cereus*) 32, 33, 176, 177

Senecio aureus (*Golden Ragwort* or *Life Root*) 88, 121, 128, 129, 201, **263**, 310

Senecio jacobaea (*Ragwort*) 103, 176, **305**

Serenoa serrulata (*Saw Palmetto Berries*) 130, 135, 156, 177, 179, **312**

Silybum marianum (*Milk Thistle*) 156, 168, **285**

Smilax utilis (*Sarsaparilla*) 93, 94, 95, 103, 113, 122, 156, 175, 180, **311**

Solanum dulcamara (*Bittersweet*) 44, 198, **219**

Solidago virgauria (*Golden Rod*) 51, 52, 54, 169, 175, 176, 177, 201, 247, 251, 253, **263**, 266

Sorothamnus scoparius (*Broom*) 32, 33, 34, 35, 37, 176, 177, 199, **228**

Stachys palustris (*Woundwort*) 93, 189–90, **336**

Stellaria media (*Chickweed*) 13, 93, 95, 96, 169, 178, 180, 189, 200, 214, **240**, 335

Stillingia sylvatica (*Queen's Delight*) 175, 203, **304**

Symphytum officinale (*Comfrey*) 8, 13, 38, 39, 45, 46, 47, 48, 61, 63, 67, 68, 70, 71, 93, 95, 99, 156, 177, 178, 179, 180, 188, 189, 191, 192, 200, 216, **242–3**, 261, 278, 284, 336

Symplocarpus foetidus (*Skunk Cabbage*) 176, 178, 179, **317**

Syzygium cumini (*Jambul*) 115, **273**

T

Tanacetum parthenium (*Feverfew*) 87, **256**

Tanacetum vulgare (*Tansy*) 86, 123, 126, 143, 145, 175, 176, 178, 179, 180, 204, **322–3**

Taraxacum officinale (*Dandelion*) 13, 33, 34, 35, 39, 60, 63, 72, 73, 74, 85, 94, 96, 103, 109, 113, 125, 133, 136, 149, 156, 157, 175, 177, 178, 179, 180, 186, 200, 222, 237, **248–9**, 265, 337

Teucrium sorodonia (*Wood Sage*) **335**

Thuja occidentalis (*Thuja*) 44, 55, 93, 94, 97, 98, 108, 126, 160, 175, 177, 178, 204, **323–4**

Thymus vulgaris (*Thyme*) 44, 46, 47, 61, 62, 86, 93, 109, 142, 164, 165, 167, 175, 176, 177, 178, 179, 180, 184, 204, **324**

Tilia europea (*Lime Blossom*) 33, 35, 36, 37, 38, 48, 69, 71, 77, 83, 85, 86, 130, 156, 157, 176, 177, 184, 189, 202, 245, 268, **279**, 286, 337

Trifolium pratense (*Red Clover*) 84, 86, 93, 94, 95, 96, 113, 149, 156, 175, 179, 180, 184, 204, **306**

Trigonella foenum-graecum (*Fenugreek*) 127, 178, 179, 180, **255**

Trillium erectum (*Trillium* or *Beth Root*) 122, 124, 129, 134, 176, 178, 179, 180, 204, 261, 264, 299, **325–6**

Tropaeolum majus (*Nasturtium*) 142, 203, **291**

Turnera aphrodisiaca (*Damiana*) 77, 85, 88, 116, 122, 130, 156, 179, 180, **248**, 275, 312

Tussilago farfara (*Coltsfoot*) 13, 44, 45, 46, 47, 48, 156, 157, 166, 175, 177, 178, 179, 180, 200, 210, 211, 214,

242, 243, 245, 247, 252, 266, 271, 272, 278, 280, 281, 287, 289, 293, 319, 329

U

Ulmus fulva (*Slippery Elm Bark*) 61, 67, 69, 70, 71, 72, 93, 176, 177, 178, 179, 180, 188, 189, 191, 192, 257, 283, 284, **318**

Umbilicus rupestris (*Pennywort*) 51, **298**

Urginea maritima (*Squill*) 32, 44, 170, 177, 178, 187, **319**

Urtica dioica (*Nettle*) 12, 13, 61, 93, 95, 103, 115, 116, 126, 141, 155, 156, 157, 163, 175, 179, 180, 203, **291**, 293, 306, 312, 328

V

Valeriana officinalis (*Valerian*) 13, 34, 35, 37, 48, 61, 63, 65, 66, 67, 68, 69, 71, 74, 77, 83, 85, 86, 87, 88, 89, 94, 104, 106, 115, 122, 125, 126, 128, 130, 137, 171, 174, 175, 176, 177, 178, 179, 189, 204, 220, 230, 246, 269, 273, 276, 296, 317, **327**, 332

Verbascum thapsus (*Mullein*) 12, 45, 46, 47, 51, 156, 157, 169, 175, 176, 177, 178, 179, 180, 202, 242, 264, 287, **289–90**, 329

Verbena officinalis (*Vervain*) 53–4, 60, 73, 77, 79, 85, 88, 127, 156, 175, 176, 177, 178, 179, 180, 184, 204, **327–8**

Viburnum opulus (*Cramp Bark*) 37, 77, 108, 122, 124, 125, 126, 136, 167, 176, 178, 179, 192, 200, 220, 221, **246**, 295, 296, 327

Viburnum prunifolium (*Black Haw*) 77, 124, 126, 176, 178, 179, 180, 198, **220–1**, 246, 273

Vinca major (*Periwinkle*) 71, 72, 122, 124, 129, 149, 176, 180, 191, 203, **299**, 325

Viola odorata (*Sweet Violet*) 149, 204, **322**

Viola tricolor (*Pansy*) 95, 203, **293–4**

Viscum alba (*Mistletoe*) 33, 35, 36, 37, 38, 61, 77, 83, 88, 94, 149, 176, 178, 179, 180, 202, 268, 279, **286**, 337

Vitex agnus-castus (*Chasteberry*) 88, 121, 123, 124, 125, 128, 178, 200, **239**

Z

Zanthoxylum americanum (*Prickly Ash Bark*) 39, 97, 103, 104, 108, 177, 178, 180, 203, 246, **303**

Zea mays (*Corn Silk*) 122, 134, 135, 136, 156, 175, 177, 229, **244**

Zingiber officinale (*Ginger*) 33, 39, 60, 61, 62, 63, 72, 103, 104, 108, 142, 176, 177, 178, 179, 180, 185, 186, 189, 226, 233, 260, **261**, 289, 292, 315, 332, 337